CompTIA® A+®
Complete Practice Tests
Core 1 Exam 220-1101 and
Core 2 Exam 220-1102
Third Edition

Audrey O'Shea

Jeff T. Parker

SYBEX®
A Wiley Brand

To my life partner Rick, my rock.
—Audrey

Acknowledgments

Genuine thanks to the Sybex/Wiley team, particularly to Kenyon Brown for the opportunity to author this edition. To Kim Wimpsett and Archana Pragash, thank you for your guidance and patience, and answering all those questions. To Christine O'Connor, thank you for your support. Finally, to Chris Crayton, thank you for pointing out all the little things and providing a fresh perspective. It takes a team to create an excellent book, and the readers have these people to thank for the quality found in the pages that follow.

About the Authors

Audrey O'Shea lives along the shore of Lake Ontario and currently teaches electronics and CompTIA A+ and ITF+ courses at a technical school in upstate New York. Prior to this she taught Cisco entry-level courses and has taught courses at the community college level, including *electrical theory and practice for energy workers* and *computer information systems*. Audrey's information technology career started in 1989 as owner of a computer consulting firm, and since then she has held the positions of network administrator, tech support specialist, trainer, and consultant and has been a public speaker advocating for women to enter the tech field. She holds two degrees and a New York State teaching license.

Audrey also holds several CompTIA certifications, including CompTIA A+, ITF+, Network + Security +, Project +, CSIS, and CIOS, and she has earned several web, programming, Microsoft, and other certifications. She authored the Wiley book *A Geek Girl's Guide to Electronics and the Internet of Things* 2021, and served as the technical editor for *CompTIA A+ Complete Practice Tests, Second Edition* 2019, and appeared in Wiley Efficient Learning online courses for CompTIA A+ and Project +. Audrey can be reached at `aoshea@live.com`.

Jeff T. Parker, CISSP, Project+, CySA+, is a certified technical trainer and consultant specializing in governance, risk management, and compliance.

About the Technical Editor

Chris Crayton is a technical consultant, trainer, author, and industry-leading technical editor. He has worked as a computer technology and networking instructor, information security director, network administrator, network engineer, and PC specialist. Chris has authored several print and online books on PC repair, CompTIA A+, CompTIA Security+, and Microsoft Windows. He has also served as technical editor and content contributor on numerous technical titles for several of the leading publishing companies. He holds numerous industry certifications, has been recognized with many professional and teaching awards, and has served as a state-level SkillsUSA final competition judge.

Contents

Contents

Introduction

If you're picking up this book, there's a good chance that you want to pass the CompTIA A+ exam. It means that you're likely either an IT professional looking for certifications or someone who has a bit of computer knowledge and wants to start an IT career. The A+ exam is entry level and is often the first certification test IT technicians will take.

While still considered an entry-level credential, the exam has become more challenging compared to what it was a few years ago. The newest exam puts a slightly higher importance on operating systems, security, mobile devices, and troubleshooting. New topics include long-range fixed wireless, Wi-Fi 6, the newest USB ports, cable categories, and Windows 11. Overall, our opinion is that the industry will understand this exam to be more practical and vigorous and the credential will be even more valued. The time to gain this credential is now.

While we're confident that if you can answer all the questions in this book you can pass the exam, we encourage you to take time to read the explanations and go beyond memorizing questions and answers. One reason is that the questions on the actual exams will be different than the ones written for this book. Another (better) reason is that life isn't a multiple-choice exam. When you're in the field and trying to fix a computer, you won't have possible solutions given to you—you need to have a solid base of knowledge to work from.

CompTIA® A+® Complete Practice Tests, Third Edition, combined with the Sybex *CompTIA® A+® Complete Study Guide, Fifth Edition* (and also the Deluxe Study Guide), will help give you the foundation you need to pass the exams. Study them well and they will also give you the tools you need to navigate a myriad of technical topics and make you more valuable to prospective employers.

What Is A+ Certification?

The A+ certification program was developed by the Computing Technology Industry Association (CompTIA) to provide an industrywide means of certifying the competency of computer service technicians. The A+ certification is granted to those who have attained the level of knowledge and troubleshooting skills that are needed to provide capable support in the field of personal computers and mobile devices. It is similar to other certifications in the computer industry, such as the Cisco Certified Network Associate (CCNA) program and the Microsoft certification programs. The theory behind these certifications is that if you need to have service performed on a certain vendor's products, you would prefer to use a technician who has been certified in one of the appropriate certification programs rather than just the first "expert" that pops up in a Google search. The difference with A+ is that it's an industry-wide certification and vendor agnostic. That means by passing it, you're capable of handling different issues regardless of the software or hardware vendor.

Everyone must take and pass two exams: Core 1 (220-1101) and Core 2 (220-1102). You don't have to take the 220-1101 exam and the 220-1102 exam at the same time, but the A+ certification isn't awarded until you've passed both tests.

Tests are administered by CompTIA's global testing partner, Pearson VUE. For more information on taking the exam, visit the CompTIA website at www.comptia.org. You can also visit Pearson VUE at www.pearsonvue.com.

Who Should Buy This Book?

If you want to pass the A+ exam, this book is definitely for you. This book is an exam prep book. If you're an experienced computer professional, a book like this may be all you need to pass the exam.

However, a book of exam questions isn't designed to give you all the background you need to truly understand the basics of personal computers, mobile devices, and virtualization. If you're newer to the industry, we encourage you to buy a study guide as well, such as the Sybex *CompTIA A+ Complete Study Guide Fifth Edition*. The study guide will provide more depth and context to help you acquire the skills and knowledge you need to be successful. This book then becomes a great companion as you prepare to take the exam.

How to Use This Book and the Interactive Online Learning Environment and Test Bank

This book includes 1,500 practice test questions, which will help you get ready to pass the A+ exam. The interactive online learning environment that accompanies *CompTIA A+ Complete Practice Tests, Third Edition* provides a robust test bank to help you prepare for the certification exams and increase your chances of passing them the first time! By using this test bank, you can identify weak areas up front and then develop a solid studying strategy using each of these testing features.

The test bank also offers two practice exams. Take these practice exams just as if you were taking the actual exam (without any reference material). When you've finished the first exam, move on to the next one to solidify your test-taking skills. If you get more than 90 percent of the answers correct, you're ready to take the certification exams.

You can access the Sybex interactive online test bank at www.wiley .com/go/Sybextestprep.

Like all exams, the A+ certification from CompTIA is updated periodically and may eventually be retired or replaced. At some point after CompTIA is no longer offering this exam, the old editions of our books and online tools will be retired. If you have purchased this book after the exam was retired or are attempting to register in the Sybex online learning environment after the exam was retired, please know that we make no guarantees that this exam's online Sybex tools will be available once the exam is no longer available.

Tips for Taking the A+ Exams

Here are some general tips for taking your exams successfully:

- Bring two forms of ID with you. One must be a photo ID, such as a driver's license or passport. The other can be another ID with your name or a recent photo. Both IDs must have your signature. These requirements sometimes change, so be sure to check for updates on the Candidate ID Policy page of www.comptia.org before scheduling your test.

- Arrive early at the exam center so you can relax and review your study materials, particularly tables and lists of exam-related information.

- Read the questions carefully. Don't be tempted to jump to an early conclusion. Make sure you know exactly what the question is asking.

- Don't leave any unanswered questions. Unanswered questions are scored against you.

- There will be questions with multiple correct responses. Be sure to read the messages displayed to know how many correct answers you must choose.

- When answering multiple-choice questions you're not sure about, use a process of elimination to rule out the obviously incorrect answers first. Doing so will improve your odds if you need to make an educated guess.

- On form-based tests (nonadaptive), because the hard questions will eat up the most time, save them for last. You can move forward and backward through the exam.

- For the latest pricing on the exams and updates to the registration procedures, visit CompTIA's website at www.comptia.org.

Exam Objectives

CompTIA goes to great lengths to ensure that its certification programs accurately reflect the IT industry's best practices. Exam content comes from surveying and receiving feedback from companies and people currently working in the industry, as well as input from subject matter experts (SMEs). This ensures that the test objectives and weightings truly reflect the job requirements.

The SMEs' work in focus groups to write and review hundreds of test items. The process is estimated to take over 5,000 SME hours to develop a single exam. And, in many cases, they must go back to the drawing board for further refinements before the exam is ready to go live in its final state.

CompTIA also uses a trained psychologist/psychometrician to ensure that the test and test development process exceed the certification industry's standards.

CompTIA ensures that their tests are developed with impartiality and objectivity, and they take security of the exam contents very seriously. By maintaining exam question confidentiality, the certification retains its validity and value in the computer industry.

So, rest assured, the content you're about to learn will serve you long after you take the exam.

A+ Certification Exam Objectives: Core 1 (220-1101)

The following table lists the domains measured by this examination and the extent to which they are represented on the exam:

Domain	Percentage of Exam
1.0 Mobile Devices	15%
2.0 Networking	20%
3.0 Hardware	25%
4.0 Virtualization and Cloud Computing	11%
5.0 Hardware and Network Troubleshooting	29%
Total	100%

2.0 Networking

Domain	Chapter(s)

2.1 Compare and contrast Transmission Control Protocol (TCP) and User Datagram Protocol (UDP) ports, protocols and their purposes.   2, 10

Ports and protocols   2, 10
- 20/21 – File Transfer Protocol (FTP)
- 22 – Secure Shell (SSH)
- 23 – Telnet
- 25 – Simple Mail Transfer Protocol (SMTP)
- 53 – Domain Name System (DNS)
- 67/68 – Dynamic Host Configuration Protocol (DHCP)
- 80 – Hypertext Transfer Protocol (HTTP)
- 110 – Post Office Protocol 3 (POP3)
- 137/139 – Network Basic Input/Output System (NetBIOS)/ NetBIOS over TCP/IP (NetBT)
- 143 – Internet Mail Access Protocol (IMAP)
- 161/162 – Simple Network Management Protocol (SNMP)
- 389 – Lightweight Directory Access Protocol (LDAP)
- 443 – Hypertext Transfer Protocol Secure (HTTPS)

445 – Server Message Block (SMB)/Common Internet File System (CIFS)   2,10
- 3389 – Remote Desktop Protocol (RDP)

TCP vs. UDP   2, 10
- Connectionless
    - DHCP
    - Trivial File Transfer Protocol (TFTP)
- Connection-oriented
    - HTTPS
    - SSH

2.2 Compare and contrast common networking hardware.   2, 10

Routers   2, 10

Switches   2, 10
- Managed
- Unmanaged

Access points   2, 10

Domain	Chapter(s)
Motherboard form factor	3, 10
- Advanced Technology eXtended (ATX)	
- Information Technology eXtended (ITX)	
Motherboard connector types	3, 10
- Peripheral Component Interconnect (PCI)	
- PCI Express (PCIe)	
- Power connectors	
- SATA	
- eSATA	
-Headers	
- M.2	
Motherboard compatibility	3, 10
-CPU sockets	
- Advanced Micro Devices, Inc. (AMD)	
- Intel	
-Server	
-Multisocket	
-Desktop	
-Mobile	
Basic Input/Output System (BIOS)/Unified Extensible Firmware Interface (UEFI) settings	3,10
- Boot options	
- USB permissions	
- Trusted Platform Module (TPM) security features	
- Fan considerations	
- Secure Boot	
- Boot password	
Encryption	3, 10
- TPM	
- Hardware security module (HSM)	

Domain	Chapter(s)
Cloud characteristics	4, 10
- Shared resources	
- Metered utilization	
- Rapid elasticity	
- High availability	
- File synchronization	
Desktop virtualization	4, 10
- Virtual desktop infrastructure (VDI) on premises	
- VDI in the cloud	
4.2 Summarize aspects of client-side virtualization.	4, 10
Purpose of virtual machines	4, 10
- Sandbox	
- Test development	
- Application virtualization	
- Legacy software/OS	
- Cross-platform virtualization	
Resource requirements	4, 10
Security requirements	4, 10
5.0 Hardware and Network Troubleshooting	
5.1 Given a scenario, apply the best practice methodology to resolve problems.	5, 10
Always consider corporate policies, procedures, and impacts before implementing changes.	5, 10
1. Identify the problem.	5, 10
- Gather information from the user and identify user changes, and if applicable, perform backups before making changes.	
- Inquire regarding environmental or infrastructure changes.	
2. Establish a theory of probable cause (question the obvious).	5, 10
- If necessary, conduct external or internal research based on symptoms.	

Domain	Chapter(s)
3. Test the theory to determine cause.	5, 10
- Once the theory is confirmed, determine the next steps to resolve the problem.	
- If the theory is not confirmed reestablish a new theory or escalate.	
4. Establish a plan of action to resolve the problem and implement the solution.	5, 10
- Refer to the vendor's instructions for guidance.	
5. Verify full system functionality and, if applicable, implement preventive measures.	5, 10
6. Document findings, actions, and outcomes.	5, 10
5.2 Given a scenario, troubleshoot problems related to motherboards, RAM, CPUs, and power.	5, 10
Common symptoms	5, 10
- Power-on self-test (POST) beeps	
- Proprietary crash screens (blue screen of death (BSOD)/pinwheel)	
- Black screen	
- No power	
- Sluggish performance	
- Overheating	
- Burning smell	
- Intermittent shutdown	
- Application crashes	
- Grinding noise	
- Capacitor swelling	
- Inaccurate system date/time	
5.3 Given a scenario, troubleshoot and diagnose problems with storage drives and RAID arrays.	5, 10

Domain	Chapter(s)
Common symptoms	5, 10

- Light-emitting diode (LED) status indicators
- Grinding noises
- Clicking sounds
- Bootable device not found
- Data loss/corruption
- RAID failure
- Self-monitoring, Analysis, and Reporting Technology (S.M.A.R.T.) failure
- Extended read/write times
- Input/output operations per second (IOPS)
- Missing drives in OS

5.4 Given a scenario, troubleshoot video, projector, and display issues.	5, 10
Common symptoms	5, 10

- Incorrect data source
- Physical cabling issues
- Burned-out bulb
- Fuzzy image
- Display burn-in
- Dead pixels
- Flashing screen
- Incorrect color display
- Audio issues
- Dim image
- Intermittent projector shutdown

5.5 Given a scenario, troubleshoot common issues with mobile devices.	5, 10

Domain	Chapter(s)
5.7 Given a scenario, troubleshoot problems with wired and wireless networks.	5, 10
Common symptoms	5, 10

- Intermittent wireless connectivity
- Slow network speeds
- Limited connectivity
- Jitter
- Poor Voice over Internet Protocol (VoIP) quality
- Port flapping
- High latency
- External interference

A+ Certification Exam Objectives: Core 2 (220-1102)

The following table lists the domains measured by this examination and the extent to which they are represented on the exam.

Domain	Percentage of Exam
1.0 Operating Systems	31%
2.0 Security	25%
3.0 Software Troubleshooting	22%
4.0 Operational Procedures	22%
Total	100%

Domain	Chapter(s)
2.8 Given a scenario, use common data destruction and disposal methods.	7, 11
Physical destruction	7, 11
- Drilling	
- Shredding	
- Degaussing	
- Incinerating	
Recycling or repurposing best practices	7, 11
- Erasing/wiping	
- Low-level formatting	
- Standard formatting	
Outsourcing concepts	7, 11
- Third-party vendor	
- Certification of destruction/recycling	
2.9 Given a scenario, configure appropriate security settings on small office/home office (SOHO) wireless and wired networks.	7, 11
Home router settings	7, 11
- Change default passwords	
- IP Filtering	
- Firmware updates	
- Content filtering	
- Physical placement/secure locations	
- Dynamic Host Configuration Protocol (DHCP) reservations	
- Static wide-area network (WAN) IP	
- Universal Plug and Play (UPnP)	
- Screened subnet	

Domain	Chapter(s)
Licensing/digital rights management (DRM)/end-user license agreement (EULA)	9, 11
- Valid licenses	
- Non-expired licenses	
- Personal use license vs. corporate use license	
- Open-source license	
Regulated data	9, 11
- Credit card transactions	
- Personal government-issued information	
- Personally identifiable information (PII)	
- Healthcare data	
- Data retention requirements	
4.7 Given a scenario, use proper communication techniques and professionalism.	9, 11
Professional appearance and attire	9, 11
- Match the required attire of the given environment	
- Formal	
- Business casual	
Use proper language and avoid jargon, acronyms, and slang, when applicable	9, 11
Maintain a positive attitude/project confidence	9, 11
Actively listen, take notes, and avoid interrupting the customer	9, 11
Be culturally sensitive	9, 11
- Use appropriate professional titles, when applicable	
Be on time (if late, contact the customer)	9, 11
Avoid distractions	9, 11
- Personal calls	
- Texting/social media sites	
- Personal interruptions	

Exam objectives are subject to change at any time without prior notice and at CompTIA's sole discretion. Please visit the certification page of CompTIA's website at www.comptia.org for the most current listing of exam objectives.

Where the term *Windows* is used in the text, it refers to both Windows 10 and Windows 11, which are the two Microsoft operating systems on this version of the CompTIA A+ exam. Where necessary, differences between the two versions of the operating system are noted. Keep in mind that like the CompTIA A+ exam objectives, Microsoft operating systems are subject to change at their discretion.

COMPTIA A+ CORE 1 EXAM 220-1101

- Mobile Devices
- Networking
- Hardware
- Virtualization and Cloud Computing
- Hardware and Network Troubleshooting

Chapter

1

Mobile Devices

THE COMPTIA A+ 220-1101 TOPICS COVERED IN THIS CHAPTER INCLUDE THE FOLLOWING:

✓ **1.1 Given a scenario, install and configure laptop hardware and components.**

- Hardware/device replacement

  - Battery

  - Keyboard/keys

  - Random-access memory (RAM)

  - Hard disk drive (HDD)/solid-state drive (SSD) migration

  - HDD/SSD replacement

  - Wireless cards

- Physical privacy and security components

  - Biometrics

  - Near-field scanner features

✓ **1.2 Compare and contrast the display components of mobile devices.**

- Types

  - Liquid crystal display (LCD)

    - In-plane switching (IPS)

    - Twisted nematic (TN)

    - Vertical alignment (VA)

  - Organic light-emitting diode (OLED)

- Mobile display components

- Wi-Fi antenna connector/placement

- Camera/webcam

- Microphone

- Touch screen/digitizer
- Inverter

✓ 1.3 Given a scenario, set up and configure accessories and ports of mobile devices.

- Connection methods
    - Universal Serial Bus (USB)/USB-C/ microUSB/miniUSB
    - Lightning
    - Serial interfaces
    - Near-field communication (NFC)
    - Bluetooth
    - Hotspot
- Accessories
    - Touch pens
    - Headsets
    - Speakers
    - Webcam
- Docking station
- Port replicator
- Trackpad/drawing pad

✓ 1.4 Given a scenario, configure basic mobile-device network connectivity and application support.

- Wireless/cellular data network (enable/disable)
    - 2G/3G/4G/5G
    - Hotspot
    - Global System for Mobile Communications (GSM) vs. code-division multiple access (CDMA)
    - Preferred Roaming List (PRL) updates
- Bluetooth
    - Enable Bluetooth
    - Enable pairing

1. You are configuring the mail app on an iPhone to use an `Outlook.com` email address. What configuration information do you need to enter to establish connectivity?

   A. Email address and password

   B. Email address, password, and server name

   C. Email address, password, server name, and mail protocol

   D. Email address, password, server name or IP address, and mail protocol

2. Which type of smartphone display has fewer layers, providing more flexibility, a better viewing angle, and excellent color as compared to other technologies?

   A. IPS

   B. OLED

   C. LED

   D. TN

3. In which scenario would you use the Fn key and the F10 key?

   A. To turn the screen brightness down

   B. To turn the screen brightness up

   C. To turn the speaker volume down

   D. To turn the speaker volume up

4. You are purchasing a mobile device that allows you to use multi-finger gestures to interact with the device. What type of touchscreen technology does this device most likely use?

   A. Capacitive

   B. Infrared

   C. SAW

   D. Resistive

5. You are using a public Wi-Fi hotspot and believe that someone is trying to hack into your laptop. Which laptop feature should you use to immediately turn off all wireless connections?

   A. Silent mode

   B. Quiet mode

   C. Airplane mode

   D. Connectionless mode

6. You have been asked to purchase a new camera for the company photographer. Some of the cameras are marketed as "smart" cameras. What key feature does this likely mean the camera includes?

   A. Wi-Fi

   B. RJ-45

   C. Separate video processor

   D. Internal hard drive

7. Your friend's iPhone 13 will no longer charge. They have tried replacing the charging block and cable with compatible ones and tested the wall outlet. What should be done next?

   A. Purchase a new phone.

   B. Purchase a new battery.

   C. Take the phone to a repair shop.

   D. Use a wireless charging pad.

8. Your customer brought you a laptop with an internal battery that will no longer charge. You have told them that replacing the battery will be no problem at all. Which of the following will you need to do first?

   A. Remove the back cover.

   B. Remove the keyboard.

   C. Disconnect the external power.

   D. Disconnect the LCD panel.

9. A coworker is having a problem with their laptop and has asked you to fix it. When an external keyboard is plugged in, the laptop works just fine, but without it strange characters appear on the screen when typing. Which of the following are likely causes? (Choose two.)

   A. The driver is corrupted and needs to be updated/replaced.

   B. The ribbon cable is partially disconnected and needs to be reseated.

   C. The laptop needs to be replaced.

   D. There is debris under the keys.

10. You're working as the IT support person at an accounting firm. One of the accountants dropped their keyboard, and the number 5 key is no longer there. This is a critical problem for an accountant. What is the most cost-effective way to get them up and running again?

   A. Replace the laptop with a new one.

   B. Replace the entire keyboard.

   C. Replace the missing key.

   D. Give them a desktop computer to use.

11. Your boss has asked you to maximize the RAM in their laptop computer. You check the specifications and discover that the maximum system RAM is 32 GB of DDR4 RAM. The laptop currently has 16 GB onboard RAM and one empty slot. Which of the following RAM modules will you purchase?

   A. One 16 GB SODIMM

   B. One 32 GB SODIMM

   C. One 16 GB DIMM

   D. One 32 GB DIMM

12. A friend is trying to install an update on their iPod, but they're receiving a message about insufficient space. They want to know if you can upgrade their storage. What will you tell them?

   A. Sure, bring it over later today.

   B. Storage can't be upgraded. You'll need to buy a new iPod.

   C. Storage can't be upgraded, but you may be able to offload some apps you no longer use.

   D. Just purchase more space on iCloud; it's the same thing.

13. You need to replace a failed SATA hard drive on a 10-year-old laptop. The user has asked that the new drive be as fast as possible, regardless of disk space or cost. What type of drive should you install?

   A. SSD

   B. Magnetic

   C. Hybrid

   D. NVMe

14. You need to replace a failed hard drive in a user's laptop, and it's a model you are unfamiliar with. You look at the bottom of the laptop and see no obvious entrance points. Which component will you most likely need to remove to access the hard drive bay?

   A. Plastics/frames

   B. Battery

   C. System board

   D. Keyboard

15. You are on the phone talking to a technician who is trying to upgrade a laptop. The technician is having trouble identifying the Mini PCIe card. How wide should you tell the technician that the card is?

    A. 27 mm

    B. 30 mm

    C. 51 mm

    D. 60 mm

16. Which mobile connection type allows you to share your cellular Internet connection with a Wi-Fi enabled device?

    A. Hotspot

    B. NFC

    C. Bluetooth

    D. IrDA

17. Your friend wants to be able to use their phone to pay for purchases at a popular coffee shop. They noticed that the phone needs to be about 4″ from the coffee shop's reader. What radio wave communication type do you need to configure for your friend?

    A. NFC

    B. Wi-Fi

    C. IrDA

    D. Bluetooth

18. You're working from a home office and need to be able to type on your keyboard while talking with clients, so you purchase a wireless headset. What wireless technology will you need to enable on your laptop to ensure that the headset and laptop can communicate?

    A. Wi-Fi

    B. IR

    C. Bluetooth

    D. NFC

19. You are wearing your smart watch, which allows you to make payments like a credit card. What type of connection technology does this service use?

    A. Bluetooth

    B. NFC

    C. Wi-Fi

    D. IR

20. You're upgrading the Wi-Fi card in a manager's laptop and notice that the antenna cable is frayed, so you need to replace that too. What will you likely need to do to replace the antenna?

   A. Wrap the antenna with electrical tape.

   B. Open the display to replace the cable.

   C. Attach a dongle for the new cable.

   D. Just install the new card because the antenna is part of the card.

21. Your boss has asked you to make sure that each of the company's laptops has a biometric scanner as an extra measure of security. Which of the following are biometric devices that are commonly found and can be configured on laptops? (Choose two.)

   A. ID card scanner

   B. Face ID

   C. Fingerprint reader

   D. Retina scanner

22. Your company is producing posters for an upcoming public relations campaign. The project leader wants to embed information into an NFC Type 4 tag in the poster. How much information can this tag hold?

   A. 16 KB

   B. 32 KB

   C. 1.4 MB

   D. 2.4 MB

23. Your customer has an iPhone 8 and wants to read and write NFC tags with it. What advice will you give them? (Choose two.)

   A. Their iPhone will only work with Apple Pay.

   B. They need to upgrade to iPhone X to write NFC tags.

   C. With iOS 13 or better on their device, they'll be able to read and write NFC tags using a third-party app.

   D. iPhone 12 and iPhone 13 can read NFC tags simply by holding the phone over the tag.

24. You've been asked by the company president what can be done with NFC in addition to paying for coffee. What will you tell them? (Choose three.)

   A. Securely share data with someone you're having lunch with.

   B. Beam data to someone 10 feet away.

   C. Transfer files, photos, and videos.

   D. Add information or URLs to business cards, making it easier for customers to learn about your products or services.

25. You are investigating new laptops for your company. You want the laptop displays to have a wide viewing angle. Which technology standard is best suited for your needs?

    A. LED

    B. SVA

    C. IPS

    D. TN

26. Which type of LCD has the best contrast, meaning the darkest black and lightest white?

    A. TN

    B. IPS

    C. VA

    D. OLED

27. Of the laptop LCD technologies, which consumes the least amount of power?

    A. LED

    B. IPS

    C. TN

    D. VA

28. What type of display uses organic materials that themselves light up so that no backlight is needed, meaning true black and greater contrasts can be achieved?

    A. QLED

    B. Mini-LED

    C. LED

    D. OLED

29. You have recently purchased a laptop computer with a touchscreen. It allows you to draw images on the screen and save them on the computer. Which device is responsible for converting the input into the image that you see and save?

    A. Inverter

    B. Touchpad

    C. Digitizer

    D. Touchscreen

30. Which two components of a laptop or other mobile device are the most useful when making a videoconference call? (Choose two.)

    A. Digitizer

    B. Webcam

    C. Microphone/speaker

    D. Inverter

31. Of the laptop components listed, which one is least likely to be built into the display?

    A. Wi-Fi antenna

    B. Speakers

    C. Webcam

    D. Digitizer

32. Which mobile device component can take input from a stylus or your finger, depending on the sensor type, and convert it into an image on the laptop or other mobile device?

    A. Digitizer

    B. Touchpad

    C. Point stick

    D. Inverter

33. What is this device, which can be found inside an iPhone 10 along the bottom, connected with a small ribbon cable?

    A. Wi-Fi antenna

    B. Digitizer

    C. Haptics connector

    D. Stylus sensor

34. In which scenario would you use the Fn key and the F4 key shown here?

 A. To turn the touchpad on or off
 B. To change the video output to an external display
 C. To change the screen orientation from landscape to portrait
 D. To turn the keyboard backlight on or off

35. Which type of mobile device is known for using electrophoretic ink?

 A. E-reader
 B. Smart watch
 C. Smart glasses
 D. Tablet

36. Which display component is capable of discharging energy and causing severe injuries to technicians?

 A. Screen
 B. Backlight
 C. Inverter
 D. LCD

37. Which of the following is not a type of LCD?

 A. OLED
 B. IPS

    C. TN

    D. VA

38. What types of networking will smart cameras often have built into them? (Choose two.)

    A. Bluetooth

    B. IrDA

    C. RJ-45

    D. Wi-Fi

39. What component or characteristic on most mobile phones has its ability measured in megapixels?

    A. Brightness

    B. Contrast

    C. Camera

    D. Digitizer

40. What three components of a mobile display are often connected in such a way that if one fails, you must replace the other two with it? (Choose three.)

    A. Glass cover

    B. LCD

    C. Wi-Fi antenna

    D. Digitizer

41. An artist in your company's marketing department just received the new drawing pad that they ordered. What might you need to do to configure it? (Choose three.)

    A. Install an alternate operating system.

    B. Plug the device into an appropriate port, likely USB.

    C. Enable Windows Ink or other software settings.

    D. Calibrate the device.

42. A coworker just started working with their new laptop yesterday, and today they're complaining that the trackpad won't work. You suspect that they accidentally turned it off. What key or key combination based on the graphic will remedy the problem?

A. Fn and F8

B. Fn and F9

C. F7

D. F9

43. One of your coworkers has purchased an external Bluetooth trackpad to use with their tablet. They've turned to you, the company IT person, to install and configure it for them. What actions will you need to take? (Choose two.)

A. Plug the device into a USB port.

B. Install drivers.

C. Put the device in pairing mode and open Bluetooth settings on the tablet, then tap the trackpad.

D. Go to Settings to configure speed and scrolling features.

44. What type of connection are you using if you use a USB cable to connect your laptop to your cell phone in order to use the cellular wireless connection from the laptop?

A. Hotspot

B. Tethering

C. USB networking

D. Phoning

45. You often work remotely, in your favorite coffee shop. What device can you use to physically protect your laptop from theft if you step away from the table for a minute?

A. Docking station

B. Protective cover

C. Cable lock

D. LoJack

46. The company president misplaced their charging cable for their iPhone 13. You tell them it's no problem, and hand them a new one. What type of connector does this iPhone use for charging?

A. Thunderbolt

B. Lightning

C. ApplePower

D. USB-C

47. What type of mobile device connector is shown here?

    A. USB-C

    B. Lightning

    C. Micro-USB

    D. Thunderbolt

48. Your significant other just purchased a new car and wants you to configure their cell phone to work through the car using voice commands. You must initiate pairing on the phone and choose to search for pairing devices on the car. What protocol is being used by the car and the device?

    A. 802.11a

    B. Lightning

    C. Bluetooth

    D. Wi-Fi Enabled

49. A laptop user wants to have a full-sized display and keyboard, as well as an external hard drive, and speakers available to them at their desk. Which accessory can they purchase to avoid plugging each of these devices separately into their laptop every time they return to the desk? (Choose two.)

    A. KVM switch

    B. Port replicator

    C. Desktop station

    D. Docking station

50. A user needs ports for external devices in addition to what their laptop is capable of connecting. The user would like these devices to have connectivity with each other whether or not the laptop is there. Which of the following will provide that option?

    A. Docking station

    B. Port replicator

    C. KVM switch

    D. Docking port

51. Which laptop expansion port technology was developed by Apple and Intel and supports a wide variety of peripheral devices?

    A. USB

    B. DisplayPort

    C. eSATA

    D. Thunderbolt

52. You're upgrading a user's laptop from 802.11n to 802.11ac. What port will you most likely use inside the laptop?

    A. PCI

    B. PCIe

    C. Mini PCIe

    D. Mini PCIe x16

53. You've been handed a device to install. The cable looks like the one here. What type of connector does this device use?

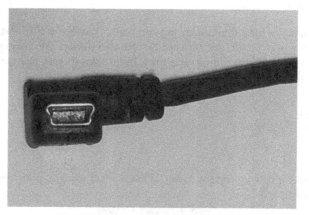

    A. USB-C

    B. miniUSB

    C. microUSB

    D. Thunderbolt 3

54. What port looks identical to a Thunderbolt 3 connector but will not charge a connected device as quickly?

    A. USB-C

    B. miniUSB

    C. USB A

    D. microUSB

55. You've been handed a device to install. The cable looks like the one here. What type of connector does this device use?

    A.   USB-C

    B.   miniUSB

    C.   microUSB

    D.   Thunderbolt 3

56. You're the IT manager for a manufacturing company. One of the corporate executives is questioning why you're buying serial instead of parallel devices. You explain that serial transmits only one bit of information at a time, but it does so very fast compared to parallel. Which of the following will you tell them is not a serial connection?

    A.   Centronics

    B.   Thunderbolt

    C.   Lightning

    D.   USB-C

57. You're configuring a new laptop for a user. What devices can you plug into the port shown here? (Choose two.)

    A.   Speaker

    B.   Headphones

    C.   Webcam

    D.   Touch pen

58. A technician has a failed Lenovo laptop and suspects the motherboard is bad. They have several other laptops available from which they can harvest parts. Which of the following statements is most likely true regarding the replacement motherboard that is selected?

   A. The motherboard is not replaceable.

   B. Any laptop motherboard will work.

   C. A motherboard from any other Lenovo laptop will work.

   D. Only a motherboard from that same model of Lenovo laptop will work.

59. What type of connector is used on Android smartphones? (Choose two.)

   A. Lightning

   B. Thunderbolt

   C. USB-C

   D. USB Micro-B

60. You will be traveling to another country for work and will have a 10-hour airplane flight. You need to work on your laptop while on the flight, but your battery won't last that long. What should you buy to allow you to use the auxiliary power outlets on the airplane?

   A. AC adapter

   B. DC adapter

   C. Power inverter

   D. Docking station

61. The AC adapter for your laptop is not working properly, and you are searching for a replacement. Which two factors should be most important when selecting a new AC adapter? (Choose two.)

   A. Polarity

   B. Same wattage as the original

   C. Brand of the adapter

   D. Size of the adapter

62. How do modern docking stations connect to laptops? (Choose two.)

   A. USB 2

   B. USB-C

   C. Thunderbolt 3 or 4

   D. HDMI

63. You have enabled the GPS service in your tablet. What is the minimum number of GPS satellites your tablet needs to be in contact with to determine its location?

   A. One

   B. Two

   C. Three

   D. Four

64. What is the name of the OS used by the Apple Watch, which was designed specifically for the watch?

    A. iOS

    B. OS X mobile

    C. watchOS

    D. Tizen

65. A technician needs to replace a failed laptop hard drive. Which of the following form factors could it use?

    A. 1.3″

    B. 2.0″

    C. 2.5″

    D. 3.5″

66. What type of wearable technology device is specifically designed to track a user's movements and heart rate and may include features such as GPS?

    A. Smart watch

    B. Fitness monitor

    C. Smart glasses

    D. Smart headset

67. You want to play video games on your tablet computer. Which accessory would you purchase if you wanted to play the game much like you would on a gaming console?

    A. Docking station

    B. Touch pad

    C. Point stick

    D. Game pad

68. Your new laptop has 4 GB system RAM and an integrated video card. The default setting specifies 512 MB of video memory. How much RAM is available for the processor to use?

    A. 4 GB.

    B. 3.5 GB.

    C. 3 GB.

    D. It's variable.

69. Oculus, Samsung, and HTC are manufacturers of what specific type of wearable technology devices?

    A. Smart glasses

    B. Smart headsets

    C. Smart watches

    D. VR/AR headsets

70. Tablet computers feature touchscreens that are approximately what size?

    A. Between 5″ and 7″

    B. Between 3″ and 5″

    C. Between 7″ and 12″

    D. Between 12″ and 24″

71. What type of connectors are the two shown in the center here?

    A. Lightning

    B. Thunderbolt

    C. DisplayPort

    D. PCIe x 1

72. Which type of network connection is least likely to be found on a tablet computer?

    A. Wi-Fi

    B. Bluetooth

    C. RJ-45

    D. Cellular

73. What type of device would use a Lightning connector to charge and transfer data?

    A. Samsung smartphone

    B. Fitbit watch

    C. Intel based laptop

    D. Apple iPhone

74. You are upgrading a laptop with a Mini PCIe card. What type of connector does Mini PCIe use?

    A. 52-pin

    B. 68-pin

    C. 144-pin

    D. 200-pin

75. What is the likely type of Wi-Fi antenna connector you will find as an external connector on a laptop?

    A. SMA-female-RP

    B. N-male

    C. SMA-male-RP

    D. N-female

76. A warehouse manager at a factory is required to supervise productivity while walking around and taking notes. They find their laptop awkward to type on while walking but do not want to use two devices. What would you recommend they do?

    A. Get a small tablet to synchronize with the laptop.

    B. Place accessible workstations throughout the factory.

    C. Get a laptop with a rotating or removable screen.

    D. Get a smaller laptop.

77. After enabling your device for communication using the IEEE 802.15.1 standard, what is the next step?

    A. Enter the PIN code.

    B. Find a device for pairing.

    C. Enable pairing.

    D. Open port 802.15.1.

78. You've enabled Bluetooth on your new headset and your laptop and enabled pairing on both. They have discovered each other, so what is the typical next step?

    A. Pressing and holding a Bluetooth button

    B. Entering the Bluetooth password

    C. Entering the Bluetooth PIN code

    D. Exiting out of any running Bluetooth applications

79. You're configuring private email on a coworker's cell phone. They want to make sure all of their mail will be only on their phone. Which mail protocol keeps all emails stored on a single device and can only be accessed from one device?

    A. IMAP

    B. SMTP

    C. POP3

    D. S/MIME

80. You're configuring company email on a coworker's phone. The company needs to keep a copy of every email on their server, even after it's accessed by the user. Which mail protocol keeps all emails stored on the server, allowing messages to be synchronized between multiple devices?

    A. IMAP

    B. SMTP

    C. POP3

    D. S/MIME

81. What service is built into Apple-developed devices and permits users and subscribers to store documents, media, and contact information off their devices?

    A. iStore

    B. OneDrive

    C. iCloud

    D. CloudOnline

82. What is the hosted messaging version of Microsoft's Exchange mail server that saves customers email off-site?

    A. Google Inbox

    B. Exchange Online

    C. iExchange

    D. On-Prem Exchange

83. What configuration settings are commonly used when setting up email from an online provider on a device?

    A. Active Directory domain name

    B. Port and TLS settings

    C. Email server name

    D. Username and password

84. What type of update is done to mobile devices over the air?

    A. PRI and PRL

    B. IMEI

    C. Screen resolution

    D. IMSI

85. Which number that is a part of the GSM system is hard-coded into the phone and identifies your physical phone hardware to the cellular tower?

    A. PRI

    B. IMSI

    C. IMEI

    D. MAC

86. Which unique mobile number identifies you as a user and is coded into the SIM card if you're on a GSM network, or otherwise linked to your account, allowing you to transition from one phone to another?

    A. PRI

    B. IMSI

    C. IMEI

    D. MAC

87. A user is traveling to a country that employs content blocking technology on the cellular network. What would you suggest setting up to bypass the content blocking as well as keep the user's mobile browsing more private?

   A. S/MIME

   B. PRL

   C. Baseband

   D. VPN

88. What best practice can save someone from losing the data such as calendar entries and contacts on their mobile device if the device is lost?

   A. Synchronization

   B. VPN

   C. Encryption

   D. Updating

89. A user wants a list of favorite websites to be readily available between multiple devices, including their mobile device. What is the best option?

   A. Email weblinks to self.

   B. Send links to a URL shortening service.

   C. Synchronize bookmarks.

   D. Print web URLs to carry.

90. When two parents wish to share appointment dates and times between devices, what is their best option?

   A. Synchronizing calendars

   B. Sharing calendar passwords

   C. Texting calendar data to each other

   D. Emailing calendar invites to each other

91. What Windows app is used to synchronize data between a user's mobile devices like smartphones and their desktop computers?

   A. MSync

   B. ActiveSync

   C. SyncTime

   D. Timewarp

92. What technology lets you minimize how often a user must log in for multiple services?

   A. SSO

   B. SMTP

   C. Synchronization

   D. Nonrepudiation

93. You're installing Bluetooth speakers in a conference room and just entered the pin to connect the two devices. What is your next step?

 A. Enable pairing.

 B. Search for the Bluetooth device.

 C. Enable Bluetooth.

 D. Test connectivity.

94. The owner of a company that solely provides transportation from the airport to various hotels wants to employ a software that will tell them where every vehicle is at all times. All of the vehicles use satellite-based navigation systems. What technology is most likely being used to track where they are?

 A. Global Positioning System (GPS)

 B. Mobile Device Management (MDM)

 C. Cellular location services

 D. Mobile Application Management (MAM)

95. You're going hiking this weekend in unfamiliar territory and have installed an application on your phone that shows you where you are on the map in relation to the trails and surrounding areas. What two types of location technology might this app use? (Choose two.)

 A. GPS

 B. MDM

 C. Cellular location services

 D. RFID

96. Your coworker wants to be able to use maps with their phone but is unhappy that other applications are also tracking their physical location. They ask for your help. Which of the following is not true?

 A. If location services are turned off for one purpose, they are turned off for all services.

 B. When you're installing an application, most likely it will ask you when it is allowed to use location services.

 C. Some applications won't work without location services.

 D. You can turn location services on or off for applications in the settings of your device.

97. You're at home binging on a popular Internet movie service and suddenly notice that the spinning wheel is showing up often, taking more time to download the movie than normal. What is likely the problem?

 A. Your router needs to be reset.

 B. You have reached your data cap.

 C. Your laptop is overheating.

 D. The service is overwhelmed with requests.

98. The executives at your company are concerned about employees using their personal devices for work. They worry that someone may leave and take proprietary information with them. You calm their fears by telling them that there are settings in place that protect company data that is accessed by employees. What are those settings called? (Choose two.)

    A. MDM

    B. MAM

    C. GSM

    D. CDMA

99. Which of the following is not a type of two-factor authentication?

    A. Sending an access code via text message

    B. Using an authenticator application

    C. Needing a password and physical security key

    D. Needing a username and password

100. Which cellular communication technology is known as Long-Term Evolution (LTE)?

    A. 2G

    B. 3G

    C. 4G

    D. 5G

101. Which of the following display types refers not to how the liquid crystals are arranged, but rather to the type of backlight being used?

    A. LED

    B. OLED

    C. IPS

    D. TN

102. You are responsible for replacement parts within your company's IT department. Because of the critical nature of your business, you need to have replacement parts on hand in the event of a hardware failure. Your company uses four different types of laptops, two HP and two Dell. How many different types of motherboards do you most likely need to stock?

    A. One

    B. Two

    C. Three

    D. Four

103. Tech support has recommended that you update the OS on your iPad to resolve a problem you're having with it. What OS will you be updating?

    A. iPadOS

    B. OS X mobile

    C. watchOS

    D. iOS

104. Your client is frustrated that their Bluetooth earpiece that was working yesterday is no longer working, and they've asked for your help. What is the likely source of the problem?

   A. The earpiece has paired to a different device.

   B. The earpiece is broken.

   C. The Wi-Fi signal is weak.

   D. Bluetooth connectivity was lost.

105. The Wi-Fi connection between your laptop and network has failed. Upon examining Device Manager you notice that the network card is not listed. You've reseated the card and it still isn't found in Device Manager, so you've decided to replace it. Which of the following card types will you likely need to purchase?

   A. PCIe

   B. PCI

   C. M.2

   D. PCMCIA

106. A technician needs to replace a hard drive that failed in their new laptop. What type of drive will they likely need? (Choose two.)

   A. M.2

   B. mSATA

   C. 2.5²

   D. 3.5²

Networking

THE COMPTIA A+ 220-1101 TOPICS COVERED IN THIS CHAPTER INCLUDE THE FOLLOWING:

✓ **2.1 Compare and contrast Transmission Control Protocol (TCP) and User Datagram Protocol (UDP) ports, protocols, and their purposes.**

- Ports and protocols
    - 20/21 – File Transfer Protocol (FTP)
    - 22 – Secure Shell (SSH)
    - 23 – Telnet
    - 25 – Simple Mail Transfer Protocol (SMTP)
    - 53 – Domain Name System (DNS)
    - 67/68 – Dynamic Host Configuration Protocol (DHCP)
    - 80 – Hypertext Transfer Protocol (HTTP)
    - 110 – Post Office Protocol 3 (POP3)
    - 137/139 – Network Basic Input/Output System (NetBIOS)/NetBIOS over TCP/IP (NetBT)
    - 143 – Internet Mail Access Protocol (IMAP)
    - 161/162 – Simple Network Management Protocol (SNMP)
    - 389 – Lightweight Directory Access Protocol (LDAP)
    - 443 – Hypertext Transfer Protocol Secure (HTTPS)
  - 445 – Server Message Block (SMB)/Common Internet File System (CIFS)
    - 3389 – Remote Desktop Protocol (RDP)
  - TCP vs. UDP
    - Connectionless
      - DHCP
      - Trivial File Transfer Protocol (TFTP)
    - Connection-oriented

- HTTPS
- SSH

✓ **2.2 Compare and contrast common networking hardware.**

- Routers
- Switches
    - Managed
    - Unmanaged
- Access points
- Patch panel
- Firewall
- Power over Ethernet (PoE)
    - Injectors
    - Switch
    - PoE standards
- Hub
- Cable modem
- Digital subscriber line (DSL)
- Optical network terminal (ONT)
- Network interface card (NIC)
- Software-defined networking (SDN)

✓ **2.3 Compare and contrast protocols for wireless networking.**

- Frequencies
    - 2.4 GHz
    - 5 GHz
- Channels
    - Regulations
    - 2.4 GHz vs. 5 GHz
- Bluetooth
- 802.11

- a
- b
- g
- n
- ac (WiFi 5)
- ax (WiFi 6)
- Long-range fixed wireless
  - Licensed
  - Unlicensed
  - Power
  - Regulatory requirements for wireless power
- Near-Field Communication (NFC)
- Radio-frequency identification (RFID)

✓ **2.4 Summarize services provided by networked hosts.**

- Server roles
  - DNS
  - DHCP
  - Fileshare
  - Print servers
  - Mail servers
  - Syslog
  - Web servers
  - Authentication, authorization, and accounting (AAA)
- Internet appliances
  - Spam gateways
  - Unified threat management (UTM)
  - Load balancers
  - Proxy servers

- Legacy/embedded systems
    - Supervisory control and data acquisition (SCADA)
- Internet of Things (IoT) devices

✓ **2.5 Given a scenario, install and configure basic wired/wireless small office/home office (SOHO) networks.**

- Internet Protocol (IP) addressing
    - IPv4
        - Private addresses
        - Public addresses
    - IPv6
    - Automatic Private IP Addressing (APIPA)
    - Static
    - Dynamic
    - Gateway

✓ **2.6 Compare and contrast common network configuration concepts.**

- DNS
    - Address
        - A
        - AAAA
    - Mail exchanger (MX)
    - Text (TXT)
        - Spam management
        - (i) DomainKeys Identified Mail (DKIM)
        - (ii) Sender Policy Framework (SPF)
        - (iii) Domain-based Message Authentication, Reporting, and Conformance (DMARC)
- DHCP
    - Leases
    - Reservations
    - Scope

- Virtual LAN (VLAN)
- Virtual private network (VPN)

✓ **2.7 Compare and contrast Internet connection types, network types, and their features.**

- Internet connection types
    - Satellite
    - Fiber
    - Cable
    - DSL
    - Cellular
    - Wireless Internet service provider (WISP)
- Network types
    - Local area network (LAN)
    - Wide area network (WAN)
    - Personal area network (PAN)
    - Metropolitan area network (MAN)
    - Storage area network (SAN)
    - Wireless local area network (WLAN)

✓ **2.8 Given a scenario, use networking tools.**

- Crimper
- Cable stripper
- WiFi analyzer
- Toner probe
- Punchdown tool
- Cable tester
- Loopback plug
- Network tap

1. You are installing a fiber-optic cable between two buildings. To install the cable, you must run it through a conduit between the buildings, and access to the conduit is not easy. Before you run the cable, you want to ensure that it's working properly. Which tool should you use?

   A. Cable tester

   B. Multimeter

   C. Loopback plug

   D. Tone generator and probe

2. Which TCP/IP protocol, designed to download email, allows for multiple clients to be simultaneously connected to the same mailbox?

   A. SMTP

   B. POP3

   C. IMAP

   D. SMB

3. You are using your laptop on the company network. In your web browser, you type www.google.com and press Enter. The computer will not find Google. You open the browser on your phone, and using your cellular connection, you can open Google without a problem. Your laptop finds internal servers and can print without any issues. What is the most likely reason you can't open Google?

   A. DNS server problem

   B. DHCP server problem

   C. Missing subnet mask

   D. Duplicate IP address

4. Which one of the following TCP/IP protocols was designed as a replacement for Telnet?

   A. SMB

   B. SSH

   C. SFTP

   D. FTPS

5. Which of the following network connectivity devices operates at Layer 2 of the OSI model?

   A. Hub

   B. Switch

   C. Cable

   D. Router

6. Which of the following TCP/IP protocols is connection-oriented and attempts to guarantee packet delivery?

   A. IP

   B. TCP

   C. UDP

   D. ICMP

7. Which TCP/IP protocol allows a user to log into a remote computer and manage files as if they were logged in locally?

   A. FTP

   B. SFTP

   C. SMB

   D. RDP

8. Which Wi-Fi standard is the fastest, operating in both the 2.4 and 5 GHz frequencies?

   A. 802.11a

   B. 802.11ac

   C. 802.11ax

   D. 802.11n

9. Bob has a device that operates at 5 GHz. He is unable to connect his device to a LAN that he hasn't accessed before, although he has verified that he has the correct password. What type of network might pose this problem?

   A. 802.11g

   B. 802.11n

   C. 802.11ac

   D. 802.11ax

10. Which TCP/IP protocol is used to provide shared access to files and printers on the network?

   A. FTP

   B. SSH

   C. SMB

   D. SMTP

11. What port does the Telnet protocol use?

   A. 21

   B. 22

   C. 23

   D. 25

12. You have just installed a wireless 802.11ac network for a client. The IT manager is concerned about competitors intercepting the wireless signal from outside the building. Which tool is designed to test how far your wireless signal travels?

   A. Tone generator and probe

   B. Protocol analyzer

   C. Packet sniffer

   D. Wi-Fi analyzer

13. Some of your network users are concerned about submitting confidential information to an online website. What should you tell them?

    A. It's fine, because all Internet traffic is encrypted.

    B. If the website address starts with `TLS://`, it should be OK to submit confidential information to a trusted site.

    C. If the website address starts with `HTTPS://`, it should be OK to submit confidential information to a trusted site.

    D. Don't ever submit confidential information to any online website.

14. Which TCP/IP Internet layer protocol is responsible for delivering error messages if communication between two computers fails?

    A. ICMP

    B. IP

    C. TCP

    D. UDP

15. Which type of IPv6 address identifies a single node on the network?

    A. Multicast

    B. Anycast

    C. Unicast

    D. Localcast

16. What type of network covers large geographical areas and often supports thousands of users, often using lines owned by other entities?

    A. LAN

    B. WAN

    C. PAN

    D. MAN

17. Which TCP/IP protocol, developed by Microsoft, uses port 3389 to connect to a remote computer?

    A. RDP

    B. SMB

    C. CIFS

    D. Telnet

18. What port does the SSH protocol use?

    A. 21

    B. 22

    C. 23

    D. 25

19. Which of the following IP addresses is not routable on the Internet?

   A. 10.1.1.1

   B. 11.1.1.1

   C. 12.1.1.1

   D. 13.1.1.1

20. Which network connectivity device does not forward broadcast messages, thereby creating multiple broadcast domains?

   A. Hub

   B. Switch

   C. Bridge

   D. Router

21. What type of address does a router use to get data to its destination?

   A. IP

   B. MAC

   C. Memory

   D. Loopback

22. You have a desktop computer that is behaving erratically on the network. The wired connection will often disconnect without warning. Which tool should you use to troubleshoot the network adapter?

   A. Multimeter

   B. Tone generator and probe

   C. Loopback plug

   D. Cable tester

23. Your company just expanded and is leasing additional space in an adjacent office building. You need to extend the network to the new building. Fortunately, there is a conduit between the two. You estimate that the cable you need to run will be about 300 meters long. What type of cable should you use?

   A. CAT-5e

   B. CAT-7

   C. CAT-8

   D. MMF

24. You want to ensure that client computers can download email from external email servers regardless of the protocol their email client uses. Which ports do you open on the firewall to enable this? (Choose two.)

   A. 23

   B. 25

   C. 110

   D. 143

25. You are installing network cabling in a highly secure facility. The cables need to be immune to electronic eavesdropping. What type of cable should you use?

   A. Fiber-optic

   B. UTP

   C. STP

   D. Coaxial

26. Which networking device is capable of reading IP addresses and forwarding packets based on the destination IP address?

   A. Hub

   B. Switch

   C. NIC

   D. Router

27. Which network device is designed to be a security guard, blocking malicious data from entering your network?

   A. PoE injector

   B. EoP device

   C. Firewall

   D. Router

28. You are manually configuring TCP/IP hosts on the network. What configuration parameter specifies the internal address of the router that enables Internet access?

   A. Subnet mask

   B. DHCP server

   C. DNS server

   D. Default gateway

29. Which of the following devices will be found in a telecommunications room and provides a means to congregate horizontal wiring, terminating each run in a female port?

   A. Patch panel

   B. Multiplexer

   C. Rack U

   D. Demarcation point

30. What type of network is most commonly associated with Bluetooth devices such as wireless keyboards, mice, and headphones, and covers a small area?

   A. LAN

   B. WAN

   C. PAN

   D. MAN

31. When troubleshooting a network connectivity issue, you discover that the local computer has an IPv4 address of 169.254.2.2. What do you immediately know about this local computer?

    A. It is working fine.

    B. It can't find a DHCP server.

    C. It isn't on the network.

    D. It has an invalid IP address.

32. Which of the following IPv6 addresses is automatically assigned by the host when it boots and is only usable on the broadcast domain that it exists in?

    A. 2000::/3

    B. FC00::/7

    C. FE80::/10

    D. FF00::/8

33. You need to configure a wireless router for an office network. The office manager wants new devices to be able to automatically join the network and announce their presence to other networked devices. Which service should you enable to allow this?

    A. DHCP

    B. NAT

    C. QoS

    D. UPnP

34. You are troubleshooting a computer with an IPv6 address that is in the FE80::/10 range. Which of the following statements are true? (Choose two.)

    A. The computer will not be able to get on the Internet using that IP address.

    B. The computer will be able to get on the Internet using that IP address.

    C. The computer is configured with a link-local unicast address.

    D. The computer is configured with a global unicast address.

35. You have set up your web server to function as an FTP server as well. Users on the Internet complain that they are not able to access the server using FTP clients. What port should they be trying to access the server on?

    A. 21

    B. 22

    C. 23

    D. 80

36. Which TCP/IP protocol allows you to access data such as employee phone numbers and email addresses that are stored within an information directory?

    A. SNMP

    B. SMTP

    C. CIFS

    D. LDAP

37. What port is associated with the LDAP protocol?
    A. 22
    B. 139
    C. 389
    D. 3389

38. You are configuring network hosts with static IP addresses. You have chosen to use a Class B network address. What is the default subnet mask that you should configure on the hosts?
    A. 255.0.0.0
    B. 255.255.0.0
    C. 255.255.255.0
    D. 255.255.255.255

39. You are installing a new network and working in a telecommunications room. You need to attach several network cables to a 110 block. Which tool should you use to perform this task?
    A. Crimper
    B. Cable stripper
    C. Cable tester
    D. Punchdown tool

40. Which of the following Internet connection types offers the fastest download speeds?
    A. Cable
    B. DSL
    C. Fiber-optic
    D. Satellite

41. Which of the following are public IPv4 addresses? (Choose two.)
    A. 69.252.80.71
    B. 144.160.155.40
    C. 172.20.10.11
    D. 169.254.1.100

42. Which TCP/IP protocol uses port 445?
    A. FTP
    B. SSH
    C. SMB
    D. SNMP

43. What rendition of SMB was used by Windows servers and NAS servers but is no longer often used?

A. CIFS

B. Samba

C. NFS

D. SMB3

44. For IPv6, which of the following statements are true? (Choose two.)

A. Each IPv6 interface can have only one address.

B. Each IPv6 interface is required to have a link-local address.

C. IPv6 addresses are incompatible with IPv4 networks.

D. IPv6 does not use broadcasts.

45. Which network connectivity device is seldom used in modern networks, except to extend a network?

A. Bridge

B. Hub

C. Switch

D. Router

46. There is a TCP/IP protocol that should only be used locally because it has virtually no security. It may be used as a part of a preboot execution environment (PXE) or with thin clients booting from a network drive. It uses very little memory and is good for transferring boot files or configuration data between computers on a LAN, and it is connectionless. Which file transfer protocol is this?

A. FTP

B. TFTP

C. FTPS

D. SMTP

47. Which of the following IPv6 addresses is equivalent to 127.0.0.1 in IPv4?

A. ::0

B. ::1

C. ::127

D. 2000::/3

48. You are asked to perform consulting work for a medium-sized company that is having network connectivity issues. When you examine the patch panel, you notice that none of the dozens of UTP cables are labeled. Which tool can you use to identify which cable goes to which workstation?

A. Cable tester

B. Loopback plug

C. Punchdown tool

D. Tone generator and probe

49. Which TCP/IP protocol is responsible for dynamically assigning IP addresses to client computers?

    A. DNS

    B. DHCP

    C. RDP

    D. LDAP

50. Which networking device has multiple ports, each of which is its own collision domain, and examines the header of the incoming packet to determine which port the packet gets sent to?

    A. Hub

    B. Switch

    C. Bridge

    D. Router

51. Which TCP/IP port will an email client use to push email to its email server?

    A. 23

    B. 25

    C. 110

    D. 143

52. A technician is going to set up a Wi-Fi network using standard omnidirectional antennae. Because of the building configuration, transmitting signals for the greatest distance is the technician's primary criterion. Which standard should they choose?

    A. 802.11a

    B. 802.11g

    C. 802.11n

    D. 802.11ac

53. You are troubleshooting an intermittently failing Cat 6 network connection. You suspect that there is a short in the connection. Which tool can you use to determine this?

    A. Tone generator and probe

    B. Loopback plug

    C. Cable tester

    D. Crimper

54. What marks the boundary of a IPv4 broadcast domain?

    A. Hub

    B. Switch

    C. Router

    D. Modem

55. Which TCP/IP protocol gathers and manages network performance information using devices called agents?

   A. SNMP

   B. SMTP

   C. LDAP

   D. SMB

56. Which Internet connection type, once popular for home use, offers asymmetrical download and upload speeds and is implemented over common phone lines?

   A. POTS

   B. Cable

   C. DSL

   D. ISDN

57. You are installing an 802.11n Wi-Fi network with five wireless access points. The access points are set up so their ranges overlap each other. To avoid communications issues, what principle should you follow when configuring them?

   A. Configure all access points to use the same channel.

   B. Configure all access points to use adjacent channels.

   C. Configure all access points to use nonoverlapping channels.

   D. Channel configuration will not cause communications issues.

58. You need to configure email settings for use with IMAP. Which port will you be configuring?

   A. 25

   B. 80

   C. 110

   D. 143

59. Which of the following technologies will enable you to install networking devices that need power to function, in a location that has no power outlets?

   A. EoP

   B. PoE

   C. WAP

   D. Hub

60. You have been asked to install a Wi-Fi network in a building that is approximately 100 meters long and 25 meters wide. Because of cost considerations, you will be using 802.11ac. At a minimum, how many wireless access points will you need?

   A. Two

   B. Three

   C. Four

   D. Six

61. What two tools will you need to connect an RJ45 connector to an appropriate cable? (Choose two.)

    A. Punchdown tool

    B. Network tap

    C. Crimper

    D. Cable stripper

62. You are installing network cabling in a drop ceiling of an office space. The ceiling area is used to circulate breathable air. What type of cable must you install?

    A. Coaxial

    B. UTP

    C. Fiber-optic

    D. Plenum

63. You need to install a wireless access point in a drop ceiling where there is no access to a power source. Which technology will allow you to get power to that device?

    A. EoP

    B. PoE

    C. Hub

    D. Repeater/extender

64. Which of the following IP addresses is not a private address and therefore is routable on the Internet?

    A. 10.1.2.3

    B. 172.18.31.54

    C. 172.168.38.155

    D. 192.168.38.155

65. You are configuring a wireless 802.11ax router. The office manager insists that you configure the router such that traffic from her computer receives higher priority on the network than other users' traffic. Which setting do you need to configure to enable this?

    A. QoS

    B. UPnP

    C. Screened subnet

    D. Port forwarding

66. If you are connecting to a website that encrypts its connection using TLS, what port does that traffic travel on?

    A. 21

    B. 80

    C. 143

    D. 443

67. Your network is currently running a mix of 802.11b and 802.11g devices. At the end of the year, you have extra budget to upgrade some, but not all, of the wireless infrastructure. You want to upgrade to the newest technology possible but still maintain backward compatibility. Which standard should you choose?

    A. 802.11g

    B. 802.11ac

    C. 802.11ax

    D. 802.11r

68. What type of network spans multiple buildings or offices, possibly even crossing roads, but is confined to a relatively small geographical area?

    A. LAN

    B. WAN

    C. PAN

    D. MAN

69. Which of the following shorthand notations corresponds to the CIDR subnet mask 255.255.224.0?

    A. /19

    B. /20

    C. /21

    D. /22

70. You are configuring hosts on a network running IPv4. Which elements are required for the computer to connect to the network?

    A. IP address

    B. IP address and subnet mask

    C. IP address, subnet mask, and default gateway

    D. IP address, subnet mask, default gateway, and DNS server address

71. You work at a tech support company and a customer called reporting that they received an error, something about a duplicate IP address. Why are they getting this message? (Choose two.)

    A. All hosts on a network must have a unique IP address.

    B. A PC is manually configured with an IP that is in the DHCP scope.

    C. A PC is manually configured with an IP that is not in the DHCP scope.

    D. None of the PCs have been manually configured.

72. You're setting up a network for a customer. The network uses a DHCP server, but the customer needs an IP address for their print server that does not change. What are two possible solutions? (Choose two.)

   A. Let the DHCP server assign a number because once assigned, it will not change.

   B. Manually configure the print server to have a static IP address.

   C. Configure a reserved IP address on the DHCP server for the print server.

   D. Static and dynamic IP addresses can't exist on the same network. You'll have to manually configure everything.

73. Which obsolete Wi-Fi encryption standard uses a static key, which is commonly 10, 26, or 58 characters long?

   A. WPA3

   B. WPA2

   C. TKIP

   D. WEP

74. You've been asked to set up a device that will be monitored using an SNMP agent and manager. What port will the SNMP manager use when polling the agent?

   A. TCP 143

   B. UDP 143

   C. TCP 161

   D. UDP 161

75. Because of a recent security breach, your IT team shut down several ports on the external firewall. Now, users can't get to websites by using their URLs, but they can get there by using IP addresses. What port(s) does the IT team need to open back up to enable Internet access via URLs?

   A. 20/21

   B. 53

   C. 67/68

   D. 80

76. All your network hosts are configured to use DHCP. Which IP address would indicate that a host has been unable to locate a DHCP server?

   A. 192.168.1.1

   B. 10.1.1.1

   C. 172.16.1.1

   D. 169.254.1.1

77. You have reason to believe that several network users are actively browsing prohibited content on unsecured sites on the Internet. Which port can you disable on the firewall to immediately stop access to these websites?

   A. 53

   B. 67

   C. 80

   D. 443

78. Which TCP/IP protocol is designed to help resolve hostnames to IP addresses?

   A. ARP

   B. RARP

   C. DHCP

   D. DNS

79. You need to install an Internet connection for a forest ranger outlook tower, located far away from electrical lines. Which option would be best for broadband Internet access?

   A. Cable

   B. DSL

   C. Fiber

   D. Satellite

80. Your customer will be moving their small office to a remote mountain village where there is no cable Internet access. They have heard that there is a wireless option available in the area that is faster than satellite but that requires an antenna and line-of-sight to a tower. What option have they heard about?

   A. Satellite

   B. DSL

   C. WISP

   D. Cellular hotspot

81. Which TCP/IP host-to-host protocol makes its best effort to deliver data but does not guarantee it?

   A. IP

   B. TCP

   C. UDP

   D. ICMP

82. What type of network is typically defined as being contained within a single office or building?

   A. LAN

   B. WAN

   C. PAN

   D. MAN

83. You are installing a wireless network for a small company. The management wants to have 1 Gbps or better wireless transmission rates. Which of the following standards will allow you to provide this? (Choose two.)

    A. 802.11ac

    B. 802.11ax

    C. 802.11g

    D. 802.11n

84. Which of these standards operate in both the 2.4 GHz and 5 GHz frequencies? (Choose two.)

    A. 802.11ac

    B. 802.11ax

    C. 802.11g

    D. 802.11n

85. What legacy network protocol allows NetBIOS-dependent computer applications to communicate over TCP/IP?

    A. TFTP

    B. HTTPS

    C. NetBT

    D. BGP

86. Which of the following features does not require a managed network switch?

    A. Priority of traffic

    B. VLAN configuration

    C. Direct packets out the proper port

    D. Port mirroring

87. The senior network administrator struggles to configure company network devices spanning several cities. It's a challenge because they are required to be on premises for the network infrastructure of each building. What would be a cost-effective solution?

    A. Employ network administrators at each building.

    B. Go to a flat network.

    C. Train a local sales associate.

    D. Employ a cloud-based network controller.

88. What port(s) does DHCP use?

    A. 67/68

    B. 137/139

    C. 80

    D. 445

89. What is the maximum distance allowed between a power over Ethernet injector and the Ethernet device running on a 1000BaseT network?

  A. 50 meters

  B. 100 meters

  C. 250 meters

  D. 450 meters

90. Which of the following protocols uses port 137 and 139?

  A. DNS

  B. SMB

  C. NetBT

  D. SSH

91. When setting up a small office, home office (SOHO) network, how do the end-user devices know what IP address they need to use to connect with the network?

  A. The network switch broadcasts configuration settings.

  B. Devices utilize service location protocol.

  C. The NIC is set with a static address or DHCP-served.

  D. End users configure IP addresses as needed.

92. You've been asked to set up a wireless network for a SOHO that will only allow five specific devices to connect. How do you accomplish this?

  A. Disable the router's SSID.

  B. Configure port forwarding.

  C. Set a DHCP scope with only five addresses.

  D. Configure MAC address filtering.

93. What is the most likely way for a homeowner's IoT devices to connect to their wireless network?

  A. DNS

  B. AD

  C. SSO

  D. DHCP

94. What type of communication technology is being used at a fast-food restaurant when a customer places their phone next to a device to pay for their purchase?

  A. RFID

  B. NFC

  C. Wi-Fi

  D. HAV

95. What communication technology allows for low-power, passive reading of a small tag or patch on an object that may be a few feet to dozens of feet away?

    A. RFID

    B. NFC

    C. Wi-Fi

    D. RFI

96. What type of server provides Internet access to company-provided information such as how to contact a company, products or services for sale, and other information?

    A. FTP server

    B. Proxy server

    C. File server

    D. Web server

97. A friend is showing you how they can control their thermostat at home from their cell phone while at work. What type of device do they have at home?

    A. IoT

    B. SQL

    C. DoS

    D. EFS

98. What server would function as a central repository of documents and provide network shared file storage for internal users?

    A. FTP server

    B. Proxy server

    C. File server

    D. Web server

99. You work as a network administrator for a school district. The district is required to provide access to the Internet for students but also required to protect the network and the students from malicious network traffic and inappropriate websites. What type of server do you need to configure?

    A. FTP server

    B. Proxy server

    C. File server

    D. Web server

100. What type of server can host files for easy access and downloading, similar to how a web server serves web pages?

    A. FTP server

    B. Proxy server

    C. File server

    D. DNS server

101. You're a network administrator and just added a device to your network that allows multiple users to access several printers. What have you attached to the network?

    A. Syslog server

    B. DNS server

    C. Print server

    D. Authentication server

102. What server is used to resolve domain names to IP addresses to facilitate web browsing or locating a directory resource on the network?

    A. Syslog server

    B. DNS server

    C. Print server

    D. Authentication server

103. What server is accessed each time it's necessary to challenge and validate a user's credentials in order for the user to access a network resource?

    A. Syslog server

    B. DNS server

    C. Print server

    D. Authentication server

104. What service can collect and journal all the system-generated messages produced by servers and network devices?

    A. Syslog server

    B. DNS server

    C. Print server

    D. Authentication server

105. You're configuring your phone to download and upload email. What type of server are you configuring your phone to use?

    A. Web server

    B. Authentication server

    C. Mail server

    D. FTP server

106. Which of the following are connection-oriented protocols? (Choose two.)

    A. DHCP

    B. TFTP

    C. HTTPS

    D. SSH

107. A company wanting to monitor network traffic or host system behavior to identify suspect activity will install what type of service?

    A. Proxy server

    B. IDS

    C. UTM

    D. ATM

108. What is the primary difference between an IDS and an IPS?

    A. IDS works both on a host and a network.

    B. IDS will not actively alert on suspect activity.

    C. IPS works in pairs.

    D. IPS will actively react to suspect activity.

109. Managing security on your growing network has become difficult, so you ask your peers what they are doing to manage their networks. They recommend a device that will allow you to manage your security in one place. What have they recommended?

    A. IDS

    B. IPS

    C. UTM

    D. UTP

110. A switch is overheating, and the SNMP agent is sending an SNMP trap to an SNMP manager. Which of the following are true? (Choose two.)

    A. It is a managed switch.

    B. It is an unmanaged switch.

    C. It is communicating on port 161.

    D. It is communicating on port 162.

111. Your cousin is a nature photographer, traveling the country and living in their Class A motorhome. Much of the time their motorhome is parked in a national park, but seldom is Wi-Fi available. Your cousin uploads photos from their camera to a laptop, modifies them, and needs to upload them to their publisher, various magazines, and their website on a regular basis. What is a viable networking option for your cousin?

    A. Satellite

    B. Cellular

    C. WISP

    D. DSL

112. Based on the drawing, what is the device labeled A?

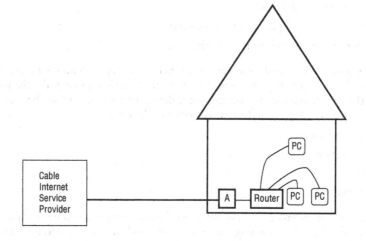

A. Switch

B. Hub

C. Cable modem

D. Cable multiplexer

113. What is the device in the image used for?

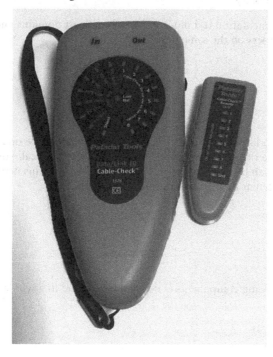

    A. It multiplexes several signals into one.

    B. It's a network cable tester.

    C. It's for attaching RJ45 connectors to cable.

    D. It's for testing Wi-Fi signal strength.

114. You are a network administrator. Currently there is no wireless access to the business network, but the company is purchasing tablets so that employees can take their work with them as they move around the facility. What device will you install so that employees will be able to connect to the wired network with wireless devices?

    A. Ethernet router

    B. Proxy server

    C. WAP

    D. NFC hub

115. Last weekend you installed and booted several more computers to be ready for Monday morning. Later Monday morning you hear from employees as they come in that they cannot log in. Their desktops don't seem to want to connect. You investigate and find that each faulty workstation has a `169.254.x.x` IP address. What might you look at next?

    A. DHCP scope

    B. LAN connector broken

    C. Windows patch unable to install

    D. Corrupted Registry

116. What network segmentation technique reduces broadcast domains and provides a layer of security between users on the same network?

    A. VPN

    B. VLAN

    C. UPS

    D. SQL

117. One of your network users must work remotely from their office on an extremely confidential project. Their team is concerned about security so they call you, the IT department head, to see what can be done. What will you set up between this network user and the company server so that the communications are secure?

    A. VPN

    B. SDN

    C. VLAN

    D. SRAM

118. Which of the following components is not typically found in a wireless LAN (WLAN)?

    A. WLAN router

    B. WLAN gateway

    C. WLAN server

    D. WLAN client

119. You need to configure dynamic IP addressing on your network to cut down on management time. How will you do this? (Choose two.)

    A. Enable DHCP settings on the router.

    B. Configure each NIC to obtain an IP address automatically.

    C. Configure each NIC to a specific IP address.

    D. Configure each NIC to obtain DNS server addresses automatically.

120. Your network admin needs to add a computer to an IPv6 subnet. Which of the following IPv6 addresses is on the same subnet as `2601:0:0:0f:1a:308c:2acb:fee2`?

    A. `2601::0f:308c:47:4321`

    B. `2601::0f:ab:cd:123:4a`

    C. `fe80:ab:bc:0f:1a:308c:2abc:fee5`

    D. `2601:0:0:0x::2acb:ac01`

121. Dylan is troubleshooting his IPv4 network. The network's subnet mask is `255.255.192.0`. Which of the following IP addresses is *not* on the same network as the others?

    A. `130.200.65.5`

    B. `130.200.130.1`

    C. `130.200.100.4`

    D. `130.200.125.5`

122. Which of the following is a PoE standard?

    A. 802.3bt

    B. 802.3b

    C. 802.11

    D. 802.11ax

123. Your friend has purchased a PoE device for their home. It is a type 2 device. Which of the following PoE switches will be compatible with this device? (Choose two,)

    A. 802.3af-compliant switch

    B. 802.3at-compliant switch

    C. 802.3bt-compliant switch

    D. 802.11b-compliant switch

124. Which of the following is true of an ONT? (Choose two.)

    A. It stands for optical network terminator.

    B. It converts fiber-optic light signals to electrical (Ethernet) signals.

    C. It is user installed.

    D. It requires external power to work properly.

125. Which of the following is not a benefit of software-defined networking (SDN)?

    A. Dynamic load balancing

    B. Reduced infrastructure costs

    C. Requires a cloud-based network

    D. Centrally manage physical and virtual routers

126. Which type of WISP radio frequency has the advantages of no fees, less expensive equipment, and a wide pool of practical knowledge so help is easier to find?

    A. Licensed

    B. Unlicensed

    C. Limited

    D. Unlimited

127. You are working with your customer, a doctor's office, to develop a network that will allow the doctor's staff to work with their tablet PCs in any room of the office without having to worry about network cabling. What type of network will you establish for the doctor's office?

    A. LAN

    B. VLAN

    C. WLAN

    D. WAN

128. Which of the following is a network of storage devices that a server can access as if it were a locally connected drive?

    A. NAS

    B. SAS

    C. SAN

    D. WAN

129. Which of the following is true of a network TAP? (Choose two.)

    A. TAP stands for terminal access point.

    B. It is solely used by hackers to intercept packets.

    C. It is part of a router.

    D. It allows network admins to monitor network traffic.

130. What software runs on a machine where data files to be accessed are housed and controls access to those files as requested by a client?

    A. CAL

    B. Fileshare server

    C. Fileshare client

    D. SAN

131. A friend is having some issues with the wireless network in their apartment dropping the connection or running very slowly. What tool can be used to determine the best channel to use?

    A. WAP

    B. Wi-Fi analyzer

    C. Toner probe

    D. Cable tester

132. In the United States, the Federal Communications Commission (FCC) imposes rules that govern radio communications. What is the maximum EIRP (watts) that can be transmitted in the 2.4 GHz band for a point-to-multipoint WISP connection?

    A. 2 watts

    B. 4 watts

    C. 158 watts

    D. 125 mw

133. Using which Wi-Fi channels does not require that your router has Dynamic Frequency Selection (DFS) and Transmit Power Control (TPC) built into the router?

    A. Channels 36 to 48

    B. Channels 52 to 64

    C. Channels 100 to 144

    D. Channels 149-165

134. Which broadband network communications technology became more competitive with other types of service when, in 2021, the FCC ruled to include it in the Over-The-Air-Reception Devices Rule (OTARD), which protects the rights of those organizations to place antennas where they are needed?

    A. Fios

    B. Long-range fixed wireless

    C. DSL

    D. Satellite

135. What is the host number in an IP address of `192.168.2.200` and a subnet mask of `255.255.255.0`?

    A. `192.168`

    B. `192.168.2`

    C. `2.200`

    D. `200`

136. What are the three A's employed by authentication servers?

    A. Authentication, activation, acceptance

    B. Authorization, access, allocation

    C. Accept, access, accounting

    D. Authentication, authorization, accounting

137. Which Internet appliance is used to distribute incoming traffic over resources, such as multiple web servers?

    A. Proxy servers

    B. Spam gateways

    C. Load balancers

    D. UTM device

138. What type of system, consisting of both hardware and software, is used to control and monitor industrial machines and processes?

    A. SCADA

    B. IrDA

    C. UTM

    D. RADIUS

139. Your friend owns a restaurant and provides free Wi-Fi to their clientele. Lately they have been receiving complaints that the Wi-Fi isn't working. It seems to work for customers already connected but not for people trying to connect. What can be configured on the router to release an IP address and make it available for other users after a couple of hours?

    A. MAC address filtering

    B. Port forwarding

    C. DHCP lease duration

    D. SSID broadcast

140. What type of address is known as a DNS AAAA address?

    A. IPv4

    B. IPv6

    C. MAC

    D. Physical

141. What type of entry in a DNS record can be used for load balancing of incoming mail?

    A. MX

    B. DX

    C. AAAA

    D. TXT

142. What type of DNS record contains a list of users (IP addresses) that are authorized to send email on behalf of a domain?

    A. DKIM

    B. SPF

    C. DMARC

    D. A

143. What is the interface ID of the IP address `2001::1a3:f1a:308:833`?

    A. `2001:0:0:0:`

    B. `2001`

    C. `1a3:f1a:308:833`

    D. `833`

144. What two terms are used to identify an Internet provider that may connect to the Internet using T1 or T3 lines, or fiber optic, for example, and uses point-to-point millimeter-wave or microwave links between its towers for its backbone or to extend its service area, and point-to-multipoint wireless to provide Internet access to its customers?

    A. WISP

    B. ISP

    C. Demarcation point

    D. Long-range fixed wireless

145. Your friend is again considering the network configuration in their apartment. They've asked you the difference between channels on the 2.4 GHz and 5 GHz networks that are available on their Internet connection. What will you tell them? (Choose two.)

    A. If they are using the 2.4 GHz network, they should choose channel 1, 6, or 11 because they don't overlap each other.

    B. The 5 GHz network channels provide greater bandwidth, so data could be transferred faster, but they may have more interference with their neighbors.

    C. The 5 GHz frequency is considered obsolete, so the 2.4 GHz frequency should be used.

    D. All of the 5 GHz frequencies overlap, so there will be greater interference.

146. Which IEEE Wi-Fi standard is also known as Wi-Fi 6?

    A. 802.11a

    B. 802.11ac

    C. 802.11ax

    D. 802.11n

Chapter

3

Hardware

THE COMPTIA A+ 220-1101 TOPICS COVERED IN THIS CHAPTER INCLUDE THE FOLLOWING:

✓ **3.1 Explain basic cable types and their connectors, features, and purposes.**

- Network Cables
  - Copper
    - Cat 5
    - Cat 5e
    - Cat 6
    - Cat 6a
    - Coaxial
    - Shielded twisted pair
      - (i) Direct burial
    - Unshielded twisted pair
  - Plenum
  - Optical
    - Fiber
  - T568A/T568B
- Peripheral cables
  - USB 2.0
  - USB 3.0
  - Serial
  - Thunderbolt
- Video cables
  - High-Definition Multimedia Interface (HDMI)
  - DisplayPort

- Digital Visual Interface (DVI)
- Video Graphics Array (VGA)
- Hard drive cables
  - Serial Advanced Technology Attachment (SATA)
  - Small Computer System Interface (SCSI)
  - External SATA (eSATA)
  - Integrated Drive Electronics (IDE)
- Adapters
- Connector types
  - RJ11
  - RJ45
  - F type
  - Straight tip (ST)
  - Subscriber connector (SC)
  - Lucent connector (LC)
  - Punchdown block
  - microUSB
  - miniUSB
  - USB-C
  - Molex
  - Lightning port
  - DB9

✓ **3.2 Given a scenario, install the appropriate RAM.**

- RAM types
  - Virtual RAM
  - Small outline dual inline memory module (SODIMM)
  - Double Data Rate 3 (DDR3)
  - Double Data Rate 4 (DDR4)
  - Double Data Rate 5 (DDR5)
  - Error correction code (ECC) RAM

- Single-channel
- Dual-channel
- Triple-channel
- Quad-channel

✓ **3.3 Given a scenario, select and install storage devices.**

- Hard drives
  - Speeds
    - 5,400 rpm
    - 7,200 rpm
    - 10,000 rpm
    - 15,000 rpm
  - Form factor
    - 2.5
    - 3.5
- SSDs
  - Communications interfaces
    - Non-volatile Memory Express (NVMe)
    - SATA
    - Peripheral Component Interconnect Express (PCIe)
  - Form factors
    - M.2
    - mSATA
  - Drive configurations
    - Redundant Array of Independent (or inexpensive) Disks (RAID) 0, 1, 5, 10
  - Removable storage
    - Flash drives
    - Memory cards
    - Optical drives

✓ **3.4 Given a scenario, install and configure motherboards, central processing units (CPUs), and add-on cards.**

- Motherboard form factor
    - Advanced technology eXtended (ATX)
    - Information Technology eXtended (ITX)
- Motherboard connector types
    - Peripheral Component Interconnect (PCI)
    - PCI Express (PCIe)
    - Power connectors
    - SATA
    - eSATA
    - Headers
    - M.2
- Motherboard compatibility
    - CPU sockets
        - Advanced Micro Devices, Inc. (AMD)
        - Intel
    - Server
    - Multisocket
    - Desktop
    - Mobile
- Basic Input/Output System (BIOS)/Unified Extensible Firmware Interface (UEFI) settings
    - Boot options
    - USB permissions
    - Trusted Platform Module (TPM) security features
    - Fan considerations
    - Secure Boot
    - Boot password

- Encryption
    - TPM
    - Hardware security module (HSM)
- CPU Architecture
    - x64/x86
    - Advanced RISC Machine (ARM)
    - Single-core
    - Multicore
    - Multithreading
    - Virtualization support
- Expansion cards
    - Sound card
    - Video card
    - Capture card
    - Network interface card (NIC)
- Cooling
    - Fans
    - Heat sink
    - Thermal paste/pads
    - Liquid

✓ **3.5 Given a scenario, install or replace the appropriate power supply.**

- Input 110-120 VAC vs. 220-240 VAC
- Output 3.3 V vs. 5 V vs. 12 V
- 20-pin to 24-pin motherboard adapter
- Redundant power supply
- Modular power supply
- Wattage rating

✓ **3.6 Given a scenario, deploy and configure multi-function devices/printers and settings.**

- Properly unboxing a device – setup location considerations
- Use appropriate drivers for a given OS
    - Printer Control Language (PCL) vs. PostScript
- Device connectivity
    - USB
    - Ethernet
    - Wireless
- Public/shared devices
    - Printer share
    - Print server
- Configuration settings
    - Duplex
    - Orientation
    - Tray settings
    - Quality
- Security
    - User authentication
    - Badging
    - Audit logs
    - Secured prints
- Network scan services
    - Email
    - SMB
    - Cloud services
- Automatic document feeder (ADF)/flatbed scanner

✓ **3.7 Given a scenario, install and replace printer consumables.**

- Laser
  - Imaging drum, fuser assembly, transfer belt, transfer roller, pickup rollers, separation pads, duplexing assembly
  - Imaging process: processing, charging, exposing, developing, transferring, fusing, and cleaning
  - Maintenance: Replace toner, apply maintenance kit, calibrate, clean
- Inkjet
  - Ink cartridge, print head, roller, feeder, duplexing assembly, carriage belt
  - Calibration
  - Maintenance: Clean heads, replace cartridges, calibrate, clear jams
- Thermal
  - Feed assembly, heating element
  - Special thermal paper
  - Maintenance: Replace paper, clean heating element, remove debris
  - Heat sensitivity of paper
- Impact
  - Print head, ribbon, tractor feed
  - Impact paper
  - Maintenance: Replace ribbon, replace print head, replace paper
- 3D printer
  - Filament
  - Resin
  - Print bed

1. Identify the cable connector in the picture. It is threaded and screws into place.

   A. F-type
   B. BNC
   C. SC
   D. FC

2. Of the following fiber connectors, which are used for duplex (two strands instead of one)? (Choose two.)
   A. ST
   B. SC
   C. FC
   D. LC

3. What twisted pair connectors are commonly used with telephone wire?
   A. RJ-45
   B. Coaxial
   C. RJ-11
   D. FC

4. Using the T568B wiring standard on both ends of a cable would produce what type of network cable?
   A. T568B on both ends is not a working network cable.
   B. T568B is a telephone wiring standard.
   C. T568B on both ends is a crossover network cable.
   D. T568B on both ends is a straight-through network cable.

5. You're looking at a connector that has eight wires with colors in the order of green stripe, green, orange stripe, blue, blue stripe, orange, brown stripe, brown. What type of cable do you have?
   A. Twisted pair, T568A standard
   B. Twisted pair, T568B standard
   C. LC
   D. SC

6. You need to install a memory upgrade in a laptop computer. The computer's documentation says that the laptop uses DDR4 SODIMMs. How many pins will be on the SODIMM?

   A. 262

   B. 200

   C. 204

   D. 260

7. The most common RAM slots used in desktop and laptop computers, respectively, are what?

   A. SODIMM and DIMM

   B. Micro-DIMM and DIMM

   C. DIMM and Mini-DIMM

   D. DIMM and SODIMM

8. Which laptop expansion port was designed as an industry standard to replace VGA and DVI ports and is backward compatible with both standards?

   A. DisplayPort

   B. VideoPort

   C. Thunderbolt

   D. HDMI

9. You have a MacBook Pro computer with a Thunderbolt 4 port. What is the maximum throughput of a device plugged into this port?

   A. 5 Gbps

   B. 10 Gbps

   C. 20 Gbps

   D. 40 Gbps

10. Which motherboard form factor measures 4.7" × 4.7"?

    A. Mini-ITX

    B. Nano-ITX

    C. Pico-ITX

    D. Mobile-ITX

11. Which of the following statements are true regarding CPUs and operating systems? (Choose two.)

    A. A 32-bit OS can run only on a 32-bit CPU.

    B. A 64-bit OS can run only on a 64-bit CPU.

    C. A 64-bit OS can run on a 32-bit CPU or a 64-bit CPU.

    D. A 32-bit OS can run on a 32-bit CPU or a 64-bit CPU.

12. The DC power supply (DCPS) within a laser printer converts AC power into what three voltages? (Choose three.)

    A. +5 VDC

    B. –5 VDC

    C. +24 VDC

    D. –24 VDC

13. Identify the cable type shown here.

    A. Component

    B. Composite

    C. Coaxial

    D. RCA

14. A technician is considering whether to buy a new LCD. Which type of LCD has faster response times than the others?

    A. TN

    B. VA

    C. IPS

    D. Plasma

15. Which type of storage device is composed of a conventional magnetic hard drive and a substantial amount of solid-state storage?

    A. SSD

    B. HDD

    C. Mesh

    D. Hybrid

16. You need to share printers on your network with multiple client operating systems, such as Windows, macOS, and Linux. Which of the following services will best meet your needs?

   A. Bonjour

   B. AirPrint

   C. TCP printing

   D. Virtual printing

17. Which one of the following connector types are you most likely to find on the end of a Cat 6a cable?

   A. RJ-11

   B. RJ-45

   C. BNC

   D. SATA

18. Identify the video connector shown here.

   A. DVI

   B. VGA

   C. HDMI

   D. Composite

19. What type of printer technology will often use a roll of paper as opposed to individual sheets?

   A. Inkjet

   B. Thermal

   C. Laser

   D. Fax machine

20. Which of the following types of printers does not require the replacement of some sort of ink or toner?
    A. Laser
    B. Thermal
    C. Impact
    D. Inkjet

21. You are working on repairing a defective laser printer. Which of the following is a true statement regarding the imaging drum in a laser printer?
    A. It can hold a high negative charge only when it's not exposed to light.
    B. It can hold a high negative charge only when it's exposed to light.
    C. It can hold a high negative charge regardless of light exposure.
    D. It is not required to hold a charge.

22. What are the dimensions of a mini-ITX motherboard?
    A. 12" × 9.6"
    B. 9.6" × 9.6"
    C. 6.7" × 6.7"
    D. 3.9" × 2.8"

23. When discussing video displays, what is the term used to describe the number of pixels used to draw the screen?
    A. Refresh rate
    B. Frame rate
    C. Aspect ratio
    D. Resolution

24. You have three hard disks, each 1 TB in size. After installing them as a RAID-5 array in a computer, how much usable storage space will you have?
    A. 1.5 TB
    B. 2 TB
    C. 2.5 TB
    D. 3 TB

25. What hardware device is used to store encryption keys, making them safer because they are never directly loaded into a server's memory?
    A. HSM
    B. BIOS
    C. ITX
    D. TPM

26. You need to enable clients to scan documents and place them on network accessible storage regardless of the multifunction device's location worldwide. Which service will best suit your needs?

    A. Bonjour

    B. AirPrint

    C. Virtual printing

    D. Cloud services

27. What is the most important consideration when installing a network connected multifunction device that is capable of directly scanning and emailing?

    A. Print quality

    B. Duplexing

    C. Security

    D. Speed

28. What protocol is often used when scanning documents from a large multifunction device and sending them to the corporate server?

    A. TPM

    B. HSM

    C. SNMP

    D. SMB

29. Identify the computer component shown here.

    A. CPU heat sink and fan

    B. Passive CPU heat sink

    C. Power supply fan

    D. Secondary cooling fan

30. What features are included in modern networked MFDs? (Choose all that apply.)

    A. Email

    B. Scanning

    C. Printing

    D. Faxing

31. Which of the following connectors transmit analog signals? (Choose two.)

    A. VGA

    B. RJ-45

    C. RJ-11

    D. HDMI

32. Your partner wants to know what this port is on the back of their computer. What will you tell them?

    A. eSATA

    B. DisplayPort

    C. DVI port

    D. HDMI port

33. You have a motherboard that supports up-plugging. Which of the following statements regarding PCIe are true? (Choose two.)

    A. You can put an x1 card into an x8 slot.

    B. You can put an x8 card into an x16 slot.

    C. You can put an x8 card into an x1 slot.

    D. You can put an x16 card into an x8 slot.

34. A technician needs to increase the fault tolerance of their computer's storage system, and they have two hard drives available. Which of the following options is their best choice?

    A. Install both drives and configure them as separate volumes.

    B. Install both drives and implement RAID-0.

    C. Install both drives and implement RAID-1.

    D. Install both drives and implement RAID-5.

35. During which step of the laser printer imaging process does a fluorescent lamp discharge the photosensitive drum?

  A. Cleaning

  B. Charging

  C. Exposing

  D. Developing

36. What type of front-panel or top-panel connector uses a standard 3.5 mm jack to make connections?

  A. USB

  B. Audio

  C. FireWire

  D. Thunderbolt

37. The motherboard in your desktop computer supports dual-channel memory. Which of the following statements regarding RAM in this motherboard are true? (Choose two.)

  A. The RAM will work only if it's installed in pairs.

  B. The RAM will work only if it's installed in pairs or if one double-sided RAM module is used.

  C. The RAM will work if only one module is installed but not in dual-channel mode.

  D. The RAM will work in dual-channel mode if two identical modules are installed.

38. A customer wants you to upgrade their motherboard so that they can have the fastest video connection possible. They want to know how fast PCIe 4 is. What will you tell them the data rate of a single lane of PCIe 4 is?

  A. 250 MBps

  B. 500 MBps

  C. 1 GBps

  D. 2 GBps

39. A technician needs to replace a failed power supply in a desktop computer. When choosing a replacement power supply, which two specifications are most important to consider? (Choose two.)

  A. Wattage

  B. Multiple rail

  C. Dual voltage options

  D. Number and type of connectors

40. You need to replace the magnetic hard drive in your manager's laptop. They want a high-speed, high-capacity drive. What are the most common issues associated with their request? (Choose two.)

    A. Increased battery usage

    B. Increased heat production

    C. Decreased component life span

    D. Decreased space for other peripherals

41. You have a motherboard with a white expansion slot, that has a divider on the opposite end of a PCIe connector like the two shown in the image. What type of expansion slot is this?

    A. PCIe x1

    B. VESA

    C. PCI

    D. AGP

42. A designer from the corporate office is visiting your field office. The user tries to print from their MacBook Pro to a networked printer, but it does not work. Local users in the office are able to print to the device using their Windows computers. What would most likely solve the problem?

    A. Select the Enable Mac Printing option in the print server configuration settings.

    B. Select the Enable Bonjour option in the print server configuration settings.

    C. Install a macOS printer driver on the print server.

    D. Stop and restart the print spooler service.

43. A user that you support needs to replace this cable. What type of peripheral connector, shown here, will you be looking for?

- **A.** USB Type A
- **B.** USB Type B
- **C.** USB Standard mini-B
- **D.** Thunderbolt

44. Which of the following are advantages of using a CPU liquid cooling system over an air-based system? (Choose two.)
- **A.** Easier to install and maintain
- **B.** More efficient
- **C.** Quieter
- **D.** Safer for internal components

45. You need to perform preventive maintenance on an impact printer. What are two areas you should examine that you would not need to on most inkjet printers? (Choose two.)
- **A.** Ink cartridges
- **B.** Output tray
- **C.** Printhead
- **D.** Tractor feed mechanism

46. Which expansion bus technology uses lanes, which are switched point-to-point signal paths between two components?
- **A.** PCI
- **B.** PCI-X
- **C.** PCIe
- **D.** Mini-PCI

47. A large display with a wide viewing angle is needed for a small conference room. Which type of LCD would be best?

   A. VA

   B. IPS

   C. LED

   D. Plasma

48. You have a user who needs recommendations for installing a home server PC. They want their family to be able to share files and videos on their home network. They also want their data to be protected in the event of a hard drive failure. Which components do you recommend the system include? (Choose two.)

   A. Dedicated print server

   B. RAID array

   C. Gigabit NIC

   D. Dual processors

49. Your motherboard has 3 PCIe x16 v 4.0 slots and the motherboard does not support up-plugging for PCIe adapter cards. Which of the following statements is true?

   A. You can't put an x8 card into an x16 slot.

   B. You can put an x8 card into an x16 slot, but it will run at x1 speed.

   C. You can put an x8 card into an x16 slot, and it will run at x8 speed.

   D. You can put an x8 card into an x16 slot, and it will run at x16 speed.

50. Which system component enables the use of Secure Boot technology?

   A. BIOS

   B. UEFI

   C. AMI

   D. SATA

51. Motherboard documentation for a desktop computer mentions 240- pin DIMM slots. What type of DIMM is used on this motherboard?

   A. DDR3

   B. DDR4

   C. DDR5

   D. SODIMM

52. DDR4 and DDR5 DIMMs have the same number of pins. How, then, can you tell the difference between the two?

   A. Placement of the module key (notch).

   B. Color of the module.

   C. Size of the module.

   D. DDR5 have heat sinks; DDR4 don't.

53. Which CPU technology allows for the assignment of two logical cores for every physical core present?

  A. Multicore

  B. 32-bit vs. 64-bit

  C. Integrated GPU

  D. Multithreading

54. You are adding paper to a printer that uses tractor-feed paper, which requires lining the holes up with pins on the paper-forwarding mechanism. What type of printer are you maintaining?

  A. Impact

  B. Thermal

  C. Laser

  D. Inkjet

55. Which motherboard form factor is common in desktop computers and measures 12″ × 9.6″?

  A. ATX

  B. MicroATX

  C. Mini-ITX

  D. ITX

56. An inkjet printer doesn't seem to be moving the printhead to the right area. What two components within an inkjet printer are responsible for moving the printhead into proper position and therefore could be the problem?

  A. Carriage and belt

  B. Roller and belt

  C. Carriage motor and roller

  D. Carriage motor and belt

57. You need to configure Hyper-V on one of your Windows-based desktop computers with an Intel processor. Which of the following must be true? (Choose three.)

  A. The CPU must have SLAT.

  B. The CPU must have Intel VR.

  C. The processor must be 64-bit

  D. You need to enable virtualization in the BIOS/UEFI.

58. An analog LCD is most likely to have what type of connector?

  A. DisplayPort

  B. RCA

  C. VGA

  D. BNC

59. You have a peripheral that needs a data speed of 20 Gbps and 9 W of power to be supplied by the connection to the PC. Which PC peripheral connection type is it most likely to use?

   A. Thunderbolt

   B. USB 3.0

   C. eSATA

   D. DisplayPort

60. In the laser printer imaging process, which step immediately follows the exposing step?

   A. Charging

   B. Fusing

   C. Developing

   D. Transferring

61. What are the two power requirements that a PCI expansion bus may have in a desktop computer? (Choose two.)

   A. 1.7 V

   B. 3.3 V

   C. 5 V

   D. 6.6 V

62. Which of the following is a standard for a secure cryptoprocessor that can secure hardware (and the system boot process) using cryptographic keys?

   A. TPM

   B. LoJack

   C. Secure Boot

   D. BitLocker

63. In a laser printer, what is the function of the transfer corona assembly?

   A. It transfers a positive charge to the paper.

   B. It transfers a positive charge to the imaging drum.

   C. It transfers the toner from the imaging drum to the paper.

   D. It transfers the image from the laser to the imaging drum.

64. What type of connector is shown here?

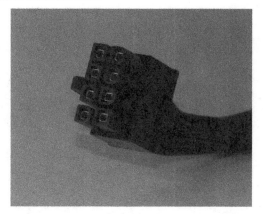

   A. Molex

   B. SATA

   C. PCIe

   D. ATX

65. A technician has installed a printer driver on a Windows client computer. What is the best next step the technician can take to ensure that the printer is installed properly?

   A. Ping the printer's IP address.

   B. Check the printer status and ensure that it says "Ready."

   C. Stop and restart the spooler service.

   D. Print a test page.

66. Which component within a laser printer converts AC current into usable energy for the charging corona and transfer corona?

   A. LVPS

   B. HVPS

   C. ACPS

   D. Transfer corona assembly

67. You have been asked to install and configure a RAID-10 storage array for a computer. What is the minimum number of hard disks required for this configuration?

   A. Two

   B. Three

   C. Four

   D. Five

68. Identify the peripheral connector shown here.

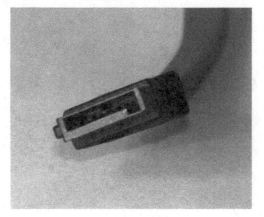

   A. HDMI

   B. PATA

   C. SATA

   D. eSATA

69. A graphic designer in your office needs two displays to do their work. Which of the following should you install to set up their desktop computer for this configuration?

   A. A video splitter

   B. A second video driver

   C. A second video card

   D. A video replicator

70. You have a motherboard designed to hold DDR3 1600 memory. What will happen if you attempt to install DDR4 2400 memory into the motherboard?

   A. It won't fit.

   B. It will operate at 667 MHz.

   C. It will operate at 1133 MHz.

   D. It will operate at 1600 MHz.

71. What happens during the transferring step of the laser printer imaging process?

   A. The image is transferred to the imaging drum.

   B. The toner is transferred to the imaging drum.

   C. The toner is transferred to the paper.

   D. A strong, uniform negative charge is transferred to the imaging drum.

72. One of your users needs to print several copies of a 20-page document. They want to ensure that the document's pages are printed on both sides of the paper to conserve paper. Which option do they need to set properly in their printer configuration settings?

A. Duplexing

B. Collating

C. Print Quality

D. Orientation

73. A technician needs to install an optical disk system with capacity to burn disks storing about 60 GB of data at one time. What is the minimum technology required to get over this threshold?

A. DVD-10

B. DVD-18

C. Triple BDXL

D. Quad BDXL

74. Which home and office printing technology typically employs a reservoir of ink, contained in a cartridge that sometimes needs replacing, as its medium to form images on paper?

A. Laser

B. Thermal

C. Inkjet

D. Impact

75. You have been asked to purchase new RAM for three workstations. The workstations call for DDR4 3600 chips. What throughput will these modules support?

A. 450 Mbps

B. 1,800 Mbps

C. 3,600 Mbps

D. 28,800 Mbps

76. A technician needs to purchase new RAM for a motherboard. The motherboard specifications call for 5,200 MHz DDR5 RAM. Which RAM modules should the technician use?

A. PC 5200

B. PC 41600

C. PC5 41600

D. PC5 5200

77. On your network, users want to print easily from their iPads and iPhones. Which service supports this?

A. Bonjour

B. AirPrint

C. TCP printing

D. Virtual printing

78. You have a new computer that needs to communicate with other computers on a wireless network. What type of expansion card do you need to install?

A. WAP

B. NIC

C. KVM

D. WPA

79. When printing, which component is responsible for converting the data being printed into the format that the printer can understand?

A. PDL

B. Printer driver

C. Print queue

D. Print spooler

80. You're installing a new printer and notice that the manufacturer has provided two drivers with the printer. One is a PostScript driver and the other is a Printer Control Language (PCL) driver. The user will mainly be printing graphics. Which driver should you install?

A. Allow Windows to install its default driver.

B. Install the PCL driver.

C. Install the PostScript driver.

D. Either driver will work equally well.

81. What type of printer driver is best to use if you'll be printing mostly documents and want to have the PC released to do other jobs more quickly?

A. Allow Windows to install its default driver.

B. Install the PCL driver.

C. Install the PostScript driver.

D. Driver choice won't have an effect.

82. You notice that a fan on a power supply has stopped turning and you will need to replace it. Which of the following statements best describes the function of a typical power supply fan?

A. It cools the power supply by blowing in air from outside the case.

B. It cools the power supply by blowing hot air out the back of the power supply.

C. It cools the computer by blowing in air from outside the case, through the power supply, and into the computer.

D. It cools the computer by pulling hot air from inside the case, through the power supply, and blowing it out the back of the power supply, which in turn draws cooler air in through vents in the case.

83. A technician needs to install a new hard drive for their client. Access speed is far more important to this client than disk space. What type of hard drive is best suited for this client?

   A. SSD

   B. HDD

   C. SD

   D. BD-R

84. What is the maximum data rate for a USB 3.0 connection?

   A. 12 Mbps

   B. 480 Mbps

   C. 5 Gbps

   D. 10 Gbps

85. A technician has been asked to install and configure a RAID-10 array in a working computer that contains one hard drive. How many additional hard drives, at a minimum, do they need to bring to the job?

   A. One

   B. Two

   C. Three

   D. Four

86. You've been tasked with making a system faster, so you implement a RAID solution that does only that. What level of RAID will you implement?

   A. RAID-0

   B. RAID-1

   C. RAID-5

   D. RAID-10

87. Which CPU architecture term describes a CPU with multiple physical processor dies in the same package?

   A. Multicore

   B. 64-bit

   C. Integrated GPU

   D. Multiprocessor

88. Which of the following optical disk standards provides the highest capacity?

   A. DVD-R SS, SL

   B. DVD-R DS, SL

   C. DVD-R SS, DL

   D. DVD-R SS, TL

89. Your company recently shipped five desktop computers from Germany to the United States. After switching the power cord to an American-style plug, you try to power one on and it doesn't work. You try the others and none of them power on either. What is the most likely cause?

    A. All of the computers were damaged during shipping.

    B. German power supplies work only with German power cords.

    C. The power supplies won't work because they expect 50 Hz frequency from the wall outlet and the United States standard is 60 Hz.

    D. The power supply voltage switch needs to be moved.

90. What are the dimensions of a mobile-ITX motherboard?

    A. 9.6″ × 9.6″

    B. 6.7″ × 6.7″

    C. 3.9″ × 2.8″

    D. 2.4″ × 2.4″

91. Which of the following printer types is an impact printer?

    A. Laser

    B. Inkjet

    C. Dot-matrix

    D. Thermal

92. Which two CPU sockets are capable of supporting Intel Core i9 processors? (Choose two.)

    A. LGA1700

    B. LGA2066

    C. Socket AM3+

    D. Socket FM2

93. You are discussing data storage needs with a client who is a videographer and media producer. They need to store dozens of large files and need immediate access to them for editing. What is the most appropriate storage technology for them to use?

    A. NAS

    B. SSD

    C. SD

    D. BD-R

94. You are searching for a new display on the Internet and find a used digital LCD for sale. What are the two most likely types of connector you will find on this display? (Choose two.)

    A. Composite

    B. DVI-D

    C. HDMI

    D. VGA

95. Which of the following are typical formats supported by virtual printing? (Choose three.)

    A. Print to PDF

    B. Print to XPS

    C. Print to DOC

    D. Print to image

96. A PCIe x1 v 3.0 lane provides how much data throughput?

    A. 250 MBps

    B. 500 MBps

    C. 1 GBps

    D. 2 GBps

97. The toner is falling off every paper that comes out of a user's laser printer. Which component, responsible for heating up and melting the toner into the paper, do you need to replace?

    A. Transfer corona assembly

    B. Pickup rollers

    C. Exit assembly

    D. Fuser assembly

98. During which step in the laser printer imaging process does a wire or roller apply a strong, uniform negative charge to the surface of the imaging drum?

    A. Charging

    B. Conditioning

    C. Exposing

    D. Transferring

99. You are installing two new RAM modules into a dual-channel motherboard. Which of the following is true?

    A. Both RAM modules need to have the same parameters.

    B. The RAM modules can be different sizes but must be the same speed.

    C. The RAM modules can be different speeds but must be the same size.

    D. The RAM modules can have different speeds and sizes, as long as they are the same type.

100. Which of the following printer components is not found in a laser printer?

    A. Fuser assembly

    B. Imaging drum

    C. Transfer roller

    D. Carriage motor

101. What type of common printer can potentially release harmful ozone into the atmosphere and therefore may contain an ozone filter?

    A. Laser

    B. Inkjet

    C. Thermal

    D. Impact

102. There are four servers in your server closet. You need to access each of them, but not at the same time. Which device will allow you to share one set of input and output devices for all four servers?

    A. Touchscreen

    B. Docking station

    C. Set-top controller

    D. KVM switch

103. A user on your network has a laser printer that is several years old with no Ethernet connection. It's connected to their computer and shared on the network for others to use. Now, the user no longer wants the printer, but others still need to use it on the network. What would be the best upgrade to install in this printer to allow others to send print jobs to it directly over the network?

    A. A network card

    B. A print server

    C. TCP/IP printing

    D. AirPrint

104. A technician needs to perform maintenance on an inkjet's dirty paper pickup rollers. What should they use to clean them?

    A. Rubbing alcohol

    B. Mild soap and water

    C. A dry, lint-free cloth

    D. Compressed air

105. During which step in the laser printer imaging process is toner attracted to the imaging drum?

    A. Exposing

    B. Transferring

    C. Fusing

    D. Developing

106. You are installing and configuring a magnetic hard drive and have several models to choose from. Which hard drive is most likely to have the highest data throughput rates?

   A. 500 GB, 7,200 rpm

   B. 750 GB, 5,400 rpm

   C. 750 GB, 10,000 rpm

   D. 1 TB, 7,200 rpm

107. Identify the white connector on the section of motherboard shown here.

   A. RAM

   B. PATA

   C. Mini-PCI

   D. ATX

108. Your manager tells you to buy a high-capacity magnetic hard drive with the highest data transfer rate possible. Which hard drive parameter do manufacturers modify to increase hard drive data transfer rates?

   A. Read/write head size

   B. Connector size

   C. Spin rate (rpm)

   D. Platter size

109. Three of these four motherboard form factors can be mounted in the same style of case. Which ones are they? (Choose three.)

   A. ATX

   B. MicroATX

   C. Mini-ITX

   D. Nano-ITX

110. Which RAM feature can detect and possibly fix errors within memory?

  A. Parity

  B. Non-parity

  C. ECC

  D. Non-ECC

111. You have a client who needs a hot-swappable, nonvolatile, long-term storage technology that lets them conveniently carry data from one location to another in their pocket. Which technologies can you recommend? (Choose two.)

  A. USB flash drive

  B. Hybrid SSD

  C. PATA

  D. SD

112. What type of expansion slots are the first, third, and fifth slots (from the top down) on the motherboard shown here?

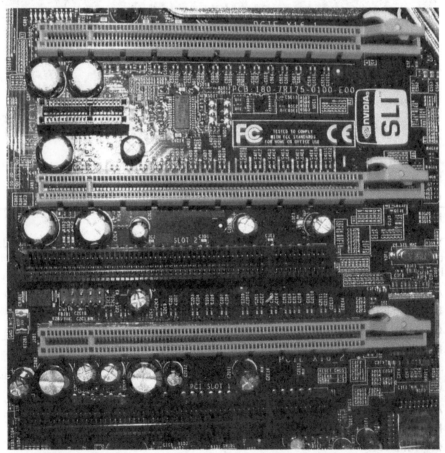

A. PCIe x1

B. PCIe x8

C. PCIe x16

D. PCI

113. You have been asked to assemble 20 new desktop PCs for a client. When you look at the first motherboard, you see four memory slots. The one closest to the CPU is colored blue. Then in order they are white, blue, and white. Which of the following statements are true? (Choose two.)

A. This is a quad-channel motherboard.

B. This is a dual-channel motherboard.

C. For optimal performance, you should install RAM modules into the two slots closest to the CPU.

D. For optimal performance, you should install RAM modules into the two blue slots.

114. You have a computer running Windows 10. Every time you boot, the computer insists on trying to boot from the USB drive. Where can you change the setting to have the system boot to the hard drive first?

A. BIOS/UEFI

B. Windows Configuration

C. System Manager

D. Device Manager

115. Which of the following types of connectors are generally found on the front or top panel of the computer? (Choose two.)

A. SATA

B. PCIe

C. Power button

D. USB

116. Your manager is excited because they just purchased a fast USB 3.2 Gen 2x2 external hard drive for their work team. They want to set it in the middle of the cubicles and let everyone have access to it. Some of the cubicles are about 15 feet away from each other. What is the recommended maximum cable length for this type of device?

A. 3 meters

B. 5 meters

C. 10 meters

D. 15 meters

117. A technician has just installed an automatic document feeder (ADF) on a laser printer. The ADF was sold by the manufacturer and is compatible with the printer. However, the printer doesn't pull the papers from the feeder. What might resolve the issue?

A. Removing and reinstalling the duplexing assembly

B. Turning the printer off and back on

C. Upgrading the printer's firmware

D. Stopping and restarting the spooler service

118. A medical office needs to make all old records available electronically. What device can they install on their printer to make scanning hundreds of documents go more quickly?

A. High-capacity paper tray

B. Flatbed scanner

C. Duplexing assembly

D. Automatic document feeder

119. You have a desktop computer with three PCI expansion slots. What will happen when you mix cards of different speeds on the same motherboard?

A. The cards will operate at their original speeds.

B. None of the cards will function.

C. The cards will all operate at the faster speed.

D. The cards will all operate at the slower speed.

120. Which of the following statements accurately explains what happens during the exposing step in the laser printer imaging process?

A. A laser reduces areas of the drum from a strong negative charge to a slight positive charge.

B. A laser reduces areas of the drum from a strong negative charge to a slight negative charge.

C. A laser increases areas of the drum from a slight negative charge to a strong negative charge.

D. A laser increases areas of the drum from a slight positive charge to a strong positive charge.

121. Which of the following is the defining characteristic of a passive heatsink cooling system for a CPU?

A. It uses water.

B. It uses heat pipes.

C. It uses liquid nitrogen or helium.

D. It does not require a fan or power.

122. Which of the following system settings are configurable in the UEFI? (Choose three.)

    A. Date and time

    B. Enabling and disabling services

    C. CPU fan speeds

    D. Power-on password

123. Which level of cache is typically the smallest and closest to the processor die in a computer?

    A. L1

    B. L2

    C. L3

    D. L4

124. Which computer component gets power from the connector shown here?

    A. Motherboard

    B. Hard drive

    C. Expansion card

    D. Secondary case fan

125. Which of the following are types of CPU sockets? (Choose two.)

    A. LGA

    B. CGA

    C. IGA

    D. PGA

126. Your office has a laser printer, and your manager asks if it can be upgraded to print on both sides of the paper. What type of device can add this functionality?

    A. Flipping assembly

    B. Dual-paper feed assembly

    C. Duplexing assembly

    D. Rear paper feed assembly

127. Which component in a laser printer is responsible for converting AC current into usable energy for the logic circuitry and motors? (Choose two.)

    A. LVPS

    B. HVPS

    C. DCPS

    D. ACPS

128. What types of RAM modules are shown here, from top to bottom?

    A. DDR3 and DDR4

    B. DDR5 and DDR3

    C. DDR4 and DDR3

    D. DDR4 and DDR5

129. The Acme company has a laser printer in its Chicago office that has been used for three months. A technician needs to ship the printer to the Detroit office for use there. What, if any, preparations should be made for the toner cartridge?

A. No preparations are needed for the toner cartridge before shipping.

B. Insert a toner blocker into the toner cartridge before shipping.

C. Seal the toner cartridge with tape before shipping.

D. Remove the toner cartridge from the printer before shipping.

130. A client wants you to upgrade their desktop computer to have two video cards. You want to be sure that this computer can support the extra adapter. What type of open internal expansion slot should you look for?

A. PCIe

B. ISA

C. VGA

D. DVI

131. Which step immediately precedes the cleaning step in the laser printer imaging process?

A. Processing

B. Transferring

C. Exposing

D. Fusing

132. Which of the following are services created by Apple to allow for the automatic discovery of printers on local networks? (Choose two.)

A. Bonjour

B. AirPrint

C. TCP printing

D. Virtual printing

133. After installing a new print cartridge in an inkjet printer, what process must be run before printing to the device?

A. Degaussing

B. Driver installation

C. Rasterizing

D. Calibration

134. Which type of printing technology might require replacing a heating element if it is no longer making images on waxy paper?

A. Laser

B. Inkjet

C. Thermal

D. 3D printer

135. You have a laser printer that is displaying the message "Perform user maintenance." What should you do to resolve this situation?

  A. Apply a maintenance kit and clear the message.

  B. Use compressed air to blow out the inside of the printer and clear the message.

  C. Turn the printer off and back on again to clear the message.

  D. Replace the toner cartridge and clear the message.

136. Identify the connectors shown here, from left to right.

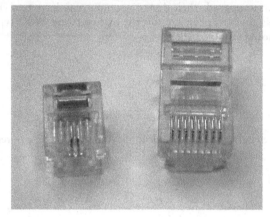

  A. ST and SC

  B. SC and ST

  C. RJ-45 and RJ-11

  D. RJ-11 and RJ-45

137. Identify the connector shown here.

  A. ST

  B. SC

  C. LC

  D. MFF

138. You need to create several UTP cables from a roll of bulk cable. Your company uses the T568B standard. What is the correct order for wires in the connectors?

    A. White/orange, orange, white/green, blue, white/blue, green, white/brown, brown

    B. White/orange, orange, white/green, green, white/blue, blue, white/brown, brown

    C. White/orange, green, white/green, blue, white/blue, orange, white/brown, brown

    D. Orange, white/orange, white/green, blue, white/blue, green, white/brown, brown

139. You are installing network cable that will support digital cable television signals. What type of cable should you install?

    A. RG-6

    B. RG-8

    C. RG-58 A/U

    D. RG-59

140. You need to replace a faulty 250-foot section of RG-6 cable, but all you have available is RG-59. Which of the following statements is true?

    A. The replacement cable will not work because the distance exceeds RG-59 specifications.

    B. The replacement cable will not work because RG-6 and RG-59 use different connectors.

    C. The replacement cable will not work because RG-6 and RG-59 have different impedance.

    D. If the replacement cable works, it won't work as well. RG-6 should be purchased.

141. You have been asked to design a new network that requires 10 Gbps transmission speeds. Which cable types will meet the minimum specifications? (Choose two.)

    A. MMF

    B. Cat 5

    C. Cat 5e

    D. Cat 6a

142. What characteristic differentiates STP from UTP?

    A. STP uses RJ-45s connectors instead of RJ-45.

    B. STP follows the T568A wiring standard.

    C. STP does not produce poisonous gas when burned.

    D. STP has a layer of foil shielding inside the cable insulation.

143. You are investigating remnants of a network setup in an unused building. At the end of a conduit, all you see are the connectors shown here. What type of cable do you expect these connectors to be attached to?

    A. Coaxial

    B. STP

    C. UTP

    D. Fiber-optic

144. Identify the connector shown here.

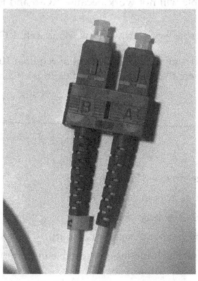

    A. ST

    B. SC

    C. LC

    D. MFF

145. While cleaning out a storage room, a technician finds several rolls of Cat 5e network cable. The technician thinks they might be able to use it to create replacement cables for their network. What is the maximum speed that this cable will support?

A. 100 Mbps

B. 1 Gbps

C. 10 Gbps

D. 20 Gbps

146. You are replacing cabling in a network. The existing cable was only capable of 100 Mbps maximum speed. What type of cable are you replacing?

A. Cat 5

B. Cat 5e

C. Cat 6a

D. Single mode

147. You are installing UTP network cable for a client. The client's policies require that network cables do not produce poisonous gas when burned. What type of cable do you need to install?

A. Plenum

B. PVC

C. STP

D. Cat 5e or higher

148. You are trying to replace a hard drive in an older system. The connector has 68 pins, along two rows. You believe from the printing on the motherboard that it is a 16-bit connection. What type of drive do you have to replace?

A. SATA

B. ATA

C. SCSI

D. NVMe

149. A technician has a tablet whose documentation says it can connect to an HDMI display. However, the tablet has a port far smaller than HDMI. What type of video connection would be typical for this small form factor device?

A. USB-C

B. RS-232

C. DB-9

D. Mini-HDMI

150. What was the connectivity port/cable end Apple used to replace the 30-pin dock connector beginning in 2012?

    A. RS-232

    B. Mini-HDMI

    C. Micro-USB

    D. Lightning

151. With what connection standard is the Apple Thunderbolt 3 cable fully compatible?

    A. USB-C

    B. Mini-HDMI

    C. Micro-USB

    D. DB9

152. Which of the following connection types can be inserted or first flipped over and inserted?

    A. DB9

    B. RS232

    C. Micro-USB

    D. USB-C

153. What serial connector type was commonly used for communication, keyboards, mice, or game controllers before USB became popular?

    A. SCSI

    B. PS/2

    C. DB9

    D. Lightning

154. Which of the following does not apply with triple channel memory?

    A. Triple the 64-bit communication path to the CPU

    B. Triple the speed with which memory is accessed

    C. Requires installation of three matched memory modules

    D. Triple the memory access latency

155. What form factor for solid-state hard drives measures 22 mm wide with lengths varying between 30 mm, 42 mm, 60 mm, and longer?

    A. NVMe

    B. SATA

    C. PCIe

    D. M.2

156. What form factor for solid-state hard drives has dimensions that mirror the older, platter-type magnetic drives?

    A. M.2

    B. mSATA

    C. 2.5″

    D. NVMe

157. You want to connect a 3.5″ external hard drive to your computer. What port is used to connect external drives to the SATA bus?

    A. NVMe

    B. eSATA

    C. M.2

    D. mSATA

158. You wish to protect your system from someone not authorized to start the OS. What is your best option?

    A. Password-protect the locked screen.

    B. Password-protect in the BIOS/UEFI settings.

    C. Encrypt the hard drive.

    D. Use a 12-character login password.

159. What is used to ensure an efficient and effective heat exchange away from the CPU?

    A. Thermal paste

    B. High-tension clamps to heat sink

    C. Dihydrogen monoxide coolant

    D. Lower CPU speeds

160. If you require more USB ports than your system can provide, what is your most cost-effective option?

    A. Install a USB expansion card.

    B. Swap peripherals for those requiring different connectors.

    C. Replace the motherboard for one with additional USB ports.

    D. Swap out peripherals as you use them.

161. What technology allows you to generate a tangible product from a computer-aided drafting application?

    A. Smartcard reader

    B. 3D printer

    C. Touchpad

    D. VR headset

162. You need to purchase RAM for a computer. Which factors determine the speed of memory you should purchase? (Choose two.)

    A. CPU speed

    B. RAM speed supported by the motherboard

    C. RAM speed supported by the processor

    D. RAM speed supported by the TPM chip

163. You installed a new motherboard because the previous one failed. Your new motherboard doesn't have a VGA display port; it has onboard HDMI. Your display only uses VGA. What is the least expensive option to resolve this dilemma?

    A. Purchase a new display.

    B. Return the motherboard and choose a different one.

    C. Purchase a video card with a VGA port on it.

    D. Purchase an HDMI-to-VGA adapter.

164. What type of printer will most likely have an extruder as one of its components?

    A. 3D printer

    B. Impact

    C. Thermal

    D. Laser

165. Your company owns a 3D printer and has asked you to order the consumable materials for it. It is an extrusion type printer that is used to make small plastic parts. What is the material called that you'll order for it?

    A. Toner

    B. Ink

    C. Filament

    D. Resin

166. You've been asked to replace some UTP network cable with other UTP cable that is capable of 10 Gbps. The longest drop is 75 meters from the network rack. What is the lowest category of cable that can meet your needs?

    A. Cat 5

    B. Cat 5e

    C. Cat 6

    D. Cat 6a

167. You need to update a twisted pair cable that runs between two networking closets. The total distance is only 20 meters, and it needs to run at 10 Gbps. What is the lowest category of cable that you can replace it with?

    A. Cat 6

    B. Cat 6a

    C. Cat 7

    D. Cat 8

168. Your friend wants to run cable for a PoE WAP in their workshop, which is about 100 feet from the network connection in their house. They're not sure how to go about it, but they know that they don't want to have wires overhead. They also want to make sure it is shielded. What type of cable can you suggest that can go that far and has superior insulation and a water blocking layer?

    A. Cat 7

    B. Direct burial STP

    C. UTP Cat 10

    D. Cat 6e

169. What are advantages of UTP over STP? (Choose two.)

    A. UTP is more flexible.

    B. UTP can run faster.

    C. UTP can be buried.

    D. UTP is less expensive.

170. What type of network cable uses pulses of light to transmit data instead of an electrical charge?

    A. STP

    B. Coaxial

    C. Plenum

    D. Fiber-optic

171. What type of data cable transmits data only one bit at a time, but very fast?

    A. Plenum

    B. Serial

    C. Parallel

    D. Ethereal

172. What type of connector is the one shown?

    A. SATA

    B. eSATA

    C. HDMI

    D. SATAe

173. What type of data cable shown here was a parallel standard for connecting multiple hard drives to the motherboard?

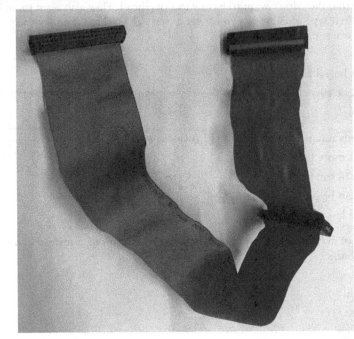

- **A.** UPS
- **B.** SATA
- **C.** IDE
- **D.** eSATA

174. You have a motherboard that has 16 RAM slots. It is a quad-channel, with four RAM slots for each channel. The slots are all black, but they are labeled A1, A2, A3, A4, B1, B2, B3, B4, and so on. To take advantage of the quad-channel feature, how will you install the RAM modules?

- **A.** Any four slots will work for quad channel.
- **B.** Install them all in the "A" slots.
- **C.** Install them in A1, B2, C3, and D4.
- **D.** Install them in A1, B1, C1, and D1.

175. You've maxed out the physical RAM on a motherboard but need more to run a particular app. The operating system will let you adjust a setting so that you can use some of the hard drive as if it were physical RAM, and the OS will swap data between RAM and the hard drive in a unit called a page. What type of memory are you using?

- **A.** Virtual
- **B.** DIMM
- **C.** SODIMM
- **D.** Cache

176. What network connectivity device is shown here?

- **A.** Hub
- **B.** Switch
- **C.** Router
- **D.** Punchdown block

177. What is the purpose of a Molex connector?
- **A.** Parallel data communications
- **B.** Serial data communications
- **C.** Power connections
- **D.** Fan connectors on the motherboard

178. You have an extruder type 3D printer. What two components of the printer are likely to move as the print job progresses? (Choose two.)
- **A.** Extruder nozzle
- **B.** Print bed
- **C.** Platform
- **D.** Resin tray

179. What are the two types of connectors shown here, left to right?

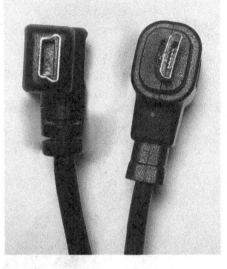

    A. MicroUSB, miniUSB

    B. MiniUSB, microUSB

    C. USB-A, USB-B

    D. USB-C, USB4

180. What type of drive is likely to be a 15,000 rpm drive?

    A. NVMe

    B. SSD

    C. Blu-ray

    D. Magnetic

181. What type of hard drives are not available in a 3.5″ form factor?

    A. SSD

    B. mSATA

    C. SATA

    D. Magnetic

182. What keys are used for M.2 slots? (Choose two.)

    A. A

    B. B

    C. E

    D. M

183. Which version of SATA ties SATA drives into the PCIe bus on the motherboard, boosting the data throughput far beyond 600 MBps?

   A. SATA 1

   B. SATA 2

   C. SATA 3.2

   D. SATA 4

184. Which of the following are AMD socket types? (Choose two.)

   A. Socket AM4

   B. LGA 1200

   C. Socket TR4

   D. LGA 2066 Socket R4

185. What connects in the motherboard socket shown here?

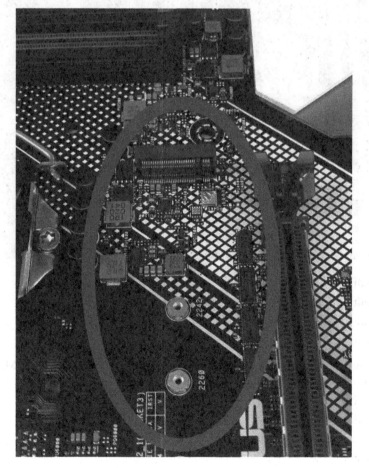

A. Network card
B. Hard drive
C. RAM
D. TPM

186. The server motherboard shown here has a processor on the right and a place for a second processor to be inserted on the left. What term describes this type of motherboard?

A. Multicore
B. Multithreaded
C. Coprocessor
D. Multisocket

187. What type of motherboard may have multiple processors and plenty of RAM, and can sometimes be found mounted in a networking rack?

A. Server
B. Workstation
C. Desktop
D. Mobile

188. Which of the following processors are you more likely to find in a server than a workstation? (Choose two.)

  A. Intel Atom

  B. Intel Xeon

  C. AMD EPYC

  D. AMD Ryzen 3

189. What type of motherboard is designed to be very compact and is generally proprietary?

  A. Server

  B. Workstation

  C. Desktop

  D. Mobile

190. Which of the following are true about ARM architecture? (Choose two.)

  A. It's licensed by ARM Holdings to many chip manufacturers.

  B. It uses Complex Instruction Set Computing (CISC).

  C. It uses Reduced Instruction Set Computing (RISC).

  D. It is only found in smartphones.

191. You work in a secure environment and it's your responsibility to ensure that no data leaves the network. You've just received a batch of new computers in. What can you do in the UEFI to help ensure users can't copy data to a USB drive?

  A. Look for a setting to disable USB ports and disable them.

  B. Put USB ports first in the boot options.

  C. Remove USB from the boot options.

  D. Look for a setting to enable USB ports and enable them.

192. What are the four motherboard connectors shown here?

    A. USB

    B. SATA

    C. EEPROM

    D. Power

193. You're building a SAN for your company. Which of the following will you most likely need to install in your server to attach the server to the SAN?

    A. NIC

    B. Modem

    C. Fibre Channel HBA

    D. WAP

194. Your friend is looking over your shoulder as you work on a computer. They ask what all the pins sticking up are. Some are labeled USB1, some USB2, and others are labeled front panel. What is the generic term for these pins on the motherboard?

    A. Ports

    B. Pins

    C. Standoffs

    D. Headers

195. What is the purpose of the connector shown here in white?

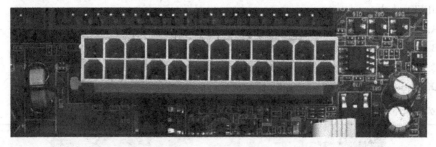

    A. PCIe

    B. ATX motherboard power

    C. ATX12V motherboard power

    D. RAID drive

196. What type of CPU is considered long obsolete?

    A. Single-core

    B. Multicore

    C. ARM

    D. Intel

197. You need a PC solution that is capable of accepting video footage from a gaming console or video camera and saving it in a file. You also want to ensure that it won't skip, lag, or freeze. Which of the following would be the best solution?

  A. Webcam

  B. FireWire card

  C. Capture card

  D. Screen-capture software

198. A business has a PC that a user needs to work with in a room that is not air-conditioned, but the computer keeps shutting down because the processor is overheating. You've checked the cooler and thermal paste and it's fine. What can you do in this PC to help it run cool enough?

  A. Add case fans.

  B. Add heat monitoring software.

  C. Remove the chassis cover.

  D. Set it inside a refrigerator.

199. You are replacing the power supply in a computer system that uses a 24-pin P1 connector. You have a few power supplies in the closet to choose from. Which one with the following connections will work? (Choose two.)

  A. 20-pin P1 connector and P4 connector

  B. 20-pin+4-pin P1 connector

  C. An ATX12V PSU

  D. An ATX12VO power supply

200. You're considering a power supply that has interchangeable cables that plug into and out of the power supply so that you can have exactly the connectors you need and not have extra cables taking up space in the case. What type of power supply is this?

  A. ATX

  B. ATX12V

  C. Molex

  D. Modular

201. You're setting up a server that can't possibly have downtime. Which of the items below do you need to make sure you have connected to it?

  A. HBA

  B. Redundant power supply

  C. Display

  D. Dual rail power supply

202. Your new tech is unboxing a new printer and you see them open the top and flip the box upside-down, then pull the box off the printer. What will you say? (Choose two.)

    A. Great job, that's exactly how I would do it.

    B. That's not the right way to unbox a printer.

    C. It's better to lay the box on its side and pull the materials out.

    D. Please use a box cutter next time to cut the corners from top to bottom.

203. You just purchased a network-enabled multifunction device. Which one of the following connection types are likely not built into it?

    A. Bluetooth

    B. Wi-Fi

    C. Ethernet

    D. RFID

204. You have a client that wants to use carbonless, multipart forms with their new printer. What type of printer will you recommend for them?

    A. Laser

    B. Inkjet

    C. Impact

    D. Thermal

205. The administrative assistant at your company needs to be able to choose between printing on letterhead or plain paper for each print job. You're training them how to do this. What settings will you be showing them?

    A. Orientation

    B. Duplexing

    C. Quality

    D. Tray settings

206. Which types of printers require calibration as a part of maintenance? (Choose two.)

    A. Laser

    B. Thermal

    C. Impact

    D. Inkjet

207. What printer feature will store documents on the printer and not print them until the user enters a password or scans an ID card on the print device?

    A. Secured prints

    B. Snap prints

    C. User authentication

    D. Auditing

208. What type of connectivity device is used to terminate network runs in a telecommunications closet?

   A. Punchdown block

   B. Switch

   C. Router

   D. Terminator

209. What two consumable materials are used by 3D printers? (Choose two.)

   A. Resin

   B. Paper

   C. Filament

   D. Extruder nozzle

210. What are three communication interfaces that are used by SSDs to send data across a motherboard? (Choose three.)

   A. NVMe

   B. SATA

   C. PCIe

   D. IDE

211. What is the (approximate) maximum theoretical bandwidth of a PCIe x16 slot, version 5.0?

   A. 500 MBps

   B. 1,000 MBps

   C. 64 GBps

   D. 128 GBps

Chapter

4

Virtualization and Cloud Computing

THE COMPTIA A+ 220-1101 TOPICS COVERED IN THIS CHAPTER INCLUDE THE FOLLOWING:

✓ **4.1 Summarize cloud-computing concepts.**

- Common Cloud Models
  - Private cloud
  - Public cloud
  - Hybrid cloud
  - Community cloud
  - Infrastructure as a service (IaaS)
  - Software as a service (SaaS)
  - Platform as a service (PaaS)
- Cloud Characteristics
  - Shared resources
  - Metered utilization
  - Rapid elasticity
  - High availability
  - File synchronization
- Desktop virtualization
  - Virtual desktop infrastructure (VDI) on premises
  - VDI in the cloud

✓ **4.2 Summarize aspects of client-side virtualization.**

- Purpose of virtual machines
  - Sandbox
  - Test development

- Application virtualization
- Legacy software/OS
- Cross-platform virtualization
- Resource Requirements
- Security Requirements

1. What type of cloud service offers the best security?

    A. Community

    B. Private

    C. Public

    D. Hybrid

2. Your manager tells you to purchase cloud-based services. Your network needs extra processing power and file storage. What type of service should you purchase?

    A. PaaS

    B. IaaS

    C. SaaS

    D. FWaaS

3. Your company has decided to purchase cloud services from Google. They will be getting infrastructure with on-demand computing services including processing power, storage and bandwidth over the Internet. Anyone can purchase these same services from Google, and a third party is responsible for maintaining and managing the hardware. What type of cloud is Google providing for your company?

    A. Public

    B. Private

    C. Hybrid

    D. Community

4. Your company produces software and employs about 20 developers. They need to program apps for different operating systems. You decide to purchase cloud-based services to support the development team. What type of service should you purchase so that they can develop their programs and then test them in environments other than where they were developed?

    A. IaaS

    B. SaaS

    C. PaaS

    D. NaaS

5. Which type of cloud service provides your company with application hosting such as productivity applications, calendaring software, and development tools, that the employees can access over the Internet from wherever they are?

    A. PaaS

    B. FWaaS

    C. IaaS

    D. SaaS

6. Which feature of cloud service allows you to instantly obtain additional storage space or processing power as your company needs it?

   A. Ubiquitous access

   B. Rapid elasticity

   C. Resource pooling

   D. Measured service

7. You are installing virtualization on a workstation that needs to support multiple operating systems. Which type of hypervisor is best suited for this environment?

   A. Type 1.

   B. Type 2.

   C. Either Type 1 or Type 2 will function in the same way.

   D. Virtual machine manager.

8. You are configuring client-side virtualization on an existing Windows 10 64-bit workstation. You will be running a second installation of Windows 10 64-bit in the virtual environment as a test system. The bare minimum RAM required for each OS is 2 GB. Each Windows installation needs 20 GB of disk space. What are the absolute minimum hardware requirements for this workstation?

   A. 4 GB of RAM, 40 GB of disk space

   B. 2 GB of RAM, 20 GB of disk space

   C. 2 GB of RAM, 40 GB of disk space

   D. 4 GB of RAM, 20 GB of disk space

9. You are setting up virtualization on a server that will be running four instances of Windows Server 2019. Four different departments will be using one instance each, and all departments have been promised 32 GB of RAM. Using resource pooling and using a bare-metal hypervisor, what is the minimum amount of physical RAM needed on the server?

   A. 32 GB

   B. 64 GB

   C. 128 GB

   D. 16 GB

10. Your company has an application developer who creates programs for Windows, Linux, and macOS. What is the most cost-effective solution for them to be able to test their programs in multiple operating systems as quickly as possible?

   A. Buy workstations for each of the OSs they will be writing code in.

   B. Set up their workstation to dual-boot.

   C. Set up their workstation with virtual machines.

   D. Create one version of each application that will run in all three OSs.

11. Your company wants to begin transferring particular services to the cloud, but the team cannot yet decide on the migration schedule. Management wants to pay for cloud computing based on usage, not a fixed flat fee. What payment model would you recommend?

A. On-demand

B. Resource pool

C. Metered utilization

D. Shared resources

12. A client complains about the occupied space, abundant power usage, and hardware costs of the multiple machines used in its small data center. Still, the client does not wish to lose control over any of the machines. What might you recommend to the client to resolve all of those issues?

A. Establish clusters for high availability.

B. Create virtual machines.

C. Outsource to an IaaS provider.

D. Shut down the nonessential machines.

13. Which term describes physical and virtual servers, storage, and software that are used by multiple clients in a cloud computing environment?

A. Measured resources

B. Shared resources

C. Private cloud

D. Community cloud

14. What are potential problems associated with the shared resource structure of public cloud computing? (Choose two.)

A. Security and confidentiality

B. Flexibility

C. Poor application performance

D. Increased hardware costs

15. Network control and security management of cloud assets is the difference between what two types of shared resources?

A. Internal vs. external

B. Private vs. public

C. Hybrid vs. community

D. Synchronized vs. unsynchronized

16. A company using cloud services wishes to better prepare for surges for what it needs. What sort of capacity provisioning by its cloud provider should the company ask for?

A. Rapid metering

B. Infrastructure as a service

C. Metered utilization

D. Resource pooling

17. You're setting up a virtual machine for one of your customers who needs a legacy OS to run software for a paper-cutting machine in an envelope factory. Windows 10 64-bit is the host OS. The legacy client OS requires a minimum 1 GB of RAM and the software running on it requires a minimum of 2 GB of RAM. What is the absolute minimum RAM needed on the virtual machine?

    A. 1 GB

    B. 4 GB

    C. 5 GB

    D. 10 GB

18. The company's sales manager wants to ensure that the laptop files of its traveling sales engineers stay consistent with the files on the company cloud. What sort of applications could assist with that business need?

    A. File security monitoring

    B. File virtualization

    C. File emulator

    D. File synchronization

19. What service allows a user to access a virtual OS either in the cloud using a browser or client on their local devices or from a local virtualization server?

    A. On-demand desktop (ODD)

    B. Binary application desktop (BAD)

    C. Virtual desktop infrastructure (VDI)

    D. Desktop streaming (DTI)

20. An employee travels between multiple offices, using a desktop system in each office. What technology would ensure that the employee's desktop icons, files, and applications stay uniform across systems in all the offices?

    A. On-demand desktop

    B. VDI in the cloud

    C. Desktop emulation

    D. Synchronized folders

21. When running a hypervisor, what enables a guest machine to connect to a network?

    A. Cat 5 network cable

    B. Guest applications

    C. Virtual NIC

    D. Host operating system

22. How can an organization permit employees who need to run an application on one mobile device to instead run it from multiple devices?

  A. Application virtualization

  B. Wrapping

  C. Binary application desktop

  D. On-demand desktop

23. In setting up and configuring client-side virtualization, what is necessary to consider before purchasing computing and storage hardware?

  A. Resource requirements

  B. Management response

  C. Resale value

  D. Physical size

24. What must be defined when wanting to maintain confidentiality, integrity, and availability of the system resources, and should be a part of the decision when choosing a cloud solution?

  A. Scalability

  B. Emulation

  C. Elasticity

  D. Security requirements

25. In setting up and configuring client-side virtualization, what is necessary to consider before configuring a VLAN?

  A. Network requirements

  B. Emulation demands

  C. Cloud service providers

  D. Storage capacity

26. When considering how efficiently a hypervisor runs, which of the following is best when it is minimized?

  A. Storage

  B. Emulator requirements

  C. Memory

  D. Scalability

27. Which of the following is not considered to be a major category of cloud computing?

  A. SaaS

  B. PaaS

  C. IaaS

  D. XaaS

28. Which of the cloud computing models combines on premises infrastructure and Internet accessed resources?

    A. Private cloud

    B. Public cloud

    C. Hybrid cloud

    D. Combined cloud

29. With today's more mobile workforce, what technology provides the benefits of centralized security, ease of configuring new desktops for remote workers, and scalability regardless of where a user is or works from? (Choose the best answer.)

    A. IaaS

    B. SaaS

    C. VDI in the cloud

    D. VDI on premises

30. A group of real estate agents has realized that they have similar computing resource needs. They've reached out collectively to your IT services company and asked if there is a solution that will let them pool their resources and save money, possibly sharing industry-specific software, but still have their servers and information held securely and locally. What will you recommend?

    A. Community cloud

    B. Public cloud

    C. Private cloud

    D. VDI in the cloud

31. Which of these terms is a benefit of cloud computing that means the information is available constantly, regardless of location?

    A. Shared resources

    B. High availability

    C. Rapid elasticity

    D. File synchronization

32. A graphic artist at your company needs to manipulate files in both Linux and Windows environments. You, as the IT support person, want as few physical machines to support as possible. What technology allows both OSs to run on a single machine?

    A. File sharing.

    B. Cross-platform virtualization.

    C. Dual-boot system.

    D. It can't be done.

33. You've received a file from a salesperson who recently separated from your company. You want to open this file and see what it contains without subjecting your computer to possible malicious content. What Windows 10 Pro feature can you turn on that will create a protected environment for opening this file?

A. Shared Files

B. System Information

C. Sandbox

D. File Manager

34. Your friend is a software developer. They have Windows 10 Pro installed on their SOHO computer. They are creating an application that needs to run smoothly on both Windows and Linux machines, so it will need to be tested in both of those environments. What would be the best solution for your friend?

A. Windows 10 sandbox

B. Dual-boot system

C. Two separate machines

D. Virtual machines on their PC

35. A manufacturing client has a piece of equipment that is running on a Windows 7 OS. The equipment-specific software won't run on any other OS, and the client is concerned about what they will do when the Windows 7 computer inevitably crashes. Cost is always a concern. What is a viable, cost-effective solution for your client?

A. Have the programmers rewrite the code to run on Windows 10.

B. Migrate the software to a Windows 7 VM running on a Windows 10 host.

C. Wait until the hardware crashes, then shut the equipment down permanently.

D. Tell the client they need to upgrade their manufacturing equipment to something more modern as soon as possible.

36. Why would a company prefer to run multiple applications each on its own VM rather than on a single server?

A. Security

B. Scalability

C. Less maintenance

D. Less cost

37. Which of the following would essentially be the same whether running an OS on a virtual server or a physical server? (Choose two.)

A. Security configuration

B. Hardware

C. Licensing

D. Portability

38. Which cloud model offers the greatest control over data and security?

    A. Private cloud

    B. Public cloud

    C. Hybrid cloud

    D. Community cloud

39. You are a manager in a call center that employs 300 people who may be working any of three shifts on any given day, taking whichever of your 100 seats is available. Company regulations require that all information remain hosted locally. What technology can you use so that their files, folders, and desktop icons all appear the same regardless of which computer they log on to?

    A. On-demand desktop

    B. VDI in the cloud

    C. Desktop emulation

    D. VDI on premises

40. Which of these is not an advantage of cloud computing?

    A. Reduced capital expenditures

    B. Frees IT employees time for other needs

    C. Complete control over data

    D. Rapid elasticity (dynamic growth)

Hardware and Network Troubleshooting

THE COMPTIA A+ 220-1101 TOPICS COVERED IN THIS CHAPTER INCLUDE THE FOLLOWING:

✓ **5.1 Given a scenario, apply the best practice methodology to resolve problems.**

- Always consider corporate policies, procedures, and impacts before implementing changes

  - 1. Identify the problem

    - Gather information from the user, identify user changes, and, if applicable, perform backups before making changes

    - Inquire regarding environmental or infrastructure changes

  - 2. Establish a theory of probable cause (question the obvious)

    - If necessary, conduct external or internal research based on symptoms

  - 3. Test the theory to determine the cause

    - Once the theory is confirmed, determine the next steps to resolve the problem

    - If the theory is not confirmed, re-establish a new theory or escalate

  - 4. Establish a plan of action to resolve the problem and implement the solution

    - Refer to the vendor's instructions for guidance

- 5. Verify full system functionality and, if applicable, implement preventive measures
- 6. Document the findings, actions, and outcomes

✓ **5.2 Given a scenario, troubleshoot problems related to motherboards, RAM, CPU, and power.**

- Common symptoms
  - Power-on self-test (POST) beeps
  - Proprietary crash screens (blue screen of death [BSOD]/pinwheel)
  - Black screen
  - No power
  - Sluggish performance
  - Overheating
  - Burning smell
  - Intermittent shutdown
  - Application crashes
  - Grinding noise
  - Capacitor swelling
  - Inaccurate system date/time

✓ **5.3 Given a scenario, troubleshoot and diagnose problems with storage drives and RAID arrays.**

- Common symptoms
  - Light-emitting diode (LED) status indicators
  - Grinding noises
  - Clicking sounds
  - Bootable device not found
  - Data loss/corruption
  - RAID failure
  - Self-monitoring, Analysis, and Reporting Technology (S.M.A.R.T.) failure
  - Extended read/write times
  - Input/output operations per second (IOPS)
  - Missing drives in OS

✓ **5.4 Given a scenario, troubleshoot video, projector, and display issues.**

- Common symptoms
    - Incorrect data source
    - Physical cabling issues
    - Burned-out bulb
    - Fuzzy image
    - Display burn-in
    - Dead pixels
    - Flashing screen
    - Incorrect color display
    - Audio issues
    - Dim image
    - Intermittent projector shutdown

✓ **5.5 Given a scenario, troubleshoot common issues with mobile devices.**

- Common symptoms
    - Poor battery health
    - Swollen battery
    - Broken screen
    - Improper charging
    - Poor/no connectivity
    - Liquid damage
    - Overheating
    - Digitizer issues
    - Physically damaged ports
    - Malware
    - Cursor drift/touch calibration

✓ **5.6 Given a scenario, troubleshoot and resolve printer issues.**

- Common symptoms
    - Lines down the printed pages

- Garbled print
- Toner not fusing to paper
- Paper jams
- Faded print
- Incorrect paper size
- Paper not feeding
- Multipage misfeed
- Multiple prints pending in queue
- Speckling on printed pages
- Double/echo images on the print
- Incorrect chroma display
- Grinding noise
- Finishing issues
  - Staple jams
  - Hole punch
- Incorrect page orientation

✓ **5.7 Given a scenario, troubleshoot problems with wired and wireless networks.**

- Common symptoms
  - Intermittent wireless connectivity
  - Slow network speeds
  - Limited connectivity
  - Jitter
  - Poor Voice over Internet Protocol (VoIP) quality
  - Port flapping
  - High latency
  - External interference

1. You are an avid fan of Twitch, the streaming application where you entertain yourself as you watch other people play games. Twitch works well at your house and at your friend's house. However, when you visit the website at work, the website looks fine, but you can't watch anyone play games. You've tried this on both your phone and your laptop. Which of the following should you suspect as the reason?

    A. Your immediate supervisor

    B. Your company's Wi-Fi connection bandwidth

    C. Your company data retention policy

    D. Your company firewall

2. A user approaches you and asks for a CPU upgrade so their Lenovo laptop will run faster. What is most likely the easiest way to meet this user's needs?

    A. Remove the CPU and replace it with a faster one that fits the same socket.

    B. Replace the laptop with one that has a faster CPU.

    C. Replace the motherboard with a generic laptop motherboard with a faster processor.

    D. Replace the motherboard with a Lenovo laptop motherboard with a faster processor.

3. You are using a USB flash drive to transfer files from a laptop. You plug the USB drive in and then copy the files to it. What is the recommended way to remove the drive?

    A. Unplug the drive.

    B. Use the Safely Remove Hardware icon in the system tray, stop the drive, and then unplug it.

    C. Close the drive's window in File Explorer and unplug it.

    D. Use the Shut Down Hardware icon in the system tray, stop the drive, and then unplug it.

4. You have decided to start playing video-intensive games on your laptop computer. The video appears jumpy and slow to respond. What should you do first to try to increase the performance during game play?

    A. Upgrade the video card.

    B. Install additional video memory.

    C. Use Windows Control Panel to increase the amount of video memory available.

    D. Use the system BIOS/UEFI to increase the amount of video memory available.

5. A guest presenter plugs an external projector into their laptop using the HDMI port on the back of the laptop. They then use the Fn key and video toggle switch; the projector displays the presentation, but the laptop screen goes dark. What should they do if they want to see the presentation on both the projector and the laptop?

    A. Install a second video driver and then use the video toggle key to switch the video output to both screens.

    B. Unplug the projector and plug it back in to synchronize it with the laptop.

    C. Unplug the projector, use the video toggle key to switch the video output, and then plug the projector back in.

    D. Press the video toggle key again until the presentation is shown on both screens.

6. A user has a laptop that is intermittently locking up. Initial diagnostics indicate that the processor is overheating. What can you do to try to remediate the issue? (Choose two.)

   A. Leave the case open while the system is running to allow for better airflow and cooling.

   B. Lower the CPU voltage in the system BIOS/UEFI.

   C. Lower the CPU clock speed in the system BIOS/UEFI.

   D. Run the laptop on AC power instead of battery power.

7. A client has a laptop with an integrated video card. The system seems to boot but produces no video, even with an external display hooked up. What can you do to fix this?

   A. Add an external USB video card and connect the display to it.

   B. Remove the existing video card, and replace it with a new internal video card.

   C. Replace the motherboard.

   D. Leave the existing card in the system, and add an internal Mini PCIe video card.

8. A user has brought their laptop to you because the screen is intermittently flickering. Which display component is most likely causing this?

   A. Backlight

   B. LCD

   C. Screen

   D. Inverter

9. An administrator ordered replacement printer paper that is a thicker caliper than recommended by the printer manufacturer. What is the biggest risk in using this paper?

   A. Images will not print.

   B. Paper will not feed.

   C. Paper will jam.

   D. Images will not print.

10. You have an OLED display that you just plugged into a desktop computer. One of your coworkers changes the resolution from 1920×1080 to 1920×1200, but then the image looks highly distorted. What is the most likely cause of this?

    A. The video driver does not support 1920×1200 resolution.

    B. The display has a native resolution of 1920×1080.

    C. The video adapter has a native resolution of 1920×1080.

    D. The monitor is plugged into the wrong display interface to support the new resolution.

11. A user has a display that flashes a black screen every few seconds. What is likely set incorrectly and causing the problem?

    A. Refresh rate

    B. Frame rate

    C. Native resolution

    D. Aspect ratio

12. A friend who plays video games has asked you how they can fix tearing on their display. What will you tell them?

    A. They need a new display.

    B. The refresh rate is set too low.

    C. The screen's refresh rate is set too high.

    D. It's a software defect.

13. What is the name of the boot routine that verifies the size and integrity of the system memory, among other tasks?

    A. RAMCheck

    B. BIOS

    C. UEFI

    D. POST

14. You upgraded the RAM on your system and are now having boot issues. The manufacturer's website recommends updating the BIOS. What is the easiest way to do this?

    A. Replace the BIOS chip.

    B. Replace the CMOS battery.

    C. Install a new motherboard.

    D. Flash the BIOS.

15. You moved a projector from an old conference room to a new one. The projector was working fine in the other room, but the image seems dim in the new room. Before you purchase a new projector, which of the following should you try?

    A. Increase the frame rate.

    B. Lower the native resolution.

    C. Adjust the aspect ratio.

    D. Turn the brightness up.

16. Your friend has just finished building a computer. After installing the operating system, all seems fine except that they found that flash drives placed in the USB ports on the top of the case do not get noticed by the OS. Where do you suspect the problem is?

    A. Device drivers outdated

    B. USB settings misconfigured

    C. Motherboard's internal USB connector disconnected

    D. System clock

17. You are troubleshooting a Mac running macOS. Intermittently, the computer will completely lock up and display a rotating pinwheel instead of the mouse cursor. It happens when different applications are running. What is most likely causing this problem?

    A. CPU

    B. RAM

    C. Motherboard

    D. Faulty application

18. You're at a friend's house when you notice a burning smell from their computer. What is the first thing you should do?

    A. Grab a fire extinguisher.

    B. Unplug the computer.

    C. Call the fire department.

    D. Tell your friend to get a new computer.

19. You are troubleshooting a desktop computer that is prone to unexpected shutdowns. They seem to happen randomly, sometimes shortly after the computer starts, other times after several minutes. The user reports that no error messages appear before the computer shuts down. Which two things are most likely to cause this type of problem? (Choose two.)

    A. Failing hard drive

    B. Bad RAM

    C. BIOS/UEFI misconfiguration

    D. Improperly seated chips

20. You're troubleshooting a computer that the user says shuts down after 10 minutes, every time they start the computer. If they wait a few minutes and restart it, the same thing happens. What is most likely the problem?

    A. RAM

    B. Hard drive

    C. Processor

    D. Motherboard

21. A user calls the IT help desk in a panic because they have a BSOD on the screen. You ask them if there is a specific error message displayed, and if they have installed any hardware or software lately. They haven't. What would be a good first step to resolve the BSOD?

    A. Try rebooting the system; Windows will try to fix it.

    B. Refresh the operating system.

    C. Reinstall the operating system.

    D. Restore to a previous version.

22. You have just replaced faulty RAM in a desktop computer. You reboot the computer, and after a few seconds it beeps once. What does this indicate?

    A. The RAM is faulty.

    B. The motherboard needs to be replaced.

    C. The system BIOS detected an error in the POST routine.

    D. The system BIOS completed the POST routine normally.

23. You are troubleshooting a computer that will not boot. It tells you that there is no bootable device. You check the BIOS, and it does not show any installed hard drives. What should you do next?

   A. Run `bootrec /fixmbr`.

   B. Replace the hard drive with an external drive.

   C. Flash the BIOS.

   D. Check the hard drive connections.

24. A technician just replaced a failed internal hard drive in a desktop computer with an empty hard drive. They need to boot to the network to connect to an imaging server to restore the computer. How should they do this?

   A. During boot, press the F2 key to boot to the network.

   B. During boot, enter the BIOS/UEFI and change the boot sequence to boot to the network.

   C. Let the boot complete normally. When the UEFI does not find a bootable partition on the hard drive, it will boot from the network.

   D. During boot, press the F7 key to edit the boot sequence menu.

25. A user's laptop computer does not show anything on the screen, although the power light and other indicator lights are on. You plug in an external display and it does not show an image either. Which component is most likely causing the problem?

   A. Inverter

   B. Backlight

   C. Screen

   D. Integrated video

26. You are troubleshooting a computer making a loud whining noise. Looking at the exhaust fan, you see a thick coating of dust. What should you do next?

   A. Use compressed air to clean the fan.

   B. Use a computer vacuum to clean the fan.

   C. Use a damp cloth to clean the fan.

   D. Replace the power supply.

27. A user reports that their laptop battery does not charge when the laptop is plugged into an AC outlet. What is the best resolution to try first?

   A. Replace the battery.

   B. Replace the AC adapter.

   C. Remove and reinsert the battery.

   D. Drain the battery completely and then recharge it.

28. A technician has determined that they need to replace a motherboard in a laptop. Which of the following procedures should be followed? (Choose two.)

   A. Never use a power screwdriver with a laptop.

   B. Document and label screw locations.

   C. Refer to the manufacturer's instructions.

   D. Remove the keyboard before removing the motherboard.

29. You are troubleshooting a computer that has been randomly rebooting, and now it refuses to boot properly. Upon boot, you receive one long beep and three short beeps but no video on the screen. What tool should you use to troubleshoot the situation?

   A. Multimeter

   B. Power supply tester

   C. Loopback plug

   D. POST card

30. You are troubleshooting a computer that has been randomly rebooting, and now it refuses to boot properly. Upon boot, you receive one long beep and three short beeps but no video on the screen. You don't have a POST diagnostic card that will work with this motherboard. What tool should you use to troubleshoot the situation?

   A. Motherboard documentation

   B. Power supply tester

   C. Loopback plug

   D. Multimeter

31. Over time, the hard drive performance of your computer has gotten slower. A quick check of Performance Monitor shows that your disk read/writes are taking more time as compared to the baseline. What should you do to resolve this issue?

   A. Run Optimize and defragment the drive.

   B. Format the hard drive and restore the data.

   C. Delete the partition, create a new one, and restore the data.

   D. Run chkdsk.

32. A user's computer has failed. When you try to boot it up, you hear a loud, rhythmic clicking sound, and the system does not boot properly. What is most likely the issue?

   A. HDD failure

   B. SSD failure

   C. RAM failure

   D. Power supply fan failure

33. A laser printer you are working with consistently produces images with white streaks running down the page. What can you do first to resolve this issue?

   A. Clean the transfer corona wires.

   B. Clean the EP drum.

   C. Clean the fusing assembly.

   D. Gently shake or replace the toner cartridge.

34. The laser printer in your office recently started creasing papers and producing paper jams. Which of the following are likely to cause these problems? (Choose three.)

   A. Bits of paper in the paper path

   B. Paper tension settings

   C. Using the wrong paper

   D. Damaged rollers

35. You power on a desktop computer, and you hear the fan spinning. However, you do not see any indicator lights or get a POST beep. Which component is likely causing the problem?

   A. CPU

   B. RAM

   C. PSU

   D. HDD

36. Your computer is making an intermittent grinding noise. What component is most likely failing?

   A. Magnetic hard drive

   B. Solid state drive

   C. Processor fan

   D. RAM

37. You just replaced the toner cartridge on the laser printer in your office. Now you're getting an error message displayed on the screen. What should you try first?

   A. Call the printer company's tech support.

   B. Remove and reinsert the toner cartridge.

   C. Install a maintenance kit.

   D. Replace the printer.

38. Your office uses an inkjet printer. Recently, it started having problems picking up paper. Which component is likely to cause this problem?

   A. Transport rollers

   B. Pickup rollers

   C. Corona wire

   D. Transmission rollers

39. Your office uses an impact printer and multipart carbonless forms. The office manager noticed that the bottom copies of the forms are readable, but the top copy is too light to read. What needs to be replaced?

    A.   Toner cartridge

    B.   Printhead

    C.   Ink ribbon

    D.   Ribbon advance motor

40. Your network uses 802.11ac for all client computers. Recently, several users moved from one office space to another, increasing the users in the area from 20 to about 50. Now, both new and old users are reporting very slow network transfer speeds. What is most likely the cause of the problem?

    A.   802.11ac can't support that many concurrent users.

    B.   It's too far from the wireless access point.

    C.   There are too many users for one wireless access point.

    D.   The new users all have 802.11n network cards.

41. You have installed an 802.11ac wireless access point for a company. To cut costs, the company wanted only one central access point in the building, which is about 150 feet long. Users at both ends of the building report intermittent wireless connectivity drops and slow access. What is most likely the cause of the problem?

    A.   Low RF signal

    B.   Oversaturated WAP

    C.   SSID not found

    D.   IP address conflicts

42. A customer complains that although they installed a 10 Gb Ethernet card in their server and their cable supports 10 Gbps, the network connection is still running at 1 Gbps. What is most likely the problem?

    A.   Debris in the PCIe slot

    B.   Faulty network cable

    C.   Slower switch

    D.   Slower PC

43. You get a call from the accounting department that their printer is printing something very strange. There are unexpected characters and text is missing. Which of the following are likely culprits? (Choose two.)

    A.   Loose or defective printer cable

    B.   Overheating

    C.   Wrong language keyboard

    D.   Incorrect or corrupted printer driver

44. You're having lunch with a friend. They are charging their phone and you notice that the phone is swelling. What action should be taken first?

  A. Nothing, it's fine.

  B. Disconnect the power, and turn it off.

  C. Turn it off, and remove the battery if possible.

  D. Replace the battery.

45. You have a laptop that the user says won't charge up since they dropped it on the floor while it was plugged in. It hit on the side with the charger, but it was running fine until the battery ran out. What might be the most expedient solution?

  A. Replace the motherboard.

  B. Replace the power connector.

  C. Solder the power jack back onto the motherboard.

  D. Solder the power cord to the motherboard.

46. A user complains that their laptop charges only when they wiggle the connector and get it at a certain angle. What will you most likely need to do?

  A. Solder the port back into place.

  B. Replace the port.

  C. Replace the charger.

  D. This can't be fixed.

47. Lately your friend's phone hasn't been charging very well from the wall outlet. It charges very slowly, if at all. Once it's charged it seems to work OK, but when they connect it to their laptop, the laptop doesn't recognize the phone. What will you try first to remedy the situation?

  A. Check for debris in the charging port.

  B. Spray a port cleaning solution into the phone.

  C. Replace the phone battery.

  D. Replace the charger block and cord.

48. Your phone is not charging properly. When you look inside the port you can see corrosion on the connectors. What should you do?

  A. Replace the phone.

  B. Replace the port.

  C. Use lint-free swabs with a small amount of isopropyl alcohol to gently clean the connection.

  D. Use a toothbrush dampened with isopropyl alcohol to brush the connector clean.

49. The laser printer in your office recently started producing images that are not completely set. When the images come out, people are smudging them as they pick them up. What is causing this problem?

    A. Fusing assembly

    B. Exit rollers

    C. Drying assembly

    D. Charging corona

50. Guests in the lobby of your office are complaining that the wireless connection is often dropped and seems to be very slow (high latency). The company president wants their visitors to be happy, so they've asked you to take care of the situation. You analyze the wireless signal strength in the lobby, and it is very weak compared to the rest of the building. What are the two best solutions? (Choose two.)

    A. Install wired connections in the lobby for visitors.

    B. Install a WAP in the lobby.

    C. Buy a faster WAP.

    D. Install a wireless range extender.

51. A technician is troubleshooting a computer configured for wired network connection that can't connect to the network. They verified that the cable is plugged in, but there are no lights lit on the network card. The computer could connect yesterday, and no other users report an issue. Which of the following are most likely to be causing this problem? (Choose two.)

    A. Faulty network cable.

    B. Faulty network card driver.

    C. Incorrect TCP/IP configuration.

    D. The cable is unplugged at the other end.

52. You are troubleshooting network connectivity issues in one section of the building. After a few hours, you come to the conclusion that the network cables in the wiring closet must be mislabeled. Which tool is most appropriate to test your theory?

    A. Multimeter

    B. Cable tester

    C. Punchdown tool

    D. Tone generator and probe

53. You have just installed a new HP LaserJet printer on your network. You've plugged it directly into a Cat 6a network cable. You try to install the printer on a client using the printer's IP address, but you are unable to connect. The printer is in Ready state. What should you do next?

    A. Double-check the printer's IP configuration information.

    B. Stop and restart the spooler service.

    C. Take the printer offline and bring it back online.

    D. Turn the printer off and back on to save the IP configuration information.

54. Your network has recently grown from 50 client computers to about 90. All workstations on the network are connected using Cat 6 or better cabling, and all network devices support at least 1 Gbps data transfers. Users have been reporting very slow network speeds since the expansion, and complaints are now coming more frequently. Which of the following actions is most likely to help resolve the issue?

    A. Add another hub to the network.

    B. Upgrade all the cabling to Cat 8.

    C. Upgrade the existing router to support 10 Gbps data transfers.

    D. Add another switch to the network.

55. Your junior IT administrator has identified a port on your Cisco switch that is changing between up and down repeatedly. What have they observed?

    A. Port flapping

    B. Port toggling

    C. Port flashing

    D. Port flagging

56. Users have been complaining that a network resource has intermittent connectivity. You've identified the problem; the switch port is flapping. The connected device is not EEE compliant, and users need it to be available. What should you do?

    A. Configure link flap prevention settings.

    B. Replace the offending device.

    C. Disable EEE on the switch.

    D. Disable EEE on the device.

57. A user calls you about a printer not working. The user is standing next to the printer while you are in the next building. What can the user do to be helpful in your diagnosing the problem?

    A. Turn the printer off and on.

    B. Read the printer error code.

    C. Remove the jammed paper.

    D. Check the network link light.

58. A user calls to report that they can't access the Internet or a corporate server. However, they are still able to print to a printer nearby. They have not received any error messages. Other users in the area are also unable to access the Internet. What is most likely the problem?

    A. IP address conflict

    B. Default gateway down

    C. Incorrect subnet mask

    D. Network card failure

59. A workstation is sending print jobs directly to a printer that has a stapler as a finishing option. When they retrieve the print job, the document is not stapled. Which of the following could be the problem? (Choose three.)

    A. The stapler is empty.

    B. The staples are in backward.

    C. A different printer driver is needed.

    D. The stapler is not enabled.

60. A message has appeared on the office copier/printer that says "Stapler Jam." Which of the following are true? (Choose three.)

    A. The jam must be cleared before anything else is printed.

    B. Print jobs not involving the stapler may still work.

    C. This can be caused by trying to staple too many pages.

    D. The manufacturer documentation should be consulted for procedures to follow.

61. You set your phone in a cubby on the dashboard of your car while you're driving. It's a cold winter day in upstate New York, so you have the car's heat on fully. When you get to your destination and grab your phone, you discover that it has shut down and it won't turn on again. What do you need to do?

    A. Buy a new phone.

    B. Heat the phone with a blow dryer.

    C. Let the phone cool down before turning it on again.

    D. Remove the battery and reinstall it.

62. A user reports that their smartphone is always overheating and constantly locks up. What should you advise them to do?

    A. Replace the battery.

    B. Open the Power app and set the phone to operate on the low voltage setting.

    C. Turn off the phone and let it cool down.

    D. Replace the phone.

63. A user reports that the video on their desktop computer does not display properly. There are several places where the screen will not light up; those spots are always black dots. What is this a symptom of?

    A. Artifacts

    B. Dead pixels

    C. Backlight failure

    D. Overheating

64. A user calls the help desk stating that the icons on their computer screen are huge. They can see only about six of them, and they can't see the Start menu. What most likely caused this issue?

A. Failing backlight

B. Incorrect video resolution

C. External interference, such as a fan or a motor

D. Incorrect video driver

65. You are troubleshooting a desktop computer and receive S.M.A.R.T. errors. To which component do these errors refer?

A. SSD

B. RAM

C. CPU

D. Network card

66. You are troubleshooting a computer system that received a S.M.A.R.T. error. Which of the following will you do first?

A. Check that the system has adequate cooling/ventilation.

B. Back up the system's data.

C. Run a drive diagnostic tool.

D. Run a RAM diagnostic tool.

67. You're troubleshooting a computer that isn't booting properly. When the computer is turned on, the power supply fan spins, but the computer will not POST. When you remove the cover, you notice the swollen capacitor in the center of the image below. What should you do?

    A. Replace the power supply.

    B. Replace the capacitor.

    C. Replace the motherboard.

    D. Discharge the capacitor.

68. A technician is troubleshooting a desktop computer that they suspect has a network card problem. They have tested their theory to determine the cause of the problem. According to the best practice methodology to resolve problems, which step should they take next?

    A. Conduct external or internal research based on symptoms.

    B. Document findings, actions, and outcomes.

    C. Verify full system functionality.

    D. Establish a plan of action to resolve the problem and implement the solution.

69. The desktop computer you are troubleshooting will not retain the proper time and date. You set the time and date, power the system down, and power it back on. Again, the settings are incorrect. Which component is likely causing the issue?

    A. CMOS battery

    B. UEFI

    C. Hard drive

    D. RAM

70. Your friend's iPhone always has the wrong time. You tell them it's a simple fix. What should they do?

    A. Trade in the phone for a new one.

    B. Go to Settings, select the General tab, and for Date And Time choose Set Automatically.

    C. Replace the phone's battery.

    D. Update the iOS to the latest version.

71. A technician is troubleshooting a RAID 5 array with four hard disks. One of the disks has failed. What can the technician do to recover the array?

    A. Replace the failed disk and rebuild the array.

    B. Replace the failed disk and restore from backup.

    C. Rebuild the failed disk and restore from backup.

    D. Remove the failed disk and rebuild the array.

72. The corporate finance team is getting ready for a presentation in the conference room in about an hour. They frantically called you because the image the projector is putting on the screen is fuzzy. Which of the following is the least likely cause?

    A. The projector's lens needs to be cleaned.

    B. The projector focus needs to be adjusted.

    C. The contrast setting is too high.

    D. The PCs resolution is too high for the projector.

73. A user reports that regardless of what is showing on their LCD desktop display, they can always see an outline of another image that never changes. What is the solution to this problem?

   A. Replace the video card.

   B. Degauss the display.

   C. Replace the display.

   D. Clean the screen.

74. A user claims that on their laptop, the mouse cursor will occasionally jump to different areas of the screen when they are typing. It is causing problems with their work because they end up typing in different fields than they need to. What can you suggest that will help this issue?

   A. Disable the point stick.

   B. Replace the keyboard.

   C. Replace the motherboard.

   D. Disable the touchpad.

75. A user is complaining that the mouse drifts away on its own while they are working on their company laptop. They have changed the batteries, gotten a new mouse pad, and cleaned the mouse's sensor. What should they try next to resolve the issue? (Choose two.)

   A. Remove and reinstall the mouse driver.

   B. Get a new mouse.

   C. Plug the mouse into a different USB port.

   D. Disable the mouse in control panel.

76. A coworker comes to you for help with their iPhone. When they touch the screen, it acts as if they touched it somewhere else. They have already cleaned the touchscreen with a microfiber cloth. What will you do to help them?

   A. Download a calibration app.

   B. Adjust the touch accommodations settings.

   C. Suggest they get the digitizer replaced.

   D. Suggest they get a new phone.

77. You're about to refer to a vendor's instructions for guidance. What step of the best practice methodology to resolve problems should you be in?

   A. Establish a theory of probable cause.

   B. Identify the problem.

   C. Establish a plan of action to resolve the problem and implement the solution.

   D. Document the findings, actions, and outcomes.

78. Your Surface Pro tablet running Windows 10 is not responding properly to your touch gestures. What will you do?

   A. Buy a new tablet.

   B. Use the built-in calibration software.

   C. Replace the digitizer.

   D. Replace the device.

79. Your smartphone slipped into the ocean when you were taking pictures. You retrieved it after a minute or so, but it was wet. What do you do?

   A. Place it in a bag of rice.

   B. Use a hairdryer to dry it out.

   C. Nothing. It's fine.

   D. Immediately turn it off.

80. A customer comes into your shop with a smartphone that is acting strangely. The sound is distorted, and there is static when they plug in the headphones. You look into the sim card slot and see a red line. What will you tell the customer? (Choose two.)

   A. This phone may have water damage.

   B. This phone has been exposed to high temperatures.

   C. There is no way to fix your phone.

   D. We can replace corroded components, but the fix may not last.

81. You are troubleshooting a laptop that you suspect was infected with malware. You have established your plan of action and implemented the solution. According to the best practice methodology to resolve problems, which step should you take next?

   A. Test the theory to determine the cause.

   B. Determine next steps to solve the problem.

   C. Verify full system functionality and, if applicable, implement preventive measures.

   D. Document findings, actions, and outcomes.

82. A coworker is getting an error message that says Paper Mismatch. What do you tell them to do? (Choose three.)

   A. Verify that the setting is correct in printer properties or tray properties depending on the printer.

   B. Ensure they've selected the right paper size in their software.

   C. Remove and replace the paper in the tray, and verify the paper guides are properly placed.

   D. Change their orientation in the software.

83. You've recently doubled the number of employees in your call center. Users of your company's VoIP phones have been complaining that the calls sound like the person on the other end is stuttering, if they can understand them at all. What can you do to remedy this situation? (Choose two.)

   A. Add more RAM to each VoIP phone.

   B. Set up a VLAN for the phones.

   C. Configure QoS to prioritize phones.

   D. Configure WoL.

84. Laser printer users are complaining that their print jobs aren't printing. They're using an accounting package that won't let them reprint the reports they have printed. When you look at the print queue you see their print jobs just sitting there. What will you do? (Choose two.)

   A. Ensure the printer is turned on.

   B. Ensure there is paper in the printer.

   C. Stop and restart the print server service.

   D. Delete and reinstall the printer in the OS.

85. A presenter using a projector is near the end of a lengthy presentation when an audible pop is heard, and the image goes dark. What will you do to fix the situation?

   A. Allow the projector to cool down awhile.

   B. Unplug the projector, wait 30 seconds, and plug it back in.

   C. Reset the lamp timer.

   D. Replace the projector bulb.

86. A user has called the help desk complaining that their computer won't boot. You've asked them what changes, if any, have been made to the system. What step of the troubleshooting methodology are you working in?

   A. Identify the problem.

   B. Establish a theory of probable cause.

   C. Test the theory to determine cause.

   D. Establish a plan of action to resolve the problem.

87. A user has a hard drive that needs to be replaced. Before you establish a plan of action to resolve the problem and implement the solution, what should you do?

   A. Verify full system functionality.

   B. Refer to the corporate policy for handling hard drive data.

   C. Document the findings, actions, and outcomes.

   D. None of these.

88. You have a NAS system and have observed alternating blinking red and white LEDs. What is happening?

    A. The array is ready to receive data.

    B. The drives are booting up or shutting down.

    C. The RAID is synchronizing, or software is updating.

    D. You're not sure but will check the vendor's documentation.

89. Your home computer was working fine yesterday but today you get an error stating bootable device not found. Which of the following is most likely?

    A. The hard drive has failed.

    B. The OS was deleted.

    C. The POST is faulty.

    D. A USB drive is in a USB port.

90. Which two of the following are finishing processes that can cause problems with print jobs?

    A. Paper orientation

    B. Staple

    C. Hole punch

    D. Paper size

91. Users on your network are experiencing VoIP calls where they only hear every other word. What is this a symptom of?

    A. Jitter

    B. High bandwidth

    C. Packet loss

    D. Low latency

92. A user is trying to print and hole-punch reports on the shared office printer/copier, but every time the documents come out without holes. Which of the following would be related to this problem? (Choose two.)

    A. The hole punch waste tray is full.

    B. The user didn't properly select Hole Punch.

    C. A document was left in the ADF.

    D. The hole punch feature is not enabled.

93. Which of the following is not a symptom of a projector bulb that is burning out?

    A. Pop sound

    B. Dim image, even in a dark room with the projector brightness up

    C. Muddled (not crisp) colors being projected

    D. A fan running when you're done projecting

    E. Flickering projector image

94. You're working on a server RAID array and observe that the drive is blinking first green, then amber, then off. What does this tell you?

    A. The drive is preparing to be ejected.

    B. You're not sure but will check the vendor documentation.

    C. The drive has failed.

    D. The drive is online and is working fine.

95. You have a multitude of USB drives that you use for different storage purposes, but whenever you leave one in your PC, the computer tries to boot to the USB port instead of your Windows hard drive and gives you an error message about no boot device found. What can you do to remedy this situation?

    A. Enter BIOS/UEFI and change the boot order so that USB is disabled or last.

    B. Put USB locks on all the USB ports.

    C. Install the OS on a USB.

    D. Install Linux.

96. A user has called the helpline, and you're helping them troubleshoot a failed computer. Upon questioning the user, you discover that there was a lightning storm in their area last night. What step of the best practice methodology to resolve problems will you perform next?

    A. Identify the problem.

    B. Establish a theory of probable cause.

    C. Establish a plan of action.

    D. Document the findings, actions, and outcomes.

97. You've just built a new system with an SSD drive. It POSTs just fine, but it's telling you that the hard drive is not found. What should you do first?

    A. Replace the SSD with an HDD.

    B. Format the hard drive.

    C. Ensure that the hard drive's data and power cable are plugged in.

    D. Install the OS.

98. You are troubleshooting a Windows 10 computer that has crashed. It displays a blue screen with the error "UNEXPECTED_KERNEL_MODE_TRAP" on it. Which component most likely caused this problem?

    A. RAM

    B. CPU

    C. SSD

    D. PSU

99. Your computer has been intermittently rebooting when you play an online video game. You install a hardware monitoring utility and notice in the log that the CPU temperature spikes before the system shuts down. Which action should you take first to help resolve the issue?

    A. Use the system BIOS to overclock the CPU.

    B. Replace the CPU and heat sink.

    C. Reseat the CPU heat sink.

    D. Replace the power supply.

100. A user reports that their tablet computer will work on battery power for only about 20 minutes, even after the battery icon says it's full. They claim that it initially worked on battery power for several hours. What is the most likely cause of the problem?

    A. The user is running too many apps.

    B. The user is constantly using the Wi-Fi connection.

    C. The battery needs to be charged longer.

    D. The battery is failing.

101. A user complains that when they turn their desktop computer on, nothing appears on the screen. It sounds like the computer's fan is running, and the user reported hearing one beep when the computer powered on. What is the first thing you should check?

    A. Is the display plugged into the video port?

    B. Did the computer complete the POST properly?

    C. Is the display turned on?

    D. Does another display work on this computer?

102. The AC adapter for your laptop has a green LED indicator on it. When you plug the adapter into a wall outlet, the light does not illuminate. What could be the reasons for this? (Choose two.)

    A. The laptop is off.

    B. The wall outlet is defective.

    C. The AC adapter is defective.

    D. The voltage selector for the AC adapter is set incorrectly.

103. You have downloaded a scheduling app for your Android tablet. After two months of use, it will not load. You reboot your tablet, and the app still will not open. Other apps appear to work normally. What should you do?

    A. Reset the tablet to factory specifications.

    B. Reinstall the app.

    C. Ensure that the app is configured to run in Settings.

    D. Replace the tablet.

104. You have a macOS desktop computer that does not produce an image on the screen when it boots. You hear a chime sound and normal indicator lights are on. The display is connected to the computer and the power light is on. What should be your next troubleshooting step?

    A. Try the display on another computer or another display on this computer.

    B. Replace the video card.

    C. Switch the display to another video connector on the video card.

    D. Replace the motherboard.

105. The desktop computer you are troubleshooting will not boot. When you push the power button, no status light indicators come on, and you do not hear a fan. You verify that the outlet is working and try a power cord that you know works, but it doesn't help. Which component is most likely causing the problem?

    A. RAM

    B. PSU

    C. CPU

    D. HDD

106. While plugging in a VGA display, a user bent some of the pins on the connector. You attempted to straighten them, but two broke off. If you use this display, what will most likely happen?

    A. It will work properly.

    B. It will display incorrect colors.

    C. It will display a distorted image.

    D. It will produce dim or flickering images.

107. You have a macOS computer that is beeping during startup. It beeps once every 5 seconds. What do you need to do?

    A. Reseat the RAM.

    B. Replace the motherboard.

    C. Replace the video card.

    D. Nothing. It's updating firmware.

108. You're troubleshooting a printing problem. The user selected to print in landscape mode in the software, but it comes out as a small box in the middle of a portrait mode page. What can you do to attempt to fix this? (Choose two.)

    A. Tell the user to change their setting to portrait mode.

    B. Verify that the printer is set to print in landscape mode.

    C. Have the user select a different printer tray.

    D. Take the paper out of the printer tray and turn it 90 degrees.

109. Your child has a new 3D printer. They've been having fun printing all sorts of things, but today it's making a grinding noise and not moving. What can you do quickly that might fix it? (Choose two.)

  A. Ensure that the cable moving the printhead moves freely.

  B. Check for blockages and debris.

  C. Replace the printer's ink ribbon.

  D. Replace the printhead.

110. The advertising group in your company is complaining that their printer is not printing the correct colors. Which of the following can you try to correct this problem? (Choose two.)

  A. Change the print orientation.

  B. Dispose of generic print cartridges and use those made by the manufacturer for this printer.

  C. Reinstall the printer.

  D. Change the printer settings to better quality, not faster speed.

111. A laser printer you are servicing has been producing ghosted images. That is, regardless of whatever prints, you can always see a faint copy of a previous image that was printed. What can be causing this? (Choose two.)

  A. Dirty charging corona wire

  B. Broken cleaning blade

  C. Broken fusing assembly

  D. Bad erasure lamps

112. The desktop computer you are troubleshooting will not boot. When you push the power button, no status light indicators come on, and you do not hear a fan. You verify that the outlet is working and try a power cord that you know works, but it doesn't help. What two things will you do next? (Choose two.)

  A. Push the power button in for 10 seconds.

  B. Check the I/O switch on the back of the PSU.

  C. Check the 115/220 switch on the back of the PSU.

  D. Reseat the motherboard's RAM.

113. You charged your laptop overnight, but in the morning, it will not power on. You remove and reinsert the battery, but still it will not power on. The system will power on when you use the wall adapter, but not the battery, and the battery icon indicates that it's full. What is the most likely problem?

  A. The battery is defective.

  B. The AC adapter is not properly charging the battery.

  C. The battery charging icon is not properly reading the battery life.

  D. The DC converter between the battery and the motherboard is defective.

114. A user complains of a burning smell coming from their desktop computer. You instruct them to immediately shut the system down. What should be your next step?

 A. Replace the power supply.

 B. Replace the motherboard.

 C. Test the power supply with a multimeter.

 D. Inspect the inside of the computer for visible signs of damage.

115. You have a Xerox color multifunction printer that is making a grinding noise. What is the first thing you'll try to fix the problem?

 A. Replace the toner cartridge.

 B. Clean the printhead lenses.

 C. Perform a software reset.

 D. Gently shake the toner cartridge.

116. The company's advertising department has been printing documents for an upcoming seminar all day. They've called you because they noticed that the last few printouts have lighter images of the print job displayed under the original one. What component will you clean or replace?

 A. The photosensitive drum

 B. The corona wire

 C. The fusing roller

 D. The HVPS

117. Users are printing to a laser printer, but nothing is coming out. When you look at the print queue, you see several jobs backed up. The printer is online, has paper, and says Ready. What should you do to resolve the problem?

 A. Turn the printer off and back on.

 B. Stop and restart the print spooler.

 C. Press the Reset button on the printer.

 D. Use the printer's display to clear out the oldest job, take it offline, and put it back online.

118. You are troubleshooting an inkjet printer. Users report that the printer is printing in the wrong colors. The problem just started happening recently. What could be causing it? (Choose two.)

 A. Incorrect paper

 B. Leaking ink cartridges

 C. Malfunctioning fusing assembly

 D. Malfunctioning stepper motor

119. Lately print jobs have been pulling multiple sheets from the tray instead of just one. You've verified that the paper is the correct weight and that the tray is properly adjusted, and you've fanned the paper's edges, but it still happens. What component will you likely need to replace in the printer?

    A. Fusing assembly

    B. Paper tray

    C. Pickup roller or separation pad

    D. Primary corona

120. People are complaining that the output from the company's multifunction device has little spots all over it, and it's been getting gradually worse. What will you do to correct this? (Choose two.)

    A. Replace the HVPS.

    B. Ensure the correct paper is being used.

    C. Thoroughly clean the printer.

    D. Blow debris out of the printer with canned air.

121. A user is upset because their Android tablet does not ring whenever they receive a phone call. What is the first thing you should have them check?

    A. If the tablet is configured to receive voice calls

    B. If the tablet is in Airplane mode

    C. If the tablet is set to silent mode

    D. If the tablet's speakers are working in another application

122. You are troubleshooting a laptop with an integrated wireless networking card. The user reports that the laptop will not connect to the Internet. When you look at the network activity lights, the connection and activity lights alternate blinking, in a steady pattern. What is the most likely cause of the problem?

    A. No network connection

    B. Incorrect TCP/IP configuration

    C. Failed network card

    D. Unable to reach a DNS server

123. A user calls to report that they can't access the Internet or any other network resources. The IP address on their computer is 169.254.1.102. Which of the following is most likely to have caused this?

    A. Unable to reach a DNS server

    B. Unable to reach a DHCP server

    C. Unable to reach the default gateway

    D. Unable to read the local host configuration file

124. The inkjet printer in your office is producing consistently faded prints. What should you do to resolve the problem?

    A. Replace the paper feed mechanism.

    B. Turn up the color dithering.

    C. Replace the ink cartridge.

    D. Adjust the printhead to be closer to the paper.

125. The day after an electrical thunderstorm, you are troubleshooting a computer. After you power it up, it flashes information briefly on the screen and then reboots. It continuously reboots itself after this. Which components are most likely to cause this problem? (Choose two.)

    A. Hard drive

    B. Power supply

    C. Motherboard

    D. CPU

126. Within the last five minutes, several users in one part of the building have called in to report that they have lost their network connection. The connection had been working earlier in the day. What is most likely the cause of the problem?

    A. Faulty network card drivers

    B. Incorrect TCP/IP configuration

    C. Bad network cable

    D. Faulty switch

127. A user reports that they cannot see their network shares or email, or even connect to the printer, but local applications are working fine. You ask what has changed since the last access, and the user mentions cleaning their desk. What might be the problem?

    A. The user might not have logged in.

    B. The printer, email, and file server could be offline.

    C. The network cable may not be connected.

    D. The Group Policy was reconfigured.

128. During a meeting, the manager mentions the projector has been problematic since the start of the meeting. They tried running the projector from a few laptops with no success. Multiple pop-ups were occurring, but it's unknown what the pop-up windows reported. What might be your next step?

    A. Open the log for information on failed jobs.

    B. Check the light source for failure.

    C. Verify that cables were attached.

    D. Allow the projector to cool down and try again.

129. A user reports the wireless Internet connection will randomly shut down in the afternoon. You check the Internet router by the window to find it still has power. What is the most likely cause of this problem?

    A. Network overloaded

    B. Printer queue full

    C. Wireless router overheating

    D. Workstation requires patching

130. A technician is troubleshooting a suspected hard drive issue. They are following the troubleshooting methodology. As part of identifying the problem, what should they do?

    A. If necessary, conduct external or internal research based on symptoms.

    B. Question the user and identify user changes to the computer.

    C. Document findings, actions, and outcomes.

    D. Determine next steps to resolve the problem.

131. A billing clerk just moved from their normal office out to a new office separated from the loading dock by a cement block wall. The shipping clerk on the loading dock doesn't have a problem with wireless connectivity, but the billing clerk can't get reception in their new office. When they step out onto the loading dock, their laptop works just fine. Why are they losing connectivity in their office?

    A. They're too far from the WAP.

    B. The cement walls block the signal.

    C. The shipping clerk's PC interferes with the signal.

    D. The billing clerk accidentally turned their Wi-Fi off.

132. Your spouse just began working from home. They've decided that they like to work on the kitchen island, so they moved the router into the kitchen to get a better signal. Now the Wi-Fi connection gets dropped periodically no matter where they are in the home. What is going on?

    A. Your service provider is limiting the bandwidth.

    B. The router is old and needs replacing.

    C. The motors in the kitchen appliances are interfering with the Wi-Fi signal.

    D. Your spouse needs a better laptop to work from home.

133. You've moved to a new two-story townhouse and are trying to decide where to put your router. The townhouse is a rather open concept with the dining room near its center. Which of the following options would be best?

    A. On a stand in the corner of the dining room.

    B. Next to the metal staircase, so they'll be a good signal upstairs.

    C. Hide it behind the sofa.

    D. Set it on a sunny windowsill to reflect the signal back in.

134. Your friend dropped their iPad and it landed on its corner, on a rock. Now the screen has three large cracks from the corner radiating outward. The icons are still visible, and the home button works, but the screen only responds in some places to touch, and they cut their finger. What will you tell them? (Choose two.)

    A. Recycle it and get a new one.

    B. If possible, back up the device.

    C. The digitizer and glass need replacing.

    D. The display assembly needs replacing.

135. You are troubleshooting a difficult network connectivity problem. You have tested your theory to determine cause and found that you were wrong. According to troubleshooting theory, you have two choices for next steps. What are they? (Choose two.)

    A. Tell the user that the problem has been fixed, and document it as such.

    B. Verify full system functionality and document findings, actions, and outcomes.

    C. Escalate the issue.

    D. Establish a new theory of probable cause.

136. You are troubleshooting a desktop computer that is exhibiting erratic behavior. As part of establishing a theory of probable cause, what step should you take, as part of the best practice methodology to resolve problems?

    A. Question the user and identify user changes to the computer.

    B. Determine next steps to resolve the problem.

    C. Establish a plan of action to resolve the problem.

    D. If necessary, conduct external or internal research based on symptoms.

137. You're at your favorite coffee shop. You want to use their Wi-Fi, but your smartphone didn't automatically connect like it usually does. What do you suspect?

    A. Their WAP is down.

    B. Airplane mode is on.

    C. Their DNS server is down.

    D. Your phone is damaged.

138. You're in an office building and need to make a phone call, but when you look at your phone, you have half of a bar. What should you do?

    A. Ask to join their Wi-Fi and use it to make a call.

    B. Move toward an outside wall.

    C. Move closer to the elevator.

    D. Go to a lower floor.

139. You are troubleshooting a computer with a RAID 0 array using four disks. One of the disks fails. What can you do to recover the array?

    A.   Rebuild the failed disk and restore from backup.

    B.   Replace the failed disk and rebuild the array.

    C.   Replace the failed disk and restore from backup.

    D.   Remove the failed disk and rebuild the array.

140. You are troubleshooting a Windows desktop computer that appears to be having driver issues. According to troubleshooting methodology, when is the appropriate time to perform backups of the system?

    A.   After verifying full system functionality and implementing preventive measures

    B.   Before making changes

    C.   After documenting findings, actions, and outcomes

    D.   Before identifying the problem

141. The laser printer in your office is about eight years old. Recently, when you print, you occasionally get "low memory" error messages. What should you do to fix the problem?

    A.   Stop and restart the print spooler.

    B.   Implement printing priorities for the most important users.

    C.   Upgrade the printer's memory.

    D.   Upgrade the printer's hard drive.

142. You are troubleshooting a recently installed three-disk RAID array. The original technician left notes that they were concerned about creating multiple points of potential failure in the system. Which type of RAID array creates more points of potential failure than a single hard drive?

    A.   RAID 10

    B.   RAID 1

    C.   RAID 0

    D.   RAID 5

143. You've been working awhile and decide to restart your Windows 10 computer, but instead of booting into the OS, the screen flashes on and off several times and seems to restart. What is likely happening?

    A.   The OS is performing updates.

    B.   The display is about to fail.

    C.   The hard drive is about to fail.

    D.   The display cable is loose.

144. A technician is troubleshooting a Windows laptop that won't boot properly. They have established a theory of probable cause. According to troubleshooting methodology, what should they do next?

  A. Identify the problem.

  B. Test the theory to determine cause.

  C. Establish a plan of action to resolve the problem and implement the solution.

  D. Document findings.

145. The display on your laptop seems to go off and on whenever you move it. What's happening?

  A. The video cable is loose.

  B. The laptop is failing.

  C. The battery is failing.

  D. The motherboard is failing.

146. Your employer has a heavily used conference room with a ceiling mounted projector. The projector connects to users' laptops with an HDMI cable. Lately users are complaining that no matter what computer is connected to the projector, the sound is muffled. What will you try first to fix it?

  A. Replace the lamp assembly.

  B. Replace the HDMI cable.

  C. Clean the speakers.

  D. Clean the lens.

147. A day-long training is happening in your company's conference room. The group took a break for lunch and when they returned, the projector was off. The presenter has called you for help. What has most likely happened?

  A. The projector overheated.

  B. The projector entered standby.

  C. The power cable is loose.

  D. The lamp has burned out.

148. You are about to begin troubleshooting a laptop with no display. According to the best practice methodology to resolve problems, what should you always consider before you begin troubleshooting?

  A. The user's feelings

  B. The cost associated with hardware replacement

  C. The implications of delivering bad news to management

  D. The corporate policies, procedures, and impacts before implementing changes

149. You just installed an additional new hard drive in your Windows 10 desktop computer, but when you turn the computer back on, the drive shows in the BIOS/UEFI but not in File Explorer. What is your next step?

   A. Replace the new drive.

   B. Check the drive's data and power cables.

   C. Partition and format the drive.

   D. Reinstall the OS.

150. Your friend's home theater projector is turning off unexpectedly. Which one of the following is not a possible cause?

   A. The power cable is loose.

   B. The unit is overheating.

   C. The filter needs cleaning.

   D. The HDMI cable is loose.

151. Over time, the hard drive performance of your computer has gotten slower. A quick check of Performance Monitor shows that your disk read/writes are taking more time as compared to the baseline. What should you do to resolve this issue?

   A. Format the hard drive and restore the data.

   B. Enable write caching on the drive.

   C. Delete the partition, create a new one, and restore the data.

   D. Run chkdsk.

152. Your server's drive read/write times are a bottleneck in your system, and you're concerned about downtime in the event of a drive failure. Which of the following will improve performance and fault tolerance?

   A. Replace the HDD with an SSD.

   B. Install RAID 0.

   C. Install RAID 1.

   D. Install RAID 5.

153. You've been troubleshooting a network connectivity issue for a user at your company and just resolved it. You've verified that the system is fully functioning again and talked to the user about how to prevent this problem in the future. What is your next step?

   A. Hand them the bill.

   B. Document the finding, actions, and outcomes.

   C. Consider corporate policies and procedures.

   D. Thank them for their patience.

154. You are troubleshooting a computer that will not boot properly. When you power it on, it produces a series of beeps. Which components are most likely to be causing this to happen? (Choose two.)

A. BIOS

B. Hard drive

C. Network card

D. RAM

155. You are working on a laptop that appears to be frozen. You press the Num Lock key several times, but the indicator light remains on. What should you do to try to resolve this issue?

A. Push and hold the power button until the laptop turns off, and reboot.

B. Remove the battery and disconnect the laptop from an AC power source, and reboot.

C. Press and hold the Num Lock key until the light turns off.

D. Press Ctrl+Alt+Del to reboot the laptop.

156. A user reports that their mobile phone is extremely hot and appears to be locked up. What should you instruct them to do?

A. Plug the phone into a wall outlet or USB port to charge it.

B. Turn the phone off and let it cool down.

C. Perform a factory reset of the phone.

D. Open the Power app and set the phone to operate on the low voltage setting.

157. You have an Android phone and it's running slowly. The problem seems to be isolated to one app in particular. You check and you have plenty of free memory. You have rebooted the phone several times and the app is still slow. What should you try next?

A. Hold the power button and the Home button simultaneously for 10 seconds, and the phone will reset.

B. Reset the phone to factory specifications.

C. Uninstall and reinstall the app.

D. Get a new phone.

158. The desktop computer in your office's lobby plays a welcome video for guests. Recently, the audio started intermittently failing. You replaced the speakers, and it still happens. What is the next step you should take in troubleshooting the issue?

A. Replace the motherboard.

B. Reseat the speakers.

C. Replace the sound card.

D. Reseat the sound card.

159. You have just used administrative privileges to install a printer on a user's workstation. When the user tries to print to the printer, they get an error message saying access denied. What is the cause of this problem?

    A. The printer is offline.

    B. The printer is out of memory.

    C. The print spooler needs to be restarted.

    D. The user does not have the security permissions to print.

160. The inkjet printer in your office jams a lot and produces many crinkled papers. What is the most likely cause of this?

    A. Incorrect paper tension settings

    B. Dirty printheads

    C. Obstructed paper path

    D. Paper that is too dry

161. While replacing a toner cartridge in a laser printer, a technician spilled toner on and around the printer. What should be used to clean up the spill?

    A. A damp cloth

    B. Compressed air

    C. A toner vacuum

    D. Denatured alcohol

162. You are disassembling a defective laptop to replace the motherboard. Which of the following steps are recommended? (Choose two.)

    A. Place the screws in a multicompartment pill box and label where they go.

    B. Remove the hard drive before removing the motherboard.

    C. Label where the cables plug into the motherboard.

    D. Use needle-nose pliers to remove the motherboard from the spacers.

163. A user reports that their LCD display is flickering constantly. What is the easiest course of action to resolve this problem?

    A. Replace the video card.

    B. Replace the display.

    C. Remove external interference such as fans or motors.

    D. Degauss the display.

164. You are having problems printing to a networked printer from your Windows workstation. Several jobs were sent, but none printed. You just tried to print a test page and nothing came out. What should you do?

    A. Check your connections and stop and restart the print spooler.

    B. Turn the printer off and back on.

    C. Use the printer's display to clear out the oldest job, take it offline, and put it back online.

    D. Press the Reset button on the printer.

165. A user reports that none of the keys on their laptop keyboard seem to work. They have rebooted the computer and the problem has not gone away. They need to finish an important paper before lunch. What should you do next?

   A. Replace the keyboard.

   B. Check to ensure that the internal keyboard is still connected properly.

   C. Connect an external keyboard using the USB port.

   D. Clean under the keys of the keyboard with compressed air.

166. At random times, your computer will completely lock up, requiring a hard reboot. Which two components are most likely to cause this type of problem? (Choose two.)

   A. CPU

   B. RAM

   C. PSU

   D. GPU

167. You are consulting with a user who has a failed hard drive in a Windows computer. The user needs to get critical data off the drive but did not make a backup. Are there any options to recover the data?

   A. There is no way to recover data from the failed drive.

   B. Use the Windows Disk Repair tool to create a backup and then restore the backup to a new hard drive.

   C. Use a file recovery service or software package to try to recover the data.

   D. Install a second hard drive of the same or larger size. During Windows installation, choose Recover Contents Of Hard Drive from the Advanced Options menu.

168. In the morning, a user calls from their desk and reports that their laptop will not connect to the wireless network. They have never had a problem connecting to the wireless network from that location. When you look at their wireless adapter, you notice that there are no lights illuminated. What is most likely the problem?

   A. They are not receiving a Wi-Fi signal.

   B. The SSID cannot be found.

   C. Their wireless card is disabled.

   D. There is a conflict between the wireless card and wired network port.

169. Your iPhone 11 has appeared to lock up. The touchscreen is unresponsive. You press and hold a volume button and the side button, but it does not turn off. What should your next step be?

   A. Press and release the volume up button, press and release the volume down button, and press and hold the side button.

   B. Use a paper clip to press the recessed reset button on the bottom of the phone to reset the phone.

   C. Hold the side button and the up and down volume buttons simultaneously for 10 seconds and the phone will reset.

   D. Get a new phone.

170. You frequently need to carry your laptop around the building as you troubleshoot computer issues. In several places, you notice that the Wi-Fi connection drops completely. What is the most likely cause of this problem?

   A. You are walking too fast for the Wi-Fi to stay connected.

   B. Low RF signal.

   C. Oversaturated WAP.

   D. Failing Wi-Fi antenna in the laptop.

171. You have just installed a printer on a client computer. When you print to the printer, the output is completely garbled characters. What is the most likely cause of this problem?

   A. The print spooler

   B. The printer's memory

   C. The printer driver

   D. The print queue

172. A user's laptop computer does not display anything on the screen, although the power light and other indicator lights are on. You plug in an external display, and after you toggle the LCD cutoff switch, an image appears on the external display. Which components are most likely causing the problem? (Choose two.)

   A. Video driver

   B. Backlight

   C. Screen

   D. Video card

173. You have an Android phone and it's running very slowly. The apps aren't working as fast as they used to, but you still have plenty of free memory. You have rebooted the phone several times and it's still slow. You tried running only one app at a time and it's still slow regardless of what app you're running. What should you try next?

   A. Hold the power button and the Home button simultaneously for 10 seconds, and the phone will reset.

   B. Back up the phone, then reset it to factory specifications.

   C. Uninstall and reinstall all apps.

   D. Get a new phone.

174. The laser printer you are using has started producing all-black pages. What should you do to fix the problem?

   A. Use the display to initiate a self-cleaning cycle.

   B. Use a maintenance kit to clean the printer.

   C. Replace the toner cartridge.

   D. Turn the printer off and back on again.

175. You have installed an internal RAID controller and configured a RAID-5 array on it with four hard disks. It has been operating normally. Today when you boot up, you receive an error message saying, "RAID not found." Which component is most likely causing this issue?

   A. One of the four hard disks

   B. The RAID controller

   C. The system BIOS/UEFI

   D. The onboard hard drive controller

176. One of your friends complains that when playing action games on their computer, the screen is slow to refresh and the motion is often jerky. Their system has a video card; their graphics are not integrated with the CPU. What should be done to resolve this problem? (Choose two.)

   A. Buy a display with a faster refresh rate.

   B. Increase system RAM.

   C. Increase video memory.

   D. Lower the screen resolution.

177. A user shows you their mobile device, and the screen is constantly flickering. They have turned the device off and on again, and it still happens. Which component is likely causing the problem?

   A. Display

   B. Video card

   C. Backlight

   D. Converter

178. You are troubleshooting a laptop computer that has a pointing stick in the center of the keyboard. If nobody is moving the external mouse, the cursor will slowly drift up and to the right. You have tried a different external mouse and the problem still happens. What should you do to resolve the problem?

   A. Replace the laptop keyboard.

   B. Recenter the laptop's point stick.

   C. Recenter the laptop's touchpad.

   D. Replace the laptop motherboard.

179. A remote workstation can't connect to the network. You want to narrow down the problem to the UTP cable or the network card. Which tool can help you determine whether the cable is causing the problem?

   A. Multimeter

   B. OTDR

   C. Cable tester

   D. Crimper

180. An iPhone user just downloaded a new app that requires the use of GPS. It doesn't function properly. Another app they have on their phone also needs GPS, and it also does not work. How do they configure the phone to let the new app work properly?

    A. Enable GPS under Settings ➢ Privacy.

    B. Enable Location Services under Settings ➢ Privacy.

    C. Enable GPS under Settings ➢ Location Services.

    D. Enable Location Services under Settings ➢ GPS.

181. A technician just replaced the toner cartridge in a laser printer. Now the printer only prints blank pages. What should you do to resolve the problem?

    A. Stop and restart the print spooler.

    B. Reinstall the printer driver.

    C. Replace the toner cartridge with a new toner cartridge.

    D. Remove the toner cartridge, remove the sealing tape, and then reinstall the cartridge.

182. A user just started having intermittent network access problems. While you're trouble-shooting, a message pops up saying Windows has detected an IP address conflict. Your network has a DHCP server. You open the user's TCP/IP properties and it's configured as shown here. What do you need to do to resolve the issue?

    A. On the DHCP server, exclude the user's IP address from the scope.

    B. On the user's computer, run `ipconfig /release` and `ipconfig /renew`.

    C. On the user's computer, set it to Use The Following IP Address and assign them a different address.

    D. Use a packet sniffer to determine the computer with the duplicate address, and change that computer to obtain an IP address automatically.

183. You are troubleshooting network connectivity issues from a Linux workstation. Which command should you use to check the computer's IP address and subnet mask?

   A. `ping`

   B. `ipconfig`

   C. `ifconfig`

   D. `netstat`

184. You are troubleshooting a Windows 10 computer that appears to be unresponsive. You press the Caps Lock key on the keyboard, but the Caps Lock light on the keyboard does not light up. What is most likely happening?

   A. The keyboard has malfunctioned.

   B. The system is waiting for a process to finish and will respond soon.

   C. The motherboard has failed.

   D. The system has locked up and needs to be rebooted.

185. A user reports that their computer is running slowly. When you investigate, you notice that the free disk space is at 5 percent. What is the first solution to try?

   A. Add more RAM.

   B. Remove old files or applications.

   C. Format the hard drive and reinstall from backup.

   D. Replace the hard drive.

186. About a dozen network cables were unplugged from the patch panel, and none of them is labeled. You are at the one workstation that needs to be reconnected, and another technician is in the wiring closet. You want to set this computer to persistently check network connectivity so that you know when the other technician plugs in the right cable. Which command should you use?

   A. `ping -t`

   B. `ping -p`

   C. `ping -l`

   D. `ping -n`

187. You are troubleshooting a laptop, and some of the keys on the left side of the keyboard are constantly sticking. The user says that a little soda might have spilled on the keyboard. What should you do first to resolve the issue?

   A. Use a slightly dampened cotton swab to clean under the keys.

   B. Remove the keyboard and rinse it with soap and water in a sink.

   C. Replace the keyboard.

   D. Hold the keyboard upside down and shake it.

188. A user complains that sometimes their computer will not open files, and it happens in different programs. Which component is most likely to cause this problem?

   A. RAM

   B. CPU

   C. HDD

   D. Motherboard

189. The LCD display you use with your desktop suddenly became very dim. You have attempted to adjust the brightness settings, but even on the highest setting the picture is still dim. What will most likely resolve the issue?

   A. Degauss the display.

   B. Replace the backlight.

   C. Replace the screen.

   D. Replace the inverter.

190. The lines of print on your inkjet printer are unevenly spaced. Some are too close together, while others are too far apart. What is the most likely cause of this problem?

   A. Paper feed mechanism

   B. Exit rollers

   C. Print cartridge

   D. Stepper motor

191. A user calls the help desk to complain that they're getting an error message stating "SSID not found." Then you get a second call for the same reason. Both users were connected from the same locations the day before. What is most likely the problem?

   A. Low RF signal.

   B. Oversaturated WAP.

   C. SSID broadcast is disabled.

   D. The WAP is down.

   E. The user's NIC is not working.

192. You have sent several print jobs to a networked printer and nothing has printed. You do not have printer administrator access. What can you do to see whether your Windows computer is communicating properly with the printer?

   A. Send the print job in RAW format.

   B. Stop and restart the print spooler.

   C. Print a test page.

   D. Print a blank document from Notepad.

193. You are troubleshooting a laptop that has a poor battery life. It will work for only about 30 minutes on a full charge. Which two things should you try first? (Choose two.)

    A. Replace the battery.

    B. Perform a battery calibration.

    C. Drain the battery completely and then charge it fully.

    D. Open the Power Management app and set the laptop to run on low energy mode.

194. A user is unable to connect to your Wi-Fi network. When you look at their device, there is nothing to indicate that Wi-Fi is working, and Airplane mode is off. You next look in Device Manager and see a yellow exclamation point next to the Wi-Fi NIC. What will your next step be?

    A. Replace the NIC.

    B. Replace the device.

    C. Update the driver.

    D. Provide a USB NIC.

195. You have installed a PCIe RAID controller and want to create a RAID-5 array with three disks. You plug the disks in and boot up the computer. The RAID array is not detected. Where should you go to set up or troubleshoot the RAID array?

    A. Windows Device Manager

    B. Windows Disk Management

    C. The RAID controller's BIOS

    D. System BIOS/UEFI

196. A user complains of a loud whining noise coming from their computer. It occurs whenever the computer is on and is relatively constant. Which component is most likely to cause this problem?

    A. RAM

    B. SSD

    C. CPU

    D. PSU

197. You have just upgraded the RAM in a desktop computer. After you power on the computer, no video appears on the screen, and the computer produces a series of three long beeps. What does this indicate?

    A. The system BIOS detected an error in the POST routine.

    B. The system BIOS completed the POST routine normally.

    C. The RAM is faulty.

    D. The motherboard needs to be replaced.

198. A user with an 802.11ac network adapter is trying to join your 802.11ax network. Their laptop is next to yours, which is connected to the network. However, they are unable to locate the SSID. What is the most likely cause of the problem?

  A. 802.11g is not compatible with 802.11n.

  B. SSID broadcasting is disabled on the wireless access point.

  C. The user is out of range of the wireless access point.

  D. The SSID has been changed.

199. A user's Android 7 phone has been crashing and they complain that their data usage has gone way up although their phone habits haven't changed. What will you suspect is the problem?

  A. Bad battery

  B. Water damage

  C. Malware

  D. Loose data cable

200. You are troubleshooting a laser printer that keeps producing vertical black lines running down the page. Which component is most likely causing this problem?

  A. Fusing assembly

  B. Pickup rollers

  C. Exit rollers

  D. EP drum

201. A user reports that the screen on their tablet computer is very dim and difficult to see. They've adjusted it to the maximum brightness and it's still dim. Which component is likely causing the problem?

  A. Backlight

  B. Converter

  C. Display

  D. Video card

202. You have been troubleshooting a computer, and you believe the power supply has failed. Which of the following tools can you use to test the integrity of the power supply? (Choose two.)

  A. Power supply tester

  B. Loopback plugs

  C. POST card

  D. Multimeter

203. A user is trying to display a presentation on a projector, but nothing appears on the external screen. They try toggling their LCD cutoff switch, and it doesn't help. Another user had just presented on the projector, and it worked fine. Which component is most likely causing the problem?

    A. Backlight

    B. Display

    C. Video port

    D. Inverter

204. A mobile phone user is unable to connect the phone to their wireless headset so they can make hands-free calls. Their iPhone screen is shown here. What is most likely the problem?

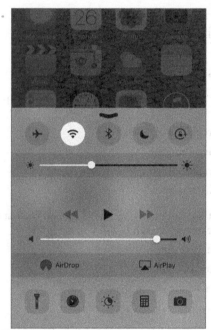

    A. His wireless headset is turned off.

    B. Bluetooth is disabled.

    C. AirPlay is disabled.

    D. Airplane mode is enabled.

205. Your corporate office has sent a memo that all remote offices must use a security protocol that your WAP doesn't support. What should you do first?

    A. Update the WAP's firmware.

    B. Replace the WAP.

    C. Buy all new devices.

    D. Keep using the old security protocol.

206. You're considering storage devices for a NAS. Some drives are HDD, and some are SSD. You need to balance drive speeds and price. What will you use to compare the drive speeds?

   A. RPM

   B. IOPS

   C. Mbps

   D. Gbps

207. Your client is running a NAS with ten 16 TB HDDs for a total capacity of 160 TB. They are complaining that the storage array's average IOPS isn't enough to keep up with company demands. What might they replace the HDDs with to maintain capacity but increase performance? (Choose two.)

   A. A single 160 TB HDD

   B. Twenty 8 TB HDDs

   C. Ten 16 TB SSDs

   D. Five 20 TB HDDs

208. A routine check of IOPS of your NAS reveals that it has dropped significantly. What is a likely cause? (Choose two.)

   A. The HDDs were replaced by SSDs.

   B. Usage patterns have changed.

   C. The HDDs were replaced with M.2 drives.

   D. A drive in the array has failed.

209. A user complains that they can barely see the image on their smartphone. Everything seems to work fine, but they can't see it. What will you do first?

   A. Check the brightness settings.

   B. Replace the display assembly.

   C. Turn on location settings.

   D. Replace the battery.

210. You're at a friend's house. Your phone was working fine before you got here, and it usually works fine when you are here, but now it's taking forever to try to load a web page, and then it times out and asks if you want to use cellular data. You're at your data plan's limit. What should you do?

   A. Tell it to forget this network and ask your friend for the new password.

   B. Use your cellular data and pay the overcharges.

   C. Check for problems with their router.

   D. Try a different website.

211. You just installed and configured a new WAP to provide better network connectivity in a remote part of the building. When you turn your laptop on to check the connectivity, there are only a couple of bars even though you're looking up at the WAP. What do you need to do?

    A. Increase the signal strength.

    B. Broadcast its SSID.

    C. Turn on your laptop wireless.

    D. Adjust the antennas.

212. You're taking a walk around the exterior of your office building when your Wi-Fi analyzer shows that your network is visible in the parking lot. You're concerned that an unauthorized person can connect to your wireless network. What should you do?

    A. Enable SSID broadcast.

    B. Lower the WAP's power setting.

    C. Increase the WAP's power setting.

    D. Turn off the WAP's broadcast.

213. Your Wi-Fi network is experiencing some interference, which is causing poor performance and making it unstable. Which of the following might help? (Choose two.)

    A. Enable SSID broadcast.

    B. Disable SSID broadcast.

    C. Increase the WAP's power setting.

    D. Choose a different channel.

PART

II

COMPTIA A+ CORE 2 EXAM 220-1102

- Operating Systems
- Security
- Software Troubleshooting
- Operational Procedures
- Practice Exam 1 (220-1101)
- Practice Exam 2 (220-1102)

Chapter 6

Operating Systems

THE COMPTIA A+ 220-1102 TOPICS COVERED IN THIS CHAPTER INCLUDE THE FOLLOWING:

✓ **1.1 Identify basic features of Microsoft Windows editions.**

- Windows 10 editions
    - Home
    - Pro
    - Pro for Workstations
    - Enterprise
- Feature differences
    - Domain access vs. workgroup
    - Desktop styles/user interface
    - Availability of Remote Desktop Protocol (RDP)
    - Random-access memory (RAM) support limitations
    - BitLocker
    - gpedit.msc
- Upgrade paths
    - In-place upgrade

✓ **1.2 Given a scenario, use the appropriate Microsoft command-line tool.**

- Navigation
    - cd
    - dir
    - md
    - rmdir
    - Drive navigation inputs:
        - C: or D: or x:

- Command-line tools
  - ipconfig
  - ping
  - hostname
  - netstat
  - nslookup
  - chkdsk
  - net user
  - net use
  - tracert
  - format
  - xcopy
  - copy
  - robocopy
  - gpupdate
  - gpresult
  - shutdown
  - sfc
  - [*command name*] /?
  - diskpart
  - pathping
  - winver

✓ **1.3 Given a scenario, use features and tools of the Microsoft Windows 10 operating system (OS).**

- Task Manager
  - Services
  - Startup
  - Performance
  - Processes
  - Users

- Microsoft Management Console (MMC) snap-in
    - Event Viewer (eventvwr.msc)
    - Disk Management (diskmgmt.msc)
    - Task Scheduler (taskschd.msc)
    - Device Manager (devmgmt.msc)
    - Certificate Manager (certmgr.msc)
    - Local Users and Groups (lusrmgr.msc)
    - Performance Monitor (perfmon.msc)
    - Group Policy Editor (gpedit.msc)
- Additional tools
    - System Information (msinfo32.exe)
    - Resource Monitor (resmon.exe)
    - System Configuration (msconfig.exe)
    - Disk Cleanup (cleanmgr.exe)
    - Disk Defragment (dfrgui.exe)
    - Registry Editor (regedit.exe)

✓ **1.4 Given a scenario, use the appropriate Microsoft Windows 10 Control Panel utility.**

- Internet Options
- Devices and Printers
- Programs and Features
- Network and Sharing Center
- System
- Windows Defender Firewall
- Mail
- Sound
- User Accounts
- Device Manager
- Indexing Options

- Administrative Tools
- File Explorer Options
  - Show hidden files
  - Hide extensions
  - General options
  - View options
- Power Options
  - Hibernate
  - Power plans
  - Sleep/suspend
  - Standby
  - Choose what closing the lid does
  - Turn on fast startup
  - Universal Serial Bus (USB) selective suspend
- Ease of Access

✓ **1.5 Given a scenario, use the appropriate Windows settings.**

- Time and Language
- Update and Security
- Personalization
- Apps
- Privacy
- System
- Devices
- Network and Internet
- Gaming
- Accounts

✓ **1.6 Given a scenario, configure Microsoft Windows networking features on a client/desktop.**

- Workgroup vs. domain setup
    - Shared resources
    - Printers
    - File servers
    - Mapped drives
- Local OS firewall settings
    - Application restrictions and exceptions
    - Configuration
- Client network configuration
    - Internet Protocol (IP) addressing scheme
    - Domain Name System (DNS) settings
    - Subnet mask
    - Gateway
    - Static vs. dynamic
- Establish network connections
    - Virtual private network (VPN)
    - Wireless
    - Wired
    - Wireless wide area network (WWAN)
- Proxy settings
- Public network vs. private network
- File Explorer navigation - network paths
- Metered connections and limitations

✓ **1.7 Given a scenario, apply application installation and configuration concepts.**

- System requirements for applications
    - 32-bit vs. 64-bit dependent application requirements
    - Dedicated graphics card vs. integrated

- Video random-access memory (VRAM) requirements
- RAM requirements
- Central processing unit (CPU) requirements
- External hardware tokens
- Storage requirements
- OS requirements for applications
  - Application to OS compatibility
  - 32-bit vs. 64-bit OS
- Distribution methods
  - Physical media vs. downloadable
  - ISO mountable
- Other considerations for new applications
  - Impact to device
  - Impact to network
  - Impact to operation
  - Impact to business

✓ **1.8 Explain common OS types and their purposes.**

- Workstation OSs
  - Windows
  - Linux
  - macOS
  - Chrome OS
- Cell phone/tablet OSs
  - iPadOS
  - iOS
  - Android
- Various filesystem types
  - New Technology File System (NTFS)
  - File Allocation Table 32 (FAT32)

- Third extended filesystem (ext3)
- Fourth extended filesystem (ext4)
- Apple File System (APFS)
- Extensible File Allocation Table (exFAT)
- Vendor life-cycle limitations
  - End-of-life (EOL)
  - Update limitations
- Compatibility concerns between OSs

✓ **1.9 Given a scenario, perform OS installations and upgrades in a diverse OS environment.**

- Boot methods
  - USB
  - Optical media
  - Network
  - Solid-state/flash drives
  - Internet-based
  - External/hot-swappable drive
  - Internal hard drive (partition)
- Types of installations
  - Upgrade
  - Recovery partition
  - Clean install
  - Image deployment
  - Repair installation
  - Remote network installation
  - Other considerations
    - Third-party drivers
- Partitioning
  - GUID [globally unique identifier] Partition Table (GPT)
  - Master boot record (MBR)

- Drive format
- Upgrade considerations
  - Backup files and user preferences
  - Application and driver support/backward compatibility
  - Hardware compatibility
- Feature updates
  - Product life cycle

✓ **1.10 Identify common features and tools of the macOS/desktop OS.**

- Installation and uninstallation of applications
  - File types
    - .dmg
    - .pkg
    - .app
  - App Store
  - Uninstallation process
- Apple ID and corporate restrictions
- Best practices
  - Backups
  - Antivirus
  - Updates/patches
- System Preferences
  - Displays
  - Networks
  - Printers
  - Scanners
  - Privacy
  - Accessibility
  - Time Machine

- Features
    - Multiple desktops
    - Mission Control
    - Keychain
    - Spotlight
    - iCloud
    - Gestures
    - Finder
    - Remote Disc
    - Dock
- Disk Utility
- FileVault
- Terminal
- Force Quit

✓ **1.11 Identify common features and tools of the Linux client/desktop OS.**

- Common commands
    - ls
    - pwd
    - mv
    - cp
    - rm
    - chmod
    - chown
    - su/sudo
    - apt-get
    - yum
    - ip
    - df

- grep
- ps
- man
- top
- find
- dig
- cat
- nano
- Best practices
  - Backups
  - Antivirus
  - Updates/patches
- Tools
  - Shell/terminal
  - Samba

1. You want to transfer files from your computer to a remote server. To do this, you want to connect to a shared directory on the server and copy the files. Which command-line utility will allow you to do this?

   A. `netstat`

   B. `net`

   C. `netshare`

   D. `netdom`

2. A technician is troubleshooting a computer that occasionally will not read data from the hard drive. What should they try first?

   A. Run Defragment and Optimize Drives.

   B. Run `chkdsk` at a command prompt.

   C. Format the hard drive and reinstall the OS.

   D. Replace the hard drive.

3. You have replaced a failed hard drive and need to prepare the new drive for data storage. Which utility will you use first?

   A. `format`

   B. `chkdsk`

   C. `diskpart`

   D. `gpupdate`

4. You are at a Windows computer with the Command Prompt open. You believe that a user is improperly accessing files on a shared folder named `docs`. On the Windows computer, the `D:\userfiles` folder is shared as docs. Which command will immediately stop the sharing of this folder?

   A. `net share D:\userfiles /delete`

   B. `net share D:\userfiles /stop`

   C. `net share docs /delete`

   D. `net share docs /stop`

5. You want to use BitLocker to encrypt the company president's laptop drive, but when you go into Control Panel to find it, it isn't there. What Windows 10 edition does this computer have?

   A. Home

   B. Pro

   C. Pro for Workstations

   D. Enterprise

6. Which of the following Windows editions support ReFS (Resilient File System)? (Choose two.)

    A. Home

    B. Pro

    C. Pro for Workstations

    D. Enterprise

7. You just purchased a new computer that has four CPUs. What edition of Windows will you need, at a minimum, to take advantage of the computer's processing capability?

    A. Home

    B. Pro

    C. Pro for Workstations

    D. Enterprise

8. An employee wants to bring their Windows device to use at work. At work they will need to log into a domain. Which reason below will prohibit the employee from using their device on the domain?

    A. Their device only has one processor.

    B. Their device OS is Windows Home.

    C. Their device only has 8 GB of RAM.

    D. Their device must be Windows Enterprise.

9. One of your technicians needs to use the Task Manager utility. What are ways they can open Task Manager? (Choose two.)

    A. Press Ctrl+Alt+Delete and then click Task Manager.

    B. Press Ctrl+Shift+T.

    C. Press Ctrl+Alt+T.

    D. Press Ctrl+Shift+Esc.

10. You need to configure Internet connections on a Windows workstation. Which tabs of the Internet Options utility in Control Panel would you use to set the home page and enable the pop-up blocker?

    A. Connections, Security

    B. General, Security

    C. General, Privacy

    D. Connections, Privacy

11. A network connection doesn't seem to be working as it should. You've verified that the cables are good from end to end. Where can you quickly look in the OS to see if there is a problem with the onboard NIC driver?

    A. Device Manager

    B. Programs and Features

    C. File Explorer Options

    D. Ease of Access

12. A salesperson in your company travels regularly to foreign countries, through different time zones. They have asked you if there is a way to set their Windows 10 PC so that it will always show the time and date for their location. How can this be done?

    A. In Windows Settings, choose Time & Language, then Date & time, and select Set time automatically.

    B. In Control Panel, choose Date and Time, then select Set Time Zone Automatically.

    C. In Windows Settings, choose Date And Time, then select Synchronize Your Clock.

    D. In Windows Settings, choose Time & Language, then choose Date & time, and select Set time automatically and Set time zone automatically.

13. One of your Windows 10 users has limited eyesight and has asked you to enable voice activation for as many applications as possible. Where can this be done?

    A. In Control Panel, Default Programs

    B. In Windows Settings, under Privacy, Notifications

    C. In Windows Settings, under Privacy, Voice Activation

    D. In Control Panel, Indexing Options

14. You are working with a customer that has a small workgroup (peer-to-peer) network with Windows 10 PCs. The employee computers have a program that requires using the X: drive. Several computer users need to be able to access this drive, which is actually a shared folder located on the manager's PC. What can you do to make this drive available for other computers to access as drive X:? (Choose two.)

    A. On each client computer, open File Explorer, click This PC, then click Map network drive. Choose drive letter X, then navigate to the shared resource.

    B. On the manager's PC, navigate to the shared folder, then right-click it and choose Map network drive.

    C. On the manager's PC, ensure that each user who will connect to the manager's PC has a user account.

    D. On the client computer, create a folder called `Drive X:`, then on the manager's PC, map `Drive X:` to that folder.

15. You are setting up a network for a very small company. They have a total of 10 computers running a mix of Windows 10 Home and Windows 10 Pro computers, and they have a network-attached printer. What will you use to allow them to share files and their printer?

   A. Domain

   B. Workgroup

   C. Homegroup

   D. Crossover cables

16. A user's Windows workstation seems to be using an excessive amount of memory. Which management tool could you use to identify the application that is causing the problem?

   A. Performance Monitor

   B. Computer Management

   C. Windows Memory Diagnostics

   D. Processes tab of Task Manager

17. The CEO will be attending several meetings whose discussions must remain confidential. They want to ensure that the microphone on their Windows 10 PC is not available while they are using certain apps. Where can these settings be configured?

   A. In Windows Settings, choose Privacy, then Microphone.

   B. Device Manager.

   C. Computer Management.

   D. In Windows Settings, choose Personalization.

18. You are manually configuring IPv4 addresses on a computer. The IP address is `200.100.1.10`, and the network number is 200.100.0.0. What is the appropriate subnet mask for this computer?

   A. `200.100.0.0`

   B. `255.255.0.0`

   C. `0.0.255.255`

   D. `192.168.0.0`

19. You are configuring a Windows client computer on a network that has a DHCP and DNS server attached. Where will the computer get its IP address and subnet mask?

   A. You will manually configure them in Windows Settings by choosing Personalization.

   B. You will manually configure them in Windows Settings, by choosing Network & Internet.

   C. It will automatically get them from the DHCP server.

   D. It will automatically get them from the DNS server.

20. You have been told to configure a static IP of `110.110.1.5` for a server. This server will need to be able to access the Internet. Which one of the following is not a required setting to configure?

    A. Default gateway

    B. IP address

    C. Proxy server

    D. Subnet mask

21. Considering the graphic, what is most likely the IP address of a router?

```
Administrator: Command Prompt                                           —    □    ×

Wireless LAN adapter Wi-Fi:

    Connection-specific DNS Suffix  . : lan1
    Description . . . . . . . . . . . : Intel(R) Dual Band Wireless-AC 7265
    Physical Address. . . . . . . . . : 48-45-20-C1-12-BD
    DHCP Enabled. . . . . . . . . . . : Yes
    Autoconfiguration Enabled . . . . : Yes
    Link-local IPv6 Address . . . . . : fe80::308c:fee2:2acb:8337%17(Preferred)
    IPv4 Address. . . . . . . . . . . : 192.168.1.229(Preferred)
    Subnet Mask . . . . . . . . . . . : 255.255.255.0
    Lease Obtained. . . . . . . . . . : Saturday, November 20, 2021 12:42:51 PM
    Lease Expires . . . . . . . . . . : Saturday, December 4, 2021 6:46:11 AM
    Default Gateway . . . . . . . . . : 192.168.1.1
    DHCP Server . . . . . . . . . . . : 192.168.1.1
    DHCPv6 IAID . . . . . . . . . . . : 172508448
    DHCPv6 Client DUID. . . . . . . . : 00-01-00-01-28-99-BB-10-48-45-20-C1-12-BD
    DNS Servers . . . . . . . . . . . : 192.168.1.1
    NetBIOS over Tcpip. . . . . . . . : Enabled

Ethernet adapter Bluetooth Network Connection:

    Media State . . . . . . . . . . . : Media disconnected
    Connection-specific DNS Suffix  . :
    Description . . . . . . . . . . . : Bluetooth Device (Personal Area Network)
    Physical Address. . . . . . . . . : 48-45-20-C1-12-C1
    DHCP Enabled. . . . . . . . . . . : Yes
    Autoconfiguration Enabled . . . . : Yes

C:\WINDOWS\system32>
```

    A. `192.168.1.229`

    B. `192.168.1.1`

    C. `48-45-20-C1-12-BD`

    D. `255.255.255.0`

22. You're creating a network diagram for a company that has just hired you as a network admin. Which of the following could be the default gateway on the company's network? (Choose two.)

    A. Web server

    B. Proxy server

    C. Router

    D. Switch

23. What is the purpose of a subnet mask?
    A. Identifies the network portion of an IPv4 address
    B. Identifies the network portion of an IPv6 address
    C. Masks (hides) part of the IP address from a hacker
    D. Masks (hides) the host number from a hacker

24. You've been asked to help with a network for a company that has 50 computers. They've been using workgroups, but it is getting too difficult. There is an assortment of Windows editions on the computers, including Windows Home, Windows Pro, and Windows Pro for Workstations. What will you do to set up their new network? (Choose two.)
    A. Upgrade all the Windows Home PCs to Windows Pro.
    B. Install a server with Active Directory.
    C. Downgrade all the Windows Pro for Workstations to Windows Pro.
    D. Upgrade all the workstations to Windows Enterprise.

25. You work for a multinational corporation that is using Windows 10 laptops. All the company laptops are configured to use United States English, but a worker that speaks Bajan (Barbados English) would prefer to see apps and websites in their native language. Is this possible?
    A. No, this is not possible.
    B. Yes, Add English (Barbados) in the Control Panel, Programs and Features utility.
    C. Yes, add English (Barbados) in Windows Settings, Time & Language, Language section.
    D. Yes, but it will require reinstalling the OS in Bajan.

26. A Windows workstation has an application that appears to be locked up, but the keyboard is responsive in other applications. What system tool can you use to terminate the nonresponsive application?
    A. Event Viewer
    B. Task Manager
    C. Computer Management
    D. `msconfig.exe`

27. Which of the following Control Panel utilities enables configuration of a proxy server?
    A. Internet Options
    B. File Explorer Options
    C. Device Manager
    D. Security and Maintenance

28. Considering the graphic, what do you know about the network configuration of this computer? (Choose three.)

```
■ Administrator: Command Prompt                                          —   □   ×

Wireless LAN adapter Wi-Fi:

    Connection-specific DNS Suffix  . : lan1
    Description . . . . . . . . . . . : Intel(R) Dual Band Wireless-AC 7265
    Physical Address. . . . . . . . . : 48-45-20-C1-12-BD
    DHCP Enabled. . . . . . . . . . . : Yes
    Autoconfiguration Enabled . . . . : Yes
    Link-local IPv6 Address . . . . . : fe80::308c:fee2:2acb:8337%17(Preferred)
    IPv4 Address. . . . . . . . . . . : 192.168.1.229(Preferred)
    Subnet Mask . . . . . . . . . . . : 255.255.255.0
    Lease Obtained. . . . . . . . . . : Saturday, November 20, 2021 12:42:51 PM
    Lease Expires . . . . . . . . . . : Saturday, December 4, 2021 6:46:11 AM
    Default Gateway . . . . . . . . . : 192.168.1.1
    DHCP Server . . . . . . . . . . . : 192.168.1.1
    DHCPv6 IAID . . . . . . . . . . . : 172508448
    DHCPv6 Client DUID. . . . . . . . : 00-01-00-01-28-99-BB-10-48-45-20-C1-12-BD
    DNS Servers . . . . . . . . . . . : 192.168.1.1
    NetBIOS over Tcpip. . . . . . . . : Enabled

Ethernet adapter Bluetooth Network Connection:

    Media State . . . . . . . . . . . : Media disconnected
    Connection-specific DNS Suffix  . :
    Description . . . . . . . . . . . : Bluetooth Device (Personal Area Network)
    Physical Address. . . . . . . . . : 48-45-20-C1-12-C1
    DHCP Enabled. . . . . . . . . . . : Yes
    Autoconfiguration Enabled . . . . : Yes

C:\WINDOWS\system32>
```

    A. The PC is configured to obtain an address dynamically.

    B. This computer is getting its address from a DHCP server.

    C. The IPv4 address is a routable address.

    D. The internal network number is `192.168.1.0`.

29. Given the IP address of `fe80::308c:fee2:2abc:8337`, what do we know about this address? (Choose two.)

    A. It is an IPv4 address.

    B. It is an IPv6 address.

    C. The subnet mask is 0.

    D. It is not routable.

30. You see an IP address with /48 after it. What does the /48 tell you? (Choose two.)

    A. There are 48 PCs on this network.

    B. The prefix length is 48 bits.

    C. This network uses the IPv6 addressing scheme.

    D. This network uses the IPv4 addressing scheme.

31. Which of the following IPv6 address types are routable?

   A. Global unicast

   B. Link-local

   C. Loopback

   D. Unique local

32. You are on a Windows computer that is joined to a workgroup. You're going home and ready to shut your computer down but want to be certain that no one is using the shared files on the computer first. Where would you go to check?

   A. Task Manager

   B. Users and Groups

   C. Performance Monitor

   D. Control Panel ➤ Networking

33. You have a workstation with a 64-bit processor and no operating system. When you install an operating system on the workstation, which of the following is true?

   A. You can only install a 64-bit operating system.

   B. You can only install a 32-bit operating system.

   C. You can install either a 64-bit or 32-bit operating system.

   D. You can install a 64-bit operating system or a 32-bit operating system running in compatibility mode.

34. A customer has a PC from 2017 on which they would like to install Windows 10 Pro. What is the minimum processor speed they must have to install Windows 10 64-bit?

   A. 1 GHz

   B. 2 GHz

   C. 3 GHz

   D. 10 GHz

35. Which of the following is not a Windows 10 edition?

   A. Home

   B. Enterprise

   C. Pro Artist

   D. Pro Workstation

36. What information do you need to connect to a PC using Remote Desktop?

　　A. The IP address of the PC

　　B. The password to the network that the PC resides on

　　C. The name under "How to connect to this PC" when Remote Desktop was enabled

　　D. The password of the signed-on PC user

37. You're troubleshooting a PC and want to see what ports TCP is connected on and the IP addresses of those connections. What command-line utility can you use to see statistics on network interfaces?

　　A. `ping`

　　B. `nbtstat`

　　C. `nslookup`

　　D. `netstat`

38. A new technician asked you how to use a Windows command. In the spirit of sharing knowledge with others, you show them how to get help on many commands instead of just one. Which one of the following does not work with any commands?

　　A. `help [command name]`

　　B. `[command name] help`

　　C. `[command name] /?`

　　D. `/? [command name]`

39. Which Windows utility allows you to view error messages generated by system events, applications, or login failures?

　　A. System Information

　　B. Windows Defender

　　C. Event Viewer

　　D. Disk Management

40. To learn how much RAM is in this system, what command did you type in the search bar and launch to quickly bring up the window shown in the graphic?

```
System Information
File  Edit  View  Help

System Summary           Item                      Value
  Hardware Resources     System SKU                ASUS-NotebookSKU
  Components             Processor                 Intel(R) Core(TM) i7-6500U CPU @ 2.50GHz, 2592 Mhz, 2 C...
  Software Environment   BIOS Version/Date         American Megatrends Inc. Q524UQ.301, 4/18/2019
                         SMBIOS Version            3.0
                         Embedded Controller V...  255.255
                         BIOS Mode                 UEFI
                         BaseBoard Manufacturer    ASUSTeK COMPUTER INC.
                         BaseBoard Product         Q524UQ
                         BaseBoard Version         1.0
                         Platform Role             Mobile
                         Secure Boot State         On
                         PCR7 Configuration        Elevation Required to View
                         Windows Directory         C:\WINDOWS
                         System Directory          C:\WINDOWS\system32
                         Boot Device               \Device\HarddiskVolume1
                         Locale                    United States
                         Hardware Abstraction L... Version = "10.0.19041.1151"
                         User Name                 HOT-CHOCOLATE\Audrey
                         Time Zone                 Eastern Standard Time
                         Installed Physical Mem... 12.0 GB
                         Total Physical Memory     11.9 GB
                         Available Physical Mem... 1.79 GB
                         Total Virtual Memory      23.4 GB
                         Available Virtual Memory  3.36 GB
                         Page File Space           11.5 GB
                         Page File                 C:\pagefile.sys
                         Kernel DMA Protection     Off
                         Virtualization-based se... Not enabled
                         Device Encryption Supp... Elevation Required to View

Find what:  [_____]   Find    Close Find
  Search selected category only   Search category names only
```

- **A.** msinfo32.exe
- **B.** resmon.exe
- **C.** msconfig.exe
- **D.** devmgmt.msc

41. You find that you are often using System Configuration, Disk Cleanup, and Event Viewer. What Windows 10 Control Panel utility gives you quick access to these and more tools?

- **A.** Computer Management
- **B.** Resource Monitor
- **C.** Administrative Tools
- **D.** Task Scheduler

42. Your manager has a laptop running Windows. They want to configure the laptop so that when it is on battery power, the display shuts off after five minutes of inactivity. When the laptop is plugged in, the display needs to stay active for up to 45 minutes of inactivity. Which Control Panel utility is used to configure these settings?

   A. Power Options

   B. Computer Management

   C. Performance Monitor

   D. System Configuration

43. You need to work at a command prompt on a Windows PC. When you open the prompt, you are at `C:\window\system32`. You need to work on the second partition, which is listed as drive D:. How will you navigate to drive D:? Assume you press Enter after the command.

   A. `root D:`

   B. `D:`

   C. `cd D:`

   D. `cd D:\`

44. Which Windows 10 Editions support up to four CPU sockets? (Choose two.)

   A. Home

   B. Pro

   C. Pro for Workstations

   D. Enterprise

45. You have a workstation with a 32-bit processor and no operating system installed. When you install an operating system on the workstation, which of the following is true?

   A. You can only install a 32-bit operating system.

   B. You can install a 64-bit operating system but it will run in compatibility mode.

   C. You can install either a 32-bit or 64-bit operating system and either will run fine.

   D. You can install a 64-bit operating system but it will only run half as fast.

46. You are installing the Windows 10 Home 64-bit operating system on a friend's computer. What is the minimum storage space that must be available for the OS installation?

   A. 1 GHz

   B. 2 GHz

   C. 16 GB

   D. 20 GB

47. You are in the Windows 10 Command Prompt, using Run as administrator. There is a directory named `d:\files` that you want to delete. It currently has six subdirectories and dozens of files in it. Which command should you use to delete `d:\files`?

   A. `del d:\files /s`

   B. `del d:\files /q`

   C. `rmdir d:\files /s`

   D. `rmdir d:\files /q`

48. You've installed several identical new PCs and want to capture a baseline of their performance for future troubleshooting. What tool would be best suited for that purpose?

    A. Event Viewer

    B. Performance Monitor

    C. System Information

    D. System Configuration

49. A user has called the help desk saying that the Internet is down on their Windows computer. After asking a few questions, you want to examine their network configuration to determine the cause of their computer's connectivity problem. You've talked them through accessing the Windows Command Prompt. What command will you have them type so they can read the computer configuration to you?

    A. `ipconfig /all`

    B. `ipconfig /renew`

    C. `ip`

    D. `tracert`

50. A computer user that you support is having difficulty reading the words on the screen because they have a visual impairment that makes distinguishing colors difficult for them. What can you change in Windows Settings to make their screen more readable?

    A. Go to Personalization, then Fonts.

    B. Go to Personalization, then Background, and choose High contrast settings.

    C. Select System, then Display, then Nightlight.

    D. Select Accounts, then choose High Contrast Settings.

51. You need to work at a command prompt on a Windows PC. When you open the prompt, you are at `C:\window\system32`. You need to be at the root of the C: drive for what you'll be doing. How do you get to C:\? Assume you would press Enter after the command.

    A. `cd c:`

    B. `cd\`

    C. `C:\`

    D. `cd root`

52. A laptop user has traveled to visit a client and forgot their power adapter. The user is heading to lunch with the client and wants to conserve battery power but enable the fastest possible startup when they get back, with the applications already open. Which power mode will conserve battery life but enable the fastest startup?

    A. Shut down

    B. Sleep

    C. Hibernate

    D. Resting

53. Which of the following operating systems is open source, allowing its users to customize it as they wish to suit their individual needs?

   A. Windows

   B. Linux

   C. macOS

   D. Chrome OS

54. What does Keychain provide for the user in macOS?

   A. Password management

   B. Local file sharing

   C. Certificate management

   D. Screen protection

55. You're installing Windows 10 Pro edition on a workstation. How much memory must there be? (Choose two.)

   A. 20 GB for the 64-bit version

   B. 16 GB for the 32-bit version

   C. 1 GB for the 32-bit version

   D. 2 GB for the 64-bit version

56. Which Windows 10 edition supports up to 2 TB of RAM?

   A. Home

   B. Pro

   C. Pro for Workstations

   D. Enterprise

57. You work at home with a computer that has a Windows Home edition installed. You're trying to run gpedit.msc to establish group policies on the computer that will limit what your children can do on it. For some reason, gpedit.msc won't launch. What do you do?

   A. Reboot the computer, then run gpedit.msc.

   B. Upgrade to Windows Pro edition.

   C. Install Windows Active Directory.

   D. Launch it from Administrative Tools.

58. You are at a Windows command prompt, on the C: drive. You need to create a directory named files on the D: drive. What is the proper command and syntax to do this?

   A. cd d:\files

   B. cd files d:\

   C. md d:\files

   D. md files d:\

59. You will be installing several new resource-intensive applications on a Windows workstation, and the user has concerns over system performance. You want to monitor memory and CPU performance and set up the workstation so that it logs performance over time. Which utility should you use to set this up?

A. Resource Monitor

B. Performance Monitor

C. Task Viewer

D. Event Viewer

60. You don't like the pictures that are on your desktop and change from time to time. Where will you go in Windows Settings to change this setting?

A. Accounts

B. Apps

C. Personalization

D. System

61. What operating system developed by Google is used on tablets or laptops used mainly for accessing the Internet and using Android applications?

A. Ubuntu

B. iOS

C. Windows 11 Pro

D. Chrome OS

62. On your laptop running macOS, what is the name of the utility used to browse through files and folders?

A. Spotlight

B. Remote Disc

C. iCloud

D. Finder

63. You're troubleshooting a network connectivity issue and want to see if the local computer can reach a particular server on the web. What command will you use?

A. ping

B. tracert

C. ipconfig

D. pathping

64. Which command in a Linux environment is used to display the full path to the current directory?

A. ls

B. pwd

C. cp

D. yum

65. One of the users you support has a MacBook. They're finding that their desktop is too cluttered. What can they use to have quick access to what they want and help them organize their desktop? (Choose two.)

A. Finder

B. Time Machine

C. Spaces

D. Multiple desktops

66. What is the name of the bar on the bottom of the screenshot shown in the graphic, where shortcuts to commonly used programs and utilities are kept in the macOS?

A. Taskbar

B. Dock

C. File Explorer

D. Finder

67. What Windows feature best describes Event Viewer (`eventvwr.msc`), Disk Management (`diskmgmt.msc`), and Certificate Manager (`certmgr.msc`)?

A. Services

B. Processes

C. Policies

D. Snap-ins

68. Your laptop battery is getting older and won't hold a charge as long as it once did, so you want to ensure that, when you walk away from it for a period of time and it isn't plugged in, it will not use any power but save everything and let you pick up where you left off working. What power state will work for this scenario?

A. Always On

B. Sleep

C. Hibernate

D. Hyper-V

69. You are at a command prompt on a Windows PC, at C:\, and need to get to C:\Windows\ system32. Which command listed will get you there? Assume you press Enter after the line. (Choose two.)

A. `c:\windows cd system32`

B. `cd C:\windows\system32`

C. `cd windows\system32`

D. `cd system32 windows`

70. Your system is running sluggishly, and you want to know why. Which application, as shown in the graphic, shows CPU usage by core and allows you to end problematic processes and stop running services?

> **A.** `eventvwr.msc`
>
> **B.** `lusrmgr.msc`
>
> **C.** `perfmon.msc`
>
> **D.** `resmon.exe`

71. You have installed Windows 10 32-bit on a desktop computer that has a 32-bit processor. It seems to be working fine, but when you install more RAM, bringing the total up to 12 GB, the operating system doesn't recognize anything above 4 GB. What is the problem?

> **A.** You need to tell the BIOS that the extra RAM is there.
>
> **B.** A 32-bit OS can support a maximum of only 4 GB of RAM.
>
> **C.** You need to go to Device Manager to add the RAM.
>
> **D.** You need to replace the motherboard.

72. You're at a friend's house when a manager at your company calls to say they are having a problem with their Windows Pro PC while working at home. You listen and tell them you can easily fix it using Remote Desktop to take over their computer for a minute or two. Which of the following would not be an option to use Remote Desktop from where you are?

> **A.** Use your friend's Windows Home PC.
>
> **B.** Use your friend's Windows Pro PC.
>
> **C.** Use Remote Desktop Mobile on your iOS device.
>
> **D.** Use Remote Desktop Mobile on your Android device.

73. You are at a Windows workstation and have a command prompt open. Which of the following commands is used to refresh Group Policy settings and force their changes to take effect?

> **A.** `gpedit`
>
> **B.** `gpresult`
>
> **C.** `gprefresh`
>
> **D.** `gpupdate`

74. You've been having trouble with network communications to one of your company's offices. You want to determine the source of latency on the connection. What command will you use in the Windows Command Prompt to see where the latency is?

> **A.** `grep`
>
> **B.** `pathping`
>
> **C.** `tracert`
>
> **D.** `mv`

75. Your spouse is trying to work at home but has started to complain about the constant notifications appearing on the computer and interrupting their work. What category can you access in Windows Settings to turn them off?

> **A.** System
>
> **B.** Gaming
>
> **C.** Update and Security
>
> **D.** Apps

76. Which of the following commands is used by an administrator on a Red Hat Linux system to update software?

A. pwd

B. ls

C. cp

D. yum

77. A macOS user is complaining that their MacBook has been acting strangely lately, and it's very slow to start. What utility will you use to repair any potential disk errors?

A. FileVault

B. Terminal

C. Disk Utility

D. Force Quit

78. You've created a batch file that needs to run every day before the employees arrive. What can you use to ensure that this batch file is run every weekday at 6 a.m.?

A. Task Scheduler

B. Event Viewer

C. Device Manager

D. Local Users And Groups

79. A smartphone user recently found their phone on an EOL list. They asked you what this means. Why will you recommend they purchase a new phone?

A. They can't download any more apps.

B. Their phone will stop working by the date on the list.

C. Their phone may not receive any more security updates.

D. Their phone will no longer connect to cellular service.

80. You are on a Windows computer working at a command prompt and need to see a list of files in the directory that you are working in. What command will you type?

A. dir

B. ls

C. pwd

D. grep

81. A user with a Windows workstation recently received a second hard drive. Another administrator created a partition on the hard drive, and it's ready for use. The user will store the raw video files they create on that drive and insists that it be called the R: drive. Which of the following statements is true?

A. You can use Disk Management to change the drive letter to R:.

B. You can use Disk Management to change the drive letter to R:, but only if it's a dynamic disk.

    C. You can use Disk Management to change the drive letter to R:, but only if it's in an extended partition.

    D. You will need to use Disk Management to delete the partition first, then re-create it as R:.

82. A salesperson at your company travels with their macOS laptop every week. You want to encrypt the data on their startup disk to ensure data security. What macOS utility will you use?

    A. Finder

    B. Time Machine

    C. FileVault

    D. BitLocker

83. A user wants to perform a backup on their MacBook. Which software utility should be used to make backups?

    A. Image Recovery

    B. Time Machine

    C. iBackup

    D. Accessibility

84. One of your network users has a MacBook Pro. Where should this user go to see whether there are any OS updates available?

    A. Open the App Store and click Updates in the toolbar.

    B. Open Safari and click Updates in the toolbar.

    C. Open System Preferences and click Updates in the toolbar.

    D. Open Finder and click Updates on the menu bar.

85. What command will bring up the screen shown in the graphic?

About Windows

Windows 10

Microsoft Windows
Version 20H2 (OS Build 19042.1288)
© Microsoft Corporation. All rights reserved.

The Windows 10 Home operating system and its user interface are protected by trademark and other pending or existing intellectual property rights in the United States and other countries/regions.

This product is licensed under the Microsoft Software License Terms to:

    user name
    org name

OK

    A. `winver`

    B. `version`

    C. `osver`

    D. `build`

86. Which of the following commands was used to display the screen snippet shown in the graphic?

```
Select Administrator: Command Prompt                    —    □    ✕

RSOP data for HOT-CHOCOLATE\Audrey on HOT-CHOCOLATE : Logging Mode
-----------------------------------------------------------------

OS Configuration:            Standalone Workstation
OS Version:                  10.0.19042
Site Name:                   N/A
Roaming Profile:             N/A
Local Profile:               C:\Users\Audrey
Connected over a slow link?: No


USER SETTINGS
-------------

    Last time Group Policy was applied: 11/28/2021 at 12:21:18 PM
    Group Policy was applied from:      N/A
    Group Policy slow link threshold:   500 kbps
    Domain Name:                        HOT-CHOCOLATE
    Domain Type:                        <Local Computer>

    Applied Group Policy Objects
    ----------------------------
        N/A

    The following GPOs were not applied because they were filtered out
    ------------------------------------------------------------------
        Local Group Policy
            Filtering:  Not Applied (Empty)

    The user is a part of the following security groups
    ---------------------------------------------------
        High Mandatory Level
        Everyone
        Local account and member of Administrators group
        BUILTIN\Administrators
        BUILTIN\Users
        NT AUTHORITY\INTERACTIVE
        CONSOLE LOGON
        NT AUTHORITY\Authenticated Users
        This Organization
        aoshea@live.com
```

    A. `gpedit`

    B. `gpresult`

    C. `gprefresh`

    D. `gpupdate`

87. Which Linux command is used to copy files, groups of files, or whole directories from one place to another?

    A. mv

    B. cp

    C. find

    D. cat

88. Despite your great objections, someone you know is still running a Windows OS that pre-dates Windows 10 and has reached its end of extended support. The software they regularly use on it still works, and they have an antivirus installed. Why should they update to a newer OS? (Choose two.)

    A. They will not receive security updates.

    B. They will not receive feature updates.

    C. Their apps will stop working.

    D. Their OS will stop working at end-of-life.

89. A smartphone user has come to you for help. They would like a laptop so they can use a big-ger screen but don't know what to choose. They're accustomed to doing their work online with Google Docs and their smartphone and saving it to the cloud. They would like to be able to use some of the same apps that they have available on their Android phone. Cost is a factor. What type of laptop would you recommend for this user?

    A. Windows Home

    B. Linux

    C. macOS

    D. Chromebook

90. A user called the help desk because they were denied access to a secure server and received a message that they have an invalid certificate. Their computer was recently updated. Where can you go to manage their certificates?

    A. Device Manager

    B. Local Users and Groups

    C. Certificate Manager

    D. Group Policy Editor

91. Which desktop operating system is a proprietary product of Apple?

    A. Apache

    B. Red Hat Linux

    C. macOS

    D. FreeBSD

92. A user on your network complains that they are unable to type a human-friendly name like Sybex.com into their browser to reach a website, but typing an IP address in the browser works. What client network configuration setting do you suspect is the problem?

- **A.** Authentication server
- **B.** DNS server
- **C.** DHCP server
- **D.** Proxy server

93. You need to start a new shell on a Linux workstation with root permissions. Which command should you use to do this?

- **A.** su
- **B.** sudo
- **C.** apt-get
- **D.** ps

94. A user wants to change the resolution on their MacBook. Which System Preferences pane would they use to do that?

- **A.** Printers & Scanners
- **B.** Desktop & Screen Saver
- **C.** Accessibility
- **D.** Displays

95. You want to be able to access your Windows Pro desktop PC at home no matter where you are. Which of the following do you not need to do?

- **A.** Upgrade to Windows Enterprise.
- **B.** Enable Remote Desktop on your PC.
- **C.** Open Remote Desktop Connection, provide the PC name, and click Connect.
- **D.** Install the Remote Desktop App on your smartphone.

96. You are at a Windows command prompt. You believe that some of the Windows system files are corrupted. Which command should you use to scan and repair problematic system files?

- **A.** sfc /scanfile
- **B.** sfc /scannow
- **C.** sfc /verifyfile
- **D.** sfc /verifyonly

97. You are at a Windows command prompt. Which command allows you to copy files and directories, copy NTFS permissions, and mirror a directory tree?

- **A.** copy
- **B.** xcopy
- **C.** robocopy
- **D.** copyall

98. The hard drive performance on your Windows workstation has deteriorated over time. To attempt to improve performance, you want to ensure that files on the hard drive are written in contiguous blocks. Which Windows tool should you use to make this happen?

A. Disk Management

B. Optimize Drives

C. Disk Optimizer

D. Device Manager

99. Your client is taking over a business and wants to upgrade the computer systems, which are currently all legacy Windows machines. They will be using Microsoft 365 along with accounting and manufacturing software that is part of the business. They are concerned about compatibility of other files with their customers, vendors, and historical company data. What operating system would you recommend for them?

A. Chrome OS

B. Linux

C. macOS

D. Windows

100. In macOS, where can the menus Displays, Printers, and Privacy be found and settings changed?

A. System Preferences

B. Accessibility

C. Settings

D. App Store

101. Your friend has a Windows 10 PC and has never made a backup. You provide them with an external drive to use. What category will you choose in Windows Settings to turn on automatic backups for your friend every hour?

A. System

B. Apps

C. Update & Security

D. Network & Internet

102. Your company has a DHCP server to automatically assign IP addresses to any nodes that connect to it. Which of the following would you want to assign a static IP address to? (Choose two.)

A. Workstation

B. File server

C. Printer/MFD

D. Local printer

103. You're installing an application that requires 4 GB of RAM on a Windows 10 64-bit work-station. The workstation has 4 GB of RAM. Will you need to make any configuration changes to the system to install this application?

    A. No, since the system already has 4 GB of RAM.

    B. No, because the OS and the Application won't be running at the same time.

    C. Yes, you'll need at least 4 additional GB of RAM.

    D. Yes, you'll need at least 2 additional GB of RAM.

104. Which of these filesystem types is used when running a Linux distribution?

    A. FAT32

    B. NTFS

    C. ext4

    D. APFS

105. You are going to install Windows on a workstation from an image located on a server. What does the workstation need to support to install Windows this way?

    A. netboot

    B. Unattended installation

    C. PXE boot

    D. USB boot

106. You're in a secure environment where the workstations are not allowed to have USB ports or DVD drives. You've just received 10 new bare-metal workstations, with PXE support, that need to have Windows installed. How will you install the Windows OS on these 10 PCs?

    A. Optical media

    B. External drive

    C. Internet based

    D. Network

107. You need to run just one command as root. What will you use?

    A. su

    B. sudo

    C. apt-get

    D. ps

108. You're working in a school district in a computer lab full of Windows workstations, setting up an application that uses the name of the computer to identify it on the application. What command can you use at a workstation to determine its name? (Choose two.)

    A. nslookup

    B. clientname

    C. hostname

    D. ping localhost

109. You're at a Windows workstation, troubleshooting a connectivity problem with a computer in another office of your campus area network. You need to determine where packets between the two are being dropped. Which command will tell you the last router the packet traversed?

    A. `ipconfig /all`

    B. `ping`

    C. `ip`

    D. `tracert`

110. You're setting up a computer for a user with limited vision, who would like to have the contents of the screen read to them. What Control Panel utility will you use to accomplish this?

    A. Devices and Printers

    B. Programs and Features

    C. Ease of Access Center

    D. Sound

111. The Linux workstation you are using seems slow. You want to see what processes are running on the computer. Which command should you use?

    A. `su`

    B. `sudo`

    C. `apt-get`

    D. `ps`

112. Which of the following is not an advantage that the ext4 filesystem has over ext3 filesystem?

    A. Supports larger volumes and files

    B. Compatible with macOS and Windows

    C. Unlimited number of subdirectories

    D. Faster filesystem checks

113. A user installed a new headset, but the audio is still playing through the speakers. Where can you go to change that configuration? (Choose two.)

    A. Control Panel, Security and Maintenance

    B. Windows Settings, Devices

    C. Control Panel, Sound

    D. Windows Settings, Apps

114. A user wants to know if it's possible to change what happens when they close the lid on their Windows 11 laptop. Currently closing the lid does nothing, but they would like the laptop to hibernate when the lid is closed. Where can this setting be changed?

    A. Control Panel, Power Options utility

    B. Control Panel, Devices and Printers utility

    C. Windows Settings, System group, choose Power & Battery

    D. Windows Settings, Devices group, choose Power Options

115. Which of the following Windows operating systems and editions cannot be upgraded to Windows 10 Pro directly from the desktop by performing an in-place upgrade? (Choose two.)

    A. Windows 7 Enterprise

    B. Windows 8.1 (core)

    C. Windows 10 Home

    D. Windows 8 Pro

116. You need to uninstall an app that is on your Linux computer. What command will you use?

    A. su

    B. sudo

    C. apt-get

    D. ps

117. You are working at a Windows command prompt. Which command should you use to copy directories and subdirectories but not empty directories?

    A. xcopy /e

    B. xcopy /s

    C. xcopy /h

    D. xcopy /a

118. You're having trouble with a new digitizing pad that the operating system doesn't seem to be recognizing. Which MMC (Microsoft Management Console) would you use to trouble-shoot the problem?

    A. Event Viewer

    B. Performance Monitor

    C. Device Manager

    D. Disk Management

119. You suspect that one of your running services is causing problems with the operating system. What is the tool, shown in the graphic, that lets you choose a diagnostic startup on the next restart?

A. Event Viewer

B. Performance Monitor

C. System Information

D. System Configuration

120. You need to check the integrity of key Windows system files on the C: drive, which are hidden from view by default. Which Control Panel utility allows you to view hidden files?

A. Programs and Features

B. File Explorer Options

C. Indexing Options

D. System

121. What is the name of the macOS command-line user interface?

A. Terminal

B. Finder

C. Command Prompt

D. File Explorer

122. You're setting up an online storage system for backing up your data, but the remote storage company said that you need to open up your software firewall to allow it to communicate with your computer. Where in the Windows Control Panel can you do this?

    A. Programs and Features

    B. Internet Options

    C. Windows Defender Firewall

    D. Network and Sharing Center

123. You have a Windows command prompt open. You are in the D:\users directory and want to copy all 20 of the files with a .docx extension into the D:\files directory. Which of the following statements is true?

    A. You need to copy the files one at a time.

    B. You can use the command copy *.docx d:\files.

    C. You can use the command copy all.docx d:\files.

    D. You can use the command copy .docx d:\files.

124. In Linux, what is the name of the interpreter between the user and the operating system?

    A. Terminal

    B. Command Prompt

    C. GUI

    D. Shell

125. You are working on a Linux file server. Which command would you use to see the amount of free disk space on a volume?

    A. grep

    B. df

    C. ps

    D. dig

126. A user wants to ensure that the hard drive in their Windows PC is encrypted for maximum data security. What are two commands you can have the user type into the Run box (Windows Key+R) or Windows Command Prompt to see whether the BitLocker Drive Encryption Service is enabled and running? (Choose two.)

    A. services.msc

    B. perfmon.exe

    C. compmgmt.msc

    D. diskmgmt.msc

127. You're setting up security for a company that is expanding rapidly. Part of your plan is to create groups to manage permissions to folders, and then add users to those groups to grant them the permissions they need. What utility will let you add users to groups?

A. Device Manager

B. Local Users and Groups

C. Certificate Manager

D. Group Policy Editor

128. One of your users has a MacBook Air, and an application appears to have crashed. What can they use to compel the app to close?

A. Task Manager

B. Force Quit

C. Terminal

D. Time Machine

129. You would like to monitor CPU, memory, and Wi-Fi usage in real time on a Windows computer. Which of the following options will provide you with that information? (Choose two.)

A. The Task Manager Performance tab

B. Administrative Tools, System Information

C. Event Viewer

D. Resource Monitor

130. You are on a Linux computer working in Terminal and need to see a list of files in the directory that you are working in. What command will you type?

A. dir

B. ls

C. pwd

D. grep

131. What Linux utility is like the Windows Command Prompt?

A. Time Machine

B. Mission Control

C. Terminal

D. Shell

132. A system has been doing some quirky things and you think it might have something to do with a temporary file. A best practice to avoid malware is to remove files and programs that aren't being used. Which tool, shown in the graphic (with the name redacted), will you use to delete temporary and unused files from a computer system?

- **A.** Resource Monitor (`resmon.exe`)
- **B.** Disk Management (`diskmgmt.msc`)
- **C.** Registry Editor (`regedit.exe`)
- **D.** Disk Cleanup (`cleanmgr.exe`)

133. You are at a Windows command prompt. A remote Windows workstation named advertising4 is misbehaving and needs to be shut down and rebooted. What is the proper syntax to shut down this remote system?

- **A.** `shutdown /r /m \\advertising4`
- **B.** `shutdown /s /m \\advertising4`
- **C.** `shutdown /r /c \\advertising4`
- **D.** `shutdown /s /c \\advertising4`

134. You have recently deployed a custom application to several Windows workstations on your network. The application appears to have a bug, and the developer suggests you edit the Registry to fix it. Which administrative tool would you use to do this?

- **A.** `msinfo32`
- **B.** `command`
- **C.** `regedit`
- **D.** `notepad`

135. A couple of applications that run at startup are causing problems with a computer. Where can you change settings so that those programs won't automatically start when the computer does?

   A. Task Manager, Services tab

   B. Task Manager, Startup tab

   C. Services console

   D. Task Scheduler

136. You are working on a computer with macOS, and about a dozen applications are open. Which feature allows you to easily see all of them and switch to your desired application?

   A. Spotlight

   B. Keychain

   C. Mission Control

   D. Finder

137. You have a Windows Pro computer with multiple printers installed. Which Control Panel utility allows you to manage multiple print servers and printers from a single interface?

   A. Devices and Printers

   B. Programs and Features

   C. Network and Sharing Center

   D. Device Manager

138. One power state will close applications and files, and log off users like a full shutdown would, then save the kernel state and system session to a hibernation file before shutdown. Then, when the computer is restarted, it will automatically and quickly restore that file, saving some of the time involved in a normal boot. Which of the following states is being described?

   A. Hibernate

   B. Sleep

   C. Selective Suspend

   D. Fast Startup

139. You're troubleshooting a computer that is unable to resolve domain names to IP addresses. What command-line utility can help identify what DNS server the computer relies on?

   A. `nslookup`

   B. `netstat`

   C. `ping`

   D. `tracert`

140. A user recently left the company, and you need to change ownership of their files on the Linux server to a new user. Which command should you use to do this?

    A. chown

    B. chmod

    C. cat

    D. cp

141. You need to configure a virtual private network (VPN) for an employee working remotely on a Windows Pro computer. What category group in Windows Settings provides options for establishing dial-up or VPN connections?

    A. Network and Sharing Center

    B. Network & Internet

    C. System

    D. Accounts

142. While using your Windows laptop remotely, you want to set up a secure connection over a Wi-Fi network. What type of connection do you need to establish?

    A. VPN

    B. Dial-up

    C. Fios

    D. Hotspot

143. A print queue has stalled, so you're going to stop and restart the Print Spooler service. Where can you do this? (Choose two.)

    A. The Services console

    B. Task Manager, Services tab

    C. Disk Management, Services tab

    D. Task Scheduler

144. A user types their username and password into a workstation that is configured in a domain. What examines their information and determines whether they are allowed access to network resources?

    A. Local operating system

    B. File server

    C. Authentication server

    D. DHCP server

145. Your spouse takes gaming seriously and has complained that restart notifications some-times pop up on the screen at crucial moments, disrupting their game. What settings group can you use to stop restart notifications from appearing and stop unnecessary programs from running in the background?

   A. System

   B. Gaming

   C. Update and Security

   D. Apps

146. What type of operating system is found on an Apple iPhone?

   A. iPhone OS

   B. iOS

   C. Android

   D. Windows for iPhone

147. You want to find and download a new application to use for network monitoring on your MacBook. Where can you do this in the macOS?

   A. Finder

   B. App Store

   C. Mission Control

   D. FileVault

148. You work as the IT manager of a telephone call center. Your company just purchased one hundred computers in anticipation of a large wave of hiring, and you need to configure them all with the OS, applications, and settings that your company uses. What type of installation will you do?

   A. Upgrade

   B. Recovery partition

   C. Repair installation

   D. Image deployment

149. A MacBook user has a program that they no longer use. What are their options for removing it from their computer? (Choose two.)

   A. Use Finder, then Applications to locate the app, then right-click and choose Delete.

   B. Use Finder, then Applications to locate the app's folder, then look for an uninstaller and run it.

   C. Use Finder, then Applications to find the app, then drag the app from the Applications folder to the trash.

   D. Click Apple, then Uninstall, and then choose the app.

150. You're on a Linux system and need to change a user's access to a file. Which command will you use to do this?

  A. chown

  B. chmod

  C. cat

  D. cp

151. You just got a new MacBook for a child, but they said the text on the screen is too hard to read. What system preference would you use to help them?

  A. Accessibility options

  B. Displays

  C. Privacy

  D. Time Machine

152. An application on a user's Windows Pro workstation has become corrupted. Where can you go in Control Panel to attempt to repair or reinstall the application?

  A. Devices and Printers

  B. Programs and Features

  C. Network and Sharing Center

  D. Device Manager

153. A Wi-Fi user at your company said that their MacBook isn't connecting to the network. What option will you choose from Preferences in the Apple menu to turn Wi-Fi on and select Automatically join this network?

  A. Ethernet

  B. Wi-Fi

  C. Network

  D. Accessibility

154. You are at a Linux workstation and need to search for text within several files. Which command should you use?

  A. sudo

  B. grep

  C. cp

  D. ls

155. You need to install Windows on a new machine. Which of the following is not an installation option?

  A. USB

  B. Network

  C. External drive

  D. CD

156. Which of the following is not a best practice for hardening your macOS against attack?

  A. Use Time Machine to back up your Mac.

  B. Use BitLocker to encrypt your drive.

  C. Install updates and patches as soon as they are available.

  D. Turn on the firewall in the Security & Privacy pane.

157. Which of the following file extensions indicates a drive image that can be mounted in macOS and treated like a drive?

  A. .pkg

  B. .bat

  C. .dmg

  D. .app

158. The graphics department of your company just purchased a new printer, and now you need to install it. What System preference pane can you use to install new printers in macOS?

  A. Printers

  B. Printers & Scanners

  C. Devices

  D. Sharing

159. You want to find and download a new Wi-Fi analyzer application to use on your Android phone. Where on your phone would you do this?

  A. Finder

  B. App Store

  C. Mission Control

  D. Play Store app

160. Your friend just bought a new iPad. What type of operating system will it have?

  A. iPhone OS

  B. iOS

  C. iPadOS

  D. Android

161. You would like to see the contents of a file named bogus.txt. What command will you use to view the file's contents?

  A. chown

  B. chmod

  C. cat

  D. cp

162. Your customer, an artist, uses their Windows 10 tablet PC to enter sales and accept customer payments. They walk around the gallery with it and want to conserve as much power as possible. What Control Panel utility will you use to enable USB Selective Suspend? (Choose two.)

   A. Power Options

   B. Device Manager

   C. Programs and Features

   D. Indexing Options

163. Your company just purchased five new MacBook computers for employee use. You will be providing tech support for them. What filesystem will they have?

   A. HFS+

   B. APFS

   C. ext4

   D. NTFS

164. Your friend wants a new phone but has told you that they are not fond of Apple products. They've decided to buy a Microsoft Duo product. What operating system will likely be on their new phone?

   A. iPadOS

   B. iOS

   C. Android

   D. Windows

165. On a Mac using macOS 10.6 or later, what is the best way to protect the system against viruses and other malware? (Choose two.)

   A. Install an antivirus from a vendor you trust.

   B. Ensure the system data files and security updates are set to run automatically.

   C. Only install software from reliable sources.

   D. Use Finder to find and delete viruses and malware.

166. A user calls the hotline saying that they can't get directions and Siri can't give them the weather. What System Preferences pane do they need to use to remedy the situation?

   A. Security & Privacy

   B. Mission Control

   C. Accessibility

   D. Networks

167. A salesperson will be working remotely, and you need to set up a virtual private network (VPN) for them. What Control Panel utility will you use to do this?

   A. Devices and Printers

   B. Programs and Features

   C. Network and Sharing Center

   D. User Accounts

168. A user brought you a laptop that wouldn't boot into the OS. After trying some troubleshooting techniques, you inform them that you will need to reinstall the operating system. After ensuring that they have a backup of their files, you restart the computer, press F10, and the OS installation begins. What type of installation are you doing?

   A. Upgrade

   B. Recovery partition

   C. Repair installation

   D. Image deployment

169. A second person is going to be using the Windows computer at your desk when you're not there. What would you choose in Windows Settings to create their user account?

   A. Accounts

   B. User Accounts

   C. Personalization

   D. System

170. You're working in the Linux Terminal and need to locate a file. Which command lets you locate and perform actions on a file?

   A. find

   B. ps

   C. man

   D. nano

171. A user wants to install an application that requires a 1 GHz processor on a Windows 10, 64-bit installation. What is the minimum speed processor that their computer must have?

   A. 1 GHz

   B. 2 GHz

   C. 3 GHz

   D. 4 GHz

172. Which of the filesystems listed is compatible with more operating systems than the others?

   A. FAT32

   B. exFAT

   C. NTFS

   D. ext4

173. What operating systems can be found on a smartphone? (Choose two.)

    A. iOS

    B. macOS

    C. Android

    D. Windows 11

174. Before you upgrade your Windows 8.1 OS to Windows 10, you want to create a backup of your Windows 8.1 system configuration so that you can restore it if something goes wrong. What should you create?

    A. Restore point

    B. System restore

    C. Windows backup

    D. Shadow copy

175. A friend has a game that they love on their macOS desktop computer, and they want to put it on the Windows laptop that they travel with. What will you tell them?

    A. Sure, it's no problem to install it.

    B. They can only install it if both are 64-bit systems.

    C. They can install macOS software on a Windows machine, but not Windows software on a Mac.

    D. They will need to find a Windows-compatible version of the software to install it on their Windows laptop.

176. You're looking at the specifications for a new computer and notice that it says, "Intel® UHD Graphics 630 with shared graphics memory." What is true about this graphics card? (Choose two.)

    A. The GPU is on an expansion card.

    B. The GPU is located on the processor.

    C. It uses part of the system's RAM.

    D. It has its own VRAM.

177. You want to uninstall an app on a Windows computer. Where will you go in Windows Settings to uninstall it?

    A. System

    B. Apps

    C. Update And Security

    D. Gaming

178. You just built your first computer from components. What type of operating system installation will you perform?

    A. Upgrade installation

    B. Recovery partition

    C. Clean installation

    D. Image deployment

179. You're upgrading your Windows 10 Home edition to Windows 10 Pro. What utility will you use to make a backup of your data before upgrading the system? (Choose two.)

    A. File History

    B. Windows Update

    C. Recovery

    D. Backup

180. You're buying a new graphics-intensive program that says it must have a GPU with 256 MB of dedicated VRAM. Your existing graphics adapter's properties are shown in the graphic. What is your best option?

    A. Purchase a new graphics card that meets the requirement.

    B. Replace the CPU with one that has an integrated GPU.

    C. Add VRAM to your graphics card.

    D. Add RAM to your system.

181. You're working in the Linux Terminal and aren't sure how to use the `ps` command. Which of the following will show you detailed information about the command?

    A. `find ps`

    B. `ps man`

    C. `man ps`

    D. `nano ps`

182. You're moving your Windows 8.1 computer to Windows 10. What type of installation are you doing?

    A. Upgrade installation

    B. Recovery partition

    C. Clean installation

    D. Image deployment

183. You're considering upgrading your Windows 8.1 PC to Windows 10. Which of the following does not need to be done before upgrading?

    A. Backups of user files and preferences

    B. Operating system refresh

    C. Check application and driver compatibility

    D. Check hardware compatibility

184. You're purchasing a software that says it uses 32-bit processing. Your computer has a 64-bit processor. Can you use this software on your computer?

    A. Yes, a 32-bit software can run on a 64-bit processor.

    B. No, a 32-bit software must have a 32-bit processor.

    C. Yes, if you replace the processor with a 32-bit one.

    D. Yes, it will just need more RAM.

185. Which of the following commands, when entered into a Linux terminal, will open a text editor?

    A. find

    B. ps

    C. man

    D. nano

186. You would like to know the IP address of a website. What Linux tool will you use?

    A. chown

    B. dig

    C. top

    D. ip

187. Which of the following is not true regarding managed Apple IDs?

    A. They are created by a company for its employees.

    B. They can't make purchases.

    C. An IT administrator can remove or update your account.

    D. You can reset your own password.

188. Your accounting department uses an application that requires they enter a username and password, then insert a fob into a USB port on the computer in order to move money between accounts at the bank. Which of the following are true? (Choose two.)

A. They are using two-factor authentication.

B. They are using an external software token.

C. They are using an external hardware token.

D. Their bank account can never be hacked.

189. Which of the following filesystems is optimized for flash drives?

A. FAT32

B. NTFS

C. ext4

D. exFAT

190. You are working on a Linux workstation. A file named `docs` needs to be renamed to `newdocs`. What is the right command to do this?

A. `ren docs newdocs`

B. `mv docs newdocs`

C. `cp docs newdocs`

D. `rm docs newdocs`

191. Which of the following software packages lets Linux, Windows, and other operating system platforms use shared files, shared printers, and other resources across a network or the Internet?

A. Spotlight

B. Time Machine

C. Samba

D. FileVault

192. You have Control Panel open and want to quickly check how much RAM is installed in the system and what processor it has. Which Control Panel utility will you use to view this information?

A. System

B. Device Manager

C. Devices And Printers

D. Programs And Features

193. You downloaded a new application that you want to install on your Windows 10 PC and noticed that it has only one file, and that file has an .iso extension. Which of the following is true regarding this file?

A. Double-click it and let it run to install the application.

B. Right-click the file and choose Mount. Windows will then see and treat the file as a disk in an optical drive.

C. You will need a third-party utility to open this file.

D. Right-click and choose Extract to install the software.

194. You're considering installing a new software for monitoring network traffic. You know that it will generate additional network traffic of its own. Which of the following should be considered before purchasing the software? (Choose three.)

A. Impact to the network

B. Impact to operations

C. Impact to the software company

D. Impact to business

195. An application that you're installing requires 20 GB of space plus storage for data files of 400 GB. What is the absolute minimum size your hard drive must be if you're running Windows 10 64-bit, which requires 20 GB of storage?

A. 20 GB

B. 400 GB

C. 420 GB

D. 440 GB

196. You're working at a Linux command prompt (that is, you're in the Linux Terminal) and need to delete a file called oldstuff.txt. Which of the following commands will work?

A. rm oldstuff.txt

B. del oldstuff.txt

C. er oldstuff.txt

D. rd oldstuff.txt

197. Which of the following extensions indicates a file that can be extracted or opened with an installer app to install an application?

A. .pkg

B. .bat

C. .dmg

D. .app

198. Which of the following is not an advantage of downloadable software distribution over using physical media to distribute software?

   A. It's always current.

   B. It costs the distributor less.

   C. It works on a system without a DVD drive.

   D. It works on all bare-metal systems.

199. You're working on a Windows computer that is having some trouble booting. After trying System File Checker (SFC) and other troubleshooting techniques, you decide that you need to reinstall the operating system files. What type of installation will you be doing?

   A. Upgrade

   B. Repair

   C. Clean

   D. Remote

200. You need to quickly view the network configuration on a Linux computer. What command will you use?

   A. `ipconfig`

   B. `ipconfig /all`

   C. `ip`

   D. `cfg`

201. You purchased a Windows 10 laptop and notice that it immediately resumes when you open the lid. What allows it to do that?

   A. Hibernate

   B. Idle mode

   C. Modern Standby

   D. Auto off

202. You're at a command prompt in Windows and need to quickly add a user named student. What command will you use?

   A. `net user student * /add`

   B. `net use /add student *`

   C. `net user student *`

   D. `user /add student`

203. What shortcut keys can you use to quickly access many of the technician tools used in Windows operating systems?

   A. Press Windows Key+D.

   B. Press Windows Key+L.

   C. Press Windows Key+I.

   D. Press Windows Key+X.

204. A friend just installed Windows 10 on their bare-metal machine. They called you because everything works except for their network. What do they need to do?

    A. Reinstall the operating system.

    B. Install third-party drivers.

    C. Remove and reinstall the network card.

    D. Replace the faulty network card.

205. What Linux command is used to display the partial dynamic table shown in the graphic?

```
16:10:38 up  3:06,  1 user,  load average: 0.12, 0.06, 0.02
Tasks: 202 total,   1 running, 201 sleeping,   0 stopped,   0 zombie
%Cpu(s):  0.3 us,  0.2 sy,  0.0 ni, 99.5 id,  0.0 wa,  0.0 hi,  0.0 st,  0.0 s
MiB Mem :   3831.9 total,    1797.2 free,    783.4 used,    1251.3 buff/cache
MiB Swap:   2048.0 total,    2048.0 free,      0.0 used.    2696.4 avail Mem

  PID USER      PR  NI    VIRT    RES    SHR S  %CPU  %MEM     TIME+
 3545 audrey    20   0   20492   3864   3364 R   0.7   0.1   0:02.49
  914 audrey    20   0  761080  47404  23116 S   0.3   1.2   0:26.34
    1 root      20   0  167732  11748   8508 S   0.0   0.3   0:02.77
    2 root      20   0       0      0      0 S   0.0   0.0   0:00.00
    3 root       0 -20       0      0      0 I   0.0   0.0   0:00.00
    4 root       0 -20       0      0      0 I   0.0   0.0   0:00.00
    6 root       0 -20       0      0      0 I   0.0   0.0   0:00.00
    8 root       0 -20       0      0      0 I   0.0   0.0   0:00.00
    9 root      20   0       0      0      0 S   0.0   0.0   0:00.00
   10 root      20   0       0      0      0 S   0.0   0.0   0:00.00
   11 root      20   0       0      0      0 S   0.0   0.0   0:00.27
   12 root      20   0       0      0      0 I   0.0   0.0   0:01.21
   13 root      rt   0       0      0      0 S   0.0   0.0   0:00.06
   14 root     -51   0       0      0      0 S   0.0   0.0   0:00.00
   16 root      20   0       0      0      0 S   0.0   0.0   0:00.00
   17 root      20   0       0      0      0 S   0.0   0.0   0:00.00
   18 root     -51   0       0      0      0 S   0.0   0.0   0:00.00
```

    A. chown

    B. dig

    C. top

    D. ip

206. A Mac user accidentally deleted an app and wants to reinstall it. They believe that the file to install the software again is still on their computer. What file extensions will you be looking for? (Choose two.)

    A. .pkg

    B. .bat

    C. .dmg

    D. .app

207. What feature, known more for mobile devices than desktops, is available for the desktop macOS by using a trackpad or Magic Mouse?

A. SDK

B. Power options

C. Gesture-based interactions

D. Emergency notifications

208. You have a workgroup with all Windows Home PCs. One of the computers is sharing a folder with two users who don't have an account on this PC. What Control Panel utility will you use to add the users and their passwords to this computer?

A. Administrative Tools

B. User Accounts

C. Local Users and Groups

D. Mail

209. You need to check the integrity of key Windows system files on the C: drive, which are hidden from view by default. Which tool can you use to allow you to view hidden files and their extensions?

A. Computer Management

B. System Configuration

C. Local Security Policy

D. File Explorer

210. On your personal computer, it seems that searching through files has gotten slower and slower. What utility will organize data so searches run faster?

A. In Control Panel, choose the Indexing Options utility.

B. In Windows Settings, choose the System group.

C. In Windows Settings, choose the Apps group.

D. In Control Panel, choose the Default Programs utility.

211. You are on a domain controller and need to share a folder of data files for some users and not others. Where will you configure access to the folder? (Choose two.)

A. On a domain controller.

B. In Windows Active Directory.

C. Configure Sharing on individual workstations.

D. Run a batch file to copy the files to each user who needs access.

212. On your network, a few users have been accessing material on inappropriate websites. What type of server can you install to block content from a list of prohibited websites?

    A. DNS server

    B. Authentication server

    C. Proxy server

    D. Web server

213. You're installing Windows 11 Enterprise in a bare-metal system. What is the maximum amount of RAM you can put into this system?

    A. 128 GB

    B. 2 TB

    C. 6 TB

    D. 256 TB

214. You are creating a network for a small office with Windows Pro computers. They do not want centralized security, but they want it to be easy to share printers and files, including libraries. What type of network setup should you recommend?

    A. Workgroup

    B. Homegroup

    C. Personal area network

    D. Domain

215. Which File Explorer layout shows filename, data modified, type, and size of the file?

    A. Extra large icons

    B. Details

    C. List

    D. Content

216. Which of the following is not a best practice for updating/patching Red Hat Linux?

    A. Keep installed software updates current.

    B. Verify that installed packages have a valid signature.

    C. Update packages quarterly.

    D. Download packages only from trusted sources.

217. What Linux program includes security features that can be used to find, list, and install security updates?

    A. chmod

    B. man

    C. find

    D. yum

218. You're using the Mail utility of Control Panel to configure a new user's computer so that their Microsoft Outlook mail will automatically be downloaded onto their Windows computer. What pieces of information will you need to set up their profile? (Choose two.)

   A. The protocol the server uses

   B. The user's email address

   C. The user's password

   D. The server port number

219. You have a MacBook Pro and want to share files with a small group of Mac users. Because your team edits the files frequently, you want to make sure everyone has access to the same version of the files online. What storage solution should you use?

   A. iCloud

   B. Finder

   C. Remote Disc

   D. Spotlight

220. Which of the following is not a best practice for backing up Linux (or any) desktop systems?

   A. Follow the 3-2-1 rule.

   B. Make only monthly backups.

   C. Carefully document backups.

   D. Periodically verify that backups are not corrupted and can be restored.

221. You're working at a Windows command prompt and need to prepare a volume on a hard drive to receive data using the NTFS filesystem. The volume should be designated as drive X. Which command would you use at a command prompt to do this?

   A. `format x: /fs:ntfs`

   B. `initialize x: /fs:ntfs`

   C. `format x: /ntfs`

   D. `initialize x: /ntfs`

222. You're running a computer with macOS. Which of the following will protect your data against accidental deletion?

   A. Mirrored drives

   B. An online utility

   C. Time Machine

   D. Nothing

223. You are a junior IT administrator, and the senior IT administrator has just set up a proxy server, so you need to add settings for it to every workstation. What information do you need to properly set up the proxy server in the Network & Internet group of Windows Settings? (Choose two.)

    A. The proxy server's IP address

    B. The router's IP address

    C. The DHCP server's IP address

    D. The port number to use for the proxy server

224. You are working on a MacBook Pro and need to search the computer for a document you wrote a few months ago. Which feature should you use to search the hard drive?

    A. Keychain

    B. Spotlight

    C. Finder

    D. Siri

225. Which of the following is not a best practice for avoiding viruses/malware in a Linux system?

    A. Create a different user and disable the root user.

    B. Install antivirus and update it regularly.

    C. Use sudo instead of su.

    D. Only use eight-character alphanumeric passwords.

226. You are installing a new network for a small office. They are concerned about security and therefore want it managed by one computer. When installing the Windows computers, what type of network setup will you choose?

    A. Workgroup

    B. Homegroup

    C. Personal area network

    D. Domain

227. You are viewing the screen shown in the graphic. Which of the following is not true about the network connection from this screen?

A. It is a public network.

B. File And Printer Sharing is likely enabled.

C. It is likely a network you or your company controls.

D. Network Discovery is likely enabled.

228. A user has shared a folder with you. Working in File Explorer, how can you configure access to this shared network location each time you log in without reentering the path? (Choose two.)

A. Left-click This PC and choose the network share.

B. Select This PC on the left then click Map Network Drive icon in the File Explorer ribbon and follow the onscreen prompts, ensuring that you choose Reconnect at sign-in.

C. Use File Explorer to drill down to the shared network resource. Right-click the shared resource, then choose Map Network Drive and follow the onscreen prompts, ensuring that you choose Reconnect at sign-in.

D. Click Quick Access and choose the network share.

229. You're on your private wired network at home and notice that your mouse is moving across the screen but you aren't moving it. Also, your computer seems to be running slowly, so you suspect someone with malicious intent has hacked into it. You want to immediately block access through the local machine's firewall. Where can you quickly do this?

    A. Search for Firewall. Choose Firewall & Network Protection, click Private, then click Block All Incoming Connections, including those in the list of allowed apps.

    B. Start typing Windows in the search box, choose Windows Defender Firewall, then click Private Networks and Disable.

    C. Search for **air**, click Turn Airplane mode on or off, then turn Airplane mode on.

    D. Search for Windows Defender Firewall and choose it, then turn the firewall off.

230. You have a Windows Pro computer set up in a workgroup, and you need to perform some routine management tasks on it. Before you do, you want to see what shares already exist on the local computer. What utility can you use to do this?

    A. In Windows Settings, choose Network & Internet.

    B. In Windows Settings, choose Ease Of Access.

    C. In Computer Management, choose Shared Folders, then double-click Shares.

    D. In the Network And Sharing Center utility of Control Panel, click Change Advanced Sharing.

231. Your laptop is equipped with a WWAN card, and you've arranged for service with a cellular provider. Where in Windows 10 can you connect to the network? (Choose two.)

    A. Click the wireless network icon on the taskbar and choose the network with the cellular network icon (vertical bars) in the list.

    B. In the Network & Internet group of Windows Settings, click Mobile Hotspot.

    C. In the Network & Internet group of Windows Settings, click Wi-Fi.

    D. In the Network & Internet group of Windows Settings, click Cellular.

232. You want to block an application from communicating through your Windows Defender Firewall. What will you set up for this application?

    A. An exception

    B. A restriction

    C. A mapped drive

    D. A network share

233. You need to connect to the Internet, but you regularly are working in remote areas, and your only option is to use a cellular network. What type of network are you establishing when you connect to the Internet?

    A. PAN

    B. CAN

    C. WWAN

    D. LAN

234. You're working on your laptop at a friend's house and click your browser to research something, but a window pops up saying No Internet. How do you resolve this? (Choose two.)

    A. Right-click the browser shortcut and choose New Window.

    B. Start typing **network** in the search box, then choose Network Status, then Show Available Networks, and get the network name and password from your friend.

    C. Click the taskbar icon that looks like a globe, then choose your friend's network and ask for the password.

    D. Type **firewall** in the search box and choose Firewall & Network Protection, then click Private Network.

235. You need to allow Open Office to communicate through the local Windows computer's firewall. Where is this configured? (Choose two.)

    A. In the Search box, type **Firewall & Network Protection**, then choose it from the results and click Allow An App Through Firewall.

    B. In Windows Settings, choose the Apps group.

    C. In Control Panel, choose Windows Defender Firewall, then select Allow An App Or Feature Through Windows Defender Firewall.

    D. In Control Panel, open the Programs And Features utility.

236. A user has a laptop that they think has WWAN capabilities. Where can you quickly check?

    A. Disk Management

    B. Device Manager

    C. Apps & Features

    D. Programs And Features

237. A user wants to use a WWAN connection to the Internet because they travel and Ethernet and Wi-Fi networks aren't always available to connect to. What will this user need? (Choose two.)

    A. A Wireless NIC

    B. A WWAN card or device

    C. A cellular service provider

    D. An RJ-45 connector

238. A user at your company just signed up for WWAN service through their cellular provider. Their data is capped at 10 GB per month. It's very costly if they go over, so they've asked you if there is a way for them to avoid going over their data limit. What will you do for them?

    A. Set up their cellular WWAN as a metered service.

    B. Use Performance Monitor to track their WWAN use.

    C. Switch them to a VPN so it won't cost anything.

    D. Use a proxy server so their data downloads won't count.

239. A junior network administrator wants to know the fastest way to access File Explorer, because they use it often. What do you tell them?

   A. Press Windows Key+F.

   B. Press Windows Key+M.

   C. Press Windows Key+E.

   D. Press Windows Key+X, then choose File Explorer from the menu.

240. You need to establish a wired connection between a newly installed Windows Pro computer and an Ethernet home network. The router is next to the desk and provides DHCP services. What will you need to connect a desktop computer to this network? (Choose two.)

   A. Patch cable

   B. Wireless NIC

   C. NIC with RJ-45 port

   D. IP address and subnet mask

241. You need to know the path to a network resource. How can you locate it?

   A. Type **mynetworkdrives** in a browser window to see them.

   B. In File Explorer, right-click the resource, choose Properties, then click the Sharing tab.

   C. In File Explorer, select This PC, Network Drives, and their path will show under Network Locations.

   D. Select Computer Management ➤ Shared Folders ➤ Shares.

242. You're installing Windows 10 64-bit on the only drive in a computer that uses BIOS, not UEFI. You'll be booting from this drive. Which of the following are true? (Choose two.)

   A. The partition scheme must be MBR.

   B. The partition scheme must be GPT.

   C. The partition must be less than 2 TB.

   D. You won't be able to boot from this drive.

243. You've installed a new hard drive in a Windows PC and need to partition the drive and format the volumes. What tools can you use to format it? (Choose two.)

   A. `diskmgmt.msc`

   B. `diskpart`

   C. `perfmon.msc`

   D. `services.msc`

Chapter

7

Security

THE COMPTIA A+ 220-1102 TOPICS COVERED IN THIS CHAPTER INCLUDE THE FOLLOWING:

✓ **2.1 Summarize various security measures and their purposes.**

- Physical security
    - Access control vestibule
    - Badge reader
    - Video surveillance
    - Alarm systems
    - Motion sensors
    - Door locks
    - Equipment locks
    - Guards
    - Bollards
    - Fences
- Physical security for staff
    - Key fobs
    - Smartcards
    - Keys
    - Biometrics
        - Retina scanner
        - Fingerprint scanner
        - Palmprint scanner
    - Lighting
    - Magnetometers
- Logical security

- Principle of least privilege
- Access control lists (ACLs)
- Multifactor authentication (MFA)
  - Email
  - Hard token
  - Soft token
  - Short message service (SMS)
  - Voice call
  - Authenticator application
- Mobile device management (MDM)
- Active Directory
  - Login script
  - Domain
  - Group Policy/updates
  - Organizational units
  - Home folder
  - Folder redirection
  - Security groups

✓ **2.2 Compare and contrast wireless security protocols and authentication methods.**

- Protocols and encryption
  - Wi-Fi Protected Access 2 (WPA2)
  - WPA3
  - Temporal Key Integrity Protocol (TKIP)
  - Advanced Encryption Standard (AES)
- Authentication
  - Remote Authentication Dial-In User Service (RADIUS)
  - Terminal Access Controller Access-Control System (TACACS+)

- Kerberos

- Multifactor

✓ **2.3 Given a scenario, detect, remove, and prevent malware using the appropriate tools and methods.**

- Malware

  - Trojan

  - Rootkit

  - Virus

  - Spyware

  - Ransomware

  - Keylogger

  - Boot sector virus

  - Cryptominers

- Tools and methods

  - Recovery mode

  - Antivirus

  - Anti-malware

  - Software firewalls

  - Anti-phishing training

  - User education regarding common threats

  - OS reinstallation

✓ **2.4 Explain common social-engineering attacks, threats, and vulnerabilities.**

- Social engineering

  - Phishing

  - Vishing

  - Shoulder surfing

  - Whaling

  - Tailgating

- Impersonation
- Dumpster diving
- Evil twin

- Threats
    - Distributed denial of service (DDoS)
    - Denial of service (DoS)
    - Zero-day attack
    - Spoofing
    - On-path attack
    - Brute-force attack
    - Dictionary attack
    - Insider threat
    - Structured Query Language (SQL) injection
    - Cross-site scripting (XSS)

- Vulnerabilities
    - Non-compliant systems
    - Unpatched systems
    - Unprotected systems (missing antivirus/ missing firewall)
    - EOL OSs
    - Bring your own device (BYOD)

✓ **2.5 Given a scenario, manage and configure basic security settings in the Microsoft Windows OS.**

- Defender Antivirus
    - Activate/deactivate
    - Updated definitions
- Firewall
    - Activate/deactivate
    - Port security
    - Application security

- Users and groups
    - Local vs. Microsoft account
    - Standard account
    - Administrator
    - Guest user
    - Power user
- Login OS options
    - Username and password
    - Personal identification number (PIN)
    - Fingerprint
    - Facial recognition
    - Single sign-on (SSO)
- NTFS vs. share permissions
    - File and folder attributes
    - Inheritance
- Run as administrator vs. standard user
    - User Account Control (UAC)
- BitLocker
- BitLocker To Go
- Encrypting File System (EFS)

✓ **2.6 Given a scenario, configure a workstation to meet best practices for security.**

- Data-at-rest encryption
- Password best practices
    - Complexity requirements
        - Length
        - Character types
    - Expiration requirements
    - Basic input/output system (BIOS)/Unified Extensible Firmware Interface (UEFI) passwords

- End-user best practices
  - Use screen saver locks
  - Log off when not in use
  - Secure/protect critical hardware (e.g., laptops)
  - Secure personally identifiable information (PII) and passwords
- Account management
  - Restrict user permissions
  - Restrict login times
  - Disable guest account
  - Use failed attempts lockout
  - Use timeout/screen lock
- Change default administrator's user account/password
- Disable AutoRun
- Disable AutoPlay

✓ **2.7 Explain common methods for securing mobile and embedded devices.**

- Screen locks
  - Facial recognition
  - PIN codes
  - Fingerprint
  - Pattern
  - Swipe
- Remote wipes
- Locator applications
- OS updates
- Device encryption
- Remote backup applications
- Failed login attempts restrictions
- Antivirus/anti-malware

- Firewalls
- Policies and procedures
  - BYOD vs. corporate owned
  - Profile security requirements
- Internet of Things (IoT)

✓ 2.8 Given a scenario, use common data destruction and disposal methods.

- Physical destruction
  - Drilling
  - Shredding
  - Degaussing
  - Incinerating
- Recycling or repurposing best practices
  - Erasing/wiping
  - Low-level formatting
  - Standard formatting
- Outsourcing concepts
  - Third-party vendor
  - Certification of destruction/recycling

✓ 2.9 Given a scenario, configure appropriate security settings on small office/home office (SOHO) wireless and wired networks.

- Home router settings
  - Change default passwords
  - IP filtering
  - Firmware updates
  - Content filtering
  - Physical placement/secure locations
  - Dynamic Host Configuration Protocol (DHCP) reservations

- Static wide-area network (WAN) IP
- Universal Plug and Play (UPnP)
- Screened subnet
- Wireless specific
  - Changing the service set identifier (SSID)
  - Disabling SSID broadcast
  - Encryption settings
  - Disabling guest access
  - Changing channels
- Firewall settings
  - Disabling unused ports
  - Port forwarding/mapping

✓ **2.10 Given a scenario, install and configure browsers and relevant security settings.**

- Browser download/installation
  - Trusted sources
    - Hashing
  - Untrusted sources
- Extensions and plug-ins
  - Trusted sources
  - Untrusted sources
- Password managers
- Secure connections/sites – valid certificates
- Settings
  - Pop-up blocker
  - Clearing browsing data
  - Clearing cache
  - Private-browsing mode
  - Sign-in/browser data synchronization
  - Ad blockers

1. Which type of security device requires the user to insert some type of identification card to validate access?

   A. PIN code

   B. Badge reader

   C. Security token

   D. Biometrics

2. Someone has configured an external server with an IP address that should belong to one of your sister company's servers. With this new computer, they are attempting to establish a connection to your internal network. What type of attack is this?

   A. Spoofing

   B. On-path attack

   C. Zombie/botnet

   D. Non-compliant system

3. What type of security device often incorporates RFID technology to grant personnel access to secure areas or resources?

   A. Smartcard

   B. Security token

   C. Access control vestibule

   D. Key fob

4. You are configuring a wireless network for a small office. What should you enable for the best encryption possible for network transmissions?

   A. WPS

   B. WEP

   C. WPA

   D. WPA3

5. You work for a company that has employees fill out and manually sign personnel documents. Once the signed documents are scanned into a system, the paper copies are no longer needed. What should be done with the paper documents?

   A. Place them in the recycle bin.

   B. Shred them.

   C. Place them in the trash.

   D. Keep them in a locked cabinet.

6. Which types of security threats involve the attacker attempting to directly contact a potential victim? (Choose two.)

   A. Spoofing

   B. Phishing

   C. Social engineering

   D. Brute-force attacking

7. An employee uses their security badge to enter the building through a secured door. Another person tries to enter the building behind them before the door closes without swiping a badge. What type of behavior is the second person demonstrating?

   A. Shoulder surfing

   B. On-path attack

   C. Brute-force

   D. Tailgating

8. You have a Windows domain network and want to ensure that users are required to meet password complexity requirements. What is the best way to implement this on the network?

   A. Use a firewall.

   B. Use a VPN.

   C. Use Group Policy.

   D. Use DLP.

9. You are planning security protocols for your company's new server room. What's the simplest way to help physically keep potential attackers away from your servers?

   A. Lock the door.

   B. Use cable locks.

   C. Install an access control vestibule.

   D. Implement biometrics.

10. A user on your network reported that their screen went blank and a message popped up. It's telling them that their files are no longer accessible, and if they want them back, they need to enter a credit card number and pay a $200 fee. Which type of malware has infected this system?

   A. Rootkit

   B. Ransomware

   C. Trojan

   D. Spyware

11. You are setting up a new wireless router for a home office. Which of the following should you change immediately when initially configuring the network? (Choose two.)

   A. The router's default administrator username and password

   B. The default SSID

   C. The radio power level

   D. The guest account password

12. You are configuring a router for a small office network. The network users should be able to access regular and secure websites and send and receive email. Those are the only connections allowed to the Internet. Which security feature should you configure to prevent additional traffic from coming through the router?

   A. MAC filtering

   B. Content filtering

   C. Port forwarding/mapping

   D. Port security/disabling unused ports

13. On a Windows 10 workstation, there are two NTFS volumes. The Managers group has Modify access to the D:\mgmt directory. You move the folder to the D:\keyfiles folder, to which the Managers group has Read access. What level of permissions will the Managers group have to the new D:\keyfiles\mgmt directory?

   A. Full Control

   B. Modify

   C. Read & Execute

   D. Read

14. For users to log on to your network from a remote location, they are required to supply a username and password as well as a code from an RSA token. What type of security is being used?

   A. Firewall

   B. Multifactor authentication

   C. Access control list

   D. Principle of least privilege

15. You want to recycle some hard drives that your company no longer uses but want to ensure that other people will not be able to access the data. Which methods of removing the data are acceptable for your purposes? (Choose two.)

   A. Formatting the drive

   B. Using an overwrite utility

   C. Using a drive wipe utility

   D. Using electromagnetic fields

16. You have installed Windows 11 Pro on a workstation. For better security, which user account should you ensure is disabled?

   A. Administrator

   B. DefaultAccount

   C. Power User

   D. Guest

17. Which type of network attack involves an intermediary hardware device intercepting data and altering it or transmitting it to an unauthorized user?

    A. On-path attack

    B. Non-compliant system

    C. Zombie/botnet

    D. Spoofing

18. You are implementing new password policies for your network, and you want to follow guidelines for password best practices. Which of the following will best help improve the security of your network? (Choose two.)

    A. Require passwords to expire every 180 days.

    B. Require passwords to be a minimum of 8 characters.

    C. Require passwords to have a special character.

    D. Require passwords to be no more than 10 characters long.

19. What does NTFS use to track users and groups and their level of access to resources?

    A. ACLs

    B. Tokens

    C. Badges

    D. Control rosters

20. You have created a user account for a contract employee on a Windows 11 PC. The contractor will be with the company for one month. Which user group should this user's account be placed in?

    A. Power Users

    B. Administrators

    C. Standard Users

    D. Guest

21. On your network, there are multiple systems that users need to access, such as a Windows domain, a cloud site for storage, and order processing software. You want to configure the network such that users do not need to remember separate usernames or passwords for each site; their login credentials will be good for different systems. Which technology should you use?

    A. EFS

    B. MDM

    C. SSO

    D. UAC

22. A user discovers a strange text file at the root of their user directory. It contains everything they have typed over the past few days, including their credentials. What is the likely cause of the text file?

   A. System auditing enabled

   B. Keylogger installed

   C. Email application in debug mode

   D. Backup file

23. What security solution would protect a user from unwanted network traffic probing their workstation?

   A. Software firewall

   B. Antiphishing training

   C. Anti-malware

   D. Antivirus

24. A user wants to use multifactor authentication at their PC but does not want to carry a key fob and is strongly against biometrics. What method can you suggest?

   A. Second password

   B. Hardware token

   C. Software token

   D. Fingerprint reader

25. What wireless protocol used in WPA compensates for the weak encryption of WEP?

   A. VLAN

   B. TKIP

   C. VPN

   D. AES

26. Which of the following Active Directory concepts can help enforce security settings? (Choose two.)

   A. EFS

   B. Group Policy/updates

   C. Port security

   D. Login scripts

27. What 128-bit block encryption that uses an encryption key of 128, 192, or 256 bits is used in WPA2 and is more secure than TKIP?

   A. AES

   B. VPN

   C. RADIUS

   D. Kerberos

28. What protocol was designed to authenticate remote users to a dial-in access server?

   A. TKIP

   B. TACACS+

   C. VPN

   D. RADIUS

29. A user is complaining that they can no longer sign into their account because of too many bad attempts. What basic Active Directory function is at work here?

   A. Failed login attempts restrictions

   B. Antivirus/anti-malware

   C. A bollard

   D. A rootkit

30. What concept in Active Directory creates a directory subdivision within which may be placed users, groups, computers and other objects?

   A. User

   B. Domain

   C. Organizational unit

   D. Home folder

31. Which of the following authentication encryption protocols is older than the others and was developed by Cisco but became an open protocol in the 1990s and can be found on Linux distributions?

   A. AES

   B. TACACS+

   C. Kerberos

   D. RADIUS

32. Your data center recently experienced a theft of a server from the rack. Which security mechanisms would protect servers from future theft? (Choose two.)

   A. Equipment locks

   B. Security token

   C. Alarm systems

   D. Hard token

33. What other security devices are often employed in an access control vestibule? (Choose two.)

   A. Bollard

   B. Motion sensors

   C. Guards

   D. Video surveillance

34. Normally, a company places a user's profile and folders on the local machine. Now, the organization would like a few users to be able to log in from other computers. What concept in Active Directory allows a user's profile folders to be placed in storage somewhere else on the network?

   A. Home folder

   B. Folder redirection

   C. Organizational unit

   D. VPN

35. What wireless encryption protocol replaced WPA and uses both TKIP, for backward compatibility, and AES?

   A. WEP

   B. WPA2

   C. WPA3

   D. RADIUS

36. When should OS and application patches be applied to a system to prevent it from becoming vulnerable?

   A. Every 6 months

   B. Every 3 months

   C. Once a month

   D. As soon as they are available

37. You have a Windows workstation and want to prevent a potential hacker from booting to a USB drive. What should you do to help prevent this?

   A. Require strong Windows passwords.

   B. Restrict with user permissions.

   C. Set a BIOS/UEFI password.

   D. Change the default administrator password.

38. Which type of security solution generally functions as a packet filter and can perform stateful inspection?

   A. VPN

   B. EFS

   C. Antivirus/anti-malware

   D. Firewall

39. Which of the following are examples of physical security methods? (Choose two.)

   A. Biometric locks

   B. Multifactor authentication

   C. Keys

   D. Firewalls

40. A user on your network reported that they received a phone call from someone in the IT department saying the user needed to reset their password. The caller offered to do it for them if the user could provide the IT worker with their current password. What is this most likely an example of?

- **A.** The IT department helping the user to reset their password
- **B.** A spoofing attack
- **C.** A social engineering attack
- **D.** A brute-force attack

41. Your corporate IT department has decided that to enhance security they want to draft a mobile device management (MDM) policy to require both a passcode and fingerprint scan to unlock a mobile device for use. What is this an example of?

- **A.** An authenticator application
- **B.** Biometric authentication
- **C.** Full-device encryption
- **D.** Multifactor authentication

42. Several employees at your company have been tailgating to gain access to secure areas. Which of the following security methods is the best choice for stopping this practice?

- **A.** Door lock
- **B.** Entry control roster
- **C.** Access control vestibule
- **D.** ID badges

43. A user has joined your company as a network administrator. Let's assume their user account name is AOShea. What is the recommended way to give AOShea the administrative privileges they need?

- **A.** Add the AOShea user account to the Administrators group.
- **B.** Create an account called AdminAOShea. Add that account to the Administrators group. Have the new administrator use the AOShea account unless they need administrative rights, in which case they should use the AdminAOShea account.
- **C.** Copy the Administrator account and rename it AOShea.
- **D.** Add the AOShea user account to the Power Users group.

44. You are designing a security policy for mobile phones on your network. Which of the following is a common method of biometric authentication used with mobile devices?

- **A.** Fingerprint scan
- **B.** Retina scan
- **C.** Swipe lock
- **D.** DNA lock

45. An administrator is transferring confidential files from one Windows Pro workstation to another, using a flash drive. Policy dictates that the files on the flash drive must be encrypted. Which technology should be used?

   A. BitLocker

   B. BitLocker To Go

   C. EFS

   D. AES

46. Which type of security system uses physical characteristics to allow or deny access to locations or resources?

   A. ID badges

   B. Bollards

   C. Biometrics

   D. Tokens

47. You have just transformed a Windows workgroup into a small domain and are configuring user accounts. Which of the following is considered a best practice for managing user account security?

   A. Require every user to log on as a Guest user.

   B. Allow all users Read and Write access to all server files.

   C. Follow the principle of least privilege.

   D. Place all user accounts in the Administrators group.

48. A security consultant for your company recommended that you begin shredding or burning classified documents before disposing of them. What security risk is the consultant trying to protect the company from?

   A. Shoulder surfing

   B. Dumpster diving

   C. Social engineering

   D. Brute-force attack

49. Several workstations on your network have not had their operating systems updated in more than a year, and your antivirus software is also out-of-date. What type of security threat does this represent?

   A. Non-compliant systems

   B. Zombie/botnet

   C. Brute-force attack

   D. Zero-day attack

50. On the Internet, you get a news flash that the developer of one of your core applications found a security flaw. They will issue a patch for it in two days. Before you can install the patch, it's clear that the flaw has been exploited and someone has illegally accessed your network. What type of attack is this?

   A. Zombie/botnet

   B. Non-compliant system

   C. Zero-day attack

   D. Brute-force attack

51. UserA is a member of the Dev group and the HR group. They are trying to access a local resource on an NTFS volume. The HR group has Full Control permission for the `payroll` folder, and the Dev group has Deny Read permission for the same folder. What is UserA's effective access to the `payroll` folder?

   A. Full Control

   B. Read

   C. Write

   D. Deny

52. Which default Windows group was designed to have more power than normal users but not as much power as administrators, and is now kept for backward compatibility only?

   A. Superuser

   B. Standard Users

   C. Power Users

   D. Advanced Users

53. You have assigned a Windows workstation to a workgroup. Which of the following are recommended best practices for maximizing security regarding the Administrator account? (Choose two.)

   A. Disable the Administrator account.

   B. Rename the Administrator account.

   C. Remove the Administrator account from the Administrators group.

   D. Require a strong password.

54. You're at home using a digital security method to connect to your corporate network. This security method wraps data in encryption (encapsulating it) to transfer the data across a public network (the Internet), and your connection gets a corporate IP address just as if you were sitting in the office. What type of connection is this?

   A. VPN

   B. Firewall

   C. BitLocker

   D. EFS

55. Which of the following are advantages of using NTFS permissions over using share permissions? (Choose two.)

 A. NTFS permissions will override share permissions if there is a conflict.

 B. NTFS permissions affect users at the local computer, but share permissions do not.

 C. NTFS permissions are more restrictive in their access levels than share permissions.

 D. NTFS permissions can be set at the file level, but share permissions cannot.

56. Someone has placed an unauthorized wireless router on your network and configured it with the same SSID as your network. Users can access the network through that router, even though it's not supposed to be there. What type of security threat could this lead to?

 A. Zombie/botnet

 B. Spoofing

 C. Non-compliant system

 D. On-path attack

57. Which type of security method is worn by employees and usually has a picture on it?

 A. Key fobs

 B. ID badges

 C. Smartcards

 D. Biometrics

58. You're working at a high-security server farm and must ensure that vehicles stay a certain distance away from the building. What physical security methods can be used for this purpose? (Choose two.)

 A. Bollards

 B. Motion sensors

 C. Fences

 D. Lighting

59. Between you and your family members, there are several mobile devices, including phones, laptops and smart watches. Someone generally forgets where they put their phone, or it may be stolen, and it would be nice to easily find it. In addition, you want to see where other family members are when they are around town. Which type of app will allow you to do this?

 A. Trusted source app

 B. Remote control app

 C. Locator app

 D. Firewall app

60. Which security mechanism specifies permissions for users and groups as well as the type of activities the users or groups can perform?

   A. ACL

   B. EFS

   C. VPN

   D. PIN

61. You need to know which files have been modified in a folder. Which of the following is not a way to see when files have been modified?

   A. Right-click each file and choose Properties, and then Advanced to see whether the archive bit is set.

   B. Open the folder in File Explorer and click Date Modified to sort the files by the date they were last modified.

   C. Type **archive** at a command prompt.

   D. Type **attrib** at a command prompt.

62. You want to create a new policy to encrypt all company drives using BitLocker. Which operating system will need to be upgraded?

   A. Windows 10 Pro

   B. Windows 11 Home

   C. Windows 11 Pro

   D. Windows 10 for Workstations

63. Software was installed on a laptop without the user's knowledge. The software has been tracking the user's keystrokes and has transmitted the user's credit card information to an attacker. What type of threat is this?

   A. Zombie/botnet

   B. Spoofing

   C. Spyware

   D. Ransomware

64. A new user has joined your company as a network administrator. Which of the following statements is most correct regarding their network access?

   A. They should have just one user account, with administrator-level permissions.

   B. They should have just one user account, with standard user-level permissions.

   C. They should have two user accounts: one with user-level permissions and one with administrator-level permissions.

   D. They should have three user accounts: one with user-level permissions, one with administrator-level permissions, and one with remote access administrator permissions.

65. Which types of security threats are direct attacks on user passwords? (Choose two.)

    A. Brute-force

    B. Zombie/botnet

    C. Dictionary attack

    D. Spoofing

66. You read corporate email on your smartphone and do not want others to access the phone if you leave it somewhere. What is the first layer of security that you should implement to keep others from using your phone?

    A. Multifactor authentication

    B. Full-device encryption

    C. Screen lock

    D. Remote wipe software

67. You use your smartphone for email and extensive Internet browsing. You want to add an additional level of security to always verify your identity online when accessing various accounts. Which type of app do you need?

    A. Authenticator app

    B. Trusted source app

    C. Biometric authenticator app

    D. Account encryption app

68. You have instructed users on your network to not use common words for their passwords. What type of attack are you trying to prevent?

    A. Brute-force

    B. Dictionary attack

    C. Social engineering

    D. Shoulder surfing

69. Which type of malware is designed to look like a different program and, when installed, creates a back door for an attacker to access the target system?

    A. Trojan

    B. Spyware

    C. Virus

    D. Whaling

70. You have been asked to dispose of several old magnetic hard drives. What are you doing if you use a large magnet to clear the data off a hard drive?

    A. Overwriting

    B. Zero writing

    C. Degaussing

    D. Incineration

71. If you check the Read-only or Hidden box on the graphic, what feature of the folder is being changed?

myfolder Properties ✕

General Security Previous Versions Customize

myfolder

Type:	File folder
Location:	C:\Users\aoshe\Desktop
Size:	0 bytes
Size on disk:	0 bytes
Contains:	0 Files, 0 Folders
Created:	Saturday, December 18, 2021, 4:22:18 AM

Attributes: ☐ Read-only (Only applies to files in folder)
☐ Hidden   Advanced...

OK   Cancel   Apply

- **A.** Archive bit
- **B.** NTFS permissions
- **C.** Attributes
- **D.** Share permissions

72. You're setting up a Windows 11 Pro machine and want to encrypt the entire hard drive, including startup files. Which technology best meets your needs?
- **A.** Windows OSs do not allow full-drive encryption.
- **B.** BitLocker
- **C.** BitLocker to Go
- **D.** EFS

73. Which type of security threat gains administrative-level access for an attacker to perform another attack, and then hides its presence from system management tools?
- **A.** Virus
- **B.** Whaling
- **C.** Rootkit
- **D.** Ransomware

74. A computer user wants to encrypt a few files on an NTFS volume on their Windows Pro workstation. They do not have administrative rights to the computer. Which of the following statements is correct?

   A. They can only use device encryption.

   B. They can use BitLocker.

   C. They can use BitLocker To Go.

   D. They can use EFS.

75. Which type of digital security is designed to protect your network from malicious software programs by both preventing them from entering the system and removing them if they are found?

   A. Firewall

   B. Anti-malware

   C. EFS

   D. UAC

76. Your company has hired a consultant to intentionally send emails asking for login information from your employees. What is your company engaging in?

   A. Phishing

   B. Whaling

   C. Zero-day attack

   D. Anti-phishing training

77. On a Windows workstation, there is one volume formatted with NTFS. The Developers group has Modify access to the `C:\dev` directory. You copy the folder to the `C:\operations` folder, to which the Developers group has Read access. What level of permissions will the Developers group have to the new `C:\operations\dev` directory?

   A. Read & Execute

   B. Read

   C. Full Control

   D. Modify

78. You are configuring NTFS and share permissions on a Windows 11 workstation. Which of the following statements is true regarding permissions?

   A. Both NTFS and share permissions can be applied only at the folder level.

   B. NTFS permissions can be applied at the file or folder level, and share permissions can only be applied at the folder level.

   C. NTFS permissions can be applied only at the folder level, but share permissions can be applied to files and folders

   D. Both NTFS and share permissions support inheritance.

79. Which type of security device displays a randomly generated code that the user enters for access to computer resources?

    A. ID badge

    B. RFID badge

    C. Smartcard

    D. Key fob

80. You recently noticed a change on your computer. Now when you open your web browser, no matter what you search for, you get a dozen unsolicited pop-up windows offering to sell you items you didn't ask for. What type of problem does your computer have?

    A. Spyware

    B. Ransomware

    C. Zombie/botnet

    D. Trojan

81. A computer user wants to encrypt the data on their Windows 10 Home device. They have administrative rights to the computer. Which of the following statements is correct?

    A. They may be able to use Windows device encryption.

    B. They can use BitLocker.

    C. They can use BitLocker To Go.

    D. They can use EFS.

82. Which of the following is true about the permissions shown in the graphic? (Choose two.)

A. They are only in effect when accessed via a network.

B. They are NTFS permissions.

C. This type can be used on files and folders.

D. Everyone can read files inside this folder.

83. Which of the following statements are true regarding file and folder attributes on a Windows 11 workstation? (Choose two.)

A. File attributes are available only on NTFS volumes.

B. Only members of the Administrators group can change file/folder attributes.

C. Attributes can be accessed by right-clicking the file/folder and choosing Properties and then selecting the General tab.

D. Compression is an advanced file/folder attribute.

84. Which type of digital security needs to have constant updates to best protect your network or computer?

A. Antivirus

B. Firewall

C. Access control list

D. NTFS permissions

85. You are at work and receive a phone call. The caller ID indicates it's coming from your manager's desk. You can see your manager's desk and no one is sitting there. Which of the following is likely happening?

A. Zombie/botnet attack

B. Impersonation attack

C. Zero-day attack

D. Phishing attack

86. A user is working on a Windows workstation. Their user account is a member of the Managers group, and they are trying to access a folder named `reports`, located on a different computer. The NTFS permissions for the `reports` shared folder on that computer for the Managers group are Read and Write. The folder's share permissions for the Managers group is the Read permission. What are the user's effective permissions on the `reports` folder?

A. Full Control

B. Read and Write

C. Read

D. No access

87. Which NTFS permission overrides all the others?

A. Full Control

B. Deny

C. List Folder Contents

D. Read

88. A system administrator is concerned about Windows users inadvertently installing malware from DVD-ROMs and USB thumb drives that contain malicious code. What can they do to help prevent this from happening?

   A. Set restrictive user permissions.

   B. Enable BIOS/UEFI passwords.

   C. Disable AutoRun and AutoPlay.

   D. Enable data encryption.

89. Someone has placed an unauthorized wireless router on your network and configured it with the same SSID as your network. Users can access the network through that router, even though it's not supposed to be there. What is this router configuration known as?

   A. Zombie/botnet

   B. Evil twin

   C. Non-compliant system

   D. On-path attack

90. Which of the following is true about the information shown in the graphic? (Choose two.)

   A. The graphic shows share permissions.

   B. The graphic shows NTFS permissions.

   C. These permissions will be inherited by any folder created on the C drive.

   D. These permissions are only effective when someone accesses them over a network.

91. Your office has recently experienced several laptop thefts. Which security mechanism, as pictured in the graphic, is designed to protect mobile devices from theft?

   A. Security token

   B. Laptop lock

   C. Key fob

   D. Magnetometer

92. Which of the following is an open source authentication encryption protocol that is widely used and that uses a third party to verify user credentials?

   A. AES

   B. TACACS+

   C. Kerberos

   D. RADIUS

93. Your company allows employees to use their own devices, and as the IT director, you are naturally concerned with the security of corporate information on those devices. Which technology should you require in this situation?

    A. EFS

    B. MDM

    C. SSO

    D. UAC

94. Which of the following is not a logical security method of delivering a code for multifactor authentication?

    A. Voice call

    B. Email

    C. Bollards

    D. SMS

95. Which of the following is an example of a hard token? (Choose two.)

    A. Key fob

    B. Retina scanner

    C. Smartcard

    D. Motion sensor

96. Which of the following devices. often found in smartphones and other mobile devices, is used to pinpoint a person's location on Earth, and therefore can be used for multifactor authentication?

    A. Magnetometer

    B. Retina scanner

    C. Key fob

    D. Hard token

97. Which of the following is not a physical security measure for protecting computer systems and access to them?

    A. Lighting

    B. Equipment locks

    C. Motion sensors

    D. Soft token

98. Which of the following is not a biometric identification device?

    A. Fingerprint reader

    B. Retina scanner

    C. Hard token

    D. Palmprint scanner

99. A user is worried about others shoulder surfing. What should they use to help avoid this problem?

    A. Access control vestibule

    B. Video surveillance

    C. Display privacy filter

    D. Smartcard

100. Which type of malware will often cause critical files to disappear, often while displaying a taunting message, and requires user intervention (usually inadvertent) to spread from computer to computer?

    A. Botnet

    B. Virus

    C. Trojan

    D. Rootkit

101. A computer user in the accounting department received a phone call from someone who claimed to be from the company's bank. They had a partial account number and needed the user to verify the full account number, their username, and password before they could discuss the reason for their call with the user. The user said they would call them back, and the caller on the other end hung up abruptly. They contacted you in the IT department because it seemed like such a strange call. What kind of attempted attack will you tell them just happened?

    A. Phishing

    B. Vishing

    C. Whaling

    D. Evil twin

102. Your company allows employees to use their personal devices for company work, because it will save the company money on hardware. What is this called?

    A. BYOD

    B. MDM

    C. SSO

    D. UAC

103. Why is an EOL OS a security threat?

    A. There will be no more security updates.

    B. There will be no more feature updates.

    C. There will be no more company support.

    D. The software will stop working on the EOL date.

104. What type of malware is dangerous because it is loaded during system startup before the antivirus software is able to load?

    A. Spyware

    B. Ransomware

    C. Boot sector virus

    D. Keylogger

105. Which of the following is not a type of malware that needs to be eradicated from a computer system?

    A. Keylogger

    B. Virus

    C. WinRE

    D. Spyware

106. You believe your computer has contracted a boot sector virus. Which command-line tool permits someone to make changes to the operating system without having to boot up Windows?

    A. WinRE

    B. RADIUS

    C. Administrative tools

    D. Active Directory

107. You're reviewing the Event Viewer logs and notice repeated failed attempts to access the corporate bank account information. The attempts are coming from someone with a company login, and in fact, you are able to catch the person, an employee hired only a month ago, in the act. What type of attack is this?

    A. Insider threat

    B. Eval twin

    C. Whaling

    D. Social engineering

108. Your web server just crashed because there was a flood of responses to a packet that looks like it was from your server but your server didn't send it. What just happened?

    A. Whaling attack

    B. Denial-of-service attack

    C. Distributed DoS attack

    D. Evil twin attack

109. A computer user on your network is trying to access a folder named `Projects` on a local NTFS volume. Their user account is in the Developers group. The Developers group has Read & Execute permissions to the folder, and the user's user account has Full Control. What is the user's effective access to the `Projects` folder?

    A. Full Control

    B. Read & Execute

    C. Read

    D. No access

110. You've discovered that a system on your network has had its firewall turned off and antivirus disabled. What type of vulnerability does this present?

    A. Zero-day attack

    B. SQL injection

    C. Unprotected system

    D. Cross-site scripting

111. What Active Directory security measure moves a user's data to a server and off the local drive so that if a laptop is lost or stolen and someone gains access to it, they won't have access to information in the user's data files?

    A. Home folder

    B. Security group

    C. Organizational unit

    D. Login script

112. You notice that your computer seems to be working more than the normal updating that it does when you're not actively using it. It also seems to be running more slowly than normal. What type of malware, instead of stealing your data, uses your computing power?

    A. Spyware

    B. Ransomware

    C. Keyloggers

    D. Cryptominers

113. Which of the following is not important in preventing malware from damaging your computer system?

    A. User education regarding common threats

    B. Installing a keylogger

    C. Keeping anti-malware signatures up-to-date

    D. Keeping operating systems and applications patches up-to-date

114. A user on your network wants to install an interesting browser extension that they found on a download site neither you nor they have used before. They got a warning before going to the site but clicked an option to continue. What type of website is this?

    A. Spoofed

    B. Trusted source

    C. Untrusted source

    D. Certified

115. As the IT person in a small firm using Windows operating systems, you would like a window to pop up whenever apps try to make changes to a system and when the user makes changes to the system so that an administrator password will be required to be entered. What utility will you use to configure that setting?

    A. UAC

    B. Windows Defender Firewall

    C. Facial recognition

    D. Personalization

116. A friend is considering purchasing an antivirus program. You let them know that there is one included with the Windows operating system. What settings should they look for in Windows Settings?

    A. Windows Defender Firewall

    B. Virus & threat protection

    C. Windows Update

    D. Device Security

117. Your company's website has been a victim of a botnet attack, causing your server to crash. What type of attack did the botnet attack cause?

    A. Brute-force

    B. Zero-day

    C. Distributed denial of service

    D. Non-compliant system

118. What type of attack is like a SQL injection, except that it uses a website and HTML or JavaScript instead of a database, where malicious code is injected into the website (which is normally trusted by the user), and then used to gather data from the website user's computer because their systems don't see the normally trusted website as a threat?

    A. Zero-day attack

    B. SQL injection

    C. Unprotected system

    D. Cross-site scripting

119. Your company has different locations, each with its own management needs, but it wants a cohesive way to manage all the users, computers, and other resources on the network. What will you group those users, computers, and resources into that will provide a centralized point of control for each location?

   A. Active Directory

   B. Domain

   C. Security groups

   D. Home folders

120. The company's vice president just called you in the IT department because they received an email from you requesting their username and password. The VP didn't respond because they thought you should know them already. What kind of attack was just attempted?

   A. Phishing

   B. Vishing

   C. Whaling

   D. Evil twin

121. What is the software used to control access to resources in a Windows domain?

   A. Home folder

   B. Security group

   C. Organizational unit

   D. Active Directory

122. You've been reading about a recent malware that is causing problems for other companies and want to verify that the Windows built-in antivirus definitions are up-to-date. Where is this done?

   A. Virus & Threat Protection in the Settings app

   B. Virus & Threat Protection in Control Panel

   C. Windows Defender Firewall in the Settings app

   D. Windows Defender Firewall in Control Panel

123. You are a junior IT administrator, and your supervisor has asked you to ensure that all workstations have the built-in Windows firewall activated. Where can you go to do that? (Choose two.)

   A. Firewall & Network Protection in the Settings app

   B. Firewall & Network Protection in Control Panel

   C. Windows Defender Firewall in the Settings app

   D. Windows Defender Firewall in Control Panel

124. Your company has started using a new software in the cloud, but your users are finding that they can't use the software. Their computers are running Windows 11. What can you do to ensure that the software can be used remotely by the employees? (Choose two.)

    A. Click Allow An App Through Firewall in the Firewall & Network Protection settings of the Settings app.

    B. Click Allow An App Through Firewall in the Virus & Threat Protection settings of the Settings app.

    C. Add a new rule in the Advanced settings of Windows Defender Firewall, which can be found in Control Panel.

    D. Add a new rule in Administrative Tools in Control Panel.

125. Employees in your company work on very confidential projects. All employees have been instructed to lock their screens whenever they walk away from their computer, even if it is only for a minute. What key sequence will immediately lock their desktop and require a password to reenter?

    A. Windows Key+X

    B. Windows Key+L

    C. Windows Key+Right Arrow

    D. Windows Key+D

126. Your employees have all been trained on end-user best practices, including locking their laptop when they walk away from it. What can be done to ensure that each employee's laptop and its data will remain with the company and not fall into someone else's hands? (Choose two.)

    A. Use a cable lock to secure the laptop to the desk.

    B. Use MDM software to wipe the laptop remotely if stolen.

    C. Place the laptop in a desk drawer when the employee walks away.

    D. Ask a stranger to watch the laptop when they use the restroom at a coffee shop.

127. You're setting up authentication for new users of Windows 10 and Windows 11 machines. Which of the following Windows logon methods requires specific hardware? (Choose two.)

    A. Username and password

    B. PIN

    C. Fingerprint

    D. Facial recognition

128. You're setting up new users on your network and have let them know that they will need to change their user password the first time they log in and that it must meet complexity requirements. Which of the following is not true about password best practices?

    A. Password minimum length is eight characters.

    B. Longer passwords are better.

    C. At least one of each of these should be used: upper- and lowercase letters, numbers, and special characters.

    D. Passwords that are four characters long are okay if they are complex.

129. You've just hired a new employee who will be working at a Windows workstation on your network. You're helping the user understand what their password should be like. Which of the following are best practices for passwords? (Choose two.)

    A. Enforce password complexity.

    B. Passwords should be easy to guess in case you forget, like your dog's name.

    C. Passwords expire after 45 days.

    D. Passwords expire after 180 days.

130. Your company has a Windows domain managed by a domain controller. Following best practices, what feature of the domain controller is used to apply permissions to users?

    A. Active Directory

    B. User accounts

    C. Security groups

    D. Home folders

131. You're configuring password requirements such as length and expiration for several Windows 11 Pro workstations. What utility can you use on the workstation to configure the password requirements?

    A. Users Accounts in Control Panel

    B. Local Users and Groups

    C. Administrative Tools

    D. Local Security Policy

132. A user of a computer that you administer on your Active Directory domain has forgotten their logon password. What can be done to get them back into the system?

    A. Reset the password on the local computer.

    B. Reset the password on the domain controller.

    C. Reinstall the OS and re-create their user.

    D. Make them a new account with a new username.

133. A computer user is setting up a new Windows 11 Home computer for the first time. They called you because they can't figure out how to set it up with a local account. What will you tell them?

    A. That option is not available. They must use a Microsoft account.

    B. Press F10 during bootup to create a local account.

    C. They must switch to the Pro edition if they want to use a local account after setup.

    D. Local accounts are never available in Windows 11.

134. When using a Microsoft account to log in to your Windows 11 computer, which of the following is not true?

    A. Your username is your email.

    B. There are more recovery options if you use a Microsoft account rather than a local account to access your computer.

    C. You won't be able to use your computer if your Internet access is down.

    D. You can access information stored on OneDrive from another computer if you log in with your Microsoft account.

135. Your friend wants to change the password for another user who is unable to log into the PC because they forgot their password. When they try to access User Accounts in Control Panel, they are unable to access it. What will you tell them?

    A. They need administrator access to change or create another user's account, and they are only a standard user.

    B. They can change it in Local Users and Groups.

    C. They need to use the command-line utility to change the user's password.

    D. They can't change the password but they can add a new username for the password and make that user an administrator so that they can access their data.

136. You are disposing of used hard drives, and a network administrator recommends performing a low-level format. What is the difference between a low-level format and a standard format?

    A. Low-level formats are performed at the factory, and standard formats are performed using the `format` command.

    B. Standard formats are performed at the factory, and low-level formats are performed using the `format` command.

    C. A modern low-level format fills the entire drive with zeros, returning it to factory mode. A standard format creates the file allocation table and root directory.

    D. A standard format records the tracks and marks the start of each sector on each track. A low-level format creates the file allocation table and root directory.

137. You have been instructed to destroy several old hard drives that contained confidential information, so you take them to a local company that specializes in this process. The IT director wants confirmation that the drives were properly destroyed. What do you need to provide him with?

    A. Hard drive fragments

    B. Photos of the destroyed hard drives

    C. A notarized letter from the disposal company

    D. A certificate of destruction

138. You work for a bank whose policy is to physically destroy, rather than recycle, hard drives that are no longer needed. Which of the following is not a physical destruction method for hard drives?

    A. Incinerating

    B. Drilling

    C. Zero-filling

    D. Shredding

139. A friend is getting overwhelmed with the number of passwords they need to remember and has been writing them down, but the passwords aren't very complex, and your friend has used the same ones on several sites. You offer to help them. What will you do?

    A. Clear their browser cache.

    B. Clear their browsing data.

    C. Update their certificates.

    D. Install a password manager.

140. You work for a company that is trying to be green. They want to repurpose their old PCs by giving them to a charitable organization rather than destroying or recycling them. What should you do before you give them away? (Choose two.)

   A. Wipe all drives.

   B. Restore the computer to its factory default condition.

   C. Create a new user for the charity and delete your user.

   D. Delete users and all their files and leave a generic administrator account active.

141. You're donating a Windows 10 PC to a charity, but first want to remove all your data and restore the PCs OS to a factory install. You've booted into WinRE. What does Microsoft call the recovery option to reinstall the OS and delete all user files and data?

   A. Refresh Your PC

   B. Reset Your PC

   C. Restore Your PC

   D. Repair Your PC

142. You are setting up a Windows 11 Pro computer that will house data shared by many people. How will you establish security for this group?

   A. Use the Local Users and Groups app to create groups such as Accounting, Office, and so on. Then set up permissions for each group on shared files. Add and remove users to the group as needed.

   B. In Control Panel, User Accounts, make all users administrators so they can do what they need.

   C. Use the Local Users and Groups app to create groups such as Accounting, Office, and so on. Then set up permissions for each person on the shared files. Add users to the groups just for organizational purposes.

   D. Groups are only used on servers, so set up each person with their specific NTFS permissions on the shared data folders.

143. You're providing system training to a new employee, and they want to know where they should keep their password. What will you tell them? (Choose two.)

   A. Write the password on a sticky note attached to the bottom of their keyboard.

   B. Passwords will be saved in password manager software, and multifactor authentication is used for network access.

   C. Tape the password to the monitor so they can see it.

   D. They need to memorize their password and not write it down.

144. Which of the following are best practices for managing user accounts? (Choose two.)

   A. Restrict user permissions.

   B. Restrict login times.

   C. Enable the Guest account.

   D. Give all users administrative access.

145. Workers have been instructed to lock their computers whenever they walk away from them, but as you walk around the company, you notice computers unlocked and no one sitting there. What is the best solution to mitigate this problem? (Choose two.)

    A. Fire people who won't lock their computer.

    B. Enforce screen saver locks after a short time of inactivity.

    C. Train users on the importance of locking their PC.

    D. Set the PC to shut down after 2 minutes of inactivity.

146. Data encryption has been established for data that travels across the network, but you work in a secure environment and want to encrypt all the data on users' storage drives, including laptop drives, to prevent dissemination of information if the drives are compromised or stolen. Which of the following would not be a good solution to encrypt this data-at-rest?

    A. Use EFS and let the employee choose what to encrypt.

    B. Use a third-party encryption solution.

    C. Use MDM software.

    D. Use BitLocker on desktop systems.

147. You have a new smartphone that can authorize a transaction by using your phone's camera while you are simply looking at it. What is this technology called?

    A. Pin code

    B. Fingerprint scanner

    C. Device encryption

    D. Facial recognition

148. Which method of logging into a mobile device may make it easy for someone to guess your password based on marks left by the oils in your skin?

    A. Facial recognition

    B. Fingerprint

    C. Pattern

    D. Swipe

149. Which of the following is the least secure way to access a mobile device whose screen is locked?

    A. Facial recognition

    B. PIN code

    C. Swipe

    D. Pattern

150. You just installed a security camera that communicates on port 4150. The video camera is connected to your SOHO router. With the camera set up, you can view the video stream from your computer that is on the same SOHO router, but not remotely on your phone or another computer. What did you forget to do?

  A. Configure port forwarding on the router.

  B. Close port 4150.

  C. Connect the camera to the router.

  D. Disable the firewall.

151. You are installing a SOHO router and a wired network for a small office. The manager is concerned that employees will visit websites with objectionable material. Which feature should you look for in a router to help prevent such access?

  A. Content filtering

  B. Disabling ports

  C. VPN access

  D. Port forwarding/mapping

152. Your office is in a building with several other companies. You want to configure the wireless network so that casual users in the building are not able to easily see your network name. What should you do to configure this?

  A. Enable WPA3.

  B. Enable MAC filtering.

  C. Disable SSID broadcasts.

  D. Reduce radio power levels.

153. You're changing some configuration settings on your SOHO router and notice that WPA3 is not available. What might you be able to do to resolve this issue?

  A. Configure port forwarding.

  B. Configure content filtering.

  C. Update the SSID.

  D. Update the router's firmware.

154. Which of the following are very fast and very secure ways to access your mobile device? (Choose two.)

  A. PIN code

  B. Fingerprint scanner

  C. Swipe

  D. Facial recognition

155. You're setting up a SOHO network that uses DHCP but would like the IP address for a printer to remain consistent. What will you configure on the router to achieve this?

    A.   DHCP scope

    B.   DHCP reservations

    C.   APIPA scope

    D.   Loopback address

156. What method of securing a mobile device requires entering a series of numbers?

    A.   PIN code

    B.   Fingerprint scanner

    C.   Pattern

    D.   Facial recognition

157. You've been using a drawn pattern on your phone to unlock it for some time, and now it simply won't work. What might quickly resolve this issue? (Choose two.)

    A.   Clean the screen.

    B.   Wipe the phone and do a factory reset.

    C.   Restart the phone.

    D.   Use your Google credentials to gain access.

158. You own a small company with a SOHO router and a web server that is used to sell your products. You don't want the IP address of your web server to change, so you've paid the ISP for a specific IP address that is yours and will not change. What would you configure on your router for your ISP connection?

    A.   Dynamic WAN IP

    B.   Static WAN IP

    C.   UPnP

    D.   Screened subnet

159. What is the protocol that allows devices on your LAN, such as your laptop and printer, to find each other?

    A.   WPA3

    B.   WPA2

    C.   PIN

    D.   UPnP

160. You are configuring a new SOHO router that replaced a failed one. Your network has a mixture of devices purchased several years ago and newer ones purchased in 2022. Which of the following encryption options should you choose?

    A.   WPA3

    B.   WPA2

    C.   WPA2/WPA3

    D.   WEP

161. You perform very confidential work as a government contractor, and you work from home. Your contract specifies that the only external computers your computers can communicate with are the government computers involved in the project. What can you configure on your router to block all other computers from communicating with your network?

   A. IP address filtering

   B. Untrusted sources

   C. Hashing

   D. Port filtering

162. Your company has decided to allow users to use their own devices for company business. This decision will save the company money on hardware. To use their personal devices, the company will require that employees sign an agreement. What would this agreement be called?

   A. BYOD policy

   B. MDM policy

   C. Cell phone policy

   D. Remote work policy

163. Your iPhone requires a passcode to unlock it. Because of recent phone thefts around your office, you want to set your phone so that all data is destroyed if incorrect passcodes are entered 10 times in a row. Which feature allows you to do this?

   A. Failed login attempts restrictions

   B. Screen locks

   C. Remote wipes

   D. Locator applications

164. You own a small company with a SOHO router and a web server that is used to sell your products. You are concerned about the security of your LAN, so your IT consultant is going to set up a two-router system like the one shown in the graphic, to protect the LAN from web server traffic. What is this arrangement called?

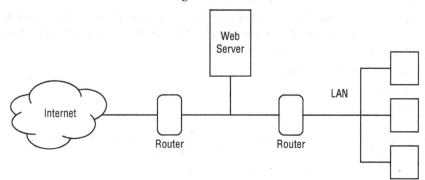

A. Dynamic WAN IP

B. Static WAN IP

C. UPnP

D. Screened subnet

165. You turned your back for a minute in the coffee shop and your mobile device is missing. Which one of the following is not a way to achieve a remote wipe on a mobile device?

A. Exceeding failed login restrictions

B. Using Google Find My Device or Find iPhone app

C. Using MDM software

D. Disabling guest access

166. You are setting up a router and network for a SOHO business. The router has wired and wireless connections. Which of the following is not a method for securing the router and network?

A. Place the router in the kitchen area for easy access.

B. Disable any guest accounts on the network. If guests need access, set up a separate VPN for them.

C. Ensure that the Wi-Fi signal doesn't extend beyond the required area, and if it does, lower the power of the Wi-Fi signal.

D. Place the router in an area that can be locked.

167. There seems to be a great deal of interference on your wireless network. You determine that it's due to the network in the office next door. What should you do to keep your network safe and reliable? (Choose three.)

A. Change the channel your router uses.

B. Turn your Wi-Fi signal power to maximum power to drown out theirs.

C. Turn your signal power down to decrease interference.

D. Try moving the router or using a different band.

168. A user needs to download a new video card driver for their HP laptop. They find the driver on the HP site and ask you if they can download it. The HP site is an example of what?

A. Part of an access control list

B. An authenticator website

C. A trusted software source

D. An untrusted software source

169. You are planning a wireless network for a small office. Which of the following is a good rule of thumb when considering access point placement?

A. Place them in walls or ceilings for protection.

B. Place them near metal objects so the signal will reflect better.

C. Place them in the center of the network area.

D. Place them at the edge of the network area and focus them in the proper direction.

170. You receive an email from an overseas bank notifying you that a relative has left you a large sum of money. You need to respond with your bank routing information so they can electronically transfer the funds directly to your account. What is this most likely an example of?

   A. Phishing

   B. Ransomware

   C. Spoofing

   D. Whaling

171. All of the following are methods to keep your mobile device safe except for one. Which one is that?

   A. Use a swipe to unlock a mobile device.

   B. Accept and install OS updates as soon as possible.

   C. Install antivirus/anti-malware.

   D. Use a remote backup application to safeguard your data in the event that you must wipe your phone.

172. Your wireless network has been working just fine, but today you're flooded with calls that employees can't access the network. You suspect that an unhappy employee who was recently fired is perpetrating a DoS attack by causing network interference. Which of the following might temporarily solve the problem?

   A. Set your router to use a different channel.

   B. Have everyone log off their computers and back on.

   C. Reset the router.

   D. Restore the router to factory defaults.

173. Your data center recently experienced a theft of a server from the rack. Which security mechanism would protect servers from future theft?

   A. Security token

   B. Server lock

   C. Key fob

   D. Firewall

174. A user is complaining that they have so many ads popping up on their screen when they are doing Internet research that they can't get their work done. What can you configure in their browser to mitigate this problem?

   A. Private-browsing mode

   B. Pop-up blocker

   C. Password manager

   D. Certificate

175. You work as a contractor for a government entity that requires proof of data destruction when decommissioning old hard drives and computers. What is the best way to do this?

    A. Hire a third-party vendor to do the destruction and provide a certificate of destruction and recycling.

    B. Have the recycling center give you a receipt for the drives.

    C. Destroy them within your company and show pictures of the destroyed drives.

    D. Zero-write all the drives.

176. What type of technology used in security devices requires bringing a smartcard or ID close to but not touching a card reader to gain access to an area?

    A. Access control vestibule.

    B. Key fob.

    C. Biometrics.

    D. RFID.

Chapter

8

Software Troubleshooting

THE COMPTIA A+ 220-1102 TOPICS COVERED IN THIS CHAPTER INCLUDE THE FOLLOWING:

✓ **3.1 Given a scenario, troubleshoot common Windows OS problems.**

- Common symptoms
  - Blue screen of death (BSOD)
  - Sluggish performance
  - Boot problems
  - Frequent Shutdowns
  - Services not starting
  - Applications crashing
  - Low memory warnings
  - USB controller resource warnings
  - System instability
  - No OS found
  - Slow profile load
  - Time drift
- Common troubleshooting steps
  - Reboot
  - Restart services
  - Uninstall/reinstall/update applications
  - Add resources
  - Verify requirements
  - System file check
  - Repair Windows

- Restore
- Reimage
- Roll back updates
- Rebuild Windows profiles

✓ **3.2 Given a scenario, troubleshoot common personal computer (PC) security issues.**

- Common symptoms
    - Unable to access the network
    - Desktop alerts
    - False alerts regarding antivirus protection
    - Altered system or personal files
        - Missing/renamed files
    - Unwanted notifications within the OS
    - OS update failures
- Browser-related symptoms
    - Random/frequent pop-ups
    - Certificate warnings
    - Redirection

✓ **3.3 Given a scenario, use best practice procedures for malware removal.**

- 1. Investigate and verify malware symptoms
- 2. Quarantine infected systems
- 3. Disable System Restore in Windows
- 4. Remediate infected systems
    - a. Update anti-malware software
    - b. Scanning and removal techniques (e.g., safe mode, preinstallation environment)
- 5. Schedule scans and run updates
- 6. Enable System Restore and create a restore point in Windows
- 7. Educate the end user

✓ **3.4 Given a scenario, troubleshoot common mobile OS and application issues.**

- Common symptoms
    - Application fails to launch
    - Application fails to close/crashes
    - Application fails to update
    - Slow to respond
    - OS fails to update
    - Battery life issues
    - Randomly reboots
    - Connectivity issues
        - Bluetooth
        - Wi-Fi
        - Near-field communication (NFC)
        - AirDrop
    - Screen does not autorotate

✓ **3.5 Given a scenario, troubleshoot common mobile OS and application security issues.**

- Security concerns
    - Android package (APK) source
    - Developer mode
    - Root access/jailbreak
    - Bootleg/malicious application
        - Application spoofing
- Common symptoms
    - High network traffic
    - Sluggish response time
    - Data-usage limit notification
    - Limited Internet connectivity
    - No Internet connectivity

- High number of ads
- Fake security warnings
- Unexpected application behavior
- Leaked personal files/data

1. A coworker is having problems with the Bluetooth connection between a device and their laptop. Which of the following can you do to check connectivity between the laptop and the device? (Choose two.)

    A. Ensure that Bluetooth is turned on in Settings.

    B. Ensure that Airplane mode is on.

    C. Ensure that Airplane mode is off.

    D. Go to a command prompt or terminal and type **Bluetooth** to enable it.

2. You just installed a new sound card in a Windows workstation. Now, the computer has crashed and given you a blue screen of death. You turn the computer off. What should you try to resolve the issue?

    A. Reinstall Windows.

    B. Boot to the Windows installation media and start the WinRE.

    C. Boot to safe mode and uninstall the sound card driver.

    D. Remove the sound card from the computer and reboot.

3. An iPad user reports that when they are in a certain part of the building, their wireless connection intermittently drops. What are the two most likely causes of this? (Choose two.)

    A. Poor wireless buffering in the iPad

    B. Interference with the wireless signal

    C. Weak signal strength from the wireless access point

    D. Retracted Wi-Fi antenna on the iPad

4. A technician is troubleshooting a Windows 10 computer that is acting strangely, and they suspect that it's infected with a virus. They have followed the best practices for malware removal and remediated the computer. What should they do next?

    A. Schedule scans and run updates.

    B. Educate the end user.

    C. Enable System Restore and create a restore point.

    D. Disable System Restore in Windows.

5. A technician is working on a Windows 10 workstation that seems to be unstable. They want to ensure that system files have not been altered. Which command should they use to scan and fix corrupted system files?

    A. `sfc /scanfix`

    B. `sfc /scanfile`

    C. `sfc /verifyonly`

    D. `sfc /scannow`

6. On your MacBook Pro, you use the Safari browser to surf the Internet. Yesterday a friend borrowed your laptop. Today, when you try to browse the web, no matter what site URL you type into the address bar, you are sent to a different website. What is most likely happening to your computer?

    A.   A practical joke by your friend.

    B.   Browser redirection.

    C.   Rogue antivirus.

    D.   It has been infected with spam.

7. Your company purchases a custom database software package from an outside vendor. You install the client software on a Windows workstation, and it crashes when you try to open it. You remove the software and reinstall it, but again it crashes when you open it. What should you do next?

    A.   Run an antivirus remediation on the workstation.

    B.   Contact the vendor to see whether an update or patch is available.

    C.   Delete and reinstall Windows.

    D.   Enable Software Compatibility through Control Panel.

8. An iPhone user reports that his phone will not connect to his wireless headset for hands-free phone calls. His headset is powered on and has worked previously. His iPhone screen is shown here. What is most likely the problem?

    A.   The headset is not paired with the iPhone.

    B.   Bluetooth is turned off.

    C.   Wi-Fi is turned off.

    D.   Airplane mode is turned on.

9. You are troubleshooting a Windows 11 workstation that could have malware on it. To follow the best practices for malware removal, what is the first step you should take?

    A. Quarantine the infected system.

    B. Update the anti-malware software.

    C. Enable system restore and create a restore point.

    D. Investigate and verify malware symptoms.

10. A user reports that his Windows 10 Start menu looks wrong. You know the environment relies on roaming profiles. What is a reliable solution to the user's problem?

    A. Rebuild the desktop image.

    B. Rebuild the Windows user profile.

    C. Delete the Registry on the local machine.

    D. Reboot the machine.

11. While working on a Windows 11 workstation, a user receives a flashing pop-up message saying that their computer has been infected with a virus and they need to download a virus scanner now to fix it. What will most likely happen when they click the button to download the recommended virus scanner?

    A. It will download a virus to their computer.

    B. It will download an antivirus program to their computer and remediate the virus.

    C. The antivirus program they download will scan their computer and find nothing because their company already uses an antivirus program.

    D. It will take them to a website that will allow them to purchase an antivirus program to remediate the virus.

12. You have 20 Windows 11 workstations on your network. You want to create bootable media that will allow you to fix Windows boot issues. Where can you create this media?

    A. Use Windows Security in the Settings app.

    B. Back up and sync your settings in the Settings app.

    C. Download and use Microsoft's media creation tool.

    D. Copy the contents of the C drive to a USB.

13. Your Windows system doesn't appear to be stable. It's slow to respond when you want it to open a file. You just installed a new software application yesterday. What should you do to fix this problem?

    A. Reinstall Windows.

    B. Restore from a recent system restore point.

    C. Use the WinRE to reformat the drive.

    D. Remove the new drivers.

14. Your Windows system is running sluggishly. When you look at the hard drive, you notice that there is very little space available. Which tool should you run to attempt to free some space on the hard drive?

    A. Optimize and defragment drive

    B. Disk Cleanup

    C. `regedit`

    D. SFC

15. A user reports that a Word document they need will not open. Other documents open as they should. They have not made a backup of this file. Which of the following statements is true?

    A. The file is probably corrupted, and its contents are lost.

    B. They can use a restore point to get the file back.

    C. They can use the command-line utility to open the document.

    D. They can use WinRE to repair the file and then open it.

16. You've been working very hard and have several Word documents open on your desktop. Luckily, you've been saving them often because suddenly the Word app is showing all sorts of strange characters on the screen, even in the ribbon at top. It appears to be corrupted and it won't respond to any commands, including Close. How can you force the app to close so you can reopen the saved files and continue your work? (Choose two.)

    A. Double-click the program file.

    B. Right-click anywhere in the program window and choose Close.

    C. Open Task Manager and select the Processes tab. Then right-click the program name and choose End task.

    D. Reboot the computer.

17. Your iPad is experiencing slow performance. What are the best two options to increase performance speed? (Choose two.)

    A. Close open apps.

    B. Perform a reset to the factory default.

    C. Increase the RAM.

    D. Perform a soft reset.

18. You just downloaded an app for your bank on your mobile device. You weren't sure which app to choose, so you picked the one that looks most like your bank. After installing the app something just didn't look right and you noticed misspelled words on the screen where it's asking for your username and password. What should you do next?

    A. Enter your username and password.

    B. Call the bank and ask them about the app.

    C. Uninstall the app immediately and run a virus scan.

    D. Run spell check on the app.

19. You are visiting a website using your favorite browser, and without you clicking anything, a new browser window opens in front of it with an advertisement. Which of the following is the most likely explanation?

  A. Your computer has been infected with adware.

  B. Your computer has been infected with spyware.

  C. Your computer has been infected with a virus.

  D. The website is programmed to show a pop-up advertisement.

20. You are talking to a friend about purchasing a gift, and they recommend a website to purchase it. When you put the website's secure address into your browser, you receive a message stating that there is an invalid certificate. What should you do?

  A. Visit the website anyway; it's probably OK.

  B. Do not visit the website.

  C. Visit the secure version of the website by changing the address to start with HTTPS://.

  D. Visit the unsecure version of the website by changing the address to start with HTTP://.

21. You are training technicians on the creation and use of restore points. Restore points can sometimes fix problems with slow or unresponsive systems. Which of the following is not a way in which restore points are created?

  A. Windows creates them automatically by default.

  B. You can manually create them.

  C. Windows creates them before a system crash.

  D. Some installation utilities will create them before installing a new program.

22. You are troubleshooting a workstation on your network and believe it has malware. To follow the best practices for malware removal, after you investigate and verify malware symptoms, which step should you take?

  A. Update the anti-malware software.

  B. Disable System Restore.

  C. Quarantine the infected system.

  D. Scan for and remove the malware.

23. Your favorite restaurant locator app on your iPhone won't load. You closed it and tried to reopen it a few times and it still doesn't work. What should you try next?

  A. Remove and reinstall the app.

  B. Perform a factory reset.

  C. Force-stop the app.

  D. Reboot the phone and try the app again.

24. You are using an iPhone. When is it generally necessary to close running apps on the iPhone?

   A. When you receive out-of-memory errors

   B. When the phone is sluggish

   C. When an app locks up

   D. When you are done using them for the day

25. You receive an email warning you of a new form of ransomware. It contains a link to receive more information on how to protect yourself from this terrible threat. What should you do next?

   A. Click the link to receive more information.

   B. Check www.us-cert.gov for information on the threat.

   C. Check to ensure that your system has a rogue antivirus installed.

   D. Forward the email to everyone in your contacts list.

26. Mobile device users on your network are required to use a VPN app to connect to the corporate network when they are out of the office. A user reports that the app will not open for them. They turned the tablet off and back on again, and the app still will not open. What should be tried next?

   A. Cycle the power.

   B. Reset to factory defaults.

   C. Uninstall and reinstall the app.

   D. Perform a force-stop.

27. A network user with an Android tablet wants to back up and synchronize their data with their phone. Which service should they use to perform these tasks?

   A. Google Sync

   B. Google Cloud

   C. Android Sync

   D. Android Cloud

28. A client has a Windows 11 computer with a virus on it. They have quarantined the system from the rest of their network. To follow malware removal best practices, what should be done next?

   A. Investigate and verify malware symptoms.

   B. Disable System Restore in Windows.

   C. Enable System Restore and create a restore point in Windows.

   D. Update anti-malware software.

29. Your Windows desktop system is running sluggishly. You have a magnetic hard drive and an M.2 drive. What could you do that might improve system performance? (Choose two.)

   A. Run Optimize and defragment drive on the magnetic media drive.

   B. Run Disk Cleanup on both drives.

   C. Run Optimize and defragment drive on the M.2 drive.

   D. Run SFC.

30. You are visiting a website using your favorite browser. You haven't clicked anything, yet you can barely read the page because there are so many pop-ups. Which of the following is the most likely explanation?

  A. Your computer has been infected with adware.

  B. Your computer has been infected with spyware.

  C. Your computer has been infected with a virus.

  D. The website is programmed to show a pop-up advertisement.

31. On your network, you are concerned about mobile users accidentally granting unauthorized account access or root access. What step should you take to help prevent these security problems?

  A. Apply patches and upgrades as soon as they are available.

  B. Monitor resource utilization and remediate high usage.

  C. Install mobile firewalls on all devices.

  D. Disable location tracking, the camera, and the microphone.

32. Client computers on your network connect to the Internet through a proxy server. Recently, a Windows client was infected with adware and a browser redirector. You have removed the malware, and now the computer will not connect to the Internet. What should you do to resolve the problem?

  A. Disable the network card. Reboot and enable the network card.

  B. Perform malware remediation again.

  C. Disable the proxy server configuration to connect directly to the Internet.

  D. Check the IP configuration to ensure it's pointing to the correct proxy server address.

33. A technician just updated the network card driver for a Windows workstation. Now, the network card does not appear to work. They reboot the computer and log back in, and it still does not work. What should be done next to resolve the issue?

  A. Reboot into safe mode and uninstall the network card driver.

  B. Reinstall Windows.

  C. Open Device Manager, find the network card, and roll back the driver.

  D. Replace the malfunctioning network card.

34. Your company has recently made changes to infrastructure services such as DNS. The new DNS information is available but not yet propagated to all workstations. Since then, a number of users have reported that they are no longer able to browse for internal servers. What should each affected user do? (Choose two.)

  A. Reboot.

  B. Manually update network settings.

  C. Disable software firewall.

  D. Boot to safe mode.

35. Your Windows PC is acting poorly after you installed a few poorly written applications. Now the system will not function properly. You want to refresh your Windows installation but keep your personal files. Where can this be done from? (Choose two.)

A. System Recovery Options

B. Safe mode

C. Emergency repair disk

D. WinRE

36. Your system has become infected with malware. You verified the symptoms, quarantined the system, and disabled System Restore. Now you need to eradicate the virus. What would be a good choice to do next? (Choose two.)

A. Boot into safe mode to clean out virus files.

B. Boot Windows as normal.

C. Rebuild the registry.

D. Use installation media to boot into the preinstallation environment.

37. A Windows user's antivirus software has crashed. They reboot the computer and try to open it again, and it crashes again. What should be done next to solve the problem? (Choose two.)

A. Look for a patch or update on the manufacturer's website.

B. Delete the antivirus software and reinstall it.

C. Remove and reinstall Windows.

D. Repair the antivirus installation through Programs and features in Control Panel.

38. A user reports that an application has been crashing on their mobile device. They said an error pop-up window flashes on the screen briefly, but they are unable to read it. What would be your next step?

A. Wait for the next crash to read the error pop-up yourself.

B. Install and run a screen recorder to capture the next pop-up.

C. Reinstall the application.

D. Check the application log for error messages.

39. A user reports that the battery life on their smartphone is very short. It works for only about three hours before it needs to be recharged. What can you recommend they do to extend the battery life? (Choose two.)

A. Turn off unnecessary wireless connections.

B. Perform a reset to factory defaults.

C. Set the screen to automatically dim.

D. Install an antivirus app.

40. A user is unable to access the network and is getting an error message that a duplicate IP exists on the system. You are confused because you have a DHCP server. What do you need to do next?

 A. Manually configure the IP address.

 B. Ensure that this computer is set to obtain an IP address automatically.

 C. Ping the IP address from another computer to find out the name of the duplicate computer.

 D. At a command prompt, enter `ipconfig /release`, then `ipconfig /renew`.

41. A user reports the printer was working fine yesterday but is no longer. Last night, they updated their printer drivers assuming they should always have the most up-to-date drivers installed. What is the likely fix for this problem?

 A. Roll back the printer driver.

 B. Update the boot order.

 C. Update the network settings.

 D. Restart the print spooler.

42. You have just purchased an Android mobile phone and are concerned about security threats. Which of the following statements is true?

 A. There are no viruses for Android-based mobile phones.

 B. Android-based phones come with an automatically enabled antivirus app.

 C. You should download and install an antivirus app.

 D. As long as you automatically install OS patches, you will not get an Android virus.

43. You are working on your Windows computer and a security alert pops up, as shown here. What should your next action be?

 A. Click the Protect Now button.

 B. Click the X in the upper-right corner to close the alert.

 C. Shut down your computer. Reboot, and initiate a virus scan using your antivirus software.

 D. Use System Restore to create a snapshot and then click the Protect Now button.

44. You have a Windows workstation that is spontaneously shutting down and restarting. What should you do to troubleshoot and resolve the issue?

    A. Check the system BIOS/UEFI settings to ensure that the boot order is set properly.

    B. Boot to the Windows installation media and navigate to the WinRE command prompt.

    C. Boot into safe mode and see if the problem still persists.

    D. Reinstall Windows.

45. A Windows desktop computer always shuts down about 10 minutes after the user boots it up. The computer works fine for those first 10 minutes, and if they boot up again a few minutes after a shutdown, it works fine again for 10 minutes. How might you fix this? (Choose two.)

    A. Reinstall Windows.

    B. Use compressed air or an ESD vacuum to clean dust and debris from the system.

    C. Use SFC to search for and repair corrupted system files.

    D. Replace the thermal paste on the processor.

46. Your Windows computer was working fine yesterday, but today it is exhibiting slow performance. Which of the following tools should be used to check for a potential problem causing the slowdown? (Choose two.)

    A. Anti-malware software

    B. Event Viewer

    C. Task Manager ➤ Processes tab

    D. Programs and Features in Control Panel

47. A user on your Active Directory domain is complaining that their profile is taking a long time to load. They've been waiting several minutes. Upon questioning, you find out that this is their first logon at a different computer. What is happening here?

    A. They are not listed as a user on this computer.

    B. Their roaming profile is downloading to this computer, and it takes longer the first time a user logs onto a different PC.

    C. A peripheral is not connected as it should be, causing a loop in the boot process.

    D. They entered the wrong password.

48. A Windows user at your office receives the message in the graphic when trying to print a document. They know that there were two printers listed yesterday. What is likely the problem?

Adobe Acrobat

(i) Before you can perform print-related tasks such as page setup or printing a document, you need to install a printer.

OK

A. Someone has deleted their printers.

B. Both of the printers are offline.

C. Both printers are out of paper.

D. The print spooler service needs to be restarted.

49. The time on your Windows computer is always off by a few minutes to an hour. You need to ensure that it will keep the right time because an incorrect time will not allow it to log into your server. Which of the following actions will not help?

A. In Settings, select Time & Language, then Date & time, and ensure that Set Time Automatically and Set Time Zone Automatically are set to On.

B. Right-click on the time on the taskbar and choose Internet Time, then choose a different time server.

C. Open the Services console and ensure that the Windows Time service start is set to Automatic and that the service is started.

D. In Settings, select Time & Language, then Date & time, and click Sync now.

50. A Windows 10 workstation that is set to boot from the C: drive, and normally boots just fine, will not boot properly. Instead, there is an error message stating that no OS is found. What steps could you take to fix this problem?

A. Boot to installation media, navigate to a command prompt, type **startup repair**, and press Enter.

B. Boot to the installation media, open SFC, and choose Startup Repair.

C. Boot to the installation media, then choose Repair your computer ➤ Troubleshoot ➤ Startup Repair and follow the onscreen prompts.

D. Boot to Safe Mode ➤ System Recovery Options ➤ Startup Repair and follow the onscreen prompts.

51. A Windows workstation is running slowly. You have already verified that there is no malware in the system. What will you check next? (Choose two.)

A. Check available physical memory.

B. Check available virtual memory.

C. Roll back the OS update to a prior one.

D. Restore from a restore point.

52. An application on your Windows workstation isn't working properly and when you research the error message online, the result is that you need to update the application. Where can you go to do this? (Choose two.)

A. Check for an update option in the software.

B. In Control Panel, click Programs and Features.

C. Check the application's website.

D. In the Settings app, select Apps, then Apps & features.

53. You're trying to launch an application on your Windows workstation, but the application won't load. You've tried uninstalling and reinstalling the application, but it didn't help. Which of the following should you do next?

    A. Check the application's website for updates.

    B. Verify that your system meets the application requirements.

    C. Choose a different application that does the same thing.

    D. Reinstall Windows.

54. You're in Microsoft Word and want to open a file that you used yesterday. You know that you saved the file, and it shows in the list of recently used files, but when you click on it a message says that the file can't be found. You go the folder where the file is stored and see that the file extension has been changed. What should you immediately suspect?

    A. The drive is corrupted and you need to reinstall Windows.

    B. The Word program is corrupted and you need to reinstall Word.

    C. A coworker has been playing with your computer and opened and saved your file using a different program.

    D. Your computer has been infected by malware.

55. A Windows computer user receives an error message that a needed service failed to start. Where can that user go to start the service? (Choose two.)

    A. Services tab of Task Manager

    B. Computer Management

    C. The Services console

    D. Device Manager

56. A Windows system is running slowly. Which of the following is not likely to be the culprit?

    A. The PC has too little RAM.

    B. The paging file is too large.

    C. The system is infected with malware.

    D. The hard drive is too large.

57. You are trying to apply Windows Updates to a Windows client computer. The update fails and gives you an error message. What should you do next?

    A. Run the Windows Update Troubleshooter in the Settings app.

    B. Wait until the next Windows update comes out in 6 months.

    C. Reinstall the operating system.

    D. Purchase an updated computer.

58. A technician is fixing a Windows workstation that has contracted a virus. They are following the best practices for malware removal and have enabled System Restore and created a restore point. What is the next step that should be taken?

    A. Educate the end user.

    B. Disable System Restore.

    C. Quarantine the infected system.

    D. Remediate the infected system.

59. You work for a government entity and they insist that you use the government time server, `time.NIST.gov`, to sync the time on your computer system. Where will you go to do this?

    A. In the Settings app, select Time & Language, then Date & time, and ensure that Set time automatically and Set time zone automatically are set to On.

    B. Open the Services console and ensure that the Windows Time is set to `time.NIST.gov` and that the service is started.

    C. In Control Panel, select Date and Time, and on the Internet Time tab, click Change settings, then under Server, choose `time.NIST.gov`.

    D. Double-click the time in the task bar and on the Internet time tab under servers, choose `time.NIST.gov`.

60. A Windows user complains that every day they get a message that a service they need for a particular program is not started, and they must open the Services console and start it every day. What will you tell the user?

    A. Some services behave that way. You'll need to start it every day.

    B. Open the Services console, double-click the service, and on the General tab, change the startup type to Automatic.

    C. Open the Services console, double-click the service, and on the General tab, change the startup type to Manual.

    D. Open the application and look for a place to have it start the service for the user.

61. You've noticed that lately your games freeze or crash more often, and you received a message stating that your computer is low on memory. What can you do to resolve this? (Choose two.)

    A. Increase virtual memory.

    B. Decrease virtual memory.

    C. Increase physical memory.

    D. Buy a bigger hard drive.

62. An application you want to install says that it needs 4 GB of RAM. Where will you go to see if you have sufficient RAM to run this application? (Choose two.)

    A. Open the case and see how many modules are installed.

    B. Use the System Information utility.

    C. Use the Performance tab in Task Manager.

    D. In Control Panel, select Memory.

63. A user reports the PC was fine until an OS update was installed. Believing that all updates are necessary, the user voluntarily updated the system on their own. However, the update was not yet tested and is found to be incompatible with a needed business application. What is your next step?

    A. Roll back the update.

    B. Update the business application.

    C. Do nothing; have the user take awareness training.

    D. Kill the updated task.

64. You are troubleshooting a Windows workstation that has contracted a virus. According to the best practices for malware removal, which two steps are part of remediating the infected system? (Choose two.)

    A. Disable system restore in Windows.

    B. Schedule scans and run updates.

    C. Update anti-malware software.

    D. Scan for and remove the malware.

65. While booting up a Windows PC, you find it takes a long time at the Welcome screen. The message "Your roaming profile isn't synchronized with the server. . ." appears. Which two of the following are true? (Choose two.)

    A. The User Profile service detected a slow connection.

    B. A locally cached profile was loaded.

    C. User Profile Service is not running.

    D. Screen resolution is not compatible with the user profile.

66. You just installed new external speakers on a Windows computer, and you've received an error message saying, "Not enough USB Controller Resources." What would most likely be causing this error? (Choose two.)

    A. The motherboard is damaged.

    B. USB devices are drawing more power than the limit.

    C. There are too many devices on a USB 3.0 hub controller.

    D. The speaker drivers are conflicting with the USB hub controller drivers.

67. A smartphone user has complained that their phone won't let them look at anything in landscape—no matter how they turn it, it will not automatically rotate. You look at their screen and it appears as in the graphic. Why isn't their phone letting them look at pictures in landscape view?

A. Their Bluetooth is off.

B. Their focus is off.

C. Their camera is not on.

D. Their orientation is locked.

68. Mobile device users on your network report that the network has very slow data speeds. Which of the following are likely contributors to this problem? (Choose two.)

A. Low battery life

B. Signal interference

C. Unintended Wi-Fi connections

D. Weak signal

69. Several mobile device users have reported that when they eat lunch in the garden next to the office building, they have limited Internet connectivity. What is the most likely fix for this?

A. Boost WAP signal strength.

B. Have all the users reboot their devices.

C. Reboot the WAP.

D. Have the users turn on Wi-Fi on each of their devices.

70. You've been looking for a specific Android app and found it at an amazing price. It almost seems too good to be true, which makes you pause to consider whether it is the real app or not. Which of the following should you check before paying for and downloading this app? (Choose three.)

    A. Check the reviews and number of reviews.

    B. Check the developer's name and how long the app has been available.

    C. Verify the spelling of the app name.

    D. Install the free version and see if there are any problems.

71. A user on your network complains that they see a message for a long time that says "Waiting for the User Profile service" and their profile is very slow to load. What could be the problem?

    A. There is a slow link between the domain controller and the client, but it was not correctly detected by the User Profile service.

    B. The user has never logged into this computer before.

    C. Windows needs to be updated.

    D. The user entered an invalid password.

72. You're working on a Windows client and have received an error message saying, "Not enough USB Controller Resources." Which of the following is not a possible remedy for this situation?

    A. Plug a USB cable from a power block into one of the USB ports on the motherboard.

    B. Purchase an external hub or docking station that is separately powered and plug devices into it.

    C. Move devices that don't need USB 3.X speed to USB 2.0 ports.

    D. Disable the XHCI Mode option in the BIOS/UEFI settings.

73. Your friend has complained that they can't connect their phone to their Wi-Fi network at home and they've used all their cellular data. You look at their screen and it appears as in the graphic. What is the problem?

    A.   Airplane mode is on.

    B.   Their Bluetooth is turned off.

    C.   Their Wi-Fi is turned off.

    D.   Their cellular service is turned off.

74. You're using the most recent version of Microsoft Edge to browse the Internet on your Windows workstation. Today when you visit any website, you receive an error message that there is an invalid certificate. It happens regardless of the site you visit. What should you do?

    A.   Check your computer's time and date.

    B.   Refresh your certificate through the Security settings in Control Panel.

    C.   Set your security level to low for the Internet Zone in Internet Properties in Control Panel.

    D.   In Microsoft Edge, turn off Enhance Your Security On The Web.

75. You use an iPad and an iPhone at work. Which of the following represents the greatest threats to leaking personal files or data? (Choose two.)

    A.   Unauthorized root access

    B.   Unintended Wi-Fi connections

    C.   Unauthorized location tracking

    D.   High resource utilization

76. You receive a notice from your wireless provider that you are about to exceed your data transmission limit for the month. What type of risk does this present?

    A.   Your account may be deactivated.

    B.   You may incur a security breach.

    C.   You may have to pay high fees.

    D.   Your phone may be locked out of the system.

77. Your Android-based phone has recently started rebooting randomly. Which of the following might be the cause? (Choose two.)

    A.   A poorly written app.

    B.   Battery is at room temperature.

    C.   Auto-restart is enabled.

    D.   Typing too fast on the keyboard.

78. A smartphone user calls to report that their phone has no wireless connectivity. What is the first thing you should tell them to do?

    A.   Turn the phone off and back on again.

    B.   Check whether Airplane mode is on.

    C.   Perform a reset to factory default.

    D.   Adjust the Wi-Fi signal receptivity.

79. You are troubleshooting a Windows system that was infected with malware. You've worked through all of the best practice procedures for malware removal up to and including scheduling scans and running updates. What do you need to do next?

    A. Enable System Restore and create a restore point in Windows.

    B. Disable System Restore in Windows.

    C. Remediate infected systems.

    D. Educate the end user.

80. Your network has several dozen mobile device users. Several of them have reported that there are areas within your office where network access is very slow. What can you use to test wireless access?

    A. Cell tower analyzer

    B. Wi-Fi analyzer

    C. Hot spot analyzer

    D. Data transmission analyzer

81. A user on your network is suddenly receiving an overwhelming number of pop-up ads on their mobile device. What is likely happening?

    A. They contracted a virus.

    B. They were the victim of shoulder surfing.

    C. They are the victim of an adware attack.

    D. They are the victim of a keylogger attack.

82. An Android phone user just received a new Bluetooth headset for phone calls. They've reported that it does not work with their phone. Both devices are powered on and appear to be operational. What is most likely the problem?

    A. Bluetooth is turned off on the Android device.

    B. Bluetooth is turned off on the mobile headset.

    C. The devices need to be paired.

    D. Airplane mode is on.

83. You have an unlimited data plan with your cellular provider, but today you receive a notice from your provider that you are about to exceed your data transmission threshold for the month. What will likely happen?

    A. Your account may be deactivated.

    B. You may incur a security breach.

    C. Your data transmissions will be slower than normal.

    D. Your phone may be locked out of the system.

84. A user complains that their Apple device is randomly restarting. They haven't installed any new software recently. What steps will you take to troubleshoot the problem? (Choose two.)

    A. Ensure that the iOS or iPadOS and apps are up-to-date.

    B. Check your battery health in Settings ➢Battery➢ Battery Health.

    C. Replace the battery.

    D. Reset the phone to factory default.

85. A very serious looking pop-up appears on your mobile device screen and says to click it for an update to your anti-malware software that will eradicate a virus your device has contracted. Which of the following should you not do?

A. Click the link to update your anti-malware.

B. Restart the device in safe mode if that is an option on your device.

C. Update your anti-malware as you normally do and run a scan.

D. Check online for information about this fake security warning.

86. A smartphone user is concerned about their privacy and wants to ensure that others can't hack into their phone and track down their location or access their personal data and pictures. Which of the following actions will provide them with some protection to help prevent this from happening? (Choose two.)

A. Install an anti-malware app.

B. Install OS updates as soon as they are available.

C. Disable Location Services.

D. Enable sync with a cloud provider.

87. A step in the malware removal best practices is to manually create a restore point in Windows. What will the restore point do?

A. Create a copy of the entire hard drive.

B. Create a copy of the Users folder and system configuration data.

C. Create a copy of system configuration data.

D. Create a bootable media with copies of key system files.

88. You're trying to pay for coffee at your favorite shop using their NFC reader and Apple Pay, but your phone isn't communicating with it. What could be the problem? (Choose two.)

A. Wi-Fi is disabled.

B. NFC isn't enabled.

C. Airplane mode is on.

D. Bluetooth is disabled.

89. You're attempting to share files with an iPad user by using AirDrop. You both have Wi-Fi turned on, but you can't seem to connect. Which of the following could be causing the problem? (Choose two.)

A. One of you does not have Bluetooth turned on.

B. You are not listed in their contacts.

C. They have their AirDrop Receiving setting set to Everyone.

D. They turned off their hotspot.

90. A mobile device user on your network is suddenly receiving an overwhelming number of pop-up ads on their mobile device. Immediately you're concerned that they've been infected with spyware. While performing the best practices for malware removal, what should be installed on their device to mitigate this threat?

    A. Antivirus software

    B. Anti-malware software

    C. A firewall

    D. A proxy server

91. You're attempting to update the iOS on your iPhone, but the update fails and you receive the message, "Unable to install update. Software update requires a network connection." What should you do first?

    A. Retry the update using the same network connection.

    B. Connect the iPhone to your PC and update it that way.

    C. Remove apps or data to make enough room on your phone for the update.

    D. Plug an Ethernet card into your iPhone.

92. An application failed to update on a user's phone. Which of the following are likely to be the problem? (Choose two.)

    A. The phone is plugged into power.

    B. There is insufficient space on the phone.

    C. You're using Wi-Fi instead of Ethernet.

    D. The Internet connection is weak.

93. A user reports that their mobile phone has been experiencing high resource utilization for about a week. What two things should you immediately suspect could be causing the problem? (Choose two.)

    A. Unauthorized root access

    B. Failing battery

    C. Excessive number of open apps

    D. Stuck sync operation

94. You are visiting a customer's office in a large city high-rise building. You need to make a call on your mobile phone, but you have only one bar. The call will not complete. What should you do?

    A. Wait a few minutes and try again.

    B. Cycle the power off and on.

    C. Reset to factory defaults.

    D. Step outside or near a window.

95. The GPS app on your mobile phone keeps popping up randomly on the screen, and your phone seems to be running very slowly. Which choice will likely not help in this situation?

   A. Restart the phone in safe mode.

   B. Force-stop the application.

   C. Perform a malware scan.

   D. Uninstall the app.

96. While driving through the remote countryside, you notice that your mobile phone battery has been quickly drained of power. What is the most likely cause of this?

   A. The battery needs to be replaced.

   B. The phone has been searching for a signal.

   C. You need to cycle the power off and on again.

   D. You need to replace the phone.

97. A user wants to use developer mode on their Android device to make some tweaks to the system. What setting will you tell them they should not leave on? (Choose two.)

   A. USB configuration

   B. Show Touches

   C. Developer mode

   D. Debugging

98. You're attempting to share pictures with a friend using Apple's AirDrop. You both have Wi-Fi and Bluetooth turned on. Neither of you is using your phone as a hotspot. They have you in their contacts list and their AirDrop Receiving setting is set to Contacts Only, yet you still can't share files with them. Which of the following could be causing the problem? (Choose two.)

   A. You are set to receive from Everyone.

   B. Your contact card on their phone doesn't have your Apple ID email or phone number.

   C. You are not within Bluetooth range of each other.

   D. They turned off their hotspot.

99. You're trying to update your iPhone's iOS, but there is not enough free space on your phone to do the update. Which of the following should you do? (Choose two.)

   A. Use your computer to perform the update.

   B. Remove content and apps that you don't use.

   C. Purchase more internal memory for your iPhone.

   D. Purchase an SD card for your iPhone.

100. You're trying to install an update to Google Chrome on your Android mobile device, but the update isn't working. Which of the following might be the problem? (Choose two.)

   A. The Play Store cache is empty.

   B. The network speed is too fast.

   C. The date and time on your device is wrong.

   D. There are other downloads or updates pending in the Play Store queue.

101. A user is complaining that they see a lot of ads popping up on their screen in the bottom right (the notifications area). They have run a scan using their anti-malware software and it says their computer is clean. The constant pop-ups are interfering with their work, and they ask you what can be done about it. Which of the following is not true?

    A. These are push notifications, not pop-ups.

    B. Nothing can be done about them.

    C. You allowed them at some point.

    D. You can disable or block all or some.

102. You're attempting to update an Android phone but receive an error message that the update failed. Which of the following could be the problem? (Choose two.)

    A. The device has insufficient storage space.

    B. There is a good Wi-Fi connection.

    C. There is insufficient battery power.

    D. The device is plugged into its charger.

103. You're considering installing a desktop alert system for your business, which has both in-house and remote workers. Which of the following are true regarding desktop alerts? (Choose two.)

    A. Desktop alerts are limited to desktops.

    B. Desktop alerts provide an excellent emergency communication system such as weather alerts.

    C. Desktop alerts are text only, not graphics.

    D. Desktop alert software can be made interactive and can become a security threat.

104. A friend asks you what jailbreaking a device is and if they should do it. Which of the following is not true about jailbreaking?

    A. Jailbreaking is like cracking software or gaining root access to a phone, which makes your device more vulnerable to attack.

    B. Jailbreaking might be illegal depending on where you are in the world.

    C. Jailbreaking is a safe way to get more out of your device.

    D. Jailbreaking gives the user full access to the device, and on an iPhone, it allows the user to download apps not approved by Apple.

105. A user is attempting to install new features for an app from the developer's website instead of from the Google Play app store, where they originally downloaded the app. The update with the new features fails to install. Why? (Choose two.)

    A. The signatures don't match.

    B. The update is an APK format.

    C. Only Google can write apps for Android devices.

    D. The website is likely spoofed.

106. Recently you've noticed a suddenly high volume of traffic on the VLAN that is used by mobile devices at your business. You know that the number of mobile devices hasn't increased that much. What should you suspect?

    A. A mobile device is malfunctioning.

    B. One or more mobile devices is infected with malware.

    C. Devices are experiencing limited connectivity.

    D. Your monitoring software is infected.

107. What is one of the best ways to prevent malware being spread by desktop alerts?

    A. Educate the end users.

    B. Block all desktop alerts.

    C. Always log in as an administrator.

    D. Update anti-malware once a month.

108. You're attempting to boot a computer that worked fine yesterday, but today it says "OS not found." What will you do first?

    A. Verify the boot options in BIOS/UEFI.

    B. Verify there are no media inserted into optical or USB drives.

    C. Restart the computer.

    D. Remove the USB drive.

109. A user complains that their Windows 11 laptop seems to be unstable. They had installed some software and although they have removed it, the system is still behaving strangely. You have examined the system and determined that it is not infected with malware. What will you do next?

    A. Boot to installation media and reformat the hard drive, then reinstall the operating system.

    B. Hold the Shift key and restart the computer. The computer will restart in WinRE.

    C. Perform a system restore from the restore point created right before the software was installed.

    D. Delete the Registry and restart the computer.

110. You are donating some Windows computers and old mobile devices to charity. What should you do before you give them away?

    A. Replace the storage media with new media and destroy the old storage media.

    B. Delete all your personal/company files.

    C. Perform an in-place update.

    D. Perform a Factory Image Restore.

111. Your company uses an Active Directory domain to control resources on your network. They also use a PC image to prepare computers for first use within your organization. One of your computer users complains that they can't print, and a few other activities are working strangely. You have determined that there is no malware on the system. What will you do to restore this computer to working order?

A. Back up the user files and reinstall the operating system.

B. Reinstall the company's PC image.

C. Boot into WinRE and reset the PC, keeping the user files.

D. Boot into WinRE and perform a Factory Image Restore.

112. When booting a Windows workstation, a user receives an error message about a missing DLL file. However, Windows still loads. Which utility should you use to attempt to fix the error?

A. SFC

B. Recovery Console

C. regedit

D. services.msc

113. You are training a class on the installation and repair of Windows 10 and 11. What is the purpose of the Windows PE? (Choose two.)

A. Runs as an operating system on thin clients

B. Collects information during a Windows installation

C. Launches the WinRE for troubleshooting

D. Repairs system files if any become corrupted

114. A Windows user has noticed that some of their files are missing or renamed. They want to know who has successfully logged into their PC recently. What Event Viewer log file will you look at?

A. Security

B. System

C. Software

D. Authentication

115. Your Windows workstation is having problems at startup. Too many applications are loading, and it is slowing the system down considerably. Which tool should you use to disable programs from loading automatically at startup?

A. Registry Editor

B. System Configuration

C. System Information

D. Task Manager

Chapter

9

Operational Procedures

THE COMPTIA A+ 220-1102 TOPICS COVERED IN THIS CHAPTER INCLUDE THE FOLLOWING:

✓ **4.1 Given a scenario, implement best practices associated with documentation and support systems information management.**

- Ticketing systems
    - User information
    - Device information
    - Description of problems
    - Categories
    - Severity
    - Escalation levels
    - Clear, concise written communication
        - Problem description
        - Progress notes
        - Problem resolution
- Asset management
    - Inventory lists
    - Database system
    - Asset tags and IDs
    - Procurement life cycle
    - Warranty and licensing
    - Assigned users
- Types of documents

- Acceptable use policy (AUP)
- Network topology diagram
- Regulatory compliance requirements
  - Splash screens
- Incident reports
- Standard operating procedures
  - Procedures for custom installation of software package
- New-user setup checklist
- End-user termination checklist
- Knowledge base/articles

✓ **4.2 Explain basic change-management best practices.**

- Documented business processes
  - Rollback plan
  - Sandbox testing
  - Responsible staff member
- Change management
  - Request forms
  - Purpose of the change
  - Scope of the change
  - Date and time of the change
  - Affected systems/impact
  - Risk analysis
    - Risk level
  - Change board approvals
  - End-user acceptance

✓ **4.3 Given a scenario, implement workstation backup and recovery methods.**

- Backup and recovery
  - Full

- Incremental
- Differential
- Synthetic
- Backup testing
  - Frequency
- Backup rotation schemes
  - On-site vs. off-site
  - Grandfather-father-son (GFS)
  - 3-2-1 backup rule

✓ **4.4 Given a scenario, use common safety procedures.**

- Electrostatic discharge (ESD) straps
- ESD mats
- Equipment grounding
- Proper power handling
- Proper component handling and storage
- Antistatic bags
- Compliance with government regulations
- Personal safety
  - Disconnect power before repairing PC
  - Lifting techniques
  - Electrical fire safety
  - Safety goggles
  - Air filtration mask

✓ **4.5 Summarize environmental impacts and local environmental controls.**

- Material Safety data sheet (MSDS)/documentation for handling and disposal
  - Proper battery disposal
  - Proper toner disposal
  - Proper disposal of other devices and assets

- Temperature, humidity-level awareness, and proper ventilation
  - Location/equipment placement
  - Dust cleanup
  - Compressed air/vacuums
- Power surges, under-voltage events, and power failures
  - Battery backup
  - Surge suppressor

✓ **4.6 Explain the importance of prohibited content/ activity and privacy, licensing, and policy concepts.**

- Incident response
  - Chain of custody
  - Inform management/law enforcement as necessary
  - Copy of drive (data integrity and preservation)
  - Documentation of incident
- Licensing/digital rights management (DRM)/end-user license agreement (EULA)
  - Valid licenses
  - Non-expired licenses
  - Personal use license vs. corporate use license
  - Open-source license
- Regulated data
  - Credit card transactions
  - Personal government-issued information
  - PII
  - Healthcare data
  - Data retention requirements

✓ **4.7 Given a scenario, use proper communication techniques and professionalism.**

- Professional appearance and attire
  - Match the required attire of the given environment
    - Formal
    - Business casual
- Use proper language and avoid jargon, acronyms, and slang, when applicable
- Maintain a positive attitude/project confidence
- Actively listen, take notes, and avoid interrupting the customer
- Be culturally sensitive
  - Use appropriate professional titles, when applicable
- Be on time (If late, contact the customer)
- Avoid distractions
  - Personal calls
  - Texting/social media sites
  - Personal interruptions
- Dealing with difficult customers or situations
  - Do not argue with customers or be defensive
  - Avoid dismissing customer problems
  - Avoid being judgmental
  - Clarify customer statements (ask open-ended questions to narrow the scope of the problem, restate the issue, or question to verify understanding)
  - Do not disclose experience via social media outlets
- Set and meet expectations/time line and communicate status with the customer
  - Offer repair/replacement options, as needed

- - Provide proper documentation on the services provided
  - Follow up with customer/user at a later date to verify satisfaction
- Deal appropriately with customers' confidential and private materials
  - Located on a computer, desktop, printer, etc.

✓ **4.8 Identify the basics of scripting.**

- Script file types
  - .bat
  - .ps1
  - .vbs
  - .sh
  - .js
  - .py
- Use cases for scripting
  - Basic automation
  - Restarting machines
  - Remapping network drives
  - Installation of applications
  - Automated backups
  - Gathering of information/data
  - Initiating updates
- Other considerations when using scripts
  - Unintentionally introducing malware
  - Inadvertently changing system settings
  - Browser or system crashes due to mishandling of resources

✓ **4.9 Given a scenario, use remote access technologies.**

- Methods/tools
    - RDP
    - VPN
    - Virtual network computer (VNC)
    - Secure Shell (SSH)
    - Remote monitoring and management (RMM)
    - Microsoft Remote Assistance (MSRA)
    - Third-party tools
        - Screen-sharing software
        - Video-conferencing software
        - File transfer software
        - Desktop management software
- Security considerations of each access method

1. You have a client who needs to plug three workstations and displays into a wall outlet that has only two plugs. They're looking for the least expensive solution available. What should you recommend they purchase?

    A. UPS

    B. Voltage conserver

    C. Surge protector

    D. Power strip

2. Which of the following is a way to provide proof that a computer user agrees to the acceptable use policy (AUP) and any changes to it every time they log into a computer connected to your network?

    A. Incident report

    B. Splash screen notice

    C. The act of logging in

    D. Signature on an AUP

3. You are upgrading a video card in a desktop computer. You are following appropriate safety procedures. When you open the case, what is the most common danger that you should watch out for?

    A. Electrical shock

    B. Sharp edges

    C. Burns

    D. Flying debris

4. A user needs to send a file to a coworker. The user has no working USB ports, disk drives, or network shares. The file is too large for email. What third-party software feature is the user requiring?

    A. USB share

    B. Encryption

    C. File share

    D. VPN

5. You open a desktop computer case and discover some dust, particularly around the fans. What should you use to clean the fans out?

    A. Denatured isopropyl alcohol

    B. Demineralized water

    C. Computer vacuum

    D. Compressed air

6. What feature of third-party software would allow a technician to demonstrate to a user how to use an application on the local desktop?

    A. File sharing

    B. SSH

    C. Browsing

    D. Screen-sharing

7. Which of the following is both a protocol and a suite of utilities that allow network administrators to remotely access and manage systems while maintaining the confidentiality of authentication credentials and data?

    A. RDP

    B. SSH

    C. HTTPS

    D. SFTP

8. You are installing a new piece of software on your computer, and you do not agree with terms in the end-user license agreement (EULA). Which of the following statements is true?

    A. You can skip the EULA and continue the installation.

    B. You will not be able to install the software unless you agree to the terms in the EULA.

    C. You can click that you agree with the EULA and then provide notes to the parts you disagree with and will not be bound to those terms.

    D. You can install the software but will be provided with limited functionality.

9. Your company has a policy prohibiting illegal content on work computers. You have seized a workstation from an employee after finding illegal content. How do you ensure that the illegal material is managed in the correct way and that it is delivered to the proper authorities?

    A. Use documentation.

    B. Follow the chain of custody policy.

    C. Drive the computer to the proper law enforcement agency.

    D. Remove the hard drive and preserve it in a locked safe.

10. You just got off a repair job at a customer's site, and it was difficult. To make matters worse, the customer was argumentative and difficult to work with. Which of the following should you not do?

    A. Document the situation in your work log.

    B. Try to put the experience out of your mind and focus on your next call.

    C. Call your manager and explain the situation.

    D. Post the experience on social media.

11. You are fixing a broken printer on the second floor of your office building. When you get the printer running again, you notice that it's printing off employee paychecks. What should you do?

    A. Take pictures of the paychecks and post them on social media.

    B. Look to see how much everyone gets paid compared to what you get paid.

    C. Ignore the information and focus on making sure the printer is fixed.

    D. Text your friends and tell them that you make more than they do.

12. When you are working at a client's site, which of the following is the most appropriate behavior you should exhibit?

    A. Taking personal calls

    B. Taking notes and asking questions

    C. Visiting social media sites

    D. Talking to coworkers

13. You are in the field replacing a defective PCIe network card in a desktop computer. You realize that you forgot your ESD strap. The computer needs to be fixed quickly. What is the best way to put yourself at the same electrical potential so that you won't damage the equipment with ESD?

    A. Touch the ground before working on the PC.

    B. Touch the plastic front of the case while working on the PC.

    C. Stay in contact with the computer's desk while working on the PC.

    D. Stay in contact with the metal part of the case while working on the PC.

14. What Microsoft protocol allows you to connect your local system to a different Microsoft client, complete with a graphical user interface?

    A. RDP

    B. SSH

    C. SFTP

    D. VPN

15. When working with a customer, which of the following demonstrates proper communication technique and professionalism?

    A. Staring at religious artifacts hanging on the wall

    B. Imitating the client's accent when speaking to them

    C. Using the client's professional title when speaking to them

    D. Laughing at the client's choice of clothing

16. You are practicing appropriate safety procedures as you fix computers. Which of the following are times you should wear an ESD strap? (Choose two.)

    A. Working inside a desktop case

    B. Working inside a power supply

    C. Working inside a laser printer

    D. Working inside a laptop case

17. While cleaning out an old filing cabinet, you discover a box filled with discarded batteries. What is the proper way to dispose of them?

    A. Burn them.

    B. Throw them in the trash.

    C. Crush them.

    D. Recycle them.

18. Your company has a policy prohibiting illegal content on work computers. A user reports that another user has illegal content, and you are the first responder at the scene. What is the first step you should take as the first responder?

    A. Follow the chain of custody.

    B. Preserve the data or device.

    C. Identify the illegal content that violates policy.

    D. Ask the user to delete the material.

19. When communicating with customers, which of the following should you do?

    A. Use jargon and acronyms to provide your abilities.

    B. Interrupt and ask questions often to clarify.

    C. Use appropriate professional titles.

    D. Assume you know what the customer wants, even if it's not what they said.

20. You are transporting several sticks of RAM and a few video cards from one of your offices to another. Which safety device should you use to help avoid electrically damaging the components?

    A. Antistatic bags

    B. ESD strap

    C. ESD mat

    D. Rubber gloves

21. Your company has a policy prohibiting illegal content on work computers. You have identified illegal content on a user's computer, you have reported the incident through proper channels, and the workstation has been removed from the user's desk. What is the right next step in the incident response process?

    A. Document the situation.

    B. Notify the proper authorities.

    C. Follow the chain of custody.

    D. Delete the illegal material.

22. You are working on-site and trying to fix a client's workstation. Their computer has a defective video card, and it will take about three days to get a new one in. Which of the following is the best course of action for you to take?

    A. Tell them it will take three days for the video card to arrive, and you will return then to replace it.

    B. Tell them that the video card is defective, not fixable, and it will take a week for the new one to arrive. Then when you replace it in three days, you will have overdelivered versus exceeded their expectations.

    C. Tell them it will take three days for the new video card to arrive. Offer to supply a loaner computer that they can use in the meantime.

    D. Tell the customer that the computer is not working, and you'll be back to fix it whenever you can fit it into your schedule.

23. You are troubleshooting a difficult problem that you have never seen before. Even after an hour, you're still not sure what is causing the problem. The customer asks what's wrong. What should you tell them?

    A. You have no idea, and it's a hard one. This is going to take a while.

    B. You're not sure yet, but you're confident that you'll get it figured out soon.

    C. It's bad. It's really bad. You're not sure if you will ever get it fixed.

    D. Not even your escalation line could figure it out, so you're about ready to just give up.

24. You are advising a startup that handles payment transactions to employ additional security controls on credit card information. What type of compliance affects how these security controls are implemented?

    A. PII

    B. PCI DSS

    C. VPN

    D. SSH

25. You are working on an LCD that has a flickering display. Which component inside the display poses the biggest risk for delivering an electrical shock?

    A. Backlight

    B. Capacitors

    C. Inverter

    D. Screen

26. Your office uses five HP LaserJet printers. An administrator has placed used toner cartridges in boxes and stacked them in the storage room. Which of the following statements is true regarding toner cartridge disposal?

    A. Toner is not harmful, but because they contain plastic, they should be recycled.

    B. Toner is not harmful and the cartridges are made of biodegradable plastic, so they can be thrown away.

    C. Toner will make a mess if it gets out of the cartridge, so to avoid making a mess, cartridges should be burned.

    D. Toner is a carcinogen, so cartridges should be taken to an authorized recycling center.

27. A desktop computer you are working on has a failed power supply. Another technician suggests that it could just be a failed capacitor inside the power supply and you could fix it. What should you do?

    A. Open the power supply, and test the capacitors with a multimeter.

    B. Do not open the power supply; dispose of it properly.

    C. Open the power supply and test the capacitors with a voltmeter.

    D. Open the power supply and test the capacitors with an electrical probe.

28. You are having a conversation with your manager about corporate security best practices. They ask what the company should do if users are found to have adult content or content that advocates hate crimes on their workstations. How should you answer?

    A. Users should be allowed to keep it if it is for personal use only.

    B. The company should implement a policy that forbids such material and specifies consequences for violating the policy.

    C. The company should not condone adult or hate crime–related content but can't legally prevent users from having it.

    D. The company should ignore the content that users have on their workstations.

29. You are training a new group of technicians on power issues. One asks if an under-voltage event or complete power failure can affect the company's computer systems. What should you say? (Choose two.)

    A. A complete power failure can damage electrical components.

    B. An under-voltage event will not be detected by computer equipment because there is not complete power loss, so equipment won't be damaged.

    C. Both complete power failures and under-voltage events can damage electrical components.

    D. An under-voltage event might cause a monitor to flicker, but it won't damage electrical components.

30. When dealing with a customer, which of the following demonstrates the communication technique for using proper language?

    A. Use computer jargon.

    B. Use acronyms.

    C. Use slang terms.

    D. Use basic terms.

31. You have downloaded open source software onto your personal laptop. Which of the following statements are true regarding open source licenses? (Choose two.)

    A. You can modify the application in any way you like.

    B. You do not need to pay for the application.

    C. You can make changes only to the applications that are approved by the originator.

    D. You pay a fee for every user of the application.

32. You want to install an electrical device that lets you plug in multiple devices at the same time. It should have a fuse in it so that if there is a power surge (over-voltage event), the fuse will be blown and the electronics plugged into it won't be damaged. It does not need a battery backup. What type of device do you need?

    A. UPS

    B. Power strip

    C. Battery backup

    D. Surge suppressor

33. When dealing with a customer and demonstrating proper communication techniques, what is meant by actively listening? (Choose two.)

    A. Taking notes and making eye contact

    B. Repeating back to the customer what you believe they just said, starting with something like, "If I understand you correctly. . ."

    C. Walking to the computer with the problem and starting to open it while listening

    D. Answering texts while listening

34. You are troubleshooting a desktop computer that is prone to shorting out and rebooting. When you open the case, there is a layer of grime on all the internal components. When you remove the expansion cards and memory, what should you use to clean the metal contacts on the cards?

    A. Demineralized water

    B. Mild soap and water

    C. Denatured isopropyl alcohol

    D. Compressed air

35. You are installing a server for a small company. They want to be sure that the server can be shut down properly in the event of a power failure, so they don't lose data. Which device should you recommend they plug the server into?

    A. Battery backup

    B. Voltage regulator

    C. Surge suppressor

    D. Power strip

36. You need to upgrade the RAM in a desktop computer. Which of the following should you do before beginning the procedure?

    A. Leave the computer running.

    B. Put the desktop into hibernate mode.

    C. Turn the PC off and unplug the power cord.

    D. Put the desktop into standby mode.

37. You are moving computer equipment from an old office to a new office. Which of the following are good personal safety measures to follow to avoid injuries? (Choose two.)

   A. Bend at the knees and lift with your legs.

   B. Bend at the waist and lift straight up.

   C. For heavy items, get a partner to help you lift and/or use a cart to move the item.

   D. When lifting, lift objects as high as possible to avoid running into things.

38. You have opened a desktop computer case and will be upgrading the memory. To help prevent ESD, you put an ESD strap on your wrist. Where should you connect the other end?

   A. The RAM

   B. The motherboard

   C. The metal case

   D. The plastic table

39. You are purchasing new spreadsheet software for your company. Your manager has instructed you to ensure that you purchase enough licenses for everyone in the office to use the product. What type of license will you likely purchase, designed for large groups of users? (Choose two.)

   A. Corporate

   B. Single user

   C. Concurrent

   D. Shareware

40. You have several old computers that you want to dispose of. What should you do with them?

   A. Throw them in the trash.

   B. Remove the hard drives to avoid having someone steal confidential data and then throw them in the trash.

   C. Donate or dispose of them in compliance with government regulations.

   D. Put them at the curb for someone to take for free.

41. You fixed a customer's laptop about three days ago. Which of the following demonstrates proper communication techniques and professionalism?

   A. Call the customer to see whether they are satisfied with the repair.

   B. Post "Another satisfied customer!" on your social media sites with a picture of their office building.

   C. Provide an accurate bill for services provided.

   D. Call the customer and ask if they have additional work you can do.

42. You are troubleshooting problems in a client's office, and the client starts arguing with you as to what the problem is. What should you do?

   A. Avoid arguing and becoming defensive.

   B. Argue back to prove that you are correct.

   C. Tell the client that they are making you uncomfortable and leave immediately.

   D. Tell the client that if they know so much, they can fix it themselves. Then leave.

43. Your company has a policy prohibiting illegal content on work computers. You have identified illegal content on a company-owned workstation. What is your next step?

   A. Get someone else to verify.

   B. Report through proper channels.

   C. Ask the user to delete the material.

   D. Preserve the data or device.

44. You are going to be upgrading the RAM on several desktop computers. Which of the following environmental conditions increases the risk of ESD damaging computer components?

   A. High temperature

   B. Low temperature

   C. High humidity

   D. Low humidity

45. Your company has a policy prohibiting illegal content on work computers. You have found illegal content on a user's workstation. What is the proper way to preserve the data or device?

   A. Ask the user to not delete the data from the device.

   B. Take a picture of the illegal content and email it to your manager.

   C. Take a picture of the illegal content and email it to yourself.

   D. Remove the data or device from the possession of the offending user and preserve it in a safe location.

46. Your company maintains a database of customers' names, vehicle license plate numbers, and driver's license numbers. What type of policy should your company have regarding this information?

   A. This information can't be used in any damaging way; therefore, no special policy is needed.

   B. This information is related to motor vehicle operation, and no special policy is needed.

   C. This information is public information, and no special policy is needed.

   D. This is PII and personal government-issued information and should be kept confidential and secure.

47. You are looking for a new software application for your company's financial data users, but you have a limited budget. Which of the following types of software licensing would you expect to not have to pay for? (Choose two.)

   A. Corporate

   B. Open source

   C. Single user

   D. Freeware

48. You are setting up a repair shop for PCs. To reduce the risk of damaging computer components with static electricity, which of the following devices should you use? (Choose two.)

   A. Magnetic screwdrivers

   B. ESD mats

   C. ESD straps

   D. A dehumidifier

49. You have chosen to use compressed air to clean away dirt and debris from the inside of a desktop computer case. What is the recommended safety gear you should wear?

   A. Safety goggles and an air filtration mask

   B. Safety goggles and a respirator

   C. Safety goggles, a respirator, and a hair net

   D. A biohazard suit

50. What type of information likely needs access safeguards per regulatory requirements as it relates to an individual's medical records?

   A. Personally identifiable information

   B. Protected healthcare data

   C. Driver's license number

   D. Place of employment

51. You need to dispose of a chemical solvent but are unsure how to properly do so. Where will you find information on this as well as the potential dangers the solvent possesses?

   A. MSDS/SDS

   B. OSHA

   C. Warning label

   D. Bottom of the container

52. You are discussing the placement of several new computers with one of your coworkers. Which of the following are the best places to put them? (Choose two.)

   A. In the corner of a room that is typically about 15 degrees warmer than room temperature

   B. In an open area at room temperature

   C. In the corner of a room that is typically about 15 degrees colder than room temperature

   D. In an enclosed kiosk so that no users can damage the system

53. A user's work area is littered with debris and crumbs, and they report that keys on their keyboard stick or sometimes make a crunching sound. What should be the first option for cleaning this keyboard?

    A. Denatured isopropyl alcohol

    B. Demineralized water

    C. Computer vacuum

    D. Compressed air

54. You are performing a safety audit for your company and are examining the company's fire extinguishers. Which type of fire extinguisher is designed to put out electrical fires?

    A. A

    B. B

    C. C

    D. D

55. You have a set meeting time with a client to upgrade their computer. Your prior service call runs long, and you will be late to the meeting. What should you do?

    A. Get to the meeting as soon as you are able.

    B. Take your time; you're already late and a few more minutes won't matter.

    C. Don't show up. Call the client later and tell them you were tied up.

    D. Call the client, apologize for being late, and explain that your last call went over. You will be there as soon as possible or can reschedule if they would prefer.

56. You are asked to help a client who is unable to send or receive email. When you get to the client's desk, what should you do?

    A. Tell them that this problem is nothing and you have dealt with far worse issues today.

    B. Ask what they did to cause the problem.

    C. Tell them that you would rather be working on updating the server, but you suppose you'll deal with this problem first.

    D. Clarify the scope of the problem and verify that you understand exactly what isn't working correctly.

57. Which of the following small devices should not be disposed of at a normal landfill but instead regarded as containing toxic chemicals? (Choose two.)

    A. Cell phone

    B. Phone packaging

    C. Light cardboard

    D. Tablet

58. While changing a laser printer toner cartridge, a technician spilled toner on a desk. What should they use to clean the mess up?

   A. Compressed air

   B. Mild soap and water

   C. Toner vacuum

   D. Denatured isopropyl alcohol

59. You are holding a laptop for someone who will be out of the country for a year or so. What is the best way to store their laptop battery to preserve its life?

   A. Store it in a cool, dry area.

   B. Store it in a closet.

   C. Store it at room temperature.

   D. Store it in a freezer.

60. You are repairing a desktop PC and upgrading the memory. What is the most important reason that equipment grounding is an important safety procedure?

   A. To prevent an electrical shock to yourself

   B. To prevent an electrical shock from damaging components

   C. To prevent fire from starting inside the case

   D. To prevent the desktop PC from slipping off the workspace

61. What type of script has the filename extension `.ps1`?

   A. PowerShell

   B. Bash

   C. JavaScript

   D. Python

62. What type of editor would you normally use to view a script with the filename extension `.vbs`?

   A. Vi

   B. Notepad

   C. Emacs

   D. CoffeeCup

63. What file extension is used with a plain-text script file that can be run or edited in a Windows command prompt?

   A. `.js`

   B. `.sh`

   C. `.py`

   D. `.bat`

64. What programming language uses files with the .js extension?

A. JavaScript

B. Java

C. Juice

D. Joomla

65. What best practice assists the administrator to track the boundaries and perimeters of data flow through the environment they are responsible for?

A. Asset tagging

B. Change management

C. Password policy

D. Network topology diagrams

66. What best practice helps the administrator keep track of the hardware found throughout the workplace?

A. Knowledge base articles

B. Asset tagging

C. Password policy

D. Network topology diagrams

67. What describes the best practice of documenting learned experience and helpful content to be shared with others?

A. Brown bagging

B. Knowledge base article writing

C. Change board documentation

D. Change management policy

68. The operations manager wants to employ asset management but does not wish to spend funds on equipping all hardware with RFID tags. What is an appropriate but less expensive option?

A. Sharpie

B. Color coding

C. Association to user by name and role

D. Barcodes/QR codes

69. What change management detail is not necessary to document?

A. Purpose of the change

B. Scope of the change

C. Unaffected applications

D. Approval

70. In considering an anticipated change, what highlights how the change will be received by a sample of the employees?

    A. Rollback plan

    B. Plan for change

    C. Risk analysis

    D. End-user acceptance

71. A network administrator wrote and documented business continuation procedures, including backup schedules. Finally, critical data was backed up as required. What should be done next before the implementation can be considered reliable?

    A. Backup testing

    B. Documenting a checklist

    C. End-user acceptance

    D. Approval of the policy

72. In a geographical area prone to tornados, what option for storing backups seems most sensible?

    A. Tape backups in the basement

    B. Tapes distributed among offices

    C. Cloud storage off-site

    D. Storage on a server against an inside wall.

73. Your company uses a ticketing system to keep track of repair calls. Which of the following might not be included in the information gathered for the ticketing system when the client/customer calls?

    A. User information

    B. Device information

    C. Description of the problem

    D. Inventory lists

74. What change-management document describes the procedures that will occur if you reach a critical go/no-go point in a project that makes a change to your network and decide that it's a no-go?

    A. Sandbox testing

    B. Rollback plan

    C. Request forms

    D. Risk analysis

75. What type of backup is done that will include all files, whether or not the archive bit is set?

    A. Complete backup

    B. Incremental backup

    C. Full backup

    D. Differential backup

76. On Sunday, your system will automatically create a full backup of your data. At the end of each weekday, Monday through Friday, a differential backup is created. It is now Thursday morning, and you discover that your system crashed during the night. You need to restore your data. Which backups will you need to restore to get all of your data back?

  A. Only Wednesday's backup

  B. Sunday and Wednesday backups

  C. Sunday, Monday, Tuesday, and Wednesday backups

  D. Sunday and Thursday backups

77. Which of the following statements comparing differential and incremental backups are true? (Choose two.)

  A. Incremental backups are created faster than differential.

  B. Differential backups are created faster than incremental.

  C. Incremental backups are more fault tolerant than differential backups.

  D. Differential backups are simpler to restore than incremental.

78. Which of the following is true about how computer components such as expansion cards and processors should be stored?

  A. In antistatic bags, with protective packing material

  B. In zippered plastic bags, stacked on plastic shelves

  C. In antistatic bags, neatly stacked up on a grounded shelf

  D. On top of antistatic bags, on a shelf in a closet

79. What should always be done before moving a laser printer?

  A. Remove the printhead.

  B. Remove stapler assembly.

  C. Remove the toner cartridge(s).

  D. Remove the paper.

80. A manufacturing facility asked to have a computer installed on the floor for workers to access so they can check production information. About a week later, they have called you down because the computer isn't working. When you arrive, you find that someone has wrapped the computer in plastic to protect it from the dust, and it's about a hundred degrees Fahrenheit on the plant floor. Why did the computer quit working? (Choose two.)

  A. Too much dust on the plant floor.

  B. Lack of ventilation/airflow.

  C. Overheating.

  D. It is unplugged.

81. You are about to retire a computer because it's being replaced with a faster one that the new updated software needs. Which of the following needs to be done with this computer before it is recycled or donated? (Choose two.)

A. Ensure that all data is removed/destroyed.

B. Take it to the sandbox testing area.

C. Remove it from the asset management inventory list.

D. Install the new software update.

82. You work as the lead IT network engineer at an IT services company that designs and installs networks for your Fortune 500 clients. Today you're meeting with the CIO of a large accounting firm. Which of the following are likely to be appropriate attire for your position and interaction with clients? (Choose two.)

A. Matching suit coat and pants/skirt, tie if appropriate

B. Khaki pants and polo shirt

C. Business casual attire

D. Business formal attire

83. You've just finished repairing a customer's printing problem and shown them how to avoid the problem in the future. What steps do you still need to take before the job is considered complete? (Choose two.)

A. Provide documentation on the services provided.

B. Tell them if they call you directly, they can get the same service for less money in the future.

C. Follow up with the customer a few days later to ensure that they are satisfied.

D. Leave without saying anything.

84. A coworker has called the help desk because they have a problem with their PC. When you start to sit down at their desk, you see a job application there. What do you do?

A. Ask them politely if they would mind moving their paperwork while you are working there; explain that you don't want to see anything that might be confidential.

B. Go to their boss and tell them that the person is looking for another job.

C. Snap a picture of the job application to post on social media.

D. Ask them about the job they are applying for.

85. Your company needs an occasional full backup, but your data is so large that the time it takes is considerable. Rather than do a full backup daily, you have elected to use software that combines incremental backups and a prior full backup to create a new full backup. What type of backup is this?

A. Incremental

B. Differential

C. Synthetic

D. Grandfather

86. You know that a backup is only good if you can restore from it, so the backups need to be tested periodically to ensure that data can, in fact, be restored from them. Which of the following is not true regarding testing data backups?

  A. Test whenever there have been big system changes like new software, major updates, or major data changes.

  B. Test after every single backup.

  C. Test whenever there are going to be big system changes like merging databases, or installing or updating software.

  D. Test once a month.

87. You work for an IT services company and today you're acting as the lead network installer. In this job you'll be running wires through ceilings and walls, and possibly interacting with your customer. What would be the appropriate attire to wear?

  A. Casual, graphic T-shirt and jeans

  B. Sneakers

  C. Business formal

  D. Company logo polo shirt and casual pants

88. In the United States there is a government entity that oversees safety in the workplace and has the authority to shut down businesses that don't comply with these safety standards. Who is that entity?

  A. OSHA

  B. The NEC

  C. FEMA

  D. IRS

89. Which information technology rule states that you need three copies of data, on two different media, and one copy off-site?

  A. Grandfather-father-son (GFS)

  B. On-site/off-site backup rule

  C. The rule of 78

  D. The 3-2-1 backup rule

90. You forgot a file that you need for a presentation today. It's on your Windows Pro computer at home. Which of the following could you use to retrieve it?

  A. RMM

  B. VPN

  C. VNC

  D. MRSA

91. You're having a first meeting with a potential customer at a company that you have been told wears jeans and t-shirts to work, even the CEO. What would be the appropriate attire for this meeting?

   A. Jeans and a t-shirt with their company logo

   B. Casual attire

   C. Business casual

   D. Business formal

92. What is the term that means a company follows state, local, federal and even international government rules and regulations that relate to their work?

   A. Disobedience

   B. Regulatory compliance

   C. Information Technology Governance

   D. Information security

93. Which backup scheme ensures that there are short-term, medium-term, and long-term backups that a business could restore from, and in theory they would never lose more than a day's worth of data and would always have a year's worth of backups?

   A. Grandfather-father-son (GFS)

   B. On-site/off-site backup rule

   C. Moore's law

   D. The 3-2-1 backup rule

94. Part of the HIPAA regulations state that if a document is created it must be maintained for a minimum period of six years from when it was created or last in effect. What is this an example of?

   A. IT governance

   B. Data retention requirements

   C. GFS

   D. License agreement

95. You and your best friend intend to start a managed services provider (MSP) company, providing technical computer support to business clients. What software will you need to invest in that will enable you to manage those clients and fix many software-related issues without leaving your office?

   A. RMM

   B. VPN

   C. VNC

   D. RDP

96. An employee has a personal-use license for some free diagramming software that they feel would be beneficial for your company. You have evaluated the software and determined that the software company also has corporate licenses for more than one user, for an annual licensing fee. Which of the following is most likely what the employee is allowed to do under the terms of their personal use license?

- **A.** Make as many copies as they want.
- **B.** Bring it into work for everyone to use.
- **C.** Sell the software for download online.
- **D.** It depends on the exact terms of the software license, but most likely, use the software on their personal computer(s) at home only.

97. What technology lets authors, musicians, artists, and other creators of copyrighted material control access to their content so that it is not stolen or illegally shared?

- **A.** Personal licenses
- **B.** Digital rights management
- **C.** Corporate licenses
- **D.** Nonexpired licenses

98. Which of the following may be undesirable results of using scripts? (Choose two.)

- **A.** Unintentionally introducing malware
- **B.** Installing applications
- **C.** Inadvertently changing system settings
- **D.** Initiating updates

99. What remote access technology allows the users to co-control a desktop instead of the remote user taking over?

- **A.** MSRA
- **B.** RDP
- **C.** SSH
- **D.** RMM

100. One of your management employees works from home most days, but they need to have access to the server as if they were sitting there in the office, and the connection must be secure. What technology will you employ to do this?

- **A.** RMM
- **B.** VPN
- **C.** RDP
- **D.** VNC

101. Which of the following would not be a possible consequence of failure to maintain compliance with government regulations?

A. Fines and fees

B. Business shutdown

C. Extra paid holidays

D. Lives lost

102. Which of the following is not an example of regulated data?

A. Credit card transactions

B. Software licensing data for software that you use

C. Healthcare data

D. Personally Identifiable Information

103. Which of these third-party tools allows multiple users in diverse locations to see one another, possibly share a screen, and discuss information with one another as if they were in the same room?

A. Screen-sharing software

B. File transfer software

C. Desktop management software

D. Videoconferencing software

104. Which of the following file extensions is used by a software in the Linux/Unix environment?

A. .sh

B. .py

C. .vbs

D. .ps1

105. Which of the following is not a type of information, recorded in a ticketing system, that needs to have very clear, concise, written communication?

A. Problem descriptions

B. Progress notes

C. Valid licenses

D. Problem resolution

106. What is used to initiate the change management process?

A. Affected systems/impact

B. Request form

C. Risk analysis

D. Change board approval

107. Which of the following would not be included in change management documentation?

  A. End-user acceptance

  B. Responsible staff member

  C. Affected systems and the impact on them

  D. Scope of the change

108. What type of software includes programs like batch files, Visual Basic, PowerShell, and so on, and is used for activities like basic automation, remapping network drives, automating backups, gathering information/data, and restarting machines based on triggers?

  A. Remote monitoring and management (RMM)

  B. Screen-sharing software

  C. Scripting programs

  D. Remote access technologies

109. You are newly hired at the help desk of your company. Which one of the following are types of information that need not be included on each ticket in a ticketing system?

  A. Category of the problem

  B. Severity of the problem

  C. Escalation levels

  D. Procurement life cycle

110. Which process is designed to enable changes that benefit an organization with as little disruption as possible to the IT services for an efficient function of that organization?

  A. Asset management

  B. Change management

  C. Ticketing systems

  D. Knowledge bases and articles

111. What part of asset management includes processes such as a request for information (RFI), a request for proposal (RFP), and identifying the business need?

  A. Database system

  B. Assigned users

  C. Procurement life cycle

  D. Warranty and licensing

112. What feature of change management examines all the possible positive and negative events that may impact a project, then identifies a response plan if the event occurs and assigns a score to the possible event?

  A. Scope of the change

  B. Change board approval

  C. Risk analysis/risk level

  D. Sandbox testing

113. What items can be used to facilitate onboarding (new hires) and offboarding (people leaving) of employees to ensure that new employees have everything they need to do their job and exiting employees aren't able to damage systems or take company information with them? (Choose two.)

    A. Incident report

    B. New-user setup checklist

    C. End-user termination checklist

    D. Splash screens

114. Your company has recently installed a server with HR information on it. The server, as with most systems, possesses input/output (I/O) ports and disk bays and is connected via network cable to the local client network. However, since the data center was full, the new server is temporarily placed in the printer room. What should be a primary concern of the responsible administrator?

    A. Security considerations of each access method

    B. I/O transfer bottleneck

    C. Ambient noise from server fans

    D. Scalability of the server while in the printer room

115. You want to ensure that employees aren't installing whatever software packages that they want to because of licensing concerns and possible impacts to your network. What document will you use to identify and explain what the procedures are for custom installation of software packages?

    A. End-user termination checklist

    B. New-user setup checklist

    C. Network topology diagram

    D. Standard operating procedures document

116. Which of the following is not important to keep track of as part of your inventory management system, and to ensure compliance with local, regional, national, or perhaps international regulations?

    A. Valid licenses in use by your company

    B. Nonexpired licenses in use by your company

    C. Technical jargon used by your company

    D. Open source licenses being used by your company

117. Which of the following would not constitute an invalid, and quite possibly illegal, use of software?

    A. Using a personal license in a corporate setting

    B. Having more users of the software than the license allows

    C. Using software whose license has expired

    D. Modifying open source software

Chapter

10

Practice Exam 1
(220-1101)

1. You have a laptop with a dead hard drive. You want to replace it with a newer SSD but have a few concerns. What disadvantages do SSDs have versus HDDs? (Choose two.)

   A. They produce more heat.

   B. They are more expensive.

   C. They are more susceptible to damage.

   D. They cost more per gigabyte.

2. Your friend is an artist and they have recently purchased a new convertible laptop. It can be used as a regular laptop or folded into a tablet computer. You've recommended they purchase a touch pen to use with their new computer. Which of the following is not an advantage of a touch pen?

   A. They don't leave greasy fingerprints on your screen.

   B. There are never compatibility issues.

   C. They can make more precise lines than fingers can.

   D. You can use them in cold weather and have gloves on your hands.

3. In a tablet computer with an LCD, which component is responsible for providing the right kind of energy to light the display?

   A. Inverter

   B. LCD

   C. Backlight

   D. Screen

4. A friend just purchased a touch pen that uses Bluetooth connectivity. They aren't very tech savvy so you have offered to set it up for them. What step of the Bluetooth connection process will you do after the laptop has found the touch pen for pairing?

   A. Enable pairing.

   B. Test connectivity.

   C. Enter the appropriate PIN code.

   D. Enable Bluetooth.

5. You're hiking in the mountains and have brought along a mobile device that has an app with all the maps of local trails on it to ensure that you don't get lost. You look at the map and notice that the blue dot indicating where you are hasn't moved since you left home. What do you need to enable in your mobile device for the app to work properly?

   A. Airplane mode

   B. GPS

   C. Wi-Fi

   D. Location services

6. What protocol/type of protocol guarantees delivery of a packet of information across a network or networks and will resend the packet if its arrival is not acknowledged? (Choose two.)

A. TCP

B. UDP

C. Connectionless

D. Connection-oriented

7. Which two port numbers need to be opened to enable communications for FTP (File Transfer Protocol)?

A. 20/21

B. 21/22

C. 22/23

D. 23/25

8. Which Internet appliance stands between a PC and the Internet and can include stateful packet inspection (packet filtering), and act as a gateway, translating traffic between networks or protocols? (Choose two.)

A. Spam gateway

B. Unified threat management (UTM)

C. Load balancers

D. Proxy servers

9. In IPv6, which of the following identifies the multicast range?

A. ::1

B. 2001;dba:45c:1::5/64

C. FE80::abc:1:2/64

D. FF00::/8

10. Several Bluetooth devices are connected in an ad hoc (without a hub, switch, or WAP) network. Which acronym best describes this type of network?

A. LAN

B. WAN

C. PAN

D. MAN

11. Users on your network complain of poor wireless network access in a certain part of your building. They say that the connection is slow and disconnects frequently. You are using 802.11ac wireless routers and access points. What tool should you use to troubleshoot the situation?

A. Wi-Fi analyzer

B. Loopback plug

C. Tone generator and probe

D. Multimeter

12. What type of audio/video connector is shown in the graphic?

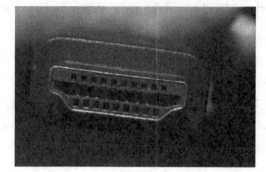

- **A.** DisplayPort
- **B.** DVI
- **C.** HDMI
- **D.** VGA

13. The computer users in your accounting department have called saying that their laser printer keeps jamming and have asked that you resolve the issue. Which of the following are common reasons for this that you can check? (Choose two.)

- **A.** Incorrect paper thickness or tray too full
- **B.** Ink cartridges need cleaning
- **C.** Debris in the paper path
- **D.** Printhead needs cleaning

14. About four computer users in the HR area of the building are complaining that their Wi-Fi connection is very slow. You use your Wi-Fi analyzer and find out that they are on the same channel as your neighbors in the office next door. What can you do?

- **A.** Set the radio signal to maximum.
- **B.** Change the channel that the WAP uses.
- **C.** Add another wireless access point.
- **D.** Check the cable from the WAP to the router.

15. Which type of connector, shown in the graphic, is used for network connections?

    A. RJ11

    B. RJ45

    C. F type

    D. ST

16. You're reading the documentation for a desktop motherboard and it says it uses 240 pin DIMMs. What type of DIMM does it use?

    A. DDR3

    B. DDR4

    C. DDR5

    D. SODIMM

17. You are investigating computer specifications for a new desktop workstation. If the specifications include 256 KB of L2 cache, approximately how much L1 cache would it be reasonable to expect the computer to have?

    A. 64 KB

    B. 256 KB

    C. 512 KB

    D. 12 MB

18. A user reports that their smartphone will not make any sounds. They have turned the phone off and back on, and the problem is still there. You check the settings, and the phone is not on silent mode and the volume is set to maximum. What can you do to fix this problem?

    A. Reset the phone to factory specifications.

    B. Replace the speakers.

    C. Replace the sound card.

    D. Replace the phone.

19. A laser printer you are working on is producing images that have vertical black streaks running the length of the page. Which of the following could be causing this? (Choose two.)

    A. There is a scratch in the EP drum.

    B. The fusing assembly is not heating up properly.

    C. The paper exit rollers are worn.

    D. The charging corona wire is dirty.

20. The motherboard documentation you are reading says that the RAM modules for this motherboard must be purchased in identical sets of 4. What type of motherboard is this?

    A. Dual channel

    B. Triple channel

    C. Quad channel

    D. Single channel

21. You have installed an 802.11ac Wi-Fi network. The network has three overlapping wireless access points. What channel width should the access points be set to in order to avoid communications problems while providing the best bandwidth?

    A. 20 MHz.

    B. 40 MHz.

    C. 80 MHz.

    D. It doesn't matter in 802.11ac.

22. A user complains that their desktop computer randomly reboots. No error messages are displayed before it happens, and there is not a specific program that triggers the reboot. Which of the following components is most likely to be causing this problem?

    A. RAM

    B. Storage drive

    C. BIOS/UEFI

    D. Network adapter

23. A user calls the help desk to report that their display is black. It was working yesterday, but when the desktop computer was booted this morning, nothing showed on the display. They did hear a beep like normal when the computer booted up. What is the first thing you should do?

   A. Reseat the plug on the video card.

   B. Replace the video card.

   C. Ask the user to press the display's power button.

   D. Refresh the operating system.

24. In your company's lobby, there is a desktop computer with an LCD that plays a continuous loop of a welcome video. The display is enclosed in a cabinet. Recently, the display will shut itself down near the end of the day for no apparent reason. What is likely causing this problem?

   A. Backlight failure

   B. Incorrect video resolution

   C. Display card failure

   D. Display overheating

25. One of your network users develops software for multiple operating systems. They have asked for a specialized computer that will allow them to run multiple operating systems at the same time in virtualized environments. Which two components should you optimize in their computer? (Choose two.)

   A. CPU

   B. RAM

   C. HDD

   D. GPU

26. The design of the micro-ATX motherboard makes which of the following statements true?

   A. It will fit in standard ATX cases.

   B. It will fit in standard ATX cases when used with a mounting adapter kit.

   C. It will fit in standard ATX cases but can't support full-length expansion cards.

   D. It will not fit in standard ATX cases.

27. You are examining an existing coaxial cable installation and notice that the previous technician installed a splitter. Which of the following statements is true?

   A. The splitter will cause the network connection to fail.

   B. The splitter will increase the distance the network signal will travel.

   C. The splitter will degrade the quality of the network signal.

   D. The splitter will have no effect on the network signal.

28. A desktop computer will not retain the system time or date. The user always needs to reset them after the system is powered off. What should you do to fix the problem?

    A. Flash the BIOS/UEFI.

    B. Replace the BIOS/UEFI chips.

    C. Replace the CMOS battery.

    D. Use the jumper on the motherboard to reset the BIOS/UEFI to factory settings.

29. A new technician trainee just turned a computer on and it beeped once. They had heard about motherboard beep codes and ask you what that single beep means. What will you tell them?

    A. Bad RAM

    B. CPU issue

    C. Video isn't working

    D. POST completed successfully

30. A user has turned in a tablet computer that has a swollen battery. What should you do to resolve the problem?

    A. Turn the tablet off, let it cool down, and then return it to the user.

    B. Order a new tablet for the user, drain the excess electrolyte from the battery, and then dispose of the defective one in the trash.

    C. Order a new tablet for the user and take the defective one to a recycling center.

    D. Order a new tablet for the user and throw the defective one in the trash.

31. You are troubleshooting a laptop computer that will not boot properly. When you power it on, there is nothing on the display, and you hear beeps in a pattern of 1-3-3. What two things could you use to troubleshoot the problem? (Choose two.)

    A. Manufacturer's website

    B. PCIe POST card

    C. USB POST card

    D. BOOT tester

32. Your motherboard supports up-plugging for PCIe adapter cards. Which of the following statements is true?

    A. You can't put an x8 card into an x16 slot.

    B. You can put an x8 card into an x16 slot, but it will run at x1 speed.

    C. You can put an x8 card into an x16 slot, but it will run at x8 speed.

    D. You can put an x8 card into an x16 slot, and it will run at x16 speed.

33. What is the first step of the laser printer imaging process?

    A. Cleaning

    B. Charging

    C. Fusing

    D. Processing

34. Your coworker needs to transfer files from a mobile device using a memory card reader and an SD memory card. They quickly discover that the maximum capacity on their SD card is 1 TB. Which technology does the coworker have?

    A. SD

    B. SDXC

    C. SDHC

    D. SDLC

35. A user reports that when they press the L key on their laptop keyboard, the L character repeats across the screen and doesn't stop until the L key is pressed several more times. When you look at the laptop, it does not appear that the key is physically sticking. What should you do next?

    A. Replace the keyboard.

    B. Replace the L key.

    C. Clean under the key with compressed air.

    D. Reboot the laptop.

36. You're working on a stormy night and the power in your house goes out, but your cellular service (smartphone) is working. You have a report on your laptop that absolutely must be submitted tonight, and luckily your laptop is fully charged. What can you to do submit your report?

    A. Connect your laptop to your car's antenna to send via Wi-Fi.

    B. Use your smartphone's hotspot feature.

    C. Go out in the storm and drive to the nearest place with power that has public Wi-Fi.

    D. Call and let them know that the report won't be submitted because your power is out.

37. You have determined that you need to replace the Wi-Fi antenna in your laptop. Where will you most likely find it?

    A. In the housing with the display

    B. Under the keyboard

    C. Under a removable panel on the back/bottom of the laptop

    D. Plugged into a USB port

38. Which of the following is a cloud application that can be used to synchronize data on all of your devices, including smartphones, laptops, desktop computers, and other devices?

    A. Calendar

    B. Contacts

    C. Microsoft 365

    D. Mail

39. You pay a premium for faster Internet service at home but have noticed that the download times have slowed considerably, and you see the spinning wheel more than normal. What is likely the problem?

    A. You have reached a data cap.

    B. You didn't pay your last bill, so they're slowing the service down.

    C. You're synchronizing too much data all at once.

    D. The Internet is down.

40. You have a small office with frequent visitors and want to provide a separate VLAN to segregate the visitor traffic from your network traffic for security reasons. What is the minimum connectivity device needed to accomplish this?

    A. Hub

    B. Bridge

    C. Managed switch

    D. Unmanaged switch

41. On an IPv6 network, you want to send a single message to a group of computers at the same time. What type of address class do you need to use?

    A. Multicast

    B. Anycast

    C. Unicast

    D. Broadcast

42. Which of the following IP addresses is not routable on the Internet?

    A. 192.169.1.1

    B. 192.168.1.1

    C. 168.192.1.1

    D. 169.192.1.1

43. When setting up your network, you configured your clients to obtain IP addressing information automatically from a DHCP server. You set the group of numbers that it can assign from 192.168.100.11 to 192.168.100.211. What is this group of assignable numbers called?

    A. APIPA

    B. Leases

    C. Scope

    D. Reservations

44. You're considering setting up a WISP. What is an advantage of using an unlicensed frequency versus using a licensed frequency?

    A. The frequencies are not congested.

    B. The radiated power is unlimited by regulations.

    C. The performance is better than licensed frequencies.

    D. Equipment is readily available.

45. What type of port is shown in the graphic?

    A. USB-C

    B. Molex

    C. SC

    D. LC

46. Which of the following would most likely use NVMe technology?

    A. 5,400 rpm drive

    B. HDD

    C. m.SATA

    D. M.2

47. Which level of RAID will provide both better performance and fault tolerance with the least number of drives possible?

    A. RAID 0

    B. RAID 1

    C. RAID 5

    D. RAID 10

48. You purchased an expansion card for your desktop that fits in a PCIe x1 slot. The documentation says that the card supports USB 3.0 with a 5 Gbps maximum transfer rate. What version of PCIe is the card?

    A. PCIe 1.0

    B. PCIe 2.0

    C. PCIe 3.x

    D. PCIe 4.x

49. A user complains of a burning smell and smoke coming from their computer. After shutting it down, you notice that the motherboard has burn marks on it. You replace the motherboard. The next day, the user complains of more smoke, and you see this motherboard is burnt as well. What should you do next?

    A. Replace the motherboard.

    B. Replace the power supply.

    C. Replace the motherboard and power supply.

    D. Plug the computer into a different wall outlet.

50. You are installing an ATX12V (sometimes called ATX2) power supply with a 24-pin main power connector. Which of the following is not a voltage provided by the power supply?

   A. −3.3 VDC

   B. +5 VDC

   C. +12 VDC

   D. −12 VDC

51. You have a Windows 10 desktop computer that is connected directly to your office printer. Your office is running a workgroup (not a domain). You want to share the office printer with a new user. What are two places you can do this? (Choose two.)

   A. Search for printers, right-click the desired printer, and choose Share.

   B. In the Settings app choose Devices, then Printers & scanners. Select the printer to share and click the Manage button, then on the window that displays, choose Printer properties and choose the Sharing tab.

   C. In Control Panel, choose Devices and Printers. Right click the printer to share and select Printer properties, and choose the Sharing tab

   D. In Device Manager, click the printer and select the Sharing tab.

52. Your company produces software and employs about 20 developers. They need to program apps for different operating systems. You decide to purchase cloud-based services to support the development team. What type of service should you purchase so that they can develop their programs and then test them in environments other than where they were developed?

   A. IaaS

   B. SaaS

   C. PaaS

   D. NaaS

53. What is the name of the virtual desktop software that is built into Windows 10 and 11?

   A. Azure Virtual Desktop

   B. VMware Fusion

   C. VirtualBox

   D. Hyper-V

54. What feature of cloud computing means that you can expand your network immediately as needed?

   A. Shared resources

   B. Metered utilization

   C. Rapid elasticity

   D. File synchronization

55. A client complains about the occupied space, abundant power usage, and hardware costs of the multiple machines used in its small data center. Still, the client does not wish to lose control over any of the machines. What might you recommend to the client to resolve all of those issues?

   A. Establish clusters for high availability.

   B. Create virtual machines.

   C. Outsource to an IaaS provider.

   D. Shut down the nonessential machines.

56. A user on your network has called you with an issue involving their hard drive. Before you make any changes to their computer, what will you always do?

   A. Consider corporate policies, procedures, and impacts.

   B. Establish a plan of action.

   C. Document findings, actions, and outcomes.

   D. Verify full system functionality.

57. You have configured two hard drives so that when you write to one, it makes an exact copy on the other, and it looks like one drive in your operating system. What level of RAID is this?

   A. RAID 0

   B. RAID 1

   C. RAID 5

   D. RAID 10

58. A technician is troubleshooting a computer in the field and calls you to report that they are getting a S.M.A.R.T. error ID 188 and command timeout. Which component is likely to be causing this error?

   A. CPU

   B. RAM

   C. Motherboard

   D. HDD

59. You just took a new display out of the box and set it up. Now you notice that it has two dead pixels. What do you do?

   A. Return the display for a refund.

   B. Keep the display but ask for a discount.

   C. Calibrate the display.

   D. Keep the display; it is fine.

60. A user complains that the color on their display is strange. It was working fine yesterday. What will you do first?

   A. Check for a loose cable connection at both ends.

   B. Replace the display.

   C. Turn the display off and back on.

   D. Check the settings on the display itself.

61. A mobile device user dropped their smartphone and now the charging port is damaged. The device is fairly new, but they didn't pay for a warranty to cover user error. They don't typically plug it into a computer or anything else. What should you do first?

    A. Take the phone apart and replace the charging port.

    B. Return the phone to the store for a refund.

    C. See if the device supports wireless charging.

    D. Replace the phone.

62. A grinding noise is coming from your office printer. You know that can't be good, and you just put new toner in two days ago. What do you do?

    A. Try replacing the toner cartridge.

    B. Take all the paper out and reload it.

    C. Thoroughly clean the printer.

    D. Check for any loose rollers or gears.

63. Several users who access the network through the same WAP are complaining that they have limited connectivity. They can see each other on the network but not any network resources like printers and servers. Everything was working fine yesterday, and network users in other parts of the building are not having problems. What should you troubleshoot first?

    A. The power of the radio signal from the WAP

    B. The connection between the WAP and the router

    C. Their IP configuration

    D. The default gateway

64. You just bought a new laptop and were told that it uses biometrics to log you in. Which of the following might they be? (Choose two.)

    A. Face scanner

    B. Entering your password

    C. Fingerprint reader

    D. Entering a code from your phone

65. There is a white streak down all of the printouts of your inkjet printer. What will you do to fix it? (Choose two.)

    A. Change the toner cartridge.

    B. Perform a nozzle cleaning routine.

    C. Clear debris from the paper path.

    D. Use different paper.

66. You're troubleshooting a computer issue and have implemented a solution. What are the next steps that you will take? (Choose two.)

    A. Verify full system functionality, and if applicable, implement preventive measures.

    B. Document the findings, actions, and outcomes.

    C. Establish a new theory of probable cause.

    D. Gather information from the user.

67. Users at your workplace are complaining that the audio over their VoIP phones is often choppy and difficult to understand. Which of these would help with that and could be done fairly quickly? (Choose two.)

    A. Configure QoS to give the VoIP phones priority.

    B. Upgrade the cabling on the network.

    C. Set up the VoIP phones on their own VLAN.

    D. Set up the VoIP phones using a VPN.

68. You notice that your friend's smartphone is swollen. They said that it happens all the time. What should be done?

    A. Replace the battery.

    B. Replace the device.

    C. Unplug it and let it cool down, then plug it back in.

    D. Use a different power outlet.

69. What are the benefits of virtualization? (Choose two.)

    A. Saves power

    B. Requires more licenses

    C. Less hardware to pay for

    D. Distributed management

70. All of the users on your network, wired and wireless, are complaining that they're getting a limited connectivity message. Where will you start troubleshooting? (Choose the best answer.)

    A. The WAP

    B. The default gateway

    C. The switch

    D. The router

71. You're shopping for a wireless speaker to use with your smartphone and considering different connection methods. Which of the following wireless connection types generally has a functional communication distance of 10 meters?

    A. NFC

    B. IR

    C. Bluetooth

    D. Wi-Fi

72. What type of display is increasingly being used in smaller mobile devices for its picture quality, lower power consumption, and foldability?

    A. IPS

    B. OLED

    C. LED

    D. VA

73. Your company is allowing workers to use their personal devices for company business. What will you, as the IT director, use to ensure that company information is safe on those personal devices? (Choose two.)

    A. MDM

    B. MAM

    C. PRL

    D. GSM

74. Which of the following would not be considered authentication in a two-factor authentication system?

    A. Key fob

    B. Authenticator app

    C. Username

    D. Soft token

75. Which two TCP/IP protocols are designed to download email from mail servers? (Choose two.)

    A. SMTP

    B. POP3

    C. IMAP

    D. SMB

76. Which TCP/IP protocol is responsible for resolving IP addresses to MAC addresses?

    A. IP

    B. SSH

    C. DHCP

    D. ARP

77. You need a wireless access point (WAP) in a loading dock, but there is not an appropriate power receptacle close enough to plug it into, so you decided to use a PoE WAP. The problem is that your switch is not PoE compliant. Which of the following will you need to purchase in addition to the PoE WAP?

    A. A very long extension cord

    B. A PoE injector

    C. A new switch

    D. A new router

78. Which wireless networking (Wi-Fi) standards can use both the 2.4 GHz and 5 GHz frequencies? (Choose two.)

    A. 802.11g

    B. 802.11n

    C. 802.11ac (Wi-Fi 5)

    D. 802.11ax (Wi-Fi 6)

79. When setting up your network, you configured your clients to obtain IP addressing information automatically from a DHCP server. Which of the following configuration items can the DHCP server provide?

A. IP address

B. IP address and subnet mask

C. IP address, subnet mask, and default gateway

D. IP address, subnet mask, default gateway, and DNS server address

80. A computer on your network is not able to reach the DHCP server. The DHCP server assigns addresses in the 200.100.1.11 to 200.100.1.110 range. What address might this computer get when it boots up? (Choose two.)

A. APIPA

B. Class C

C. 169.254.1.101

D. 200.100.1.15

81. Which of the following is not true about DNS servers?

A. They translate IP addresses to domain names like Sybex.com.

B. AAAA DNS records identify IPv6 addresses.

C. A records identify IPv4 addresses.

D. There is a setting in IP configuration to identify the DNS server to use.

82. A UTP cable just failed, and you need to replace it. You have a spool of cable and connectors but no premade cables. Which tool do you need to use to make a new cable?

A. Toner probe

B. Punchdown tool

C. Multimeter

D. Crimper and cable stripper

83. You need to create several UTP patch cables from a roll of bulk cable. Your company uses the T568A standard. What is the correct order for wires in the connectors?

A. Orange stripe, orange, green stripe, blue, blue stripe, green, brown stripe, brown

B. Orange stripe, green, green stripe, blue, blue stripe, orange, brown stripe, brown

C. Green stripe, green, orange stripe, blue, blue stripe, orange, brown stripe, brown

D. Green stripe, green, orange, blue, blue stripe, orange stripe, brown stripe, brown

84. You need a cable that will run a distance of 200 feet and support speeds up to 10 Gbps. Which cable will you use?

A. Cat 5e

B. Cat 6

C. Cat 6a

D. Plenum

85. A new technician on your team has been asked to replace memory in a laptop. They removed a card and brought it to you; it's shown here. What did they remove?

    A. SODIMM

    B. ECC

    C. DIMM

    D. M.2

86. The people in your office want a printer that will print on both sides of the paper automatically. What feature is this?

    A. Duplex

    B. Orientation

    C. Tray settings

    D. Print quality

87. What type of printer uses special paper that turns dark when subjected to heat? These printers are often used for receipt printers.

    A. Inkjet

    B. Impact

    C. 3-D printer

    D. Thermal

88. You are troubleshooting a computer for a user on your network. You have established a theory of probable cause. What is your next step according to the best practice methodology to resolve problems?

    A. Establish a plan of action.

    B. Verify full system functionality.

    C. Test the theory.

    D. Implement preventive measures.

89. You are purchasing a mobile device that requires the use of a touch pen (stylus) to input information; it does not respond to the touch of a finger. What type of touch screen technology does this device use?

   A. Tempered

   B. Resistive

   C. Capacitive

   D. Object-oriented

90. Identify the connectors shown here.

   A. ST

   B. SC

   C. LC

   D. BNC

91. A technician has two hard drives and wants to increase the data access speed of the computer. You tell them to install both drives, but which of the following configurations is their best option?

   A. Configure them as separate volumes.

   B. Implement RAID 0.

   C. Implement RAID 1.

   D. Implement RAID 5.

92. You're setting up a virtual machine for a developer who needs three instances of Windows 11, plus the host OS, which is also Windows 11. How many licenses will you need?

   A. One

   B. Two

   C. Four

   D. None

93. What are the three major categories of cloud computing? (Choose three.)

   A. SaaS

   B. DaaS

   C. PaaS

   D. IaaS

94. You are troubleshooting a video issue for a user. You have just interviewed the user to find out more about the problem. Which step of the best practice methodology to resolve problems do you do next?

   A. Test the theory to determine cause.

   B. Establish a theory of probable cause.

   C. Establish a plan of action.

   D. Document findings, actions, and outcomes.

95. What type of memory is an area on a hard drive, called a paging file, that Windows uses as if it were physical memory?

   A. VirtualBox

   B. Virtual memory

   C. SODIMM

   D. ECC

96. What part of the laser printer imaging process uses heat and pressure to permanently adhere toner to the paper?

   A. Charging

   B. Exposing

   C. Transferring

   D. Fusing

97. What must be defined when wanting to maintain confidentiality, integrity, and availability of the system resources and should be a part of the decision when choosing a cloud solution?

   A. Scalability

   B. Security requirements

   C. Elasticity

   D. Emulation ability

98. A company using cloud services wishes to better prepare for surges for what it needs. What sort of capacity provisioning by its cloud provider should the company ask for?

   A. Rapid metering

   B. Infrastructure as a service

   C. Metered utilization

   D. Resource pooling

99. A group of real estate agents has realized that they have similar computing resource needs. They've reached out collectively to your IT services company and asked if there is a solution that will let them pool their resources and save money, possibly sharing industry-specific software, but still have their servers and information held securely and locally. What will you recommend?

   A. Community cloud

   B. Public cloud

   C. Private cloud

   D. Hybrid cloud

100. An employee travels between multiple offices, using a desktop system in each office. What technology would ensure that the employee's desktop icons, files, and applications stay uniform across systems in all the offices?

   A. On-Demand Desktop Streaming

   B. VDI in the cloud

   C. Desktop emulation

   D. Synchronized folders

Chapter
11

Practice Exam 2 (220-1102)

1. You're at a favorite coffee shop using their Wi-Fi, when suddenly you notice that your mouse is moving, and you aren't moving it. You knew using this unsecured Wi-Fi was a bad idea, and now you've been hacked and want to stop the attacker as soon as possible, but you need time to save your files. What is the best course of action?

   A. Turn on Airplane mode.

   B. Unhook the network cable.

   C. Close the lid on the laptop.

   D. Turn the laptop's power off.

2. You are on-site fixing a client's laptop that will not load the OS. You are waiting to hear about your friend's awesome party that they are hosting this weekend, and your phone starts to vibrate. And it keeps vibrating. You're sure that all your friends are texting information about the party. What should you do? (Choose two.)

   A. Turn your phone off and apologize to the client. Tell them that the phone was distracting you from your job, but it won't be a problem now.

   B. Ignore your phone.

   C. Text your friends back and tell them that you are working.

   D. Call your friend and tell them to wait until after this job before planning all the details because you want to help.

3. You are planning on formatting a hard drive with NTFS that will be used to share files between Windows 10 and Windows 11 Pro computers. Which of the following features are present in NTFS? (Choose two.)

   A. Linux OS support

   B. File compression

   C. File and folder encryption

   D. Enhanced flash drive support

4. You are logged into a Linux workstation with a regular user account. You need to execute a command with root permissions. Which command do you need to use?

   A. su

   B. sudo

   C. grep

   D. man

5. A security consultant recommends that your secure facility implement biometrics as a form of building access control. Which of the following systems might they be referring to?

   A. RFID badges

   B. Key fobs

   C. Palmprint scanner

   D. Guards

6. You are looking online to find pictures to use as part of promotional materials your company wants to make. Which of the following statements is true regarding online content?

   A. Online content is considered open source; therefore, you may use whatever you find.

   B. Online content can be protected through the use of DRM.

   C. Online content is protected through the use of the EULA.

   D. Online content is protected through terms established by Microsoft.

7. In which type of security threat will someone try to gain access to a secure area without credentials by following someone else, who used their access rights, into the secured area?

   A. Brute-force

   B. Shoulder surfing

   C. Evil twin

   D. Tailgating

8. A management directive requires that you keep hard copies of all your workstations' system configurations. You have all Windows workstations. Which command can you use to easily gather this information for remote workstations and save a report as a text file?

   A. `msinfo32`

   B. `compmgmt`

   C. `mmc`

   D. `perfmon`

9. You have a situation that requires installing Windows 11 from installation media. You'll be launching Setup on the media while you are on the existing Windows 10 desktop. Which of the following is not an option?

   A. Full Upgrade

   B. Keep Data Only

   C. Forensic install

   D. Clean Install

10. You are configuring a wireless router for a home office. Which of the following changes will have the least impact on improving the security of the network?

   A. Disabling guest access

   B. Disabling the SSID broadcast

   C. Configuring WPA3

   D. Changing the default username and password

11. You are going to move a desktop computer from one office location to another. It's on the floor, underneath the desk. Which of the following are good personal safety procedures to follow? (Choose two.)

   A. Bend at the waist and lift straight up.

   B. Bend at the knees and lift with your legs.

   C. Tie back any loose jewelry, long hair, or neckties.

   D. Leave the computer plugged in to avoid ESD.

12. You have just installed a second and third hard drive into a Windows Pro workstation. Each drive is 500 GB. The user wants to combine the two drives into one 1 TB volume. What should you create from those two drives to accomplish this and give the user a disk read and write performance boost?

    A. Simple volume

    B. Spanned volume

    C. Striped volume

    D. Mirrored volume

13. Which feature of Windows Pro or higher editions is designed to encrypt storage volumes, must be activated by an administrator, and can encrypt operating system startup files?

    A. BitLocker

    B. EFS

    C. OneDrive

    D. ShadowDrive

14. Your iPhone has been stolen. To ensure that the thief does not have access to your data, what should you do?

    A. Perform a remote backup.

    B. Enable full-device encryption.

    C. Enable BitLocker.

    D. Perform a remote wipe.

15. You have installed a second hard drive in a Windows workstation. In Disk Management, what type of partition can you create that will allow you to create an unlimited number of logical partitions in it?

    A. Extended

    B. Dynamic

    C. Logical

    D. GPT

16. You have some older drives that you intend to donate to a nonprofit organization. You want to set all data on the drive to be nothing but 0s. What should you use to accomplish this?

    A. Drive-wiping software

    B. `format` command

    C. Degaussing

    D. Incinerating

17. A small business has two servers in their telecommunications room. They've come seeking your advice because the area has frequent power outages and they have lost important data on their servers as a result. What will you recommend for them to protect against this issue?

    A. Surge suppressor

    B. Power strip

    C. Battery backup

    D. Line conditioner

18. You are working on a Windows workstation that is operating very slowly. You want to quickly check system CPU and RAM usage to see whether anything appears amiss. Which two utilities can you use to do this? (Choose two.)

   A. Resource Monitor

   B. Performance Monitor

   C. Control Panel ➤ System

   D. Control Panel ➤ Device Manager

19. As the network administrator, you have set account lockout policies so that an account is locked out after five unsuccessful login attempts. What type of security threat will this deter?

   A. Shoulder surfing

   B. Brute-force attack

   C. Zero-day attack

   D. Spear phishing

20. Occasionally when visiting websites using Google Chrome, you receive a pop-up window in front of your browser. Generally, it's an advertisement trying to sell you something. Which of the following actions will stop this from happening?

   A. Enable Chrome's pop-up blocker.

   B. Install an antivirus program.

   C. Install an anti-malware program.

   D. Enable Windows Firewall.

21. Your company works with confidential government files. It is illegal for employees to copy any files to flash drives. Where do you specify this as well as the penalties for not complying with the rule?

   A. APK

   B. ACL

   C. ADF

   D. AUP

22. A Windows computer user reports that their computer just completely locked up. On the screen is a message saying that the person pictured has participated in an illegal activity. The webcam turned on by itself, and the computer user was pictured. The message also says they can resolve the charges against them by paying a $500 fine. They are understandably shaken by the incident. What should you do next?

   A. Tell the user that if they performed an illegal activity with their work computer, their employment will be terminated.

   B. Boot to a bootable media from your anti-malware provider and run a remediation.

   C. Delete and reinstall Windows.

   D. Pay the fine.

23. One of your technicians just touched a plastic bottle containing chemicals you are not familiar with. Their hand starts to feel like it's burning. Where can you find information on how to properly wash the technician's hands without making the problem worse, and how to dispose of the chemical?

    A. OSHA

    B. Bottom of the container

    C. Warning label

    D. MSDS

24. You want to protect mobile device users on your network from potentially leaked files or data. Which of the following should you do to help reduce this risk? (Choose two.)

    A. Disable network autoconnect.

    B. Enforce data transmission over limits.

    C. Enable device encryption.

    D. Install mobile firewalls.

25. You are at a Windows command prompt. The folder you are in has hundreds of files, so when you view a folder listing, you want it to only show one page of files at a time. Which command should you use to do this?

    A. `dir /p`

    B. `dir /o:s`

    C. `dir /w`

    D. `dir /s`

26. You have assigned the Finance group Modify permissions on the `D:\MonthlyReports` folder. You then create a folder named `D:\MonthlyReports\January`. What level of permissions does the Finance group have to the folder `D:\MonthlyReports\January`?

    A. No access, because no permissions were explicitly set

    B. Full control, because no permissions were explicitly set

    C. Modify, because the folder inherits permissions from its parent folder

    D. Modify, because the folder inherits permissions from the Finance Group, and the Finance Group members can grant permissions to other users or groups for this folder

27. Your company has a policy prohibiting illegal content on work computers. You have identified and verified illegal content on a user's workstation. What is the next step you should take?

    A. Ask the user to delete the material.

    B. Delete the illegal material yourself.

    C. Document the situation.

    D. Report the incident through proper channels.

28. Your Windows workstation is having intermittent video issues. The manufacturer's website suggests you install the latest driver. Which utility should you use to check the driver version installed on your computer?

    A. Display Settings

    B. Device Manager

    C. Services

    D. Disk Management

29. On a MacBook Pro running macOS, what is the name of the bar of icons that runs along the bottom of the screen, allowing you to open apps?

    A. Remote Disc

    B. Finder

    C. Spotlight

    D. Dock

30. A Windows workstation is not booting properly, and you believe it's a problem with system files. Which utility can scan and repair corrupt Windows system files?

    A. chkdsk

    B. diskpart

    C. tracert

    D. sfc

31. An Android phone user reports that their phone can't connect to the Wi-Fi network, but they have a cellular signal. What is the first thing to have them try?

    A. Check whether the phone is in Airplane mode.

    B. Check whether the Wi-Fi is enabled.

    C. Adjust the Wi-Fi signal receptivity.

    D. Reset to factory defaults.

32. You are troubleshooting a Windows workstation that has malware on it. Following the best practice procedures for malware removal, you have gotten to the point where you've scheduled system scans and run anti-malware updates. What is the next step you should take?

    A. Educate the end user.

    B. Enable System Restore and create a restore point in Windows.

    C. Disable System Restore in Windows

    D. Remediate the infected system.

33. When configuring NTFS permissions on a Windows workstation, what is the recommended method?

A. Grant permissions to user accounts.

B. Put user accounts into groups. Grant folder permissions to groups and file permissions to users.

C. Put user accounts into groups. Grant folder permissions to users and file permissions to groups.

D. Put user accounts into groups. Grant permissions to groups.

34. You are at a Windows command prompt in the D:\users folder. You want to use the copy command to copy the D:\users\jdoe folder to the D:\files folder. Which of the following statements is true?

A. You can't use the copy command to perform this task.

B. You can use the command copy d:\users\jdoe*.* d:\files.

C. You can use the command copy d:\users\jdoe d:\files.

D. You can use the command copy d:\users\jdoe d:\files /y.

35. You are working on your Windows computer and a security alert pops up, as shown here. What should your next action be?

A. Click the Continue Unprotected button.

B. Click the Remove All Threats Now button.

C. Create a restore point and then click the Remove All Threats Now button.

D. Shut down your computer, reboot, and initiate a virus scan using your antivirus software.

36. You are instructing a new Mac user on the features of macOS. They ask if the system is capable of storing their passwords to various Internet sites. Which feature would they use for that?

   A. Keychain

   B. Mission Control

   C. FileVault

   D. Terminal

37. You are troubleshooting a malware problem with a Windows 11 computer and find that you need to boot into safe mode\safe boot, which loads with minimal drivers. Which management tool can you use to force the system to boot into safe mode when it reboots?

   A. Task Scheduler

   B. Computer Management

   C. System Configuration

   D. Task Manager

38. Which of the following is an advantage of using share permissions over using NTFS permissions?

   A. Share permissions will override NTFS permissions if there is a conflict.

   B. Share permissions can be enabled to secure resources across the network that are not on an NTFS partition.

   C. Share permissions apply when users access a resource across the network, but NTFS permissions apply only to local users.

   D. Share permissions are able to be set at the file level, whereas NTFS permissions can be set only at the folder level.

39. Your manager is concerned that your company could divulge PII. Which of the following types of data is not considered PII?

   A. First name

   B. Home address

   C. Family member names

   D. Employee ID number

40. You are training mobile users on potential security risks. Which of the following could make users more susceptible to an on-path attack?

   A. Unintended Wi-Fi connection

   B. Unauthorized account access

   C. Unauthorized location tracking

   D. Unauthorized camera activation

41. The network you manage has a dozen Windows workstations. You want to ensure that users do not have the ability to change the boot order so that they can't boot to an unauthorized device. Which step should you take?

    A. Disable Autorun.

    B. Restrict user permissions.

    C. Set a BIOS/UEFI password.

    D. Enable a strong password policy.

42. A user needs to travel for a presentation and wants to be sure their laptop does not run off battery power, so they want to turn it off. However, they want to leave their files and applications running, so that when they turn it back on, the applications are already open. Which of the following statements is true?

    A. The user will be unable to do this.

    B. The user should put their computer into standby mode.

    C. The user needs to activate the sleep power plan.

    D. The user should have their computer hibernate.

43. You have a Linux server on your network. You want to back up all files in the /user/ files volume without disrupting user access. What should you use to do this?

    A. Time Machine

    B. Remote Disc

    C. Snapshot

    D. FileVault

44. You have a Windows Pro workstation installed in a workgroup. There is no centralized security. Which tool should you use to help protect yourself against malicious network attacks?

    A. Windows Defender Firewall

    B. NTFS Permissions

    C. Local Security Policy

    D. Computer Management

45. You are working on a client's desktop computer, and the video card is dead. You can get a warranty replacement, but it will take three days to arrive. Or you can replace it with a more expensive card today, but the customer would need to pay the difference. Which of the following is the best way for you to continue the service call?

    A. Tell the customer that the video card is dead. It will take three days for the video card to arrive, and you will return then to replace it.

    B. Tell the customer that the video card is dead. It will take three days for a warranty replacement to arrive (at no cost), or you can replace it with an upgraded model today if they want to pay the difference in cost.

    C. Tell the customer that the video card is dead. Offer to replace it today with a more expensive video card, and they can pay the difference in cost.

    D. Tell the customer that they will be without a computer for three days, but then you will come back and fix it.

46. You are attempting to update a Windows 10 workstation using Windows Update. The update fails with this message: "Failure configuring Windows updates. Reverting changes." You reboot and try again but receive the same error. What should you try next? (Choose two.)

   A. Wait until changes are reverted. Unplug removable media from your computer and try again.

   B. Wait until changes are reverted. Run a virus scan and try again.

   C. Wait until changes are reverted. Run the Windows Update Troubleshooter.

   D. Ignore the update.

47. A user calls and complains that they can't see any printers when they try to print a document from their Windows computer. They say that they had three network printers showing yesterday, and they can access the server across the network. What will you do first?

   A. Reinstall the network printers.

   B. Check the status of the Print Spooler service.

   C. Reinstall Windows.

   D. Repair Windows.

48. A user calls the help desk because they are not able to access the Internet. After asking a few questions, you discover that if they type in IP address in the browser, then the website pops up. Other users on the same switch aren't having this problem. Where will you start looking for the problem?

   A. File server

   B. Web server

   C. DNS settings

   D. DHCP settings

49. Whenever you log into a computer at work, a screen with the company's name and some text appears. You must click OK before you can access the company network. What is a common purpose of a company's custom splash screen?

   A. Announce upcoming events

   B. Advertising their products

   C. Tracking employee time

   D. Confirming agreement to an AUP

50. Which of the following features are not available in the Home edition of Windows but are available in Pro and higher editions of Windows? (Choose three.)

   A. File compression

   B. Join a Windows Domain

   C. Group Policy Editor (`gpedit.msc`)

   D. RDP

51. You're configuring a remote connection and need a protocol or process to ensure that both parties to a transaction are who they say they are and to encrypt their user information as it passes from one to the other. Which of the following will you use?

    A. Multifactor authentication

    B. Kerberos

    C. RADIUS

    D. TKIP

52. A user called the help desk because their mouse is moving across the screen and windows are opening and closing. They believe it's not malware because they said they didn't do anything; they just opened an email with a strange subject. Which of the following will be most important to prevent malware on this computer going forward?

    A. Educate users regarding threats.

    B. Install anti-malware and set it to update automatically.

    C. Enable and configure software firewalls.

    D. Enable and configure hardware firewalls.

53. When your friend launches their new favorite game, they often get low memory warnings. Which two of the following can you do to prevent this problem from happening in the future? (Choose two.)

    A. Use Task Manager to end unnecessary programs.

    B. Increase virtual memory.

    C. Increase physical memory.

    D. Put in a faster NIC.

54. A friend is having trouble with the network connection on their Windows 10 computer, so you open Network & Internet in the Settings app. Which of the following is not an option there?

    A. Network Troubleshooter

    B. Mobile Hotspot

    C. Change Adapter Options

    D. Share A Printer

55. You need to manually configure the IP address for a server, so you go to Network and Sharing Center, click Change Adapter Settings, then right-click the connection, choose Properties, and select IPv6. Which of the following pieces of information is not needed to configure IPv6?

    A. IPv6 address

    B. Subnet mask

    C. Subnet prefix length

    D. Default gateway

56. A user is trying to use Google Chrome on their Windows computer, but they receive the error message "Unable to access the network." If they use Microsoft Edge, they are able to access websites with no problem. What do you need to do?

A. Uninstall and reinstall Google Chrome.

B. Instruct the user to only use Microsoft Edge.

C. Ensure that Google Chrome is a permitted program in Windows Defender Firewall.

D. Reinstall the operating system.

57. Which of the following is not done/created before the change board approves a change?

A. Rollback plan

B. Sandbox testing

C. Risk analysis

D. Kickoff meeting

58. Your company makes a full backup every Sunday. Monday through Friday they create differential backups. They keep the weekly backup for a month, the daily backups are overwritten each week, and they make a backup once a month that is kept for a year. What is this backup scheme called?

A. On-site/Off-site

B. Grandfather-father-son (GFS)

C. 3-2-1 backup rule

D. Synthetic

59. A user has called the help desk, and you've entered their ticket. The problem they describe is beyond your training. What do you do?

A. Hang up and tell them to call the PC manufacturer.

B. Put them on hold for an hour while you figure it out.

C. Escalate the problem to the next level.

D. Tell them to perform a factory installation of their operating system.

60. Your friend has a new Windows 11 computer, and they're getting way too many notifications while they're trying to work. What will you tell them?

A. Yes, we all do. It's just something we have to deal with.

B. I can help you fix that. It's easy.

C. We can turn them all off or all on; you don't get to choose.

D. You have to reinstall your apps and tell it no when it asks if you want to allow notifications.

61. Your client has computers using macOS and other computers that are Windows-based. They want to have a shared drive configured so that both operating systems can access it. The files are very large, some of them exceeding 4 GB. What filesystem should you use to format the shared drive?

   A. NTFS

   B. ext4

   C. exFAT

   D. FAT32

62. A user wants to have Full Control over their C: drive and all the contents of it, because they have one program that defaults to saving files in a folder there. Why will you not give them this access? (Choose two.)

   A. It is a security risk.

   B. It violates the Windows EULA.

   C. Only administrators can have access to the C: drive.

   D. It violates the principle of least privilege.

63. A user has a computer that suddenly started running very sluggishly. Upon inquiry, you find that they went to some websites yesterday that they don't normally visit, so you decide to follow the best practice procedures for malware removal. What is the first step?

   A. Quarantine infected systems.

   B. Disable System Restore in Windows.

   C. Investigate and verify malware symptoms.

   D. Schedule scans and run updates.

64. A user tells you that they received a BSOD error on a Windows 10 computer. No changes have been made to this computer recently. What is the best way to restart Windows to see whether you can isolate the issue?

   A. Boot to the Windows installation media and start the WinRE.

   B. Boot to safe mode.

   C. Boot using an anti-malware boot drive.

   D. Boot normally and see whether the error happens again.

65. A user reports that their profile is very slow to load, then they get an error message that says, "unable to load profile." What should you suspect?

   A. The profile is too large.

   B. The profile is corrupted.

   C. The user logged on using the wrong password.

   D. They need to reboot and try again.

66. An app on your Android-based device won't open. What will you try first?

    A. Check for Android updates.

    B. Check for app updates.

    C. Restart the device.

    D. Clear the app's data and cache.

67. You're installing a new video card in a computer. It was an expensive card and you want to ensure that it isn't damaged by ESD. Until you are ready to place the card in the slot, what is the safest place for the card?

    A. Lying on the antistatic mat

    B. Lying on the antistatic bag

    C. Inside its antistatic bag

    D. Lying on the edge of the computer so that it's grounded

68. Your friend in another state is having a problem with their Windows 11 Home edition computer and wants your help. What could you do to provide the quickest possible help?

    A. RDP

    B. VPN

    C. MSRA

    D. RMM

69. You are writing a script in Microsoft PowerShell to automate some processes that you perform daily. What file extension will the script file have?

    A. .bat

    B. .ps1

    C. .vbs

    D. .py

70. You need to add a new user on a Windows desktop computer. Where can you go to do this? (Choose two.)

    A. Settings ➤ Accounts

    B. Settings ➤ Users

    C. Control Panel ➤ User Accounts

    D. Control Panel ➤ Credential Manager

71. A user who is less comfortable with technology is having to navigate through File Explorer to a network shared resource several times a day. The user asks if there is an easier way. What will you configure for this user?

    A. Mapped drive

    B. Domain name

    C. Subnet mask

    D. Gateway

72. One of the users you are responsible for called the help desk because when they turned the computer on this morning, instead of booting into Windows, it showed a green screen with 1s and 0s running down it. What will you do?

   A. Turn the computer off and boot using boot media from your antivirus company.

   B. Go into WinRE and repair the operating system installation.

   C. Go into WinRE and perform a clean installation of the operating system.

   D. Boot into safe mode and restore from a recent restore point.

73. Your mobile device locks after a short inactivity period for security reasons. Which of the following are common biometric devices for opening a mobile device whose screen is locked? (Choose two.)

   A. Facial recognition

   B. Fingerprint readers

   C. PIN codes

   D. Swipe to unlock

74. A user logs onto their computer system and notices that several of their files are missing and some are renamed. What should you do?

   A. Begin the malware removal process.

   B. Reimage the machine.

   C. Restore the files from a backup.

   D. Restore from the last Restore Point.

75. A new network admin wants to try their hand at writing a PowerShell script. You tell them that's fine but to show it to you before they run it. What are possible undesirable effects of running a script file? (Choose two.)

   A. Inadvertently changing system settings

   B. Saves time in remapping network drives

   C. Browser or system crashes due to mishandling of resources

   D. Automates backups

76. You're considering purchasing new 3D printers. The printers have software that will be installed to create and print the 3D objects. There are also hardware requirements to consider. Which of the following is least likely to be a hardware requirement?

   A. CPU type/speed

   B. RAM speed or quantity

   C. Storage requirements

   D. 32-bit operating system

77. You have a macOS computer that is behaving in an unstable manner, so you press the Command+R keys while it is booting and enter Disk Utility. What option in Disk Utility will check and repair the filesystem?

   A. First Aid

   B. Partition

   C. Erase

   D. Restore

78. You need to configure encryption for the data-at-rest on a new Windows Pro workstation. Which of the following are options? (Choose two.)

   A. Kerberos

   B. EFS

   C. BitLocker

   D. RADIUS

79. You're trying to share pictures with your friends. You both have iPhones, but your AirDrop doesn't seem to be working. Which of the following might solve the problem? (Choose two.)

   A. Turn Bluetooth on.

   B. Turn Airplane mode on.

   C. Ensure both devices are discoverable.

   D. Turn on both hotspots.

80. A user has a Windows 10 Pro laptop that they have installed and tested lots of software on and now it will barely run. There is nothing that they want to save on it, and they've asked if you can just make it like new again. What is likely the easiest way to do this?

   A. Create installation media from the Microsoft website and perform a repair installation.

   B. Create installation media from the Microsoft website and perform a clean installation.

   C. Boot to a recovery partition and perform a factory installation.

   D. Install a new hard drive and perform a clean installation from Microsoft installation media.

81. You're verifying settings on your router and notice that it only has WPA2, not WPA3. Your devices have all been working with WPA2 and you have some older and some newer devices. What should your next steps be? (Choose two.)

   A. Update the router's firmware.

   B. Choose WPA2/WPA3 Transitional.

   C. Choose WPA3 Personal.

   D. Chose WPA2 Personal (AES).

82. Your client has a computer on their network that they have configured to be a secure web server. How should you configure their router to ensure that traffic for the server is going to the server? (Choose two.)

    A. Forward outgoing requests for port 443 to the web server's IP address.
    B. Forward incoming requests for port 443 to the web server's IP address.
    C. Set the router to use UPnP.
    D. Create a screened subnet for the web server.

83. You've tried to access a website that you're sure is safe, but you're getting an invalid certificate warning. What should you do?

    A. Verify the date and time on your computer.
    B. Run an antivirus.
    C. Report the website as dangerous.
    D. Delete the certificate from your computer.

84. A friend asks you what jailbreaking a device is and if they should do it. Which of the following is not true about jailbreaking?

    A. Jailbreaking is like cracking software or gaining root access to a phone, which makes your device more vulnerable to attack.
    B. Jailbreaking might be illegal depending on where you are in the world.
    C. Jailbreaking is a safe way to get more out of your device.
    D. Jailbreaking gives the user full access to the device and on an iPhone, it allows the user to download apps not approved by Apple.

85. You need to configure a VPN for a new salesperson. Where is this done in Windows 10? (Choose two.)

    A. Control Panel ➤ Network and Sharing Center
    B. Control Panel ➤ Windows Mobility Center
    C. Settings ➤ Personalization
    D. Settings ➤ Network & Internet

86. A user has a 32-bit application that they want to use on a 64-bit operating system and they have asked you if that will work. What do you tell them?

    A. 32-bit and 64-bit are interchangeable.
    B. Yes, a 32-bit application will work on a 64-bit operating system.
    C. No, the application must be 64-bit to run on a 64-bit operating system.
    D. A 64-bit application will run on a 32-bit operating system, but a 32-bit application will not run on a 64-bit operating system.

87. You are required to enter a username, password, and a code from an authenticator app on your phone before you can access the company website. What type of authentication is this?

    A. Multi sign-on

    B. Single sign-on

    C. Multifactor

    D. Domain

88. You're troubleshooting a computer that appears to have contracted a boot sector virus, following the best practice procedures for malware removal. It seems to be booting OK now, and you have created a restore point in Windows. What is your next step?

    A. Schedule scans and run updates.

    B. Quarantine the infected system.

    C. Disable System Restore in Windows.

    D. Educate the end user.

89. Computer users are often reluctant to have anything change, so gaining their acceptance prior to the change will make a transition run more smoothly. What are two ways that you can gain end-user acceptance to a change? (Choose two.)

    A. Make them fill out request forms.

    B. Involve them in the planning process.

    C. Thoroughly explain why this change is necessary.

    D. Don't tell them and just have the change done when they come in on a Monday.

90. Your company does a full backup every Sunday and incremental backups all the other days of the week at the end of the day. If you come in on Wednesday morning and your system has crashed, what backups will need to be restored so that your system will be fully recovered?

    A. Sunday only

    B. Sunday and Monday

    C. Sunday and Tuesday

    D. Sunday, Monday, and Tuesday

91. You need to make a secure connection to a remote router and make some configuration changes. What will allow you to do that securely?

    A. SSH

    B. Telnet

    C. Videoconferencing software

    D. FTP

92. What is the danger in using an operating system that has reached EOL?

    A. Lack of feature updates.

    B. Lack of security updates.

    C. There is no technical support.

    D. Technical support is very expensive.

93. You need to ensure that your Linux computer is up-to-date. Which command can be used to do this automatically?

    A. yum

    B. pwd

    C. chmod

    D. apt-get

94. You have hired a new network administrator. We'll assume their name is NewUser. How many and what type of accounts will you set up for NewUser?

    A. NewUser, an administrator account only

    B. NewUser, a standard user only

    C. NewUser_Admin, which is an administrator account and NewUser, a standard user account

    D. NewUser_Admin, which is an administrator account and NewUser_Guest, which is a guest account

95. An application on your mobile device has crashed and is unresponsive. What should be your first choice to fix it?

    A. Force-close the application.

    B. Restart the device.

    C. Revert to factory defaults.

    D. Reinstall the application.

96. You are running late because your morning appointment took longer than you thought it would. Your next client meeting is in five minutes, and they're 20 minutes away. What do you do?

    A. You get there when you get there. Your time is valuable.

    B. Skip that meeting and go on to the next so you're not late all day.

    C. Call the client and apologize. Let them know the situation, and ask if they would prefer to reschedule or see you a bit later.

    D. Call the client and tell them you're running late.

97. You have downloaded some open source license software. What are you usually allowed to do with it? (Choose two.)

    A. Modify the program to suit your needs.

    B. Resell the software to other people for a profit.

    C. Make copies but credit the original source, and redistribute it under the same license you received it under.

    D. Run only one copy on one machine.

98. You're in the middle of a major IT systems change and have gotten to a point where you realize that it's not going to work without shutting down everything for a week. This would cost the company a fortune and will put production way behind. What will you do?

    A. Let the management know and continue with the project.

    B. Follow the rollback plan.

    C. Fire the responsible staff member.

    D. Follow the AUP.

99. You're working at your desktop computer, viewing a web page you use often, when a website that you know should be updating doesn't seem to be. In fact, if you access it from a different device, the website looks different. What can you do to force the website to update on your computer? (Choose two.)

    A. Clear the browser's cache.

    B. Clear the browser's stored cookies.

    C. Uninstall and reinstall your browser.

    D. Hold the Ctrl Key and F key simultaneously while on the website.

100. You're on your smartphone and notice that the apps are all responding slowly, almost jittery when you change from one to the other. What is the first thing to do?

    A. Check the storage on the device.

    B. Close some running apps.

    C. Suspect a virus.

    D. Check the battery charge.

Appendix

Answers to the Review Questions

Chapter 1: Mobile Devices

1. **A.** When configuring a mobile email client to access a commercial email provider, you typically just need your username and password to establish connectivity. Examples include Google, Yahoo, `Outlook.com`, and iCloud.

2. **B.** Many newer smartphones are boasting OLED displays for their light weight, flexibility, color depth, and wider viewing angle. IPS is a popular type of LCD (Liquid Crystal Display) that requires backlighting to display the image. TN was the LCD technology developed first. It uses less power and has a limited viewing angle, but it supports very fast refresh rates. LEDs can be used as the backlight for LCD systems. OLED displays don't need a backlight because their carbon-based material can emit light and color.

3. **B.** Some laptop keys are consolidated into special multifunction keys to save valuable space. These keys are accessed through the standard keys by using a special function (Fn) key. Video adjustments come in two varieties: changing the video output and dimming or brightening the screen. In this case, there is a large sun icon for brightening the screen on the F10 key, so pressing the Fn key and the F10 key simultaneously would increase the brightness. Some laptops use a smaller sun to label the key for dimming and a larger sun to label the key for brightening, or they use plus and minus signs or up and down arrows next to the suns. You may also see special function keys to turn network connections on or off or to play, fast-forward, or rewind media.

4. **A.** Capacitive touchscreens are a little less accurate than resistive touchscreens but more responsive. They respond to changes in electrical current, and as such, the human fingertip works great as the facilitator of input. Resistive screens require a heavier touch and don't support multi-touch input. Infrared screens don't work with multi-touch gestures, but like resistive screens, they can be used with gloves on. Surface Acoustic Wave (SAW) is another type of touchscreen, but it is not popular.

5. **C.** Airplane mode turns off all wireless connections on a mobile device. It's common on phones and tablets, and most laptops have the feature as well.

6. **A.** Smart cameras have built-in wireless network connectivity for easy picture and video transfers. Many will include Wi-Fi, Bluetooth, and Near-Field Communication (NFC). Smart cameras, such as security cameras, can also connect via Wi-Fi to your network and the Internet, and can thus be accessed and controlled by a cell phone.

7. **C.** While it's possible that the phone could be charged with a charging pad, most often phones won't charge because the battery is worn out and needs replacing. Also, according to the Apple Support website, a phone that won't charge likely needs servicing. Your friend should take their phone to a service center. They may be able to replace the battery or fix problems they find with the phone's connector.

8. **C.** Legacy laptops may have a battery that is removable and replaceable by sliding a connector or removing a few screws from the back of the case, but you might not be able to find a compatible replacement. Modern laptops have internal batteries. Before removing the back (bottom) cover of the laptop to get to the battery, you must disconnect the power to avoid

getting shocked or damaging the laptop. You'll also want to be certain that you can purchase a compatible battery both in features and size/shape. Most do not require you to remove the keyboard or LCD panel to reach the battery, but again before doing either of those, the power should be disconnected, and you will have researched the laptop.

9. A, B. Users should be discouraged from eating cookies or toast (or anything) over their laptops. Fine crumbs or other debris can cause keys to stick, but that likely wouldn't cause the type of problem the user is experiencing. Oftentimes a laptop keyboard can be replaced fairly easily assuming a compatible one can be found, but in this case, the problem is most likely caused by a loose ribbon cable connecting the keyboard to the motherboard, or a corrupted driver.

10. C. Individual keys can be replaced on a laptop. If your company uses many of the same model of laptops, keeping one or two nonfunctioning ones in stock for parts is helpful. If a key is not readily available, they can be purchased from third-party vendors for much less than an entire keyboard. When ordering, ensure that it has the right type of clips, hinges, and possibly cup for the model being replaced. Is the short term, an inexpensive USB-connected keypad might suffice.

11. A. You will always check the device's documentation before purchasing components to ensure compatibility. In a laptop, RAM is often soldered directly onto the motherboard (onboard) and isn't meant to be replaced by most users. Since the maximum system RAM is 32 GB, you would need one 16 GB RAM module to bring it up to that total. The SO in SODIMM stands for Small Outline and is the type of RAM module used in devices like laptops and sometimes printers. DIMMs (Dual Inline Memory Modules) are used in desktop computers.

12. C. The short answer is that no, storage on an iPhone, iPad, iPod, or almost any small device can't be upgraded. When you buy one of these devices, it's best to buy as much storage as you can afford. Attaching the device to your PC and doing the upgrade there may work. If not, you may not have to buy a new iPod if you have some data that you no longer need like conversations from years ago, or if you have some apps that you no longer use and can delete. You should be able to download them again later onto a new device. iCloud is storage in the cloud, and not the same as storage on your device; however, you could store photos in iCloud Photos or use Messages in iCloud to save space on the device.

13. A. A solid-state drive (SSD) uses the same memory technology found in other forms of flash memory. They are much faster than traditional magnetic drives or hybrid drives but generally don't have as much capacity for the same price. An NVMe drive is newer technology and would have to be supported by the laptop. It also uses a different connector.

14. D. As a rule of thumb, either you can access components from the bottom of a laptop, such as the memory and Mini PCIe card, or you're going to need to remove the keyboard to access the components from the top.

15. B. Mini PCIe cards come in two sizes. The full-size cards measure 30 mm wide and 51 mm long. Half-size cards are 30 mm wide and 27 mm long.

16. A. If you have a cellular-enabled device such as a smartphone, you may be able to turn that phone into a mobile hotspot. By doing so, you can share your cellular Internet connection with Wi-Fi-enabled devices such as laptops and tablets. Near-Field Communication (NFC) devices can communicate and send data and files but only if they are within inches of each other. Bluetooth is a common wireless technology for connecting devices such as keyboards and headsets to a computer, and IrDA (infrared) communicates using light, but requires a line-of-sight.

17. A. Near-field communication (NFC) is a wireless technology that uses radio frequency (RF) signals with limited range, about 4″ (10 cm). Bluetooth and Wi-Fi have greater ranges, and IrDA uses infrared light and requires line-of-sight communications. IrDA is no longer popular.

18. C. Headsets are used for hands-free phone conversations and listening to music. Headsets can either plug into the speaker/headphone jack or be wireless. Most wireless headsets are Bluetooth. Wi-Fi is for connecting to wireless Local Area Networks (LANs). IR is infrared communication, which uses infrared light and requires line-of-sight for connections. It is seldom used. NFC (near-field communication) only works over very short distances, about 10 cm or 4″.

19. B. Near-field communication (NFC) is a wireless technology that uses radio frequency (RF) signals with limited range, about 4″ (10 cm). NFC can operate in card emulation mode, which lets the device act as a smartcard. This is useful for making payments at the site of a merchant who uses NFC. Bluetooth is a popular protocol for personal area networks (PANs) such as a laptop and headset or speakers. Wi-Fi is used for wireless Local Area Networks (LANs). IrDA uses infrared light for communication; although it was once popular, it is rarely used in PC communications.

20. B. Often in laptops, the antenna is housed in the display area of the laptop. You would most likely need to separate the display from the laptop's motherboard section to open it and replace the antenna cable. It will also likely have two different parts, a right and a left antenna, so make sure you get the right one.

21. B, C. Biometrics are using part of your body to identify you. An ID card is not biometric. Retina scanners are used in some secure environments but are not commonly found on laptops, but facial recognition like Apple's Face ID and Windows Hello are on most modern laptops. Fingerprint readers can be found on many laptops, or can be easily added.

22. B. Near-field communication (NFC) is a wireless technology that uses radio frequency (RF) signals with limited range, about 4″ (10 cm). To read an NFC tag in a poster, you would move your phone close to the tag. The phone would generate a small RF field that would power the tag, and data could then be read from the tag. There are five types of tags that vary in speed from 106 kbps to 2424 kbps and in maximum capacities from 2 KB to 32 KB. Type 4 holds the most data but is slower than Type 3.

23. C, D. The only Near-field communication (NFC) capability with devices prior to the iPhone 7 is the ability to use Apple Pay; however, with iPhone 7 and newer devices, a third-party app can be used to read and write NFC tags. iPhone 12 and newer devices can natively read NFC tags.

24. A, C, D. NFC can do so much more than pay for your coffee. In addition to the answers above, NFC tags can be set up to automate tasks instead of manually changing settings, such as silencing an alarm or logging into a PC. In some places they can allow your phone to be your bus pass. They're considered secure for communication because of the short distance between devices.

25. C. There are three types of Liquid Crystal Display (LCD) technologies listed in the A+ exam objectives: Twisted Nematic (TN), In-Plane Switching (IPS), and Vertical Alignment (VA). IPS LCDs provide better color representation as well as wider viewing angles, so that would be the best choice for this situation. Their drawbacks are somewhat slower response times and they tend to be a bit more expensive. Considering the other two types of LCD technologies, TN displays were developed first. They use less power compared to IPS and VA; however, when you start viewing them at wider angles, the picture quality suffers greatly. VA LCDs have slower response times than either IPS or TN, but they have the best contrast and image depth. SVA, or Super Vertical Alignment, is a Samsung term, not a standard, but it claims to offer better viewing angles than VA displays. LED monitors use Light Emitting Diodes as the backlight for an LCD. There are also microLED monitors and OLED monitors that create colors using LEDs with no backlight required.

26. C. OLED (Organic LED) monitors are not LCD (Liquid Crystal Display) monitors. Each of the other three has their advantages. TN (Twisted Nematic) displays have the fastest refresh rates, IPS (In-Plane Switching) displays have the best viewing angle, and VA (Vertical Alignment) displays have the best color contrast.

27. C. There are three types of Liquid Crystal Display (LCD) technologies listed in the exam objectives: Twisted Nematic (TN), In-Plane Switching (IPS), and Vertical Alignment (VA). Of those three display types, TN uses the least amount of power. TN displays also have very fast refresh rates. The issue with TN LCD screens is that when you start viewing them at wider angles, the picture quality suffers greatly. IPS LCDs provide better color representation as well as wider-angle viewing, but they tend to be a bit more expensive and have somewhat slower response times. VA LCDs have slower response times than either IPS or TN, but they have the best contrast and image depth. LED (Light-Emitting Diode) refers to a type of backlighting for LCD monitors.

28. D. The Organic LED (OLED) displays have incredible color contrast ratio because they can turn individual pixels off. They also have an excellent viewing angle. The drawback is that they may not be as bright as an LED (Light Emitting Diode) display. LED and mini-LED displays use LEDs for backlighting, but still need the LCD (Liquid Crystal Display) panel. QLED is a marketing name, but QLED displays use a quantum dot layer providing more color depth than regular LED displays. Micro-LEDs use three microscopic LEDs (red, green, and blue) to make each pixel, and each pixel can be turned on or off like an OLED TV. QLED, mini-LED, and micro-LED aren't on the CompTIA A+ objectives yet.

29. C. A digitizer is a device that can be written or drawn on and the content will be converted from analog input to digital images on the computer. Digitizers take input from a user's finger or a writing utensil, such as a stylus. Touchscreen devices and touchpads have a digitizer built into them. An inverter changes DC (Direct Current) to AC (Alternating Current) and is needed for some types of backlighting.

30. B, C. Webcams are nearly universal on laptops. The most common placement is right above the display on the laptop. Microphones are also often built into the display, next to the webcam. Both laptops and mobile devices such as smartphones are used for videoconferencing. Desktop computers can be used for videoconferencing, too, but usually will require adding a webcam and microphone. A digitizer converts touch input into digital format, and an inverter is used to convert DC (Direct Current) to AC (Alternating Current).

31. B. Common components to include in the display are the screen, Wi-Fi antenna, webcam, microphone, inverter, and digitizer. Speakers are often near the keyboard on a laptop; however, some desktop displays have built-in speakers.

32. A. A digitizer is a device that can be written or drawn on, and the content will be converted from analog input to digital images on the computer. Digitizers take input from a user's finger or a writing utensil, such as a stylus. Digitizers may be built into laptop and mobile device displays, or they can be separate devices that connect to a computer via a USB or other cable. Touchpads and pointing sticks convert your finger movement to mouse movement on the display. An inverter is used in CCFL displays to convert DC to AC.

33. A. Smartphones will have both a cellular antenna and a Wi-Fi antenna internal to the phone. Typically they connect with a ribbon cable, and they may be shaped differently or in different places depending on the particular cell phone model. These are not considered user-replaceable parts, but as an IT technician, you may be asked to replace them. Special tools, often plastic, may be needed to open a cell phone case without causing damage. The digitizer is a thin layer of electronic material that is usually fused between the glass and the LCD. Haptics are the ability of the device to interact through touch, such as vibration when they ring or feeling like you're pressing a physical button even though you're not. Stylus sensors are not actual devices.

34. B. Because of the much smaller space available for keys, some laptop keys are consolidated into special multifunction keys. These keys are accessed through the standard keys by using a special function (Fn) key. Nearly every laptop has a video connector on the back or the side to plug in an external display or a projector. You will need to use the video toggle key to get this external port to work. This is done by pressing the Fn key and the video toggle key simultaneously.

35. A. Most e-reader displays use a technology called electrophoretic ink, or E Ink, which is a proprietary type of electronic paper. Although E Ink is available in color, many consider its best applications to be in grayscales or pure black and white. Additionally, E Ink uses almost no power to keep print on the page until the print is changed.

36. C. The job of the inverter is to store and convert energy from DC to AC. Inverters have the potential to discharge that energy and can be dangerous to technicians, so be careful when working with them. A backlight provides light that shines through the Liquid Crystal Display (LCD) to create pictures on the screen.

37. A. OLED technology uses organic material that lights up and creates colors without the use of backlighting or an LCD (Liquid Crystal Display). IPS, TN, and VA are all types of LCDs.

38. A, D. Smart cameras have built-in wireless network connectivity for easy picture and video transfers. Many will include Wi-Fi, Bluetooth, and NFC (Near-field Communication). IrDA uses infrared light for communication and is not popular, and RJ-45 is a type of networking connector.

39. C. Megapixels are a measure of how many unique points a digital camera is capable of storing. It's more a measure of detail than quality, but for most of us it's a quick way to compare a smartphone's photographic capabilities. Brightness and contrast are settings that affect the display, whereas the digitizer accepts analog input and converts it into digital format.

40. A, B, D. The digitizer on a mobile device is a thin layer of electronic material that is glued or fused onto the back of the glass. Popular new smartphones are fusing all three together, so if the ability to communicate with the smartphone through touch fails, you must replace not only the digitizer but the glass cover and LCD (Liquid Crystal Display) as well. If the glass cover shatters, then the digitizer and LCD are replaced as well because it is sold as one unit. The Wi-Fi antenna is usually a discrete part inside the case.

41. B, C, D. Some drawing pads simply plug into the USB port of a laptop and they work just fine. Higher-end devices will likely need more setup but will pay off in quality. Some will need special software installed, including drivers, and that software will need to be configured. Most likely you'll want to enable and configure Windows Ink. You may need to calibrate a drawing pad when you first connect it or only if the movement of the stylus is off from the movement on the screen. It's unlikely that you'll need a different operating system to use it.

42. B. Most keyboards will have an Fn (function) key used in combination with the F keys across the top to perform various tasks. In this case, the user likely accidentally turned off the trackpad, also called a touchpad. We know that F9 is the trackpad button because the graphic shows the pad with the two mouse-click areas on the bottom.

43. C, D. Configuring a new Bluetooth trackpad is a fairly simple procedure. You first need to pair the device with the tablet, then configure it for speed and clicking and such. The CompTIA A+ objectives list the steps for connecting Bluetooth devices as follows:

1. Enable Bluetooth.

2. Enable pairing.

3. Find a device for pairing.

4. Enter the appropriate PIN code.

5. Test connectivity.

44. B. Tethering is connecting a device to a mobile hotspot. The term used to be reserved only for when you were connected via USB cable, as opposed to connecting via wireless. Some devices will not function as a mobile hotspot but will allow you to tether a mobile device to it with a USB cable so that the mobile device can share the cellular Internet connection.

45. C. To physically secure your laptop, use a cable lock. Essentially, a cable lock anchors your device to a physical structure, making it nearly impossible for someone to walk off with it. LoJack is software that can help secure data but does not prevent physical theft. A protective cover will help protect your device from damage if it gets dropped (and some are water-proof too), but it won't stop someone from stealing it. Docking stations are usually used in your home office or corporate office to provide a mobile device, such as a laptop, tablet, or smartphone, with access to external devices that can provide charging, speakers, and other features.

46. B. The iPhone 13 series uses the proprietary connector called the Lightning connector. They can also use a compatible wireless charging pad.

47. B. The connector shown is the Apple Lightning connector used by iPhones since the iPhone 5.

48. C. To connect Bluetooth devices, a user must initiate the pairing process on both devices. Bluetooth is used to create a PAN (personal are network) also known as a piconet. The range for a Bluetooth network is only about 30 feet. 802.11a is a Wi-Fi standard, Lightning is a type of connector, and Wi-Fi enabled refers to a device that uses a Wi-Fi connection. The CompTIA A+ objectives list the steps for connecting Bluetooth devices as follows:

1. Enable Bluetooth.

2. Enable pairing.

3. Find a device for pairing.

4. Enter the appropriate PIN code.

5. Test connectivity.

49. B, D. A docking station often replicates the functions of the ports on the back of a laptop so that peripherals such as displays, keyboards, printers, and so on that don't travel with the laptop can remain connected to the dock and don't all have to be unplugged physically each time the laptop is taken away. Docking stations effectively turn a laptop computer into a desktop computer, and the docking station may offer its own devices, such as an optical drive and speakers. It may have a generic connector such as USB-C or a proprietary connector. Docking station can also mean a charging cradle for a smartphone or tablet to plug in ver-tically that provides other functions such as built-in speakers for music playback or a clock. Two examples are Android Radio and Music Dock or Apple's Universal Dock. This differs from a port replicator, whose main function is to let the user connect several devices at once and doesn't require the laptop to be connected to offer connectivity between the devices. A KVM switch enables you to use one keyboard, video device, and mouse (hence the name, KVM) with two or more system units. *Desktop station* is not an actual term.

50. B. A port replicator is an attachment that provides the same ports as or additional ports to a laptop. The devices can communicate with each other via the port replicator whether or not the laptop is there. Docking stations are similar to port replicators because they provide a single connection to a laptop that will connect several devices, but the point of the docking station is to effectively make a laptop function as a desktop PC. Whereas a docking station may (or may not) be a proprietary device, a port replicator is not, and will generally provide a connection to the external devices via a USB or similar port. Docking station can also mean a charging cradle for a smartphone or tablet. KVM switches allow multiple system units to share a keyboard, video and mouse. Docking port is not an actual term.

51. D. Thunderbolt was co-developed by Apple and Intel as an offshoot of the DisplayPort technology. Apple added support for PCIe and launched it in 2011. In terms of versatility, it's second only to USB. You will find video devices, hard drives (both HDD and SSD), printers, laptop docking stations, audio devices, and PCIe expansion enclosures that use Thunderbolt. Thunderbolt 3 is compatible with USB-C.

52. C. Mini PCIe is just for small devices like laptops. PCI and PCIe are found on desktop PCs. PCIe x16 (x16 is pronounced as *by 16*) is often used for video at blazing speeds. PCIe x1 is popular for all sorts of devices. There is no Mini PCIe x16.

53. B. There are several different types of USB connectors. The one shown here is a miniUSB.

54. A. USB-C uses an oval port that looks identical to Thunderbolt 3, and both can be used to transfer data and power to a device, but Thunderbolt 3 does it much faster, at 40 Gbps. To tell them apart, look for the lightning bolt on a Thunderbolt cable or port.

55. C. There are several different types of USB connectors. The one shown here is a microUSB.

56. A. Centronics is a common name for a parallel port. Parallel ports are now legacy because serial communications are so much faster. Thunderbolt, Lightning, and USB-C all use serial communications, and they are very fast.

57. A, B. This is an audio output port and can be used to connect either speakers or headphones. A microphone can use a port that looks the same but is color-coded pink.

58. D. Laptop motherboards are nearly always proprietary, meaning they are not interchangeable between manufacturers or even between models from the same manufacturer. When a laptop motherboard needs to be replaced, you most likely need a laptop motherboard from the same make and model.

59. C, D. Older Android devices used the USB Micro-B connector, while newer Android smartphones use the USB-C connector. Lightning is the connector used by iPhones, and Thunderbolt has a connector whose shape looks identical to a USB-C, but Thunderbolt is much faster.

60. B. A DC power adapter allows a user to plug the laptop into the DC power source (usually called an auxiliary power outlet) inside a car or on an airplane. AC power adapters are for plugging into standard wall outlets. Some airplanes now provide AC power outlets to their passengers as well.

61. A, B. You should choose an AC adapter rated for the same wattage as the original. You must also pay special attention to the voltage and polarity of the plug that interfaces with the laptop. If the laptop requires the positive lead to be the center conductor, for instance, then you must take care not to reverse the polarity. It's best to find one that advertises compatibility with the device it will be charging.

62. B, C. Legacy docking stations would have a proprietary port that would align with a connector, usually on the bottom or back of a laptop. The docking stations would be proprietary, meaning they can only work with specific equipment. Modern docking stations connect with the fast USB-C or Thunderbolt ports, and sometimes USB-A ports. They often supply their own power and can make a laptop seem like a desktop by plugging in one cable that connects your laptop to multiple monitors, gigabit Ethernet, audio, or almost any other port type. Docking station can also mean a charging cradle for a smartphone or tablet to plug in vertically that provides other functions such as built-in speakers for music playback or a clock. Two examples are Android Radio and Music Dock or Apple's Universal Dock.

63. C. GPS systems were designed to require multiple satellites. Receivers use a process called triangulation, which they use to calculate the distance between themselves and the satellites (based on the time it takes to receive a signal) to determine their location. They require input from four satellites to provide location and elevation or three to provide location.

64. C. The Apple Watch uses watchOS. It's similar to iOS (used on iPhones) but was developed specifically for the watch. Its features are similar to iOS, but it includes features more tailored toward a smaller device. There is also iPadOS, which is, as you've likely surmised, for iPads. OS X mobile is a fictitious term, and Tizen is an open source mobile device OS.

65. C. An older laptop hard drive will be one of two form factors (sizes): 1.8″, which is now considered legacy, or 2.5″. Modern laptops most likely use either mSATA or M.2 drives, which are thinner than a RAM module and much smaller. Desktop computers have historically used 3.5″ hard drives.

66. B. A fitness monitor is normally worn on the wrist, and it tracks a user's movements and heart rate. Some fitness monitors will be able to track sleep patterns and have a clock, alarm, and other features such as GPS. All fitness monitors have the ability to sync to a device such as a smartphone, laptop, or desktop.

67. D. A good game controller can make your mobile device feel a bit more like a gaming console. Most of the game pads will look like standard console controllers and connect via Bluetooth. Touchpads and pointing sticks are input devices like a mouse. Touchpads are usually rectangular areas on a laptop where your finger movements replace moving a mouse. A pointing stick will usually be in the middle of a keyboard and is controlled with a single finger pushing the stick in any direction. A docking station lets a laptop connect to multiple devices with a single connection on the laptop, enabling the user to use it easily with full-sized devices like a desktop PC.

68. B. Many laptops use shared video memory, meaning that system RAM is divided up for use between the processor and the video card. On these types of systems, the amount of RAM available for video is configured in the BIOS/UEFI. Anything reserved for the video card is unavailable to the processor. In this case, subtracting half a gigabyte from 4 GB leaves the CPU with 3.5 GB.

69. D. Oculus VR specializes in virtual reality and augmented reality headsets (VR/AR headsets). Samsung and HTC, while manufacturing smartphones, also produce VR/AR headsets.

70. C. Tablet screen sizes typically fall anywhere between 7″ and 12″, although you can find much larger ones with 24″ displays.

71. B. The two center connectors are Thunderbolt connectors. They have the characteristic lightning bolt icon. Thunderbolt is an offshoot of DisplayPort technology and supports many types of peripherals.

72. C. RJ-45 is an 8-pin connector commonly used to connect computers to a local area network (LAN). Tablets are designed for mobile communication. As such, most tablets come equipped with Wi-Fi and Bluetooth, and many have cellular capabilities as well.

73. D. iPhones since the iPhone 5 have used a proprietary connector called the Lightning connector. Samsung smartphones and Fitbit watches most likely use a USB-C cable, whereas Intel-based laptops use a variety of charging jacks depending on the device.

74. A. Mini PCIe cards use a 52-pin connector. The Mini PCIe cards are 30 mm wide and come in full length (50.95 mm) and half length (26.8 mm). 68-pin connectors are used with SCSI devices, whereas 144-pin and 200-pin are SODIMM connector sizes.

75. A. The overwhelming majority of Wi-Fi antenna connectors for indoor-rated antennas found on laptops are type SMA (SubMiniature version A). On the device will be an SMA-female. What makes a connector "male" is the center pin and threads on the inside, while a "female" connector will have a receptor for the pin and threads on the outside. RP (reverse polarity) means that the pin and receptor are in opposite positions with regard to connector gender while the outside housing remains the same. SMA-RP and SMA are therefore not compatible with each other. N-type connectors look similar but are weatherproof and larger than SMA connectors.

76. C. Laptops with a rotating or removable screen allow the touchscreen to function like a tablet. This allows the warehouse manager to take notes with a tablet while keeping the laptop for their desk.

77. C. The IEEE standard 802.15.1 is commonly known as Bluetooth. The CompTIA A+ objectives list the steps for connecting Bluetooth devices as follows:

 1. Enable Bluetooth.

 2. Enable pairing.

 3. Find a device for pairing.

 4. Enter the appropriate PIN code.

 5. Test connectivity.

Not all Bluetooth devices require entering a pin. Opening a port is done on a router to allow a particular type of traffic to pass through the router to a connected network.

78. C. When pairing two Bluetooth devices, depending on the security settings, it is sometimes necessary to enter a Bluetooth PIN code. In security configuration menus, the PIN is sometimes referred to as the Bluetooth passcode or passkey. The CompTIA A+ objectives list the steps for connecting Bluetooth devices as follows:

 1. Enable Bluetooth.

 2. Enable pairing.

 3. Find a device for pairing.

4. Enter the appropriate PIN code.

5. Test connectivity.

79. C. POP3 (Post Office Protocol 3) keeps emails stored on one device. This means both sent and received messages are stored on that one device, so all email is accessed from that device. The IMAP (Internet Message Access Protocol) downloads mail but leaves a copy on the server. SMTP (Simple Mail Transfer Protocol) is a protocol for sending (not receiving) mail. S/MIME (Secure Multipurpose Internet Mail Extensions) is an encryption standard for securing email.

80. A. Internet Messaging Access Protocol (IMAP) keeps a copy of emails on the server. This allows someone to view and work with their email from more than one device. SMTP (Simple Mail Transfer Protocol) is a protocol for sending (not receiving) mail. POP3 (Post Office Protocol 3) downloads mail to a device and does not leave a copy on a server. Once downloaded, mail can only be read on that device. S/MIME (Secure Multipurpose Internet Mail Extensions) is an encryption standard for securing email.

81. C. Apple's cloud service called iCloud is for users and subscribers to store their media, contacts, and so on. OneDrive is Microsoft's online cloud user storage.

82. B. Exchange Online is the cloud service version of Microsoft Exchange and part of Microsoft Office 365.

83. D. If you use a common email provider such as Google, Yahoo, Outlook, or iCloud, then setting up email on a device should be simple. Often all you need is your username and password. If setting up a corporate account or if you must manually configure email, then you'll need more information such as the protocol (IMAP [Internet Message Access Protocol] or POP3 [Post Office Protocol version 3]) and the server names for sending and receiving email. You may also need the port number and security settings.

84. A. The Preferred Roaming List (PRL) and Product Release Instructions (PRI) deal with how your phone connects to the correct mobile tower and network. Updates to this information on the phone is typically done over the air. Your IMEI (International Mobile Equipment Identity) and IMSI (International Mobile Subscriber Identity) and screen resolution can't typically be changed. IMEI identifies the exact device, and IMSI uniquely identifies the account holder.

85. C. The International Mobile Equipment Identity (IMEI) is a unique number assigned to the physical phone. This unique identifier is hard-coded into the device. The Product Release Instructions (PRI) describe how your device connects to the network. An IMSI (International Mobile Subscriber Identity) number uniquely identifies the account holder, and a MAC (Media Access Control) address uniquely identifies a network interface card.

86. B. The International Mobile Subscriber Identity (IMSI) is a unique number that identifies you, the user, to the cellular service. If you're on a GSM network, it is on your SIM card and can easily be transferred from one phone to another. If you're on a CDMA network, you must transfer from one phone to another by activating the phone on your account. The International Mobile Equipment Identity (IMEI) is a unique number assigned to the physical phone. This unique identifier is hard-coded into the device. The Product Release Instructions (PRI) describe how your device connects to the network, and a MAC (Media Access Control) address uniquely identifies a network interface card.

87. D. A virtual private network (VPN) will keep browsing confidential as well as bypass any local content blocking efforts. S/MIME (Secure Multipurpose Internet Mail Extensions) is an encryption standard for securing email. Baseband is a type of signaling technology that only allows for one signal on a medium at a time (Ethernet uses this). The Preferred Roaming List (PRL) ensures that your cellphone connects to the most appropriate tower based on your location and provider.

88. A. Synchronization means to duplicate or back up the data from the device. Synchronization can be done to the local desktop, to the cloud service off premises, or even to an automobile. A VPN (virtual private network) uses encryption protocols to safeguard communications across a shared transmission medium (like the Internet) and mimics the network connection you would have if you were in the same building as your server. Encryption is using algorithms to change data so that it can't be read by unauthorized people or devices, thus protecting your data and logins. Updating is a generic term for modernizing and adding features to something.

89. C. When you synchronize bookmarks between devices, the website addresses are copied and readily available. The same synchronization can be done for several media types, such as videos, music, pictures, and documents.

90. A. Synchronizing calendars between devices and users is an easy and reliable option for ensuring that all parties have the same information.

91. B. ActiveSync was developed by Microsoft to make synchronization of data easier and allow users to access their data even when they're not online.

92. A. Single sign-on (SSO) is the authentication feature of users logging into their device, which in turn uses their authorization and credentials to authenticate to other systems or services. This is implemented through Active Directory (AD) or another centralized service that could store a user's privileges. Since the user was authenticated through the service (like Active Directory) and that service is trusted by the other software, the user is not required to log into the other software. SMTP is a protocol for sending email, synchronization means updating between systems, and nonrepudiation is proof of delivery or access such that a party can't later say they didn't access or see something. Nonrepudiation is a principle of information security.

93. D. As with any device installation in IT, the last step is to verify that the device works as intended. The CompTIA A+ objectives list the steps for connecting Bluetooth devices as follows:

1. Enable Bluetooth.
2. Enable pairing.
3. Find a device for pairing.
4. Enter the appropriate PIN code.
5. Test connectivity.

94. A. Any device that has a GPS receiver has the ability to ping satellites, which will correspond with at least two others to triangulate the position of the device, and they are quite accurate. (A fourth satellite is needed to determine elevation.) This is a common way for devices to provide turn-by-turn directions. While cellular location services work the same way, that wouldn't be the answer unless the vehicle has its own cellular service. MDM and MAM are methods of data security in a corporate environment.

95. A, C. Both GPS and cellular location services can be used to pinpoint the location of any device on Earth that has a GPS receiver or cellular service. GPS finds your location by pinging satellites whereas cellular location services use two or more cell phone towers. MDM is a type of data security for mobile devices, and RFID is radio frequency ID, which is often used for inventory management.

96. A. Some applications need to know your location to work properly. Others don't. Luckily turning off location services is not an "all or nothing" situation. You can turn location services off and on by application, and maintain discrete control over who is allowed to see where you are and who is not in the privacy settings of your phone.

97. B. While it's possible that the server has too many requests, the more likely culprit to your slow downloads is that you've reached your Internet service's data cap and your service has slowed down. This can happen whether it's a home service or a cell phone. Some services may cut you off completely and others merely send you a text message that you've reached your limit so they'll be slowing your connection or billing you more. If the router needed to be reset, the symptoms would be different. If the laptop was overheating, it would most likely shut down.

98. A, B. Mobile Application Management (MAM) protects corporate data while being used on employee's personal devices. It can force employees to save all work files in the company's OneDrive, encrypt files and delete them after a period of time, and restrict employees from downloading company content. It can even delete company files when a device has become inactive. Mobile Device Management (MDM) systems can be used to wipe data from a device and restore it to factory settings. GSM and CDMA are cellular communication systems.

99. D. A username is identification, and a password is authentication, but two-factor authentication, as the name implies, requires another method of authentication. Authentication can be based on something you know (like a password), something you have (a security card or cell phone, for example), something you are (biometrics: fingerprint readers, face scanners), or somewhere that you are. Sending an access code to a cell phone via text message after you've entered your username and password is one type of two-factor authentication. Authenticator applications on your laptop or phone generate codes that last usually only for seconds. The code is a combination of a key that was likely scanned from a QR code on the website or software and the time. A physical security key is something only you have that can communicate via USB, Bluetooth, a scanner, or even Wi-Fi.

100. C. The fourth generation of cellular services (4G) also known as LTE, was introduced to the world in the 2000s. It boasted downstream rates as fast as 53.3 Mbps. Prior to that, 2G came out in 1991 and added text-based SMS services (messaging). 3G was released in 2001 and transmits up to 7.2 Mbps. 5G, which is still being implemented, employs the use of different software and radio transmitters, is backward compatible, and is estimated that it will be able to reach transmission rates of 20 Gbps.

101. A. LED (Light-Emitting Diode) refers to the light source used as backlighting for an LCD (Liquid Crystal Display). OLED displays do not need backlighting because their carbon-based diodes emit both light and colors. IPS, TN, and VA are all types of LCD monitors that need a backlight. Not on the CompTIA A+ exam yet are micro-LED displays, where the LED produces the color and the light similar to an OLED, and mini-LED monitors that provide backlighting for LCDs but use a much smaller LED, allowing for better color specificity.

102. D. Laptop motherboards are nearly always proprietary, meaning they are not interchangeable between manufacturers or even between models from the same manufacturer. When a laptop motherboard needs to be replaced, you most likely need a laptop motherboard from the same make and model.

103. A. Apple iPads use iPadOS. Its features are similar to iOS, but it includes additional features such as keyboard support and multitasking capabilities, such as Split View. watchOS is for Apple Watches and OS X mobile doesn't exist.

104. D. It's most likely that Bluetooth connectivity was lost between the earpiece and the once-paired device, probably a phone. You'll examine the phone and troubleshoot connectivity between the phone and the earpiece.

105. C. Most likely you'll need to purchase an M.2 Wi-Fi card, and it's the only option listed that would work. Before you purchase a replacement, verify that your laptop has an internal connector and note what type it is. Then disable the onboard Wi-Fi, if there is one, before installing the new card. Mini-PCIe is a laptop connector standard that was largely replaced by M.2 connectors. PCIe and PCI are for desktop computers; PCI having been replaced by the newer, faster PCIe. PCMCIA is a legacy type of laptop connector. If there is no internal connector for a Wi-Fi card, you could purchase a USB Wi-Fi card, but it will take up one of your ports and may get bumped, and it was not listed as an option for this question.

106. A, B. Modern laptops most likely use either mSATA or M.2 drives, which are thinner than a RAM module and much smaller. Legacy laptops used 1.8" or 2.5" drives, and desktop computers have historically used 3.5² hard drives.

Chapter 2: Networking

1. A. Cable testers are indispensable tools for any network technician. Usually you would use a cable tester before you install a cable to make sure it works. Of course, you can test them after they've been run as well. Multimeters are used to test power supplies and wall outlets. Loopback plugs are used to test network interface cards, and tone generators and probes are used to locate a wire among other wires.

2. C. Internet Message Access Protocol (IMAP) is a secure protocol designed to download email. It has several advantages over the older Post Office Protocol 3 (POP3). First, IMAP4 works in connected and disconnected modes. Second, it lets you store the email on the server, as opposed to POP3, which requires you to download it. Third, IMAP4 allows multiple clients to be simultaneously connected to the same inbox. Simple Mail Transfer Protocol (SMTP) is used for sending mail, and Server Message Block (SMB) is used in sharing files across a network.

3. A. The Domain Name System (DNS) server is responsible for resolving hostnames, such as www.google.com, to IP addresses to enable communication. If it's not working properly or you can't connect to it, you won't be able to browse the Internet using friendly website names. Dynamic Host Configuration Protocol (DHCP) is used to assign IP addresses to network clients. The subnet mask might be incorrect, but it wouldn't be missing, and a duplicate IP address would provide an error message stating that.

4. B. Secure Shell (SSH) can be used to set up a secure session over port 22 for remote logins or for remotely executing programs and transferring files. Because it's secure, it was originally designed to be a replacement for the unsecure telnet command. Server Message Block (SMB), File Transfer Protocol (FTP), and FTP Secure (FTPS) protocols are used for sharing files across a network.

5. B. A switch operates at layer 2 of the open systems interconnection (OSI) model. Layers of the OSI model are (1) physical, (2) datalink, (3) network, (4) transport, (5) session, (6) presentation, and (7) application. The physical layer encompasses transmission media such as unshielded twisted pair (UTP), shielded twisted pair (STP), fiber optic, and so on. The datalink layer deals with transmitting frames on a LAN, so it includes the network interface card (NIC) and switch. Routers operate on OSI layer 3, because they transmit data between networks. Hubs work on OSI layer 1 because they merely connect devices in the same collision domain without regard to packet header information. The OSI model is not listed as an objective on the CompTIA A+ exam, but understanding it will help you understand network communications.

6. B. Transmission Control Protocol (TCP) guarantees packet delivery through the use of a virtual circuit and data acknowledgments, and User Datagram Protocol (UDP) does not. Because of this, TCP is often referred to as connection-oriented, whereas UDP is connectionless. Internet Protocol (IP) is used to get packets to their destination across the Internet, and Internet Control Message Protocol (ICMP) is used by connectivity devices to diagnose problems and send messages.

7. D. Remote Desktop Protocol (RDP) is a replacement for the older Telnet protocol, which is not secure. RDP, as its name implies, lets users log into a local machine and use a remote machine almost as if they were sitting at it. RDP uses port 3389. File Transfer Protocol (FTP), Secure File Transfer Protocol (SFTP), also called Secure Shell (SSH) FTP, and Server Message Block (SMB) protocols are all used for sharing files across a network.

8. C. 802.11ax (Wi-Fi 6) is considered a replacement for 802.11ac (Wi-Fi 5). 802.11ac operates in the 5 GHz frequency, while 802.11ax can operate between 1 and 7.125 GHz frequencies, encompassing the 2.4 GHz and 5 GHz bands. 802.11ac can send data at over 1 Gbps, while 802.11ax can be several times that. 802.11a was adopted in 1999. It operates at 54 Mbps in the 5 GHz frequency band. 802.11n was adopted in 2008. It operates at 600 Mbps in both the 2.4 GHz and 5 GHz ranges.

9. A. If Bob is trying to connect to an 802.11g network, his device will not be able to connect because 802.11g operates on the 2.4 GHz frequency only. 802.11n and 802.11ax both operate on 2.4 GHz and 5 GHz. 802.11ac operates only on the 5 GHz frequency.

10. C. Server Message Block (SMB) is a protocol used to provide shared access to files, printers, and other network resources. In a way, it functions a bit like File Transfer Protocol (FTP), only with a few more options, such as the ability to connect to printers and more management commands. Secure Shell (SSH) uses encryption to create a secure contact between two computers, and Simple Mail Transfer Protocol (SMTP) is used for sending email.

11. C. Telnet lets users log into another machine and "see" the remote computer in a window on their screen. Although this vision is text only, users can manage files on that remote machine just as if they were logged in locally. Telnet uses port 23. Telnet has been largely replaced by Secure Shell (SSH), and SSH (over port 22) is more secure than Telnet. Port 21 is used by File Transfer Protocol (FTP), and port 25 is used by Simple Mail Transfer Protocol (SMTP).

12. D. A wireless locator, or a Wi-Fi analyzer, can be either a handheld hardware device or specialized software that is installed on a laptop, smartphone, or other mobile device and whose purpose is to detect and analyze Wi-Fi signals. It can detect where signals are strong or weak to determine whether there are potential security issues. A tone generator and probe are used for locating a wire. Protocol analyzers and packet sniffers are tools used for capturing and analyzing network traffic.

13. C. Internet traffic is not encrypted by default. Websites that are secure and encrypt their transmissions will start with HTTPS:// rather than HTTP://. These sites can be trusted to encrypt the data, and their identity is verified.

14. A. The main Internet layer protocol is Internet Protocol (IP), and it's the workhorse of TCP/IP. Another key protocol at this layer is Internet Control Message Protocol (ICMP), which is responsible for delivering error messages. If you're familiar with the ping utility, you'll know that it utilizes ICMP to send and receive packets. Transmission Control Protocol (TCP) and User Datagram Protocol (UDP) are both communication protocols; TCP guarantees delivery but UDP does not.

15. C. There are three types of addresses in IPv6: unicast, anycast, and multicast. A unicast address identifies a single node on the network. An anycast address refers to one that has been assigned to multiple nodes, and a packet will be delivered to one of them. A multicast address is one that identifies multiple hosts, and a packet will be sent to all of them.

16. B. A wide area network (WAN) covers large geographical areas and often supports thousands of users. A WAN can be for different locations of a single company, or a WAN may connect several different companies together to share information. WAN lines are often leased from a WAN provider. The Internet is considered to be a very large WAN. A local area network (LAN) covers a relatively small area such as a home or business. A personal area network (PAN) is usually used by one person and consists of their computer and its Bluetooth devices. A metropolitan area network (MAN) is similar to a WAN, but the area covered is much smaller, such as a university or a city.

17. A. Developed by Microsoft, the Remote Desktop Protocol (RDP) allows users to connect to remote computers and run programs on them as if they were sitting at the computer. It uses port 3389. A port is associated with a specific protocol and must be "opened" on a router to allow traffic from the program or protocol to enter the LAN. The combination of an IP address and a port is considered a socket. The IP address gets the data to the right destination, and the port number tells the transmission layer of the OSI model which application the data is to be sent to. Server Message Block (SMB) and Common Internet File System (CIFS) are used in sharing files across a network. Telnet is an unsecure protocol that has been largely replaced by the Secure Shell (SSH) protocol.

18. B. Secure Shell (SSH) can be used to set up a secure session for remote logins or for remotely executing programs and transferring files. SSH uses port 22. SSH has largely replaced the insecure Telnet, which uses port 23. Port 21 is used by File Transfer Protocol (FTP), and port 25 is used by Simple Mail Transfer Protocol (SMTP).

19. A. Private IP addresses are not routable on the Internet. IPv4 network numbers were arranged in classes, and classes A, B, and C each have their own private range. The private IP address range for Class A networks is 10.0.0.0/8. The /8 means that the first 8 bits of the subnet mask denote the network number. Expressing a subnet mask this way is known as CIDR (pronounced cider) notation. CIDR stands for classless interdomain routing. While the term CIDR doesn't appear on the objectives for this CompTIA A+ exam, you may still run into it while working in IT.

20. D. One of the key features of routers is that they break up broadcast domains. Broadcast traffic from one port of the router will not get passed to the other ports, which greatly reduces network traffic. Bridges, hubs, and switches will all forward broadcast packets.

21. A. Routers are OSI model Layer 3 devices. They keep a chart containing the IP address of the device connected to each port, whether that device is a computer or another router's external address. A media access control (MAC) address is the address of a network interface card (NIC). Memory addresses identify where information is stored, and a loopback address is used to test TCP/IP on the local host. The loopback address for IPv4 is 127.0.0.1, and for IPv6 it is ::1.

22. C. A loopback plug is for testing the ability of a network adapter to send and receive. The plug gets plugged into the network interface card (NIC), and then a loopback test is performed using troubleshooting software. You can then tell whether the card is working properly. Multimeters are used for testing power supplies and wall outlets, a tone generator and probe help the technician to find a specific wire, and a cable tester checks that an Ethernet wire was configured correctly and that it can make an end-to-end connection.

23. D. Category 5, 6, and 7 UTP cables are limited to 100 meters, while Category 8 is limited to only 100 feet, so none of the UTP cables listed will work. You need fiber, and multimode fiber (MMF) can span distances of 300 meters. MMF is also known as OM1, OM2, OM3, OM4, and OM5. OM stands for optical mode. Specifications for each type of multimode fiber are available in the ISO/IEC 11801 standard.

24. C, D. Simple Mail Transfer Protocol (SMTP, port 25), Post Office Protocol 3 (POP3, port 110), and Internet Message Access Protocol (IMAP, port 143) are all email protocols. SMTP is for sending email. POP3 and IMAP are for downloading (receiving) email. Port 23 is used by Telnet. Option B is incorrect because the question specifically asks about downloading (not sending) email.

25. A. Fiber-optic cabling uses pulses of light instead of electric voltages to transmit data, so it is immune to electrical interference and to wiretapping. UTP, STP, and coaxial are all copper cables, which use electricity to transmit data and so can be subjected to electronic eavesdropping.

26. D. Routers operate at the Network layer (Layer 3) of the OSI model. Because of this, they make their decisions on what to do with traffic based on logical addresses, such as an Internet Protocol (IP) address. Switches use media access control (MAC) addresses and are OSI Layer 2 devices. Hubs and NICs operate primarily at the physical layer (Layer 1). The OSI model is not listed as an objective on the CompTIA A+ exam, but understanding it will help you understand network communications.

27. C. A firewall is a hardware or software solution that serves as your network's security guard. Firewalls can protect you in two ways: they protect your network resources from hackers lurking in the dark corners of the Internet, and they can simultaneously prevent computers on your network from accessing undesirable content on the Internet or sending out data that they shouldn't. PoE stands for Power over Ethernet, and EoP stands for Ethernet over Power. Neither has to do with protection. While a router may incorporate a firewall, it is not, by itself, a firewall. Routers are responsible for communications with other networks or broadcast domains. A firewall may be a discrete physical network appliance or software incorporated into another device like a router.

28. D. The default gateway is the address to the network's router on the LAN side of the router. The router allows the host to communicate with hosts who are not on the local network. The default gateway is also called the router's internal address. The `ipconfig /all` command can be used to see the default gateway address that the local computer is currently configured to use. The router will also have an external address, which is used to communicate with networks outside the LAN. Virtually all modern routers use a process called network address translation (NAT), which will substitute the router's external address for a host's IP address when requesting information from a remote network. The router knows which host requested the information and will pass it on to the correct host when it is received. This is one of the ways that the router protects the local hosts from the outside world.

29. A. A patch panel can be found in a telecommunications room (also called a wiring closet), usually mounted in a networking rack. On the back will be connections to "punch down" wires into. On the front will be a female port, usually an RJ45 type. A multiplexer is a device that aggregates several connections into one. A rack U is simply a measurement of the height of a device mounted into a rack (e.g., my patch panel is 4U). Each U is equal to 1.75 inches. The demarcation point is where responsibility for a network changes from the ISP to its customer.

30. C. A personal area network (PAN) is a small-scale network designed around one person within a limited boundary area. The term generally refers to networks that use Bluetooth technology. A local area network (LAN) covers a larger area such as a house or perhaps one floor of a building and likely uses the Ethernet protocol. A metropolitan area network (MAN) covers a larger area such as a city or university campus, and a wide area network (WAN) covers a very large geographic area such as one connecting distant cities or different countries.

31. B. The `169.254.0.0/16` range in IPv4 is the automatic private IP addressing (APIPA) range. APIPA comes into play when the host is unable to locate a Dynamic Host Configuration Protocol (DHCP) server, and the network connection is configured to acquire an IP address dynamically. Since the computer is unable to get a dynamic IP address from the DHCP server, the operating system automatically assigns a random IP address in the APIPA range.

32. C. An IPv6 address in the FE80::/10 range is called a link-local address and is similar to an IPv4 automatic private IP addressing (APIPA) address. (The 169.254.0.0/16 range in IPv4 is the APIPA range, used for automatic configuration if the host can't locate a Dynamic Host Configuration Protocol [DHCP] server.) Link-local addresses are generated by the PC when it boots up. Packets using a link-local address cannot be forwarded by a router.

33. D. Universal Plug and Play (UPnP) is a standard designed to simplify the process of connecting devices to a network and to enable those devices to automatically announce their presence to other devices on the network. In a truly secure environment, UPnP would be disabled, but it is often left enabled on home networks. Dynamic Host Configuration Protocol (DHCP) automatically assigns an IP address to a device when it is powered on, attached to a network, and configured to obtain an address dynamically. Network address translation (NAT) is a feature of routers used to hide the IP addresses of computers on the local network side of the router from the other networks and computers on the outside of the network. Quality of Service (QoS) can be configured to give desired devices preference over others for using network bandwidth.

34. A, C. Addresses in the FE80::/10 range are link-local unicast addresses. A link-local address is assigned to each IPv6 interface but is not routable on the Internet. If this is the only address the host has, it will not be able to get on the Internet.

35. A. The File Transfer Protocol (FTP) is optimized for downloading files from servers. It uses port 21. Secure Shell (SSH) uses port 22, Telnet uses port 23, and Hypertext Transfer Protocol (HTTP) uses port 80.

36. D. The Lightweight Directory Access Protocol (LDAP) is a directory services protocol based on the X.500 standard. LDAP is designed to access information stored in an information directory typically known as an LDAP directory or LDAP database. This often includes employee phone numbers and email addresses. Simple Network Management Protocol (SNMP) is used in network monitoring, Simple Mail Transfer Protocol (SMTP) is used in sending email, and Common Internet File System (CIFS) is a filesystem for providing shared access between diverse clients.

37. C. Lightweight Directory Access Protocol (LDAP) is designed to access information stored in an information directory typically known as an LDAP directory or LDAP database. LDAP uses port 389. Port 22 is used by Secure Shell (SSH,) 139 is used by NetBIOS, and 3389 is used by the Remote Desktop Protocol (RDP.)

38. B. The default subnet mask for Class B networks is 255.255.0.0, or written in shorthand, /16. The default subnet mask for Class A networks is 255.0.0.0, or written in shorthand, /8, and for Class C it is 255.255.255.0, or written in shorthand, /24. 255.255.255.255 is an IPv4 broadcast address. As a subnet mask it is represented as /32 (in shorthand) in the classless interdomain routing (CIDR) notation.

39. D. If you're working on a larger network installation, you might use a punchdown tool. It's not a testing tool but one that allows you to connect (that is, punch down) the exposed ends of a twisted pair wire into wiring harnesses, such as a 110 block or patch panel. A crimper is used to connect wires to an RJ45 connector, a cable striper removes the outer cover from wires, and a cable tester is used to verify the integrity of a cable.

40. C. Fiber-optic broadband Internet offers fast speeds (often in the 1–2 Gbps range) but is also the most expensive. Cable may have download speeds up to 1 Gbps (typically 10 to 500 Mbps), but upload speeds are typically only around 5 to 50 Mbps, while fiber-optic upload speeds may be in the 1 Gbps range. Digital Subscriber Line (DSL) uses plain old telephone service (POTS) lines and is slow. Satellite networks can be faster than DSL, but still only offer speeds up to about 150 Mbps.

41. A, B. IPv4 specifies private (nonroutable) IP address ranges for each class as follows: Class A: 10.0.0.0 to 10.255.255.255, Class B: 172.16.0.0 to 172.31.255.255, and Class C: 192.168.0.0. to 192.168.255.255. Other nonroutable numbers are 127.0.0.1, which is the loopback address, and 169.254.0.0 to 169.254.255.255, which is the automatic private IP addressing (APIPA) range. Class A addresses have a first octet from 0 to 127. Class B's first octet ranges from 128 to 191. Class C's first octet ranges from 192 to 223. Numbers above Class C are reserved.

42. C. Server Message Block (SMB) is a protocol used to provide shared access to files, printers, and other network resources. It originally ran on NetBIOS over UDP using ports 137/138 and over TCP using ports 137 and 139, but it's now part of the TCP/IP stack and uses port 445. Running on NetBIOS allows SMB to facilitate file sharing on a single network, while being part of TCP/IP allows it to facilitate file sharing across the Internet. By itself, SMB is not secure, so it needs other network appliances or software to secure the data being sent over its port(s). File Transfer Protocol (FTP) uses ports 20/21, Secure Shell (SSH) uses port 22, and Simple Network Management Protocol (SNMP) uses ports 161/162.

43. A. All of the answer choices are communications protocols for sharing resources. The Common Internet File System (CIFS) is Microsoft's version of Server Message Block (SMB.) Once upon a time CIFS was used extensively for file sharing over a network, but it has since fallen out of favor. While CIFS and SMB both facilitate file sharing, SMB does it better and has other features as well. Samba and Network File System (NFS) facilitate sharing files between clients and servers in Linux distributions. Samba will allow mixed environments with both Windows and Linux machines to share files. NFS will not.

44. B, D. Each IPv6 interface can and often does have multiple addresses assigned to it. IPv6 is backward compatible with IPv4 by using tunneling, dual stack, or translation. IPv6 uses multicast addresses in place of broadcast addresses, and a link-local address is established either automatically when a computer boots up or by manually configuring it, but either way the link-local address must be present.

45. B. Hubs were once used extensively in Ethernet networks, but they have fallen out of favor because they have a large disadvantage when compared to switches. A hub forms a single collision domain with all of their ports. On a switch, each port is its own collision domain. A switch keeps a table of its ports and the media access control (MAC) address that can be reached from each port. A switch will only forward a packet to a specific port, whereas a hub will forward a packet to all of its ports. The exception is that a broadcast packet will be sent to all switch ports. Switches are faster and more accurate than hubs and are used almost exclusively as the connectivity device within a local area network (LAN.)

46. B. The Trivial File Transfer Protocol (TFTP) is a very simple connectionless protocol. It has little overhead, meaning that it doesn't take much memory to run it. This makes it perfect for booting a thin client across a network. It can be used to transfer the needed boot files to devices that don't have hard drives. It should not be used to transfer files across the Internet because it is not secure. File Transfer Protocol (FTP) is more robust than TFTP. File Transfer Protocol Secure (FTPS) is a secure version of FTP. Simple Mail Transfer Protocol (SMTP) is used to send email messages.

47. B. 127.0.0.1 is the IPv4 loopback address, used to ping the local network interface. The IPv6 equivalent is ::1.

48. D. If you need to trace a wire in a wall from one location to another, a tone generator and probe is the right tool to use. To use it, attach one end to one end of the cable, such as the end at the computer. Then go to the patch panel with the other end of the probe to locate the cable. These tools are lifesavers when the cables are not properly labeled. A cable tester is used to confirm the integrity of a cable and verity that it is wired correctly. A loopback plug is used to test a network interface card (NIC,) and a punchdown tool is used to terminate wires into a patch panel.

49. B. Dynamic Host Configuration Protocol (DHCP) dynamically assigns IP addresses and other IP configuration information to network clients. The Domain Name System (DNS) translates human-readable names to their associated IP addresses, the Remote Desktop Protocol (RDP) allows a user to access a computer remotely as if they were sitting there, and Lightweight Directory Access Protocol (LDAP) is used for retrieving information from a database.

50. B. Switches provide centralized connectivity for a LAN. Switches examine the header of incoming packets and forward each to only the port whose associated media access control (MAC) address matches the receiving MAC address in the header. Hubs are seldom used now because the entire hub is one collision domain and when a packet is received, the hub sends the packet out to all of its ports indiscriminately. Bridges are used to connect different networks to work as one, and routers are used to forward packets from one network to other networks.

51. B. Email is pushed from clients to servers using the Simple Mail Transfer Protocol (SMTP). SMTP uses port 25. When trying to remember if SMTP is sending or receiving email, think S for Send. Port 23 is used by Telnet, now considered insecure and obsolete. Port 110 is used by POP3 (Post Office Protocol 3), and port 143 is used by IMAP (Internet Mail Access Protocol), both of which are used to retrieve email.

52. C. Of the Wi-Fi standards listed, 802.11n has the longest range by default, at roughly 70 meters indoors and 250 meters outdoors. 802.11ac is newer and faster than 802.11n, but it transmits exclusively in the 5 GHz range, which restricts its functional distance. 802.11a, which is legacy and uses the 5 GHz frequency range, could only send a signal about 30 meters, and 802.11g, which is also legacy but uses the 2.4 GHz frequency range, could only send a signal about 50 meters.

53. C. A cable tester typically uses lights to indicate that the cable is working correctly, and if there is a short, then the indicators for two wires would light up at the same time. Cable testers can range from basic ones that are only a few dollars to very sophisticated ones that are hundreds of dollars. Some of the better ones can tell you how many feet from you that the problem in the cable occurs. A tone generator and probe are used to trace a wire or find a specific wire from a group, a loopback plug is used to test a network interface card (NIC), and a crimper attaches a network wire to its terminator, usually an RJ45 plug.

54. C. Hubs send every communication they receive out every connected port. Switches will send broadcast packets out every port, but otherwise will send packets to a specific port based on the MAC address. A router will not forward any broadcast packet; therefore a router is the boundary of an IPv4 broadcast domain. A modem (modulator/demodulator) converts signals from one type to another, such as from an analog signal to a digital one.

55. A. Simple Network Management Protocol (SNMP) gathers and manages network performance information. A management device called an SNMP server can be set up to collect data from these devices (called agents) and ensure that your network is operating properly. SMTP is a mail protocol, LDAP is for accessing database information, and SMB is for file sharing.

56. C. Although Digital Subscriber Line (DSL) is being dropped by some providers in favor of fiber-optic lines, it is still a viable Internet connectivity solution in rural areas that fiber has not yet reached. DSL utilizes existing phone lines and provides fairly reliable access while carrying voice and data on the same lines. Most DSL subscriptions are asymmetrical, meaning they offer faster download speeds than upload speeds. POTS stands for Plain Old Telephone Service, an acronym from dial-up days. Cable connectivity is provided by cable TV companies. ISDN is Integrated Services Digital Network, a now obsolete technology that allowed voice and data communication on the same existing telephone lines, similar to DSL.

57. C. When setting up wireless access points, it's good practice to have their ranges overlap to ensure that there is no loss of communication when roaming in the network's area. However, to avoid problems, it's best to set up the access points with nonoverlapping channels; in this way, the overlapping ranges ensure continuous signal coverage while the nonoverlapping channels avoid interference from one WAP to another in the overlapping areas.

58. D. Internet Mail Access Protocol (IMAP) is used to download mail via port 143. Port 80 is for unsecured web page traffic. Ports 25 and 110 are email ports, but they are associated with SMTP and POP3, respectively.

59. B. Power over Ethernet (PoE) enables placement of equipment in areas that otherwise would not be able to accept it. Only four of the eight wires in twisted pair wiring are used for communication. The power is sent over the wires that are not used in communication. If the devices on both ends don't support PoE, then an injector can be used to add power to the line on the way to its destination. Compatibility is important, and there are limits to the amount of power that can be transmitted this way. Ethernet over Power (EoP) is not in the CompTIA A+ objectives, but it uses special devices to send Ethernet communications over existing wiring such as in a household. A wireless access point (WAP) is a device that is used to connect wireless devices to a wired network or to each other. Some WAPs support PoE. A hub is a very simple network connectivity device.

60. B. The 802.11ac standard has an indoor range of approximately 35 meters. At a minimum, you will need three access points. Depending on coverage and indoor interference, such as thick walls, you might need more.

61. C, D. Punchdown tools are used to connect unshielded twisted pair (UTP) and shielded twisted pair (STP) to a patch panel. A network tap is used to monitor network traffic. The crimper and cable stripper are both needed to add an RJ45 connector to the end of a twisted pair cable. Often both tools are included in one. The stripper removes the outer insulation from the group of wires so that they can be individually inserted into the RJ45 jack. Once the wires are properly inserted, the crimping tool is used to force metal teeth into each wire so that an electrical connection can be made.

62. D. The cable can be any of the three major types, coaxial, twisted pair, or fiber, but it needs to be plenum rated. Normal cables have a PVC coating, which produces a poisonous gas when burned. Plenum-rated cables have a Teflon coating, which is not toxic when burned.

63. B. Power over Ethernet (PoE) allows you to power an Ethernet device (such as a switch) through one of the Ethernet ports. For it to work, the access point and the device it plugs into both need to support PoE. Further, both the access point and device need to be compatible with each other. EoP, while not on the current A+ objectives, is a technology that allows the user to transmit Ethernet signals over existing power lines. This can be useful in a place where running Ethernet wires is impossible, but more often Wi-Fi is used in those situations instead. A hub can be used to regenerate a signal, but they also need a power source and are not a wireless access point. A repeater/extender is essentially the same as a hub. It requires power to regenerate a signal and send it on its way.

64. C. The private IP address ranges are `10.0.0.0/8`, `172.16.0.0/12`, and `192.168.0.0/16`. The address `172.168.38.155` is outside the private IP address range and is a public (routable) address.

65. A. By configuring Quality of Service (QoS), an administrator can set different priorities for one or more types of network traffic based on different applications, data flows, or users. UPnP allows devices to identify and connect to other devices on a network. A screened subnet is a secure area established using a router or routers to protect an internal network from traffic coming to a web-facing server. Port forwarding is configured on a router to send specific traffic to a specific device on a network.

66. D. To encrypt traffic between a web server and client securely, Hypertext Transfer Protocol Secure (HTTPS) can be used. HTTPS connections are secured using either Secure Sockets Layer (SSL) or Transport Layer Security (TLS). HTTPS uses port 443. Port 21 is used by File Transfer Protocol (FTP), port 80 is used by Hypertext Transfer Protocol (HTTP), and port 143 is used by Internet Mail Access Protocol (IMAP).

67. C. 802.11b/g transmits in the 2.4 GHz frequency, as does 802.11n, so they are compatible. The newer 802.11ac is a 5 GHz standard and therefore is not backward compatible with 802.11b/g. 802.11ax transmits in both the 2.4 GHz and 5 GHz frequencies, up to 7 GHz. 802.11r is not a standard related to Wi-Fi speed and is not in the A+ exam objectives.

68. D. Networks that are larger than a LAN but confined to a relatively small geographical area are metropolitan area networks (MANs). A MAN is generally defined as a network that spans a city or a large campus. LAN stands for local area network. PAN (personal area network) is the smallest of the types of networks, and a WAN is the largest type of network. It could connect faraway cities or even other countries.

69. A. A subnet mask of 255.255.224.0 has 8 bits in each of the first 2 octets set to on, and it has 3 bits in the third octet on. Therefore, it corresponds to /19 in shorthand. In the binary number system (base two), each bit has two possible values, 0 or 1. Each bit in an octet going from right to left increments by an exponent of two, making the bits of the octets worth the decimal values as follows: | 128 |64 |32 |16 | 8 | 4 | 2 | 1 |. Bits for the subnet mask are always used from left to right, so one bit would be equal to a decimal value of 128. Two bits would be equal to a decimal value of 192 (128 + 64). Three bits would be equal to a decimal value of 224 (128 + 64 + 32), and so on. When all 8 bits of the octet are used for the subnet mask, the equivalent decimal value is 255. For this example, the first 2 octets (8 bits each) are completely on, and in the third octet, only 3 bits are on, making a total of 19 bits in the subnet mask turned on to indicate the network number (8 + 8 + 3 = 19).

70. B. To communicate on an IPv4 network, a host must be configured with a valid IP address and a subnet mask. A default gateway is needed only if the host will connect to a remote network. DNS servers are optional but useful, because they resolve hostnames to IP addresses.

71. A, B. No two nodes on any network, whether IPv4 or IPv6, can have the same IP address because the host portion (or interface ID) of the IP address is what identifies the individual computer on the network. If the network has some machines manually configured, which is generally done with servers, and the remainder of the computers are configured to use Dynamic Host Configuration Protocol (DHCP), you would need to ensure that the manually configured numbers are outside of the DHCP scope (the numbers the DHCP server will automatically assign) but within the bounds of the network. For example, in an IPv4 network, if the network number is 200.100.1.0, the router, which is also acting as a default gateway, might be assigned 200.100.1.1, and numbers from 200.100.1.2 through 200.100.1.20 could be reserved for static configuration on devices that need an IP address that does not change. The DHCP scope would need to *not* include those numbers. If the network needed an available 180 IP addresses, then 200.100.1.21 to 200.100.1.200 could be safely assigned to the DHCP scope, avoiding any IP address duplication.

72. B, C. Certain devices on a network, such as printers and servers, should have an IP address that doesn't change (static) so that the other nodes on the network can always find the device. Option A is incorrect because if the DHCP lease on the IP address expires, the print server would be assigned a different IP address the next time it logs in. A static IP could be configured on the printer server, or the IP address could be configured as reserved on the DHCP server for that print server. Either choice would work. Static and dynamic IP addresses almost always exist on the same network, because each is needed to have a network that runs smoothly.

73. D. Wired Equivalent Privacy (WEP) was one of the first security standards for wireless devices. It uses a static key; the keys are commonly 10, 26, or 58 hexadecimal characters long. WEP was depreciated in 2004 because it was no longer secure and was replaced temporarily by WPA, which was quickly replaced by WPA2. WPA3 is the current and most secure standard.

74. D. Simple Network Management Protocol (SNMP) uses UDP port 161. User Datagram Protocol (UDP) is considered connectionless, so it does not guarantee delivery of data packets and has a lower network overhead than Transmission Control Protocol (TCP), a connection-oriented protocol, does. Port 143 is used for IMAP.

75. B. Clients are unable to get to the DNS server, which resolves hostnames (or URLs) to IP addresses. DNS uses port 53. Ports 20 and 21 are used for File Transfer Protocol (FTP). Ports 67 and 68 are used by Dynamic Host Configuration Protocol (DHCP). Port 80 is used for Hypertext Transfer Protocol (HTTP), and port 443 is HTTP Secure (HTTPS).

76. D. Automatic Private IP Addressing (APIPA) is a TCP/IP standard used to automatically configure IP-based hosts that are unable to reach a Dynamic Host Configuration Protocol (DHCP) server. APIPA addresses are in the 169.254.0.0/16 range. If you see a computer that has an IP address beginning with 169.254, you know that it has configured itself.

77. C. Normal (unsecured) websites are accessed on port 80, which is the port that Hypertext Transfer Protocol (HTTP) uses. Shut it down, and no one will be able to access websites, except secure sites that use HTTPS, which is on port 443.

78. D. The Domain Name System (DNS) is responsible for resolving hostnames to IP addresses. This is used millions of times daily on the Internet; when someone types in a website name, such as www.sybex.com, DNS will resolve that to an IP address to enable communication. Address Resolution Protocol (ARP) maps Internet addresses to hardware addresses. Reverse ARP (RAPR) does the opposite, and Dynamic Host Configuration Protocol (DHCP) assigns IP addresses to hosts automatically.

79. D. Satellite Internet is not much like any other type of broadband connection. Instead of a cabled connection, it uses a satellite dish to receive data from an orbiting satellite and relay station that is connected to the Internet. Because it requires a clear line of sight between the transmitter and receiver, it can be referred to as "line of sight" wireless. Mobile hotspot (cellular) devices are also an option, but they may not be able to reach the speed of a satellite connection and they depend on a strong cellular signal. For an installation far from civilization (and cell towers), satellite may be the only option. Cable, DSL, and fiber rely on lines that would not run as far as a forest ranger lookout tower.

80. C. Wireless Internet Service Providers (WISPs) use fixed wireless technology, which requires antennas to send radio waves between your location and a fixed hub on a tower or other tall structure similar to a cellular tower. Download speeds can be up to 1 Gbps. Satellite is an option in very remote areas but has the latency involved with traveling thousands of miles between the connection to the satellite and back again. Digital Subscriber Line (DSL) uses telephone lines to create an Internet connection, but many carriers no longer offer DSL. A cellular hotspot can be used in many remote locations but depends on connection to a cellular tower and is not as fast as satellite.

81. C. The two host-to-host protocols are Transmission Control Protocol (TCP) and User Datagram Protocol (UDP). TCP guarantees packet delivery through the use of a virtual circuit and data acknowledgments, and UDP does not. Because of this, TCP is often referred to as connection-oriented, whereas UDP is connectionless. IP and ICMP are not considered host-to-host protocols.

82. A. A local area network (LAN) is often defined as being contained in a single building, office, or home. The types of network based loosely on geography, from smallest to largest are PAN, LAN, MAN, WAN.

83. A, B. 802.11a and 802.11g provide throughput that is only 54 Mbps, 802.11n (Wi-Fi 4) provides throughput over 100 Mbps (theoretically up to 300 Mbps), but 802.11ac (Wi-Fi 5) and 802.11ax (Wi-Fi 6) have far surpassed these standards with throughputs, over 1 Gbps and multiple Gbps, respectively.

84. B, D. 802.11ac operates in the 5 GHz frequency only. 802.11g is only 2.4 GHz. 802.11n and 802.11ax operate in both frequencies.

85. C. NetBIOS over TCP/IP (NetBT) is for older applications still reliant on NetBIOS, the legacy network protocol intended for very small networks. NetBT lets such applications communicate over TCP/IP. Trivial File Transfer Protocol (TFTP) is a basic connectionless protocol that allows file transfer functions without user interaction. Hypertext Transfer Protocol Secure (HTTPS) is a secure connection-oriented protocol that runs over port 443.

86. C. An unmanaged switch will simply perform the basic task a switch should do: direct network traffic out the correct destination port. Prioritizing traffic, configuring virtual LANs (VLANs), and mirroring ports are all jobs that are done using managed switches.

87. D. Migrating network configuration to the cloud would allow the network administrator to perform their duties without requiring travel.

88. A. DHCP uses ports 67/68. Ports 137/139 are for NetBIOS/NetBT. Port 80 is for HTTP, and port 445 is for SMB.

89. B. The distance for Power over Ethernet (PoE) is limited by the maximum distance set by the Ethernet cabling: 100 meters (328 feet). The power injector, the device that sources the electrical power to certain wires in the cable, can be as much as 100 meters from the powered device. The injector also needs to have sufficient power to match device needs, and devices must be compatible. PoE devices such as powered switches can provide a few watts or well over 100 watts, depending on the device.

90. C. NetBT is NetBIOS over TCP/IP, an older protocol for applications that still rely on NetBIOS. It uses ports 137 and 139, and it's still on the CompTIA A+ certification objectives. DNS uses port 53, SMB uses port 445, and SSH uses port 22.

91. C. The end-user devices are configured to at least request a DHCP-assigned IP address or they are preconfigured with a static IP, gateway, subnet mask, and DNS information.

92. D. MAC address filtering uses the physical address of a NIC to determine whether or not to allow a device to connect to the router. Disabling the SSID will hide the network from neighbors, but it won't keep them from connecting if they discover the network. Port forwarding redirects requests for a specific port to a specific device on the network. The DHCP scope can be set up to only allow five machines to connect, but it may not be the right five machines.

93. D. Unless an Internet of Things (IoT) device possesses an end-user accessible management interface, that device will likely connect at least initially using Dynamic Host Configuration Protocol (DHCP) to obtain an IP address. Domain Name System (DNS) resolves names like Wiley.com to an IP address. AD is Active Directory, which is a Microsoft client-server security solution, and Single Sign-On (SSO) allows a user to enter their credentials once to access several resources.

94. B. Near-field communication (NFC) requires devices to be within about 10 centimeters of each other to transmit data. In this case, the devices are working in card emulation mode, but NFC can also be used to transmit between two like devices, such as two cell phones, or to read a smart tag. Radio frequency identification (RFID) is another technology that uses radio waves to transfer information. Wi-Fi is 802.11-based wireless networking, and hardware-assisted virtualization (HAV) is virtualization that allows the virtual machine (VM) more direct access to the physical processor's capabilities.

95. A. Radio frequency identification (RFID) can be implemented to detect and read a "passive" (no power) tag that is essentially an antenna as it passes within a few feet in range. RFID tags are often used in industry and retail for inventory tracking. The distance for RFID implementation depends on the size and polarization of the antenna, and the frequency and power used, among other features. NFC requires a distance of only a few centimeters. Wi-Fi is 802.11-based wireless networking. Radio frequency interference (RFI) is a nuisance that can disrupt network communications.

96. D. A web server consists of hardware and software used to provide information to remote clients via the Internet. The main protocols for web servers are HTTP and HTTPS, but they can use other protocols as well. File Transfer Protocol (FTP) servers are used for downloading files quickly, and while they may have a graphical user interface (GUI), they have much less overhead than a web server. Proxy servers are a security measure between an internal user and the web and are used to monitor and filter information going into or out of a network. File servers are often used on a LAN to provide access to the same files by multiple users.

97. A. Internet of Things (IoT) devices allow a multitude of personal and industrial devices to connect and communicate over the Internet. Structured Query Language (SQL) is a method of retrieving information from a database. Denial of service (DoS) is a type of network attack, and Encrypting File System (EFS) allows the user to encrypt individual files, folders, or volumes.

98. C. The file server is a centralized repository for users, typically company employees. File Transfer Protocol (FTP) servers are used for downloading files quickly, and while they may have a graphical user interface (GUI), they have much less overhead than a web server. Proxy servers are a security measure between an internal user and the web, and they are used to filter information going into or out of a network, whereas web servers may provide information about a company or its products to the general public.

99. B. Proxy servers act as a gateway through which Internet access requests are handled, monitored, and, if need be, filtered. File Transfer Protocol (FTP) servers are used for downloading files quickly, and while they may have a graphical user interface (GUI), they have much less overhead than a web server. File servers are often used on a LAN to provide access to the same files by multiple users, whereas web servers may provide information about a company or its products to the general public.

100. A. The File Transfer Protocol (FTP) server hosts files for easy access, allowing users to browse it and download and upload files. Proxy servers monitor and filter traffic into and out of a network. File servers are a repository of files accessed by multiple users on a network. A DNS server resolves human-readable names such as Wiley.com to an IP address.

101. C. A print server can be either a physical device or software configured on a computer. The print server provides centralized availability of print services to authorized users on the network. It accepts print jobs, and the documents are printed according to order of receipt or some configured priority. A syslog server gathers event information from devices on a network, creating a central repository for a network administrator to monitor and respond to events. A DNS server resolves domain names to IP addresses, and an authentication server verifies identity before allowing access to a network.

102. B. If a user types www.sybex.com into a web browser, the Domain Name System (DNS) server will resolve the domain name to an IP address. Similarly, DNS servers will resolve a fully qualified domain named (FQDN) network directory resource on the network to make locating that resource possible. Syslog servers provide a repository of events on the network to aid in network management. Print servers provide and manage access to one or more printers by multiple users on a network, and an authentication server verifies identity before granting access to resources on a network.

103. D. The authentication server facilitates the challenge/response service for validating someone's credentials. Syslog servers provide a repository of events on the network to aid in network management. DNS servers resolve URLs to IP addresses, and print servers provide and manage access to one or more printers by multiple users on a network.

104. A. The syslog server operates with the Syslog protocol, which is used by many different operating systems and devices. These system-generated messages vary from the mundane "System started" to critical alerts. DNS servers resolve domain names to IP addresses. Print servers facilitate and manage printing by multiple users to one or more printers on a network, and authentication servers verify identity before granting access to a resource.

105. C. Mail servers are used to send, receive, and sometimes store and manage emails. They operate on ports 25, 110, and 143. Often devices will need to be configured with the name or IP of the server and the proper protocol or port for sending and receiving email. Web servers provide web pages over the Internet. Authentication servers verify identify before allowing access to resources, and FTP servers are used to quickly locate, download, and upload files.

106. C, D. Connection-oriented protocols work over TCP, which guarantees delivery of packets. This guarantee requires greater resources than UDP, which is connectionless, therefore not requiring that a packet be resent if not received. HTTPS and SSH are connection-oriented protocols, whereas Trivial File Transfer Protocol (TFTP) and DHCP are connectionless protocols.

107. B. An intrusion detection system (IDS) will monitor and alert you on suspect behavior. The IDS can be a network-based device or host-based, meaning it runs as a process in the background. Proxy servers are used to control traffic into and out of a network. Unified Threat Management (UTM) provides multiple security features on a single appliance. ATM (Asynchronous Transfer Mode) has to do with transferring different types of traffic (i.e., voice and data) over the same communication lines at the same time.

108. D. The intrusion detection system (IDS) will alert on suspect activity, but it will not react or actively attempt to block the activity. The intrusion prevention system (IPS), however, should attempt to block the activity.

109. C. Unified Threat Management (UTM) systems can be hardware networking devices, virtual devices, or an off-premises service. UTM's role is to combine several security features and services into a single device, allowing for easier management and compatibility. IDSs (intrusion detection systems) will only notify an admin if a threat is detected. Intrusion protection systems (IPSs) will detect and respond to security threats. UTP is unshielded twisted pair, a type of network cabling.

110. A, D. A Simple Network Management Protocol (SNMP) trap is unrequested information being sent from an SNMP agent, in this case running on a managed switch. SNMP traps are sent via port 162.

111. B. Cellular is the only type of network connection that allows for the type of mobility that this photographer needs. A cellular hotspot device from a mobile provider would work well. Satellite would require repositioning of the dish on a regular basis and may not work well because of obstructions. WISP requires being within a few miles of a tower and line-of-sight between the antenna and tower, so that wouldn't work well either. DSL requires a stationary phone line.

112. C. Cable Internet service requires a cable modem to separate the Internet signal from TV channels and to convert the signal into one that your computer can use. A switch is used on a LAN as a central connection point. A hub for networking is an obsolete device that would send any signal it received out of all of its ports. A cable multiplexer connects several signals into one for transmission over a cable, such as input from multiple security cameras.

113. B. This device is for testing cables that are terminated with an RJ45 connector.

114. C. You need to add a wireless access point (WAP), which will have an RJ45 port to connect to the company server and Wi-Fi antennas to provide wireless connectivity. An Ethernet router is wired. A proxy server is a security device. NFC, although wireless and using radio waves, is for connecting devices within a few centimeters of each other.

115. A. With many new systems added and already booted, it is likely that the DHCP scope, which is a valid range of IP addresses that are available to client-based systems on a particular subnet, is now too small for the number of systems requesting IP addresses. Expand the DHCP scope to solve the problem.

116. B. Virtual LANs, or VLANs, will segment your network into smaller broadcast domains. Multiple VLANs can exist on the same physical switch. Traffic is isolated to only the paths determined by how you have identified VLANs on your managed switches. A VPN (virtual private network) uses tunneling protocols to secure a private connection across a public network. A UPS (uninterruptable power supply) is a battery backup with other features used to maintain power to a device when the main power goes down, and SQL (Structured Query Language) is used to retrieve information from a database.

117. A. A virtual private network (VPN) uses encryption to secure a transmission across a public network. SDN (software-defined networking) is a network architecture designed to make managing a network easier and more flexible. A VLAN separates a LAN into separate broadcast domains and is used for security purposes. SRAM, or static RAM, is often found in processor cache.

118. C. Wireless LAN (WLAN) networks commonly have three types of nodes: a client, a router, and a gateway. They typically don't include a server and often are of fluid nature, where devices come and go as needed. They may include a printer. A WLAN can be used to connect wireless users to a wired network.

119. A, B. A NIC can be configured either with a specific (static) IP address, or to obtain an IP address from an available Dynamic Host Configuration Protocol (DHCP) server. Many routers have the capability to provide DHCP services. When a device with a properly configured NIC attempts to join a network, a request for an address will be sent to the DHCP server, and the DHCP server will lease an address to that device, if one is available.

120. B. Option B, 2601::0f:ab:cd:123:4a, and the address in the question both have a subnet of 0f. IPv6 addresses consist of 128 bits, divided by colons (:) into 8 hextets. Therefore, each hextet represents 16 bits. Leading 0s can be omitted, and in one place in each address, consecutive groups of 0s can be omitted, represented by double colons (::). The last 64 bits (4 hextets) of an IPv6 address are the Interface ID, identifying the unique computer. The first 64 bits are called the prefix. ISPs and very large organizations are assigned /48 prefixes. The next 16-bits (the fourth hextet) are used to define subnets. Option A has a fourth hextet of 0. Option C is a link-local address. Option D is an invalid number because hex numbers only go to letter f.

121. B. The third octet's subnet mask of 192 means that the first 2 bits of the octet are used to identify the network number, so the network can be broken down into four subnets using those first 2 bits of the octet. The subnets would be 00000000, 01000000, 10000000, and 11000000. IP addresses within each range would be 0 to 63, 64 to 127, 128 to 191, and 192 to 255. The first and last IP in each range would not be used because they would represent the subnet itself and the broadcast numbers. Options A, C, and D all fall in the second subnet's range. Option B is in the third subnet.

122. A. The PoE standards are IEEE 802.3af (PoE), 802.3at (PoE+), and 802.3bt (PoE++). A main difference between the standards is how much power per port can be provided. 802.3af can supply up to 15.4 watts per port, 802.3at can provide up to 30 watts per port, and 802.3bt can provide 60 watts (Type 3) or 100 watts (Type 4). The power that actually reaches the devices is less due to voltage loss over distance. 802.3b is a legacy broadband Ethernet standard. 802.11 and802.11ax are Wi-Fi standards.

123. B, C. PoE devices providing power are backward compatible with older devices, meaning that while 802.3bt is rated at 60W for Type 3 and 10W for Type 4, an 802.3bt device will work with an 802.3at (Type 2) device. Option A would not provide enough power for your friend's device. Option D is a Wi-Fi standard, not a PoE standard.

124. B, D. ONT (optical network terminal) is installed by a fiber-optic ISP, and it's typically a small box on an outside wall. The terminal is a transducer, converting between copper/electrical signals and fiber-optic/light signals. It does require power, and the terminal may have an indicator light to signal whether it is receiving power.

125. C. Software-defined networking (SDN) has many advantages over traditional networking. It can work with virtual and physical networks using SDN-compatible devices, providing centralized control of the entire network and the ability to reconfigure networks often without having to physically touch a router or switch.

126. B. Frequencies for wireless Internet service providers (WISPs) can be licensed or unlicensed. (The FCC is the licensing body.) Most WISPs use the unlicensed frequencies because they are free to use.

127. C. A wireless LAN (WLAN) would be the best solution for this office. A WLAN is a group of devices in the same location that communicate via radio waves instead of cables. WLANS can have multiple wireless access points (WAPs), preferably overlapping so that users won't experience signal drop. Wi-Fi is a type of WLAN. A LAN is incorrect because it would require disconnecting and reconnecting cables in each room. A VLAN (virtual LAN) is established using security protocols to segregate a network. WAN is incorrect because this is a network in a single office, not geographically distant computers.

128. C. A storage area network (SAN) is a high-speed network whose purpose is to provide fast access by servers to storage. Network attached storage (NAS) differs from a SAN in that it is not a separate high-speed network but a single storage device attached to a LAN. SAS is statistical analysis software, and WAN is wide area network.

129. A, D. A network terminal access point (TAP) connects to a network in an area of concern and creates a copy of traffic, sending it on to monitoring devices. It can be an integral part of network management. TAPs can be active or passive. Passive TAPs do not require power or management, but active TAPs do.

130. B. A fileshare server handles requests from fileshare clients for access to data stored on the server. The fileshare server resides on the same machine as the data. A client access license (CAL) is a license allowing one machine to connect to a server, and SAN is a storage area network, both of which are unrelated to the question.

131. B. A wireless access point (WAP) provides wireless LAN (WLAN) connectivity, but it may not help with the problems on this network. Your friend needs to determine what wireless channel has the least traffic and configure their Wi-Fi to use that channel. For that they need a Wi-Fi analyzer, which can be a separate device or as simple as an app on a smartphone. A toner probe is used to figure out which network cable is connected when they are not labeled, and a cable tester determines if the cable's wires are connected properly.

132. B. Wireless Internet service providers (WISPs) that are operating in the 2.4 GHz band are limited to 4 watts of effective isotropic radiated power (EIRP) for their point-to-multipoint connections. Their point-to-point connections vary between 4 watts and 158 watts for the 2.4 GHz band. The maximum EIRP for the 5 GHz bands is 125 mw. FCC maximums can be found at www.air802.com/fcc-rules-and-regulations.html.

133. A. Channels 36 to 48 are set aside for domestic use. All channels above that require a router to have DFS and TPC. DFS will automatically switch to a different channel when weather radar and radar system signals are detected. TPC can be used to force clients to lower power so that they won't interfere with nearby users or access points on the same channel. Channel 165 is set aside for industrial, scientific, and medical (ISM) use. In the United States, the FCC and IEEE are the authorities that approve channel uses.

134. B. The FCC's ruling was expanded to include long-range fixed wireless hub or relay antennas and the customer's right to place antennas of certain sizes on their premises, putting WISP providers on a more equal footing with satellite and cellular providers.

135. D. When an IP address and subnet mask are converted to the binary numbers that the computer sees, wherever there is a 1 in the subnet mask, that tells the computer that the corresponding bit in the IP address is part of the network number. Wherever there is a 0 in the subnet mask, the corresponding bit in the IP address is part of the host number. The address in the question, 192.168.2.200/24, is a Class C private address, where, in the subnet mask, the first three octets (24 bits) are all 1s, and the last octet (8 bits) are 0s. So, the first three decimal numbers of the IP address, which is expressed in dotted decimal notation, are the network number, (192.168.2) and the last octet (.200) is the host (individual computer) address. Network numbers will always go from left to right with no breaks between.

136. D. Authentication servers provide the AAA framework for security. Authentication requires that an entity prove who they are before gaining access. Authorization grants the authenticated user access to resources. Accounting tracks user activity.

137. C. Load balancers do as their name implies. Rather than allow all incoming traffic on a port to go to one server or device, the traffic is distributed among devices. Proxy servers monitor incoming and outgoing packets, filtering them out based on specified criteria. Spam gateways don't allow spam in; rather they are used to filter it out. Unified threat management (UTM) can employ an appliance or be software-driven, or even an outside service that monitors and manages malicious activities against a network.

138. A. Supervisory Control and Data Acquisition (SCADA) systems consist of both hardware and software. Hardware is used to gather information, which is sent to a computer running software that analyzes the data and logs events. SCADA can also initiate alarms when specified conditions exist. Infrared Data Association (IrDA) is network communications via infrared light. Unified threat management (UTM) is an appliance, software, or service that combines all malware security in one place. Remote Authentication Dial-In User Service (RADIUS) is a protocol for authentication servers that encrypts transmissions between client and server.

139. C. A DHCP server will "lease" an IP address to a client for a specified period of time. The default is usually 24 hours. In a SOHO where there are few new users, the lease time could be longer, but in a restaurant where many people come and go each hour, the DHCP scope might not have enough addresses to accommodate that many users. Setting the lease time to a shorter duration will release the IP address and make it available for a new user. MAC address filtering only allows connection from computers with specific MAC addresses and would greatly limit connectivity. Port forwarding sends traffic for a specific port to a specified computer on the network. The SSID is the wireless network name and can be broadcast so that it is easily found, or it can be hidden.

140. B. The Domain Name System (DNS) uses two types of records to resolve domain names to IP addresses. Type A records resolve the domain name to IPv4 addresses. Type AAAA records resolve domain names to IPv6 addresses. MAC and Physical addresses are two names for the NIC address.

141. A. Multiple Mail Exchanger (MX) records can be set up for a domain that specify different mail servers for load balancing. Direct Connect (DX) is an Amazon Web Services dedicated connection between client and AWS. AAAA signifies an IPv6 address in a DNS record, and TXT DNS records let an administrator specify text in their DNS record. These text records can be used to prevent email spam.

142. B. Sender Policy Framework (SPF) is a technique to prevent email address spoofing. It is done using a TXT entry in a domain's DNS service. DomainKeys Identified Mail (DKIM) performs a similar function, but it uses a digital signature. Domain-Based Message Authentication, Reporting, and Conformance (DMARC) uses SPF or DKIM and in addition requires that the sender's domain be the same as the DNS domain name. Domain administrators can specify to quarantine or reject emails that fail DMARC. To use DMARC, a DMARC record must exist in the DNS.

143. C. This is an IPv6 address. It is 128 bits long, and the last 64 bits are the interface ID, which identifies the individual computer. Since there are eight groups of hex numbers, that means the rightmost four groups are the interface ID. Any leading zeros in an IPv6 address can be omitted, and the :: can be used once in an address to replace consecutive groups of all zeros, so the number in the question fully expanded would be `2001:0000:0000:0000:01a3:0f1a:0308:0833`. The interface ID is therefore `1a3:f1a:308:833`. The leftmost three sections identify the network, and the fourth identifies the subnet. In this example, `2001:0:0` is the site prefix and 0 is the subnet ID. IPv6 addresses do not need a subnet mask like IPv4 addresses do.

144. A, D. For decades now, wireless Internet service providers (WISPs) have been established by groups of individuals or small companies to provide Internet access to areas where it is not profitable for large commercial Internet providers to run, such as very rural areas. They are also called long-range fixed wireless providers. The first one was established in 1992 in the Midwest of the United States. Now there are thousands of them all over the world. In some areas of the world, where there is little or no wired infrastructure, WISPs are the only way that people can get Internet connectivity. A WISP connects to the Internet using either leased lines or microwaves, generally uses point-to-point microwaves between its towers, and uses point-to-multipoint connections between the final tower and users. An ISP is an Internet service provider, and a demarcation point is the place in a customer's premises where the responsibility for the network changes from the ISP to the customer.

145. A, B. Option A is true. Channels 1, 6, and 11 are the only ones that don't overlap in a 2.4 GHz network. Option B is also true. Each channel in a 2.4 GHz network is only about 5 MHz wide, while in a 5 GHz network the minimum is 20 MHz, but it can be configured to use 40 MHz or 80 MHz by combining channels. Option C is false. The 2.4 GHz frequency supports older devices; the 5 GHz frequency is newer. While 2.4 GHz channels overlap with the exception of 1, 6, and 11, 5 GHz channels don't overlap. Your friend needs to choose a frequency and channel that are compatible with their devices, but the router may automatically configure the channel if using the 5 GHz frequency.

146. C. The Institute of Electrical and Electronics Engineers (IEEE) 802.11ax standard is now known as Wi-Fi 6, and is considered a replacement for 802.11ac (Wi-Fi 5). 802.11n is designated as Wi-Fi 4. Prior IEEE standards (802.11b, 802.11a, and 802.11g) are not designated with official Wi-Fi X nomenclature, but working backward in time, 802.11g would be Wi-Fi 3, 802.11a would be Wi-Fi 2, and 802.11b would be Wi-Fi 1. The CompTIA A+ objectives only ask that you know what Wi-Fi 5 and Wi-Fi 6 are.

Chapter 3: Hardware

1. A. F-type connectors are threaded and screw into place. F-type connectors are often found at the end of an ISP's cable connection. BNC connectors were once used in LAN wiring but are now found in RF and video applications and test equipment such as oscilloscopes. The BNC connector locks by twisting one-quarter turn. SC and FC connectors are for fiber-optic cable.

2. B, D. Both SC and LC connectors are square and can be purchased in single or duplex connectors. SC is square and is a push/pull design. ST have a bayonet connection. FC connectors have a threaded coupling. LC connectors are smaller at 1.25 mm and have a latching mechanism to keep them in place, making them good for rack mount use. SC, FC, and ST connectors are 2.5 mm. There are other connectors on the market, but not on the A+ exam.

3. C. RJ-11 accommodates two pair of wires and is the standard for household or office wired telephone connections. RJ-45 is the four pair connector used for twisted-pair Ethernet. Coaxial is a type of network cable and would have a BNC connector (with a locking mechanism) or an F-type connector. FC is a type of fiber-optic connector.

4. D. A cable with the same T568 standard on both ends is a straight-through network cable. These are used for patch cables and network drops. If you have a T568A on one end and a T568B on the other, that's a crossover cable.

5. A. The color code listed is the T568A standard. In the T568B standard the orange and green are opposite. LC and SC are fiber-optic connectors.

6. D. DDR4 SODIMMs have 260 pins, DDR3 SODIMMs have 204 pins, and DDR5 SODIMMs have 262 pins.

7. D. Desktop computers use dual inline memory modules (DIMMs), and laptops most commonly use small outline DIMMs (SODIMMs). Another potential laptop memory form factor is the Micro-DIMM, which is used in super lightweight laptop computers.

8. A. The Video Electronics Standards Association (VESA) introduced DisplayPort in 2008. It was designed to be an industry standard and to replace VGA and DVI. It's also backward compatible with VGA and DVI by using adapters. A DisplayPort connection is intended for video devices only, but like HDMI and USB, it can transmit audio and video simultaneously.

9. D. The first version of Thunderbolt supported 10 Gbps data rates, which is fast. Thunderbolt 2.0 joins two 10 Gbps channels together for 20 Gbps throughput. But Thunderbolt 3 and Thunderbolt 4 provide 40 Gbps.

10. B. Nano-ITX motherboards are 4.7″ square, a mini-ITX motherboard is a 6.7″ square, pico-ITX motherboards are 3.9″ × 2.8″, and mobile-ITX motherboards are 2.4″ square.

11. B, D. A 64-bit OS will run only on a 64-bit processor.

A 32-bit OS can run on either a 32-bit or a 64-bit processor, although you will not be able to fully utilize the 64-bit processor's capabilities with a 32-bit OS.

12. A, B, C. The DC power supply (DCPS) converts house current into three voltages: +5 VDC and −5 VDC for the logic circuitry and +24 VDC for the paper-transport motors.

13. A. Three RCA-like connectors at the end of a cable indicate a component video cable.

14. A. TN Liquid Crystal Displays (LCDs) have the fastest response times. The IPS is quick enough for someone interested in gaming, but plasma displays would show significant blur or lag when pushed to their limits by fast-moving gameplay. VA displays are slower than IPS displays.

15. D. A hybrid hard drive is a combination of a conventional magnetic hard disk drive and solid-state storage. The goal is to increase access speed for commonly accessed data while still providing larger capacity similar to a conventional HDD.

16. C. TCP printing allows clients with different OSs to send jobs directly to printers without worrying about intra-OS conflicts. Bonjour and AirPrint are both Apple services, and virtual printing allows you to print output to documents such as PDF files. Whenever sharing printers for remote printing, be sure to set proper user authentication on the print device.

17. B. A Cat 6a cable is a twisted pair network cable, and you are most likely to find an RJ-45 connector at the end of it. RJ-11 connectors are for phone lines. BNC connectors are network connectors but are typically used with coaxial cable. SATA connectors are used with hard drives.

18. A. The connector shown is a DVI connector used for digital video. More specifically, it is a DVI-I Dual Link connector capable of sending both analog and digital signals. The analog signals are ignored unless a DVI-I to VGA adapter is used to connect the PC to an older display using VGA. This makes the DVI-I connector more versatile than DVI-D connectors, but they are both considered digital interfaces.

19. B. Thermal printers will often use a roll of paper as opposed to individual sheets. Impact printers may also use rolls of paper but with tractor feed holes on the sides. Impact printers generally use multipart forms, since printing on multiple copies at once is their unique ability.

20. B. Laser printers need toner cartridges, impact printers need ink ribbons, and inkjet printers use ink cartridges. Thermal printers heat up paper to produce images.

21. A. An imaging drum is a photosensitive drum that can hold a high negative charge if it's not exposed to light. It is dark inside an electrophotographic (EP) printer, except when the laser scanning assembly shines on particular areas of the photosensitive drum, reducing the high negative charge to a much lower negative charge. Toner itself is negatively charged and repelled by the highly negative charged areas but attracted to the areas with a very low charge. The use of varying negative charges is what facilitates the printing process. When replacing a photosensitive drum, it's best to avoid exposing it to light.

22. C. Mini-ITX motherboards are 6.7" square (or more precisely, 6.69" square). ATX motherboards are 12" × 9.6". A micro-ATX motherboard is a 9.6" square, and pico-ITX motherboards are 3.9" × 2.8".

23. D. Resolution is the number of pixels used to draw a computer screen. Refresh rate determines how many times per second the screen can be redrawn. Frame rate tells you how many frames per second the original content was filmed in. Aspect ratio defines the dimensions (width × height) of an image.

24. B. In a RAID-5 array, each stripe places data on n−1 disks, and parity computed from the data is placed on the remaining disk. The parity is interleaved across all the drives in the array so that neighboring stripes have parity on different disks. Said differently, you lose the equivalent of one hard disk worth of storage to hold the parity information. RAID stands for Redundant Array of Inexpensive (or Independent) Disks.

25. A. The Hardware Security Module (HSM) is a piece of hardware that can be removed and is used to hold encryption keys for a system. It differs from TPM (Trusted Platform Module) implementations in that TPM is a chip on the motherboard, not a separate piece of hardware, and TPM can also be software. TPM is used to encrypt hard drives. The BIOS (or UEFI) is the program the CPU uses to start up the system after being powered on. ITX is a motherboard form factor.

26. D. Many modern multifunction devices have the ability to connect to a cloud and email and store scanned documents and images directly from the device without requiring a connected PC. The documents are made accessible worldwide via services such as Dropbox, Evernote, or Google Drive.

27. C. The ability of multifunction devices to email and scan without a PC means that these devices need to be hardened the same way any other device with a network connection would. Secure protocols need to be present to protect sensitive corporate information.

28. D. Server Message Block (SMB) is the secure protocol used when scanning documents from a multifunction device to a server. TPM and HSM are security encryption devices, not protocols. SNMP is Simple Network Management Protocol, used to gather information from managed switches and other devices across a network.

29. A. Heat sinks are often made of metal, with many fins on them to increase surface area and dissipate heat faster. Many modern CPU coolers will have both a fan (which requires power) and the finned metal heat sink. Passive heat sinks do not use power (so no fan), and secondary cooling fans are generally attached to the case.

30. A, B, C, D. While faxing is not used as often as it once was, it is still a feature available on some MFDs. Email, scanning, and printing are also common features.

31. A, C. VGA is an analog video connector, and RJ-11 connectors are used with analog phone lines and modems. Modems receive a digital signal from a computer, then modulate that signal to analog to transmit over analog lines. On the other end, they demodulate the signal into a digital one again that a computer or other digital device can understand. RJ-45 connectors are used in networking, and HDMI carries digital audio and video signals.

32. B. The port shown is a DisplayPort. There is also a mini-DisplayPort, but that is not shown.

33. A, B. With up-plugging, you can put a smaller PCIe card into a larger slot, even though it does not fill it up completely. For example, you can insert an x8 card into an x16 slot. The x8 card won't completely fill the slot, but it will work at x8 speeds. It's important to note that a motherboard doesn't necessarily support this feature, so if you plan to use a smaller card in a larger PCIe slot, make sure the motherboard supports up-plugging or the card will run at 1x speed.

34. C. RAID-1 is called disk mirroring; it writes data simultaneously to both drives. If one drive fails, the other still has a working copy of the data. RAID-0 is disk striping and does not provide fault tolerance. RAID-5 is striping with parity and provides fault tolerance, but it requires a minimum of three hard disks.

35. A. During the cleaning step, a rubber blade inside the toner cartridge scrapes any toner left on the drum into a used toner receptacle, and a fluorescent lamp discharges any remaining charge on the imaging drum, making it neutral and ready to be charged again by the corona wire (or charging roller).

36. B. The audio connector on the front-panel or top-panel will use a round, 3.5 mm connector. You can plug speakers or a headset with a boom microphone into it.

37. C, D. With most dual-channel motherboards, RAM will work just fine if one module is installed. However, you will get better performance if you fill the entire bank. If there is only one RAM module installed in one channel, then you can't possibly take advantage of the dual-channel architecture.

38. D. There are five major versions of PCIe currently specified: 1.x, 2.x, 3.0, 4.0 and 5.0. Each version doubles the data transfer rate of the version before. For the four versions, a single bidirectional lane operates at a data rate of 250 MBps, 500 MBps, approximately 1 GBps, roughly 2 GBps, and nearly 4 GBps respectively. In any version of PCIe, there can be up to 16 lanes, so for example, in theory, a PCIe 4.0 x16 connector could transfer nearly 32 GB/s (1.969 GB/s per lane, x 16 lanes). You might find it helpful in your studies to locate or create a chart of the different versions and bandwidth for x1, x4, x8 and x16.

39. A, D. When installing or replacing a power supply, always make sure that it has enough wattage to power the components in the computer. In addition, it must have enough of the right connectors to connect to all the components that require their own power. Multiple rail and dual voltage are optional features.

40. A, B. Faster hard drives transfer more data than slower hard drives, but there is no specific correlation between hard drive speed and its life span. The downsides to faster hard drives can be increased battery usage and heat production.

41. C. The slot described is a PCI slot. It used a 32-bit or 64-bit bus. The first version was released in 1992, and they remained popular until PCIe was developed. Some motherboards have PCI and PCIe slots on them. PCI and PCIe are not physically compatible. VESA and AGP are legacy slots for video cards.

42. C. Print servers need to have the appropriate drivers for all operating systems that will be clients. It's possible that this print server does not have the macOS driver installed.

43. B. The connector shown is USB Type B. It will plug into the USB peripheral device and is commonly used by printers.

44. B, C. Liquid cooling systems are generally quieter than air-based systems that use fans, and they are more efficient at cooling the processor. However, they are more complex to install, and if the liquid were to leak out, it could cause damage to internal components.

45. C, D. Impact printers create images by physically striking the paper, which can wear down the printhead. Always check that. Also, impact printers most often use tractor-feed mechanisms to load the paper, and they can wear down or get bogged down by paper debris as well.

46. C. PCIe uses lanes. Each lane between any two intercommunicating devices consists of a separate pair of wires, one for each direction of traffic, which dramatically increases speed.

47. B. Of the liquid crystal display (LCD) choices given, IPS have the better viewing angle. LCDs can be twisted nematic (TN), in-plane switching (IPS), or vertical alignment (VA). VA has a greater contrast ratio, but it has a narrower viewing angle than IPS. TN is legacy technology. LED refers to a type of backlighting, and plasma displays are not a type of LCD.

48. B, C. A home server PC should be able to handle media streaming as well as file and printer sharing. A dedicated print server is not likely needed, though, as the operating system can function as a print server. A gigabit NIC will be helpful to manage the network traffic, and a RAID -1 or RAID 5 array can help recover from hard drive failure.

49. B. The x8 card won't completely fill the x16 slot, but it will work at x8 speeds if up-plugging is supported by the motherboard. Otherwise, the specification requires up-plugged devices to operate at only the x1 rate.

50. B. Secure Boot is an option enabled in system firmware. BIOS is not technically advanced enough to manage Secure Boot, but its successor UEFI is. AMI (American Megatrends) is a BIOS manufacturer, and SATA is a type of hard drive technology.

51. A. DDR3 DIMMs have 240 pins. DDR4 and DDR5 DIMMs have 288 pins, but they are not interchangeable and have notches (module keys) in different locations to prevent installing the incorrect modules into a motherboard. SODIMMs are laptop RAM, not desktop RAM.

52. A. The module key, also called a notch, on a DDR5 DIMM is at the center of the module whereas the DDR4 DIMM is slightly off center. Both are sold with heat sinks attached and come in multiple colors. Physically, they're the same size.

53. D. Multithreading is a feature of processors that divides physical processor cores into logical cores, and software processes into multiple threads that can be run concurrently on those logical cores. As a result, the operating system can schedule two processes at the same time on each physical core. Intel's implementation of multithreading is called hyperthreading.

54. A. An impact printer typically requires paper that always feeds at a consistent rate. To achieve this, the paper will have holes on the outside edges, which is fed into the printer using a tractor-feed mechanism. Thermal printers use special paper and heat to create images, whereas laser printers use the electrophotographic process. Inkjet printers spray drops of ink onto paper.

55. A. ATX motherboards are common in desktop computers and measure 12″ × 9.6″. They are the largest motherboards commonly used in personal computers today.

56. D. The motor that makes the printhead carriage move is also often called the carriage motor or carriage stepper motor. It has a belt attached to it, the carriage belt, which moves the printhead carriage back and forth.

57. A, C, D. The CPU must support VM Display Mode Extension; on an Intel processor, it's called Virtualization Technology (Intel VT). The processor must be 64-bit and have second-level address translation (SLAT). Virtualization also requires the Windows Pro edition or better. Virtualization must be enabled in the BIOS/UEFI and may be found under different names depending on the motherboard manufacturer.

58. C. The most common analog video connector is a VGA connector. It is usually blue in color, arranged in a D shape with 15 pins arranged in 3 rows.

59. A. Thunderbolt v1 and v2 both provide 20 Gbps of data bandwidth. Thunderbolt 3 doubles the data rate to 40 Gbps. Thunderbolt 3 and Thunderbolt 4 can also provide the power the device needs. USB 3.0 can only provide about 5 W of power and is much slower at 5 Gbps. eSATA is also slower and doesn't provide power, although eSATAp does. DisplayPort is also slower and provides no power, unless it's DisplayPort over USB.

60. C. The order of steps is processing, charging, exposing, developing, transferring, fusing, and cleaning.

61. B, C. PCI slots and adapters are manufactured in 3.3 V and 5 V versions. Adapters are keyed to fit in a slot based on their voltage requirements. Universal adapters are keyed to fit in slots based on either of the two voltages. PCI has largely been replaced by PCIe, but there are still implementations of it, and it is still on the CompTIA A+ exam objectives.

62. A. Trusted Platform Module (TPM) is an international standard for a dedicated security coprocessor, or cryptoprocessor. Coupled with a BIOS/UEFI, it can be configured to boot the system only after authenticating the boot device. LoJack is a feature for locating stolen or missing devices, Secure Boot is designed to prevent malicious software from loading before a PC boots, and BitLocker is a feature of Windows Pro and higher editions that is used to encrypt entire storage drives.

63. A. The transfer corona assembly is given a positive charge, which is transferred to the paper, which in turn pulls the negatively charged toner from the photosensitive imaging drum. This is the transferring phase of the laser printer imaging process.

64. C. This is an eight-pin PCIe power connector. They also come in 6-pin configurations.

65. D. After installing a new printer, it's good practice to print a test page to ensure functionality.

66. B. The high-voltage power supply (HVPS) provides the high voltages used by both the charging corona and the transfer corona during the laser printer imaging process. The printer will likely have a second power supply that provides power to the circuit boards. Caution needs to be observed when working inside any laser printer because of the danger inherent in the two power supplies.

67. C. RAID-10 (also known as RAID-1+0) provides fault tolerance to RAID-0 through the RAID-1 mirroring of each disk in the RAID-0 striped set. It requires a minimum of four hard disks.

68. C. The image is of a SATA connector, commonly used for internal hard drives.

69. C. To use a second display on a desktop computer, you need to install a second video adapter or have one video adapter with two display interfaces. Laptops often have an external display interface and are capable of providing video to the built-in screen and an external display at the same time.

70. A. DDR3 and DDR4 memory slots are both keyed, but the keys are in different places. DDR3 has 240 pins and DDR4 has 288 pins. Therefore, the memory will not fit into the slots on the motherboard.

71. C. During the transferring step, the positively charged paper pulls the negatively charged toner from the photosensitive drum at the line of contact between the roller and the paper.

72. A. Duplexing is printing on the front and back. Other common options or settings include orientation (portrait or landscape), collating (printing pages in sets such as 1, 2, 3, 1, 2, 3) and print quality (such as draft or high resolution).

73. C. A Blu-ray Disc Extra Large (BDXL) can store up to 128 GB of data, (Quad BDXL) although most for sale boast only 100 GB of storage (Triple BDXL). Blu-ray is the latest rendition of optical disks, but DVDs are still available, and come in single layer (SL), dual layer (DL), single side (SS) and dual side (DS) formats. DVD-18 (DS, DL) hold approximately 16 GB of data. DVD-10 (DS, SL) can hold approximately 9GB, and DVD-9 (SS, DL) hold approximately 8 GB of storage. DVD-9 and DVD-10 can both be DVD+R or DVD-R format but DVD-18 can only be the DVD+R format.

74. C. Inkjet printers typically use a reservoir of ink (also known as an ink cartridge), a pump, and a nozzle to print images. Empty cartridges need to be replaced.

75. D. The number designation of 3600 in DDR4 3600 indicates bus speed of 3,600 MHz. To find the throughput, multiply the bus speed by 8. DDR4 3600 therefore is the same as PC4 28,800 with a peak transfer rate of 28,800 Mbps. (3,600,000 cycles per second x 8 = 28,800,000 bits per second. Divide by 1000 to get Mbps = 28,800).

76. C. Multiply the 5200 bus speed by 8 to get the bits per second that can be transferred in and out of the RAM module. The PC5 designation means that it is DDR5, and the 41,600 means that it can (theoretically) transfer 41,600 Mbps (megabits per second).

77. B. iPads and iPhones can automatically detect AirPrint-enabled printers on their local network and print to them without requiring the installation of a driver. Bonjour is a service that works with both Macs and Windows devices but requires some configuration. TCP printing uses an IP Address to connect to a printer. Virtual printing sends the output to something else such as a .pdf file.

78. B. To communicate with other computers on a network, you need a network interface card (NIC). A wireless access point (WAP) is a wireless hub that many wireless devices communicate with, and WPA is a wireless security standard. A KVM switch allows you to have multiple systems attached to the same keyboard, video, and mouse. Other types of expansion cards (that could use the same slot as a NIC) include but are not limited to video cards, sound cards, storage cards, TV tuner cards, and riser cards.

79. B. The printer driver uses a page description language (PDL) to convert the data being printed into the format that the printer can understand. The driver also ensures that the printer is ready to print. PDL stands for page description language, which specifies the printed page layout. The print queue holds print jobs that are waiting to be printed, the print spooler manages the printing process, including locating the right printer driver.

80. C. Windows comes with many drivers for different devices, but if the manufacturer has provided a specific printer driver, it's often best to install that printer driver first, then connect the device. In this case, the user will be printing mostly graphics, so the PostScript driver will provide better printing for them. PostScript drivers are not dependent on the hardware, so the printed graphic will look the same regardless of what device it is printed on.

81. B. Printer Control Language (PCL) drivers depend on the printer hardware to create some of the effects such as filling in areas and making underlines. The PC releases the print job to the printer to finish, making the PC and application available to the user more quickly.

82. D. The power supply fan is used to cool the power supply and the inside of the computer case. This fan draws air from inside the case into vents in the power supply. This pulls hot air through the power supply so that it can be blown out of the case, which also causes cooler air to be drawn in through vents in the case.

83. A. A solid-state drive (SSD) is the best choice for a hard drive when access speed is the most important characteristic. A conventional magnetic hard disk drive (HDD) is slower. Secure Digital (SD) is a memory card format, not a hard drive type. BD-R is a Blu-ray disk format.

84. C. USB 3.0 supports 5 Gbps, USB 1.0 supports 12 Mbps, USB 2.0 supports 480 Mbps, and USB 3.1 Gen 2 supports 10 Gbps.

85. C. With RAID 10, drives are set up as mirrors, then those mirrors are striped. A minimum of two drives are needed to create a mirror, then another two to stripe the data for a total of four drives. The computer already has one drive in it. That drive would be mirrored, then striped, so three more drives are needed. RAID 10 provides both extra speed and fault tolerance.

86. A. RAID-0 uses a minimum of two drives, writing different bits of data to each drive at the same time to improve speed, but it doesn't offer any fault tolerance. RAID-1 is disk mirroring, which provides some fault tolerance but no speed improvement. RAID-5 and RAID-10 improve both speed and fault tolerance.

87. A. A processor that exhibits a multicore architecture has multiple completely separate processor dies in the same package. The operating system and applications see multiple processors in the same way that they see multiple processors in separate sockets. 64-bit refers to the width of the data bus. An integrated GPU means that the graphics processor is also on the CPU package, and multiprocessor refers to more than one physical socket on a motherboard.

88. B. All are digital video disk (DVD) technologies. A single-sided, single-layer (SS, SL) DVD provides about 4.7 GB of storage. A dual-sided (DS) disk will double that capacity to 9.4 GB. Adding a second layer, or dual-layer (DL), adds more capacity, but the technology does not double the capacity of a single layer. A single-sided, dual-layer (SS, DL) disk has a capacity of about 8.5 GB. There is no DVD-R SS, TL, but a DVD+R DS, DL holds nearly 17 GB of data. The -R refers to the encoding scheme. There is also a + R format. There are also number designations to identify how many sides and layers a DVD has. DVD-9 is single side, dual layer, DVD-10 is dual side, single layer, DVD-18 is dual side, dual layer.

89. D. Many power supplies have a two-position slider switch called a dual voltage switch. It can be set for 110–120 V or 220–240 V, depending on what local power specifications are.

90. D. Mobile-ITX motherboards are 2.4″ square, MicroATX motherboards are 9.6″ square, mini-ITX motherboards are 6.7″ square, and Pico-ITX motherboards are 3.9″ × 2.8″.

91. C. Dot-matrix printers use printheads that strike an ink ribbon, which presses up against the paper to make an image. Therefore, they are impact printers. Laser printers use a photosensitive drum to create the image, inkjet printers use an ink reservoir (cartridge) and spray nozzles to produce an image on paper using dots of ink, and thermal printers use heat to produce an image on special heat-sensitive paper.

92. A, B. Sockets that support Intel processors are currently named starting with the letters LGA, such as LGA1700 and LGA2066. Socket names that start with AM or FM will support AMD processors and not Intel processors.

93. B. A solid-state drive (SSD) will provide them with the highest capacity of the four options and also give them immediate access. Network attached storage (NAS) speaks to its connection and availability, not capacity. If the client required file sharing as well, then using a NAS would be the proper choice. Secure Digital (SD) is a memory card format and does not offer the capacity or immediacy they need. BD-R is a Blu-ray disk format. It has good storage capabilities, but not the immediacy for editing.

94. B, C. Digital displays will have a digital interface, such as DVI-D, HDMI, or mini-HDMI. Composite connectors are rarely used on displays, and VGA is analog, not digital.

95. A, B, D. The four virtual printing options are print to file, print to PDF, print to XPS, and print to image.

96. C. There are five major versions of PCIe currently specified: 1.x, 2.x, 3.0, 4.0, and 5.0. For the five versions, a single bidirectional lane operates at a data rate of 250 MBps, 500 MBps, approximately 1 GBps, roughly 2 GBps, and nearly 4 GBps, respectively. Each PCIe slot can have up to 16 lanes, the number of lanes being indicated by x1, x4, x8, x16. (The x is pronounced as *by*.) Therefore, a PCIe 3 x1 slot can support up to 1 GBps of bandwidth.

97. D. Laser printers incorporate a fuser assembly, which uses two rollers that apply pressure and heat to fuse the plastic toner particles to the paper.

98. A. During the charging step, the charging corona uses a high voltage to apply a strong, uniform negative charge (around −600 VDC) to the surface of the imaging drum.

99. A. When installing dual-channel RAM, be sure that the RAM modules both have the same parameters. In some cases, you might even need to make sure they come from the same manufacturer. RAM for channeled motherboards is often sold in packs such as a pack of two RAM modules for dual-channel motherboards, three modules for triple-channel motherboards, and four modules for quad-channel motherboards.

100. D. Carriage motors are components in inkjet printers. Laser printer components include a fuser assembly, imaging drum, transfer belt, transfer roller, pickup roller, separation pads, and a duplexing assembly.

101. A. A laser printer uses various high-voltage biases inside the case, and high voltages can create harmful ozone.

102. D. The purpose of a KVM switch is to allow you to have multiple systems attached to the same keyboard, video display, and mouse. You can use these three devices with only one system at a time, and the KVM switch will have a dial or buttons to allow you to switch between systems.

103. B. To get this printer off of the original user's desk, it probably needs to be its own print server. Installing an integrated (or stand-alone) print server with a network connection should work well in this situation. Installing a network card wouldn't take care of the sharing aspect of the problem. You need a network connection before you can use TCP/IP settings to connect to it. AirPrint is Apple's wireless printing, which would also need to have the printer connected to a wireless network.

104. B. Clean pickup rollers (and other rubber rollers) with mild soap and water and not alcohol. Alcohol can dry out the rollers, making them brittle and ineffective. A dry cloth will not remove the dirt or debris, and compressed air would just blow the debris into other internal printer components.

105. D. During the developing step, toner is attracted to areas of the drum where an image has been written by the laser. Those areas have a slight negative charge (−100 VDC) as opposed to unexposed areas of the drum and the developing roller (to which the toner is stuck), which each have a charge of −600 VDC.

106. C. The primary factor in determining data throughput for a magnetic hard drive is the spin rate, which is measured in revolutions per minute (rpm). Higher spin rates will result in faster data reads and writes and increase data throughput.

107. D. The white connector is a 20-pin ATX power connector. You will also see 24-pin versions, which have two rows of 12 pins each. The 24-pin versions are ATX12V. Whether 20 or 24 pin, these are often labeled P1.

108. C. To make information available to the rest of the computer more quickly, hard drive manufacturers increase the speed at which the hard drive platters spin, which is measured in revolutions per minute (rpm). The downside of higher speed is usually more heat generated by the drive, so faster hard drives may require additional cooling in the case.

109. A, B, C. The ATX, MicroATX, and mini-ITX motherboard form factors can all be mounted inside a standard ATX case. The mini-ITX will have only three of the four mounting holes line up with the case, but the rear interfaces are placed in the same location as those on ATX motherboards.

110. C. If memory supports ECC, check bits are generated and stored with the data. If one of the eight memory bits is in error, ECC can correct the error. ECC tends to be more expensive than non-ECC memory, so it is more often found in servers than in workstations.

111. A, D. USB flash drives and SD cards are hot swappable. (In the case of USB, be sure that the flash drive does not contain key file system files needed for the computer to run!) Hybrid SSDs might or might not be hot swappable and are larger than USB and SD drives. PATA devices are legacy technology and not hot swappable.

112. C. This SLI-ready motherboard has three PCIe x16 slots (every other slot, starting with the top one), one PCIe x1 slot (second slot from the top), and two PCI slots (first and third slots from the bottom). Notice the latch and tab that secures the x16 adapters in place by their hooks.

113. B, D. Dual-channel motherboards have two banks of two RAM slots. They are usually color-coded such that the two slots of the same color belong to different channels. For best performance, a RAM module needs to be installed into each channel, so two can be accessed at a time. It's always best to refer to the motherboard manual for proper RAM placement. Some motherboards will revert to single-channel mode if, for example, three RAM modules were placed in a dual-channel motherboard with four slots. Channels are typically marked with letters.

114. A. The boot sequence of a computer is changed in the BIOS/UEFI settings.

115. C, D. Typical front- or top-panel connectors include USB, audio, power button, power light, drive activity lights, and the reset button. SATA and PCIe connectors are found inside the case, on the motherboard.

116. A. The USB 3.0 standard doesn't specify a cable length limitation, but it does recommend a cable length of 3 meters or less. USB 2.0 cables can be up to 5 meters in length. USB4 cables should be only 0.8 meters. The manager will need a USB hub, and to extend the distance the manager could purchase active USB cables, some of which have an external power supply or extra USB A connector for extra power, or a Cat 5/Cat 6 USB extender.

117. C. Depending on the printer, you may be able to update the printer's information in Devices and Printers; otherwise, a firmware update may be needed. Firmware upgrades can offer newer features that are not available on previous versions.

118. D. An automatic document feeder (ADF) is a device that sits on top of a flatbed scanner. It is used to pull a stack of papers through and scan them one at a time without user intervention. Some MFDs will scan the front and back of the paper at the same time.

119. D. PCI is a shared-bus topology, so mixing 33 MHz and 66 MHz adapters in a 66 MHz system will slow all adapters to 33 MHz.

120. B. In the exposing step, the image is written to the photosensitive imaging drum. Wherever the laser beam touches, the photosensitive drum's charge is severely reduced from –600 VDC to a slight negative charge (around –100 VDC). As the drum rotates, a pattern of exposed areas is formed, representing the image to be printed.

428   Appendix ▪ Answers to the Review Questions

121. D. Passive cooling systems come in a variety of models, and some are very effective. The defining characteristic is that they do not use a fan or require a power source. Their advantage is that they are the ultimate in cooling system quiet because there is no fan or pump running.

122. A, C, D. The UEFI configures many hardware components and settings, such as system date and time, boot sequence, enabling and disabling devices, clock speeds, virtualization support, fans, and UEFI/Boot security.

123. A. The typical increasing order of capacity and distance from the processor die is L1 cache, L2 cache, L3 cache, RAM, and HDD/SSD. The closest caches are located on the processor die.

124. A. The picture shows a motherboard power connector that can convert between ATX (20 pin) and ATX12V (24 pin) power connectors.

125. A, D. A pin grid array (PGA) socket has holes to receive the pins that are on the CPU. The land grid array (LGA) is a newer technology that places the delicate pins on the motherboard instead of on the CPU.

126. C. A duplexing assembly is used for two-sided printing. After the first page is printed, it's fed into the duplexing assembly, turned over, and fed back into the paper feed assembly.

127. A, C. The DC power supply (DCPS), also sometimes called the low voltage power supply (LVPS), provides power for the logic boards and motors, whereas the high voltage power supply (HVPS) provides higher voltages for the toner transfer process. The printer's logic circuitry and motors require low voltages, between +5 VDC and +24 VDC. The DC power supply (DCPS) converts house current into three voltages: +5 VDC and −5 VDC for the logic circuitry and +24 VDC for the paper-transport motors. This component also runs the fan that cools the internal components of the printer.

128. A. The top module is DDR3, and the bottom one is DDR4. DDR3 has 240 pins whereas DDR4 has 288 pins. DDR5 also has 288 pins, but the DDR5 key position may vary depending on whether it is UDIMM or RDIMM.

129. D. Never ship a printer anywhere with a toner cartridge installed! The jostling that happens during shipping could cause toner to spill out of the cartridge and all over the inside of the printer, and a toner spill is difficult to clean up. Remove the toner cartridge first. You can put it in a sealed, airtight bag to ship if needed.

130. A. Most internal video adapters today are PCIe cards. You might still find PCI video cards available. ISA is a legacy expansion slot type not used today. VGA and DVI are types of display connectors, not expansion slot types.

131. D. The order of steps is processing, charging, exposing, developing, transferring, fusing, and cleaning.

132. A, B. Apple created Bonjour and AirPrint. Bonjour helps many devices find each other on a network, not just printers.

133. D. Before you print to an inkjet printer, you must ensure that the device is calibrated. Calibration is the process by which a device is brought within functional specifications. For example, inkjet printers need their printheads aligned so that they print evenly and don't print funny-looking letters and unevenly spaced lines.

134. C. Thermal printers use a heating element. It heats up spots on special waxy, heat-sensitive paper to form the image.

135. A. When a laser printer requests maintenance, it's because it has reached a certain page count. Apply a proper maintenance kit (one recommended by the manufacturer) and then clear the service message.

136. D. The connectors are a four-pin RJ-11, typically used for telephone installations, and an eight-pin RJ-45 connector, used on UTP and STP for network transmissions.

137. C. The connector shown is a type of mini form factor (MFF) fiber-optic connector called a Lucent connector (LC). It's especially popular for use with Fibre Channel adapters, fast storage area networks, and Gigabit Ethernet adapters.

138. A. The correct order for a T568B cable is white/orange, orange, white/green, blue, white/blue, green, white/brown, brown. In the T568A standard, the orange and green cables are swapped. The blue and brown wires don't change position between the two standards.

139. A. Cable television installations typically use RG-6 but may also use RG-59 cable. RG-6 is slightly thicker, can run longer distances, and supports digital signals. RG-59 is suited only for analog TV signals and is used for some security cameras.

140. D. RG-6 is a better choice because it supports digital signals and has a longer range (304 meters, or 1,000 feet). RG-59 can run up to 228 meters (750 feet). Both have impedance of 75 ohms, and both use BNC connectors or F-type connectors. RG-6 is usually better insulated and will have less signal loss. While the RG-59 might work, if it doesn't, would you want to do the job over?

141. A, D. Multimode fiber (MMF) and unshielded twisted pair (UTP) Cat 6 and newer support 10 Gbps transmission speeds. Cat 5 supports up to 100 Mbps, and Cat 5e supports up to 1,000 Mbps.

142. D. Shielded twisted pair (STP) cabling has a foil shield surrounding the wire pairs to decrease electrical interference. Some STP cables also shield individual wire pairs. Unshielded twisted pair (UTP) does not have the shielding. Both types use RJ-45 connectors, can follow the T568A wiring standard, and can be produced as plenum-rated cable that does not produce poisonous gas when burned.

143. D. The connectors shown are ST connectors, which are used with fiber-optic cable. ST connectors attach with a BNC-like locking mechanism.

144. B. The connector shown is a subscriber connector (SC), also known as a square connector because of its shape. It's a fiber-optic cable connector. ST and LC are also types of fiber-optic connectors, and MFF is multimode fiber-optic cable.

145. B. Cat 5e cable can support speeds of 1 Gbps. Cat 5 has a maximum of 100 Mbps. Cat 6 and newer can support 10 Gbps. Cat 8 cabling can support speeds around 40 Gbps, but only for short distances. To run at a given speed, all components of the network must support that speed, including NICs, cable, routers, and switches.

146. A. Cat 5 UTP can transmit data at speeds up to 100 Mbps, for a distance of 100 meters. Cat 5e is capable of 1 Gbps. Cat 6 and newer can support 10 Gbps. Single mode is a type of fiber-optic cable and is very fast.

147. A. Most network cables are coated with a plastic PVC coating, which produces toxic gas when burned. Plenum-rated cables are coated with a Teflon-like material that is not poisonous when burned.

148. C. The 16-bit SCSI drives were connected by a Molex type connector, two rows of pins, totaling 68 pins.

149. D. On small form factor devices like tablets, the video-out connector is the small version of HDMI: mini-HDMI. It resembles a USB-C but is still tapered on only one side. To connect to an HDMI display, you would need a mini-HDMI-to-HDMI adapter.

150. D. Lightning was introduced in autumn 2012 and still works on the Apple 13, released in 2021. RS-232 is a type of serial connection that dates back to 1960. Mini-HDMI is a smaller version of HDMI for smaller devices and will require a mini-HDMI-to-HDMI adapter to plug in a display. MicroUSB is a type of USB connector that was popular for a time.

151. A. Thunderbolt 3 cables work as USB-C cables and are fully compatible. Thunderbolt 3 are capable of transferring at 40 Gbps, but USB 3.1 (on USB-C) can only reach 10 Gbps. USB4 is able to reach 40 Gbps.

152. D. USB-C is the only one of these that can be inserted correctly both as you try the first time or flip over and try again. Micro-USB resembles USB-C but it is not "flippable"—one edge is slightly tapered. DB9 and RS232 are legacy serial connectors.

153. C. DB9 was the "D" format, 9-pin serial connector type that was the standard format for keyboards, mice, and other small peripherals. It was also used for communications between a PC and some managed switches. Small Computer Systems Interface (SCSI) is a type of drive connector and technology that would allow up to 15 drives on one daisy chain. The PS/2 connector, also called a mini-DIN, is newer than a DB9 connector but older than USB. It has 6 pins and was used for connecting mice (color-coded green) and keyboards (color-coded purple). Lightning connectors are used on Apple devices.

154. D. Triple channel memory is achieved when three matching memory modules are installed, permitting data to be spread and memory accessed simultaneously. The effect is lower memory latency, triple the access speed (compared to single channel), and triple the 64-bit communication path.

155. D. M.2 is a solid-state hard drive form factor, measuring 22 mm wide. Its lengths vary between 30 mm, 42 mm, 60 mm, 80 mm, and 120 mm. NVMe is a storage protocol, not a form factor. Many M.2 drives use the NVMe protocol. SATA and PCIe are bus interface standards found on a motherboard.

156. C. Solid-state drives (SSDs) come in multiple form factors, such as a "stick" resembling a memory module (M.2) or a 2.5″ box housed in metal. SSDs also come in 3.5″ form factor. M.2 and mSATA are form factors for SSDs. NVMe is a protocol for storing data that is commonly used with M.2 drives, although M.2 drives can also use the older Advanced Host Controller Interface (AHCI).

157. B. eSATA is external SATA, a type of connector for external SATA drives. Nonvolatile Memory Express (NVMe) is a protocol and communications interface designed to connect small SSD storage to the PCIe bus of a motherboard. The Advanced Host Controller Interface (AHCI) technology preceded NVMe, and was much slower. M.2 and mSATA are form factors for SSDs that connect directly to a motherboard. An mSATA drive looks similar to M.2, but the connectors are slightly different and mSATA only connects to the slower SATA bus using AHCI technology. M.2 drives can be either NVMe or AHCI, so checking documentation is important.

158. B. The system BIOS/UEFI settings include password protection to not allow system bootup unless someone enters a password. This would prohibit the OS from loading upon boot.

159. A. Thermal paste is like a grease that ensures that the heat generated from the CPU is efficiently conducted away and into the heat sink. New coolers (fan/heat sink combinations) often come with thermal pads (paste) preinstalled. Lowering the CPU speed might result in less heat generated, but it would obviously also result in degraded performance.

160. A. A USB expansion card would utilize an expansion slot on the motherboard to provide two to four additional USB ports. Not included as an option, but a USB hub is a cost-effective fix as well, and some will provide additional power for USB-powered devices.

161. B. The 3D printer can be attached locally or, if allowed by the manufacturer, accessible by shared network. There are many different methods and materials used for 3D printing, but the CompTIA A+ objectives want you to know about the following two of them. 3D printers use either an extruder and filament to create a 3D object by heating the plastic filament and extruding one layer at a time through a nozzle as the nozzle and print bed move, or they use a vat of resin that is hardened with a laser, then the excess resin washed away leaving the 3D object. A smartcard reader is used to integrate smartcards as an authentication factor for your system. A touchpad coupled with finger movement on it can be used to replace mouse input. A VR headset is used for experiencing virtual reality.

162. B, C. The speed of RAM that a computer can use is limited by the speed of the motherboard's memory bus and the speed of RAM supported by the processor, especially now that the memory controller is part of the processor. Even if faster RAM is purchased, it will run at the slower speed of the memory bus or what the processor supports.

163. D. Although the more fun answer is to purchase a new display, the question asks what would be the least expensive, and that is to purchase an HDMI-to-VGA adapter. There are adapters for almost everything on a computer system, so in a case like this, that would be the quickest and least expensive solution.

164. A. There are several types of 3D printers. Material extrusion printers work by pushing material through a nozzle as the nozzle and possibly a print bed move to place the material. The materials used are as diverse as plastic, metal, and human tissue. Vat polymerization 3D printers use a light source to harden resin in a vat. When the liquid is drained away, the hardened product remains. Powder bed fusion types deposit one thin layer of material at a time that is hardened where needed. Each of these has subtypes, and this is not an exhaustive list of the types of 3D printers.

165. C. Extrusion type 3D printers heat material called filament from a roll and force it through a narrow nozzle while the nozzle is moved to the appropriate spot to build an object layer by layer. Filament is available in different thickness and characteristics, so it's important to verify exactly what type of filament the printer uses before ordering it.

166. D. Cat 6 and newer can support 10 Gbps, but Cat 6 can only go 55 meters at 10 Gbps. To go 100 meters you'll need Cat 6a. Cat 5e's top speed is 1 Gbps, and Cat 5 is only 100 Mbps.

167. A. Category 6 cable will work for the implementation described. It is capable of 10 Gbps but only for a distance of 55 meters. Category 6a can go 100 meters at 10 Gbps. Cat 7 is not an IEEE standard, nor is it approved by TIA/EIA, and it doesn't use a standard RJ45 connector. Cat 8 is IEEE approved; it can support 10 Gbps over 100 meters and can support 40 GBps, but only over very short distances (24 meters), which makes it good for things like a storage area network (SAN). Cat 7 and Cat 8 are not on the CompTIA A+ objectives this time, so don't spend too much time on them right now.

168. B. Direct burial cable is made to go underground without any kind of conduit around it. The coating is made to be waterproof and block moisture vapor as well. A good cable will also protect against degradation from sunlight.

169. A, D. Shielded twisted pair (STP) has at least one extra layer of shielding to protect the cable from crosstalk and interference. Some types of STP have shielding around each wire. With all the extra material, STP tends to be less flexible and more expensive than unshielded twisted pair (UTP). Being shielded or unshielded doesn't affect the maximum transmission speed of a cable, and UTP is not suitable for direct burial.

170. D. Only fiber-optic cables use pulses of light to transmit data. The other three listed are types of copper cable that use electrical charges to transmit data signals.

171. B. Data transmissions can be parallel, meaning multiple bits at the same time in parallel with each other, or they can be serial, meaning only one bit at a time. It would seem that parallel transmissions should be faster, but they aren't. In fact, modern peripheral and hard drive cables all send data in series.

172. B. eSATA connectors provide a way to access the SATA bus via an external connector. Serial Advanced Technology Attachment (SATA) is a type of internal drive connection and bus that replaced the older parallel ATA (PATA). SATAe is a motherboard bus that supports both SATA and PCIe. HDMI is an audio/video interface.

173. C. Integrated Device Electronics (IDE) cables were used to connect parallel ATA (Advanced Technology Attachment) drives to a motherboard. PATA cables had 40 connector pins and could connect two hard drives per cable. Most motherboards at the time had two IDE connectors, so they were capable of connecting four IDE hard drives. PATA were replaced by serial ATA (SATA) drives and cables, which are much faster and only connect one drive per cable, simplifying installation. Several SATA connectors can be on a single motherboard.

IDE and ATA are often used interchangeably, although they aren't exactly the same. IDE was the parallel interface that used an ATA protocol. SATA is a serial, as opposed to a parallel, ATA connection. A UPS is an uninterruptible power supply, and eSATA is external SATA.

174. D. Typically in a motherboard with multichannel support, the channels will be labeled with a letter (A, B, C, D). To take advantage of the multichannel capabilities, you would install one RAM module in each channel. Lowest numbered slots are usually filled first, so you would use slot 1 (or zero, if numbering started there) of each channel. You should, of course, always consult the motherboard documentation.

175. A. A part of the hard disk drive (or SDD) being used as if it was RAM is known as virtual memory. Virtual memory works by moving a chunk of information, called a page, to a file named `pagefile.sys`. `pagefile.sys` is literally the file on the hard drive where information in virtual memory is stored. Because of this, virtual memory is sometimes called the page file or paging file. It isn't as fast to access as actual RAM, but it will allow some programs to run that wouldn't otherwise. DIMMs and SODIMMs and Cache are types of physical memory. DIMMs are used in desktop computers, SODIMMs are used in laptops, and cache resides on the processor die.

176. D. This is a punchdown block. It can be found in a telecommunications closet mounted on a networking rack. Network drops from work areas are terminated (punched down) in the back, and cables with RJ-45 connectors connect the front to a switch or router.

177. C. Molex connectors have a metal sleeve inside a plastic housing. Technically they can come in any number of connections but those used most often in computer systems are 4 pin, 6 pin, 8 pin, and 20/24 pin. They are used to provide power to various devices and the motherboard.

178. A, B. In many extruder type 3D printers, the print bed will move down as the print job progresses and may move front to back during the printing of each layer, while the extruder nozzle moves left to right, building the 3D object one layer at a time.

179. B. The connector on the left is a miniUSB, and on the right is a microUSB.

180. D. NVMe and SSD drives don't have platters that spin. Blu-ray optical discs spin, but their spin speed is not how they are measured. Only magnetic drives are measured in rpms, and 15,000 would be a very fast magnetic drive.

181. B. SSDs and magnetic drives can both be found in the 3.5″ form factor that is used in desktop computers, and often they connect via a SATA interface. mSATA and M.2 are solid-state drives consisting of a very small circuit board that connects directly to the motherboard via a slot with a screw or connector to hold it in place.

182. B, D. M.2 drives are keyed with B or M or B+M keys. A and E keys are for Wi-Fi, Bluetooth, or cellular devices such as networking cards found in laptops. In computers, a key is a device such as a notch, an indent on a circuit board, that ensures you can't plug the wrong type of device into something. Power connectors are keyed by shape, RAM modules are keyed with notches in different places, CPUs will have keys, SATA connectors have an L shape for a key, and M.2 drives are keyed as well. In an M.2, a B key is for PCIe x 2/SATA/USB and so on, and an M key is PCIe x4/SATA.

183. C. SATA 3 had a speed of 6 Gbps and a data throughput of 600 MBps, but SATA 3.2 (also called SATAe) ties compatible drives into the PCIe bus on the motherboard, decreasing overhead and taking advantage of the PCIe bus speeds which makes the data throughput multiple times better.

184. A, C. Socket AM4 and Socket TR4 are only compatible with AMD processors. The two LGA sockets listed are for use with Intel processors only.

185. B. This socket is for an M.2 drive. Notice the holes for a screw to hold the different drive lengths.

186. D. This is a multisocket motherboard, meaning that it has sockets for more than one processor. The other three terms describe characteristics of processors. Multicore is more than one core on a die. Multithreaded means each core can perform more than one string of code at a time, and a coprocessor is usually a chip designed to perform a specific function to help a processor be more efficient.

187. A. Servers often perform more work than any other computer on a network, especially in a virtualization environment. A server could be as simple as an ordinary desktop computer, but more often the server will have extra processing power and loads of RAM, and be rack-mounted for easy access by technicians in a corporate environment.

188. B, C. Intel Xeon and AMD EPYC processors are designed to be high-end server processors. The Atom processor is a small form factor processor, and the Ryzen 3 is a desktop processor.

189. D. Motherboards found in smaller devices such as laptops and cell phones tend to be very proprietary, meaning that if you can replace them, you must replace them with a board made by the same manufacturer for that precise device.

190. A, C. Arm Holdings, LTD. is the company that has developed the nine iterations of ARM processors. ARM is famous for developing Reduced Instruction Set Computing (RISC), and their intellectual property can be found in everything from embedded systems and smartphones all the way up to servers. An ARM processor is considered a SoC (system-on-a-chip) rather than a CPU because processors are built with various features around the ARM processor.

191. A. If you disable the USB ports, a user won't be able to attach a USB drive to copy files. Removing USB from the boot options will keep them from booting to it, but it won't prohibit someone from using a USB drive. You can also purchase USB drive locks, which are little plugs for the USB ports. Just don't lose your key!

192. B. The connectors shown are for data connections to SATA drives.

193. C. A SAN (storage area network) is a separate network that has only storage devices on it, but you still need a way to connect to that storage. Connecting can be done through a host bus adapter (HBA) connected through the PCIe bus on a network server's motherboard. Since Fibre Channel (FC) networks are so fast, they are often used for SANs.

194. D. These pins are called headers. The ones mentioned connect the motherboard to the case front, where you will find USB ports, power buttons, HDD status lights, and reset switches.

195. C. The image shown is a 24 pin ATX12V motherboard power connector. Original ATX motherboard power connectors were 20 pin. The color doesn't matter, but the number and shape of pins does. Technically this is a type of Molex connector, but it is commonly called P1. In addition, motherboards may use a 4-pin, 12V connector or an 8-pin power connector to supply additional power for the CPU.

196. A. All modern CPUs are multicore processors, meaning they have more than one processor on a die and can execute at least four threads at a time. ARM is a processor architecture used in many devices, and Intel is a processor manufacturer.

197. C. A webcam would be very inefficient and difficult solution at best, and FireWire would not be fast enough for today's systems. While screen-capture software might work, the best solution would be to install a capture card either as a discrete (external) unit or in a PCIe slot on a motherboard. The capture card can take some of the workload off the processor, making the video less likely to skip, lag, or freeze.

198. A. Adding case fans can draw excess heat out of a case, and cooler air into the case. Most processors won't shut down until they reach 70 to 100 degrees Celsius (158 to 212 degrees Fahrenheit), so if a person is working in that room, the ambient temperature won't be that high. Heat monitoring software lets you see what's going on but won't help cool the case. Removing the chassis cover subjects the computer to debris and dust that can cause other problems, and a refrigerator is likely to cause condensation, which can short out electrical systems. Adding case fans is the best choice given. Using a water-cooled system or adding a bigger heat sink to the processor might also help.

199. B, C. Some power supplies will have a 20-pin+4-pin connector designed to connect to a 24-pin P1 motherboard connector. An ATX12V PSU is the perfect solution. A 20-pin P1 connector plus a P4 connector is the right number of pins, but the P4 connector is not compatible with the main motherboard power. ATX12VO is a 12 volt only connector that has only 10 pins and that would not be compatible with this motherboard, unless it had other connections.

200. D. A modular power supply allows you to use only the connectors you need by plugging and unplugging compatible cables into the PSU.

201. B. If you have a system that can't have any downtime, then you need to have redundant everything. An HBA is a host bus adapter, which you only need if connecting external devices. A display doesn't have anything to do with redundancy. A dual rail power supply can still fail. For this situation you would want redundant power supplies that are hot-swappable.

202. B, C. Whenever you get new equipment for the first time, the best choice is to check for manufacturer's directions. Lacking those, flipping a printer over and pulling the box off of the printer may cause damage before you've even set it up! The best course of action is to slide the contents gently out of the box. Using box cutters could damage the printer or its cables.

203. D. Most modern network-enabled multifunction devices will have Bluetooth, Wi-Fi, and Ethernet connections. They may also have AirPrint support for Apple devices. They are not likely to have RFID as a connection type, although they may have an RFID reader for secure print job authentication.

204. C. The only type of printer that will print on all copies of multipart forms is an impact printer, usually a dot-matrix. It's the only type of printer listed that makes a mark by physically striking the paper. These multipart forms are sometimes called NCR (No Carbon Required) or carbonless multipart forms. The back of each page, except the last one, will have a coating of microencapsulated ink or dye that produces an image when it is pressed or written on.

205. D. If you have a printer with multiple trays, normally when you print there will be a setting that allows you to choose which tray to print from. Letterhead can be in one tray and plain paper in another. Orientation is whether the paper is printed in the taller or wider direction. Duplexing means printing on both sides, and quality settings let the user choose either faster or better printing.

206. A, D. Both laser and inkjet printers occasionally need to be calibrated. Exactly when depends on the printer, but often for inkjet printers it's after installing a new ink cartridge, and for laser printers, when you need to adjust colors.

207. A. Secured prints is the feature described. Secure print jobs are retrieved at the device based on user authentication by using either a password or a security badge, depending on the printer. Auditing won't prevent attacks, but it will show you when the printer is being accessed and by whom, much like Event Viewer. Other security features might include removable hard drives with the printer, overwriting documents following DoD (Department of Defense) requirements, and data encryption.

208. A. A punchdown block can be found in a telecommunications closet mounted on a networking rack. Network drops from work areas are terminated (punched down) in the back, and cables with RJ-45 connectors connect the front to a switch or router. Punchdown blocks provide a neat way to keep cables organized. Switches and routers are network connectivity devices. A terminator is another name for a terminating resistor, which is sometimes needed at the end of a length of coaxial cable.

209. A, C. Resin and filament are the consumable materials used by 3D printers to make the 3D objects. The extruder nozzle will often last the life of the printer. There may be a tape or base material that lines the print bed that is also replaced for each new print job so that the print job can be easily removed from the print bed.

210. A, B, C. Nonvolatile Memory Express (NVMe), SATA, and PCIe are all communication methods used by solid-state drives to connect to the motherboard for transferring data between the drive and CPU. IDE is a legacy connection technology that was used with the original ATA drives, parallel ATA (PATA).

211. C. There are five major versions of PCIe currently specified: 1.x, 2.x, 3.0, 4.0 and 5.0. For the five versions, a single bidirectional lane operates at a data rate of 250 MBps, 500 MBps, approximately 1 GBps, roughly 2 GBps, and nearly 4 GBps respectively. Each PCIe slot can have up to 16 lanes, the number of lanes being indicated by x1, x4, x8, x16. (The x is pronounced as *by*.) Therefore, a PCIe 5.0 x16 slot can support up to 64 GBps of bandwidth. (16 x 4 = 64).

Chapter 4: Virtualization and Cloud Computing

1. **B.** Companies can purchase virtualization software to set up individual clouds within their own network. That type of setup is referred to as a private cloud. Running a private cloud pretty much eliminates many of the features that companies want from the cloud, such as rapid scalability, and eliminating the need to purchase and manage computer assets. The big advantage, though, is that it allows the company to control its own security within the cloud. A hybrid model would be the scenario providing benefits of both public and private clouds. The community model is something akin to a shared private cloud, with responsibilities and benefits collaboratively shared.

2. **B.** Let's say that your company needs extra network capacity, including processing power, storage, and networking services (such as firewalls), but doesn't have the money to buy more network hardware. Instead, your company can purchase infrastructure as a service (IaaS), which is a lot like paying for utilities; you pay for what you use. Of the four, IaaS requires the most network management expertise from the client side. In an IaaS setup, the client provides and manages the software. PaaS is platform as a service and SaaS is software as a service. FWaaS is sometimes used to mean firewall as a service, but is not widely recognized nor on the CompTIA A+ 220-1101 objectives.

3. **A.** The traditional type of cloud that usually comes to mind is a public cloud, like the ones operated by third-party companies such as Microsoft, Google, HP, Apple, Netflix, and Amazon with its Amazon Web Services (AWS). These clouds offer the best in scalability, reliability, flexibility, geographical independence, and cost effectiveness. Whatever the client wants, the client gets. For example, if the client needs more resources, it simply scales up and uses more.

4. **C.** Platform as a service (PaaS) adds a layer to IaaS that includes software development tools such as runtime environments. Because of this, it can be helpful to software developers; the vendor manages the various hardware platforms. This frees up the software developers to focus on building their application and scaling it. The best PaaS solutions allow for the client to export its developed programs and run them in an environment other than where they were developed.

5. **D.** The highest of the three levels of cloud service is software as a service (SaaS), which handles the task of managing software and its deployment. This is the model used by Google Docs, Microsoft Office 365, and even storage solutions such as Dropbox.

6. **B.** In most cases, clients can get more resources instantly (or at least quickly or on-demand), which is called rapid elasticity. For the client, this is a great feature because they can scale up without needing to purchase, install, and configure new hardware. Ubiquitous access refers to clients being able to access the cloud ubiquitously, or from anywhere, anytime. Resource pooling, particularly when a cloud provider deals with multiple tenants, refers to the provider effectively saving money by not duplicating available capacity. Finally, when the service provided to those tenants is monitored and paid for according to their use, it's metered service or metered utilization.

7. B. A Type 2 hypervisor sits on top of an existing operating system, called the host OS. This is most commonly used in client-side virtualization, where multiple OSs are managed on the client machine as opposed to on a server. The hypervisor is also called a virtual machine manager (VMM).

8. A. If presented with a scenario for installing multiple operating systems (OS) on a computer running client-side virtualization, just add the minimum hardware requirements (or recommendations) together. Treat it as if each OS needs its own minimum (which it does) and they are just sharing the available physical hardware (which they are). Also, each OS needs its own virtual network card to participate on the network and needs its security to be individually configured based on OS requirements and user needs. Treat it as though it is a separate computer. In reality, you're never going to go with just the absolute minimum because although the OS will run, it won't run well.

9. C. If each client has been promised 32 GB of RAM, then the server must have enough RAM to give each client their allotment. This means 128 GB in this case. The assumption is that the hypervisor will require no RAM on its own. In reality, it probably will require a little but not much. Resource pooling, when a cloud provider deals with multiple tenants, refers to the provider having additional capacity available but saving money by sharing that availability.

10. C. The major feature of virtualization is breaking down that one-to-one hardware and software barrier. The virtualized version of a computer is appropriately called a virtual machine (VM). Thanks to VMs, it is becoming far less common to need dual-boot machines today than in the past. VMs allow computers to do things like run five instances of an OS or one instance each of several different OSs.

11. C. Metered utilization is synonymous with pay-as-you-use. The resources are available, but payment is calculated according to the actual usage. This is a common model for enterprise environments, especially during the early "migration of services" period. On-demand means services can be added as needed on the fly. A resource pool refers to the resources owned by a cloud provider such as RAM and storage capacity that are available to the cloud provider's clients. Shared resources refer to the idea that a cloud provider's physical resources may be shared among many different companies.

12. B. The creation of virtual machines would alleviate the issue of space, power, and most of the hardware costs associated with maintaining bare-metal systems. Virtual machines can provide much of the same services, at a fraction of the costs. Control and management of the machines would not change.

13. B. Shared resources describe the cloud infrastructure shared among clients of a cloud provider. For example, a cloud provider may have one physical server that is shared by multiple companies. Shared resources are also those resources made available to multiple employees or users on a local network. Measured resources are synonymous with pay-as-you-go services where the company pays only for the resources they are using. A private cloud negates many of the advantages of a public cloud such as rapid elasticity, but control remains with the owner of the cloud. A community cloud is shared by a small group of users with similar needs who pool their resources for a more cost-effective solution.

14. A, C. Many companies go to cloud computing and the inevitable shared resources for the advantages of lowering their hardware costs and for the flexibility of adding resources on the fly. There are, however, some concerns with cloud computing, such as who has access to the data, the potential for another cloud computing client to introduce malware, and potentially poor application performance if another application is monopolizing the shared resources. Another potential problem is Internet connection downtime.

15. A. Internal shared resources would be under local network control and local security management, perhaps provided to different units within the same organization, whereas external assets are very likely secured and controlled by an external cloud provider.

16. C. For a company needing additional cloud resources on demand, they should request metered utilization, in which a cloud service will bill much like a utility would, as resources are used. Infrastructure as a service (IaaS) refers to hardware and networking in the cloud, and resource pooling is used in cloud computing to mean that resources are pooled and delivered as needed to many clients. Rapid metering is not an IT term.

17. C. This configuration would need 2 GB for Windows 10 (the host) plus 3 GB for the client OS and running software at a minimum. In reality, more RAM would be better.

18. D. Synchronization applications work to keep all files consistent, updating from multiple locations as needed. Emulation is when one thing acts like (emulates) something else. File security is ubiquitous and is needed everywhere, but it does not address the need to keep the files consistent, whether the users are traveling or on premises. Virtualization is using a single set of hardware as if it were multiple machines to run multiple OS instances or multiple operating systems.

19. C. Virtual desktop infrastructure (VDI) can be managed/hosted on either a local server (local cloud) or over the Internet by a third party. When in the cloud and managed by a third party, it is sometimes called desktop as a service (DaaS). The advantages of VDI are savings in hardware costs and configuration time. Data sensitivity and data security may preclude using VDI in the cloud.

20. B. A virtual desktop infrastructure (VDI) moves the desktop icons, files, and folders to a server instead of the desktop originating from the local machine. When the desktop experience is hosted on a centralized server location, the icons, files, and folders are the same. With this user working from different offices, the best solution for them is VDI in the cloud.

21. C. In a virtual environment, a virtual network interface card (NIC) connects the guest machine to its local virtual network and any external networks.

22. A. Application virtualization delivers software using a virtual structure, which allows an organization to make a needed application available across multiple devices without having to install it on each of these devices. This might apply to any platform the organization needs, whether a desktop computer or a mobile device.

23. A. Before purchasing hardware of a host system to support a number of virtual systems, it is wise to consider the resource requirements of those virtual systems. The more virtual systems a single hardware system supports, the more resources are needed.

24. D. When wanting to maintain confidentiality, integrity, and availability, security requirements and regulations must first be defined. A company can then consider if an Internet cloud solution would be appropriate.

25. A. Network requirements dictate the need for and configuration of virtual local area networks (VLANs). A VLAN is a network design feature that isolates network traffic by the switch port. Just like a physical machine, a virtual machine must be compatible with the network it is intended to run on.

26. B. Emulator requirements should be as small as possible in order to keep resources free for use by the host and guest operating systems. Generally speaking, more storage and RAM lead to greater scalability, which means you can install more virtual machines on the same physical box.

27. D. While software as a service (SaaS), platform as a service (PaaS), and infrastructure as a service (IaaS) are widely considered to be the major categories of cloud computing, everything as a service (XaaS) is not.

28. C. A private cloud pools the on premises resources of a company for use within the company; there is no Internet component. A public cloud is owned by a third-party provider who delivers resources, including storage, platforms, and software via the Internet. A hybrid cloud combines the two other forms, where some resources are on premises and others are available over the Internet. The on premises resources may provide more control over data, while the Internet resources offer on-demand scalability. Different types of data could be kept in different locations depending on the company's needs.

29. C. Virtual desktop infrastructure (VDI) in the cloud, sometimes called desktop as a service (DaaS), allows a network admin to easily and almost immediately configure desktops for new users, even if they are in a remote location halfway around the world. Infrastructure as a service (IaaS) provides the physical computing, network, memory, and storage resources enabling the cloud provider's customers to set up virtual servers and networks in the cloud. IaaS can also provide server software and databases, although not all providers do. Think of IaaS as renting the entire network structure. The cloud provider is responsible for resource provisioning and maintenance needed for the organization's infrastructure. Software as a service (SaaS) provides applications but not necessarily desktops. VDI on premises offers similar advantages, but scalability is limited by local servers.

30. A. A community cloud is the solution for such situations. It allows shared cloud resources to a limited group of people or companies. The group can benefit from economies of scale but keep their resources separate from other organizations. They could even share in joint projects. Their servers could be in a data center or stored locally by one of the members. The group will have more control than they would over a public cloud but could share the maintenance costs of their cloud. A community cloud is similar to a private cloud, but with multiple members.

31. B. While all of the items listed are advantages of using cloud-computing, high availability means that data and applications are available around the clock, regardless of the users' location. Shared resources often lead to lower costs and rapid elasticity. File synchronization means that users' files are updated with the newest changes whether they're working at home or in the office.

32. B. Configuring a virtual machine using VMM software whose features include cross-platform virtualization will allow you to configure multiple desktop platforms on one physical machine regardless of the host OS. Dual-boot systems may not work well together, depending on the operating systems being used. Sharing files isn't really the question being addressed; using different operating systems is.

33. C. In general terms, a sandbox is an isolated test environment separate from your network where you can "play" with applications and settings without worrying about negative effects on your network or computers. Sandbox is also a feature that can be enabled in Windows 10 and Windows 11 Pro and higher editions. When launched, it opens a separate instance of the Windows operating system running as a virtual machine on your Windows desktop. A file can be opened in that virtual machine to help protect your computer against malicious code. When the sandbox is closed, anything running in it is discarded.

34. D. Your friend will need to run both OSs to test the software. A Windows 10 sandbox will protect their host OS from any problems the application might cause, but it won't let them test the application on a Linux OS. Dual-boot systems are clunky at best, and they require rebooting between OSs. Running two computers would cost more in utilities and hardware, not to mention precious office space. The best solution for your friend is to install virtual machines on their office PC. This would enable them to test in either Linux or Windows without shutting the PC down between, saving time while making corrections. It will also protect their machine against unintentional bad code that could otherwise cause damage.

35. B. Developing software for a specific manufacturing function is often costly and time-con-suming, so a manufacturer might want to keep that equipment and software running as long as possible. If the equipment is doing the job they need it to do, they will be disinclined to upgrade to something new. Shutting the equipment down when it fails may spell disaster for the company. The best option here is to prepare a Windows 10 PC to run the legacy OS and software within a virtual machine, and test the software. Then, during a planned shut-down, transfer the control of the manufacturing machine over to the new PC with the virtual machine, and, of course, make sure you have an image to rapidly deploy if the new machine fails in the future.

36. A. The advantage of having applications each running in their own virtual machine is that if one application's or VM's security is penetrated, the others may still be secure. Scalability would still be limited to the resources of the server. The hardware maintenance would be the same, but the security maintenance might actually be more; however, being able to set up different access for each machine may simplify security configuration. The cost would actually be more because a separate license would be needed for each OS running in its own virtual machine.

37. A, C. Regardless of whether a server is physical or virtual, it will need the same security configuration, and a license must exist for every virtual server just as it must for every physical server. While RAM and storage requirements would be the same, one of the advantages of using a virtual machine is being able to put more than one server on a single piece of computer hardware, so overall hardware cost would be less, and maintaining that hardware would be less expensive. Virtual servers are much more portable than physical servers, meaning they can easily be moved from one piece of hardware to another.

38. A. While each model has its advantages, if security is the greatest concern, then a private cloud is the best solution. Public, hybrid, and community clouds all involve other entities, which may introduce additional potential security problems.

39. D. A virtual desktop infrastructure (VDI) moves the desktop icons, files, and folders to a server instead of the desktop originating from the local machine. When the desktop experience is hosted on a centralized server location, the icons, files, and folders are the same regardless of where a user logs on. VDI on premises hosts the desktop on a local server, whereas VDI in the cloud hosts the desktop on a remote server.

40. C. Cloud computing has many advantages, including (a) reduced capital expenditures, which can help growing companies and (b) relieve IT personnel of infrastructure management so that they can focus on other objectives such as customer support, and (c) rapid elasticity, which means a company can grow its IT infrastructure on a moment's notice as needed. Also, adding new employees can be easier with cloud computing. There are a few downsides, though. Some of them are that someone else has control of your data, fees can be surprising when usage is more than expected, and moving from one IaaS provider to another might be difficult. There are more advantages and disadvantages than can reasonably be listed here.

Chapter 5: Hardware and Network Troubleshooting

1. D. Your supervisor probably prefers that you are not on Twitch but has little actual impact on the site's performance. The Wi-Fi connection would be sufficient. The company likely has a policy against watching streaming applications or against particular websites like Twitch. However, the data retention policy is not relevant. Instead, the firewall is the reason behind the streaming being denied.

2. B. Laptop processors generally are permanently attached to the motherboard. And motherboards are normally proprietary, meaning one from a certain model will not fit into a different case. Therefore, the best course of action is likely a laptop upgrade.

3. B. You need to stop the device first (this is good policy even for USB devices) using the Safely Remove Hardware icon in the system tray (it looks like a card and may have a green arrow or green check mark over it, depending on your version of Windows). Highlight the device and click Stop. Once it's stopped, you can unplug it.

4. D. Many laptops use shared video memory, meaning that system RAM is divided up for use between the processor and the video card. On these types of systems, the amount of RAM available for video is configured in the BIOS/UEFI.

5. D. Because of the much smaller space available for keys, some laptop keys are consolidated into special multifunction keys. These keys are accessed through the standard keys by using a special function (Fn) key. Nearly every laptop has a video connector on the back or the side to plug in an external display or a projector. You will need to use the video toggle key to get this external port to work. Usually there are three or four states: laptop only, external output only, duplicate, or extend the desktop (some models won't extend the desktop).

6. B, C. To combat heat, you can either slow the processor down (run it at a lower speed) or give it less juice (run it at a lower voltage). Most of the time, this is configured in the system BIOS/UEFI. For example, many Intel processors have SpeedStep technology to slow the processor down to produce less heat, and they may also have adaptive thermal management.

7. C. If the integrated video card fails, you're looking at a motherboard replacement. Some laptops do have a replaceable video card. If it fails or if you choose to upgrade it, the procedure will probably resemble replacing system memory.

8. D. If you are having problems with flickering screens or dimness, it's more likely that the inverter is the problem and not the backlight itself.

9. C. Thicker paper can cause paper jams, especially in printers with curved paper paths. Paper that is too thin may not get picked up by the printer rollers at all.

10. B. Most digital displays have a native resolution, which is a single, fixed resolution that they support. Attempting to change the resolution may result in distorted images, or the image may not display at all.

11. A. Refresh rate defines the vertical scan frequency of a display and determines how many times, in one second, an image can be redrawn on the screen. Many LCD displays have a fixed refresh rate. If the refresh rate is set faster than the video card or software can run, then problems such as a black screen every few seconds may result. The solution is to lower the refresh rate or invest in new hardware.

12. B. Often when tearing happens, a video game is sending frames to the display faster than the display can render them. Setting the refresh rate of the display higher, if it supports this, may solve the problem.

13. D. The power-on self-test (POST) is a series of system checks performed by the system BIOS when the computer is turned on. Checking the system memory is part of the POST routine.

14. D. Flashing the BIOS is the recommended way to upgrade a BIOS. It involves downloading the new BIOS and flashing software from the manufacturer and installing it on the computer. The worst-case scenario is replacing the motherboard (or in this case, the RAM, since that is what you upgraded).

15. D. If the projector worked fine in a different room, then it's something about the new conference room. If the room is brighter, you'll need to turn up the brightness of the projector or turn off lights and close shades. If these don't solve the issue, then you might need a new projector. Lumens is the measure of brightness for a projector. For a well-lit business setting, you probably want a projector rated at 5,000–6,000 lumens.

16. C. Likely the friend forgot to connect the internal USB connector on the motherboard to the USB ports of the case.

17. B. The spinning pinwheel, also known as the "Spinning Wheel of Death," can happen for several reasons. Sometimes it's a frozen app, but in this case, it's happening when different apps are running, so hardware would be suspect. Of the hardware listed, the RAM is the most likely problem. A faulty hard drive could also cause the problem.

18. B. It's rare that a computer will catch on fire, but sometimes wires are frayed and excessive dust can cause short circuits to happen. Burning electronics have an unmistakable odor. If you ever smell electronics burning, even if you don't see smoke or flame, immediately unplug the device.

19. B, D. Unexpected shutdowns are difficult to troubleshoot, as are all intermittent issues. The first thing to check is to ensure that all socketed chips are seated properly; in fact, reseating them is a good option. If that does not resolve the issue, test the RAM or replace it if possible.

20. C. Most likely, the processor is overheating. Check that the thermal paste/tape between the processor and heat sink have not dried out. If they were fine, then consider adding better or additional fans in the case. This would also be a good time to clean any dust out of the case.

21. A. Sometimes it's as simple as rebooting the system and the problem will resolve. If it doesn't, then the solution depends on any error messages received and what you find in the troubleshooting process.

22. D. Every computer has a diagnostic program built into its basic input/output system (BIOS) called the power-on self-test (POST). When you turn on the computer, it executes this set of diagnostics. If the computer doesn't perform the POST as it should, one way to determine the source of a problem is to listen for a beep code. This is a series of beeps from the computer's speaker. A successful POST generally produces a single beep.

23. D. Failure to boot at all likely means the drive is dead. But first, do your due diligence and reseat the connections and make sure the BIOS recognizes the drive before replacing it. BIOS/UEFI should autodetect the hard drive. If that autodetection fails, it's bad news for the hard drive unless there's a cable, connection, or jumper issue. If the internal hard drive is indeed dead, you might be able to get by temporarily by plugging in an external drive.

24. B. The system BIOS/UEFI contains the boot sequence for a system. Most systems probably boot to the first hard drive, but they can also be configured to boot from a secondary hard drive, the optical drive, or the network. This setting is configured in the BIOS/UEFI.

25. D. If a laptop does not display any video, it could be the screen or the integrated video. To test it, plug in an external display (that you know works) and use the function keys on the laptop to switch to external video output. If that doesn't work, it's likely that the video card is defective.

26. A. Try cleaning the fan before replacing any parts. The power supply fan has a protective grid covering it, and you won't really be able to get to it with a computer vacuum or a damp cloth. Using compressed air to blow it out is your best option. Be sure to insert something nonconductive, like a plastic knife, between the blades of the fan to keep the fan from spinning and protect the fan's motor. You will, of course, do this with the computer off.

27. C. If the battery won't charge while the laptop is plugged in, try removing the battery and reinserting it. If it still won't charge, you might want to replace the battery.

28. B, C. When repairing laptops, you should always document and label screw and cable locations, organize parts, refer to manufacturer instructions, and use appropriate hand tools. Power screwdrivers can be used. In some cases, but not all, you might need to remove the keyboard to remove the motherboard. Refer to the manufacturer's instructions.

29. D. This computer is giving you a beep code during the POST routine. One way to troubleshoot this is to use a POST card. This is a circuit board that fits into an expansion slot (PCI or PCIe) in the motherboard or connects via a USB port, and reports numeric codes as the boot process progresses. Each of those codes corresponds to a particular component being checked. If the POST card stops at a certain number, you can look up that number in the manual for the card to determine the problem.

30. A. This computer hasn't reached the video part of POST yet, so the only way it has to communicate error codes with the user is through a series of beeps. The pattern of beeps has a specific meaning. Often continuous short beeps is a RAM problem, while one short beep and three long is video, but you would need to consult the motherboard manual to be sure. A power supply tester and multimeter would be used to troubleshoot problems with power, and a loopback plug is used to troubleshoot problems with the network card.

31. A. When files are written to a hard drive, they're not always written contiguously (with all of the data in a single location). As a result, file data is spread out over the disk, and the time it takes to retrieve files from the disk increases. Defragmenting a disk involves analyzing the disk and then consolidating fragmented files and folders so that they occupy a contiguous space, thus increasing performance during file retrieval.

32. A. A rhythmic clicking sound can be made only by components with mechanical parts, such as a conventional hard disk drive (HDD). A power supply fan failure will usually result in a whining sound or no sound at all because the fan doesn't work, but it will not cause a system boot failure. Solid state drives (SSDs) and random access memory (RAM) don't make any sound when they fail.

33. D. Vertical white lines running down the page are likely due to toner that is clogged and not able to transfer properly to the drum. This is a common problem when the ambient air's humidity is too high. First remove and try gently shaking the toner cartridge to loosen the toner. If that doesn't work, you may have to replace the toner cartridge with a new one.

34. A, C, D. Printer jams and creased paper happen when something prevents the paper from advancing through the printer evenly. There are several reasons this could be happening. If the rollers that pull the paper along are damaged, they won't pick paper up properly. If the paper is too humid it can crease, jam, or tear easily. Paper that is too thick or debris in the paper path can cause paper to crease or jam.

35. C. This is most likely a problem with the power supply. Test it with a power supply tester or a multimeter. Even though the fan is spinning, the power supply might still not be providing the correct power to run the computer. Not having any indicator lights would indicate a problem with the power supply. If it were RAM, CPU, or HDD, there would at least be some lights (like the power light) on.

36. A. If you hear a grinding noise, consider yourself fortunate to have a warning that your hard drive is failing. If you don't have a good backup and a way to reinstall the operating system, you'll want to take care of that immediately then invest in a new hard drive. Solid state drives (SSDs) and RAM don't make any noise when they fail. A failing processor fan would result in an overheating CPU, which would shut the system down.

37. B. Whenever you've just replaced something and an error pops up, it's a fairly safe assumption that it had something to do with what you just replaced. A toner cartridge that isn't seated properly can cause an error message. Reseat it and the error might go away.

38. B. If your printer fails to pick up paper, it could indicate that the pickup rollers are too worn. They press up against small rubber or cork patches known as separation pads. These help to keep the rest of the paper in the tray so that only one sheet gets picked up at a time. A pickup stepper motor turns the pickup rollers.

39. C. Most likely, the ink ribbon has reached its maximum number of prints or has dried out. Since the bottom copies are printing fine, the printhead is working. Replace the worn-out ribbon and it should work fine again.

40. C. The users are connecting; it's just slower than it should be. This is likely due to too many people accessing the WAP at once. The more devices there are connected, the more likely that their signals will interfere with each other, even if the WAP hasn't reached the theoretical maximum that the manufacturer says it should support. To solve this problem, install a second WAP.

41. A. The most common reason that users on wireless networks experience intermittent connectivity issues is distance. The farther away from the WAP the user gets, the weaker the signal becomes. When the signal weakens, the transfer rates drop dramatically. Ways to fix a low RF signal range from using a more powerful transmitter, using a larger antenna, focusing the signal toward where it is needed, or moving the users closer.

42. C. Unless you replace all the network connectivity devices with faster 10 Gbps devices, the network will run at the slower speed. The customer needs to replace the switch with a 10 Gbps switch.

43. A, D. Try reseating the printer's data and power cable. The printer may need to be reset, which can sometimes be done by unplugging it for 30 seconds, then plugging the power back in. If the print jobs are still garbled, replace the printer driver.

44. B. An overheating, swelling battery has the potential to explode and should be handled carefully. If the phone is plugged in, immediately unplug it. Turn the phone off and discontinue using it. While you might be able to replace the battery, for most phones you'll need to replace the device.

45. C. Most laptops have a power jack that is soldered onto the motherboard. They have been known to be knocked loose with rough handling or when a laptop is dropped or bumped while the power cord is plugged in. If the power jack isn't damaged, you may be able to rectify the problem by simply soldering the power jack back into place. If the power jack is damaged, then you'll need to find a replacement jack.

46. B. When a charger wiggles in the port, it's usually a sign that the port has been damaged by pressure against the cord plugged in, causing the port to bend out of shape. You would, of course, check the port and the cable first, but most likely you'll need to replace the port. Soldering it back into place won't help.

47. A. Phones that are stuffed in back pockets or purses often end up with lint and other debris in the charging port. Using canned air to remove debris from ports isn't recommended. Try holding the phone with the port facing downward and gently tap the phone to remove the debris. Don't blow into the port as this can introduce moisture into the phone. You may be able to remove the debris with a small sewing needle, but this could also damage the port if you're not careful. If debris isn't the problem, you'll need to try some other solutions, such as a different block and cord or replacing the battery or the port. You would never spray cleaning solution or any liquid into the phone. If the phone is compatible with wireless charging, you could try charging the battery wirelessly to determine if the battery is the problem.

48. C. Corrosion can limit or totally prevent a phone's charger port and cable from making a connection, but you don't necessarily need to replace the port or the phone. Tread carefully when cleaning corrosion. Isopropyl alcohol is used to clean because it will dry very quickly. Ensure that the phone is powered off and remove the battery if it is one that is intended to be removed. Use as little liquid as possible on a lint-free cleaning swab, and be gentle. Never use a toothbrush to clean the phone's power port.

49. A. The fusing assembly heats up the toner, and the toner melts into the paper. If the fuser isn't heating properly, images can smudge.

50. B, D. Installing another wireless access point closer to where the users are will extend the overall range of the wireless network and give them a better signal. A wireless range extender might also do the trick. You wouldn't install wired connections for the users because not all visitors will have an RJ45 connection on their device or carry a cable with them. Buying a faster WAP won't help if the network doesn't support it, and it doesn't solve the issue of the signal being weak in the lobby.

51. A, D. If the network card doesn't have any lights, it doesn't have a connection. It could be that the cable is bad or that it's not plugged in on the other side, or it could also be a problem with the NIC or the connectivity device on the other side. If nobody else in the same area is having the same problem, that points to an issue with this computer or cable.

52. D. If you need to trace a wire in a wall from one location to another, a tone generator and probe (or toner probe) is the tool for you. It consists of two pieces: a tone generator and a probe. Because it's so good at tracking, you will sometimes hear this referred to as a "fox and hound."

53. A. For network-enabled laser printers, no connectivity can be a sign of improperly config-ured IP settings such as the IP address. While each printer is somewhat different, you can manually configure most laser printers' IP settings through the LCD control panel.

54. D. On a wired network, if you run into slow speeds or intermittent connectivity, it's likely a load issue. There's too much traffic for the network to handle, and the network is bog-ging down. Solutions include adding a switch, replacing your hubs with switches, and even creating virtual LANs (VLANs) with switches. If you want to upgrade the cabling or con-nectivity infrastructure to combat a speed issue, you should do all of it and not just cables or a router.

55. A. This is known as port flapping, also known as link flapping. It can be caused by a faulty or nonstandard network cable, non–Energy Efficient Ethernet (EEE) devices, or small form-factor pluggable (SFP) devices that are not working or synchronizing properly.

56. C. You would need to disable EEE on the switch. The port is flapping because the device connected to it is not EEE compliant. Link flap prevention settings would disable the port when port flapping is detected and require the network administrator to enable the port each time it is disabled. Eventually you may want to replace the offending device, but until that is done, disabling EEE on the switch is the best option.

57. B. Without knowing the printer's problem, it would be most helpful if the user can tell you the error code seen on the printer's display. The error code might signify a paper jam or no connectivity, but knowing the error code will save the guesswork and possibly avoid creating more problems.

58. B. You can immediately rule out client-side hardware issues because the user can connect to some resources. You need to figure out why they can't connect to others. This is most likely caused by one of two things: a configuration issue or a connectivity device (such as a router) problem. Since it's affecting multiple people, it's probably something to do with the router (default gateway).

59. A, C, D. The answer will depend on the specific printer, but common causes are that the stapler is empty, a different driver is needed, or the staple unit isn't enabled on the printer. It's usually physically impossible to put the staples in backward.

60. B, C, D. Depending on the copier/printer, you may still be able to print to it even though the stapler is jammed. Trying to staple too many pages or unsupported paper can certainly cause staple jams, as well as installing the wrong staples. Since the procedure varies by company, you'll want to consult the manufacturer's documentation for removing jammed staples.

61. C. The phone has overheated due to the car's heater blowing hot air on it and it is in an area that is not ventilated. It needs to cool down before you try to use it again. The phone wouldn't be too cold because you had the heat on. It's probably not necessary to buy a new phone. Most modern phones will shut down before damage occurs, and most modern phones don't have batteries that are intended to be removed.

62. D. If overheating is persistent, you don't have many options. The problem is most likely the battery and in modern mobile phones, the battery is not designed to be field replaceable. In this case, the only option may be to replace the device.

63. B. Dead pixels are spots on the screen that never light up. You can check for these by setting the background to white and seeing whether any spots don't light up. If the display is under warranty, you may want to return it, but otherwise there isn't much you can do to fix a dead pixel.

64. B. Oversized images and icons are related to screen resolution; it usually means that your resolution is set too low for the display or projector you are using. Set the resolution to the native setting (or higher than it was) and the problem should disappear.

65. A. Nearly every hard drive is built with Self-Monitoring, Analysis, and Reporting Technology (S.M.A.R.T.) software installed on it, which monitors hard drive reliability and theoretically can warn you in the event of an imminent failure.

66. B. Before you do anything else, you need to back up the system's drive. S.M.A.R.T. (Self-monitoring, Analysis, and Reporting Technology) errors indicate that a hard drive failure will happen. Drive failure may be averted if the error is because of excessive heat and there is a way to correct it; otherwise, expect the drive to fail sooner rather than later. The best course of action is to ensure that the system is backed up regularly until a new drive can be installed.

67. C. Almost every circuit board will have a capacitor or a few on it. Capacitors store electricity between two dielectric plates and discharge that energy as needed. When they fail, they can swell or burst and electrolyte will seep out of the top vent. If you see a swollen or weeping capacitor on a motherboard, the best option is to replace the motherboard immediately.

68. D. CompTIA's best practice methodology to resolve problems consists of the following steps:

   1. Identify the problem.

   2. Establish a theory of probable cause (question the obvious).

   3. Test the theory to determine the cause.

   4. Establish a plan of action to resolve the problem and implement the solution.

   5. Verify full system functionality, and if applicable, implement preventive measures.

   6. Document the findings, actions, and outcomes.

69. A. A common issue with the BIOS/UEFI is when it fails to retain your computer's settings, such as time and date and hard drive configuration. The BIOS/UEFI uses a small battery (much like a watch battery) on the motherboard to help it retain settings when the system power is off. If this battery fails, the BIOS/UEFI won't retain its settings. Simply replace the battery to solve the problem.

70. B. If Set Automatically is turned off, the date and time will be based on what the user set it at initially, which may or may not be correct.

71. A. If you're using RAID 5 (disk striping with parity), a single drive failure usually means that your data will be fine, provided you replace the failed drive. If you lose multiple drives at the same time, you will need to restore from backup. Incidentally, the minimum number of disks for a RAID 5 array is only three, but the additional disk to stripe across will increase speed.

72. C. Of the possible issues, the least likely is the contrast setting. Having an incorrect contrast may make the image difficult to see, but it shouldn't make it blurry. Adjusting the focus and cleaning the lens are easy fixes. The most likely, if they're using their own laptop, is that the resolution is too high for the projector. In that case, change the PCs resolution to match the native resolution of the projector if possible. Depending on the projector, you may need to adjust the sharpness setting or turn on automatic keystone adjustment. The position of the projector shouldn't matter if it's in a room where it's mounted to the ceiling and doesn't get moved; otherwise, having it too far away could also be a problem.

73. C. With artifacts, no matter what you have on your screen, you can still see the outlines of a different image. That image has been "burned" into the display (sometimes simply referred to as burn-in) and isn't going away. The only solution is to replace the display. Burn-in is also called image persistence or ghosting.

74. D. When users are typing, their palm might rest on the touchpad, causing erratic pointer behavior. This is referred to as a ghost cursor because it seems like the cursor just randomly jumps all over the screen. The touchpad can be turned off through Control Panel. Depending on the OS, you disable the touchpad under Settings. You may also be able to adjust the sensitivity of the touchpad. On a laptop, there may be a function button to turn the touchpad on and off easily.

75. A, C. A corrupted driver can make any device behave in a nonstandard way. Check the driver name in Device Manager, then locate and rename the driver file with a different extension such as .old. Again in Device Manager, remove the old driver and install a new one. The driver file being renamed keeps Windows from reusing it, and leaving it there means you'll still have the file to revert to if you must. There could also be a problem with connectivity with the mouse port. Try using a different port to see if the problem disappears.

76. C. Most smartphones use capacitive touchscreens. Calibrating the screen is not an option. You can check to see if something is pressing on the phone where it shouldn't be, but otherwise fixing this problem is likely going to require replacing the digitizer.

77. C. Step 4 of the best practice methodology, which is establish a plan of action, includes Refer to the vendor's instructions. CompTIA's best practice methodology to resolve problems consists of the following steps:

1. Identify the problem.

2. Establish a theory of probable cause (question the obvious).

3. Test the theory to determine the cause.

4. Establish a plan of action to resolve the problem and implement the solution.

5. Verify full system functionality, and if applicable, implement preventive measures.

6. Document the findings, actions, and outcomes.

78. B. If the touchscreen on a Microsoft Surface Pro is not working properly, search for calibrate and select Calibrate the screen for pen or touch, then follow the onscreen instructions.

79. D. While modern smartphones are water resistant, none of them to date are waterproof. The water-resistant feature fades over time and doesn't protect the phone against water under pressure (like a shower) or extreme temperatures. If your phone gets wet, immediately turn it off. Tap it gently with the power port facing down to remove excess water and leave it off in a well-ventilated area to allow it to dry out for several hours. A fan gently blowing cool air into the power connector may help. Wipe any visible water off the phone with a clean, soft cloth, but don't stick anything into the phone's ports. Water, especially salt water, is conductive and can cause a short in the phone that could damage or destroy it or cause the battery to swell or explode.

80. A, D. Water and electronics don't mix. A darkened screen, inability to charge, and distorted pictures and sound are all symptoms of water damage. Water inside a phone can cause a short circuit and damage the phone or the battery. Some problems might not show up until much later, when components have had time to corrode and lose their connectivity. Most phones will have some type of visible indicator, like a red line, to show when the phone has been exposed to excessive moisture.

81. C. CompTIA's best practice methodology to resolve problems consists of the following steps:

1. Identify the problem.

2. Establish a theory of probable cause (question the obvious).

3. Test the theory to determine the cause.

4. Establish a plan of action to resolve the problem and implement the solution.

5. Verify full system functionality, and if applicable, implement preventive measures.

6. Document the findings, actions, and outcomes.

82. A, B, C. Exactly what to do will depend on the printer and software being used, but most likely it's a default setting somewhere either on the printer or in the software. It could also be caused by the paper guide being inadvertently moved when paper was placed in the tray. Changing the orientation of the paper won't fix this problem as a paper mismatch or wrong paper size error means exactly that. There is a disconnect between the paper they're telling the software to print on and the paper size that the printer believes is in the tray.

83. B, C. What the users are experiencing is called jitter. There can be many causes for jitter, but setting up a VLAN for the phones to segment traffic may help as well as configuring Quality of Service (QoS) to prioritize the phone traffic. WoL is Wake-on-LAN, a feature to remotely turn on a computer. Most VoIP phones don't have user-upgradable RAM.

84. A, B. Always look for the simple things first. Is the printer turned on? Does it have the right paper in the selected tray? Restarting the print server service will delete all the jobs in the queue, which would result in some very upset accountants. So would deleting and reinstalling the printer in the OS. If one particular job is causing problems, you may be able to stop that print job and print the others, then try to resolve the problem with that one print job.

85. D. An audible pop sound and darkness is most likely the projector bulb burning out. It's time to replace the bulb. Most projectors will have an indicator light or will display a message telling you that the bulb is near its end-of-life, so hopefully you will have already purchased one and have it on hand. Projectors should not be unplugged without allowing the fan to cool the lamp down. Resetting the lamp timer would be done when the bulb is replaced so that it can keep track of remaining bulb life for you.

86. A. CompTIA's best practice methodology to resolve problems consists of the following steps:

   1. Identify the problem.

   2. Establish a theory of probable cause (question the obvious).

   3. Test the theory to determine the cause.

   4. Establish a plan of action to resolve the problem and implement the solution.

   5. Verify full system functionality, and if applicable, implement preventive measures.

   6. Document the findings, actions, and outcomes.

87. B. Before implementing any changes to computer systems or infrastructure, it's important to consider the corporate policies and procedures as well as what impact your plan of action will have in totality, not just on the system in question.

88. D. Hard drives, NAS, RAID arrays, NICs, and other devices, even motherboards, use LED codes to let you know what's going on with them. Knowing the LED codes for your particular system is important. In the device used for this question (a Seagate NAS array), alternating red and white means the RAID is synchronizing or software is updating. Blinking white happens when the drive is starting up, shutting down, or has activity. When the LED is solid white, the system is ready, but even an experienced tech wouldn't know that without checking the documentation or familiarity with the specific product.

89. D. While this error can be caused by a faulty hard drive, it's more likely that someone left a USB drive in the computer and it's set to boot to USB before the hard drive. It's unlikely that the OS was deleted unless there was an electrical event or someone sneaking in and deleting it. If the POST detected a problem with the system, you would not have gotten this far. To remedy the situation, enter the BIOS/UEFI and change the boot order so that USB ports are not included, or at the very least, so that it looks for the hard drive first.

90. B, C. Hole punch and staple are considered finishing options on printers. Both of these can occasionally cause print jobs to stall. Incorrect paper size can also cause printers to stall but is not a finishing option. Paper orientation will usually cause undesirable effects on the output and might stall a print job, but again this is not a finishing option.

91. C. Packet loss occurs when a chunk of data doesn't make it to its destination, and words cutting out is a symptom of it. Increasing bandwidth, setting up a VLAN for the phones, or updating hardware may fix it. Jitter manifests as garbled or stuttered speech. High bandwidth and low latency are always desirable features.

92. B, D. If hole punching isn't enabled, the printer/copier won't hole-punch the documents. User error could also be a problem. Ensure that users are trained on selecting finishing options. If the hole punch waste tray is full but everything else is in order, most printers will pause the print job until the tray is emptied. A document in the automatic document feeder (ADF) should have no effect on the current print job. If it were left on the scanning tray it might, depending on the printer.

93. D. Typically a fan should run a while to cool the bulb down when you've finished using a projector. A single loud pop sound, dim or flickering image, and muddy colors are all symptoms of a projector lamp that is burned out or on its way to burning out.

94. B. Most RAID arrays will have indicator lights to tell you the status of the drive. These may vary by manufacturer, but anything other than a green light is usually a cause for concern. Other statuses that the lights may tell you are when the drive is rebuilding, a rebuild is aborted, or the drive is predicted to fail.

95. A. Putting USB locks on all the USB ports would certainly prevent the PC from booting to them, but it would also prohibit you from using those ports when you need them. If the OS was installed on a bootable USB, you could likely boot from it, but that's not what you want either. You want it to boot to the hard drive. Whether it's Windows or Linux isn't the issue either. You need to change the BIOS/UEFI boot order settings or disable booting to USB.

96. B. Since inquire regarding environmental changes is part of step 1 of the best practice methodology, the next step is step 2, establish a theory of probable cause. CompTIA's best practice methodology to resolve problems consists of the following steps:

1. Identify the problem.

2. Establish a theory of probable cause (question the obvious).

3. Test the theory to determine the cause.

4. Establish a plan of action to resolve the problem and implement the solution.

5. Verify full system functionality, and if applicable, implement preventive measures.

6. Document the findings, actions, and outcomes.

97. C. You can't format or install an OS on the hard drive until the system can see that it's there. Occasionally you will find a drive that is DOA (Dead on Arrival), but it's more likely that you forgot to plug in either the data cable or the power cable for the drive. You would certainly check those before installing a different drive.

98. A. While the CPU may be the component that generated the error, the most common cause of this particular error is RAM. This is considered a fatal error in your operating system, producing the infamous blue screen of death (BSOD) in Windows or the rotating/spinning pinwheel in macOS.

99. C. If the CPU is overheating, it may be that the heat sink is not functioning properly or is not connected properly to the CPU. After the system cools down, try using new thermal paste and reseating the heat sink. Overclocking will only make the processor run hotter. If reseating the heat sink does not work, you might need to replace the processor or install a better cooler.

100. D. As batteries get older, they are not able to hold as much of a charge, and in some cases, they are not able to hold a charge at all. It might be time for a new tablet.

101. C. Check the easy fixes first. It might seem silly, but be sure that the display is plugged into a power outlet and turned on. Check to see if its power light is on.

102. B, C. Many laptop power adapters have a light on them indicating that they're plugged in. If there's no light, check to make sure that the outlet is working or switch outlets. Also, most laptops have a power-ready indicator light when plugged into a wall outlet as well. Check to see whether it's lit. If the outlet is fine, try another power adapter. They do fail on occasion.

103. B. Sometimes you will tap on an app and nothing happens. Most likely, this means that something has corrupted the app, but it could possibly be a memory issue. Try powering the device off and back on again and then try the app once more. If that doesn't resolve the problem, simply uninstall and reinstall the app.

104. A. Most macOS machines will make a chime sound on a successful bootup, so we're relatively certain the problem is not the motherboard itself. Before going that route, try another display or try this display on another computer. That will narrow it down quickly. Remember, if it's not the display, it's probably the video card.

105. B. If you try to power on the system but get no lights or fan, first check the obvious things. Is it plugged in? Does the cord work? If those all check out, then it's probably the power supply unit (PSU).

106. B. A display can present incorrect colors if the pins on the connector are damaged or if the connector isn't plugged all the way in.

107. A. One beep every five seconds indicates that the Mac isn't detecting any RAM. Sometimes RAM will creep out of place because of heating and cooling of the metal contacts. This might also happen if you just installed new RAM. If it's updating firmware, the Mac will beep three long, three short, and three long beeps. After a time, the Mac should start up normally. If it produces three beeps, a five-second pause, and three more beeps, then the RAM didn't pass its integrity check and needs to be reinstalled or replaced.

108. B, C. Depending on the printer and the settings, either choosing a different tray or changing the printer settings may do the trick. The printer may be overriding the software settings. Most printers don't have a single automatic tray that lets you turn the paper 90 degrees (it's done using multiple trays), although some manual-feed trays will.

109. A, B. Depending on your printer, there may be several reasons it's making a grinding sound, and the fixes vary by printer, but the two solutions here are fairly universal. If a cable moves along with the printhead, make sure that is it not caught on something or

obstructed in some way. Check for any blockages or debris that may be preventing moving parts from moving. It those two things don't resolve the issue, refer to the manufacturer's documentation or online resources as there are many different kinds and manufacturers of 3D printers. 3D printers don't have ink ribbons, and you wouldn't replace the printhead (Nozzle Extruder Print Head) without further troubleshooting first.

110. B, D. Sometimes using off-brand ink and toner works just fine, and other times it doesn't. It may be close enough for most of us but not for an artist's eye. Try using ink or toner made specifically for that make and model of printer. Another quick fix is to ensure that the printer is defaulting to better quality, not faster speed. The exact steps to do that depend on the specific printer being used. Paper orientation has nothing to do with color, and you might need to reinstall a corrupted printer driver, but it's unlikely that you'll need to delete and reinstall the printer to correct a color problem.

111. B, D. Two things that can cause ghosting are a broken cleaning blade or bad erasure lamps. A broken cleaning blade causes old toner to build up on the EP drum and consequently present itself in the next printed image. If the erasure lamps are bad, then the previous electrostatic discharges aren't completely wiped away. When the EP drum rotates toward the developing roller, some toner sticks to the slightly discharged areas. A third cause can be printing many copies of a document without allowing the printer to cool off between. In that case, the toner can stick onto the fusing roller.

112. B, C. The I/O switch will not allow the PSU to power on if it is in the Off position; equally, the wrong voltage being selected may prevent the computer from starting, and if it does start, using the wrong voltage would have disastrous consequences. The other two choices are irrelevant to the problem at hand.

113. A. If the laptop works while it's plugged in but not while it's on battery power, the battery itself may be the culprit. As batteries get older, they are not able to hold as much of a charge, and in some cases, they are not able to hold a charge at all.

114. D. If you smell an odd odor or see smoke coming from a computer, shut it down immediately. Open the case and start looking for visible signs of damage. Things to look for include melted plastic components and burn marks on circuit boards. If components appear to be damaged, it's best to replace them before returning the computer to service.

115. C. Modern multifunction devices (MFDs) are practically computers on their own. As such, like computers, restarting them will sometimes clear existing problems. If that fails, you could try the other three options given, but refer to the individual printer manufacturer's troubleshooting procedures.

116. C. When a fusing assembly doesn't have a chance to cool off, toner can melt onto the overheated fusing roller, causing ghost images to appear on the printed page. The roller will need to be cleaned or replaced.

117. B. If jobs aren't printing and there's no apparent reason why, it could be that the print spooler has stalled. To fix the problem, you need to stop and restart the print spooler. This is done through your operating system. The downside is that the print jobs in the queue will be deleted and users will need to reprint them.

118. A, B. Sometimes, when you print a color document, the colors might not be the same colors that you expected based on what you saw on the screen. A few different issues could cause this problem. First, ink could be bleeding from adjacent areas of the picture, causing the color to be off. A leaking cartridge can cause this, as can using the wrong type of paper for your printer. Paper that is designed for an ink-jet printer has different characteristics than paper designed for a laser printer. You should always use the right paper for your type of printer to avoid problems like incorrect colors or ink bleeding into unintended areas. Second, it could be a dirty printhead. Try running the self-cleaning routine. If that doesn't work, consider replacing the ink cartridges.

119. C. If the pickup roller or separation pads get dirty or damaged, the result can be multiple pages picked up instead of just one at a time. To remedy the situation, either clean them or replace them. The fusing assembly has to do with melting toner on the paper, and the primary corona charges the drum. It's unlikely that a paper tray would need replacing, and you've already verified that it is properly adjusted.

120. B, C. The spots are likely being caused by dirt or debris in the printer, on the scanning tray, or in the automatic document feeder (ADF). Replacing the high-voltage power supply (HVPS) is not going to fix this problem, and you would never use compressed air to blow debris out of a printer. It may cause dust and debris to go even deeper into the device or contain an explosive material that shouldn't be used with electronics. Instead, follow the manufacturer's instructions for thoroughly cleaning all parts of the machine.

121. C. There's probably a simple explanation for this one. The device may be in silent or vibrate mode. Most mobile devices will have a switch on the side that sets them to silent or vibrate mode, and that will mute the device from making a noise when it receives a call or a message. If that doesn't resolve the problem, it might also be a good idea to check their volume settings.

122. A. Some wireless cards will have their connection and activity lights alternatively blink if there is no network connection. If the card had failed, there likely would be no lights on it at all.

123. B. The address shown is one assigned by the IPv4 Automatic Private IP Addressing (APIPA) service. It autoconfigures your network card with an IP address if your computer is set to receive an IP address from the Dynamic Host Configuration Protocol (DHCP) server and that server doesn't respond. You can always tell an APIPA address because it will be in the format of 169.254.*x.x*.

124. C. Faded prints generally mean the printer is running out of ink. Replace the ink cartridge and the problem should disappear.

125. C, D. A failing motherboard or CPU often causes continuous reboots. A hard drive failure might give an error such as "No operating system found." If the power supply failed, the computer would not be booting at all.

126. D. If the problem affects multiple users, chances are that it's an issue with the central connectivity device. Suspect an issue with the switch that the computers are plugged into.

127. C. Given that the user recently cleaned their desk, it is likely cables were moved. The first thing to check would be the network cable. You know that they have logged in because they are working locally. If the servers were offline or the problem was caused by a reconfigured Group Policy, you would be receiving other complaints.

128. A. Opening the projector's log to review for relevant information is a good step to take. From the description, it doesn't sound like the culprit was loose cables, lighting, or overheating.

129. C. The most likely explanation is that the wireless router is overheating. If it randomly shuts down in the afternoon, being in the sun may contribute to overheating.

130. B. Part of identifying the problem is to gather information from the user, identify user changes to the computer, and perform backups before making changes. One could argue that doing external or internal research is part of identifying the problem as well, but in A+ troubleshooting methodology, that step is part of establishing a theory of probable cause. CompTIA's best practice methodology to resolve problems consists of the following steps:

1. Identify the problem.

2. Establish a theory of probable cause (question the obvious).

3. Test the theory to determine the cause.

4. Establish a plan of action to resolve the problem and implement the solution.

5. Verify full system functionality, and if applicable, implement preventive measures.

6. Document the findings, actions, and outcomes.

131. B. Wi-Fi signals can be blocked by thick walls, and concrete walls are very thick indeed. While the office might be a safe place for the billing clerk to work, the walls are blocking their Wi-Fi signal.

132. C. Although your spouse may want a better laptop, if it was working fine before and the only thing that has changed is router placement, that's most likely the problem. Large motors and microwaves, among other things, can cause electromagnetic interference (EMI), which can wreak havoc with Wi-Fi signals. To solve the problem, move the router and work area to another location.

133. A. Wi-Fi signals are radio waves and part of the electromagnetic spectrum. The metal staircase would act like an antenna, absorbing the energy of the signal. Sofas are thick and most have metal in them that will also absorb the signal. The sunny windowsill is out in the open, but sunlight can interfere with radio signals too, and too much heat might damage the router. The best option here is on the stand in the corner of the dining room, which is in the center of the home. While you have chairs and a table there, there would likely not be as much furniture to block the signal as behind the sofa. Placement would, of course, depend on the exact situation.

134. B, D. Newer iPads, like smartphones, have the display, digitizer, and glass front neatly bonded together, so if you must replace one, you must replace them all. If a backup has not been recently made and the device is still working, make one immediately. A bit of package sealing tape over the crack may keep it together until it can be repaired and keep your friend from cutting their finger again.

135. C, D. When troubleshooting an issue, a technician should never leave it unresolved. If the technician's first attempt at solving the problem failed, there are two acceptable next steps, depending on the situation and available resources. The first is to establish a new theory and test it. The second is to escalate the issue to a more experienced technician who may be able to solve it.

136. D. Part of establishing a theory of probable cause is to perform external or internal research based on symptoms. CompTIA's best practice methodology to resolve problems consists of the following steps:

1. Identify the problem.

2. Establish a theory of probable cause (question the obvious).

3. Test the theory to determine the cause.

4. Establish a plan of action to resolve the problem and implement the solution.

5. Verify full system functionality, and if applicable, implement preventive measures.

6. Document the findings, actions, and outcomes.

137. B. It's easy to accidentally bump the Airplane mode button on some smartphones. Airplane mode turns off cellular and Wi-Fi service on your device so that it won't interfere with a plane's controls during takeoff and landing. Luckily, turning off Airplane mode is equally easy.

138. B. Multiple walls and floors between you and the outside world, not to mention all the electronic equipment found inside an office building, may be interfering with your signal. Move toward an outside wall or window away from the interfering walls and equipment to see if the connection improves.

139. C. If you are using RAID 0 (disk striping), you have increased performance but no fault tolerance. RAID 0 has more points of failure than a single drive would, meaning that you're at a greater risk of failure versus using just one hard drive. One drive failure will cause the entire set to fail. To recover it, your only option is to replace the failed disk and restore from backup. You cannot rebuild the array as you could with RAID 1 or RAID 5.

140. B. According to troubleshooting methodology, backups should be made before making changes. This is part of the first step, which is identifying the problem. It does make a lot of sense to perform backups before making major changes to a system—just in case.

141. C. If print jobs are processed very slowly or if you are continually seeing "low memory" error messages, it might be a good time to upgrade the memory in the printer.

142. C. If you are using RAID 0 (disk striping), you have more points of failure than a single device, meaning that you're at a greater risk of failure versus using just one hard drive. One drive failure will cause the entire set to fail. If a single drive fails with RAID 1, RAID 5, or RAID 10, the system will not crash, and you can rebuild the failed drive from the information on the other drives. If the drives are hot-swappable, you may be able to do it without incurring any downtime at all.

143. A. If this happens, don't panic. Wait several minutes to see if it stops. Most likely the screen is flashing on and off several times because the operating system is updating. Flashing could indicate a display that is failing; however, it was working fine before you restarted it, so it's more likely to be an update.

144. B. CompTIA's best practice methodology to resolve problems consists of the following steps:

1. Identify the problem.

2. Establish a theory of probable cause (question the obvious).

3. Test the theory to determine the cause.

4. Establish a plan of action to resolve the problem and implement the solution.

5. Verify full system functionality, and if applicable, implement preventive measures.

6. Document the findings, actions, and outcomes.

145. A. A loose video cable may be fine while you're stationary, but wiggle enough to lose connection between the motherboard and display when the laptop is moved. Luckily, this is an easy fix. The video cable in a laptop is a very thin and delicate ribbon cable. Disassemble the laptop following manufacturer's instructions to the point where you can reseat the video cable, then carefully reseat it.

146. B. HDMI cables carry both video and audio signals. These cables can wear out over time from excessive use, plugging and unplugging, or excessive heat.

147. B. While an overheated projector will shut down, and a burned-out lamp will not project an image, the most likely cause is that the projector simply went to sleep after a time of inactivity. Usually a touch of the power button will wake it up again.

148. D. It's always good to consider the feelings of the user so that you don't make them feel worse for a situation that they likely already feel bad about. But the right answer is to consider corporate policies, procedures, and impacts before implementing changes. Perhaps considering user feelings should be part of the corporate policies and procedures for technicians.

149. C. You know that the drive's data and power cables are plugged in properly because the drive is showing in the BIOS/UEFI. The drive won't show in File Explorer until it is partitioned and formatted. There is no need to reinstall the OS or replace the drive. Neither is faulty.

150. D. A loose power cable can cause intermittent shutdown. Try reseating the cables. If the unit is overheating, it will shut down and not turn back on until it cools. Check to see if there is excessive dust in the cooling fan, and if so, clean it. Projectors also have a filter that may need periodic cleaning to avoid overheating. A loose HDMI cable would have other symptoms such as a flickering image or distorted sound.

151. B. The hard drive cache will hold information that is being used repeatedly so it can be accessed more quickly, much like the cache on a processor. It also acts as a buffer between writing data and the hard drive, improving system performance; however, if the power goes out unexpectedly, data stored in the hard drive's cache will be lost.

152. D. Replacing the mechanical drives with SSDs will improve the performance, but not the fault tolerance of the system. RAID 0 (disk striping) does the same. RAID 1 (mirroring) will provide fault tolerance but does nothing to help performance. RAID 5 provides disk striping and parity. The striping improves system read/write speed and the parity means that if one drive crashes, the system can continue working until the drive is replaced.

153. B. According to CompTIA's best practice methodology for resolving problems, the final step is to document the findings, actions, and outcomes. CompTIA's best practice methodology to resolve problems consists of the following steps:

 1. Identify the problem.

 2. Establish a theory of probable cause (question the obvious).

 3. Test the theory to determine the cause.

 4. Establish a plan of action to resolve the problem and implement the solution.

 5. Verify full system functionality, and if applicable, implement preventive measures.

 6. Document the findings, actions, and outcomes.

154. A, D. Every computer has a diagnostic program built into its basic input/output system (BIOS) called the power-on self-test (POST). When you turn on the computer, it executes this set of diagnostics. The steps include checking the CPU, checking the RAM, checking for the presence of a video card, and verifying basic hardware functionality. An error in the BIOS or one of the checked components can cause a beep code.

155. A. If the laptop is locked up, the only way to reboot it is with a hard boot. Although removing all the power sources would work, it's not necessary to do so. Simply hold down the power button for about five seconds, and the laptop will power off. If that does not work, then you might need to remove power sources.

156. B. If a mobile device is overheating, turn it off to let it cool down. It could be from overuse, or perhaps it was left in a hot environment or did not have proper ventilation. If it continues to overheat or does so for no reason, expect a problem with the battery, and if possible, replace the battery. If the battery can't be replaced, replace the phone.

157. C. If the phone is really slow but isn't completely locked up, isolate the issue. Is it one app or overall performance? It could be that apps are running in the background and need to be closed. Shutting down those apps or powering the device off and then back on is a good step. You can also check to see how much memory is available. If it's one app that's giving you problems instead of the entire device, look for updates to the app, or delete and reinstall the app. Finally, if none of these steps works, perform a restore to factory settings. If the problems persist, it's time for a new device.

158. D. One potential cause of intermittent device failures is chip creep, which happens when components such as expansion cards start to creep out of their socket. This can be caused by heating and cooling. Reseat the card (and screw it into the case!) and see whether that resolves the issue. If not, you may need to replace the sound card.

159. D. In a networked environment, users need the proper permissions both to install and to print to the printer. Not having permission will result in denied access.

160. C. Printer jams (aka "The printer crinkled my paper!") happen when something prevents the paper from advancing through the printer evenly. There are generally three causes of printer jams: an obstructed paper path, stripped drive gears, and using the wrong paper.

161. C. If you have a toner spill, don't use compressed air to blow it away. You should use a specialized toner vacuum to pick it up. Also, never use a damp cloth to try to clean up a toner spill. If a cloth is needed, use a dry one.

162. A, C. When repairing laptops, you should always document and label screw and cable locations, organize parts, refer to manufacturer instructions, and use appropriate hand tools. In some cases, but not all, you might need to remove the hard drive to remove the motherboard. To remove the motherboard, use appropriate tools recommended by the manufacturer as each system can be different.

163. B. In an LCD display, dimness or flickering is most commonly caused by the backlight starting to fail. In those cases, replace the backlight or the display.

164. A. If your printer isn't spitting out print jobs, it may be a good idea to print a test page and see whether that works. The test page information is stored in the printer's memory, so there's no formatting or translating of jobs required. If the test page works, then the problem is not communication between PC and printer. If nothing happens, double-check your connections and stop and restart the print spooler. If garbage prints, there is likely a problem with the printer or the print driver.

165. C. If a laptop keyboard is not responding, you can always plug in an external keyboard and use that. It might not be an ideal long-term solution, but it will generally get a user back up and running.

166. A, B. The most likely components are the processor and the memory. Try reseating the chips or testing them. If the problems persist, you may need to replace those components. It could also be the motherboard.

167. C. If your hard drive fails completely and you need to get critical data off it, there are third-party companies that provide file recovery software and services. These services are generally very expensive. (And your user should have been backing up the drive in the first place!)

168. C. If your wireless networking isn't working, check to make sure that the LEDs on your network card are functioning. If there are no lights, it could indicate a problem with the card itself or, on some cards, that there is no connection or signal. Considering they received a signal in that location previously, it's most likely something to do with the card. First, make sure the wireless card is enabled through the OS.

169. A. If an iPhone is entirely frozen, all you really can do is power it off and then back on. The exact buttons to press depend on the model, but the process described in this question works for iPhones X, 11, 12, and 13.

170. B. The most likely cause of this intermittent Wi-Fi issue is a low RF signal. If you get too far from a WAP, the signal will be too weak and the Wi-Fi will disconnect.

171. C. The correct printer driver needs to be installed for the printer and operating system. For example, if you have an HP LaserJet Pro M15w and a Windows 11 computer, then you need to install an HP LaserJet Pro M15w driver made for Windows 11. If this is not done, you will get garbled characters out of the printer. Often the Windows OS will have adequate drivers for your printer, but the manufacturer's driver downloads often come with other software that provides additional features for you to use with your printer, and if the output is garbled, then you certainly want to use the manufacturer's printer drivers, not those provided with Windows.

172. B, C. If a laptop does not display any video, it could be the screen or the video card/integrated video. To test it, plug in an external display (that you know works), and use the function keys on the laptop to switch to external video output. If that doesn't work, it's likely that the video card is defective. If the external display works, you know it's a problem with the display on the laptop. The backlight (or inverter) could be dead or it could be the screen.

173. B. If the phone is extremely slow but isn't completely locked up, isolate the issue. Is it one app or overall performance? It could be that apps are running in the background and need to be closed. Shutting down those apps or powering the device off and then back on is a good step. You can also check to see how much memory is available. If it's one app giving you problems instead of the entire device, look for updates to the app or delete and reinstall the app. Finally, if none of these steps works, perform a restore to factory settings. If the problems persist, it's time for a new device.

174. C. All-black pages happen when the charging unit (the charging corona wire or charging corona roller) in the toner cartridge malfunctions and fails to place a charge on the EP drum. Because the drum is grounded, it has no charge. Anything with a charge (like toner) will stick to it. As the drum rotates, all of the toner is transferred to the page and a black page is formed. Replace the toner cartridge. Other possible causes not listed include a defective DC controller PCA (printed circuit assembly) or a defective high-voltage power supply.

175. B. If the system had been operating normally but now tells you RAID not found, it's likely something is wrong with the RAID controller. Double-check to ensure that the RAID controller BIOS is configured properly and everything is connected as it should be.

176. A, C. If the screen is slow to refresh, an obvious solution is to buy a display with a faster refresh rate. Additionally, certain unacceptable video-quality issues (such as jerky refresh speeds or lags) can be remedied by increasing video card memory. Since most video cards don't have the ability to add memory, you'll likely need to purchase a new video card. Doing so generally results in an increase in both quality and performance.

177. C. Dim or flickering displays on mobile devices are usually caused by a faulty backlight in the display panel. A failing inverter can cause these problems, too.

178. B. Pointer drift is the mouse cursor slowly drifting in one direction even though you are not trying to make it move. This issue is generally related to the point stick not centering properly after it's been used. If you have pointer drift, try using the point stick and moving it back and forth a few times to get it to recenter itself. You can also try rebooting. If the problem persists, either disable or replace the point stick.

179. C. Cable testers are indispensable tools for any network technician. Usually you would use a cable tester before you install a cable to make sure it works. Of course, you can test them after they've been run as well.

180. B. The iPhone and iPad use the term *Location Services* to refer to GPS. Android devices will call it *Location*, *Location Services*, or *Location Reporting*. On an iPhone, you enable Location Services under Settings ➤ Privacy. In Android, location access settings are usually configured under Settings ➤ Location or Settings ➤ Personal ➤ Location.

181. D. Toner cartridges are often shipped with a strip of sealing tape across the cartridge to keep the toner from getting shaken out during shipment. If the user forgets to remove the tape, the printer will only print blank pages. The solution to this problem is fortunately quite easy: remove the toner cartridge from the printer, remove the sealing tape, and reinstall the cartridge.

182. D. The most common cause of an IP address conflict is if someone configures a computer with a static IP address that's part of the DHCP server's range. The DHCP server, not knowing that the address has been statically assigned somewhere, doles out the address, and now there's a conflict. Rebooting the computer won't help, and neither will releasing the address and getting a new lease from the DHCP server—it's just going to hand out the same address again because it doesn't know that there's a problem. As the administrator, you need to track down the offending user. A common way to do this is to use a packet sniffer to look at network traffic and determine the computer name or MAC address associated with the IP address in question.

183. C. The `ifconfig` command is used in Linux, Unix, and macOS to check a computer's IP configuration information. `ipconfig` is used in Windows.

184. D. Most keyboards will have status lights for the Caps Lock and Num Lock keys. If you believe a system is locked up, try pressing the Caps Lock or Num Lock key on the keyboard to see whether the lights change. If they don't, that's a sign that the system is unresponsive. Reboot the computer.

185. B. Luckily with today's large hard drives, this problem doesn't happen often. However, if a hard drive is too full and has less than 10 percent free space, it can slow down dramatically. The first solution to try is to remove files and uninstall unused apps to free up space. Then you would want to run Disk Cleanup and optimize the drive. If that doesn't resolve the issue, you may need to replace the hard drive.

186. A. The `ping` command is one of the most useful commands in the TCP/IP protocol. It sends a series of packets to another system, which in turn sends back a response. This utility can be extremely useful for troubleshooting problems with remote hosts. The `ping -t` command sets a persistent ping, which does not stop until you cancel it.

187. A. If the key physically sticks, you can try blowing out underneath the key with compressed air or use a cotton swab slightly dampened with isopropyl alcohol to clean underneath the key. Make sure to clean the entire surface underneath the sticking key. If none of this resolves the issue, you might need to replace the keyboard.

188. C. Failure to open files means that the computer can't properly read those files. In most cases, this indicates an issue with the hard drive.

189. B. In an LCD display, dimness or flickering is most commonly caused by the backlight starting to fail. In those cases, replace the backlight or the display.

190. D. Stepper motor problems on inkjet and impact printers will look similar to each other. If the main motor is damaged, lines of print will be unevenly spaced, and if the printhead motor goes bad, characters will be scrunched together.

191. D. Suspect that the WAP is down. A low RF signal would show fewer bars but should still be able to connect to the WAP, especially if they did the day before. An oversaturated WAP would show sluggish performance and dropped packets. SSID broadcast shouldn't be the issue because they've connected to this network before and likely have saved the network to their device. Since there is more than one user, the problem probably isn't the individual user. It is, most likely, that the WAP has failed.

192. C. If your printer isn't spitting out print jobs, it may be a good idea to print a test page and see whether that works. The test page information is stored in the printer's memory, so there's no formatting or translating of jobs required. It's simply a test to make sure that your printer hears your computer. If the test page works but other print jobs don't print, there could be a problem with the application or the driver.

193. B, C. Small devices sometimes suffer from an extremely short battery life. If it's a laptop, you may be able to perform a battery calibration. For all mobile devices, you can try to drain the battery completely and then charge it fully before turning the device back on. If these options don't work, then it's likely that the battery needs to be replaced.

194. C. The yellow exclamation point tells you that there is a problem with the driver, and updating the driver may be all it takes to get this user on the network.

195. C. Nearly all PCIe RAID controllers will have their own BIOS for setup, configuration, and troubleshooting. Some will have utilities available for use within an operating system as well. If a motherboard has an onboard RAID controller, you will likely need to go to the BIOS/UEFI to configure it.

196. D. The power supply is the only component listed with moving parts and therefore is the most likely component to cause a whining sound. It's more than likely a fan. Either it needs to be cleaned (desperately) or replaced. Power supplies that are failing can also sound louder and quieter intermittently because a fan will run at alternating speeds.

197. A. Every computer has a diagnostic program built into its basic input/output system (BIOS) called the power-on self-test (POST). When you turn on the computer, it executes this set of diagnostics. If the computer doesn't perform the POST as it should, one way to determine the source of a problem is to listen for a beep code. This is a series of beeps from the computer's speaker. A successful POST generally produces a single beep. If there's more than one beep, the number, duration, and pattern of the beeps can sometimes tell you what component is causing the problem. Check the documentation to determine the specific issue.

198. B. The most likely cause is that the router is configured to not broadcast SSIDs. 802.11ac and 802.11ax are compatible, and they are certainly within range if your computer is connected right next to theirs. Provide the user the SSID and password so that they can connect.

199. C. Both repeated crashes and soaring data usage could indicate malware on a phone. Typically, Android OS security updates end three years after the OS release, and without security updates an older device is more at risk of contracting malware. The best thing to do in this scenario is go to the Google Play store and download anti-malware software to check the device. It might also be time to consider an upgrade.

200. D. A groove or scratch in the EP drum can cause the problem of vertical black lines running down all or part of the page. Because a scratch is lower than the surface, it doesn't receive as much (if any) of a charge as the other areas. The result is that toner sticks to it as though it were discharged. The groove may go around the circumference of the drum, so the line may go all the way down the page.

201. A. Dim or flickering displays on mobile devices are usually caused by a faulty backlight in the display panel. A failing inverter can cause these problems, too.

202. A, D. If you're curious as to the state of your power supply, you can buy hardware-based power supply testers or multimeters to test it. Loopback plugs are for testing network interface cards (NICs), and POST cards are for testing motherboards.

203. C. If the laptop won't output a screen image to an external display or projector, it means one of two things (assuming you know that the display or projector works): either the external video port is malfunctioning or the function keys aren't working. In either case, you likely need to replace the motherboard if you want the display to appear on an external device.

204. B. Most wireless headsets use a Bluetooth connection. The first thing to check is that Bluetooth is enabled, which also means double-checking that Airplane mode is not turned on. In this case, Bluetooth is off.

205. A. Your first step is to see if a firmware update to the WAP will provide the new security protocol that you need. You'll want to try updating the devices' firmware or software as well. During transition times, WAPs will often have a transitional security setting that will support both the older and the new devices until you can get everything updated. If you can't update your old WAP, the next step would be to look for a new WAP to use during your transition.

206. B. Input/output operations per second (IOPS) is the only way to truly compare the speed when some drives are solid state and others are mechanical. Mechanical drives often use revolutions per minute (RPM), which is also known as spindle speed, as an indication of how fast they can access data. Solid-state drives (SSDs) have no moving parts, so there is no spindle speed. Regardless of the drive type, IOPS is a better way to compare drive performance, and the only way when they are not the same type of drive. Other factors to consider are how long the drive is expected to last and drive latency.

207. B, C. HDDs have a natural speed disadvantage compared to SSDs because of their moving parts. As hard drive storage gets bigger, the performance lag is exaggerated. SSDs have no moving parts, so their latency is much lower. Either replacing the existing HDDs with several smaller drives or the same size of SSDs would increase the performance, but also the cost of the drives. IOPS is the best measure to use when comparing drive performance.

208. B, D. A significant change in usage patterns can affect the IOPS on the system based on the type/size of files being transferred and the software used to do it. If a drive in the array has failed, that will also affect the maximum IOPS the system is capable of, as there is one less drive to do the work.

209. A. A dim or flickering screen can be a sign that the display assembly needs to be replaced, but before you go that route, it's best to check the brightness or auto-brightness features. Location settings and battery are irrelevant in this situation. The battery is still working because they can see something.

210. C. This error will happen when you have logged on to a familiar Wi-Fi but it is unable to connect to the Internet. If the password was the problem, you would have gotten an error about being unable to automatically connect, in which case you would forget the network and rejoin with the new password. You could use your cellular data, but it might be better to help the friend get their Internet connection working again instead.

211. D. Improperly adjusted antennas can make a big difference in wireless connectivity. In this case, take a few minutes and a Wi-Fi analyzer to check the signal strength and adjust the antenna until it's just where you want it. You would not need to adjust the WAP's signal strength because you're right under it, looking up at it. Even on the lowest power setting you should still see more bars. The SSID being broadcast or not is irrelevant.

212. B. Setting a WAP to transmit at the maximum power may cause the Wi-Fi to extend into areas you would rather it didn't. It can also cause problems like more interference causing poor performance and stability because it's picking up signals from nearby Wi-Fi networks. Enabling or disabling the SSID broadcast will have no effect on the signal strength. It may take a bit of playing with settings, antennas, and placement to get the Wi-Fi transmission exactly how you need it to be, but in this case, lowering the WAP's power setting is a good start.

213. C, D. The answer will depend on the exact situation, but if your WAP is experiencing interference from other WAPs or networks, you may want to lower, rather than raise, the signal strength. You would want to run a network analyzer and choose the channel with the least traffic, or optionally, if the WAP allows, let it choose the best channel for you. Installing an antenna with a lower gain might also work.

Chapter 6: Operating Systems

1. B. Depending on the version of Windows you are using, net can be one of the most powerful commands at your disposal. While all Windows versions include a net command, its capabilities differ based on whether it is used on a server or workstation and the version of the operating system. Commonly net share is used to create shared folders, and net use is used to connect to shared resources. The net user command allows administrators to create and manage user accounts. netstat shows what sockets (IP address plus port) are being used and by which protocols. net share is a valid command for managing shared resources, but netshare and netdom are not valid commands.

2. B. It's possible that the hard drive has some bad sectors, so run chkdsk to scan the drive and attempt to repair them. If that doesn't work, formatting is the second option, and replacing the drive is the third. If your drive is getting read/write errors, having an extra hard drive on hand would be wise.

3. C. The diskpart utility lets the user see and manage partitions on the computer's hard drives. Because of the enormous power it holds, the user must have administrator status to run diskpart. Once a partition is created, the format command will set up the filesystem on the new volume. The chkdsk command verifies the disk integrity, and gpupdate forces Group Policy changes to take effect immediately.

4. C. The net share command is used to share folders on a network as well as stop sharing folders. The proper syntax to share a folder is
net share <*share name*>=<*drive letter*>:<*path*>. To stop sharing, use
net share <*share name*> /delete. You must be running the Command Prompt as an administrator to create and delete shares.

5. A. Windows 10 Home edition does not offer BitLocker as an option. BitLocker is available in the Pro, Pro for Workstations, and Enterprise editions.

6. C, D. Resilient File System (ReFS) is a feature available on Windows Pro for Workstations and Windows Enterprise editions. ReFS will detect when data on a mirrored drive has been corrupted and will use a healthy copy of the data on other drives to attempt to correct corrupted data and protect data.

7. C. Windows Pro for Workstations is designed so that users can take advantage of the capabilities of high-end workstations. Windows Home edition can support one physical processor, Windows Pro can support up to two physical processors, while Windows Pro for Workstations can support up to four physical processors.

8. B. Windows Home does not have the capability of joining a domain, so the employee will not be able to use their personal device. Windows Pro, Pro for Workstations, and Enterprise editions are all able to log into a domain. The number of processors and amount of RAM are irrelevant to the ability to log into a domain.

9. A, D. Task Manager is a powerful tool that works in all versions of Windows, although it has different capabilities in different versions. In Windows 10 and 11 it allows you to shut down nonresponsive applications; view performance of CPU, memory, disks, Wi-Fi, and GPUs; as well as show application usage history, services, and programs that are launched at startup, users who are attached to the system, and other useful information.

10. C. The Internet Options utility in Windows Control Panel has six tabs that allow you to configure how your browser interacts with the Internet. The six tabs are General, Security, Privacy, Content, Connections, Programs, and Advanced. Not all versions of Windows have the Content tab. The General tab allows you to change the home page whereas the Privacy tab has a Turn On Pop-up Blocker option.

11. A. A quick look at Device Manager is often all you need to troubleshoot a problem with an onboard device. If the device drivers aren't installed for the device, you'll see a yellow exclamation point in Device Manager. Programs and Features allows the user to add, remove, or troubleshoot installed programs (the options will change by program) and add Windows features that are not yet installed. The File Explorer Options utility changes how File Explorer works such as showing hidden files or extensions and other view options. Ease of Access provides alternative ways to interact with the computer for differently abled users.

12. D. To always show the time and date correctly for the salesperson's location, you would need to enable both Set time automatically and Set time zone automatically, as shown in the graphic. Synchronize your clock would work in the moment but will not automatically change the time and time zone as the salesperson travels. The Date And Time utility of Control Panel will let you change the date and time, but it does not have a setting for automatically changing them as you move from place to place. In Windows 11 Time And Language appears as Time & Language, but otherwise the choices are the same.

13. C. Voice activation, found under Privacy in Windows Settings will allow the user to turn on microphone access and choose which apps are allowed to use voice activation, even when the device is locked. The choices are slightly different in Windows 11. In Windows Settings, choose Privacy & security, then Speech. The setting is on by default. The Default Programs app of Control Panel allows you to manage default applications for opening types of files such as photos or mail by opening those settings in Windows Settings. By choosing Privacy, then Notifications in Windows Settings, you can allow or deny applications to access your notifications. Control Panel's Indexing Options looks at words in files and the files' metadata to provide faster file searches.

14. A, C. In a workgroup (peer-to-peer) network, you would first need to ensure that each person who will be using the shared resource has a username and password on the manager's computer. The resource would then be shared on the manager's PC, and on each employee's computer, go into File Explorer, click This PC, then Map network drive and follow the onscreen prompts to map drive X: to that shared resource. The choices in Windows 11 are slightly different. In File Explorer, after clicking This PC you would click the three dots in the ribbon then choose Map network drive.

15. B. In order to have a domain, you would need a domain controller (DC), for which the company would need Windows Server software installed on a network connected computer. They only have Windows 10 workstations. Homegroups were a networking scheme that shared a computer's libraries with other people on the same Homegroup, but Homegroups are no longer an option. Crossover cables are not a practical way to share anything among 10 computers. By default, the computers would belong to the workgroup named workgroup. Each computer that is sharing a resource would need to have the user they are sharing with listed on that computer, then the person sharing information could right-click a folder and choose Give access to, then Specific people and choose who they want to share that particular resource with. Workgroups are great for small groups of people, but if there are more than 20 or 30 people in the group, you'll likely want to move up to a DC and centralized security.

16. D. One of Task Manager's many capabilities is allowing you to see what resources (memory, CPU, GPU, network, and disk) are being used by application, and it allows you to end the process or the entire process tree to free up those resources. Performance Monitor will show resources used but not by application. Computer Management gives access to several other resources, but not Task Manager, whereas Windows Memory Diagnostics is used to test the health of RAM modules.

17. A. In Windows Settings, choosing Privacy, then Microphone opens a window that provides granular settings for microphone use, including which apps can use the microphone. Device Manager could be used to disable the microphone, but it would be for all purposes. Computer Management provides access to several tools, but not granular microphone settings. In Windows Settings, Personalization options allow the user to change settings such as background, colors, and lock screen. In Windows 11 the only difference is that you would choose Privacy & Security, not Privacy.

18. B. The best way to understand IPv4 addressing is to convert the IP address and subnet mask to binary numbers. This is essentially what the operating system is looking at when determining the network and host portion of an IP address. What we see as dotted decimal notation is seen by the computer as four sets of eight binary bits (either a 1 or a 0). In the subnet mask, a binary 1 indicates that the position of that bit is part of the network number and a 0 indicates that it is part of the host number. Network numbers always go consecutively from left to right with no breaks between. Eight binary bits that are all ones (11111111) equates to 255 in decimal, so the maximum value of a subnet mask's octet is 255. Options A and D are invalid subnet masks because for a number to exist in the second octet from the left, the first octet would need to be all 1s, which is equal to decimal value 255. Option C is an invalid subnet mask because the ones indicating the network number would be in the first octets reading from left to right, not the last. If we then compare the IP address of 200.100.1.10 to the subnet mask in option B, 255.255.0.0, we can see that the first two octets are network number and the last two are host numbers, making the network number 200.100.0.0 for that IP address and subnet mask combination. The host computer is then 0.0.1.10.

19. C. The default setting for obtaining an IP address is automatic, which means that the computer will look for a DHCP server to assign an IP address and subnet mask. No manual configuration is required, but in Windows 10, you can verify that the connection is set to automatically obtain an IP address, as shown in the graphic, by following these steps: Open Windows Settings, then click Network & Internet. Choose Change adapter options, and right-click the network connection in question. Then choose Properties, click Internet Protocol Version 4 (TCP/IPv4), and click Properties. The process is the same for IPv6, except that you would choose IPv6 instead of IPv4. This can also be done through Control Panel by clicking Network and Sharing Center instead of Network and Internet, then the next steps are the same. In Windows 11, Windows Settings, choose Network & Internet, click Properties of the active network connection at the top of the page. This will bring you to the network's configuration page where you can ensure that the setting for IP assignment is configured to Automatic (DHCP). The Control Panel options for Windows 11 are the same as Windows 10.

20. C. An IP address on a device can be either dynamic or static. In a static IP address, the minimum amount of information that needs to be configured is the IP address, subnet mask, and, if the computer will access the Internet or other networks, a default gateway. A proxy server is an added security measure between a device and the Internet. It is used to translate between protocols and filter out certain types of traffic such as keeping inappropriate websites out and confidential data in the network.

21. B. Often on a network, especially a smaller one, the router will serve multiple purposes. In this scenario it is the default gateway, the DHCP server, and the DNS server. 192.168.1.1 is the address of the router, gateway, DHCP server, and DNS server. 192.168.1.229 is the local computer's IP address. 48-45-20-C1-12-BD is the MAC address, which is embedded in the computer's network interface card (NIC). 255.255.255.0 is the subnet mask.

22. B, C. Web servers provide web pages to users sometimes inside but often outside of the company by answering HTTP (Hypertext Transfer Protocol) or HTTPS (HTTP Secure) requests. They are often separate from the main network on a screened subnet for security reasons. A proxy server can serve as a gateway for a network because, if one exists, traffic will go through the proxy server before going into or out of the network. In the absence of a proxy server, the router serves as a gateway, forwarding traffic on to the next network or receiving external traffic and sending it to the proper device inside a network. A switch is an internal networking device that provides a central connection point for network nodes and uses the node's MAC (Media Access Control) address that is found on the NIC (network interface card) to send packets to the proper destination.

23. A. In IPv4 networking, a computer system will compare the subnet mask to the IP address to identify the network and host number of the IP address. IPv6 addresses don't use a subnet mask. IPv6 addresses consist of eight segments. The first three are a site prefix, the fourth is the subnet ID, and the last four segments are the interface ID, which is essentially the host address. The subnet mask doesn't hide anything.

24. A, B. A network with that many computers (typically more than 10) needs a domain for security management. The Windows Home edition PCs can't log into a domain, so they would need to be upgraded to at least the Pro edition. It's not necessary to upgrade them to Pro for Workstations or Enterprise editions.

25. C. It is possible to view apps and websites in many languages and dialects. In Windows Settings, choose Time & Language, then Language (see the graphic). Click Add a language to choose the appropriate language to install, then move it to the top of the language list. Apps and websites that support that language will appear in the language that is at the top of the list. The language may require downloading a Language pack. Icons to the right of the installed language are used to indicate what is available in that language. In the graphic, to the right of English (United States) from left to right the icons indication options available are as follows: Display language, Text-to-speech, Speech recognition, Handwriting, and Spell-check.

26. B. The Processes tab of Task Manager will allow you to terminate the nonresponsive application. Event Viewer keeps a log of security, application, and system events. Computer Management gives access to several other resources, but not one that lets you end wayward applications. The `msconfig.exe` application launches System Configuration, which gives you access to boot configuration settings, running services, and links to other Windows tools.

27. A. In Control Panel, choosing Internet Options, selecting the Connections tab, and then clicking LAN settings will take you to a window that enables configuration of a proxy server. Proxy server settings can also be configured through Windows Settings by choosing Network & Internet and choosing Proxy. The File Explorer Options utility is used to configure how files and folders are viewed, and how searches are conducted. Device Manager is a great utility to use when troubleshooting hardware issues, and the Security and Maintenance utility provides a quick way to see if security is configured on the PC and to see any recent messages.

28. A, B, D. The computer is configured to obtain the address dynamically because the graphic says Yes next to DHCP Enabled. If it was set to obtain an address dynamically but not able to reach the DHCP server, the operating system would have obtained an address using APIPA (Automatic Private IP Addressing) and would have been in the range that begins with 169.254.0.0, so this PC is not being assigned an APIPA address. It is set to DHCP and getting an address that is not APIPA, so we know that it is getting its address from the DHCP server. Addresses in the 192.168.*x*.*x* range are nonroutable addresses, meaning that they can only be used internally. To reach the Internet they would go through a gateway (router) that has NAT (network address translation) enabled (essentially all modern routers use NAT). We know the network number is 192.168.1.0 and that the host address is 0.0.0.229 by comparing the IP address to the subnet mask.

29. B, D. IPv4 addresses are 32 bits long and consist of 4 octets, which is a group of 8 bits each, separated by a period (.) They are normally presented in dotted decimal notation, meaning each group of 8 bits is shown as a decimal number less than 256, with a period (.) between each number, such as 192.168.1.1. IPv6 addresses are a 128-bit IP address presented as eight segments of four hexadecimal numbers each, separated by a colon (:). Where the hexadecimal number is 0 in any segment, it can be omitted and replaced simply by double colons (::). If consecutive segments are 0, they can all be replaced by a single set of double colons, but only one set of double colons can exist in any given address—otherwise you wouldn't be able to tell how many sets of zero are in each part of the IP address. In the example, fe80::308c:fee2:dabc:8337, the expanded address would be fe80:0:0:0:308c:fee2:dabc:8337. The first three segments (48 bits) are the site prefix, and the fourth segment (16 bits) is the subnet ID, also known as private topology or site topology. The site prefix and subnet number together constitute the subnet prefix. The last four segments (64 bits) are the interface ID, also sometimes called a token. The subnet ID in this case would be 0. IPv6 addresses do not have a subnet mask. The value of the first octet, fe80, tells us that this number is a link-local address, an internal number only and not routable.

30. B, C. The IP address in question must be IPv6 because IPv4 addresses are only 32 bits long. The / indicates that the number behind it is the number of bits for the network address in IPv4 or the prefix length in IPv6, both of which identify the network number of an IP address. In IPv4 we call this CIDR (Classless Inter-domain Routing) notation.

31. A. Global unicast addresses are routable, like IPv4 public addresses. That means that a global unicast address can be reached by any other PC on the Internet, unless you put security measures in place like a firewall. You would likely want a global unicast address on a web server, but not on your workstation. Link-local addresses can only be used to communicate with devices that are on the same local link. They will start with fe80 and are assigned in a manner similar to IPv4 APIPA addresses. The IPv6 loopback address is ::1, and is used for testing just like the loopback address in IPv4 (127.0.0.1). A unique local address is akin to an IPv4 private address. Unique local addresses are nonroutable, so a computer with only a unique local address and a link-local address (but no global unicast address) would need a router with IPv6 NAT in order to access the Internet.

32. A. The Task Manager's Users tab provides information about any users that are connected to the local machine. The Users tab shows the user's identification and the resources that are being used by them. Right-click and choose Expand to see what they are using on your computer. You can also disconnect them from here, but it might be nicer to message them first.

33. C. With a 64-bit processor, you can install either a 32-bit or 64-bit operating system. A 32-bit system will not be able to take advantage of the full processing power of the 64-bit processor, though.

34. A. Windows 10 minimum requirements are a 1 GHz or faster processor or SoC (System on a Chip), DirectX 9 or later with the WDDM (Windows Display Driver Model) 1.0 driver, and a minimum 800×600 display. For storage, the 32-bit version requires 16 GB and the 64-bit version requires 20 GB available for the OS. RAM requirements are 1 GB for the 32-bit operating system and 2 GB for the 64-bit operating system. Keep in mind that these are the absolute minimum requirements, and the OS will run but not as well as we have come to expect. In reality, a faster processor, more RAM, and more storage would be expected.

35. C. Windows 10 is available in many different editions. The editions on the CompTIA A+ exam (for both Windows 10 and Windows 11) are Home, Pro, Pro for Workstations, and Enterprise. Other Windows editions (not on the CompTIA A+ exam) include Education, Pro Education, Windows 10 in S mode, Windows for IoT, and Windows 10 Team.

36. C. To connect, all you need to know is the name of the device you're connecting to, but there are steps that must have already taken place. If you're using your smartphone to connect, you need Remote Desktop Mobile installed on the smartphone and Remote Desktop must be enabled on the target PC. Then you would simply open the app on your smartphone and type the name that appeared under "How to connect to this PC" when Remote Desktop was enabled on that PC.

37. D. The `netstat` command-line utility presents statistics related to the installed network interfaces. By default, on a Windows machine, running the command will display a list of connections and the associated protocol, the source and target address, and the current state of the connection. `Ping` is used to test connectivity between two computers, `nbtstat` is used for troubleshooting NetBIOS over TCP/IP, and `nslookup` is used to query a DNS server.

38. D. The `/? [command name]` syntax simply does not work. The CompTIA A+ objectives list `[command name] /?`, but there are other ways to get help at a command prompt. Typing **help** and pressing Enter at a command prompt will provide a list of commands that `help` can help you with. Armed with that information, you can type **help [command name]**, for example, **help xcopy**, and you will see the syntax, switches, and explanations for how the command works. Some commands, for example, `sfc`, will not work with that help syntax. To find help with `sfc`, you would type **sfc /?, sfc /help** or **sfc help**, but none of those options work with all commands. For example, `gpresult /?` works, but `gpresult /help` will tell you that `/help` is an invalid option. Remember that the option CompTIA wants you to know is `[command name] /?`. There are upward of 200 commands supported by Windows 10 and Windows 11. CompTIA's A+ objectives list just a few, so focus on those.

39. C. Event Viewer (`eventvwr.msc`) is a Windows tool, available in most versions, that allows you to view application error logs, security audit records, and system errors. System Information (`msinfo32.exe`) shows a plethora of information about the hardware and software of a system, but it doesn't keep a log of changes. It provides static information available at the time you launch the program. Windows Defender is a Control Panel utility that provides a software firewall for the local computer. Disk Management (`diskmgmt.msc`) is a graphic utility for creating and formatting volumes on any physical drives attached to the system. Worth noting is that Disk Management shows you the physical disks attached to the system and their volumes, whereas opening File Explorer and choosing This PC shows only the logical volumes.

40. A. The screen shown is System Information. It quickly provides a snapshot of the system's hardware and software, including the OS version, RAM, processor, motherboard, and much, much more. The program to launch it is `msinfo32.exe`. Resource Monitor's program name is `resmon.exe`. Unlike System Monitor, Resource Monitor is changing every moment, alerting you to resources that are overused or experiencing difficulty. System Configuration (`msconfig.exe`) has been appearing in Windows operating systems for many years, but Its features have changed over time. In Windows 10 and Windows 11, this utility is used to control how Windows boots up and to provide quick access to other Windows tools. Finally, `devmgmt.msc` is Device Manager, which should be your go-to app when resolving hardware issues. From there you can update or install drivers, see what isn't working, and disable hardware if need be.

41. C. Administrative Tools, which can be found in the Windows 10 Control Panel, has many of the computer management tools that are used to maintain and troubleshoot computer systems, not just the ones listed in this question. Computer Management is a Microsoft Management Console (MMC) that contains other tools as well. In it you can find Task Scheduler, Even Viewer, Shared Folders, Performance, Device Manager, and Disk Management, as well as Services and Windows Management Instrumentation (WMI) Control. In Windows Pro and above editions Computer Management also contains Local Users and Groups. Resource Monitor shows resources being used by process in real time, and Task Scheduler is just as the name sounds—it can be used to schedule other applications, even batch files, to run based on time or other predetermined events. Administrative Tools is not available in Windows 11, but the other tools listed in this question are.

42. A. A power plan needs to be created with the user's desired settings. This is done in the Power Options utility of Control Panel. Different options, such as Hibernate or Standby, can be configured for when the laptop is on battery power versus when it's plugged in. There are also power settings in Windows Settings, but they are not listed in the CompTIA A+ objectives.

43. B. The way to change to a different drive is to type the drive letter and a colon, such as `D:`, and press Enter. `cd` is the change directory command. It can take you to a different directory or change the working directory on a different drive but cannot take you to a different drive. `root` is not a Windows command.

44. C, D. Windows Pro for Workstations and Enterprise editions support up to four physical CPU sockets and 6 TB of RAM. The Home edition supports 128 GB of RAM and one CPU socket whereas the Pro edition supports 2 TB of RAM and a maximum of two CPU sockets.

45. A. A 32-bit processor doesn't have the capability to run a 64-bit operating system in any mode. It also won't be able to run a 64-bit program. It simply doesn't have a wide enough data path.

46. D. Windows 10 minimum requirements are a 1 GHz or faster processor or SoC (System on a Chip), DirectX 9 or later with the WDDM (Windows Display Driver Model) 1.0 driver, and a minimum 800×600 display. For storage, the 32-bit version requires 16 GB, and the 64-bit version requires 20 GB available for the OS. RAM requirements are 1 GB for the 32-bit operating system and 2 GB for the 64-bit operating system. Keep in mind that these are the absolute minimum requirements, and the OS will run but not as well as we have come to expect. In reality, a faster processor, more RAM, and more storage would be expected.

47. C. The cd, md, and rd commands are used to change, make, and remove directories, respectively. They're shorthand versions of the chdir, mkdir, and rmdir commands. The rd or rmdir command will only delete empty directories by default. With that command, the /s switch will remove all subdirectories and files. The /q switch is quiet mode, and when used with the /s switch, it will not ask if it's OK to remove all the files and subdirectories; it will remove them without warning. The del command is for deleting files.

48. B. Performance Monitor (perfmon.msc) offers a graphic display of a wide range of counters to track how well hardware such as RAM, drives, and CPUs are performing over time. Those reports can be printed and filed as a baseline to compare to future performance and used to identify bottlenecks in a system. Event Viewer (eventvwr.msc) keeps logs of system, application, and security events that can be used for activities such as detecting attempted unauthorized access to resources. System Information provides a snapshot of the system's hardware and software, including the OS version, RAM, processor, motherboard, and much, much more. The program to launch it is msinfo32.exe. System Configuration (msconfig.exe) has been appearing in Windows operating systems for many versions now, but its features have changed over time. In Windows 10 and Windows 11, this utility is used to control how Windows boots up and to provide quick access to other Windows tools.

49. A. The ipconfig command is used to display information about the computer's current network configurations. The /all switch will show more detailed information than ipconfig alone will, such as whether DHCP (Dynamic Host Configuration Protocol) is enabled and what the DNS (Domain Name System) settings are. Typing ipconfig /renew will request a new IP address from a DHCP server, if one is available to the host PC. The macOS equivalent of ipconfig is ip (replacing the old ifconfig command), and tracert shows the path a packet takes to get from one computer to another.

50. B. Select Windows Settings, then Personalization, choose Background, then click on High contrast settings. On the next screen click the toggle to turn on high contrast, which will make the colors more distinct and easier for visually impaired users to distinguish between them. This may make it easier for the user to read the words on the screen. Like most Windows options, there are other ways to access the High Contrast Settings. The Fonts selection under Windows Settings, then Personalization, allows the user to add fonts to the system that are not already there. While changing to a different font might help the computer user, this isn't the place to do it. The nightlight settings use warmer colors at night, which might make PC use even more difficult for this user. High contrast settings are not available under Accounts.

51. B. Typing **cd** will take you to the root of whatever drive you are on. You could also type **cd..** and press Enter to go back one directory at a time. For example, to go from C:\windows\system32 to C:\, you would need to type **cd..** and press Enter, then type **cd..** and press Enter. The other options will not get you to the root of the C: drive.

52. B. Sleep stores everything that's open in RAM and enters a low power state. The display and drives aren't using power, but power is needed to continually refresh memory so that it can retain the information. It uses very little power but "wakes up" very quickly with everything open as it was. Sleep in some computer systems and other electronic devices may be called standby or suspend. Shutting the computer down would cause the laptop to use no power but starting up would take longer. Hibernate stores open programs and data to the hard drive and once the computer is hibernated it would use no power, but it will not resume its state as quickly as using Sleep would. There is no resting power state.

53. B. Linux is free and open source, so a user can modify the operating system's source code to behave and appear however they choose. The downside is that there might not be as much support if something goes wrong as there would be with a commercial package. Windows and macOS are commercial operating systems, meaning that you pay for them and can use their utilities to configure the OS, but you don't have access to the operating system's source code. Chrome OS is a commercial, proprietary operating system found only on Chromebooks, but there is an open source version called Chromium OS.

54. A. Remembering the passwords for various websites is easily managed in macOS with Keychain.

55. C, D. Regardless of the version that is being installed, Windows 10 has the same minimum requirements, which are a 1 GHz or faster processor or SoC (System on a Chip), DirectX 9 or later with the WDDM (Windows Display Driver Model) 1.0 driver, and a minimum 800×600 display. For storage, the 32-bit version requires 16 GB, and the 64-bit version requires 20 GB available for the OS. RAM requirements are 1 GB for the 32-bit operating system and 2 GB for the 64-bit operating system. Keep in mind that these are the absolute minimum requirements, and the OS will run but not as well as we have come to expect. In reality, a faster processor, more RAM, and more storage would be expected. Windows 11 requirements are different. It requires a 1 GHz or faster processor with a minimum of 2 cores on a 64-bit processor or SoC. The minimum RAM is 4 GB, UEFI firmware (not BIOS), Trusted Platform Module (TPM) version 2.0, DirectX 12 or later with the WDM 2.0 driver, and a high-definition display greater than 9″ diagonally. The Home edition requires a Microsoft account and Internet access for installation.

56. B. Windows 10 Pro edition supports up to 2 TB of RAM and a maximum of two CPU sockets. The Home edition supports only 128 GB of RAM and one CPU socket. Windows Pro for Workstations and Enterprise editions support up to four physical CPU sockets and 6 TB of RAM.

57. B. The Local Group Policy Editor (gpedit.msc) is not available in the Home editions of Windows. It is available in the Pro, Pro for Workstation, and Enterprise editions. You don't need to have Active Directory installed on a server to use the Local Group Policy Editor, although it is available there as well. Going to Administrative Tools won't help because the Group Policy Editor is not available anywhere on Windows Home editions, and Administrative Tools is included in Windows 10 but not included in Windows 11.

58. C. The cd, md, and rd commands are used to change, make, and remove directories, respectively. They're shorthand versions of the chdir, mkdir, and rmdir commands. The syntax of the command is md [drive:]path, so the directory would appear after the drive letter when typing the command. The drive letter must be included because it is not the drive that you are on.

59. B. There are three tools that quickly show you CPU and memory usage in Windows: Resource Monitor, Performance Monitor, and Task Manager. The only one that lets you set up logs is Performance Monitor. It will collect counter information and then send that information to a console or event log. Event Viewer logs system, application, and security events, not performance.

60. C. From the Personalization menu of Windows Settings, you can change the desktop theme and background colors. Accounts enables the user to manage what accounts have access to this computer and at what level. The Apps settings deal with application-specific parameters and not operating system settings. Finally, the System settings in Windows Settings has a multitude of settings that relate to the system but not to the image that appears on the desktop.

61. D. The Google Chrome OS was developed by Google. It comes preinstalled on laptops and tablets called Chromebooks. A freeware version, Chromium OS, can be installed on tablets, smartphones, laptops, and desktops. The main user interface for Chrome OS is the Google Chrome browser. Chrome OS can also support Android apps. Ubuntu is based on the open source Linux OS kernel. iOS is Apple's proprietary operating system, and Windows 11 Pro was developed by Microsoft.

62. D. Finder in macOS is similar to File Explorer in Windows. Both allow you to browse through folders and find files, disks, and applications. Both can be used to change the view so that entries can be seen as images, a list, a column, and so on. Spotlight is the tool for searching on a Mac, and iCloud is similar to Microsoft's OneDrive for storage.

63. A. The ping (packet Internet groper) command sends a series of four packets to a remote computer and waits for a reply. If the reply is received, you know that the local computer is able to reach the remote host. It also displays how long the transaction took. ping can be used with domain names like Wiley.com or the IP address, if known. When ping localhost or ping 127.0.0.1 or ping ::1 is run, the command verifies that TCP/IP is working on the local computer. tracert shows the routers that a packet traverses to reach its destination. The ipconfig command is used to view network configuration, and pathping is a combination of the abilities of ping and tracert.

64. B. All of the answer options are Linux commands. The pwd (print working directory) command writes the full path to the current (working) directory from the root on whatever the default output device is (usually the display.) The path might be, for example, /home/audrey/documents. The ls command provides a list of all the files and folders found in the current directory, the cp command is used to copy files and directories, and yum (Yellowdog Updater Modified) is used to install, update, remove, and search for software packages.

65. C, D. If a user finds their desktop getting out of hand, they can create multiple desktops, which macOS calls Spaces, to organize their desktop objects, or simply to make more space. Multiple desktops are created using Mission Control. Once multiple desktops are created, apps can be moved from one desktop to another by dragging, similar to using a smartphone. Finder is used to drill down through the file structure to find what you're looking for, and Time Machine is used to make backups.

66. B. The macOS Dock provides quick access to the programs you'll likely use most often. Taskbar provides a similar function in Windows OSs. File Explorer and Finder are both used to drill down through the filesystem to find what you're looking for—File Explorer is the Windows utility and Finder is the macOS utility.

67. D. Event Viewer, Disk Management, and Certificate Manager are all Microsoft Management Console (MMC) snap-ins. A Microsoft Management Console provides an interface where a user can configure and easily access their own list of tools that they use most often. These tools are called snap-ins, and there are more than twenty of them available. A console contains shortcuts to the tools, and when the console is saved, it can be identified by a toolbox icon. Services are programs that run in the background on a Windows system such as a print manager and WLAN AutoConfig. Processes are parts of a program that are running, usually consisting of multiple threads. Threads are the section of code being worked on by the processor. Policies are rules for granting access such as the ability to log on locally or settings for passwords that require complexity. Policies are configured through the Group Policy Editor (`gpedit.msc`) and are not available in Windows Home editions. There are literally hundreds of policies that can be set in a Windows system. The Group Policy Editor is also an MMC snap-in.

68. C. Once the Hibernate power setting has saved everything from RAM to a system file (`hiberfil.sys`) on the hard drive, it will turn the system off and use no power. Hibernate takes longer to get back to a running state than Sleep does, but Hibernate won't use any power after it has stored the data. When the system is resumed, the contents of the system file are copied back into RAM and the user can continue where they left off. Sleep needs a small amount of power to keep the data in RAM refreshed. Always On will obviously use power continuously, and Hyper-V is Microsoft's virtualization product, not a power setting.

69. B, C. Because you are already on the C: drive, you would not need to specify the drive letter to change to a directory on that drive. If you did specify the drive (as in option B) it's not a problem, because if you were going to a directory on a different drive, you would need to specify the drive letter. Because you're already at the root of the C: drive, you can simply enter the cd command and the path (option C), **cd windows\system32**. If you were anywhere else in the C: drive, you would need to include the \ to denote the root of the drive in your command (**cd \windows\system32**). You could go to that directory with two commands, changing one directory at a time, by typing **cd windows** and pressing Enter, then typing **cd system32** and pressing Enter, but that would be inefficient and is not one of the options given.

70. D. The program `resmon.exe` launches Resource Monitor, which is shown in the graphic. Resource Monitor is a powerful performance monitoring tool. It provides more granular information than Task Manager or Performance Monitor, but it doesn't have the ability to save a log of performance. The Event Viewer can be launched with `eventvwr.msc`. The Local Users and Groups application can be launched with `lusrmgr.msc`, and Performance Monitor can be launched with `perfmon.msc`.

71. B. Any 32-bit operating system has a limit of 4 GB of RAM. The limitation is caused by the bus width. There simply aren't enough numbers available to identify memory locations above 4 GB.

72. A. Remote Desktop can only be enabled on a Windows Pro or better operating systems. Windows Home edition does not have this capability. However, using a PC with Windows Pro, Pro for Workgroups, or Enterprise edition is not the only way to access the manager's computer. The Remote Desktop Mobile app is available for iOS and Android devices.

73. D. The `gpupdate` tool is used to update Group Policy settings immediately. It refreshes, or changes, both local and Active Directory–based policies. The `gpedit` command allows the user to edit group policies, and the `gpresult` command will show the Resultant Set of Policy (RSoP) for a user or computer. RSoP is the culmination of all policies that affect the target user or computer. It is particularly helpful in troubleshooting conflicting policies. `gprefresh` is not a valid command.

74. B. The `pathping` command works like `ping` and `tracert` combined. It shows the path a packet takes from point A to point B, and then will show the time at each hop. (A hop is the number of times a packet moves from one router to another to get to its destination after it leaves the initial router.) `grep` and `mv` are Linux Terminal commands, which are used to search for text from a file, and to move files and folders, respectively. The `tracert` command shows the path a packet takes to its destination.

75. A. To turn off all notifications, or manage whether and how individual notification senders can interact with you, go to Windows Settings, choose System, then Notifications & actions. From there you can turn off all notifications or some, and choose whether or not a sound is played when they arrive. The Gaming option lets you configure the system to be optimized for gameplay and recording. Update & Security settings don't address notifications. The Apps option lets you manage where apps can be installed from, default apps for opening files, and other application configuration settings.

76. D. All of the answer options are Linux commands. The yum (Yellowdog Updater Modified) command is used to install, update, remove, and search for software packages. The syntax is `yum [options] <command> [<args?...]`. For example, to see a list of the installed packages, you would type **yum list installed**. The pwd (print working directory) command writes the full path to the current (working) directory from the root on whatever the default output device is (usually the display.) The `ls` command provides a list of all the files and folders found in the current directory, while the `cp` command is used to copy files and directories.

77. C. The macOS Disk Utility can be used to find and fix errors in the directory structure of a Mac disk. If the Mac won't boot into the OS, the utility can be accessed through macOS Recovery. Depending on the hardware your Mac is using, you would either hold the power button until startup options appear, or press and hold Command+R while the computer is starting to bring up macOS Recovery. From there choose Utilities and then Disk Utility. FileVault provides encryption, Terminal is the macOS and Linux command- line user interface, and Force Quit can be used when a single app is causing problems and refuses to close.

78. A. Task Scheduler is a Microsoft Management Console (MMC) snap-in and, as its name implies, a tool for running programs and performing tasks based on a trigger such as date, time, or events such as logon, idle, or locking the workstation. Event Viewer keeps logs of system, security, and application events. Device Manager is a tool for working with hardware and lets you update drivers and scan for newly attached devices, for example. Local Users and Groups is an MMC snap-in for creating and managing users and groups.

79. C. When an OS, smartphone, PC or any electronic device is at end-of-life (EOL), it generally is no longer sold or supported, meaning that replacement parts and product and security updates are no longer available. While you may be able to scavenge parts, not getting security updates should be a great concern. At an electronics end-of-life, the best course of action is to recycle the device and procure a newer one.

80. A. The `dir` command will show you a list of all the files and folders that are in the directory you are working in, along with the date created. Using the switches that work with `dir`, you can view much more information. `ls` is a Linux command that lists information about files in the working directory. The `pwd` Linux command prints the complete path to the working directory, and the `grep` Linux command will search for files with a pattern that you specify.

81. A. Disk Management is a Windows tool that has been available for many Windows versions. With it you can reassign or change a drive letter, create and format volumes, shrink or expand volumes, change basic drives to dynamic drives, import foreign drives, and even establish software RAID. In Windows 10 it can be launched through Control Panel by choosing Administrative Tools, then Computer Management, or you can launch it by typing **diskmgmt.msc** in the search box. Administrative Tools is not available in Windows 11, but Disk Management is. The easiest way to access Disk Management in Windows 10 or 11 is to press Windows Key+X to bring up the Quick Link menu, which is a list of commonly used tools, and click Disk Management on the list.

82. C. FileVault is the macOS utility for encrypting data. Finder is the macOS utility for drilling down through folders to find objects. Time Machine is used to create and restore backups of data on a Mac, and BitLocker is the Windows drive encryption utility.

83. B. Time Machine is the macOS backup utility. It can be accessed through System Preferences, and once set up, it will run on schedule much like any other backup software. Image Recovery and iBackup are not macOS tools. Accessibility options can be found in System Preferences and are used to adjust settings for different vision, hearing, and mobility needs.

84. A. Updates to MacOS can be found at the App Store. Open it and click Updates in the toolbar to see which updates are available. There will be an Install button to begin the installation. In System Preferences, there is generally a Software Update icon to help with updates as well. Update is not an option on the toolbar of Safari, which is the web browser. Finder is used for drilling down through directories to find files and folders.

85. A. If you are working at a command prompt and need to know the version of Windows on the PC, type **winver** and press Enter. You'll get a screen similar to the one shown in the graphic. The other options are not valid commands.

86. B. The `gpresult` command will show the Resultant Set of Policy (RSoP) for a user or computer. RSoP is the culmination of all policies that affect the target user or computer. It is particularly helpful in troubleshooting conflicting policies. The screen shown used the `/r` switch, which shows the RSoP summary for the currently logged-on user on the local computer. The `gpedit` command allows the user to edit group policies, and the `gpupdate` tool is used to update Group Policy settings. It refreshes, or changes, both local and Active Directory–based policies. `gprefresh` is not an existing command.

87. B. All of the commands listed are Linux commands. The `cp` command is used to copy files. There are three syntaxes for the `cp` command, as follows:

- `cp [option]` *source destination*
- `cp [option]` *source directory*
- `cp [option]` *source-1 source-2 source-n directory*

For example, if the copy command has two filenames, it will create a copy of the first filename and save it as the second. The command would be `cp` *file1 file2*. The `mv` command is used to move files, and the `find` command is used to find files and directories and perform operations on them. The `cat` command is a powerful tool that can be used to view contents of a file, create new files, and concatenate (put together) files.

88. A, B. Operating systems (OS) and electronics have a life cycle, just as living things do. They are introduced, grow, reach maturity (mainstream support), decline (extended support), and reach their end-of-life (EOL) which means there is no support. The last Windows OS prior to Windows 10 was Windows 8.1, which ended mainstream support on January 9, 2018, and the end of extended support date is January 10, 2023. End of mainstream support means there are no updates other than security. End of extended support means there is no support, including security updates and patches. Essentially, if (when) a vulnerability is discovered by a hacker, the user of an end-of-life OS is at risk for being attacked. Applications may continue to work just fine, but updates might not work with the OS. The OS will not magically stop working, but if a problem occurs there will be no official support available.

89. D. The Chromebook, which has Chrome OS preinstalled, is the best option for this user. It's main user interface is the Google Chrome browser, and it can run apps designed for Android smartphones. Chromebooks are also known for being less expensive laptop options. Windows Home and macOS would be fine for accessing the Internet, but they would not support the applications that the user is accustomed to using, and the user would experience a learning curve. Linux might be able to run their Android apps using third-party software, but again the user would have a learning curve.

90. C. Certificates are a way of proving who someone or a website is by means of a digital signature. A user's certificates hold the private key of a key pair for encryption. If certificates are outdated or otherwise no longer valid, then encryption doesn't happen and the transmission can be intercepted by someone with malicious intent. Normally you wouldn't need to worry about certificates, but if a problem occurs, the certificate may need to be deleted and a new one requested. Certificate Manager allows you to view and manage certificates by user or computer. Device Manager is a hardware management tool. Local Users and Groups allows for organizing users by access need and assigning permissions and access to the group rather than the user, simplifying access management. Group Policy Editor allows administrators to further control what users and computers are allowed to do on the network.

91. C. macOS is Apple's proprietary desktop operating system (OS). Apache is a popular web server OS, not a desktop OS. Red Hat Linux is a distribution of the open source Linux OS, and FreeBSD is a freeware, open source OS based on Unix.

92. B. DNS has one function on the network, and that is to resolve hostnames to IP addresses. For a computer or phone to open a website, it needs to know the IP address of that website. Each DNS server has a database, called a zone file, which maintains records of hostname-to-IP address mappings. If the network settings for DNS server on a client computer are improperly configured and the client can't reach the DNS server, then human-friendly names are not resolved to IP addresses, causing the problem this user is having. Authentication servers are used to verify whether a user has the proper credentials to gain access to resources on a network. A Microsoft domain controller is a type of authentication server. DHCP (Dynamic Host Configuration Protocol) is used to automatically provide an IP address to a client based on a list (scope) of IP addresses made available on the DHCP server. A proxy server sits between the client and the outside world and is used to filter content incoming or outgoing.

93. A. The su command (switch user, substitute user, or super user) is used to start another shell on a Linux computer. Without specifying the username, it's assumed you are trying to start a shell with super user (or root) authority. This can be dangerous because as the root, the user can do anything on the system, including delete parts of the operating system, and there is no undo or warning message. You must know the root password to run su. It's far safer to run the sudo command. The sudo command stands for superuser do, or substitute user do, and will run a single command as the alternate user. The apt-get command is used to download or remove software packages, and the ps command will list the processes that are currently running along with their process IDs (PIDs).

94. D. The Displays pane in System Preferences is used to set resolution and brightness (turn Night Shift on and off), and possibly other settings depending on whether there is a display connected. The Printers & Scanners pane is where you would add or manage a printer and its print jobs. Accessibility preferences include settings for hearing, mobility, and vision. The Desktop & Screen Saver options allow you to configure the desktop and screen saver.

95. A. Home editions of Windows do not support Remote Desktop, but the Windows business editions (Pro, Pro for Workstation, and Enterprise) do. Since you have Windows Pro, you would not need to upgrade your operating system edition. The steps to use Remote Desktop to access a PC from a smartphone are as follows:

1. Enable Remote Desktop on the PC.

2. Note the PC name.

3. Install Remote Desktop Mobile on the smartphone.

4. Open the Remote Desktop app on your smartphone.

5. Enter the name of the PC that you want to connect to.

6. Select the PC name and wait for the smartphone to connect.

96. B. The System File Checker (SFC) is a command-line utility that checks and verifies the versions of system files on your computer. If system files are corrupted, the SFC will replace the corrupted files with correct versions. The /scannow option will scan and repair files, whereas /scanfile will just check one specified file. The /verifyonly option will scan the integrity of protected system files but not attempt to repair them. The /verifyfile option will verify the integrity of a specific file.

97. C. The robocopy utility (Robust File Copy for Windows) has the big advantage of being able to accept a plethora of specifications and keep NTFS permissions intact in its operations. For example, the /mir switch, can be used to mirror a complete directory tree. copy and xcopy are both valid commands but have nowhere near the power that robocopy does. copyall is not a valid command.

98. B. When files are written to a hard drive, they're not always written contiguously or with all the data in a single location. Defragmenting a disk involves analyzing the disk and then consolidating fragmented files and folders so that they occupy a contiguous space (consecutive blocks), thus increasing performance during file retrieval. The executable for Disk Defragment is dfrgui.exe, which brings up the Optimize Drives window. By default, drives are automatically scheduled to be optimized, but it can be done here on command or the schedule settings changed. The Disk Management utility is used to create and format volumes and other tasks related to managing drives. Disk Optimizer is not a Windows tool, and Device Manager is useful in examining and troubleshooting issues with hardware.

99. D. Since the majority of business users are still using Microsoft products, and there may be compatibility concerns with data from older systems, a Windows OS would be the correct choice in this situation. Chrome OS is most appropriate where users would be working in the cloud. Linux and macOS may have compatibility issues with data from other sources. Microsoft 365 does come in a version for macOS, but the company-specific software must also be considered.

100. A. dSystem Preferences is where settings can be viewed and modified. System Preferences are divided into various panes, including Displays, Networks, Printers & Scanners, Privacy, Accessibility, Time Machine, Power, and many other selections for changing settings. Windows Settings is a part of the Microsoft Windows operating system. App Store is where you would go on macOS to find new applications to download and to update the operating system.

101. C. The Update & Security category of Windows Settings contains more than the name would suggest. In Update & Security there is, of course, Windows Update and Windows Security, but users can also find Backup, Troubleshoot, Recovery, Activation, Find my Device, For developers, and Windows Insider Program selections. To back up using File History, an additional drive (you can't back up to the drive Windows is installed on) is needed, and under More options, you'll find settings for how often to automatically back up, and you'll be able to choose which folders to back up. (In Windows 11, Windows

Settings, Backup can be found in the Accounts category and is called Windows Backup.) The Systems category contains Display, Sound, Power, and other system-related settings. The Apps category is where you can uninstall apps, set default apps, and change what apps load on startup. The Network & Internet category has Wi-Fi settings and a network troubleshooter, among other common network-related settings.

102. B, C. Typically on a network, static IP addresses, rather than dynamic, would be assigned to shared resources such as file servers and printers/MFDs to avoid problems with connecting to those resources. A user's workstation normally does not need a static IP address, and allowing it to obtain one automatically makes workstation configuration easier and avoids accidental duplication of IP addresses. A local printer, by definition, is attached to a local computer, not directly to the network, so it wouldn't even have its own IP address.

103. D. When the application is running, the operating system will also be running, so you need to add their respective RAM requirements together to determine the amount of system RAM needed. The minimum amount of RAM for a Windows 10 64-bit installation is 2 GB, and since the application's RAM requirement is 4 GB, you'll need a total of 6 GB, and since you only have 4 GB, an additional 2 GB will need to be installed. While that will run the program on this system, having only 2 GB for the operating system will not allow it to run as fast as the user is accustomed to, so in reality you'd likely want to add more.

104. C. When you install a Linux distribution, it will use an ext3 or ext4 filesystem. FAT32 is the filesystem that was used when only 32-bit processors were available, and it can still be used for compatibility issues with legacy devices, but Windows 10 and Windows 11 require NTFS (New Technology File System) for installing the OS. NTFS has been available for decades and offers security features that FAT32 doesn't have. APFS is the Apple File System and is used for macOS.

105. C. An installation can be started many ways—with a USB drive, a DVD, and so on—and an image and setup files can also be located on and installed from a network. Often called a PXE-initiated boot (for Preboot Execution Environment), it allows the workstation involved in the installation to retrieve the files from the network, as needed, and configure variables accordingly. netboot refers to booting a computer from a network drive, not installing an OS. Unattended installation is a type of installation that uses an answer file and little or no interaction from a human. While it's possible to install Windows from a USB, if you're using a USB to boot and install an image from a server, the bare-metal machine still needs PXE support.

106. D. Since the workstations don't have DVD drives, you can't use optical media to install Windows 10, and since there are no USB ports, it's unlikely that you would be able to use an external drive. Internet based installation requires that you can boot and get to the Internet, so you would need an operating system already installed, and the question states that these are bare-metal machines. You're left with a network installation using the PXE boot as the only option.

107. B. The sudo command stands for superuser do, or substitute user do, and will run a single command as the alternate user. The user can authenticate with their own password instead of the root password, which is a security feature. Another command, visudo, is used to configure exactly what each user can do when they run sudo. The visudo command is not on the CompTIA A+ objectives, but it answers the question of how you would control the access of users who are not `root`. The `su` command (switch user, substitute user, or super user) is used to start another shell on a Linux computer. Without specifying the username, it's assumed you are trying to start a shell with super user (or `root`) authority, and you need the `root` password to run it. Note the difference between `su` and `sudo`, starting a whole new shell versus running a command. The `apt-get` command is used to download or remove software packages, and the `ps` command will list the processes that are currently running, along with their PIDs (process IDs).

108. C, D. The `hostname` command returns the name of the computer that it is entered on and, while not its primary purpose, `ping localhost` will also return the name of the computer. `nslookup` will show the default DNS server and its IP address. `clientname` is not a valid command.

109. D. The `tracert` command will show the routers that a packet went through and how long each hop took, which can narrow down your search for the problem by showing how far it got. Typing **ipconfig /all** will show the current TCP/IP configuration of the local machine, such as its IP address, MAC address, and default gateway. The macOS equivalent of `ipconfig` is `ip`. The `ping` command will only show that the packet is not making the trip there and back by timing out.

110. C. Ease of Access Center has settings to help users who have limited sight, mobility, or hearing. Devices and Printers is for managing and troubleshooting printers, print jobs, and other devices like connected smartphones or keypads. Programs and Features lets you uninstall or change installed programs, and Sound is used to configure recording and playback devices, or to choose a sound scheme.

111. D. The `ps` (process status) command will list the currently running processes, along with their PIDs (process IDs), the controlling terminal for the process, the time the CPU has been used by the process, and the name of the command that started the process. The `su` command (switch user, substitute user, or super user) is used to start another shell on a Linux computer. The `sudo` command stands for superuser do, or substitute user do, and will run a single command as the alternate user. The `apt-get` command is used to download or remove software packages.

112. B. Ext4 (Extended File System, version 4) is not compatible with macOS and Windows. Neither is ext3. For compatibility between Linux, macOS, and Windows, format an external drive with exFAT or FAT32 so that it can be read by any of the three. Ext3 only supports file sizes up to 2 TB and volumes up to 16 TB, whereas ext4 supports files up to 16 TB and volumes up to 1 EB. ext3 is limited to about 32,000 subdirectories, and ext4 has no limit. ext4 also provides superior resistance to fragmentation as well as faster filesystem checking.

113. B, C. Going to Control Panel and choosing the Sound utility will enable you to change the default playback device for sound; so will opening Windows Settings and clicking Devices, where you can also configure Bluetooth, printers, and mice. Opening Windows Settings, then System and then Sound will as well, but that is not one of the options. The Security and Maintenance utility in Control Panel has settings for the firewall, malware protection, and other features. The Apps group in Windows Settings is where you would uninstall or choose default apps.

114. A. The Power Options utility in Control Panel is where you can find the setting for changing what happens when you close the lid, as well as other sleep and hibernate options. For Windows 10, in Windows Settings, in the System group, choose Power Options, then Additional Power Settings, which takes you to the Control Panel utility. Windows Settings in Windows 11 is missing this link, but in both versions of Windows, the other power settings (when to sleep, when to hibernate) are available in Windows Settings. Devices and Printers is where you would manage printers and print jobs, as well as other devices like connected cell phones. The System group in Settings controls Display, Sound, Notifications & actions, and several other areas related to the system as a whole. The Devices group in Windows 10, Windows Settings allows you to configure Bluetooth, printers, and mouse settings. In Windows 11, this group is called Bluetooth & devices.

115. A, D. A PC can be upgraded to Windows 10 Professional directly from the desktop of the PC, provided the PC is running an OS that is in the upgrade path. Surprisingly, Windows 7 Enterprise edition is the only Windows 7 edition that can't be upgraded to Windows 10 Pro. It could only be upgraded to Windows 10 Education or Enterprise editions. Windows 8.1 Enterprise and Embedded Industry editions cannot be upgraded to Windows 10, but the other Windows 8.1 editions can. No Windows 8 editions can be directly upgraded to Windows 10. They must be first upgraded to Windows 8.1, then Windows 10. Only Windows 10 Home can be upgraded to Windows 10 Pro, or an in-place upgrade from Windows 10 Pro to the same or newer version of Windows 10 Pro can be done to troubleshoot problems with the existing installation.

116. C. In many Linux distributions, the `apt-get` command is used to download or remove software packages. The syntax for this command is `apt-get [options] command`. There are too many options to explain them all here, but in the question, we are uninstalling an app, so the command could be `apt-get purge [package name]`, but remember that you would want to precede the `apt-get` command with `sudo`. If the package name were `milou`, then the command you use is `sudo apt-get purge milou`. Using `purge` deletes all configuration files as well as the package. The `sudo` command stands for superuser do, or substitute user do, and will run a single command as the alternate user. The `su` command (switch user, substitute user, or super user) is used to start another shell on a Linux computer. Without specifying the username, it's assumed you are trying to start a shell with super user (or `root`) authority. The `ps` command will list the processes that are currently running, along with their PIDs (process IDs).

117. B. The `xcopy` command is a more powerful version of `copy`. It lets you copy directories and also will copy file ownership and NTFS permissions. The `/s` switch is used to copy directories and subdirectories, except for empty ones. To copy those as well, use `/e`. The `/h` switch copies hidden and system files, and the `/a` switch copies only files with the Archive attribute set. There are many more options with the `xcopy` command. To find out more, type **xcopy /?** at a command prompt.

118. C. Device Manager is the first place to go when troubleshooting hardware. A yellow exclamation point will let you know that there is a problem that needs to be addressed. Event Viewer keeps logs of system, security, and application events. Performance Monitor helps locate bottlenecks in a system by showing resources being used in real time, and Disk Management allows for formatting, partitioning, and managing of hard drives.

119. D. System Configuration (`msconfig.exe`) has been appearing in Windows operating systems since 2006, but its features have changed over time. The General tab lets you choose a Diagnostic startup that will load just basic devices and services, which can sometimes aid in troubleshooting. The Boot tab lets you choose other boot options. Timeout, on the right of the Boot tab, can be set if you have more than one OS on the hard drive and want time to choose between them, but a more common option now is to use virtual machines when more than one OS is needed. The Services tab is where you can stop and start many services, although that can also be done through the Services console (`services.msc`), which has all the services. The Startup tab only has a link to Task Manager, and the Tools tab is used to provide quick access to other Windows tools. Event Viewer (`eventvwr.msc`) keeps logs of system, application, and security events that can be used for activities such as detecting attempted unauthorized access to resources. Performance Monitor (`perfmon.msc`) offers a graphic display of a wide range of counters to track how well components such as RAM, drives, and CPUs are performing over time. System Information provides a snapshot of the system's hardware and software, including the OS version, RAM, processor, motherboard, and much, much more. The program that launches it is `msinfo32.exe`.

120. B. Some of the most important files that you will need to work on are hidden by default as a security precaution. To make certain folders or files visible, you need to change the display properties of File Explorer. This can be done by going to the View tab of File Explorer Options in Control Panel and deselecting Hide Protected Operating System Files (Recommended). Programs and Features is for uninstalling or changing programs and turning Windows features on and off. Indexing makes a log of the metadata of files and helps search work faster. The System utility of Control Panel opens System in Windows Settings.

Note that the CompTIA A+ objectives list File Explorer Options under Control Panel utilities that you should know, so you need to know that you can access them there. But this book's author and technical editor agree that most technicians would access this through File Explorer by selecting Options, then Folder Options (or Change folder and search options, depending on the version) on the View tab. Like most things in the Windows operating system, there is more than one way to perform a task. When sitting for the CompTIA A+ exam, make sure you are familiar with the method that CompTIA has identified in their objectives.

121. A. Terminal is the name of the command-line user interface in both macOS and Linux. In it, a user can type commands to perform actions and launch programs. Often for experienced users, using a command-line terminal is faster than navigating menus. Finder is the macOS utility for drilling down through folders to find objects. Command Prompt is the name of the Windows command-line user interface, and File Explorer is the Windows rendition of Finder.

122. C. Windows Defender Firewall is a software firewall residing on the local system that provides features designed to protect your system from malware. Unfortunately, sometimes those settings interfere with other applications and need to be changed. Turning the firewall off is not advisable, but you can open it up to applications by clicking Allow an app or feature through Windows Defender Firewall. Programs and Features is used to uninstall or change applications, and to turn Windows features on and off. Internet Options affect how browsers work and can be used to connect to a VPN (virtual private network). The Network and Sharing Center is the Windows tool for viewing and configuring network connections and changing adapter settings.

123. B. The copy command makes a copy of a file in a second location. (To copy a file and then remove it from its original location, use the move command.) One useful tip is to use wildcards. For example, the asterisk (*) is a wildcard that means *everything*. So, you could type **copy *.exe** to copy all files that have an .exe filename extension, or you could type **copy *.*** to copy all files in your current directory. The other popular wildcard is the question mark (?), which does not mean everything but instead replaces one character. The **copy abc?.exe** command would only copy .exe files with four-letter names of which the first three letters are abc.

124. D. The shell is the interpreter between the user and operating system. Common Linux shells include Bash (an acronym for Bourne Again Shell), csh (C-shell), and ksh (Korn shell), but a number of others are also in use. The Terminal is akin to the Windows Command Prompt and is used to enter commands and to interface with the shell. GUI (graphical user interface) describes a type of user interface where the user clicks an icon or picture to launch a program or open a file (that is, interact with the shell).

125. B. The df (disk free) command is used to show free and used disk space on a volume. The syntax of this command is df [option] [file]. If you type df and press Enter, it will show the space that is available on all filesystems that are mounted. If you specify a particular file, it will provide information on that file. The grep Linux command will search for files with a pattern that you specify. The ps command will list the processes that are currently running, along with their PIDs (process IDs). The dig (domain information groper) command works in Linux and macOS to find information about DNS name servers, mail exchanges, and hosts.

126. A, C. There are several ways to see what services are running and to enable and disable services. They include the Services console (services.msc) and Computer Management (compmgmt.msc). Or you can open Task Manager and select the Services tab (although that has access to only a subset of the services available), and in Windows 10 only, go to Control Panel, Administrative Tools, then click Services to open the Services console. Performance Monitor (perfmon.exe) does not show running services, and Disk Management (diskmgmt.msc) does not have a link to the Services console.

127. B. Local Users and Groups allows you to organize users by access need and assign permissions and access to the group rather than individual users, simplifying access management. Incidentally, assigning NTFS permissions to groups rather than individuals is considered a best practice. Suppose your accounting manager suddenly quits and you hire a new one. Rather than set up permissions for the new manager, you would merely add their user name to the appropriate groups (and, of course, disable the former manager's account). Group Policy Editor allows administrators to further control what users and computers are allowed to do on the network, such as enforcing password complexity, disabling USB drives, and limiting what users can do in Control Panel. Device Manager is a hardware management tool, and Certificate Manager allows you to view and manage certificates by user or computer. Certificates hold the private key of a key pair used in encryption.

128. B. When an app hangs in macOS, you can use Force Quit to force it to close. Most devices, whether running macOS or iOS, offer similar options. You access Force Quit through the Apple menu or by pressing Command+Option+Esc, which is analogous to pressing Ctrl+Alt+Del on a Windows PC. Task Manager is a Windows utility, Terminal is the macOS and Linux command-line user interface, and Time Machine is used for backups.

129. A, D. Although the graphs look different in each application, both the Performance tab of Task Manager and the Resource Monitor utility will show CPU, memory, and Wi-Fi statistics in real time. In Performance Monitor, a Wi-Fi connection can be found on the Network tab. Event Viewer logs system, software, and security events. The System Information utility, which can be found in Administrative Tools, shows a snapshot of a system's configuration, but not real-time information. Note that Administrative Tools is a utility in Windows 10 but is not a part of Windows 11.

130. B. `ls` is a Linux command that lists information about files in the working directory. The `dir` command in Windows does the same. The `pwd` Linux command prints the complete path to the working directory, and the `grep` Linux command will search for files with a pattern that you specify.

131. C. The Linux Terminal is a command-driven user interface that allows the user to interact with the shell by typing command at a prompt, much like Windows Command Prompt. The command-driven user interface in macOS is also called Terminal. The shell is the part of the OS that sits between the user and the rest of the operating system, allowing the user to interact with the operating system. Time Machine and Mission Control are features of macOS used for backups and viewing all open applications, respectively.

132. D. Disk Cleanup will look through your hard drive and show how much space unused files are taking up. You then have the option to choose which files you would like to delete. Clicking a file type will provide a description of what is being deleted. On modern, large hard drives, the space saved is usually negligible. Resource Monitor shows resources being used by process in real time. Disk Management is a graphic utility for creating, formatting, and managing volumes on any physical drives attached to the system. You can even use it to configure software RAID. The Registry is a huge database that contains information about all the users, hardware, software, and configuration information in a computer. Typically, changing the Registry by using `regedit` is a last resort because changes are immediate and there is no undo button. Control Panel and Windows Settings can do much of the Registry management for you, and they're much safer.

133. A. The `shutdown` command can be used to shut down and restart computers, either the system you are on or a remote one. The `/s` switch is used to shut down a computer, and `/r` is used for a full shutdown and reboot. The `/m` switch followed by the computer name is used to specify the remote computer. The `/c` switch is for comments. There are other switches available. To find out more about the command, type **shutdown /?** at a command prompt.

134. C. Windows configuration information is stored in a special configuration database known as the Registry. This centralized database also contains environmental settings for various Windows programs. To edit the Registry, use the `regedit.exe` program. Be careful, though, because an incorrect Registry change can render a system inoperable. Changes are immediate and there is no undo. `msinfo32` is the System Information utility that provides a snapshot of the hardware, software, and some configuration information for the system; `command` is not a valid tool; and `notepad` launches the Notepad program, which is a simple text editor. Commands like these can be run using Command Prompt or the Run command (which can be accessed by pressing Windows Key+R).

135. B. To stop (disable) programs from running on startup, use the Startup tab of Task Manager. The System Configuration utility was the place to go in older versions of Windows, but now it merely has a link to Task Manager. Services are programs that run in the background and are part of the operating system, not applications that have been added. A limited subset of them can be configured on the Services tab of Task Manager, or all services can be accessed through the Services console (`services.msc`). Task Scheduler is used to automatically perform some action(s) when a trigger, such as a date, time, or other event, occurs.

136. C. On a Mac, it's possible to run a large number of things at one time, whether those things in question are apps or Windows desktops. Apple's Mission Control is an easy way to see what is open and to switch between applications. To access Mission Control, you can press the Mission Control key (identified by an image of three different-sized rectangles) on an Apple keyboard, click the Mission Control icon in the Dock (or Launchpad), or swipe up with three or four fingers on a trackpad. Spotlight is used to search for files, folders, images, and such. Keychain is the macOS password management feature, and Finder enables the user to drill down through directories to find what they're looking for, much like File Explorer in Windows.

137. A. From Devices and Printers, you can manage multiple printers and do tasks such as choosing a default printer, installing new printers, and changing printer settings. Programs and Features allows the user to add, remove, or troubleshoot installed programs (the options will change by program) and add or remove Windows features. The Network and Sharing Center is the Windows tool for viewing and configuring network connections, and changing adapter settings. Device Manager should be your go-to app when resolving hardware issues. From there you can update or install drivers, see what isn't working, and disable hardware if need be.

138. D. Fast Startup is similar to Hibernate in how it works, but instead of saving all your applications and data as you had them so that you're instantly back at work, it saves the system state. As described in the question, Fast Startup will close running apps and log off any users, then save the contents of RAM to a hibernation file. When the computer starts back up, it reads the hibernation file and loads drivers, system state, and the kernel much more quickly than it would if the system had to read all of that individually back into RAM as it would in a normal cold boot. Sleep stores everything that's open in RAM and enters a low power state. The display and drives aren't using power, but power is needed to continually refresh memory so that it can retain the information. Sleep uses very little power but "wakes up" very quickly with everything open as it was. The Hibernate option stores open programs and data to the hard drive and, once the computer is hibernated, would use no power, but it will not resume its state as quickly as Sleep would.

139. A. The nslookup utility will query the DNS server the computer is currently configured to use. The utility can be used to perform a variety of DNS queries. The netstat command shows what TCP connections exist on a computer and the port number they are using. The ping command is used to determine whether there is connectivity with a remote computer. When entered as ping localhost, it is used to determine if TCP/IP is running on the local computer. tracert displays the path (routers) that a packet took to get to a remote computer.

140. A. The chown (change owner) command is used to change ownership of files in Linux. The syntax to change the owner of a file is chown *owner-name filename*. The chmod (change mode) command is used to modify the mode of the file, meaning who has what access to the file. The cat command is a powerful tool that can be used to view contents of a file, create new files, and concatenate (put together) files. The cp command is used to copy files.

141. B. Network & Internet is the Settings category that provides options for setting up VPN or dial-up connections. Network and Sharing Center is a Control Panel utility. The System category of Settings deals with display, sound, power, notification, and other settings. The Accounts category is useful for managing users and syncing settings. In Windows 11, but not Windows 10, Windows Backup is included in the Accounts category.

142. A. A virtual private network (VPN) is a secured network connection made over an unsecure network. For example, if you wanted to connect your laptop to your corporate network over the Internet in order to read email but you also wanted to secure the connection, you could use a VPN. Dial-up is a very slow and seldom used connection that requires a telephone landline to make a connection. Fios is a vendor name for a fiber-optic connection that provides Internet access and other services, and a hotspot is sharing a cellular device's connection with other devices, essentially making the cellular device a gateway to the Internet.

143. A, B. The Services console will enable you to manage all of the computer's services. The Services tab of Task Manager is a subset of those services with a link at the bottom to the full Services console. There are several ways to see what services are running and to enable and disable services. They include the Services console, Computer Management, and the Services tab in Task Manager. In Windows 10, but not Windows 11, you can find the services console in Control Panel, Administrative Tools, and click Services. Disk Management does not have a link to the Services console, and Task Scheduler is designed to perform tasks when a trigger happens, such as a date, time, or event.

144. C. A domain uses an authentication server to determine whether a user is granted access to shared resources. In Windows, an authentication server is also known as a domain controller. Domains are not available with Windows Home editions. Windows Home editions can only use a workgroup, and in that case the operating system on the device with the shared resource would allow or deny access. A file server is a computer that provides access to shared files. A DHCP server is used to automatically assign IP addresses and configure network settings. A DHCP server is often included in the software on a SOHO router.

145. B. To turn off all notifications, or choose to manage whether and how individual notification senders can interact with you, you could go to Windows Settings, select the System group, and then click Notifications & Actions. This is not the correct answer, though, because it doesn't stop the background activity—it only stops the notifications. Game mode, found in the Gaming options group, enables you to configure the system to be optimized for gameplay and recording. In addition to preventing driver update installations and stopping restart notifications, it modifies settings affecting video frame rate. Update and Security settings don't address notifications. The Apps option lets you manage where apps can be installed from, default apps for opening files, and other application configuration settings.

146. B. iOS is the proprietary operating system for iPhones. iPhone OS and Windows for iPhone don't exist. The Android OS was developed by Google and is used on smartphones, tablets, and other touchscreen devices. Other operating systems include iPadOS for use on iPads, and of course Windows, Linux, and macOS found on desktop and laptop PCs, and Chrome OS, which is proprietary and found on Chromebooks.

147. B. The App Store is where you would go to locate and download new programs. Finder enables a user to drill down through folders to find what they are looking for. Mission Control is an easy way to see what is open and to switch between applications, and FileVault provides encryption.

148. D. Image deployments are usually done in a large-volume setting where you have many computers configured identically. One machine will have the OS and applications installed and settings configured. Then an image is created. The image can be stored on a network drive, a USB drive, or other media. When it is installed, it will include the OS, software, and settings that were configured on the original machine. An upgrade installation will keep all of your files and settings but install a different version of an OS on your computer. A recovery partition is often created on a laptop that is purchased from a major supplier. There will be a key or multiple keys to press while the computer is booting. The exact key(s) will depend on the laptop manufacturer. Using a recovery partition will erase everything that is on the drive and restore the computer to the state it was in when it was received from the manufacturer. This is sometimes called a factory reset. A repair installation will use the same OS and attempt to leave all your files and settings while fixing any of the operating system files.

149. B, C. An app can be deleted simply by dragging it to the trash, but if it has its own folder, look for an uninstall program. Right-clicking and choosing Delete is how you might remove a file in a Windows OS. There is no uninstall option from the Apple menu.

150. B. The chmod (change mode) command is used to modify the mode of the file, meaning who has what type of access to the file. The *who* is divided into file owner, group members, and others (everyone else). The permissions they can have are read, write, or execute. The command can get quite complicated, but in its basic form it is chmod [*reference*][*operator*][*mode*] *file*. As an example, if you want to restrict a user (the owner) of a file named bogus from writing to that file, the command is chmod u=r bogus. In the command, u is the reference to the user, = is the operator, and r is the mode. Then, to see the result, you enter **ls -l**. Before changing the permission on the file named bogus, running the **ls -l** command may have shown -rw-rw-r--; the first

– means it's a file, not a folder. After that, the three sets of characters (*rwx*) are first set for owner, second set for group, and third set for others. As shown in the graphic, after the chmod u=r bogus command is run, the permissions shown for the bogus file when ls -l is run should be -r--rw-r--, showing that the write permission for the owner was removed. The chown (change owner) command is used to change ownership of files in Linux. The cat command is powerful and can be used to view contents of a file, create new files, and concatenate (put together) files. The cp command is used to copy files.

```
audrey@TheOldGirl:~$ ls -l
total 48
-rw-rw-r-- 1 audrey audrey   22 Dec  4 09:29 bogus
drwxr-xr-x 2 audrey audrey 4096 Mar 17  2021 Documents
drwxr-xr-x 2 audrey audrey 4096 Mar 17  2021 Downloads
drwxr-xr-x 2 audrey audrey 4096 Mar 17  2021 Music
drwxr-xr-x 2 audrey audrey 4096 Mar 17  2021 Pictures
drwxr-xr-x 2 audrey audrey 4096 Mar 17  2021 Public
drwx------ 3 audrey audrey 4096 Mar 17  2021 snap
drwxr-xr-x 2 audrey audrey 4096 Mar 17  2021 Templates
drwxr-xr-x 2 audrey audrey 4096 Mar 17  2021 Videos
audrey@TheOldGirl:~$ chmod u=r bogus
audrey@TheOldGirl:~$ ls -l
total 48
-r--rw-r-- 1 audrey audrey   22 Dec  4 09:29 bogus
drwxr-xr-x 2 audrey audrey 4096 Mar 17  2021 Desktop
drwxr-xr-x 2 audrey audrey 4096 Mar 17  2021 Documents
```

151. A. Click Apple, then Preferences, and choose Accessibility Options to find several features that make interacting easier for people with different abilities. Zoom can enlarge text on the screen, VoiceOver will read screen contents, Sticky Keys lets the user press key combinations one key at a time, and there are several other accessibility options.

152. B. Programs and Features allows the user to add, remove, or troubleshoot installed programs (the options will change by program) and add or remove Windows features. From Devices and Printers you can manage multiple printers and do tasks such as choosing a default printer, installing new printers, and changing printer settings. The Network and Sharing Center is the Windows tool for viewing and configuring network connections and changing adapter settings. Device Manager should be your go-to app when resolving hardware issues. From there you can update or install drivers, see what isn't working, and disable hardware if need be.

153. C. The correct option is Network, where you can see all the network connections of the MacBook. Ethernet and Wi-Fi are not options in Preferences. Accessibility provides access to features that make working with a Mac easier for differently abled people.

154. B. The grep command (short for the impossibly long "globally search a regular expression and print") does just what it says it does: it searches for a string of text and then displays the results of what it found. The syntax for grep is grep [*options*] *pattern* [*files*]. The sudo command stands for superuser do, or substitute user do, and will run a single command as the alternate user. The cp command copies files, and ls provides a list of contents of the working directory.

155. D. Compact discs (CDs) don't hold enough information to be used for installation media for Windows. Windows media can be installed from a USB or an external drive, or via a network connection provided there is a way to boot to the network such as PXE support.

156. B. The program that is used to encrypt a drive on a Mac is FileVault, not BitLocker. Bit-Locker does the same in the Windows operating system. Best practices for hardening a Mac system against malware include backing up the data using Time Machine, encrypting the drive, installing patches and updates as soon as they are available, disabling remote access, turning on the software firewall, using a password manager, using a non-admin account, and setting a password-protected screen saver.

157. C. A file with a `.dmg` extension is a disk image and can be treated like a drive in macOS. It can be "mounted" like a physical hard drive, the contents read, and files opened, or applications installed. A file with a `.pkg` extension in macOS is a compressed package file. You may be able to view the contents of the file in Finder, but if not, it would need to be extracted first. Files with a `.bat` extension are batch files used in Windows to run a string of commands that have been entered into a text file, and files with an `.app` extension are applications.

158. B. The Printers & Scanners pane is where you would go to install a new printer or configure a printer in the macOS System Preferences folder. Printers and Devices are not options there, but Sharing is, and from there you can share your screen or files and choose from several other options.

159. D. Use the Play Store app on your Android phone to access Google Play, where you can find new apps to install on your Android phone. Finder and Mission Control are applications found on a computer with macOS running. The App Store is where you would go to locate and download new programs for an iPhone.

160. C. Unlike iOS for iPhones, the iPadOS has features such as Split View that allow it to use multiple applications at the same time. It also boasts support for external drives and displays. iOS is the operating system of iPhones, and the Android OS developed by Google is used on smartphones, tablets, and other touchscreen devices. iPhone OS is not a real term.

161. C. The `cat` command is powerful and can be used to view contents of a file, create new files, and concatenate (put together) files. For example, to view the line-by-line contents of the `bogus.txt` file, you would simply enter **cat bogus.txt**. To add line numbers to the output, enter the command **cat -n bogus.txt**. The chown (change owner) command is used to change ownership of files in Linux. The chmod (change mode) command is used to modify the mode of the file, meaning who has what access to the file. The cp command is used to copy files.

162. A, B. The Power Options utility in Control Panel has a setting to enable or disable USB Selective Suspend. To get there, choose Power Options, then Change Plan Settings, and then Change Advanced Power Settings; then click USB Settings in the Settings list. Note that Windows 11 does not have that option in the Control Panel Power Options utility. In Device Manager, choose Universal Serial Bus Controllers, then double-click USB Root Hub, choose the Power Management tab, and choose "Allow the computer to turn off this device to save power." Refer to the graphic. USB devices such as a card reader or signature pad may be used so seldom that it makes sense to turn them off when they are not in use, and that is exactly what USB Selective Suspend does. USB Selective Suspend is enabled by default, and this option is available in both Windows 10 and Windows 11. Programs and Features allows the user to add, remove, or troubleshoot installed programs (the options will change by program) and add or remove Windows features. Indexing Options catalogs words in files and the files' metadata to provide faster file searches.

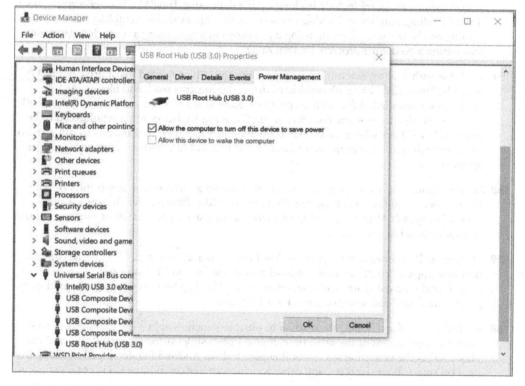

163. B. APFS, the Apple File System, has been the filesystem used by Mac computers since 2017. It supports up to 9 quintillion files and folders, full-disk encryption, and space sharing, so the free space on a drive is available to all volumes of that drive. HFS+ is an older filesystem that was used by Apple. The ext4 filesystem is used in the Linux world, and NTFS (New Technology File System) is the Windows filesystem that supports file encryption and NTFS permissions for file sharing.

164. C. Although the Duo products are made by Microsoft, they run an Android OS, not Windows. There is no Windows version for phones. iPadOS and iOS are Apple's proprietary operating systems.

165. B, C. Since Snow Leopard (macOS 10.6) Apple has included malware detection, called File Quarantine, in its software. File Quarantine will not allow a known malware file to be opened. In order to protect your system from the most recent malware, you need to ensure that updates will run automatically. This is done by choosing System Preferences from the Apple menu, selecting App Store, and selecting Automatically Check For Updates and then Install System Data Files And Security Updates. It's also good advice to only download

programs and files from reputable sources, like the App Store. You could install an antivirus or anti-malware product, but it probably isn't necessary. Finder is used to find folders and files in the directory structure, much like Windows File Explorer.

166. A. The Privacy tab in the Security & Privacy pane is where you would enable Location Services, which is how Siri knows where you are to tell you about the weather, provide maps, and give you directions. The window for each type of privacy concern will show what applications have requested Location Services. Also on the Privacy tab are Contacts, Calendars, Reminders, Photos, Accessibility, and Analytics. Mission Control will show all the open apps for quick access. Accessibility allows you to configure settings for differently abled people, and the Networks pane will show all the computer's network settings.

167. C. The Network and Sharing Center is the Windows tool for viewing and configuring network connections and changing adapter settings. From here you can also manually set up a new connection or network such as dial-up, VPN connections, or even a wireless access point (WAP). From Devices and Printers, you can manage multiple printers and do tasks such as choosing a default printer, installing new printers, and changing printer settings. Programs and Features allows the user to add, remove, or troubleshoot installed programs (the options will change by program) and add or remove Windows features. User Accounts is the utility for adding new user accounts, changing their passwords, or managing profiles as well as other user-related configurations.

168. B. This is a recovery partition installation. A recovery partition is often created on a laptop that is purchased from a major supplier. There will be a key or multiple keys to press while the computer is booting. The exact key(s) will depend on the laptop manufacturer. Using a recovery partition will erase everything that is on the drive and restore the computer to the state it was in when it was received from the manufacturer. This is sometimes called a factory reset. An upgrade installation will keep all your files and settings but install a different version of an OS on your computer. A repair installation will use the same OS and attempt to leave all your files and settings while fixing any of the operating system files. Image deployments are usually done in a large-volume setting where you have many computers configured identically. One computer will have the OS and applications installed and settings configured. Then an image of that computer is created. The image can be stored on a network drive, a USB drive, or other media. When it is installed, it will include the OS, software, and settings that were configured on the original computer.

169. A. Accounts is the group in Windows Settings that will enable you to add a new user. From there, click Family & Other Users; then, in Windows 10, click Add Someone Else To This PC. In Windows 11, you click Add Other User. User Accounts is the Control Panel utility for managing users. From the Personalization menu of Windows Settings, you can change the desktop theme and background colors. The System group in Windows Settings has a multitude of settings, including Display, Sound, Notifications & Actions, and Power.

170. A. The `find` command is used to find files and directories and perform operations on them. The syntax of the command is `find [where to look] [-options][what to find]`. For example, `find Documents -name *.jpg` will find all the files in `Documents` and its subfolders that have `.txt` at the end. Find can also search by folder, name, creation date, modification date, owner, and permissions. The `ps` command will list the processes that are currently running, along with their PIDs (process IDs); the `man` command displays a user manual for any Linux command, much like the Windows `/?` command; and `nano` is a Linux text editor.

171. B. Windows 10 64-bit requires a 2 GHz or faster processor, so that's what the system in question must already have. Unlike RAM, where you must add the requirements together, choose a processor that is at least the fastest requirement of all the running software—in this case, the 2 GHz processor that is needed for the operating system. You would not need to buy a faster processor to accommodate the new software.

172. A. File Allocation Table 32 (FAT32) is more compatible than the other filesystems. It can be read by Windows, Linux, macOS, and many game consoles. Extensible File Allocation Table (exFAT) partitions require a third-party software to be read by Linux, and New Technology File System (NTFS) doesn't play well with any operating system other than Microsoft Windows. Fourth Extended Filesystem (ext4) partitions are used in Linux. Microsoft systems can't even recognize ext4 partitions.

173. A, C. Once upon a time Microsoft had a Windows version for smartphones, but they no longer do. On modern smartphones you'll most likely find either iOS or Android, although there is also Tizen, which is a Linux, open source mobile operating system developed by Samsung. macOS and Windows 10 are for laptop and desktop computers. BlackBerry once had a smartphone operating system but now relies on Android and is known for and focused on their security software for smartphones. Bada and Symbian are other discontinued smartphone operating systems. Remember to focus on the mobile OSs that are listed on the CompTIA A+ objectives. Those are iPadOS, iOS, and Android.

174. A. A restore point is a copy of your system configuration at a given point in time. Restore points are useful for when Windows fails to boot but the computer appears to be fine otherwise, or when Windows doesn't seem to be acting right and you think it was because of a recent configuration change. In Windows 10, restore points are created on the System Protection tab of System Properties.

175. D. Software intended for macOS and Windows are not interchangeable, but some software packages come in a macOS version and a Windows version, so it's important to make sure you purchase the correct one. Windows can be run on a Mac, but not at the same time. You would need to run a program called Boot Camp to create a Windows partition on the Mac's hard drive, then install the Windows OS on that partition. At boot, you can choose either Windows or macOS, but you can't run Windows applications on macOS.

176. B, C. A video card can either be discrete or integrated. If it is integrated, then the graphics processing unit (GPU) resides on the processor, and the GPU will share RAM with the system. A discrete video card will contain a GPU and VRAM (Video RAM) and will be installed in an expansion slot.

177. B. The Apps group of Windows Settings lets you delete or update apps, choose apps to start when you log in, choose default apps for opening files, and other application configuration settings. The System group has settings for display, power, sound, and notifications, and several other options. Update And Security (Windows 10 only) has a plethora of tools, including Windows Update, Troubleshooting, Activation, Recovery, and Windows Security. (The similar Settings group in Windows 11 is Windows Update, but it is only for updates and recovery options. Troubleshooters and Activation are found in the System group, and Windows Security settings are found in the Privacy & Security group of Windows 11 Settings.) The Gaming option enables you to configure the system to be optimized for gameplay and recording.

178. C. You will be performing a clean installation. Clean installations happen on a new machine that doesn't have an operating system at all (bare metal) but can also happen when you want to completely wipe out the drive and begin fresh. An upgrade installation can only happen when there is an existing operating system, and will keep all of your files and settings but install a different version of an OS on your computer. A recovery partition is often found on laptops, and sometimes on desktop PCs, that are purchased from a major supplier. There will be a key or multiple keys to press while the computer is booting. The exact key(s) will depend on the laptop manufacturer. Using a recovery partition will erase everything that is on the drive and restore the computer to the state it was in when it was received from the manufacturer. This is sometimes called a factory reset. Image deployments are usually done in a large-volume setting where you have many computers configured identically. One computer will have the OS and applications installed and settings configured. Then an image of that computer is created. The image can be stored on a network drive, a USB drive, or other media. When it is installed on new computers, it will include the OS, software, and settings that were configured on the original computer.

179. A, D. Type **backup** in the Windows 10 search box and click Backup Settings, and you'll be taken to a screen that says "Back up using File History." You can also find the Backup window in Settings in the Update & Security group. You'll need a storage device such as an external hard drive, then from the Backup window you'll choose to automatically create backups and click More Options to choose the frequency. Every hour is the default, but the backup schedule options vary from 10 minutes up to Daily. Here you can also choose what files to back up. Windows Update checks for operating system updates, and Recovery is the utility that is used to reset a PC, meaning that the operating system is reinstalled but you can choose to keep your personal files.

180. A. VRAM is memory that is dedicated solely to be used by the graphics processing unit (GPU). The GPU takes the work of processing graphics away from the CPU. GPUs can either be integrated (on the CPU) or dedicated (on a discrete graphics card). A graphics card will have its own cooler and VRAM. VRAM on a video card can't usually be upgraded. To increase it, you would need to buy a different video card. In this scenario, you might be able to replace the CPU with one with integrated graphics, if the system supports the new processor, but that isn't the best option.

181. C. Linux has a built-in manual that can be accessed using the man command, similar to using Windows help [*command*] or [*command*] /? at a command prompt. The syntax is man [*command*]. The find command is used to find files and directories and to perform operations on them. The ps command will list the processes that are currently running, along with their PIDs (process IDs), and Nano is a Linux text editor. [*command*] --help can also be used at a Linux Terminal prompt to get help on a specific command.

182. A. You will be performing an upgrade installation. An upgrade installation can only happen when there is an existing operating system. It will keep all of your files and settings but install a different version of an OS on your computer. A recovery partition is often found on a laptop (and some desktops) that is purchased from a major supplier. There will be a key or multiple keys to press while the computer is booting. The exact key(s) will depend on the laptop manufacturer. Using a recovery partition will erase everything that is on the drive and restore the computer to the state it was in when it was received from the manufacturer. This is sometimes called a factory reset. Clean installations happen on a new machine that doesn't have an operating system at all (bare metal) but can also happen when you want to completely wipe out the drive and begin fresh. Image deployments are usually done in a large-volume setting where you have many computers configured identically. One computer will have the OS and applications installed and settings configured. Then an image of that computer is created. The image can be stored on a network drive, a USB drive, or other media. When it is installed on the new computers, it will include the OS, software, and settings that were configured on the original computer.

183. B. To refresh an OS (operating system) you would reinstall the same version over the existing one to correct issues with OS files. You don't need to do that when you are upgrading a system to a new OS. Whenever you're doing an upgrade, it is important to consider several things. Backups must be made in case something goes wrong. Before you start the upgrade, you'll want to ensure that the applications you run are compatible with the new OS and that compatible drivers are available for your hardware. You'll also want to ensure that the hardware you have will work with the new OS.

184. A. You can run a 32-bit software on a 64-bit processor—it just doesn't take advantage of the 64-bit processor's full capabilities. However, you cannot run a 64-bit software on a 32-bit processor.

185. D. Nano is a user-friendly text editor available in many Linux distributions. The Nano software is launched using the nano command. Other text editors such as Vim and Emacs may also be available, but Nano is easier to use. The find command is used to find files and directories and perform operations on them. find can also search by folder, name, creation date, modification date, owner, and permissions. The ps command will list the processes that are currently running, along with their PIDs (process IDs), and the man command displays a user manual for any Linux command, much like the Windows [*command name*] /? command.

186. B. The dig command can be used to retrieve the IP address of a website; for example, dig Sybex.com +short will return the IP address of Sybex.com. The chown (change owner) command is used to change ownership of files in Linux. The top command displays dynamic information about the running processes, and the ip command is used to display configuration information for network interfaces.

187. D. With managed Apple IDs, your company, not you, can reset your password. Your company owns a managed Apple ID, so there are restrictions in place. A managed ID is created by a company for use in company business. Since it's linked to your company, your managed Apple ID can't be used to make purchases, and an IT administrator at your company can restrict access to your account, remove it, or update it.

188. A, C. Requiring multifactor or two-factor authentication has become somewhat standard for applications that require a high level of security. By entering a password (something you know) and requiring the fob (something you have), the application is requiring two-factor authentication. An example of a software token would be a code emailed to you that you can check on the same device you are using to access the application. An external hardware token is anything physical that you must have in your possession, such as a key fob that must be inserted into the computer, a key fob that generates a code that changes every 30 seconds, or your cell phone with an authenticator app.

189. D. Extensible File Allocation Table (exFAT) is optimized for flash drives because it has low overhead like the File Allocation Table 32-bit (FAT32) filesystem (as opposed to New Technology File System [NTFS]). However, like NTFS it will support much larger file sizes than FAT32, which is limited to 4 GB. exFAT is less compatible with non-Microsoft operating systems than FAT32 is, but more compatible than NTFS. For example, macOS can only read NTFS partitions, but it can read and write to exFAT partitions.

190. B. In Linux, the mv (move) command is used to rename files. As shown in the answer, the syntax is mv [old-file-name] [new-file-name]. The cp command copies a file, but that is a different process than moving it. rm is short for remove, and it deletes files. ren is a Windows command to rename files.

191. C. Samba is a widely used freeware program based on SMB (Server Message Block) and CIFS (Common Internet File System) that lets operating systems communicate despite their differences. A request for resources is sent from a client to a Samba server, which forwards the request to the host. The host can either accept or deny the request. Spotlight, Time Machine, and FileVault are macOS tools for finding files, folders, and programs; making backups; and file encryption, respectively.

192. A. The System utility of Control Panel provides a link to the System Settings group, where you can choose the About option in Windows Settings. The screen that pops up by default shows information about the PC such as its name, the specific processor it has, how much physical RAM is installed, the Windows version and edition, and so on. Device Manager is used for troubleshooting hardware and installing device drivers. Devices And Printers is used for managing printers and multifunction devices, as well as other devices that are connected to the computer. Programs And Features helps in uninstalling applications and adding or removing Windows features.

193. B. Files with an .iso extension are disk image files. In order to install the software they contain, you need to first mount the image. You may be able to double-click it; if not, right-click and choose Mount, or locate the file in File Explorer. Select the file, then click Mount under Disk Image Tools. Once mounted, the operating system will treat the file as a disk in an optical drive. You'll look for an installer or autorun file to start the software installation. When you're done using the image, right-click it and choose eject. Extract is an option for zipped files, not ISO files.

194. A, B, D. Whenever you're considering a new software purchase, there are many things to consider. The technical aspects such as OS and application compatibility and hardware concerns are only a part of it. You must also consider what impact this will have on any devices, the network, how internal systems work and the operation of the business, and the business as a whole—how will it affect the company's bottom line? In the case of the network monitoring software presented in the question, consider whether the additional network overhead will cause a significant enough impact on the network to cause adverse effects on production, and will it decrease company profits by slowing production, or is it a wise investment because it can help protect against malware? Will it work well with routers, switches, and other network hardware? Do the positive impacts outweigh the negative ones?

195. D. With today's hard drives measured in TB, storage is seldom a problem, but in an industrial setting it might be. When determining how big a hard drive needs to be, add together the storage requirements of everything that will be on that drive, including the operating system, the applications that will be installed, and all the data that will be generated by those applications. With RAM, you need to consider what will be running at the same time, but with storage, consider all the applications and all the data whether or not they are all working at the same time. It's also important to consider what type of data files will be stored. Word documents take up much less space than video files do.

196. A. In Linux, rm (remove) is the command for deleting files and directories. As shown, the syntax is rm [option] [what-to-remove]. If you're removing more than one file at a time, list the files after the remove command such as rm file1.ext file2.ext. By using options, the rm command can also remove directories and work in verbose mode, meaning that it will tell you what it's doing. del is used to delete one or more files at a Windows command prompt. er is not a known command in either Linux or Windows, and rd is a Windows command to remove directories.

197. A. A file with a .pkg extensions in macOS is a compressed package file. You may be able to view the contents of the file in Finder, but if not, it would need to be extracted first. It can be installed by double-clicking it or opening it with an installer. A file with a .dmg extension is a disk image and can be treated like a drive in macOS. It does not need to be extracted. It can be "mounted" like a physical hard drive, the contents read, and files opened or applications installed. Files with an .app extension are applications, and files with a .bat extension are batch files used in Windows to run a string of commands that have been entered into a text file.

198. D. A bare-metal system is one that doesn't have any software yet, including the operating system. It would not be able to download software to install. It could be used for a network installation of an OS if it supported Preboot Execution Environment (PXE) booting to the network, but that would be using a LAN to distribute software as opposed to downloadable distribution, which by definition uses the Internet. Distributing software via download means that it could be the most up-to-date version of the software. It costs less because no one must pay for the USB or DVD to distribute it, and it only requires an Internet connection, not a DVD drive. Many new PCs don't have optical drives.

199. B. A repair installation (or repair upgrade, as Microsoft calls it) means that you're installing the same version of the same operating system over on top of the existing operating system. A repair installation can be done from within the existing operating system or from other media. It will go through a licensing screen and some others, eventually showing a screen where you will choose to keep Windows settings, personal files, and apps. An upgrade installation will also keep your files, apps, and settings, but you will be using a newer version of the operating system. A clean installation wipes out everything on the hard drive. A remote installation is done across a network and could be any of the other three types.

200. C. The ip command is used to configure and view network settings in modern Linux distributions, replacing the former ifconfig command. Like most Linux commands, there is a multitude of objects and options that can be used. Likely the most frequently used one is ip addr show, which will show all the network interfaces and their respective IP addresses. `ipconfig` and `ipconfig /all` are Windows commands for viewing IP configuration. `cfg` isn't an actual command.

201. C. Windows supports a feature called Modern Standby. Modern Standby must also be supported by the hardware. With Modern Standby, the system will wake from the lowest power to allow short bursts (milliseconds) of software execution as the system needs them. The system uses just enough power to process background tasks but still preserves battery life. The result is that when in sleep mode, a computer can stay connected to a LAN and reacts much like a smartphone with instant on/instant off ability.

202. A. The `net user` command can be used at a command prompt to add a user on the fly. The syntax is `net user username [password | *] /add [options] [/domain]`. In this example, we are adding a user named student, and the * replacing `password` tells the system to prompt us for a password. If no domain is specified, the command assumes the user is added to the local computer. As soon as this command is executed, the named user will appear in the Users utility of Control Panel.

203. D. Pressing Windows Key+X will open the Quick Link menu. On it, in Windows 11 you will find shortcuts to Apps And Features, Mobility Center, Power Options, Event Viewer, Device Manager, Network Connections, Disk Management, Computer Management, Task Manager, Settings, File Explorer, Search, and Run. The Windows 10 Quick Link menu includes links to Windows PowerShell and Windows PowerShell (Admin). You can also click Shut Down or Sign Out from the Quick Link menu, or click Desktop, which will display or hide all open applications on the desktop. Pressing Windows Key+D will also hide or display all open applications. Pressing Windows Key+L is a quick way to lock the computer, and pressing Windows Key+I brings you to Windows Settings.

204. B. The Windows operating system contains many drivers that will help make setting up a new operating system easy, but it would be impossible for the installation media to have all drivers for all the devices that are available. When you have a device whose driver, or a compatible one, doesn't automatically install, you'll have to install the driver from a third party, such as the motherboard manufacturer. Often these drivers can be downloaded from an online source.

205. C. The `top` command provides a dynamic chart of the running processes with the details as shown in the graphic. The top section of the screen shows resources used and process statistics. The bottom shows the processes that are currently running. The `dig` command can be used to retrieve the IP address of a website. The `chown` (change owner) command is used to change ownership of files in Linux, and the `ip` command is used to display configuration information for network interfaces.

206. A, C. A file with a `.pkg` extension in macOS is a compressed package file. You may be able to view the contents of the file in Finder, but if not, it would need to be extracted first. It can be installed by double-clicking it or by opening it with an installer. A file with a `.dmg` extension is a disk image and can be treated like a drive in macOS. It can be "mounted" like a physical hard drive, the contents read, and files opened, or applications installed from it. Files with an `.app` extension are applications, and files with a `.bat` extension are batch files used in Windows to run a string of commands that have been entered into a text file.

207. C. Modern touchpads/trackpads can accept multiple finger gestures that function similarly to gestures on a smartphone or tablet, such as swipe left or right to move between pages. To see what gestures are available, choose System Preferences from the Apple menu, then select Trackpad. Software development kit (SDK) is more of a programming term. Emergency notifications and power options have little to do with a trackpad or Magic Mouse. Incidentally, gestures are also available in Windows. To view or modify multi-finger gestures on your Windows 10 PC, in Windows Settings, choose Devices, then Touchpad. In Windows 11, from Windows Settings, choose Bluetooth & Devices, then Touchpad.

208. B. You would use the User Accounts Control Panel utility to add new accounts for the users. If you were on a Windows Pro or better computer, you could use the Local Users and Groups app, but that is not available in Windows Home editions. It also isn't listed as a separate Control Panel utility, but in Windows 10 Pro and higher editions (not Windows 11) it can be accessed through Administrative Tools (choose Computer Management, then Local Users and Groups). The Administrative Tools utility doesn't have a link to the Control Panel User Accounts utility, which is not as versatile as Local Users and Groups. The Mail utility is where you would configure user profiles for use with Microsoft Outlook.

209. D. Some of the most important files that you will need to work on are hidden by default as a security precaution. To make certain folders or files visible, you need to change the view properties of Windows File Explorer. This is generally done by going to the View tab and selecting Hidden Items in the Show/hide group. Here you can also hide or show file extensions. The same window can be accessed through File Explorer Options in Control Panel. Computer Management is a collection of tools, including Disk Management and System Tools. System Configuration has settings for changing how the computer boots and links to other tools. Local Security Policy allows you to configure options like password complexity and duration.

210. A. Control Panel's Indexing Options looks at words in files and the files' metadata to provide faster file searches. The System group of Windows Settings enables you to configure notifications, power, and many other settings, but not Indexing. The Apps group of Systems is where you can choose default programs and remove applications that you no longer need. The Default Programs app of Control Panel allows you to manage default applications for opening types of files such as photos or mail by opening those settings in Windows Settings.

211. A, B. When a computer logs into a domain, access to resources is controlled through Active Directory. The server that Active Directory resides on is called a domain controller (DC). In a workgroup, sharing would be configured on the computer that was providing access to the files. Running a batch file to copy the files to each user would result in multiple copies of the files, likely with all different information after a time, not a single file repository where the files are shared among users.

212. C. A proxy server makes requests for resources on behalf of a client. Proxy servers are known for three things. One, the proxy server can cache the information requested, speeding up subsequent searches. Two, the proxy can act as a filter, blocking content from prohibited websites and blocking sensitive data from leaving the network. Three, the proxy server can modify the requester's information when passing it to the destination, blocking the sender's identity and acting as a measure of security; the user can be made anonymous. A DNS server resolves IP addresses to domain names. An authentication server verifies the identity of a user and their access to resources, and a web server provides information in files that can be read by a web browser, whether internal to the company or on the Internet.

213. C. Windows 11 maximum RAM limits are 128 GB for the Home edition, 2 TB for the Pro edition, and 6 TB for the Pro for Workstations and Enterprise editions. They are the same limits for Windows 10 64-bit, but the maximum RAM for any 32-bit Windows operating system is only 4 GB.

214. A. You would want a workgroup. By default, Windows 10 computers will join a workgroup called workgroup, making it easy to share files, printers, and other resources. Access to resources is configured on each workstation that is sharing a resource. The drawbacks of a workgroup are that security is configured on each PC, and it's only appropriate for very small networks. Homegroup was a networking scheme in prior versions of Windows that shared libraries. A personal area network (PAN) consists of a PC and its wireless devices, usually paired Bluetooth devices such as printers, headphones, and input devices. A domain is a network where access to resources is configured on a central server that all users of the resources must log into.

215. B. Select File Explorer, then the View tab and the Layout group. Here the Details will show the filename, file size, date last modified or created, and other data. The Extra large icons shows each file as a picture. The List option will show a list of the filenames and folders with no other details, and the Content option shows the file's metadata.

216. C. Updating packages only quarterly would be disastrous to the security of your systems. It's important to plan for updates and follow the plan. If your system has many Linux installations, test package updates in a sandbox before installing on all systems. Managing patches can be time-consuming, which is why companies providing patch management services exist for both Linux and Windows installations. Checking for patches can be scripted using the yum command. Updates should only be downloaded from reliable sources, and if using Red Hat Linux, verify that the packages are signed by Red Hat.

217. D. The yum command can be used to install security updates. The command to check for security updates can be used in scripts, making it easy to run automatically and daily. The command is yum `check-update --security`. If there are none, the command returns a value of 0. The command yum `update --security` can be used to install security updates. The chmod (change mode) command is used to modify the mode of the file, meaning who has what access to the file; the man command displays a user manual for any Linux command, much like Microsoft Windows [*command*] /? command; and the find command is used to find files and directories and to perform operations on them.

218. B, C. To enable a user to retrieve their email from Microsoft Outlook using the Mail utility in Control Panel, you would only need the user's email address and password. If the server is other than a Microsoft Outlook server, then you might need more information such as the protocol the server uses and the server address. You don't need to know the port number.

219. A. One of the best ways always to have the latest version of files, regardless of the device that you are using to access them, is to have them stored and accessed in the cloud. iCloud is Apple's answer to remote storage, and you can configure your Apple devices to place files there automatically or use it for backup. Finder enables a user to drill down through folders to find what they are looking for. Remote Disc is for using a shared optical drive, and Spotlight is used to search for objects in macOS. It uses the familiar spyglass icon.

220. B. Making only monthly backups would likely not be often enough for anyone. In a business setting it's important to have a backup plan, taking into consideration how much data you're willing to lose and how long it would take to restore data if restoring from a backup were needed. The 3-2-1 rule states that you need to have three backups on two different media, and one needs to be off-site. It's also important to consider having backups that are separate from your main system so that an infection of the main system won't infect the backup. Your backup plan should include regularly verifying that the backups are able to be restored, meaning that the backups complete properly and are not corrupted, and that your restore plan works. Even emergency medical services have practice runs from time to time to ensure that when a major event happens, they will be ready. You should, too. Finally, document, document, document. If an event occurs, you need to ensure that you're restoring from the correct backups, and if the person in charge of backups is not available for any reason, a thoroughly documented backup system will make it easier for someone else to continue the process in their place and/or restore backups if needed.

221. A. The `format` command is used to format hard drives. Before you format any drive, be sure that you have it backed up or are prepared to lose whatever is on it. The `/fs:[filesystem]` switch specifies the filesystem to prepare the disk with. `initialize` is not a command.

222. C. Time Machine is a part of macOS, and it makes backups hourly daily and weekly that can be used to restore a single file from months ago if it was accidentally deleted. Mirrored drives provide redundancy if the hard drive fails, but not against human error. Online utilities are often set up to do the same. Backups should be a priority if retaining the data is important. The only drawback with Time Machine is that if the external drive being used by Time Machine gets full, it will start deleting the first backups to make room for new ones.

223. A, D. To set up a proxy server in Windows Settings, you only need the server's IP address and port number to use. You likely should also check the box that says "Don't use the proxy server for local (intranet) addresses." You would not need the router's IP address or the DHCP server's IP address unless it is also functioning as the proxy server. A router decides if a packet belongs on the LAN or another network, and a DHCP server's job is to provide IP addresses and other settings to devices that log into a network.

224. B. The search feature in macOS is Spotlight, and a magnifying glass icon in the upper-right corner of the menu bar represents it (or you can press Command+spacebar from any app). Spotlight can search for documents, images, apps, and so on. Keychain is Apple's password management system. Finder enables a user to drill down through folders to find what they are looking for. Siri is Apple's voice-activated virtual assistant.

225. D. Eight-character alphanumeric passwords are simply too easy to hack. Whether a Windows or Linux system, more complex passwords should always be required. There are other ways to keep malware and viruses out. Linux has a few advantages on that front. First and foremost, there are many, many people looking at Linux code, which means many people to catch and rectify a vulnerability that could be taken advantage of by viruses and hackers. In Linux, the user and system are more compartmentalized. If malware attacks a user, it will only have access to what that user account has access to, not system files and folders. This means if you must run commands as root, it's extremely important to, whenever possible, do so using `sudo` instead of `su`. `sudo` will run just that command as root, but `su` opens up an entire new shell as root and greater vulnerability to attack. If you're logged in as `root`, the whole system is vulnerable. Also, hackers know that `root` is the default name for the system administrator, so create another user and disable `root` so that a hacker has to guess not only the password but the username as well. It's always good advice to install an antivirus program and update it regularly. Other security actions for Linux are to configure a firewall to filter traffic on unused ports, keep the Linux packages and kernel updated, remove any software that is no longer being used, and change the `/boot` directory to read only so that it can't be changed. In addition to requiring complex passwords, force users to change them periodically and not reuse passwords. You'll also want to monitor for failed login attempts and lock accounts after a reasonable number of failed logins. Email can be encrypted, and of course, train users on the dangers of opening email from unfamiliar sources.

226. D. A domain is a group of computers that are tightly connected or associated and share a common domain name. It has a single authority (called a domain controller) that manages security and access to resources for all the computers. All users will log in to the Windows domain using their centrally created user account. If no domain is used, then by default Windows computers will join a workgroup called workgroup, making it easy to share files, printers, and other resources. Access to resources is configured on each workstation that is sharing a resource. The drawbacks of a workgroup are that security is configured on each PC and it's only appropriate for very small networks. Homegroup was a networking scheme in prior versions of Windows that shared libraries. A personal area network (PAN) consists of a PC and its wireless devices, usually paired Bluetooth devices such as printers, headphones, and input devices. A domain is a network where access to resources is configured on a central server that all users of the resources must log in to.

227. A. In the View Your Active Networks pane, you can see that this network profile is set to Private Network. A private network is one that is trusted, like where you work, or that you control, like your home network. By default, this computer will be discoverable on the network and File And Printer Sharing is enabled. To change these settings, click Change Advanced Sharing Settings. The other two types of network profiles are public and domain. To change the network type, go to Settings, choose Network & Internet, then select Status. Click Properties of the network connection that you want to change and choose the profile type. The domain profile type is detected automatically when the local computer logs in to an Active Directory domain.

228. B, C. Mapping a network drive to a share makes it easy to access that share every time you log into your computer, provided you're on the same network. Left-clicking on This PC will show the mapped drive in the right pane, after it has been set up as a mapped drive, so that you can easily choose it from there. The network share will appear on Quick Access after you've used it.

229. A. Choosing to block all incoming connections, including those in the list of allowed apps, would certainly stop all incoming connections quickly. There is no Disable option under Private Networks in the Windows Defender Firewall window. Turning Airplane mode on would stop the computer from communicating on wireless networks, but it wouldn't stop communication on a wired network, and turning off the firewall is the opposite of what you would want to do.

230. C. Choosing Computer Management, then Shared Folders, and Shares will show all of the resources that are shared on the local computer. Some are created by default. Hidden shares will have a $ at the end of the name and can only be accessed if you know the share name. Network & Internet deals with configuring network connections, not network shares. Ease Of Access enables alternate configurations that work better for differently abled people. Network And Sharing Center is used to configure networks, and it has settings to turn sharing on and off but no way to show all the current network shares.

231. A, D. The simplest way to connect to your WWAN, once it has been set up, is to choose it from the available wireless networks shown when clicking the wireless network icon on the taskbar. Or, go to Windows Settings, choose Network & Internet, then Cellular to choose your network. A mobile hotspot is when you share the Internet connection on your device with other devices that are near you. Choosing Wi-Fi in the Network & Internet group of Windows Settings will not show you the WWAN connection.

232. B. A network restriction means that you will not allow an application to communicate through a firewall, whereas an exception means that you will allow that application to communicate through the firewall. To configure a restriction in Windows Defender Firewall, open it from Control Panel and click Advanced Settings, then click Outbound Rules, then New Rule. Ensure that Program is selected and click Next. Click Browse to locate the program file, click to select it, then click Open. The program path should appear in the New Outbound Rule Wizard dialog box. Click Next, then choose Block The Connection. Click Next twice, then give your rule a name and click Finish. A mapped network drive means that you have assigned a drive letter on a local computer to a folder that is shared on a remote computer. A network share would take place on a computer with folders that you want to allow others on your network to have access to.

233. C. When you use a cellular network to connect to the Internet, you are using a WWAN. Most of us are familiar with the local area network (LAN) in our home or office and the personal area network (PAN) that we use to connect devices such as wireless keyboards, mice, and headsets to our computer. A campus area network (CAN) could exist on a property that is owned by a single entity but housed in discrete buildings. The network might even cross government-owned streets. You may be less familiar with a wireless wide area network (WWAN), which are used more and more frequently. Unlike wireless LANs that use radio, microwave, or infrared signals, WWANs take advantage of the cellular network.

You can purchase a WWAN device, often called a mobile hotspot, from a cellular service provider. They generally require a contract, but some don't. The great advantage of a WWAN is that they will work almost anywhere—the cellular network is virtually worldwide. The biggest disadvantage is likely the cost.

234. B, C. The fastest way to join your friend's network is to click the globe icon (or Wi-Fi icon) and choose the network, but going through Network Status, then Show Available Networks also works. Right-clicking a browser shortcut will show websites that you've recently been to and a few other options. Firewall & Network Protection ➤ Private Network will enable you to configure firewall settings for use with a private network.

235. A, C. You can drill down through Windows Settings to find Firewall & Network Protection Settings, but it's far easier to search for it, then choose Allow An App Through Firewall. Once there, if the app is in the list, click the Change Settings button, then select the box next to the application you want to allow access for under the listing for Private or Public network, depending on your needs. If it isn't in the list, click Allow Another App. Drilling down through Control Panel, choose Windows Defender Firewall, then An App Or Feature Through Windows Defender Firewall will take you to the same setup screen. The other two options will enable you to uninstall applications.

236. B. Opening Device Manager and clicking Network Adapters should show you what you have for network devices. Most likely you'll see a Bluetooth Device (Personal Area Network), possibly an Ethernet Local Area Network (LAN) adapter, a wireless area network (WAN) adapter and, if you have one, a wireless wide area network (WWAN) adapter. If it doesn't show there, either it isn't being detected by the system or one does not exist in your system. Disk Management is for configuring and managing drives. Apps & Features and Programs And Features both have the same job: providing a way to install or repair applications and add or remove Windows features. The former is in Settings and the, latter is in Control Panel.

237. B, C. Wireless wide area networks use the cellular system to connect to the Internet. To make a connection you would need either a WWAN card in your laptop or a WWAN device, which is sometimes called a mobile hotspot device, and a cellular service connection. Some cellular companies require a contract for this type of cellular service, but not all do. The WWAN card or WWAN device need to be compatible with your cellular provider. Wireless NICs are used for Wi-Fi connections, and an RJ-45 connector is used for wired Ethernet connections.

238. A. Metered network settings can be configured for wired, Wi-Fi, or a wireless wide area network (WWAN) connection. For example, to configure a Wi-Fi network as a metered connection, go to Settings, then choose the Network & Internet group, then click Wi-Fi, then Manage Known Networks, and select the network. In Windows 10, you need to click Properties, but in Windows 11 you're already on the Properties screen. Locate the metered connection setting and turn it on. You can then set a data limit to control data usage. Performance Monitor won't show data usage. A WWAN can connect to a virtual private network (VPN), but it will still use data. Your connection might go through a proxy server when connecting to a network, but a proxy server's job is to filter network traffic. Any time you're connecting to the Internet or a VPN via your WWAN connection, you'll be using data.

239. C. Pressing Windows Key+E will open the File Explorer window. Pressing Windows Key+X and then selecting File Explorer from the menu will also work, but it's not the fastest, most direct way. Windows Key+F will bring up a feedback window, and Windows Key+M will minimize all the open windows, leaving you at the desktop.

240. A, C. For a new Windows installation, the default network setting is to configure IP addresses dynamically, so the computer should get its IP address and subnet mask from the DHCP server. All you need is a patch cable to connect to the router and a compatible NIC installed (with its drivers, of course) with an RJ-45 port. You would not use a wireless NIC for an Ethernet network; a wireless NIC is for a Wi-Fi network. You don't need to know the IP address and subnet mask because the DHCP server will assign them automatically.

241. B. There are multiple ways to view the path to a resource. In File Explorer you can right-click the resource and then choose Properties and select the Sharing tab. The screen will say Network Path and list the path just below it. Typing **mynetworkdrives** in a browser doesn't help at all, and Shares in Computer Management shows what you are sharing, not what is being shared with you.

242. A, C. When a motherboard uses BIOS rather than UEFI to manage firmware, it must use the MBR partition type or the drive will not be bootable. A GPT partition will be able to be read but not booted to. The partition size limit for MBR is 2 TB.

243. A, B. Once a hard drive is installed, partitions must be created (even if there is only one) and the volumes must then be formatted before they will show in File Explorer and be ready for the user to store information on them. Disk Management (`diskmgmt.msc`) and `diskpart` are two excellent and powerful tools for doing just that. Disk Management is a utility that has a user-friendly GUI, whereas `diskpart` is run from the command line. `diskpart` is the more powerful of the two, and it's worth spending some time exploring. Performance Monitor (`perfmon.msc`) shows resource usage in real time, and the Services console (`services.msc`) shows all of the services available in the system and their current status.

Chapter 7: Security

1. B. A protected computer or area may have a badge reader into which you insert a smartcard. A smartcard is a type of badge or card that gives you access to resources, including buildings, parking lots, and computers. It contains information about your identity and access privileges. If using radio frequency identification (RFID), the reader is a wireless, no-contact technology and the user does not need to touch the card to the reader. A PIN (personal identification number) code is a number that would be entered to gain access to a system. A security token is something you have that is used to verify your identity; it can be a software or a hardware token. Biometrics are using part of your body as identification.

2. A. A spoofing attack is an attempt by someone or something to masquerade as someone else. This type of attack is usually considered an access attack. The most popular spoofing attacks today are IP spoofing, ARP spoofing, and DNS spoofing. This is an example of IP spoofing, where the goal is to make the data look as if it came from a trusted host when it didn't (thus spoofing the IP address of the sending host). On-path attacks occur when your data transmissions are intercepted by someone en route, then forwarded on to their destination, sometimes with changes, sometimes without. Zombie and botnet are attacks where the user of the computer doesn't know there is malware on their computer. Their computer is a zombie, and when many zombies are used to attack a system, it's known as a botnet attack. A noncompliant system is one that is not following best practices such as keeping the OS and anti-malware updated and the firewall enabled.

3. A. A smartcard is a type of badge or card that gives the holder access to resources, including buildings, parking lots, and computers. It contains information about your identity and access privileges. Each area or computer has a card scanner or a reader in which you insert your card. Radio frequency identification (RFID) is the wireless, no-contact technology used with these cards and their accompanying reader. A security token is something you have that is used to verify your identity; it can be a software or a hardware token. An access control vestibule is an area between two doors, often with a security camera. The second door grants access to a secure area. A key fob is a small device used in two-factor identification. It can generate a number or have software on it that is read to gain access.

4. D. There are generally four wireless encryption methods available. From least to most secure, they are Wired Equivalent Privacy (WEP), Wi-Fi Protected Access (WPA), and two newer versions of WPA called WPA2 and WPA3. WPA3 is the most secure and should be used unless strange circumstances prevent you from doing so, because WPA and WPA2 are no longer secure. WPS is an easy way to configure Wi-Fi for devices like printers, where a number would be generated on a printer, for example, and the number would need to be entered on the access point, or vice versa. WPS has security flaws and is not listed in the CompTIA A+ exam objectives.

5. B. Companies normally generate a huge amount of paper, most of which eventually winds up in dumpsters or recycle bins. Dumpsters may contain information that is highly sensitive in nature, and attackers may seek it out by practicing dumpster diving. In high-security and government environments, if sensitive papers are no longer needed, they should be either shredded or burned.

6. B, C. Social engineering is a process in which an attacker attempts to acquire information about your network and system by social means, such as talking to people in the organization, shoulder surfing, tailgating, or other methods. When this is done via email or instant messaging, it's called phishing. Spoofing involves pretending to be a trusted resource—for example, by using a trusted resource's IP address to gain access to something else. A brute-force attack usually involves software that keeps trying passwords or codes until it hits upon the right one to gain access.

7. D. Tailgating refers to being so close to someone when they enter a building that you can come in right behind them without needing to use a key, a card, or any other security device. Using an access control vestibule, which are devices such as small rooms that limit access to one or a few individuals, is a great way to stop tailgating. Revolving doors can also help prevent tailgating. Shoulder surfing is walking behind someone hoping to see passwords or other security information they may be entering. On-path attacks occur when your data transmissions are intercepted by someone enroute, then forwarded on to their destination, sometimes with changes, sometimes without. A brute-force attack usually involves software that keeps trying passwords or codes until it hits upon the right one to gain access.

8. C. In a Windows domain, password policies can be configured at the domain level using Group Policy Objects (GPOs). There are hundreds of variables that can be configured. Variables that can be configured relating to passwords include password complexity and length and the time between allowed changes to passwords, and a lockout policy for failed access attempts. A firewall can be configured to block certain types of traffic based on things like IP address, protocol, or MAC address. A VPN (virtual private network) is a secure path between a local and a remote device. Data loss prevention (DLP) is the process of monitoring and identifying sensitive data to make sure it is accessed only by authorized persons.

9. A. Sometimes the obvious solutions are the best ones! A key aspect of access control involves physical barriers. One of the easiest ways to prevent those intent on creating problems from physically entering your environment is to lock your doors and keep them out. Cable locks are used to secure mobile devices like laptops to a table or a fixed device so they can't be carried away. An access control vestibule is a small room between two doors, where the secure access area is beyond the second door, and biometrics are using a part of the body to identify a person.

10. B. With ransomware, software, often delivered through a Trojan, takes control of a system and demands that a third party be paid. The "control" can be accomplished by encrypting the hard drive, by changing user password information, or via any of several other creative ways. Users are usually assured that by paying the extortion amount (the ransom), they will be given the code needed to revert their systems to normal operations. Even among malware, ransomware is particularly nasty. A rootkit is software that gains access to a system as administrator, giving it full control over a system. Rootkits are adept at hiding their presence and are difficult to eradicate. A Trojan is named after the Trojan horse of mythology. Trojans are malicious software that hides in that fun game or screen saver that you just downloaded, and it installs when you install the innocent-looking files. Spyware is designed to watch what you do and where you go, hoping to gain information such as logins and passwords, and bank account numbers.

11. A, B. When configuring a new wireless router, always change the administrator's username and password first. This prevents would-be hackers from having easy access to the router. Then change the default SSID. These default values can easily be found online, and not changing them immediately makes your router vulnerable to attack. The radio power level might be changed later if you discover the signal is too weak or too strong. There is no guest account on a router.

12. D. Port security involves disabling all unneeded protocols/ports. In this case, ports 80 and 443 are needed for HTTP and HTTPS access, and ports 25, 110, 143, 465 or 587 may be needed for email. That's it. If you don't need them, remove the additional protocols, software, or services, or prevent them (disable them, or block them, as the setting is typically called on a router) from loading. Ports left open but not in use present an open door for an attacker to enter. MAC filtering is an option on most routers that will only allow devices with specific MAC addresses to access the router. Content filtering blocks undesirable traffic such as social media or hate sites on a corporate network. Port forwarding/mapping will send all traffic that comes in on a specified port number to a specific node on the network.

13. B. When you move a file or folder on the same NTFS volume, it will keep its original permissions. If you copy it or move it to a different volume, it will inherit permissions from its new parent directory.

14. B. When users log on to a computer or network, they are generally required to provide credentials such as a username or password. In multifactor authentication (MFA), the user is required to provide two or more items proving who they are. These items are generally from two of four categories: something they know (such as a password), something they have (such as a code from a security token), something they are (biometric screening), or somewhere they are (based on GPS location or Wi-Fi and cell tower triangulation). A firewall is a software or hardware device that will block traffic into or out of a network based on parameters that the administrator specifies. An access control list exists for each resource. It defines who has what level of access to that resource. The principle of least privilege states that you give a user only enough access to do what they need to do and nothing more.

15. B, C. The best methods are using either overwrite or drive wipe programs. Overwriting the drive entails copying over the data with new data. A common practice is to replace the data with 0s. Drive wipes do a similar thing. Formatting the drive does not guarantee that others can't read the data. Using electromagnetic fields (or degaussing) isn't reliable and can damage the hard drive, and it won't work at all on SSDs.

16. D. When Windows is installed, one of the default accounts it creates is Guest, and this represents a weakness that can be exploited by an attacker. While the account cannot do much, it can provide initial access to a system, and the attacker can use that to find another account or acquire sensitive information about the system. To secure the system, disable all accounts that are not needed, especially the Guest account, which is disabled by default. The Administrator account should be renamed. If a hacker knows a valid username, then they are halfway into your system. The DefaultAccount is an account that is managed by the system and is disabled by default. Power User is not an account that is installed with Windows 11, but there is a Power Users group that is kept for backward compatibility.

17. A. On-path attacks clandestinely place something (such as a piece of software or a rogue router) between a server and the user, and neither the server's administrator nor the user is aware of it. The on-path attack intercepts data, then sends the information to the server as if nothing is wrong. The on-path attack software may be recording information for someone to view later, altering it, or in some other way compromising the security of your system and session. A noncompliant system is one that is not in line with acceptable security policies and procedures. Zombie and botnet are attacks where the user of the computer doesn't know there is malware on their computer. Their computer is a zombie, and when many zombies are used to attack a system, it's known as a botnet attack. Spoofing occurs when another system pretends or appears to be a trusted system.

18. B, C. Setting strong passwords is critical to network security. They should be as long as possible. Eight or 10 characters is a good minimum. Users should also be required to use a combination of uppercase and lowercase letters, a number, and a special character such as #, @, &, or others. Passwords should also expire, but 180 days is too long. Having a 45-day or 90-day requirement would be better.

19. A. With NTFS, each file, directory, and volume can have its own security. NTFS tracks security in access control lists (ACLs) for each resource. The ACL will contain the user or group name and the level of access they have been granted. The basic permissions to choose from are Full Control, Modify, Read & Execute, List Folder Contents, Read, and Write. There are also special permissions and settings that can be applied. A token is software or hardware that is used in multifactor authentication and falls under the category of something that a user has. Badges may use RFID or other technology that is read to allow physical entry to a secure area. Control rosters are used in areas that have security guards and contain a list of people who are allowed to enter.

20. D. The Guest account is created by default (and should be disabled) and is a member of the Guests group. For the most part, members of Guests have the same rights as Users except they can't access log files. The best reason to make users members of the Guests group is to access the system only for a limited time. There is no group named Standard Users by default. There are groups created automatically called Users, Administrators, Power Users, Guests, and a few others. The Power Users group is kept for backward compatibility, but they are the same as someone in the Users group. Administrators have complete control over the systems that they are an administrator on.

21. C. One of the big problems larger networks must deal with is the need for users to access multiple systems or applications. This may require a user to remember multiple accounts and passwords. The purpose of single sign-on (SSO) is to give users access to all the applications and systems that they need when they log on. Some of the systems may require users to enter their credentials again, but the username and password will be consistent between systems. EFS is the Encrypting File System used to encrypt volumes, files, and folders in Windows OSs. MDM is mobile device management, which allows an IT department to retain some control even though users employ BYOD (Bring Your Own Device). UAC is user account control, which verifies that someone has the authority to change a Windows system before making any changes.

22. B. A keylogger seems to be running on the system, monitoring and copying all that is typed on the keyboard. Obviously, this malware needs to be removed and incident response steps taken.

23. A. A software-based firewall on the workstation would be able to stop unwanted network traffic, including port scans and probes. Antiphishing training teaches users to avoid malicious emails. Anti-malware and antivirus are software designed to recognize and quarantine or eradicate malicious code.

24. C. The software token is stored on a general-purpose device, such as the PC or a smartphone. The hardware token option would involve carrying an added key fob or device. A fingerprint reader would be unacceptable as it involves biometrics. A second password defeats the benefit of using multifactor authentication.

25. B. Temporal Key Integrity Protocol (TKIP) is an encryption protocol, used in WPA (Wi-Fi Protected Access) for wireless connections. It was intended to replace WEP's weak encryption by creating a unique key for each for each data frame. It has since been subject to wireless attacks and is not considered acceptable for big business. A VLAN (virtual LAN) occurs when devices from multiple LANs are joined together virtually and can act as if they are on the same physical network even though they are not. A VPN (virtual private network) is similar because it creates a private tunnel through a public network using encryption protocols. A VPN might be used by someone working remotely to access a corporate server. AES (Advanced Encryption Standard) is the successor to TKIP. AES and TKIP work together in WPA2 (WPA, version 2).

26. B, D. Group Policy/updates and login scripts are common ways to push and enforce security settings on Active Directory objects. EFS is the Encrypting File System, which is used to encrypt volumes, files, and folders. Port security means opening or closing ports on a router to control what type of packets traverse the router.

27. A. AES (Advanced Encryption Standard) is used in WPA2 (Wi-Fi Protected Access, version 2). VPN is a virtual private network that transmits data across a public network using encryption. RADIUS (Remote Authentication Dial-In User Service) and Kerberos are both authentication protocols.

28. D. RADIUS (Remote Authentication Dial-in User Service) was originally designed to authenticate remote users to a dial-in access server but is now used in several authentication situations. TKIP is a wireless encryption protocol used in WPA (Wi-Fi Protected Access) which made WPA more robust/secure than WEP (Wired Equivalent Privacy). TACACS+ (Terminal Access Controller Access-Control System) is an authentication protocol for centralized authentication, and a VPN (virtual private network) uses encryption to create a private connection using a public network.

29. A. Using Active Directory settings or the Local Group Policy Editor, you can restrict the number of failed login attempts before the user is locked out of their account. This is important to help prevent a brute-force attack, which attempts to guess passwords until it hits upon the right one. Antivirus/anti-malware is important to have and identifies malicious software based on its signature code but is not at work here. A bollard is a physical post to block vehicular traffic, and a rootkit is a particularly difficult malware to eradicate because it is working with administrator rights and it's good at hiding in a system.

30. C. The organizational unit (OU) is a subdivision within which may be placed users, groups, more OUs, and other objects. The OU exists on a domain, which is a group of users and resources under a single administrative control. Windows domains are managed by software called Active Directory. Active Directory is organized into organizational units, usually for security purposes. A home folder is where an individual user stores their documents and such, and in a Windows domain, that location is usually on the domain controller or another server.

31. B. TACACS+ is an authentication protocol developed by Cisco that is now an open standard. It separates the AAA (authentication, authorization, and accounting) packets and encrypts them. It was released in 1993 and RADIUS (Remote Authentication Dial-In User Service) is an authentication protocol that was released in 1997. Kerberos is an open source authentication protocol that has been around since the 1980s. AES (Advanced Encryption Standard), which is for wireless encryption and not authentication, has been around since 2001 and is the successor to TKIP (Temporal Key Integrity Protocol).

32. A, C. An equipment lock would slow down a would-be thief, and alarm systems often send thieves looking for an easier mark. A security token is involved in multifactor authentication, and a hard token is one of two types of security tokens, the other being a soft token.

33. C, D. Often an access control vestibule will have either a security guard, or video surveillance, or both. Once in the vestibule the second door could be opened remotely by someone watching through the surveillance camera or by a guard who personally clears the person trying to gain access. A bollard is a post used to block vehicular traffic. A motion sensor detects movement and is often used to trigger an alarm, turn on a light, or turn on a camera, or a combination of those.

34. B. Folder redirection allows users' profile folders to be stored off a local machine and instead placed in a more centralized location on the network. A profile stored this way is called a roaming profile. The home folder is the specific location where a user's documents and such are stored. An organizational unit is a management tool that can be used to organize Active Directory resources and can contain users, computers, and other resources. A VPN (virtual private network) is created across a public network by using strong encryption protocols.

35. B. WPA2 (Wi-Fi Protected Access, version 2) replaced WPA, which had replaced WEP (Wired Equivalency Protocol). WEP was the first wireless security protocol. WPA, which was developed next, used TKIP (Temporal Key Integrity Protocol), and WPA2 uses TKIP and the more secure AES (Advanced Encryption Standard). WPA3 was released in 2018 to replace WPA2, whose security had been broken. WPA3 also includes better security for the proliferation of IoT devices. WPA, WPA2, and WPA3 all have personal and enterprise options.

36. D. Operating system (OS) and application patches may fix vulnerabilities in the software and should be applied as soon as possible after they are released. In a corporate environment it would likely be best to test them in a sandbox first to avoid any problems. On a Windows PC, the Windows Update utility is used to manage the process for you.

37. C. A strong Windows password, restricting with user permissions, and changing the default administrator password will help protect Windows but does not protect the computer in general. If a user can get into the BIOS/UEFI (Basic Input Output System/Unified Extensible Firmware Interface), then they can change the boot sequence, boot to a USB drive, and do some damage to the system. The way to protect against this is to implement a BIOS/UEFI password.

38. D. Firewalls are among the first lines of defense in a network. They can be hardware firewalls or software firewalls and can exist on several layers of a network. The basic purpose of a firewall is to isolate one network from another or one network node from another. Firewalls function as one or more of the following: packet filter, proxy firewall, or stateful inspection firewall. VPN (virtual private network) creates a private network across a public one by using encryption protocols. EFS (Encrypting File System) is used to encrypt files and folders. Antivirus/anti-malware is used to detect malicious attackers by identifying signature lines of code or actions.

39. A, C. Biometric locks use a part of your body as identification. They are considered physical security, as are simple door keys. Multifactor authentication is security that requires identification and two or more methods of authentication, such as a password and key fob.

Authentication can be verified by something you know (passwords), something you have (key fob, smartcard), something you are (fingerprint), or somewhere you are (using GPS position or a Wi-Fi network and cell tower triangulation). Firewalls are logical security that filters incoming and outgoing packets to allow or reject them based on criteria you choose.

40. C. A person in the IT department is not likely to ask for your password. If they want you to reset it, they can use software to reset it that will make you choose a new password on next login. This is a social engineering attack. Social engineering is using kindness, coercion, or fear to get you to give up privileged information such as your password. Spoofing is when a website or server, for example, is made to look like a trusted one but in reality there is an attacker lurking there. A brute-force attack uses software to repeatedly try different passwords to break into a system.

41. D. Any time there is more than one authentication method required, it's multifactor authentication (MFA). In this case, it does involve using biometrics, but the passcode is not a biometric factor. An authenticator app can provide a code and be a part of multifactor authentication. Authenticator apps run on a device like a smartphone or PC and provide a unique key that changes every few seconds. The key proves that you have the smartphone or PC in your possession. Full-device encryption could be accomplished with a feature like Microsoft's BitLocker, which encrypts an entire drive including the boot files, or a TPM chip, which prohibits accessing a drive if the chip is not present. Multifactor authentication usually requires two of the following four types of inputs: something you know (password), something you have (smart token), something you are (biometrics), or somewhere you are (GPS or other location services).

42. C. Tailgating refers to being so close to someone when they enter a building that you can come in right behind them without needing to use a key, a card, or any other security device. Using an access control vestibule, which is a device such as a small room that limits access to one or a few individuals, is a great way to stop tailgating. With a door lock or ID badge, the tailgaters could still follow the other employee in. An entry control roster is merely a list of people who are allowed access to an area, and it isn't much use without a guard to check it.

43. B. Adding AOShea to the Administrators group will certainly work, but it's not the recommended approach. Since members of the Administrators group have such power, they can inadvertently do harm (such as accidentally deleting a file that a regular user could not). To protect against this, the practice of logging in with an Administrators group account for daily interaction is strongly discouraged. Instead, system administrators should log in with a user account (lesser privileges) and change to the Administrators group account (elevated privileges) only when necessary.

44. A. Biometric authentication requires identification of a physical feature of the user, such as a fingerprint or palmprint. Mobile devices commonly use your fingerprint to prove who you are. Most modern laptops can also use a facial scan to identify you. DNA and retina scanners are considered a form of biometric authentication, but they're not commonly used today with mobile devices. (Imagine your phone needing to collect blood or saliva to authenticate you—no thanks!) DNA and facial scans aren't on the CompTIA A+ objectives yet, but retina scanners, fingerprint, and palmprint scanners are. A swipe lock is not a type of biometrics.

45. B. BitLocker allows you to use drive encryption to protect files—including those needed for startup and logon. For removable drives, BitLocker To Go provides the same encryption technology to help prevent unauthorized access to the files stored on them. EFS is the Encrypting File System, used to encrypt volumes, files, and folders on a drive. AES is the Advanced Encryption Standard, an encrypting protocol for Wi-Fi.

46. C. Biometric devices use physical characteristics to identify the user. Biometric systems include fingerprint/palm/hand scanners, retinal scanners, face scanners, and soon, possibly, DNA scanners. To gain access to resources, you must pass a physical screening process. Bollards are vertical posts to block vehicular traffic. ID badges often use RFID (radio frequency identification) to communicate with a reader and verify your identity. Tokens can be either hard (like a key fob) or soft (software on a system) and are often used in multifactor authentication.

47. C. When assigning user permissions, follow the principle of least privilege; give users only the bare minimum that they need to do their job, nothing more. Another best practice is to assign permissions to groups rather than users, and make users members of groups (or remove them from groups) as they change roles or positions.

48. B. Companies normally generate a huge amount of paper, most of which eventually winds up in dumpsters or recycle bins. Dumpsters may contain information that is highly sensitive in nature, and attackers may seek it out by practicing dumpster diving. In high-security and government environments, sensitive papers should be either shredded or burned. Shoulder surfing is literally looking over someone's shoulder to try to see passwords or other sensitive information. Social engineering happens any time someone tries to coerce, threaten, or cajole someone into giving up privileged security information. A brute-force attack is repeatedly trying passwords in an effort to guess the correct one.

49. A. The systems are not up-to-date and therefore are more vulnerable to attacks. These systems are considered noncompliant systems. It's a violation of security best practices to fail to keep all software on your network up-to-date. Zombie and botnet are attacks where the user of the computer doesn't know there is malware on their computer. Their computer is a zombie, and when many zombies are used to attack a system, it's known as a botnet attack. A brute-force attack usually involves software that keeps trying passwords or codes until it hits upon the right one to gain access. A zero-day attack happens when a hole is found in a web browser or other software and attackers begin exploiting it the very day it is discovered by the developer, before they have time to plug the hole.

50. C. When a hole is found in a web browser or other software and attackers begin exploiting it the very day it is discovered by the developer (bypassing the one- to two-day response time that many software providers need to put out a patch once the hole has been found), it is known as a zero-day attack (or exploit). Zombie and botnet are attacks where the user of the computer doesn't know there is malware on their computer. Their computer is a zombie, and when many zombies are used to attack a system, it's known as a botnet attack. Noncompliant systems are those whose software is not up-to-date or they are not following best practices or corporate restrictions and rules. A brute-force attack usually involves software that keeps trying passwords or codes until it hits upon the right one to gain access.

51. D. When there are conflicting NTFS permissions, generally they are combined, and the most liberal is granted. The exception to that is when there is an explicit Deny. That overrides any allowed permissions.

52. C. Microsoft wanted to create a group in Windows that was powerful but not as powerful as the Administrators group, which is how the Power Users group came into being. The idea was that membership in this group would be given Read/Write permission to the system, allowing members to install most software but keeping them from changing key operating system files or accessing other users' data. However, for many current Windows versions, the Power Users group now is assigned permissions equivalent to the Standard user, a member of the Users group. There is no group called Superuser, or Standard Users, or Advanced Users.

53. B, D. You should rename the default Administrator account and always require strong passwords.

54. A. A virtual private network (VPN) is a private network connection that occurs through a public network. VPNs make use of tunneling, which sends private data across a public network by placing (encapsulating) that data into other packets. Even though a VPN is created through the Internet or other public networks, the connection logically appears to be part of the local network, although the connection will likely be a bit slower than sitting at a PC in the office. A firewall is used to filter packets, blocking or accepting them based on the port number they use, MAC address, or other criteria. BitLocker is a full-drive encryption utility. EFS (Encrypting File System) is used to encrypt volumes, individual files, and folders.

55. B, D. NTFS permissions affect users regardless of whether they are at the local computer or accessing the resource across a network. They can also be applied to individual files, whereas share permissions can be applied only to folders. One set of permissions is not inherently more restrictive than the other, as either type can be used to deny access in a given situation (at least when accessing across the network). When NTFS and share permissions affect the same folders, the most restrictive permission applies.

56. D. An unauthorized router with a seemingly legitimate configuration is specifically known as an evil twin. Those can lead to on-path attacks, which involve clandestinely placing something (such as a piece of software or a rogue router) between a server and the user, and neither the server's administrator nor the user is aware of it. The unauthorized device in the middle intercepts data and then sends the information to the server as if nothing is wrong. The unauthorized device software may be recording information for someone to view later, altering it, or in some other way compromising the security of your system and session.

57. B. An ID badge is worn by employees to identify them. Some companies use different colored badges to indicate different functions or security privileges. Most ID badges have a picture of the user on them to prevent unauthorized use. Key fobs are small devices that generate a code that changes every few seconds and are often used in multifactor authentication. Smartcards will have either an RFID tag or a chip that can be read by a reader device to allow or deny entrance to an area. Biometrics are any type of identification that uses a part of your body to identify you.

58. A, C. Bollards are vertical posts that are short and sturdy, sometimes made of cement or steel. They can be placed closely enough together so that a vehicle can't go through an area but people can. Fences can also be erected to keep vehicles and people out of an area. Motion sensors can be used to trigger alarms but won't actually keep anyone out, and good lighting is always a deterrent, but again it won't physically keep anyone out.

59. C. A locator app is what you need. Apple supplies a free app called Find My, and Google has Find My Device that, together with their respective websites, allow multiple mobile devices and to be located if powered on and attached to the Internet (via 5G, 4G, 3G, Wi-Fi, Ethernet, and so on). For Apple devices, if not attached to the Internet, nearby devices can identify your device and tell you where it is. Both Find My and Find My Device allow the device to be controlled remotely to lock it, play a sound (even if audio is off), display a message, or wipe the device clean.

60. A. File systems such as NTFS, and security devices such as firewalls, can specify security by using access control lists (ACLs). ACLs can hold permissions for local users and groups, and each entry in the ACL can also specify what type of access is given. This allows a great deal of flexibility in setting up a network. EFS is the Encrypting File System used to encrypt volumes, files, and folders, but not entire drives. VPN is a type of network connection that uses encryption to create a private network that traverses a public one. PINs (personal identification numbers) are used in many applications to identify a user.

61. C. On any individual file or folder you can right-click and choose Properties to see the Read-only and Hidden attributes, then click Advanced to see whether the file is ready for archiving (needs to be backed up). You can also open a folder in File Explorer and click Date Modified to sort the files by the last date modified. Simply typing **attrib** at a command prompt will show the file attributes for everything in that folder. Attributes are information such as whether the file is a system file (S), hidden (H), read only (R), or ready to be archived (A). To see the attributes for a single file, type **attrib** *filename*. The attrib command is not in the CompTIA A+ objectives, but file attributes are.

62. B. Professional and higher operating system editions in either Windows 10 or Windows 11 will support BitLocker. Home editions will not, regardless of what version of the Windows operating system they are.

63. C. Spyware differs from other malware in that it works—often actively—on behalf of a third party. Rather than self-replicating, like viruses and worms, spyware is spread to machines by users who inadvertently ask for it. The users often don't know they have asked for it but have done so by downloading other programs, visiting infected sites, and so on. The spyware program monitors the user's activity and responds by offering unsolicited pop-up advertisements (sometimes known as adware), gathers information about the user to pass on to marketers, or intercepts personal data such as credit card numbers. Zombies and botnets are innocent computers that are used to perpetrate an attack on someone else without the user's knowledge. An example of spoofing is using an IP address that should be someone else and pretending to be them to gain access to a system. Ransomware locks a system in some way or encrypts data and won't allow access until the system's owner pays a ransom.

64. C. The new administrator should have a nonadministrative account to use for day-to-day tasks. They also need an account with administrative privileges to perform the administrative duties. When creating user accounts, follow the principle of least privilege: give users only the permissions they need to do their work and no more. This is especially true with administrators. Those users should be educated on how each of the accounts should be used.

65. A, C. Password attacks occur when an account is attacked repeatedly with the intent of determining the password that will gain access. This is accomplished by using applications designed to break the password by sending possible passwords to the account in a systematic manner. Two types of password attacks are brute-force and dictionary attacks. Zombie and botnet are attacks where the user of the computer doesn't know there is malware on their computer. Their computer is a zombie, and when many zombies are used to attack a system, it's known as a botnet attack. A spoofing attack is an attempt by someone or something to masquerade as someone else.

66. C. All the options will increase the security of a smartphone. For just the basic level of security, though, enable a screen lock. A user will need to enter a code to gain access to the device. It's typically enough to thwart casual snoops and would-be hackers. Multifactor authentication occurs whenever you need two or more ways to prove who you are (something you know, something you have, something you are, or someplace you are). Full-device encryption would mean encoding the data and requiring a key to decrypt it. Remote wipe is a feature that can be used to remove all the personal or corporate data from a phone even though it is lost or stolen.

67. A. An authenticator app can help securely verify your identity online, regardless of the account you want to log into. Different apps work in different ways, but the general procedure is that the app will generate a random code for you to type along with your username and password. The random code helps identify you and tells the site you are logging into that you really are who you say you are. The other options are not actual application types.

68. B. A dictionary attack uses a dictionary of common words to attempt to find the user's password. Dictionary attacks can be automated, and several tools exist in the public domain to execute them. As an example of this type of attack, imagine guessing words and word combinations found in a standard English-language dictionary. The policy you have recommended could also help thwart those who may try to look over a shoulder (shoulder surfing) to see a user's password because even with a quick glance they can see whether or not it's a common word. Brute-force is trying repeatedly to guess a user's password. Social engineering is using kindness, coercion, or fear to get you to give up privileged information such as your password.

69. A. Trojans are programs that enter a system or network under the guise of another program. A Trojan may be included as an attachment or as part of an installation program. The Trojan can create a back door or replace a valid program during installation. It then accomplishes its mission under the guise of another program. A Trojan is named after the Trojan horse of mythology. Spyware watches what you do and reports back to someone. A virus is spread from computer to computer because of some contact between the machines, often through email. Whaling is phishing for "big fish," such as very wealthy or influential people. Phishing gets its name from fishing for information.

70. C. A large electromagnet can be used to destroy any magnetic media, such as a hard drive or backup tape set. The most common of these is the degaussing tool. Degaussing involves applying a strong magnetic field to initialize the media. This process helps ensure that information doesn't fall into the wrong hands. Overwriting and zero writing write random binary (or all zeros) on a magnetic hard drive using software. The process must be done several times by the software to be effective. Incineration means simply burning the drive.

71. C. Certain metadata pertaining to a file are called attributes. The most commonly used attributes are system (S), hidden (H), read only (R), and archive (A). There is a list of others that can be viewed by typing **attrib /?** at a command prompt. The attrib command can be used to view or add attributes, such as entering **attrib myfile +R** to make *myfile* read only. You can remove the read only attribute using the same command with a minus sign instead of a plus sign. In the Windows 10/11 GUI, view attributes by right-clicking a file or folder and choosing Properties. Windows 11 will display a screen like the one in the graphic. More attributes can be seen by clicking the Advanced button as seen in the graphic. The attrib command is not on the CompTIA A+ objectives, but file attributes are.

72. B. BitLocker Drive Encryption allows you to use drive encryption to protect files—including those needed for startup and logon. This is available only with Windows Pro and higher editions. For removable drives, BitLocker To Go provides the same encryption technology to help prevent unauthorized access to the files stored on them. EFS (Encrypting File System) is used to encrypt volumes, files, and folders but is not capable of encrypting the entire drive.

73. C. Rootkits are software programs that can hide certain things from the operating system; they do so by obtaining (and retaining) administrative-level access. With a rootkit, there may be several processes running on a system that don't show in Task Manager, or connections that don't appear in a netstat display may be established or available—the rootkit masks the presence of these items. Rootkits are known for being particularly difficult to eradicate. A virus is spread from computer to computer because of some contact between the machines, often through email. Whaling is phishing for "big fish," such as very wealthy or influential people. Phishing gets its name from fishing for information. Ransomware holds a machine or network hostage, making it and its data inaccessible, until a ransom is paid.

74. D. Encrypting File System (EFS) is available in most editions of Windows, and it allows for encryption/decryption of files stored in NTFS volumes. All users can use EFS, whereas only administrators can turn on BitLocker. It does not require any special hardware, while BitLocker benefits from having the Trusted Platform Module (TPM). As an additional distinction, EFS can encrypt just one file, if so desired, while BitLocker encrypts the whole volume and whatever is stored on it.

75. B. Anti-malware software will help protect computers from malicious programs. Typically, anti-malware does everything that antivirus software does as well as identify threats beyond just viruses. In fact, viruses are a type of malware. A lot of anti-malware software is marketed as antivirus software. A firewall is a hardware or software device designed to prevent certain types of traffic from entering or leaving a network. EFS (Encrypting File System) allows a user to encrypt individual volumes, files, or folders, and UAC (User Account Control) is designed to prevent users from making changes that they are not authorized to make.

76. D. Educating users to recognize phishing is one of the most important steps in preventing hackers from acquiring login credentials. One way to do this is to hire a consulting company to send phishing emails and see which employees respond when they should not and need additional training. Phishing is usually done through email and is an attempt to "fish" for information from an authorized network user such as logon information. Whaling is phishing for high-profile or wealthy targets. A zero-day attack is one that happens the same day a vulnerability is discovered, so there has not been time to rectify the vulnerability.

77. B. When a file or folder is copied on NTFS volumes, the new file or folder will inherit its NTFS permissions from its new parent folder. The old permissions will be discarded. However, when files and folders are moved versus copying them, the original permissions are retained at the new location.

78. B. Only NTFS permissions can be applied to individual files. Both NTFS and share permissions can be applied to volumes and folders. Share permissions are only effective when the resource is accessed via a network. NTFS permissions are effective whether the person accesses the resource locally or via a network. NTFS permissions are inherited from a parent folder. Share permissions do not have inheritance.

79. D. A key fob is a small device about the size that could usually be carried on a key chain. They generate a random number every few seconds that can be used for multifactor identification to gain access to a secure system such as a bank account. Key fobs are also a type of hard token. The other three choices—ID badge, RFID badge, and smartcard—are all something that can be carried by an employee to gain access to an area. Smartcards or RFID badges store electronic information that could be used to access equipment as well. Information on them is accessed by devices called readers.

80. A. Spyware differs from other malware in that it works—often actively—on behalf of a third party. Rather than self-replicating, like viruses and worms, spyware is spread to machines by users who inadvertently ask for it. The users often don't know they have asked for it but have done so by downloading other programs, visiting infected sites, and so on. The spyware program monitors the user's activity and responds by offering unsolicited pop-up advertisements (sometimes known as adware), gathers information about the user to pass on to marketers, or intercepts personal data such as credit card numbers. Ransomware is software that takes over a computer and won't allow access to the data until a ransom is paid. Zombies are computers that have been taken over by another party and are used to perform malicious acts. When there are many zombies acting together, they form a botnet. The computer user is generally unaware of the presence of the attacker. A Trojan is software that is downloaded when the user downloads an innocent-looking software program or digital image. Once downloaded, the Trojan loads into the computer system.

81. A. Encrypting File System (EFS) allows for encryption/decryption of individual volumes, files, and folders stored in NTFS volumes, whereas BitLocker encrypts entire drives, but neither of them is available in Home editions of Windows. If there is supporting hardware (Trusted Platform Module [TPM] enabled in BIOS/UEFI and Secure Boot enabled), then device encryption can be used instead. With device encryption, only someone with authorization to use the device will be able to decrypt it. You must be logged in as an administrator

to turn on device encryption; go to Start, choose Settings, then select Update & Security, and then select Device Encryption. If the option isn't there, then device encryption isn't available on the device. You can also see if the hardware supports it by launching the System Information utility as an administrator, then scrolling down to Device Encryption Support.

82. **A, D.** These are share permissions. Share permissions have no effect when someone logs on locally; they only take effect when being accessed via a network. (NTFS permissions apply whether logging on locally or via the network.) Share permissions can only be applied to folders, not individual files. The only share permission set on this folder is that Everyone can read it. No one has permission to change it.

83. **C, D.** File attributes are accessed in the same manner whether you are using Windows 10 or Windows 11. In the GUI, attributes are accessed by right-clicking the object and choosing Properties and then selecting the General tab. For some attributes, such as compression and encryption, you need to click Advanced in the Attributes section of the General tab. Compression uses algorithms to remove repeated characters and excess spaces, making files take up less space. The user does not need to be an administrator to change attributes. In addition to right-clicking the object, attributes can be changed using the `attrib` command.

84. **A.** Antivirus software needs continual updates of virus signatures as new viruses are unleashed daily. The updates are known as definition files and ensure that the antivirus engine will recognize new viruses. Firewalls can be software or hardware and are designed to block or allow network traffic based on certain criteria. Once established, settings are not often changed. ACLs (access control lists) are tied to objects in a system and are compared to an authenticated user's information to determine whether to grant access. These too are seldom changed once they are configured. NTFS permissions are part of what creates ACLs. NTFS permissions for an object are granted to a user and can include Full Control, Modify, Read & Execute, List Folder Contents, Read, and Write. Share permissions also affect access to a resource but only when a user accesses it via a network.

85. **B.** Impersonation is an attempt by someone or something to masquerade as someone else. You might think of impersonation attacks as affecting network systems, but they can affect phone systems as well. A zombie is a computer system that a hacker has a back door into and can use to perpetrate attacks, unknown to the computer system's legitimate user. A botnet is a system of zombie computers engaged in an orchestrated attack on a target. A zero-day attack occurs when a vulnerability is used to attack a system on the very day that the vulnerability is discovered, before preventive measures to block the vulnerability have been able to be created. In a phishing attack, the attacker uses coercion or other means to attempt to gain passwords or other privileged information.

86. **C.** Because the user is accessing the NTFS-based resource over the network, both NTFS and share permissions are applied. If there is a difference between the two of them, the most restrictive permissions are used. Therefore, the user has Read access only.

87. **B.** Regardless of what other permissions may be granted, Deny will override all of them and the effective permission will be Deny.

88. C. Disable AutoRun and AutoPlay should be selected on computers connected to the network. (It is never a good idea to put any media in a workstation if you don't know where it came from or what it is). The simple reason is that the media (CD, DVD, USB, SD) could contain malware. Compounding matters, the malware could be referenced in the autorun .inf file, causing it to be summoned when the media is inserted in the machine and requiring no other action. User permissions are not effective on optical drives whose content changes all the time. A BIOS/UEFI password would prevent the computer from being booted, and enabling data encryption can't be done on media that is subject to change.

89. B. An unauthorized router with a seemingly legitimate configuration is specifically known as an evil twin. Those can lead to on-path attacks, which involve clandestinely placing something (such as a piece of software or a rogue router) between a server and the user, and neither the server's administrator nor the user is aware of it. The on-path attacker intercepts data and then sends the information to the server as if nothing is wrong. The on-path attacker's software may be recording information for someone to view later, altering it, or in some other way compromising the security of your system and session. A zombie is a computer system that a hacker has a back door into and can use to perpetrate attacks, unknown to the computer system's legitimate user. A botnet is a system of zombie computers engaged in an orchestrated attack on a target. A noncompliant system is one that is not updated or not following company protocols regarding security.

90. B, C. These are NTFS permissions. They will be inherited by any folder created inside this folder, which happens to be the root of the C: drive. NTFS permissions are effective regardless of whether the user accesses them locally or over a network. (Share permissions are only effective when the resource is accessed via a network, they can only be applied to folders, and share permissions are not inherited.) Inheritance in NTFS is enabled by default but can be disabled by clicking the Advanced button (in the figure) and selecting Disable inheritance.

91. B. Locks and keys are some of the simplest yet effective physical security measures. The device shown in the graphic is a laptop lock. The user has a key to unlock the device. The heavy cable is looped around something solid like a table leg, and the end where the key is inserted locks into a special slot in a laptop or other mobile device. Security tokens can be either soft tokens or hard tokens. Hard tokens are objects a user carries such as a key fob. Soft tokens are software installed on a system. A magnetometer measures magnetic fields and can be used in a mobile device to determine your location with respect to Earth's magnetic north and south.

92. C. Kerberos was developed and named by computer scientists at MIT. It is an open source authentication protocol that uses a third party to verify user credentials and symmetric key cryptography to encode transmissions between parties. TACACS+ is an authentication protocol developed by Cisco that is now an open standard. RADIUS (Remote Authentication Dial-In User Service) is an authentication protocol that was originally used for dial-in access. It has morphed into a protocol used for authenticating remote Wi-Fi or on premises users. AES (Advanced Encryption Standard), which is for wireless encryption and not authentication, has been around since 2001 and is the successor to TKIP (Temporal Key Integrity Protocol).

93. B. MDM (mobile device management) is a software technology that allows an IT department to retain control over corporate data while allowing users to use their personal devices. BYOD (Bring Your Own Device) can save companies money on hardware but presents a security risk. Using MDM, an IT administrator can restrict the type of data and applications that are used with company information. They can also wipe all corporate information off a device that is lost or stolen, or if an employee leaves the company. EFS (Encrypting File System) is used to encrypt files and folders in Windows OSs, excluding Home editions. The purpose of single sign-on (SSO) is to give users access to all the applications and systems that they need when they log on. Some of the systems may require users to enter their credentials again, but the username and password will be consistent between systems. UAC (User Account Control) verifies that someone has the authority to change a system before making any changes by requiring them to enter an administrator password for certain operations.

94. C. Bollards are a method of physical security that can be used to keep vehicles out of a particular area. Voice calls, email, and SMS (short message service) can all be used to deliver a one-time code for multifactor authentication.

95. A, C. Both smartcards and key fobs are hard tokens. Hard tokens are a physical security device that can be carried about by the user. A smartcard has a chip whose data can be accessed by a reader to allow a user access to a secure area or computer system. A key fob generates a random number every few seconds that can be entered into a system as part of multifactor authentication. Retina scanners are biometric devices, because they use part of your body as authentication/identification, and while motion sensors are a part of physical security, they're generally used in conjunction with alarm systems.

96. A. A magnetometer measures magnetic fields and can be used to locate a person's position on Earth. As a part of multifactor authentication, that location is compared to an allow or block list, and if the device to be accessed is in an allowed location, access may be granted. A retina scanner is a biometric device that scans a person's eye to determine if access should be granted. A key fob will generate a code that changes every few seconds. A key fob is a type of hard token used for authentication.

97. D. A soft token is a logical, rather than a physical, security measure. An example of a soft token would be an authenticator app on your cell phone used to generate a code to access a website. Proper lighting can often deter would-be attackers, as can equipment and door locks, and motion sensors that trigger alarms.

98. C. A hard token is a security device that a computer user has in their possession, such as a key fob or smartcard. Biometric devices are those that use a part of your body to identify you and either deny or allow access to a system based on your identity.

99. C. To prevent shoulder surfing, a user could install a display privacy filter. Privacy filters are either film or glass add-ons that are placed over a monitor or laptop screen to prevent the data on the screen from being readable when viewed from the sides. Only the user sitting directly in front of the screen can read the data. In shoulder surfing, a potential attacker is literally looking over someone's shoulder to try to read what is on their screen. An access control vestibule is an area between two doors that helps to prevent tailgating. Video surveillance occurs when there are security cameras watching a secure area and a person observing the output of those cameras. Smartcards are devices that a user can carry that will authenticate them to a system as a part of multifactor login.

100. B. Many viruses will announce that you're infected as soon as they gain access to your system. They may take control of your system and flash annoying messages on your screen or destroy your hard disk. When this occurs, you'll know that you're a victim. Other viruses will cause your system to slow down, cause files to disappear from your computer, or take over your disk space. Many viruses today are spread using email. The infected system attaches a file to any email that you send to another user. The recipient opens this file, thinking it's something that you legitimately sent them. When they open the file, the virus infects the target system. A botnet is a group of computers that are used to perpetrate an attack without the knowledge of the authorized user of that computer. The computer is called a zombie and is controlled by some third-party attacker. A Trojan is malicious software that hides in that fun game or screen saver that you just downloaded, and it installs when you install the innocent-looking files. A rootkit is malware that gains access to a system as administrator, giving it full control over a system. Rootkits are adept at hiding their presence and so are difficult to eradicate.

101. B. Vishing, phishing, and whaling are variations of the same type of attack. In all of these, someone attempts to gain usernames and passwords or other information by intimidation, coercion, or other means. Then they'll use that information to attack your company's systems. They're all play-on-words for fishing. The attacker is casting a line and hoping you will bite on it. Vishing is using voice calls, phishing uses email, and whaling is phishing for powerful or wealthy fish (people). An evil twin attack happens when someone plugs an unauthorized WAP (wireless access point) into your network and gives it the same SSID (service set identifier) that your valid network has.

102. A. Bring Your Own Device (BYOD) can save companies money on hardware and make users happy, but BYOD presents a security risk. Mobile device management (MDM) is a software technology that allows an IT department to retain control over corporate data while allowing users to use their personal devices. Using MDM, an IT administrator can restrict the type of data and applications that are used with company information. They can also wipe all corporate information off a device that is lost or stolen, or if an employee leaves the company. The purpose of single sign-on (SSO) is to give users access to all the applications and systems that they need when they log on. Some of the systems may require users to enter their credentials again, but the username and password will be consistent between systems. User Account Control (UAC) verifies that someone has the authority to change a system before making any changes by requiring them to enter an administrator password for certain operations.

103. A. When an operating system is at end of life (EOL), it means that the company will no longer be supporting the software. That might not be a problem if you're an expert with the software and it meets your needs. The security problem arises because an EOL software will no longer receive security updates, making your network vulnerable to attack. The operating system won't magically stop working on the EOL date, and while you won't get any new features, that isn't a threat to security.

104. C. When a virus infects the boot sector, Master Boot Record (MBR), or partition table of a hard drive, it is called a boot sector virus. Boot sector viruses load before the operating system and security software can load. They may delete or modify files needed to boot the system, or the system may show no signs of being infected until an antivirus program is run. Removing the boot sector virus from a system may require booting to a different

OS or drive. Spyware is designed to watch what you do and where you go, hoping to gain information such as logins, passwords, and bank account numbers. Ransomware locks a system in some way or encrypts data and won't allow access until the system's owner pays a ransom. A keylogger is malware that records every keystroke and reports it back to a third party. This information might include user IDs and passwords, or even bank account numbers and login information.

105. C. Keyloggers, viruses, and spyware are all types of malware, although anti-malware and antivirus are often used interchangeably. Windows Recovery Environment (WinRE) is a tool used to repair problems with the operating system (OS). In addition to other tools such as startup repair and refreshing the OS, it provides access to a command prompt utility that can be used to correct problems without booting into the Windows operating system.

106. A. The Windows Recovery Environment (WinRE) in Windows 10/11 provides a command-line tool (among other tools) that allows the administrator the ability to copy or remove directories, enable or disable services, write a new Master Boot Record (MBR), format volumes, and much more. If you have a virus that has infected the boot sector of the hard drive, the only way to access the system before the boot sector virus loads is to boot to another drive, either a DVD or a USB that contains either the Windows installation media or an antivirus. Using the installation media is one way to enter the WinRE. Typically the system will automatically enter the WinRE if booting into Windows has failed three times in a row. You can force this to happen by turning the power off as soon as Windows starts to load, and repeating that until the system boots into WinRE. From the recovery environment main screen, choose Troubleshoot ➢ Advanced Options ➢ Command Prompt to get to the command prompt. Here you can enter commands or run antivirus software to remove a boot sector virus on the other hard drive. RADIUS is an authentication encryption protocol. Administrative Tools can be found in Control Panel of Windows 10 and is a collection of commonly used tools. Administrative Tools is not available in Windows 11. Active Directory is the database and software used to control and manage a Windows domain.

107. A. When someone who is an authorized user on your system attempts to gain access to something they should not or attempts a malicious act on your computer system, an insider threat has occurred. An evil twin is when an unauthorized wireless access point (WAP) appears on your network, using your service set identifier (SSID) and users are able to connect to the network using the unauthorized access point. Whaling is going after a big target using vishing or phishing. Social engineering is an attempt to acquire information about your network and system by social means, such as talking to people in the organization, shoulder surfing, tailgating, or other methods.

108. B. This is a type of denial-of-service (DoS) attack. Someone spoofs your IP address (making it look like you) and sends out requests all at once to multiple hosts who respond to your IP address. Your server is flooded with those responses and crashes. It's called a DoS attack because users who want to use the server for legitimate purposes such as placing an order are unable to due to all the malicious traffic. Whaling is using phishing to go after a big target. Distributed denial-of-service (DDoS) attacks happen when many computers are used, as in a botnet. An evil twin attack happens when someone plugs an unauthorized wireless access point (WAP) into your network and gives it the same service set identifier (SSID) that your valid network has.

109. A. In this case, the user has Full Control. When there are conflicting NTFS permissions, generally they are combined and the most liberal is granted. This holds true for conflicting permissions between groups or between a user's account and group memberships. The exception is Deny, which overrides all other permissions.

110. C. This system is vulnerable to attack because it is unprotected. The remedy is to turn on the system's software firewall and antivirus protection. Zero-day attacks happen the same day a vulnerability is discovered and attackers are able to evade antivirus programs because the antivirus companies have not had the time to respond to the vulnerability yet. A Structured Query Language (SQL) injection occurs when an attacker puts code into a database instead of data and the code is executed, giving the attacker access to the data in the database. Cross-site scripting (XSS) is similar to a SQL injection, except it uses a website and Hypertext Markup Language (HTML) or JavaScript instead of a database. Code is injected into the website and used to gather data from legitimate-website users because their systems don't see the normally trusted website as a threat.

111. A. Using a home folder on an Active Directory server to store the user's files adds a level of security because the user's data is not on the local drive and is less subject to being stolen. A security group is used to grant permissions to a shared resource. Organizational units are groupings that can include people, computers, and resources. Group Policies can be applied to organizational units, ensuring that all computers and users in that group are given the proper access to resources. A login script is used to automate activities when a user or computer logs into a domain.

112. D. Cryptominers are malware that want to use your computing power rather than steal your data. You may notice that the computer is performing more slowly than usual. Spyware is designed to watch what you do and where you go, hoping to gain information such as logins, passwords, and bank account numbers. Ransomware locks a system in some way or encrypts data and won't allow access until the system's owner pays a ransom. A keylogger is malware that records every keystroke and reports it back to a third party.

113. B. Installing a keylogger would be installing malware, and exactly the opposite of what you need to do to keep a system safe. Educating users about the types of malware, including recognizing them, avoiding them, and what to do with suspicious emails, phone calls, and so on, is one of the best things you can do to protect a system. Keeping antivirus/anti-malware software up-to-date so that new malware can be detected and keeping operating systems and applications up-to-date to patch vulnerabilities are key to keeping malware out.

114. C. This is an untrusted source. Not only have you never used it before, but there is a problem with the website's certificate that caused the warning message the user received. There is no evidence that is it a spoofed site, and clearly it does not have a valid digital certificate. Digital certificates are issued by certificate authorities who confirm that a website, person, or company is who they say they are.

115. A. User Account Control (UAC) settings is where you can change when the operating system requests an administrator password before making changes to the system. The options range from Always Notify to Never Notify, with Notify Me Only If Apps Try To Make Changes To My Computer the default. UAC can be found in Windows 11 by going to Control Panel and selecting System and Security, then Security and Maintenance, and finally Change User Account Control Settings, and in Windows 10 by going to Control Panel, clicking Security and Maintenance, and clicking Change User Account Control Settings. In either version of Windows, it's easier to simply search for UAC. Windows Defender Firewall is a software firewall included in Windows operating systems. Facial recognition is a logon option, and Personalization in Settings allows you to change items such as themes, colors, and backgrounds.

116. B. In both Windows 10 and 11, a quick search for Virus & threat protection will bring you to the Windows Settings for that feature. Windows Defender Firewall is a built-in firewall found in Control Panel. Windows Update, which is in the Settings app, is for keeping the operating system files patched. Device Security is also found in the Settings app and has settings and information for the security features of your computer, such as the TPM (Trusted Platform Module) chip.

117. C. A DDoS (distributed denial-of-service) attack is caused by a botnet attack. It is a denial of service because legitimate users are unable to access resources. The distributed part of the name comes from the fact that there was traffic from many infected computers (zombies) in different locations attacking your server at the same time, known as a botnet. Bots, by themselves, are but a form of software that runs automatically and autonomously and are not harmful. *Botnet*, however, has come to be the word used to describe malicious software running on a zombie and under the control of a bot-herder. Denial-of-service attacks—DoS and DDoS—can be launched by botnets, as can many forms of adware, spyware, and spam (via spambots). A brute-force attack uses software to repeatedly try to discover a password. Zero-day attacks happen the same day a vulnerability is discovered and are able to evade antivirus programs because the antivirus companies have not had the time to respond to the vulnerability yet. A noncompliant system is one that is not updated or complying with corporate security policies.

118. D. Cross-site scripting (XSS) is similar to a SQL injection, except that it uses a website and Hypertext Markup Language (HTML) or JavaScript instead of a database. Code is injected into the website and used to gather data from legitimate-website users because their systems don't see the normally trusted website as a threat. Zero-day attacks happen the same day a vulnerability is discovered and are able to evade antivirus programs because the antivirus companies have not had the time to respond to the vulnerability yet. A Structured Query Language (SQL) injection occurs when an attacker puts code into a database instead of data and the code is executed, giving the attacker access to the data in the database. An unprotected system is one that lacks normal measures of security such as a software firewall on the system and antivirus/anti-malware.

119. B. A domain is a grouping of resources, including people, computers, servers, printers, and so on, into a single centrally controlled unit. A domain is managed by Active Directory software. A best practice is to group the users into security groups and establish access to resources on the group level, which will then give that access to members of the group. Home folders provide a central place for users' documents, each with their own home folder, which gets the documents off the local computer, consolidating security for those folders into one place.

120. C. Whaling is an attack on a powerful or wealthy fish (person). Phishing uses email, and vishing is using voice calls to gain information. Vishing, phishing, and whaling are variations of the same type of attack. In all of these, someone attempts to gain usernames and passwords or other information by intimidation, coercion, or other means. Then they'll use that information to attack your company's systems. They're all play-on-words for fishing. The attacker is casting a line and hoping you will bite. An evil twin attack happens when someone plugs an unauthorized wireless access point (WAP) into your network and gives it the same service set identifier (SSID) that your valid network has.

121. D. Active Directory is the name given to the software and large database that is used to manage resources on a Windows domain. Using a home folder on an Active Directory server to store the user's files adds a level of security because the user's data is not on the local drive and is less subject to being stolen. A security group is a grouping of computers or users that need the same access to resources. Permissions are granted to the security group and passed on to the members of the group. Organizational units are groupings that can include people, computers, and resources. Group Policies can be applied to organizational units, ensuring that all computers and users in that group are given the proper access to resources.

122. A. Virus & Threat Protection can be found in the Settings app. There you can see when the last update was done and run a system scan, among other options.

123. A, D. The Windows built-in firewall can be configured either in the Setting app using Firewall & Network Protection or in Windows Defender Firewall, which is found in Control Panel.

124. A, C. The firewall can be configured to allow an application through (or block one) in both the Firewall & Network Protection settings of the Settings app or in Windows Defender Firewall's Advanced settings in Control Panel. The Virus & Threat Protection settings are for configuring antivirus. Administrative Tools is found in Windows 10, not Windows 11, and it doesn't have settings for the firewall, although it does contain a shortcut to the Windows Defender Firewall.

125. B. Use Windows Key+L simultaneously to lock the Windows desktop. Windows Key+X brings up the Power menu, which has shortcuts to many often-used tools. Windows Key+Right Arrow will snap the active window to the right half of the screen, and Windows Key+D displays the desktop by minimizing all the other apps. These keyboard shortcuts work in both Windows 10 and Windows 11.

126. A, B. A laptop cable lock uses a special slot on the side of the laptop and a very strong cable wrapped around something solid, like a desk leg, to secure the laptop to the work area. A key is used to free the laptop from the cable when you want to take it somewhere. Mobile device management (MDM) software can be used to wipe a laptop remotely if it is stolen. Placing a laptop in a desk drawer might get it out of sight, but it is still vulnerable, and you should never let a laptop out of your sight when you're in a public place.

127. C, D. Fingerprints and facial recognition are both biometric logins and require a fingerprint reader and camera, respectively. Many laptops come equipped with this hardware, but not all. Both could be added to a laptop or desktop that is missing the hardware by connecting them via a USB port. Username and password can also be used, and a personal identification number (PIN) is used. Windows gives you the option to include letters and symbols in your PIN, or just numbers.

128. D. Passwords should be a bare minimum of eight characters long, and complexity should be required using at least one upper- and one lowercase letter, number, and special character. If you must choose between a longer password or a more complex password, then longer is better.

129. A, C. Password complexity should be enforced. Passwords that are created by the user are better than randomly generated passwords because the user can remember them easily without having to write them down, but they should not be something that is easy for someone else to guess, like the dog's name or someone's birthday. Passwords should expire after a reasonable time, making it more difficult for someone to use a compromised password. One hundred and eighty days (6 months!) is too long of a time between password expiration; 45–90 days would be more reasonable.

130. C. A domain is a grouping of resources including people, computers, servers, printers, and so on, into a single centrally controlled unit. A domain is managed by Active Directory software. A best practice is to group the users into security groups and assign permissions to the security groups. Members of the security group will have the access that was assigned to the group. Home folders provide a central place for the users' documents, each with their own home folder on the server. This removes the documents from the local computer, consolidating security for those folders into one place.

131. D. Password policies such as history, password age, length, and complexity can be found in Local Security Policy ➤ Password Policy. User Accounts in Control Panel is for adding and managing users. You can set the password there, but not the password policies. Administrative Tools is available in Windows 10, but not Windows 11. Local Security Policy is in Pro editions of Windows 10 and 11 only, not Home editions.

132. B. One of the features of the domain controller and Active Directory is that there is a central place to control and manage security, including users' passwords. You can easily reset their password and allow them to create a new one at next login. Resetting it on the local computer would not work because they log into the domain. Reinstalling the OS and making a new username are simply not necessary.

133. A. When setting up a Windows 11 Home PC for the first time, you are required to use a Microsoft account. The setup will allow you to create one during setup. Pressing F10 does not change the type of account you need to set up Windows 11 Home. A local account can be used whether they have Windows 11 Home or Pro, but when setting up the Home version, it must be set up with a Microsoft account. It is possible to add a local account later and use it to log in to either Windows 11 Home or Pro.

134. C. You will be able to use your computer if you log in using your Microsoft account, even if the Internet is down. It will just use cached versions of files. All the other options are true.

135. A. Administrators have access to everything in the system, but a standard user account is limited in what they can do. They are not able to add or manage another user's account, for example. Nor are they able to access another user's files. Local Users and Groups is available in Pro or greater editions, but a standard user still won't be able to manage users there.

136. C. What is known as a low-level format now (also called a zero-fill) is drastically different than it was years ago. The intent is the same, though, and that is to erase all data on the hard drive so it's not recoverable. Technically, the low-level format needs to happen first. Then the drive is partitioned, creating one or more sections, and a standard format is used to create the file allocation table and root directory.

137. D. A certificate of destruction (or certificate of recycling) may be required for audit purposes. Such a certificate, usually issued by the organization carrying out the destruction, is intended to verify that the asset was properly destroyed and usually includes serial numbers, type of destruction done, and so on.

138. C. Zero-filling a drive will make data that was once on the drive unreadable, but it is not a physical destruction method. Methods of physical destruction include drilling, shredding, degaussing, and incinerating.

139. D. A password manager is software that uses algorithms to generate secure passwords. The passwords are encrypted in the software manager. The user only needs to remember a single password to access the password manager, not all the other passwords. Most password managers will use two-factor authentication to allow the user to log in and change any passwords. Websites that you access are stored in a cache on your computer so that the next time you visit the website, it will only download the changes and make websites load much more quickly. If a website you visit isn't updating properly, clearing the cache should resolve the issue. Certificates are issued by a certificate authority and prove that the website (or person) is who they say they are. A browser may warn you or block your access to a website whose certificate is expired or invalid.

140. A, B. Before you give a computer to someone else, you will certainly want to remove all of your data from it. The best way to do this is to zero-write (also called a low-level format) the drive, then restore it to its factory default condition. This can often be accomplished with a utility provided by the computer manufacturer, or in Windows, by using options in WinRE.

141. B. Choosing Reset Your PC will give you two options. You can choose to keep your personal files but remove apps and settings, or remove everything, including your files, and perform a fresh installation.

142. A. Option A, use the Local Users and Groups app to create groups, set up permissions for each group on shared files, then add users to the group as needed, is considered a best practice. By arranging security in this way, when someone changes jobs, leaves the company, or joins the company, all you need to do is remove the user from the group and/or add them to the group with the security access that they need. This process saves on human error as there is just one place that security is set up (for the group) instead of establishing the settings for each individual user. Local Users and Groups is available in Pro or better versions of modern Windows operating systems.

• Answers to the Review Questions

143. B, D. One of the best things you can do to protect a network is to train employees on how to handle IT information and events. All too often users put their passwords where they are easy for them to find, but they are also too easy for someone with malicious intent to find. Passwords need to meet complexity requirements but be simple enough for a user to understand. Other tools for securing passwords are to use password management software and multifactor authentication. Windows Credential Manager and macOS Keychain are two utilities that can manage passwords for users. Credential Manager is not on the CompTIA A+ objectives, but Keychain is.

144. A, B. Following the principle of least privilege, users should be given only the access that they need and nothing more. If a user needs to read files but not change them, then they should be restricted to reading those files only. Sometimes even the most careful users can make changes that they did not intend. If a user works only Monday to Friday, then they should not be able to log in on the weekend. Having their login available gives a hacker one more way to get into your system. The Guest account is disabled by default and should remain disabled. Even administrators should have a standard user account that they will use unless they are doing something that requires administrative access. Then they would only log on as an administrator while doing that activity.

145. B, C. Configuring all the computers to lock the screen saver after a short period of inactivity would help to mitigate the problem. If a user was still at their desk but doing something else, they could easily enter their password and log in again. Training employees on network and data safety is always helpful. Firing them would be a very drastic measure, but depending on the environment, it might be the company policy. Setting the PC to shut down after 2 minutes of inactivity is also a bit drastic, and you wouldn't want to risk losing whatever the employee was working on. Locking the screen saver can be just as effective.

146. A. Data-at-rest is any data that is sitting on a drive somewhere. It's not moving between network locations, but it needs to be protected. Letting the employee choose what to encrypt with EFS is not a good solution because it opens too much possibility for human error. There are third-party companies that specialize in protecting data-at-rest. Other solutions are to use MDM (mobile device management) software. Using MDM, the IT administrator can enforce encryption on remote devices, even those owned by employees who are using their personal devices for company business. If the device is lost or stolen, company data can be wiped from it using MDM software. BitLocker is a solution for encrypting entire hard drives, but it requires Pro or higher editions of both Windows 10 and 11 and a TPM (Trusted Platform Module) chip or module on the motherboard. BitLocker stores an encryption key in the TPM, and the TPM will only allow access to the key when the computer started as expected.

147. D. Facial recognition and fingerprint readers are available on an increasing number of smartphones and mobile devices. Facial recognition uses your cell phone's camera, sensors, and a dot projector to make a 3D map of your face. The phone then uses that 3D map to recognize you for future transactions. Pin codes are a number that you enter to gain access. Fingerprint scanners require that you touch a spot repeatedly to set up. Once the device has a map of your fingerprint, you can use your finger to log in or authorize certain transactions. Device encryption is not a method of identifying the user.

148. C. Some mobile devices allow the user to draw a pattern on the screen that is recognized by the device, then the user is allowed access. The problem with using this security device is that, because the pattern is repeatedly drawn on the screen, someone may see the oils left behind by your skin and be able to figure out the pattern that is drawn. Facial recognition uses the mobile device's camera to make and store a 3D map of your face. To gain access to the device, the camera reads your face again and compares it to the stored image. Fingerprint readers compare your fingerprint to one stored on the device for access. With a swipe lock, the user merely swipes across the screen to unlock it.

149. C. Most mobile devices will lock after a period of inactivity. For some, merely swiping across the device will unlock it. Since this can be done by anyone, it isn't secure. Facial recognition is a biometric (something that you are) type of identification, so it is quite secure depending on the software that is used to recognize the face. PIN codes and patterns are something that the user must know, and although a hacker may figure them out, they're still more secure than merely swiping across the device.

150. A. Since the camera communicates over port 4150, the port would need to be open and port forwarding configured so that your remote connection can access the camera, through the router, using that port. You know that the camera is properly connected to the router because you can access the video stream on it from a computer connected to the same router. Disabling the firewall should not be done because the firewall is a vital part of your network's security.

151. A. Content filtering is the process of blocking objectionable content from either websites or email. Many routers and firewalls will provide content filtering services. In many cases, a reference service is used to block websites, and filters can be implemented to scan emails for prohibited content. Disabling ports stops traffic from entering the network. It does not filter for content. VPN access means that a user can access the network remotely just as if they were sitting in the office. Port forwarding/mapping is used when you need traffic on a particular port to go to a particular network device. It is often used for gaming and security cameras.

152. C. One method of "protecting" the network that is often recommended is to turn off the SSID (service set identifier) broadcast. The SSID is the name of your network. The access point is still there and can still be accessed by those who know of it, but it prevents those who are looking at a list of available networks from finding it. This should be considered a weak form of security because there are still ways, albeit a bit more complicated, to discover the presence of the access point besides the SSID broadcast. WPA3 is a secure Wi-Fi encryption standard. MAC (Media Access Control) filtering allows or denies access to the network based on the MAC address associated with a NIC (Network Interface Card).

153. D. Just like computers, routers occasionally need their software updated to add new features or correct security holes. On a router this is called a firmware update because it is updating software that is embedded in chips on the router's circuit board (i.e., the router's firmware). Port forwarding will send traffic for a specified port number to a specified computer. Content filtering inspects packets for specified content and rejects or allows packets to enter or leave the network based on those criteria. The SSID (service set identifier) is the name of the network.

154. B, D. Facial recognition and fingerprint readers are available on an increasing number of smartphones and mobile devices, and they can identify you faster than you can enter numbers on a screen. Facial recognition uses your cell phone's camera, sensors, and a dot projector to make a 3D map of your face. The phone then uses that 3D map to recognize you for future transactions. Fingerprint readers can use capacitive, optical, or ultrasonic sensors, but regardless of the method, they make a map of your fingerprint and, like facial recognition, compare that map to your body. With either one you can gain access to a device or authorize a transaction in about one second. PIN codes are a number that you enter to gain access. They can be entered quickly but can also be guessed, so they're not as secure as biometrics (fingerprint scanning and facial recognition). Using a swipe to unlock a mobile device is fast but not secure.

155. B. Configuring a DHCP (Dynamic Host Configuration Protocol) reservation means that you're setting aside a particular IP address to be used only with a specific device. That IP address is then not one of the addresses that the DHCP server can assign to workstations attempting to connect to it and be given an IP address. The DHCP scope is the range of IP addresses that can be assigned, such as 192.168.1.100 to 192.168.1.199, which would yield 100 private class C IP addresses. There is no such thing as an APIPA scope. An APIPA (Automatic Private IP Addressing) address is not configured on a router, or anywhere. It is an address in the 169.254.x.x range and is generated by an operating system when it is unable to reach a DHCP server. The loopback address, 127.0.0.1 for IPv4 or ::1 for IPv6, is a number used to test TCP/IP on the local machine.

156. A. PIN codes are a number that you enter to gain access to a mobile device. Fingerprint scanners and facial recognition systems are biometrics, meaning that they use a part of your body to identify you. Once a 3D map of the face or finger is made, that map is compared to a new one generated when you touch the screen or look into the camera. If they match, access is granted. Drawing a pattern on the screen is sometimes used.

157. A, C. Oils on your skin can be left behind on the screen and cause it to not recognize a pattern or fingerprint. Cleaning the phone may help. If that doesn't work, another quick solution is to restart the phone, then try the pattern again. The other two options will take longer. If it is an Android phone and you still can't access it, you may be able to use your Google credentials to access the phone if you are logged into Google on the phone. Performing a factory reset would be akin to giving up and starting over.

158. B. On your router you would configure a static WAN (wide area network) IP address. That is the address that the ISP (Internet service provider) has assigned to you. Usually the ISP uses dynamic addressing, and your WAN setting would be Dynamic WAN IP, so having a static WAN IP generally involves higher fees paid to the ISP. UPnP (Universal Plug and Play) is a protocol that lets devices find and communicate with each other on your LAN (local area network) such as your laptop and your printer. Unfortunately, UPnP could also be used by malware to spread to other devices on your network. A screened subnet uses one or more routers to create a separate area on a network where servers, such as a web server, can be accessed from either inside the LAN or from the Internet. It provides greater security and protects the LAN.

159. D. UPnP (Universal Plug and Play) is a protocol that lets devices find and communicate with each other on your LAN (local area network), such as your laptop and your printer. Unfortunately, UPnP could also be used by malware to spread to other devices on your network. WPA3 (Wi-Fi Protected Access version 3) and WPA2 are wireless networking encryption protocols. A PIN is a personal identification number used to authenticate to a computer system.

160. C. WPA3 (Wi-Fi Protected Access version 3) is the newest and most secure wireless encryption protocol for your SOHO router, but the devices that you've had for a few years might not be able to work with it. For the time being, until those legacy devices can be replaced, it's best to use the WPA2/WPA3 mixed mode so that all your devices can connect to the network as securely as possible. WEP (Wired Equivalent Privacy) should no longer be used because it is not secure. Also, it is not listed in the CompTIA A+ exam objectives.

161. A. Configuring IP filtering enables you to set which IP addresses are allowed to communicate through your router and which are not. Untrusted sources are websites that your browser has deemed suspicious or dangerous, and it warns you of such. Hashing is the act of translating a character string into code. Port filtering is a way of allowing or denying access to a network based on the port number in the packet. Filtering router traffic by port is also an excellent security practice.

162. A. A company may have many policies and procedures that employees must agree to as a condition of employment. Two of the most common ones are an acceptable use agreement (AUP) and bring-your-own-device (BYOD) policies. Acceptable use policies define what you can and can't do with company technology, and the consequences if the policy is violated. The BYOD policy describes the conditions for an employee using their own device for company business. This likely includes that the company will use mobile device management (MDM) software to secure the company information on the user's device.

163. A. Failed login attempt restrictions will destroy all local data on the phone if incorrect passcodes are entered 10 times in a row. While this is recommended for users with phones that contain sensitive data and that are frequently taken into public venues or placed in compromising positions, the casual user should not turn on this feature unless they can be sure there will always be a recent backup available.

164. D. A screened subnet uses two or more routers with packet filtering to create a separate area on a network where servers, such as a web server, can be accessed from either inside the LAN or from the Internet. This arrangement provides greater security and protects the LAN from network traffic. A static WAN IP is one that doesn't change and needs to be configured on your router. UPnP (Universal Plug and Play) is a protocol that lets devices, such as your laptop and your printer, find and communicate with each other on your LAN. Unfortunately, UPnP could also be used by malware to spread to other devices on your network. A WAN IP is the IP address a company gets from the Internet service provider (ISP); it can be dynamic, meaning it changes, or static, meaning it doesn't.

165. D. Exactly how to wipe your device depends on the device. If you have configured failed login restrictions on your device, then after the prescribed number of failed attempts, the device will either lock or, in the case of an iOS device, 10 failed tries will cause the device to be erased. For Android devices you can use Google Find My Device to remotely wipe it, and for iOS devices you can use the Find iPhone app using a different iOS device. MDM software can also be used to wipe Apple, Android, or Windows devices. Disabling guest access is a good security practice, but it won't wipe the device's data.

166. A. A kitchen is one of the worst places for a router to be. First, there will be EMI (electromagnetic interference) from appliances like refrigerators and microwaves, which will interfere with the wireless signal and if they're too close to the router or wires, they could interfere with the wired signal, too. Second, having easy access to the router might be good for the IT person, but it's a terrible idea for security. For physical security, place the router in a room or an enclosure that can be locked and out of reach of people passing by. Any guest access or guest accounts should be disabled. If your company is one that needs to have Wi-Fi available for visitors, put it on a separate VLAN (virtual LAN) so that your network isn't exposed to those connections. For Wi-Fi routers, take a walk around with a Wi-Fi meter and ensure that the signal doesn't extend into areas where it should not be. If it extends too far, you may need to turn the power down or possibly move the router.

167. A, C, D. While the interference is usually more of an annoyance than a problem, having your wireless network easily accessed by others is a security issue. If you change the channel so that your Wi-Fi and theirs are on different channels, there will be less interference. Turn your signal power down to keep your Wi-Fi signal inside your office. If the offending network is already interfering with your Wi-Fi signal, turning up the power on your router's Wi-Fi signal might make it worse because there would be more crossover between your network and theirs. You could also try moving the router to an area with less interference. Finally, try using a different band to avoid interference. If you're using the 5 GHz band, try using the 2.4 GHz band instead if devices support it. Some environments employ a process called channel hopping (changing channels frequently) to avoid packet sniffing and signal jamming on their wireless networks.

168. C. There are trusted software sources that you know and work with all the time (such as Microsoft, HP, or other manufacturers' websites) and there are untrusted sources, and you should differentiate between them. Don't use or let your users use untrusted software sources. Generally, common sense can be your guide, but there are "safe lists" of trusted software vendors from authoritative watchdog companies such as Comodo.

169. C. There isn't any one universal solution to wireless access point placement; it depends a lot on the environment. As a general rule, the greater the distance the signal must travel, the more it will attenuate, but you can lose a signal quickly in a short space as well if the building materials reflect or absorb it. You should try to avoid placing access points near metal (which includes appliances) or near the ground. They should be placed in the center of the area to be served and high enough to get around most obstacles. Note that of all current 802.11 standards, only 802.11ac and 802.11ax offer directional antennae. All other standards are omnidirectional, meaning that the signal transmits in all directions.

170. A. Social engineering is a process in which an attacker attempts to acquire information about your network and system by social means, such as talking to people in the organization. A social engineering attack may occur over the phone, by email, or in person. When the attempt is made through email or instant messaging, it is known as phishing, and it's often made to look as if a message is coming from sites where users are likely to have accounts (banks, eBay, and PayPal are popular). Ransomware is software that holds your computer hostage in a logical way, such as encrypting your hard drive and refusing to give you the key until you pay a ransom. Spoofing is when someone or something pretends to be something else, such as an attacker's server using a familiar look and feel of a website, even a similar IP. Whaling is phishing for a wealthy or influential target.

171. A. Using a swipe to unlock a mobile device does not protect your device or your data. At the very least, using a PIN (personal identification number) is far safer than using a swipe to unlock a mobile device. Keeping operating systems up-to-date to plug any vulnerabilities is very important. All devices should have some form of antivirus, even if it is one that is built into the operating system. Make sure that you are using a remote backup application to ensure that if your mobile device is lost or stolen and you must remotely wipe all the data, you will be able to download it to a new device.

172. A. It doesn't take much to perpetrate a DoS (denial-of-service) attack on a wireless network. Someone nearby could use a Wi-Fi analyzer to determine what channel you're using and bombard that channel with interference, bringing your network to a halt. Changing the channel would provide a temporary fix. Use a Wi-Fi analyzer to find a less crowded channel and switch to that one. You don't want to reset your router to factory defaults. That wouldn't solve the problem and would just make more work for you.

173. B. It's a bold move to try to steal a server. But a server lock or locks on the rack door would stall future theft attempts. A key fob is a type of hard security token. A security token is something you have that authenticates who you are. A firewall can be a software or hardware device that is used to filter traffic on a network.

174. B. Pop-up blockers are available in virtually every browser to stop those annoying ads from taking over your screen. Look in the settings for the browser. Private-browsing mode, or incognito mode, will avoid keeping your browsing history or cookies, and keep your activities from being seen by others on the same Wi-Fi or later by another user of the device. Password managers provide a single login for you and are able to generate unique and complex passwords for all the sites that you use.

175. A. Data destruction contractors (third-party vendors) can be certified by groups such as NAID (National Association for Information Destruction) or can show that they follow government rules (such as HIPAA, in the United States) for data destruction. They can provide proof of destruction, which would be difficult to do on your own. Once you drop a drive off at a recycling center, you have no idea where that drive or its data may end up. While you could destroy the data on your own either physically or logically, it would be better to have a third-party vendor certify to the data destruction.

176. D. Radio frequency identification (RFID) devices use a reader to access information on a special tag that can be on a smartcard. The information can be used to allow or deny access to a secured area or device. RFID is also often used for inventory and fixed asset management. An access control vestibule is an area between two doors that is often used to prevent tailgating. A key fob is a type of hardware token; a hardware device that a person carries to identify the user. Biometrics are devices that use a part of a person's body to identify that person such as a face, palm, or fingerprint reader.

Chapter 8: Software Troubleshooting

1. **A, C.** Bluetooth must be turned on in settings before it will work. Airplane mode must be off for Bluetooth or any other wireless connection to work. Typing **Bluetooth** at a command prompt will not enable it.

2. **C.** The first thing to try when you get a blue/black screen of death (BSOD) error is to reboot. (In Windows 11, the blue screen has been replaced with a black one.) If the problem goes away, it may have been a one-time glitch. Often BSOD errors are caused by hardware or drivers, and since you just installed a new sound card and drivers in Windows, that would be the likely suspect. Use the WinRE to boot into safe mode by choosing Advanced Options ➤ Troubleshoot ➤ Advanced Options ➤ Startup Settings ➤ Enable Safe Mode. Once in safe mode, uninstall the driver and look for an updated one.

3. **B, C.** There are a number of reasons intermittent wireless connections can occur, but the two most common are lack of a good signal and interference. Increasing the number of wireless access points, or being closer to one, can address the lack of a good signal. Interference can be addressed by reducing the number of devices competing for the same channel or by moving away from walls or obstacles. A poor wireless signal can cause video buffering, not the other way around, and Wi-Fi antennas for mobile devices are often found inside the display housing, not a retractable antenna.

4. **A.** The seven steps of the malware removal process are as follows:
   1. Investigate and verify malware symptoms.
   2. Quarantine infected systems.
   3. Disable System Restore in Windows.
   4. Remediate infected systems.
      a. Update anti-malware software.
      b. Scanning and removal techniques (e.g., safe mode, preinstallation environment).
   5. Schedule scans and run updates.
   6. Enable System Restore and create a restore point in Windows.
   7. Educate the end user.

5. **D.** System File Checker (SFC) is a great tool for troubleshooting unstable systems. It scans for and corrects problems with protected system files. `Sfc /scannow` will check all system files and repair any problems it finds. `Sfc /scanfix` is not a valid command. `Sfc /scanfile` checks the integrity of the specified file only and will repair it. `Sfc /verifyonly` will check files but not repair problems that it finds.

6. **B.** This is a classic symptom of browser redirection. The perpetrator has one goal, which is to direct you to websites that they want you to visit, regardless of what you actually want to see. Removing the redirector might be as simple as uninstalling an application (by dragging it to the Trash and emptying the Trash), or it might require full-scale virus (malware) mitigation.

7. B. When an application crashes, you want to isolate the cause of the crash. It could be a compatibility issue, hardware, or a host of other problems. Once it's isolated, you can solve the issue. One step to take early on is to look for updates, patches, or fixes to the application released by the vendor. It's not likely to be a virus issue because you just installed this application and haven't mentioned any virus symptoms. Deleting and reinstalling Windows is a drastic measure that would be your last-ditch effort. Compatibility settings can be found in the Properties menu of a program file.

8. B. Lack of Bluetooth connectivity is often caused when a device is not turned on and/or has an improper setting for discoverability. Make sure the device is turned on and discoverable (checking the manufacturer's documentation if necessary).

9. D. The seven steps of the malware removal process are as follows:

    1. Investigate and verify malware symptoms.

    2. Quarantine infected systems.

    3. Disable System Restore in Windows.

    4. Remediate infected systems.

        a. Update anti-malware software.

        b. Scanning and removal techniques (e.g., safe mode, preinstallation environment).

    5. Schedule scans and run updates.

    6. Enable System Restore and create a restore point in Windows.

    7. Educate the end user.

10. B. The solution to rebuild Windows profiles will fix the issue. Roaming profiles tend to experience problems, most of which can be reliably fixed by rebuilding the Windows profile.

11. A. One of the more clever ways of spreading a virus is to disguise it so that it looks like an antivirus program. When it alerts the user to a fictitious problem, the user then begins interacting with and allowing the rogue program to do all sorts of damage. One of the trickier things for troublemakers to do is to make the program look as if it came from a trusted source—such as Microsoft—and mimic the user interface enough to fool an unsuspecting user.

12. C. If you need installation media, search for and download the Windows media creation tool, which will enable you to create a bootable USB or DVD. Copying the contents of the C drive will not create installation media, and the drive won't be bootable. Windows Security in the Settings app will bring you to several security options, but none of them can create installation media; neither does backing up and syncing your settings.

13. B. Since you just installed a new application, chances are that it is the cause of any problems you're having now. A restore point will restore any system settings that may have been changed and may uninstall the software, but your data won't be affected. Reinstalling Windows is likely not necessary. You would not want to reformat the drive unless the system could not be repaired. Drivers are a type of software that is used to control hardware, so it's unlikely that installing a new application would install any drivers.

14. B. If you save many large files, and the hard drive gets to be under 10 percent free space, its performance can slow down dramatically. The Disk Cleanup utility will show how much disk space is being taken up by temporary files, log files, the Recycle Bin, and other items that can easily be deleted. This could free up some disk space. You will possibly need to delete some files as well. Optimize and defragment drive will help with mechanical hard drives, but not solid-state drives. In fact, running it could damage a solid-state drive. Although it could help a sluggish system perform better, it doesn't free up space. The Registry Editor (regedit .exe) is a tool that should only be used when there isn't another utility that can do the same task. Improperly changing the registry could cause the operating system to crash. System File Checker (SFC) should be run if you're having problems related to system files; it won't free up space on your drive.

15. A. Sadly, if the user hasn't backed up this file, it is likely lost. A restore point backs up system configuration, not user files. If a file won't open in the GUI (graphical user interface), it probably won't open at a command prompt either. The WinRE can fix problems with the system booting or restore the entire machine from an image, but if the files aren't on the image, then WinRE can't restore or open the file either.

16. C, D. Rebooting the computer should close the app and clear anything out of RAM, but you may be able to solve the problem with less drastic measures by ending the process using Task Manager. Double-clicking the program file and right-clicking in the window won't help because the program is corrupted and not responding.

17. A, D. Slow performance is often related to RAM. Look for any apps that are running and can be closed or perform a soft reset (cycle power off and on again) to try to free up memory. Resetting to the factory default will delete all data on the device. You can't upgrade the RAM in an iPad.

18. C. Most likely this is a malicious application that is trying to steal your login information. Misspellings are a red flag that the application is an attempt by a malicious person to spoof your bank's app. Uninstall the app immediately and run a virus scan to ensure that nothing malicious was loaded on your system when you downloaded the app. Whatever you do, don't enter your username and password! You could call the bank and let them know about the app. Running spell check on the app wouldn't help you or even be possible on the app.

19. D. Pop-ups are annoying but not necessarily an indication that your computer is infected with anything. Most likely, the website is programmed to show a pop-up advertisement. Adware pop-ups usually spam your desktop with multiple (if not dozens of) windows at the same time. Spyware generally doesn't announce its presence, and viruses generally do more damage than a simple pop-up ad does.

20. B. An invalid certificate usually means that the certificate that you have (or the one the website has) has expired. It could mean that the site is fine. But it could also mean someone has set up a Trojan that imitates the site you are seeking. Do not visit the website. If it's a site you are not familiar with, the best bet is to avoid it altogether.

21. C. It's unlikely that Windows would be able to predict when a system crash is about to happen, so it isn't going to create a restore point. There are, however, common activities that can present a risk to a system, such as installing new hardware drivers or new applications. In those instances, Windows will create a restore point before the software or hardware driver is installed. A system restore point is also created by default once a week, and you can manually create them whenever you would like.

22. C. You don't want an infected system to infect others on your network! The seven steps of the malware removal process are as follows:

1. Investigate and verify malware symptoms.

2. Quarantine infected systems.

3. Disable System Restore in Windows.

4. Remediate infected systems.

    a. Update anti-malware software.

    b. Scanning and removal techniques (e.g., safe mode, preinstallation environment).

5. Schedule scans and run updates.

6. Enable System Restore and create a restore point in Windows.

7. Educate the end user.

23. D. Rebooting (powering off and back on) any device will clear what is in its memory and sometimes help with application problems, so try rebooting the phone and try the app again. If that doesn't work, you may want to remove and reload the app. Be sure to check the vendor's website for any known problems. You would not want to do a factory reset for a problem with one app because that would delete everything on your phone. Performing a force-stop on the app would close it if it were open, but in this scenario, we can't load the app.

24. C. If an app on your smartphone is locked up, then you need to force-close the app, which is done on an iPhone by swiping the app up. Apps running in the background of an iPhone aren't really running or using resources, unless you've set them up to refresh in the background. (Android apps aren't as good at this.) You likely won't get an "out of memory" error message, but you may run out of storage space. If your phone is sluggish, it's likely that the battery is low or you're running out of storage space. You don't need to close apps when you're done with them for the day. If they're in the background, they aren't using resources.

25. B. The email could be real, but most likely it's a hoax. Worse yet, it could be malware itself, and by clicking the link you will activate it on your computer. Always check a reputable source, such as www.us-cert.gov, www.cert.org, or an anti-malware vendor for information on the latest threats. At a minimum, delete the email and don't click the link!

26. C. If an app does not load, the first thing to try is rebooting. If that does not work, attempt to uninstall and reinstall the app. Be sure to check the vendor's site for any similar problems (and solutions) encountered by others. Cycling the power is turning the device off and on again. The user has already done that. A reset to factory defaults wipes the phone. That would be the last remedy you would try for repairing a phone problem. A force-stop is merely closing the app, which you can't do because it won't open.

27. A. Because problems tend to happen no matter how careful you may be, it is important to back up devices and be able to restore from those backups after an incident. Google Sync is available for backups and synchronization of data between Android-based devices and PCs that have a Microsoft Exchange account. Google Cloud is their IaaS (infrastructure as a service) platform. Android Sync and Android Cloud are not real services.

28. B. The seven steps of the malware removal process are as follows:

1. Investigate and verify malware symptoms.

2. Quarantine infected systems.

3. Disable System Restore in Windows.

4. Remediate infected systems.

    a. Update anti-malware software.

    b. Scanning and removal techniques (e.g., safe mode, preinstallation environment).

5. Schedule scans and run updates.

6. Enable System Restore and create a restore point in Windows.

7. Educate the end user.

29. A, B. If you save many large files, and the hard drive gets to be under 10 percent free space, its performance can slow down dramatically. The Disk Cleanup utility will show how much disk space is being taken up by temporary files, log files, the Recycle Bin, and other items that can easily be deleted. This could free up some disk space. Optimize and defragment drive will help with mechanical hard drives, but not solid-state drives. In fact, running it could damage a solid-state drive like your M.2. As you access and change files on a drive, the parts of the drive can end up scattered in different places. With a mechanical drive, retrieving the file will be faster if the file's pieces are all next to each other on the drive. Defragmenting the drive rearranges it and puts each file's scattered pieces together. System File Checker (SFC) should be run if you're having problems related to system files. It won't free up space on your drive.

30. A. Adware pop-ups usually spam your desktop with multiple (if not dozens of) windows at the same time. Spyware generally doesn't announce its presence, and viruses generally do more damage than a simple pop-up ad does. A website may have legitimate pop-up ads, but they won't have so many that it sends you to another website.

31. A. Security holes in mobile device operating systems can leave back doors into which users can get unauthorized account or root access. The majority of these holes are closed by patches and upgrades as soon as they are discovered, so be sure to keep operating systems current. Monitoring usage should be part of system maintenance as sudden, unexplained high usage could be caused by malware. A firewall wouldn't help in this situation, and disabling location tracking, the camera, and microphone would make the phone useless.

32. D. Malware can change more settings than you might be aware of on a computer. For example, adware might be obvious because of the pop-ups and browser redirects, but it can also change the client-side IP settings that point to a DNS or proxy server. Check the IP configuration on the client and be sure it's set properly.

33. C. Since you just updated the driver, it's most likely that the driver is the problem. Go to Device Manager (`devmgmt.msc`), find the network card and roll back the driver to the previous one, then reboot the system. It's not necessary to uninstall the card driver. It's highly unlikely that the card is malfunctioning. The problem is the driver the technician just installed.

34. A, B. Updating the network settings manually or rebooting should apply the new DNS information. Disabling the firewall or booting to safe mode will not help the issue.

35. B, D. There are options for entering safe mode. If you're able to use the OS, then go to Settings and search for advanced startup, then choose Change advanced startup options, and under Advanced startup, click Restart now. This will restart the computer and bring up the Windows Recovery Environment (WinRE). Alternately, hold the Shift key while restarting the computer. This will also cause the PC to boot into the WinRE. To access safe mode, choose Troubleshoot ➤ Advanced options ➤ Startup Settings ➤ Safe Mode.

36. A, D. Step 4 of the best practice procedures for malware removal is to remediate the infected systems. While the exact steps depend a bit on the malware and the damage done, it's easier to get rid of the malware files if you don't boot to the drive the malware is on. You could boot into safe mode, which is a limited operating system, and run an antivirus, or boot with installation media from a completely separate drive and run an antivirus on your hard drive, or boot from a bootable USB drive that was made using tools from your favorite antivirus company and run its antivirus/anti-malware eradication tools. In any case, you will want to ensure that you've downloaded the most current malware definition files available to scan and remove the threat.

37. A, D. When an application crashes, you want to isolate the cause of the crash—it could be a compatibility issue, hardware, or a host of other problems—and solve it. One step to take early on is to look for updates/patches/fixes to the application released by the vendor. You can also try to repair the installation through Control Panel. If needed, you can delete and reinstall the software, but you should try patching or repairing first. You would not want to remove and reinstall Windows.

38. D. Whatever message was appearing in the pop-up window is likely in the mobile application log. If it was too fast for the user to read, it's probably too fast for you to read too. You would not want to install any additional software until this problem is resolved, and reinstalling the application may not be necessary.

39. A, C. Tips for increasing battery life include keeping OS updates applied (they may include energy-saving patches), avoiding ambient temperatures that are too high or too low, letting the screen automatically dim, and turning off location-based services. You should also disconnect peripherals and quit applications not in use (Bluetooth, for example, uses power when enabled, even if you are not using it to connect to anything). A reset to factory defaults won't help with battery life, and you'll lose all your stuff! Installing an antivirus app also won't help here.

40. B. Every device on a network must have a unique IP address. Many networks use a DHCP server to assign IP addresses because keeping track of them manually would create a great deal of work. If there are two identical IP addresses attempting to access a network with

DHCP, then at least one of them has its IP address configured manually. Ensuring that this computer is set to obtain an IP address automatically should be your first step. If it isn't, then you have found the problem. If it is, then you could ping the IP address using ping -a *ipaddress*, substituting the duplicated IP address for the variable *ipaddress* in the command. This will return the hostname of the other computer. Every network admin should have a list of computer names and where they are located. You could then ensure that the other computer is also set to obtain an IP address automatically. Manually configuring an IP address is what caused the problem. The ipconfig /release and ipconfig /renew commands wouldn't help in this situation.

41. A. Given the description, it might be best to roll back the printer driver to a known good version. Updating the boot order and network settings have no impact on the printer working. Stopping and restarting the print spooler is not likely to help, since the driver was just updated. But if rolling back the device driver doesn't help, the problem might be related to a print job in the queue; then restarting the print spooler could be a next step.

42. C. Android, the mobile device operating system, is open source, which means that it is very flexible and, unfortunately, just as vulnerable to malware as any other operating system, maybe even more because of being open source. The Android operating system does have several built-in security features such as passwords, two-step verification, and Google Play Protect, which scans for malware daily and attempts to remove malicious apps before they are downloaded. Unfortunately, malware can come from other sources such as email, so it's important to install a reliable antivirus/anti-malware for Android devices. Android does not have a built-in antivirus app. Keeping the OS patches installed will help plug any security vulnerabilities, but it isn't enough.

43. C. Don't click anywhere on the warning! This is either a hoax or when you click on the pop-up, it will install malware. Even clicking the X to close the window may install malware, so don't do it. Your best course of action is to shut down the computer, reboot, and initiate a virus scan using your antivirus software.

44. C. Occasionally, a rogue system will begin automatically shutting down and/or restarting while in use. Although it could be indicative of a hardware problem (a malfunctioning motherboard, for example), it can also indicate a setting misconfiguration or driver problem. The most likely setting problem is with sleep settings, such as hibernation mode. If that's not it, then it could be a corrupted driver. To begin ruling out possibilities, boot the system into safe mode and see whether the problem continues. If the problem does not occur while in safe mode, then boot normally and begin testing what occurs as you eliminate drivers/devices one by one (sound, video, and so forth) until you find the culprit. The boot order in the BIOS/UEFI settings would have nothing to do with this problem. While you may need to go into WinRE to fix the problem, that would not be your next step. You certainly don't need to reinstall Windows, at least not yet.

45. B, D. Although it may appear to be a problem with the operating system, this is classic behavior for a system that is overheating. There are a few things to do here. Ensure that all vents on the system are free of dust and debris so that air can move freely through. Use compressed air or an antistatic computer vacuum to remove dust from inside the case. Dust on a motherboard can act as a blanket holding heat in, or worse, it can cause a short and damage the motherboard. Make sure there is adequate room around the case for airflow;

if the system is overclocked, revert to running the CPU at its manufacturer's recommended speed. If none of those remedy the situation, try replacing the processor's thermal paste with new thermal paste. Reinstalling Windows or checking system files is not necessary.

46. A, C. If the computer was fine yesterday and slow today, your first thought should be that it may have been attacked by malware. Malware running in the background is notorious for taking up system resources. Your first course of action should be to follow the malware removal process. If malware is not found on your system, look next at the Processes tab of Task Manager. Click Memory at the top to sort the list by how much memory each program is using. It may be software launched at startup that you don't need or another program that doesn't need to run all the time. Based on what you find there, take appropriate action.

47. B. Active Directory stores user information on the domain, including their profile. The first time a user logs onto a machine on the domain, the entire profile is downloaded, which may take a few minutes. For subsequent logons on the same machine, only the changes to the profile are downloaded, making the process much faster. If the user then logs into a different machine, the entire profile must be downloaded, so the logon won't be as fast as the user is accustomed to. They don't need to be listed as a user on this computer as long as they are a user on the Active Directory. A peripheral being connected or not should not affect the profile download, and entering the wrong password would quickly generate an error message stating that.

48. D. When the Print Spooler service is not running, a user will not be able to see or print to any of their devices. Open the Services console and restart the Print Spooler to remedy the situation. If the printers were offline or out of paper, most likely the printer would send a message stating such to the user's screen.

49. B. Occasionally the time on a computer is off because of errors in settings in Windows or a domain controller. In Windows 10 and 11, the time settings are accessed in the same way. If the time is off by exactly an hour, or exactly several hours, then most likely the time zone is set manually and incorrectly. If it's off by minutes, then it's something else causing it, but you can sync the time now and correct the settings using the Date & time options on the Time & Language tab in the Settings app. On an Active Directory domain, the domain controller uses the Windows Time service and Network Time Protocol (NTP) to synchronize the time of all the computers on the domain, so it's important to ensure that the Window Time service is running. Option B is not available in Windows 10 or 11.

50. C. If the operating system is missing, it could be due to a bad or corrupted boot sector on the hard drive, or the operating system may indeed be missing. Your first step would be to ensure that the boot files are not corrupted. To do this, boot to the installation media (you may have to set your BIOS/UEFI to boot to the installation media drive), then choose ➤ Next ➤ Repair your computer ➤ Troubleshoot ➤ Startup Repair and follow the onscreen prompts. Typing **startup repair** at a command prompt returns an error message. SFC (System File Checker) is used to verify OS files, not a program you can open and choose something in, and you wouldn't be able to boot into safe mode because the computer thinks the operating system is missing. You may be thinking it could be nonbootable media in a drive, but the question states that the computer is set to boot from the C: drive.

51. A, B. There are many reasons why a system would be running slowly. If it suddenly starts running slowly, suspect that malware might be involved and perform the malware removal process. If no malware is found, check physical and virtual memory. You may need to increase the physical RAM or change virtual memory settings. It could also be that a RAM module has failed or needs to be reseated. Other possibilities are a full hard drive (which rarely happens with today's huge hard drives) or a problem with hardware. Ensuring that the operating system is up-to-date is always a good idea. You would not roll back to a prior update, and restoring from a restore point would not necessarily help here.

52. A, C. The first place to look for updates would be an option on the application's menu. If nothing is found there, check the application's website. Programs and Features in Control Panel and Apps & features in the Settings app have options to uninstall, change, or repair, but not update, applications.

53. B. With all due respect, you should have verified that your system meets the application's minimum requirements before you even purchased or downloaded it. Remember, too, that you'll need enough RAM for all the programs that are running at the same time. If your operating system is newer than the application's required operating system, you could check the manufacturer's website for an update, but that would happen after you compare your system to the application's requirements. You certainly would not reinstall Windows because an application won't start, and although you could find a different application that meets your needs, that's not the best solution here.

54. D. Your first thought in this situation should be that there is malware on your computer. You would perform the procedures for malware removal immediately. It's unlikely that you would need to reinstall the Word program or Windows, and while it's possible that someone has been playing tricks on you, that's not the most likely reason, unless that someone is the person who wrote the malware.

55. A, C. All services can be found in the Services console (`services.msc`). A subset of those can be found on the Services tab of Task Manager. If the needed service isn't there, a link at the bottom of the page will take you to the full list of services. Computer Management does not have a link to the Services console, and Device Manager is intended for managing hardware and drivers.

56. D. The first concern when a system is running too slowly is that there may be malware. Once you've verified that there isn't any malware, if the system is still running slowly, check the page file size. The page file is the file that holds virtual memory. Virtual memory is using a part of a hard drive as if it were RAM. A larger paging file may alleviate low memory warnings, but the price is slower performance because the hard drive is slower than RAM. To change the amount of hard drive space reserved for virtual memory, search for advanced system settings, and select View advanced system settings. On the System Properties window click the Advanced tab then in the Performance box, click Settings. In the Performance Options window, choose the Advanced tab, and in the Virtual memory box, click the Change button. Deselect Automatically manage paging file size for all drives, then click Custom size. Adjust the size by typing the appropriate value in the Initial size (MB) box and Maximum size (MB) box. Then click Set. If you have a magnetic hard drive (HDD) and a solid-state drive (SSD), the SSD will be faster, but using it for virtual memory can shorten its life. If possible, it's better to increase the physical RAM than virtual memory. A hard drive being too large would not cause this problem.

57. A. In Windows 10 and 11, if the update fails to work properly, run the Windows Update Troubleshooter in the Settings app. The troubleshooter will search for and attempt to resolve any problems that may prevent updates to your operating system. When it has finished, check for updates again. You may need to run the troubleshooter more than once. It's important that the operating system is kept up-to-date because updates may be patching security holes in the system. You would not want to reinstall the system because eventually you would need to install the same update, and most likely you would not need to purchase an updated computer.

58. A. An educated end user who is aware of the signs of malware is one of the best protections against malware. The seven steps of the malware removal process are as follows:

1. Investigate and verify malware symptoms.

2. Quarantine infected systems.

3. Disable System Restore in Windows.

4. Remediate infected systems.

   a. Update anti-malware software.

   b. Scanning and removal techniques (e.g., safe mode, preinstallation environment).

5. Schedule scans and run updates.

6. Enable System Restore and create a restore point in Windows.

7. Educate the end user.

59. C. You can choose the time server to sync with by going to Control Panel, selecting Date and Time, and on the Internet Time tab, clicking Change settings, then the down arrow on the right of the entry box, and choosing the correct server in the Server box. The Date and Time options will allow you to change settings for time zone and set time automatically, but not which server you are using. In the Services app, you can choose how and if the Windows Time service runs, but again, not the time server that is being used.

60. B. Services will behave as you tell them to. Services can be set to Automatic so that they'll start automatically when the computer starts, or to Automatic (Delayed Start) so that the computer will start faster. They still start when the computer starts up, just two minutes later. Manual start is what the user is currently doing. Starting of the service would be set up in the Services console, not the application. A service can also be triggered to start by some event or other software, then closed again when it is no longer needed.

61. A, C. When you're getting messages that your computer is low on memory, you can stop some programs that are running in memory, but more likely you will need to increase physical memory and/or virtual memory. A rule of thumb is that virtual memory should be 1.5 times the physical memory, but you can make the setting larger if you wish. The downside of using more virtual memory instead of physical memory is that virtual memory resides in a page file (`pagefile.sys`) on the hard drive, and hard drives are slower than RAM, so having a larger swap file may slow the system performance. To change virtual memory, search for advanced system settings, and select View advanced system settings. On the System Properties window click the Advanced tab then in the Performance box, click Settings. Click the Advanced tab, and on the Performance Options window, in the Virtual memory box, click the Change button. Deselect Automatically manage paging file size for all drives, then click Custom size, and adjust the size by typing the appropriate value in the Initial size (MB) box and Maximum size (MB) box. Then click Set.

62. B, C. There are several places in the operating system where you can see how much physical RAM is installed in the system. Opening the case and counting the modules is neither necessary nor an accurate measure of how much RAM you have. The System Information utility (msinfo32.exe) has this and much more information about your computer. The Performance tab in Task Manager will not only show you how much physical memory you have, but it will also show you how much is being used. This can give you a better idea of whether you have enough RAM installed because it is also taking into consideration what is normally being used in your system. Another place you can see installed RAM, not shown in the options for this question, is Settings ➤ System ➤ About. There is no Memory utility in Control Panel.

63. A. Given the description, it might be best to roll back the update. Until the business application and update can be proven compatible, the update cannot be installed as is. Killing the task is not acceptable as it may be a necessary task, such as explorer.exe.

64. C, D. The seven steps of the malware removal process are as follows:

   1. Investigate and verify malware symptoms.

   2. Quarantine Infected systems.

   3. Disable System Restore in Windows.

   4. Remediate infected systems.

      a. Update anti-malware software.

      b. Scanning and removal techniques (e.g., safe mode, preinstallation environment).

   5. Schedule scans and run updates.

   6. Enable System Restore and create a restore point in Windows.

   7. Educate the end user.

65. A, B. The Windows User Profile service detects when there is a slow link between the client computer and the domain controller. The service will then load the user's profile from a copy that is cached on the local machine. If the user has used a different machine since the last time they used the current one, then the profile changes will not be on the local machine. The User Profile service is running, because it is what generates the error message. Screen resolution has nothing to do with this error message.

66. B, C. USB ports provide limited power to the devices connected to them. If that power is exceeded, one or more the devices attached to the controller may stop working and the error message "Not enough USB Controller Resources" may be generated. They also have a limited number of endpoints available on each port. Some devices use more endpoints than others and if the limit is exceeded, the same error message will be generated. A damaged motherboard could cause many things to malfunction but likely would not generate this error message, and it is highly unlikely that the speaker drivers would conflict with the USB hub controller drivers.

67. D. On the graphic, the third icon down on the left, just above Focus, is the screen orientation. Notice that the lock is closed. That means that their smartphone orientation is locked in portrait mode and will not autorotate. Bluetooth, focus, and the camera have nothing to do with this problem.

68. B, D. Slow data speeds can be caused by too much interference or by a weak signal. If there is too much interference, try changing the channel on Wi-Fi routers to less used channels; performance should increase. Solve weak signals by installing more access points or signal boosters, or by moving closer to an existing access point, or away from physical obstructions.

69. C. A limited connectivity error means that your device is able to connect to Wi-Fi but not to the Internet. The fact that this is happening with several users in the same area likely means that it is a problem with the wireless access point (WAP), not an individual device. The users are getting a limited connectivity error, so they're connecting to the WAP but not getting an IP address from the DHCP server or router. Try cycling the WAP off and back on to resolve the issue. If that doesn't work, troubleshoot the connection between the WAP and the router. You don't need to boost the signal strength because the users are able to connect to the WAP. Having all the users reboot their devices will not solve the issue, and if they're getting a limited connectivity message, then Wi-Fi on their device is already turned on.

70. A, B, C. There are many bootleg, imitation/fake, and malicious apps waiting for unsuspecting users to download them. They often have names very similar to the actual app, but there are ways to identify the spoofed apps. First, check the reviews. If you see negative comments about problems with mobile devices after installing the app, beware. Look at the number of downloads or reviews. If it's a popular app it will have a high number of both. For example, if you see a Hulu app with less than a million reviews, it is not the real app. Research the app and the company it comes from. Check the spelling of not only the app name, but the description and the screenshots as well. Misspelled words are a sign that the app is not legitimate. How long has the app been available? Popular apps will not have been released three days ago. If there is a free version, don't download it and install it without doing your due diligence first. Offering something for free is a way to get you to download it and install something malicious. If you download an app and it asks for permissions that you don't think it should need, be suspicious.

71. A. This message happens when the User Profile service incorrectly identifies the connection between the client and server as a fast connection, when it is actually slow. These settings can be configured on the domain controller. If the User Profile service detects a slow connection, it will load a cached profile from the local machine instead of the roaming profile on the server. If it's the first time the user has logged into a particular machine, then the profile will take longer to load because the entire profile is loaded, not just the changes, but it wouldn't generate this error message. It is unlikely that a failure to update Windows would affect this message, and if a user entered an invalid password, they would see a message stating that.

72. A. Plugging a USB cable from a power block into a port of the motherboard will not solve your problem, and it will likely destroy your motherboard. The first thing you should try is rearranging the devices that are using the USB ports. USB hubs have a limit as to how much power they can provide and the number of endpoints that each port can support. A device may have multiple endpoints, and devices that are heavily involved in data transfer may use many more endpoints than other devices. Using an external hub or docking station that is separately powered means that the port won't be providing power to the devices, so this may resolve the issue. Disabling the XHCI Mode option in the BIOS/UEFI may help with the resource error but will effectively turn off USB 3.0 and your hubs will behave like 2.0 ports. Other troubleshooting options could be to update the chipset drivers for the motherboard and check the power options in the BIOS/UEFI. Make sure any USB controller drivers are updated. If you have plugged and unplugged devices, try going to Device Manager to scan for hardware changes and test devices again. Also in Device Manager, uninstall all USB controllers and restart the computer. Windows will scan for hardware changes and all the USB controllers that were uninstalled should be reinstalled, which will allow the USB controllers to return an unresponsive port to a working condition.

73. C. Either Airplane mode being on or Wi-Fi turned off would keep them from connecting to their Wi-Fi, but in this case, according to the graphic, the Wi-Fi is turned off. Cellular service and Bluetooth should have no effect on their ability to connect to their home Wi-Fi network.

74. A. If your computer is set to an incorrect time and date (we're talking years off, not just a few minutes), then it can cause invalid certificate errors for the websites you want to visit. Refreshing your certificate is not an option in the Security settings in Control Panel, and there is no low option for the Internet zone in Internet Properties. It's never recommended to turn off your security settings for browsing the Internet.

75. A, B. When authorized users access devices through unintended connections or unauthorized users access absconded devices (such as with root access), they can access the data on the device. Every firm should have a policy for protecting data (encryption) and dealing with leaks when they occur.

76. C. Going over the limit on your phone's data plan is generally not a major risk, other than to your finances. Data overage charges can be high, depending on your provider and service plan. It is unlikely that your account will be deactivated, made more vulnerable to security breaches, or locked out of the cellular system.

77. A, C. The most likely cause for an Android phone randomly restarting is a poorly written app. Any apps that you're not using should be deleted from the device. Another cause may be that on some Android phones, there is an auto-restart feature as a part of a Device Care option to boost phone performance. If it is on, turn the feature off to avoid automatic restarts. Batteries that are too hot or too cold can cause problems, but room temperature batteries are just right. Typing too fast on the keyboard wouldn't cause a reboot problem. Other problems not listed might be the battery overheating or third-party cases that don't fit just right (causing a button to stick), defective hardware, or corrupted operating system files.

78. B. A common cause for lack of wireless connectivity is that the device is in Airplane mode. Ensure that the device is not in that mode, then cycle the power if necessary. If the problem persists, you'll need to perform further troubleshooting. There is no Wi-Fi receptivity setting, and you would not reset the device to factory default without exhausting all other options first.

79. A. The seven steps of the malware removal process are as follows:

1. Investigate and verify malware symptoms.

2. Quarantine infected systems.

3. Disable System Restore in Windows.

4. Remediate infected systems.

    a. Update anti-malware software.

    b. Scanning and removal techniques (e.g., safe mode, preinstallation environment).

  5. Schedule scans and run updates.

  6. Enable System Restore and create a restore point in Windows.

  7. Educate the end user.

80. B. A Wi-Fi analyzer can be used on your network to see signal strength, channels used, and various other network metrics. Any company with a wireless network should have one for troubleshooting purposes. A Wi-Fi analyzer could be as simple as an app on your phone, to a very sophisticated and expensive device.

81. C. The specific behavior exhibited most likely means that their device is the victim of an adware attack. Adware tracks your movements and targets you with advertisements, trying to get you to click on them and spend your money. Viruses move from one machine to another by some casual contact such as sending an email. Shoulder surfing is a type of social engineering where someone literally looks over your shoulder to try to gain classified information like your login and password. A keylogger records keystrokes and sends them back to a third party. They would try to hide their presence rather than announce it.

82. C. If the Bluetooth devices have not been used together previously, they need to be paired to work. Pairing is usually a simple process. CompTIA's steps to configure Bluetooth devices are:

  1. Enable Bluetooth.

  2. Enable pairing.

  3. Find a device for pairing.

  4. Enter the appropriate PIN code.

  5. Test connectivity.

83. C. Even most unlimited plans aren't truly unlimited. Most mobile or even home Internet providers will slow down your transmission rate when you exceed a specified data threshold. It is highly unlikely that your account will be deactivated, become vulnerable to security breaches, or be locked out.

84. A, B. According to Apple.com, if everything is up-to-date and your battery is healthy but the problem continues, you need to contact Apple Support. Most batteries are not user replaceable. Be sure to back up your data before contacting Apple Support, and if you reset the phone to the factory default, you will lose everything on the phone. This also isn't Apple's recommendation.

85. A. This is a typical fake security warning. If you click the message, or anywhere on the message, it will likely install the malware that it is mentioning. To ensure that your device is clean, update your anti-malware software and run a scan. It's important to keep your OS and all software updated with the latest versions. Use a reliable anti-malware software, strong passwords, or a password manager; avoid using public Wi-Fi (just because it says it's Starbucks Wi-Fi doesn't necessarily mean that it is); and do your due diligence when choosing new apps to download and install, even from places like the Google Play app.

86. A, B. Smartphones are susceptible to malware, just like any other computer device. Some malware can be configured to perform unauthorized location tracking. To help prevent this, always patch and update the OS as soon as updates are available and install anti-malware software. Some services such as maps require that location services be enabled, but if the user chooses to, Location Services can be disabled. Exactly how to do that depends on the device, but the option is most likely in the Settings menu. Enabling sync with a cloud provider will make a backup of their data, but it does nothing to protect it from being leaked.

87. C. A restore point is a copy, or snapshot, of your system configuration at a given point in time. It's like a backup of your configuration but not your data. Snapshots are created within Windows by clicking the search icon, typing **Create A Restore Point**, and selecting it from the list of results. The System Properties window opens. It should open on the System Protection tab. If not, click the System Protection tab, and near the bottom of the screen is a Create button next to Create a restore point right now for the drives that have system protection turned on. Clicking the Create button begins the process of creating a restore point.

88. B, C. To use NFC services like Apple Pay and Google Pay, you need to ensure that Airplane mode is off and NFC is enabled. For Apple devices, go to Settings, then Control Center, and click the green plus sign next to NFC Tag Reader. For Android devices, download the Google Pay app, launch it, and follow the onscreen instructions. Wi-Fi and Bluetooth have no effect on the NFC reader.

89. A, B. For AirDrop to work, you must both have Wi-Fi and Bluetooth enabled, and you need to be within Wi-Fi and Bluetooth range. If either party has a hotspot on, it must be turned off. If you are not in the receiver's contact list and they have their AirDrop Receiving setting set to Contacts Only, then you will not be able to send them information. If you are in their contacts list, then your Apple ID email or your phone number must be in the contact card. If they change their AirDrop Receiving setting to Everyone, then they can receive the file even if you are not in their contacts list.

90. B. There are many other forms of malware in addition to viruses. While a true antivirus program will scan for viruses, anti-malware programs are a superset of virus scanners and will look for more than just traditional viruses. They can scan for spyware, ransomware, adware, and other malicious programs as well. Firewalls and proxy servers can be used to mitigate attacks as well, but they likely won't be installed on the mobile device. The seven steps of the malware removal process are as follows:

1. Investigate and verify malware symptoms.
2. Quarantine infected systems.
3. Disable System Restore in Windows.
4. Remediate infected systems.
    a. Update anti-malware software.
    b. Scanning and removal techniques (e.g., safe mode, preinstallation environment).
5. Schedule scans and run updates.
6. Enable System Restore and create a restore point in Windows.
7. Educate the end user.

91. A. If the update fails once because of a lost or insufficient network connection, retry the update using the same network connection. If it fails again, connect the iPhone to your computer to perform the update. This error message has nothing to do with insufficient room on your iPhone, and there is no Ethernet card for an iPhone.

92. B, D. Regardless of the OS, if there is insufficient space on a smartphone or a weak Internet connection, an application is unlikely to update. Allowing the power to go too low or the device to turn off during an update may cause problems, so it's perfectly fine to have the phone plugged in while doing updates. Generally speaking, mobile devices use Wi-Fi instead of Ethernet, and you will want a strong Wi-Fi signal.

93. A, C. High resource utilization can be a telltale sign that a device is running more than you think it should be—perhaps the drives are being searched or the camera is recording your every move. Or, it could be that the user has too many apps open and the device is struggling with available resources. The latter tends to happen more on Android smartphones than iPhones.

94. D. Weak signals are a common culprit behind dropped signals. Before you engage in communication, signal strength on the device should be evaluated. If the signal is low (for example, no bars), then change location (step outside, drive out of the tunnel, exit the elevator, and so forth) and try for a better signal. A low battery can affect signal strength, so keep the battery charged as much as possible. Waiting a few minutes won't help if something is blocking the signal. And cycling the power off and on probably won't help either. You certainly wouldn't reset your phone to factory defaults any time that your signal was weak!

95. B. You don't need to force-stop the application because it isn't unresponsive. What you should do is suspect that your phone is infected with malware. Most Android phones have a method to restart in safe mode. Once there, perform a malware scan and uninstall the offending app. Make sure your OS and other apps are updated. If you identify any other suspicious apps (apps that are acting strangely), then they may have been infected as well and should be removed and a clean copy downloaded and installed.

96. B. While apps, usage, and so on can contribute to power drain, one of the biggest offenders is the search for a cellular signal. It's unlikely that the battery needs to be replaced, power cycled off and on, or the phone replaced. Simply recharge the battery.

97. C, D. If developer mode and the debugging feature are left on, then whenever the PC is connected to any computer, the Android device is essentially wide open, meaning that passwords, bank accounts, photos and so on are visible to anyone who accesses it. There are many features that can be manipulated in debugging mode, such as Show Touches, Pointer Location, Transition Animation Scale, and so on. Just ensure that developer mode and debugging are turned off when you are done with them.

98. B, C. For AirDrop to work, you must both have Wi-Fi and Bluetooth enabled. You need to be within Wi-Fi and Bluetooth range. If either party has a hotspot on, it must be turned off. If you are not in the receiver's contact list and they have their AirDrop set to receive from contacts only, then you will not be able to send them information. If you are in their contacts list, then your Apple ID email or your phone number must be in the contact card. If they change their AirDrop Receiving setting to Everyone, then they can receive the file even if you are not in their contacts list.

99. A, B. To update the iOS, you need to have sufficient room on your iPhone. You may be able to use your computer to do the update since files can be temporarily stored on the computer by the update while it is working. If it still won't update using your computer, then you need to make space on your iPhone by removing apps or data that you aren't using. Adding internal storage to an iPhone is not possible, and while it is possible to use an adapter and an SD card for extra storage, an SD card can't be used to hold the iOS.

100. C, D. The Play Store won't install updates or apps if your date or time is incorrect, so ensure that they are correct. Google Chrome won't update if there are other updates pending in the queue, so you'll need to cancel those updates to allow Chrome to update. Clearing the Chrome cache will free up space on your device. Other circumstances that you need for application updates in general are a good Wi-Fi connection, sufficient space on your device, and if the app is unresponsive, you need to force-close it before installing an update.

101. B. These are push notifications, not pop-ups, because they are coming up on the desktop, not in a browser. You can definitely do something about them. In order for them to show, you would have had to innocently agree to them at some point. And yes, you can disable or block all or some of them. You may want some notifications and not others. In Windows 10, open Settings ➤ System ➤ Notifications & actions to manage which notifications you see. In Windows 11, go to Settings ➤ System ➤ Notifications. Choosing which ones can also be done through your browser and how depends on the browser being used. In Chrome, look for Settings ➤ Security and Privacy ➤ Site Settings ➤ Notifications, and there you'll find the settings. In Edge, go to Settings ➤ Cookies and site permissions ➤ Notifications. Each browser (Safari, Firefox, Opera, and so on) has its own path to the settings, and they may change over time, but all will allow you to choose which notifications to see and which to block.

102. A, C. An Android device won't perform an OS update under the following conditions: if the Wi-Fi connection is not strong enough, the battery power is too low, the storage space is too low, or the device is no longer supported. If there is insufficient storage, remove apps or data that are no longer needed to make room for the update. Ensure that there is a good Wi-Fi connection. If the battery power is insufficient, plug the device in until it is fully charged.

103. B, D. It's possible that you've already signed up for desktop alerts. If you receive weather warnings on your computer or phone, or school closings, power outages, or other notifications, these are desktop alerts. Desktop alerts can be displayed on wall-mounted displays, desktops, mobile devices, and phones, and they are an excellent way to provide mass notifications to affected people. They can include text and graphics, and they can be made full screen and interactive so that the receiver can respond. But like many other useful features in computer systems, they can be abused by those with malicious intent. For example, an interactive button on a desktop alert could be used to deploy malware when the user clicks it. There are many third-party vendors for desktop alert systems.

104. C. Jailbreaking does let you do more with your device, but it isn't necessarily safe or legal. Jailbreaking is most commonly done with Apple devices because they are more locked down (closed-source) than Android (open source). Jailbreaking an iPhone, for instance, allows the user to install apps that are not approved by Apple. When you open the device up for yourself by cracking software or gaining root access, it also opens your device up more for cybercriminals to perpetrate an attack on it. Jailbreaking also voids the warranty on your device. The device may become unstable, and with the warranty voided, you are not likely to receive support in fixing problems. Jailbreaking may even be illegal depending on where you are in the world.

105. A, D. Apps from the Google Play app store are required to be signed by the developer, and any updates won't be installed unless the signatures for the update and the original software match. This is a security feature for Android devices. If the signatures don't match, an error message like "Signatures do not match previously installed version" will appear. If you've downloaded the update from somewhere other than the Google Play store and received this error, there is a good chance that the website is a spoof of the actual developer's site, and a criminal is trying to get you to install malware. Android package (APK) source is the format for Android apps on the Google Play store prior to August 2021. Updates for existing apps may still be in this format, but any newly developed apps after August 2021 on the Google Play store will be in an Android App Bundle (AAB) format.

106. B. The most likely reason for a sudden, high increase in network traffic is that there is malware on the system and that malware is using your network to do something. Luckily the mobile devices are on a VLAN, so it isn't directly affecting your main network. You need to immediately identify the source of the network traffic and perform malware removal procedures. A mobile device malfunctioning is not likely to be the source of the problem. Limited connectivity would not present as an increase in network traffic, and it is unlikely that your monitoring software being infected is the problem. High network traffic is precisely the sort of incident that your monitoring software should be designed to detect.

107. A. Desktop alerts perform a valuable function, but they can be subject to misuse by cybercriminals. The best protection for this type of attack is user education. You would not want to block all desktop alerts because they serve a purpose, and you certainly don't want to log on as an administrator unless absolutely necessary to avoid an attacker gaining administrator access and to avoid accidentally doing something as an administrator that could damage a system, since administrators can do anything in a system. Anti-malware should be updated daily.

108. B. If a computer's boot order is set to boot only to a USB or optical drive, then leaving a nonbootable media in that drive will give the error that the OS is not found, when in fact it may be perfectly fine on the hard drive. Your first course of action is to verify that there are no media inserted into optical or USB drives. If you find it there, remove the nonbootable media and restart the computer. If it starts normally, the issue is resolved, but you shouldn't stop there. Enter the BIOS/UEFI and verify the boot options. For a secure environment you will want to disable booting to drives other than the intended boot drive, usually a hard drive. It's true that booting to alternate drives may be necessary when troubleshooting, but leaving that option always available opens the system up to potential attack.

109. C. A seemingly unstable Windows installation may be repaired by using a system restore point from a time when the system was working well. If that doesn't resolve the issue, the next step would be to boot into WinRE ➤ Troubleshoot ➤ Reset this PC and choose to keep your personal files, performing an in-place update that will reinstall the Windows 11 operating system files. There is no need to reformat the drive and reinstall the OS or delete the Registry.

110. D. Whenever a device will leave your possession, whether it is being donated or recycled, you need to ensure that all data is removed from the device. The simplest way to do this is by restoring the device to its factory settings, if a restore image is available. In many Windows devices this is done through WinRE ➤ Troubleshoot ➤ Factory Image Restore. The process for a factory image restore on phones and mobile devices will be different depending on the device.

111. B. If the computer is behaving strangely, the simplest fix is to reinstall the company's PC image. This will delete any files that exist on the computer and install any software and settings that are necessary for the company. The user can then log into the domain. There is no need to back up their files because on the domain their files will be saved in a home directory on a server. Booting into WinRE to reset or perform a factory restore is not the best way to resolve the problem.

112. A. System File Checker (SFC) is a great tool to use to fix a corrupted DLL file. Numerous dynamic link library (DLL) files are required to boot, but usually the lack of or corruption of one of them produces a noncritical error. Enter an elevated command prompt and run the command **sfc /scannow** to find and repair problems with system files.

113. B, C. The Windows Preinstallation Environment (PE) is a minimal operating system, designed to prepare a computer for installation or to boot into for launching troubleshooting tools such as the Windows Recovery Environment (WinRE). It is not intended to be an operating system on a computer but rather a stepping-stone to get an OS installed or repaired.

114. A. The Windows Event Viewer utility provides information about what's been going on with the whole system to help you troubleshoot problems. Event Viewer shows warnings, error messages, and records of things that have happened successfully. It's found in all current versions of Windows. The three most commonly referenced logs are Security (which includes information about logins), System, and Application. The Security log can be used to audit successful and failed access attempts. The system log contains information about system events such as drivers started and programs running in the background. Software and Authentication are not logs in Event Viewer.

115. D. If too many applications starting up when Windows loads is causing problems such as a very slow boot and the system running slowly, use the Startup tab in Task Manager to disable them. The Registry Editor is intended for making changes to the Registry directly and is only used when absolutely necessary, as many of the same changes can be done using Control Panel or Settings apps. System configuration can be used in troubleshooting by choosing a Diagnostic or Selective startup, and System Information provides a wealth of information about the hardware and software in your system.

Chapter 9: Operational Procedures

1. D. Power strips come in all shapes and sizes and are convenient for plugging multiple devices into one wall outlet. Most of them even have an on/off switch so that you can turn all the devices on or off at the same time. Don't make the mistake of thinking that power strips will protect equipment from electrical surges, though. If there is a strong power surge through one of these inexpensive devices, the strip and everything plugged into it can be damaged.

2. B. A splash screen appears on a computer before a user logs in. It can contain information related to the acceptable use policy (AUP) or regulatory information that the user must agree and adhere to. This information is accepted by clicking a button indicating agreement to it before they can log in. The act of logging in alone does not prove acceptance of the conditions unless there is a statement telling the user that they must either accept the conditions or not continue. An incident report is filed when someone identifies a breach of company policies. A signature on an AUP should always be obtained as a part of onboarding, but it won't include any changes to the policy.

3. B. One component that people frequently overlook is the case itself. Cases are generally made of metal, and some computer cases have sharp edges inside, so be careful when handling them. You can, for example, cut yourself by jamming your fingers between the case and the frame when you try to force the case back on. Motherboards and expansion cards have sharp solder projections on the bottom that can cut as can a moving fan (which would only be on if troubleshooting a power issue). Less often injuries can occur from the power supply and processor. The power supply could provide a shock because it contains capacitors that hold a charge for a time after the power is turned off. You could be burned by a processor if removing it before it has had adequate time to cool off. Flying debris inside the case is very unlikely.

4. C. If the user has third-party software offering file sharing capability—for example, Dropbox, Microsoft Teams, or Google Chrome—then the file could be transferred to others via the file sharing software. Using encryption and establishing a VPN are not necessary. There is no need for USB sharing without a USB port.

5. D. One way to keep dust and debris out of your computer is to use an enclosure, which is basically an extra case. But if dust and debris do get inside your case, the best way to remove it is to use compressed air instead of vacuuming. Compressed air can be more easily directed and doesn't tend to produce ESD damage as a vacuum could. Simply blow the dust from inside the computer by using a stream of compressed air. However, make sure to do this outside so that you don't blow dust all over your work area or yourself, and place a pen or pencil in the fan so it won't spin while you're dusting it off. Denatured isopropyl alcohol is used to clean contacts because it dries quickly, and demineralized water would not be used inside the case, except perhaps in a liquid cooling system.

6. D. Third-party software that includes a screen-sharing feature would allow the technician to demonstrate a task using the user's own local desktop. File-sharing software facilitates the sharing of files, SSH (Secure Shell) is an encryption protocol and set of utilities for managing systems remotely, and browsing is not a type of screen-sharing.

7. B. Remote Desktop Protocol (RDP), Hypertext Transfer Protocol Secure (HTTPS), and File Transfer Protocol Secure (SFTP) provide confidentiality of network traffic, but SSH provides that and a suite of utilities that is commonly used by network administrators to remotely control and manage networks.

8. B. An end-user license agreement (EULA) is a contract between you and the entity providing the software. When you buy an application, you aren't actually buying the application. Instead, you're buying the right to use the application in a limited way as prescribed by the licensing agreement that comes with it. Don't like the terms? Too bad. No negotiation is allowed. If you don't accept the EULA, your only recourse is to return the software for a refund.

9. B. After the device or data has been preserved, someone needs to keep track of it before it's handed over to the proper authorities. The specific next step depends on your documented chain of custody policy. Depending on the situation, materials may be held in a safe, locked location at the office, or they may need to be turned over to local authorities. Have a documented procedure in place to follow, given a situation. Always document the findings, who has custody of the illegal materials, and if/when the custody is transferred to someone else.

10. D. One of the golden rules of customer service is, don't vent about customers on social media. You never know who will read it, and regardless, it's unprofessional to air dirty laundry. Depending on the situation, it may be advisable to discuss it with your manager or simply document it and move on with your day.

11. C. IT professionals often deal with confidential, private, or restricted information. Other users trust that IT professionals will treat the sensitive material as such and not spread information. Ignore the paychecks and focus on doing the job professionally.

12. B. Avoid distraction and/or interruptions when talking with customers. You need to make them feel that their problem is important and that it has your full attention. Distractions can include personal calls, texting, social media, talking to coworkers, and other personal interruptions. Taking notes and asking appropriate questions is part of good customer service.

13. D. Putting yourself at the same electrical potential is not as effective as using proper anti-ESD gear, but it makes up for that with its simplicity. Make sure the computer is turned off and unplugged. Then touch an exposed (but not hot or sharp!) metal part of the case. That will drain electrical charge from you. Better yet is if you can maintain constant contact with that metal part. That should keep you at the same electrical potential as the case.

14. A. Remote Desktop Protocol (RDP) lets you establish a connection to a remote client, showing the remote system's desktop. Secure Shell (SSH) lets administrators securely manage networks remotely, File Transfer Protocol Secure (SFTP) is for moving large files securely, and a virtual private network (VPN) uses encryption to create a private connection across a public network.

15. C. It is important for an IT technician to be culturally sensitive. Some people may have a language barrier that makes it difficult to explain their problem. (Think about how little computer language you learned in your high school language courses!) Others may have different habits or practices in their workplace. Be respectful of their world. In some cases, using the appropriate professional titles is a sign of respect and not using them is an insult.

16. A, D. To use the ESD strap, you attach one end to an earth ground (or more typically, the computer case) and wrap the other end around your wrist. This strap grounds your body and keeps it at a zero charge. Never wear an ESD strap if you're working inside a laser printer or inside a power supply. If you wear one while working on the inside of these components, you increase the chance of getting a lethal shock.

17. D. When batteries are thrown away and deposited into landfills, the heavy metals inside them will find their way into the ground. From there, they can pollute water sources and eventually find their way into the supply of drinking water. The best way to dispose of old batteries is to recycle them.

18. C. If you have your policy in place, then your incident response plan should be relatively scripted. Your first priority as the first responder is to identify the improper activity or content. Then you should always get someone else to verify the material or action so that it doesn't turn into a situation of your word against someone else's. Immediately report the situation through proper channels.

19. C. When dealing with a customer, always display professionalism. That means avoiding slang, jargon, and acronyms; not interrupting; and clarifying what the customer wants.

20. A. Static-shielding bags are important to have at your disposal when servicing electronic components because they protect the sensitive electronic devices from stray static charges. This is in contrast to the familiar pink antistatic bags, which only prohibit static buildup found in other plastic bags but do not shield from ESD. By design, the static charges collect on the outside of these silver or pink bags rather than on the electronic components. Unlike antistatic mats, antistatic bags do not "drain" the charges away, and they should never be used in place of an antistatic mat. Components should never be placed on an antistatic bag. While mats are designed to be stationary on a bench, bags are built for portability.

21. A. After the device or data has been properly secured and preserved, document everything that could be relevant to the situation. Many companies have standard documentation that is used in incident response to be sure that the responder captures important information and does not forget to ask critical questions or look for vital clues.

22. C. Set and meet—or exceed—expectations and be sure to communicate timelines and status with the customer. Customers want to know what's going on. In addition, offering different repair or replacement options will usually make the customer feel better because you are giving them an option in choosing a solution.

23. B. When dealing with customers, it's important to maintain a positive attitude and project confidence. Remember that if they have called you, they're already having a bad day, and they are counting on you to resolve the problem.

24. B. The Payment Card Industry Data Security Standard (PCI DSS) applies to any organization that handles credit card data or processes or stores payment transactions from bank cards. PII is personally identifiable information, VPN stands for virtual private network, and Secure Shell (SSH) is an encryption protocol.

25. C. LCDs do not use capacitors. Instead, they require an inverter, which changes direct current to alternating current and provides the high-voltage, high-frequency energy needed to power the backlight. The inverter is a small circuit board installed behind the LCD panel. Inverters store energy even when their power source is cut off, so they have the potential to discharge that energy if you mess with them. The screen itself does not have an electrical charge.

26. D. The toner itself is a carcinogen, and the cartridges can contain heavy metals that are bad for the environment. PC recycling centers will take old toner cartridges and properly dispose of them. Most toner cartridge manufacturers will also take them back for recycling.

27. B. Although it is possible to open a power supply to work on it, doing so is not recommended. Power supplies contain several capacitors that can hold lethal charges long after they have been unplugged! It is extremely dangerous to open the case of a power supply. Besides, power supplies are relatively inexpensive. It would probably cost less to replace one than to try to fix it, and this approach would be much safer. Only open a power supply if you have been specifically trained how to safely repair them.

28. B. Creating a policy is the most important part of dealing with prohibited content or actions. Without a policy in place that specifically defines what is and what isn't allowed and what actions will be taken when a violation of the policy occurs, you don't really have a leg to stand on when a situation happens. What is in the policy depends on the company for which you work. A good policy will also contain the action steps to be taken if prohibited content or activity is spotted. Those actions may involve disciplinary action, termination of employment, or contacting of law enforcement.

29. A, C. Both power failures and under-voltage events can damage computers and other electronic devices. Under-voltage events can sometimes go unnoticed, or your display may flicker and lights dim.

30. D. When talking with customers it's important to remember that they don't have the training that you do, so they won't understand all the terminology that technicians use. Describe the situation in terms that the user will understand, but don't be condescending. Never use jargon, acronyms, or slang terms, even if they are commonly used with your peers. It takes practice to put complex concepts in simple terms, but your customers will appreciate it. More tech-savvy customers will usually let you know that they understand and you can use more advanced terms with them as needed.

31. A, B. Open source software is free, not only is the application free, but the source code (code used by programmers) is also shared to encourage others to contribute to the future development and improvement of the application. Open source software can't be sold, although it can be bundled with commercial products that are sold. Contrast open source with commercial licenses, where you pay per user and can't modify the program except as allowed by the developer.

32. D. Devices that attempt to keep power surges at bay are called surge suppressors. They often look like a power strip, so it's easy to mistake one for the other, but suppressors are more expensive. They have a fuse inside them that is designed to blow if it receives too much current and not to transfer the current to the devices plugged into it. Surge protectors may also have receptacles for RJ-45 (Ethernet), coaxial, and USB or other connectors.

33. A, B. Active listening means paying attention to your customers (eye contact is good) and taking notes. Allow them to complete their statements and avoid interrupting them. Don't do something else like texting or walking away while they are talking to you. People like to know that they are being heard and understood, and as simple an act as it is, this can make all the difference in making them feel at ease with your work.

34. C. Compressed air won't likely blow the grime away. Electronic connectors of computer equipment should never touch water. Instead, use a lint-free swab moistened in distilled, denatured isopropyl alcohol (also known as electronics or contact cleaner and found in electronics stores) to clean contacts. You may have heard people say to use an eraser, but that could remove some of the soft gold from the contacts and damage the component, so don't use an eraser.

35. A. The best device for power protection is called an uninterruptible power supply (UPS), also known as a battery backup. These devices can be as small as a brick or as large as an entire server rack. Inside the UPS is one or more batteries and fuses. Much like a surge suppressor, a UPS is designed to protect everything that's plugged into it from power surges. They are also designed to protect against under-voltage events and even complete power failures. Energy is stored in the batteries, and if the power fails, the batteries can power the computer for a period of time so that the administrator can then safely power it down. Voltage regulators are an electronic component found on some circuit boards.

36. C. Whenever working inside the case, always off turn the power and unplug the unit from the power source. The only exception to this rule is when troubleshooting a power issue and you need to leave the computer on to figure out the problem.

37. A, C. The muscles in the lower back aren't nearly as strong as those in the legs or other parts of the body. Whenever lifting, you want to reduce the strain on those lower-back muscles as much as possible. To do that, bend at the knees and lift with your legs. Also observe weight limitations and partner-lift if needed. Better yet, partner-lift and use a cart to move items. Also, keep objects close to your body and at waist level to minimize stress on your body.

38. C. To use the ESD (electrostatic discharge) strap, you attach one end to an earth ground (typically, the computer case) and wrap the other end around your wrist. Some ESD mats have a connector for the ESD strap. This strap grounds your body and keeps it at a zero charge, which helps prevent you from accidentally damaging components with a jolt of static electricity.

39. A, C. Shareware generally does not require licensing, and payment may be handled via the honor system. But shareware is generally not a good choice for a corporate environment where you depend on the software. Some shareware will also specify that it is only free if used for personal use, but in a corporate environment, a fee must be paid. A single-user license is good for only one user. You could buy a lot of single-user licenses, but that is generally more expensive than buying a concurrent or corporate license. Corporate and concurrent licenses are designed for large groups of users.

40. C. If you can't find a way to reuse the equipment, be sure to dispose of it in compliance with government regulations. Most computers contain small amounts of hazardous substances, so they should be recycled by professionals who know how to deal with those dangers. Many municipalities, states, and countries have regulations in place specifying appropriate measures to enforce their proper disposal. Search the Internet for certified recycling programs near you.

41. A. You should always set expectations with the customer and then meet or exceed them. After resolving a customer's issue, follow up with them to ensure that they are satisfied with the services you provided. The follow-up shows professionalism and may earn you future business.

42. A. In difficult situations, it can be challenging to keep a level head. It's important to do so and avoid arguing and becoming defensive. Remember that if a client had to call you, they're likely already having a bad day and may be frustrated. Sometimes they will take their frustration out on you. Keep a level head and work to resolve the problem.

43. A. If you have your policy in place, then your incident response plan should be relatively scripted. Your first priority as the first responder is to identify the improper activity or content. Then you should always get someone else to verify the material or action so that it doesn't turn into a situation of your word against someone else's, then immediately report the situation through proper channels.

44. D. When humidity gets to be very low, around 20 percent or lower, the risk of electrostatic discharge (ESD) increases. Remember that computer components can be damaged with very little voltage, even less than the shock you feel when you touch a metal doorknob after walking across a carpet. Always use ESD protection to prevent damage to components.

45. D. If you have your policy in place, then your incident response plan should be relatively scripted. After identifying illegal content, you need to preserve that content. The method of preserving the data depends on exactly what format that data is in. For example, if the data is held in RAM, you can't turn the computer off. If it is files on the hard drive, you could turn the PC off and remove the hard drive. In any case, the data or device should immediately be removed from the possession of the offending party and preserved. This will ensure that the data doesn't mysteriously disappear before the proper parties are notified.

46. D. Personally identifiable information (PII) is anything that can be used to identify an individual person on its own or in context with other information. This includes someone's full name, address, other contact information; the names of family members; and other details that people would consider private. PII should always be kept confidential and secure. Government-issued information are data such as Social Security numbers, license numbers, passport data, and other government identifications. Be sure that this information is properly secured and can be accessed only by authorized personnel. There are rules and regulations for how this data can be stored, accessed, and used. This is known as regulated data.

47. B, D. Freeware is an easy choice, because it's free. Open source software is often also free, and you can modify the code free of charge as well (if you have the skills to do so). Some shareware is free, but it depends on the program. Single-user and corporate licenses generally cost money. The downside of freeware or open source software is that there might not be sufficient support for it if you run into any difficulties.

48. B, C. It is possible to damage a device by simply laying it on a benchtop. For this reason, you should have an ESD (electrostatic discharge) mat in addition to an ESD strap. This mat drains excess charge away from any item coming into contact with it. ESD mats are also sold as mouse/keyboard pads to prevent ESD charges from interfering with the operation of the computer. Many ESD wrist straps can be connected to the mat, thus causing the technician and any equipment in contact with the mat to be at the same electrical potential and eliminating ESD. Magnetic screwdrivers are not a good idea because they could damage a computer chip if they inadvertently come into contact with it. A dehumidifier removes excess moisture from the air. The correct air moisture content for working on computer equipment is about 50 percent. In cold climates, you're more likely to need a humidifier, to add moisture to air because too little moisture creates more static electricity. Too much moisture can cause components to corrode.

49. A. When compressed air is used, particles of dirt and debris can become airborne, and they can be inhaled or get into your eyes. Always wear proper safety gear, such as safety goggles and an air filtration mask.

50. B. A person's medical records and health information is classified as protected health information (PHI) (listed as Healthcare data on the CompTIA A+ objectives) and must be protected according to regulatory requirements such as HIPAA. A driver's license number and place of employment may be considered personally identifiable information (PII).

51. A. A safety data sheet (SDS) is required for any chemicals that are sold and include information such as the physical product data (boiling point, melting point, flash point, and so forth), potential health risks, storage and disposal recommendations, and spill/leak procedures. With this information, technicians and emergency personnel know how to handle the product as well as respond in the event of an emergency. The term material safety data sheet (MSDS) was replaced with the term safety data sheet in 2015, but you may still see it on the CompTIA A+ exam as MSDS.

52. B, C. Computers generally tolerate temperature and humidity levels about the same as humans do, except electronic devices do like it a bit colder. The general rule of thumb is room temperature or cooler, average humidity, and good ventilation.

53. D. The first option should be a few, quick blasts of compressed air, to immediately blow out the crumbs and debris. If that first option does not work, then the demineralized water should clean anything spilled on a keyboard. Bear in mind that when you use demineralized water, it will then take a few days to dry out the keyboard, and it shouldn't be used until it's dry.

54. C. Four major classes of fire extinguishers are available, one for each type of flammable substance: A for wood and paper fires, B for flammable liquids, C for electrical fires, and D (metal powder or NaCl [salt]) for flammable metals such as phosphorus and sodium. The most popular type of fire extinguisher today is the multipurpose, or ABC-rated, extinguisher. It contains a dry chemical powder that smothers the fire and cools it at the same time. For electrical fires (which may be related to a shorted-out wire in a power supply), make sure the fire extinguisher will work for Class C fires.

55. D. Be on time, or five minutes early. If you're going to be late, be sure to contact your customer. Not doing so indicates that you think their problem isn't important.

56. D. Providing good customer service involves proper communication and professionalism. Dismissing customer problems is not good. Neither is asking accusatory questions. Clarify the scope of the problem and ask clarifying questions to ensure that you understand what isn't working properly.

57. A, D. Both tablets and cell phones contain toxic chemicals such as beryllium, arsenic, and lead as well as rare-earth metals that could be recycled. None of what is inside most electronic devices belongs in a landfill. The other two options arguably belong elsewhere as well but are not considered toxic.

58. C. One unique challenge when cleaning printers is spilled toner. Getting it wet will make an inky mess. It sticks to everything and should not be blown into the air and inhaled; it's a carcinogen. Use an electronics vacuum that is designed specifically to pick up toner. A normal vacuum's filter isn't fine enough to catch all the particles, so the toner may be circulated into the air. Normal electronic vacuums may melt the toner instead of picking it up.

59. A. Extreme temperatures, either hot or cold, will negatively impact battery life. Batteries store best in cool (not frigid) temperatures. You may think that you should store it in a freezer, but that isn't good either because the freezer is likely a bit too cold, and they tend to have too much moisture. A closet is at room temperature, but someplace a few degrees cooler than room temperature and dry is the perfect storage area for a battery. You'll also want it to be about half charged when you store it, and bring it out periodically to charge and discharge, then store it again.

60. B. Enough electricity can hurt people, but tiny amounts can pose safety issues for computer components. One of the biggest concerns for components is electrostatic discharge (ESD). For the most part, ESD won't do serious damage to a person other than provide a little shock. But little amounts of ESD, smaller than you could see a spark or feel a zap, can cause serious damage to computer components, and that damage can manifest itself by causing computers or components to hang, reboot repeatedly, or fail completely.

61. A. PowerShell uses the `.ps1` filename extension. Linux-based Bash scripts use `.sh`, Python uses `.py`, and JavaScript uses `.js`.

62. B. Visual Basic scripts, which have a `.vbs` extension, are run on Windows platforms, so Notepad would work to edit them, but the Linux/Unix editors emacs and vi would not be used to view a VB script. CoffeeCup is for editing HTML files.

63. D. Batch scripting, which uses the filename extension `.bat`, is typically a series of command-line commands. Such a script file would run on the Windows systems' command line. The other filename extensions—`.js`, `.sh`, and `.py`—are JavaScript, shell, and Python, respectively. They each would require special additional software to be able to interpret the script.

64. A. JavaScript uses the `.js` filename extension. Java is a programming language. Juice is software to schedule downloading of podcasts, and Joomla is a web development platform. Of the four choices, only JavaScript is on the CompTIA A+ exam, so focus on that programming language's file extension.

65. D. Network topology diagrams will illustrate how the network connects and routes in and around the environment. Diagraming the network's hardware and paths show a topology of perimeters and boundaries.

66. B. Asset tagging hardware such as desktops and laptops can help an administrator quickly know the details of a particular asset. Inventory management is more easily accomplished with asset tagging.

67. B. Writing knowledge base articles to share with others, namely for those with similar tasks or duties in your environment, can be very helpful. Compared to the time and money spent on repeated discovery for a solution, writing knowledge base articles is a small investment. A change board is usually a group that approves of proposed changes as a part of project management. Change management policy describes the procedures to be followed if a major system change is needed. Brown bagging means bringing lunch from home.

68. D. Barcodes or quick response (QR) codes printed on physical tags that are then affixed to hardware to be managed are an inexpensive option to RFID asset tags.

69. C. Every documented change should include the reason or purpose of the change. The reason can explain the justification to those unfamiliar with the situation before the change. The scope of the change documents what is affected by the change. The approval, arguably the most important part, documents the management's support of the change. Documenting what applications are not affected by the change is an unnecessary step.

70. D. End-user acceptance isn't necessarily documented, but it means that the change is welcomed, agreed upon, and supported by end users. End-user acceptance is important to the success of any major change that affects how the end users do their job, and there are actions that can be taken to help ensure end-user acceptance such as including end users in the planning process and explaining in detail why a change that affects them needs to be made. The rollback plan documents the actions to take in the event the change must be stopped for some reason once the process has started. The plan for change documents detailed actions to take to implement the change as well as the purpose of the change, date and time of the change, the scope of the change, impact on the affected systems, and request forms and approvals. A risk analysis is performed to assess, and likely accept, any additional exposure caused by the change.

71. A. The greatest backup procedures in the world will not help if your backups are not reliable. Backups need to be tested on a regular basis to ensure that they can be restored if the need ever arises.

72. C. Depending on the disaster, the question of cloud storage versus local storage backups can significantly affect the success of recovery. For example, for a server hardware failure or a recent malware incident, local storage provides adequate security of backups. However, catastrophic collapse of the building would mean local storage is not accessible.

73. D. Inventory lists are a feature of asset management, not ticketing systems. On the initial call, a user would typically gather information about the user, such as their name and contact information, the device that has a problem, and a description of the problem.

74. B. Whenever you're planning a change to a business system, you need to have a plan in place to return to the old system if the planned change doesn't work out as thought. The plan to revert to the old system is known as a rollback plan. Sandbox testing is done before implementing changes to ensure that the changes will work. Request forms happen at the beginning of change management, and risk analysis examines whether to proceed with the change.

75. C. A full backup creates a copy of all files whether or not their archive bit is set. An incremental backup will back up files that have changed since the last backup was made. Incremental backups and full backups reset the archive bit. Differential backups will back up all changes since the last full or incremental backup was performed. Differential backups do not reset the archive bit.

76. B. When using full backups and differential backups to restore a system, you'll need the last one of each to recover all the data. Each differential backup is larger than the one before, because it includes the cumulative backup of all the changes that have happened since the last full backup. The backups are slower than incremental backups to create, but restoring them is easier because there are fewer datasets to restore.

77. A, D. Incremental backups are created faster over time than differential backups. If each weekday the same number of files were changed, an incremental backup on Wednesday would only take one-third as long as a differential backup, because the differential backup would have Monday, Tuesday, and Wednesday's changes. The Wednesday incremental backup would only have Wednesday's changes. Differential backups are easier to restore because you would only restore the last full backup and the most recent differential backup. Incremental backups are less fault tolerant than differential because there are more possible points of failure in the form of a greater number of backups that would need to be restored to achieve the same result as a differential backup. If your procedure is to perform a full backup each Sunday, and daily backups each night, and you discover on Thursday morning that your system crashed, then if you needed to restore from incremental backups you would have four backups to restore (Sunday, Monday, Tuesday, Wednesday), whereas using differential backups would only require restoring two (Sunday and Wednesday).

78. A. Static sensitive components should be stored in (not on) antistatic bags. If possible, use the protective packaging that came with them. They should not be stored in plastic bags or on plastic shelves because most plastics gather static. The exception would be shelves that are specifically made to be static free. Expansion cards should never be stacked on top of each other because doing so could damage or dislodge chips on the card. If you must store several of them, put each in its own box or a divided box made for that purpose. Antistatic bags are made to keep the static on the outside of the bag, like a mini Faraday cage, so placing sensitive components on an antistatic bag is like asking for trouble.

79. C. If you were moving a laser printer more than from one room to another, you would certainly want to check the manufacturer's recommendations for moving the equipment, but whenever you are moving a laser printer, it's important to remove the toner cartridges first. The cartridge may get jostled during the move and toner spilled inside the machine. That would create a hazardous situation for both you and the machine. Laser printers don't have printheads. The stapler assembly should be fine but again, check the manufacturer's documentation. Removing the paper is likely not necessary.

80. B, C. Computers will shut down when the CPU has exceeded an acceptable heat level. Components may start acting strangely as well if they are too warm. Not only is the ambient temperature too warm, but by wrapping it in plastic the computer can't get the necessary airflow to keep the components from overheating. They may need to move this computer to a cooled, protective enclosure.

81. A, C. When retiring equipment, there should be a checklist of things to do. First and foremost, ensure that there is no confidential data on the equipment, then remove it from the asset management inventory list. You could then donate or recycle it. A sandbox is a testing area that is set up like your systems but separate from them and used when testing a new configuration, software, or process. You would not install the new software update on this machine. If anything, this machine would be restored to the factory default.

82. A, D. If you're in a lead role where you meet with clients in larger businesses, you will likely want to dress in business formal attire, which would include matching suit coat and pants or skirt and a tie if appropriate. Business casual attire for many techs is the familiar khaki pants and polo shirt, but it's not what you would wear to impress a potential new client.

83. A, C. You need to provide the customer with the proper documentation according to your company, but usually this will include a description of the problem when and how long you were there and a "big picture" description of what was done. You also need to call them a few days later to ensure that they are still happy with the service they received. You would not tell them to call you directly and you'll charge less, or you probably wouldn't have a job for long. You also would not leave without talking to the customer. Ideally, have them test the changes that you made to ensure things are working well for them.

84. A. As a technician you'll probably come into contact with all sorts of confidential or privileged information, whether it is the business files on someone's computer or their personal photographs and documents. You do your best to mind your own business, but sometimes you're going to see things. Unless it's illegal or you're bound by company policy to report it, ignore it. Forget that you saw it and don't talk to anyone about it. You're there to do a job. That's all.

85. C. A full backup that is created from a prior full backup and one or more incremental backups is known as a synthetic backup. The advantages are that it takes much less time to create a backup because you only need to perform incremental backups, and if you must restore from a backup, it takes less time because you can always have a full backup. Incremental only backs up what has changed since the last incremental or full backup, and differential backs up whatever has changed since the last full backup. Differential backups don't reset the archive bit, but full backups and incremental backups do.

86. B. In an ideal world, it would be great to test the backup for integrity after every backup, but that would be prohibitive in terms of the time it would take. They should be tested often, at least once a month but more often if you are able, and certainly after something significant has changed in a system. You would also want to ensure that you have a good backup before you make those big changes.

87. D. You would not want to wear business formal, which is a suit and dress shoes, if you're running wires. You also don't want to be so casual that you look unprofessional. Here business casual is more appropriate and exactly what that means will depend on the policies of your company. For many technicians it's nice jeans or casual pants and a button-up shirt or a sweater, not a dress shirt, but also not a t-shirt or hoodie. Many companies will have attire with their logo that they prefer you wear. Sometimes IT techs get dirty.

88. A. In the United States, OSHA (Occupational Safety and Health Administration) oversees workplace safety and makes rules that companies must abide by, including training workers on working safely. If the company fails to make changes after an OSHA inspection, OSHA has the option to close them down. The NEC (National Electrical Code) is a document that was developed by the National Fire Protection Association (NFPA) for wiring and building buildings that are safe. Their rules have been adopted by all 50 states of the United States as a part of their building code. FEMA is the Federal Emergency Management Agency, which helps in the event of natural disasters, and the IRS (Internal Revenue Service) is responsible for collecting income taxes.

89. D. The 3-2-1 backup rule states that you need three copies of data, on two different media and one of them is off-site. Grandfather-father-son is a rotation scheme for backup media. The rule of 78 is an accounting rule used to calculate interest payments, and there is no common rule called the on-site/off-site backup rule.

90. C. A virtual network computer (VNC) allows a user to manipulate a computer remotely. Some VNC systems allow a smartphone to control a computer remotely, some allow for file transfer, but not all. Windows Remote Desktop, which uses the Remote Desktop Protocol (RDP), is a type of VNC that is part of the Windows operating system. Remote monitoring and management (RMM) is a category of software used by managed service providers to remotely manage, configure, and control the resources of many different networks. A virtual private network (VPN) allows a user to be away from their office, such as a remote worker or traveling salesperson, and connect to the company server or other resources with their laptop or other mobile computer as if they were in the company offices. Microsoft Remote Assistance (MRSA) could not be used as it would require someone at the home computer to send the invitation.

91. D. Until or unless they invite you to wear casual attire, you should dress in business formal attire. Even though they are a casual company, you still need to project a professional image, especially for a first meeting.

92. B. Regulatory compliance means that you're following all the laws that pertain to your company and its locations. These can be local, state or provincial, federal, or even international laws. Failure to be in compliance with government regulations can result in fines, company closure, or even jail time. Disobedience would be the opposite of compliance. Information technology governance means that the structures, processes, and actions of a company's IT department are in line with the overall goals and objectives of the company. Information security is ensuring the confidentiality, integrity, and availability (CIA) of an organization's information.

93. A. Grandfather-father-son is a rotation scheme for backup media. For a typical small business, the "son" backups would be labeled Monday, Tuesday, Wednesday, and Thursday. Seven days later they are overwritten. Each Friday a "father" backup is made, so there would always be four or five father backups, which would be overwritten a month later. The grandfather backups are made only once a month, so they won't be overwritten for a year. The 3-2-1 backup rule states that you need three copies of data, on two different media and one of them off-site. Moore's law says that technology doubles every two years, and there is no common rule called the on-site/off-site backup rule.

94. B. This is a data retention requirement, and only one of many that may affect an IT department and the data that they are responsible for. Data retention requirements are a part of regulated data. IT governance has to do with keeping the objectives of the IT department in alignment with the goals and objectives of the organization as a whole. GFS (grandfather-father-son) is a popular backup media rotation scheme, and a license agreement is a contract between you and the software company that is granting you a license to use their software.

95. A. Remote monitoring and management (RMM) is a category of software used by managed service providers to remotely manage, configure, and control the resources of many different IT networks. A virtual private network (VPN) allows a user to be away from their office, such as a remote worker or traveling salesperson, and connect to the company server or other resources with their laptop or other mobile computer as if they were in the company offices. A virtual network computer (VNC) allows a user to manipulate a computer remotely. Some VNC systems allow a smartphone to control a computer remotely, and Remote Desktop, which uses Remote Desktop Protocol (RDP), is a type of VNC that is part of the Windows operating system.

96. D. Personal-use software is sometimes distributed free to individuals in the hope that they will like it so much they will be willing to pay for premium features or purchase corporate licenses for their place of business. Some of these licenses allow users to make and distribute free copies of the software to their friends so that they can try it too. Most will not allow them to bring it into their company without paying for it, nor are they allowed to sell it. Exactly what you can do with a software that is licensed to you as an individual is covered in the end-user license agreement (EULA) that you agreed to when installing or downloading the software.

97. B. Digital rights management (DRM) means using technology to protect the copyrighted material created by artists and others from being stolen. Musicians, programmers, movie makers, authors, and so on put sometimes immeasurable hours and great expense into creating their work. To keep others from stealing it, they can use technology to control the number of people who can access content, or sharing, printing, saving, and so on. Some DRM software can limit access to information based on IP address, or even cause watermarks to appear when someone tries to print a document or image that they don't have the right to print.

98. A, C. Occasionally scripts have unintended results when they are run. They can include, but are not limited to, unintentionally introducing malware, inadvertently changing system settings, or causing browser or system crashes because they are using too many resources. These occasional mistakes are far outweighed by their uses, such as remotely installing applications, installing updates, automating backups, and restarting machines, just to name a few.

99. A. Microsoft Remote Assistance (MSRA) allows a user to invite someone to help them or lets them offer to help someone else. Both users can see and control the screen. This is a great way to show someone how to perform a task and have them try it while you are watching. Remote Desktop, which uses Remote Desktop Protocol (RDP), is used to control a remote computer as if you were sitting at it. Secure Shell (SSH) is both a protocol and suite of tools for an administrator for secure, remote management of networked resources. Remote monitoring and management (RMM) is a category of software used by managed service providers to remotely manage, configure, and control the resources of many different networks.

100. B. A virtual private network (VPN) allows a user to be away from their office, such as a remote worker or traveling salesperson, and connect to the company server or other resources with their laptop or other mobile computer as if they were in the company offices. This is accomplished using tunneling protocols. It differs from a virtual network computer (VNC) in that the VNC allows a user to manipulate a computer remotely. Some VNC systems allow a smartphone to control a computer remotely. Remote monitoring and management (RMM) is a category of software used by managed service providers to remotely manage, configure, and control the resources of many different it networks, and Remote Desktop, which uses the Remote Desktop Protocol (RDP), is a type of VNC that is part of the Windows operating system.

101. C. If you fail to comply with government regulations, there are usually severe consequences. Not only fines and fees, business shutdown, or possible jail time, but for example, if a failure to comply with rules meant that someone's health data was hacked, the cost could be measured in lives lost.

102. B. While it is important to maintain records of your software licenses, the way that data set is stored, moved, and used is not regulated. Credit card transactions, healthcare data, and personally identifiable information (PII) all have industry and/or governmental rules about what happens to that data. Data is worth far more than the hardware that it resides on, so ensuring the confidentiality, integrity, and accessibility (CIA) of that information is a primary concern of any IT department.

103. D. Videoconferencing software has been around for a long time. It enables people who might be on the other side of the world to take part in the same meeting, seeing the other attendees and participating in discussions. Some types of videoconferencing software allow for screen sharing as well. Screen-sharing software enables you to show others a window or your entire desktop or a section of it (such as an application window). File transfer software enables secure and quick transfer of large files from one system to another, remote system. Desktop management software is any software that allows you to manage multiple desktops remotely, often on different platforms.

104. A. A filename with an `.sh` extension indicates that this is a script for Bash, which stands for Bourne-Again Shell. The other file extensions —`.py`, `.vbs`, and `.ps1`— are used in Python, Visual Basic, and PowerShell, respectively.

105. C. Tracking valid licenses is a part of asset management, not a ticketing system. It is very important that the problem description, progress notes, and resolution be written in clear, concise language so that anyone who reads them in the future will be able to understand what transpired.

106. B. A request form is used to initiate the change management process. Risk analysis and a report of the affected systems and the impact on them is part of the document that is presented to the change board for their approval before the change is implemented.

107. A. End-user acceptance is a desirable result of meeting with and including end users in the decision-making process of change management. It is a desired result, not necessarily a part of the documentation. The responsible staff member needs to be listed in the documentation, and there will usually be a champion for the project, meaning someone in a position of power who supports the change who may or may not be listed as a responsible party.

A careful analysis of the affected systems and the impact the change will have on them needs to be done and included. The change document needs to include the scope of the change, which is an explanation of what will and will not be changed and how far-reaching the project is.

108. C. Batch files, Visual Basic, and PowerShell are all examples of scripting programs. They have many uses and are used daily by network administrators to facilitate management of their networks. Remote monitoring and management (RMM) is a type of remote access technology. Screen-sharing software lets the user show their screen to people who are working with them remotely.

109. D. Every ticket in a help desk ticketing system should include the category of the problem, severity of the problem, and any escalation levels that were used. The procurement life cycle is a part of asset management.

110. B. The aim of change management is to control change in such a way that it continues to move the organization forward with as little disruption as possible to the employees and IT processes of the organization—to effect change without causing any adverse results or negative effects to the company's bottom line. Asset management is maintaining documentation on the IT assets of a company. Ticketing systems allow for tracking of support issues and results, and knowledge bases and articles provide a wealth of information for resolving IT problems that have been previously encountered.

111. C. A database system, assigned users, and warranty and licensing, are all a part of asset management records. The procurement life cycle is also a part of asset management, and it starts with identifying a business need for what is being purchased. The exact steps may vary by company and be different for government entities, but they often include vendor analysis, request for information, and request for quote before a decision is made regarding what vendor to use and what specific products to purchase.

112. C. A part of every project should be the risk analysis with an identified risk level for each possible negative (or positive) event that may affect the project. The risk is assigned a score, the risk level, and response plans are identified so that in the event that the risk is realized, there is a clear plan of action to handle it. The scope of the change identifies what it will and will not affect. A change board approval is the last step before a kickoff meeting to initiate the change. Sandbox testing is setting up a system that mimics the production system in order to try the change in a safe environment before implementing it.

113. B, C. It's easiest to onboard and offboard employees if you have a checklist to follow. The checklists can include items such as adding the employee to security groups based on their department or job title and ensuring that their user account is disabled when they leave. An incident report should be filed whenever an IT employee observes a breach of protocol regarding acceptable use or when someone is injured. Splash screens are a way to ensure nonrepudiation of agreement to company policies each time a user logs onto a company computer system.

114. A. The security considerations of each access method seem to be overlooked for this server. A server hosting confidential data, located in an open, shared environment, is not best practice.

115. D. Procedures for custom installation of software packages should be spelled out in a standard operating procedures document. This should also be a part of an acceptable use policy (AUP). The checklists for new employees and terminated employees will help to ensure that all necessary steps take place, and a network diagram identifies the boundaries and equipment used in a network.

116. C. Valid licenses are those that are not void for any reason, such as using a personal license for corporate use, having more users than are allowed by the license, or using a software with a license that has expired. Software licensing can be so complicated that there are companies who make their living ensuring that other companies are in compliance with licensing agreements. Even open source licenses that are used by a company should be documented, and a periodic accounting of all software on all computers should be made to ensure that the company is in compliance with licensing laws and agreements. Inventorying the software used by your company is just as important as keeping an inventory of the hardware.

117. D. One of the great features of open source software is that you are allowed to modify the software code to meet your needs. The other three options for this question—using software licensed for personal use in a corporate setting, using more copies or having more users than the license allows, and using software whose license has expired—are all invalid uses of software and may subject you or your company to fines or even jail time. It's very important to keep an inventory of your software and valid, nonexpired licenses and where they are being used. You should do at least an annual accounting of all the software being used on all the computers in your organization.

Chapter 10: Practice Exam 1 (220-1101)

1. B, D. SSDs have many advantages over HDDs, including producing less heat and being less susceptible to damage from shock or overheating. However, they are more expensive per byte.

2. B. There are many benefits to using a touch pen (stylus) with your touchscreen computer. For artists especially, they can be more precise in their work than is possible with fingers. They're more sanitary than fingers and don't leave behind the oils that your skin would on the screen. They're easier to create handwritten notes than using your finger is. The only downside is that they are not all compatible with every touch screen, so you need to know what kind of touchscreen you have to ensure that your touch pen is compatible with it. Most touchscreens are capacitive, which means the touch pen needs to be constructed so that it will interrupt an electrostatic field. Resistive screens only register pressure. Their advantage is that almost any material can be used to make a touch pen and resistive screens are better for uses such as making lines darker in a drawing program. There are also Bluetooth touch pens, which use a wireless signal to communicate contact with the screen.

3. A. Fluorescent lighting, and liquid crystal display (LCD) backlights in particular, require fairly high-voltage, high-frequency energy. The component that provides the right kind of energy is the inverter. The inverter is a small circuit board installed behind the LCD panel that takes DC current and inverts it to AC for the backlight. An inverter is not needed in a display that uses LED backlighting.

4. C. The CompTIA A+ exam objectives list the steps for connecting Bluetooth devices as follows:

   1. Enable Bluetooth.
   2. Enable pairing.
   3. Find a device for pairing.
   4. Enter the appropriate PIN code.
   5. Test connectivity.

5. D. Location services on your device may use the Global Positioning System (GPS), which relies on satellites, Bluetooth, Wi-Fi, or cellular location services to determine your approximate location. Location services can be enabled, disabled, or conditionally enabled for different apps on your phone that need the service to function properly. Airplane mode turns off all network connectivity.

6. A, D. Protocols are either connection-oriented, meaning they will guarantee delivery, or connectionless, meaning they will not guarantee delivery. Connectionless protocols are used for activities such as streaming, where a missed packet here and there is less important than continuing to send the information. Connection-oriented protocols are used when it is important that each packet arrive. Some of the connection-oriented protocols are TCP, HTTPS, and SSH, whereas UDP, DHCP, and TFTP are examples of connectionless protocols.

7. A. File Transfer Protocol (FTP) uses ports 20 and 21. Port 22 is used by Secure Shell (SSH), port 23 is/was used by Telnet, and port 25 is used by Simple Mail Transfer Protocol (SMTP).

8. B, D. A unified threat management (UTM) appliance is a single device on your network that provides multiple security functions. It is usually placed between the outside world and the LAN, so it can function as a gateway as well as a security appliance. A proxy server can be a very powerful force for good on your network. Proxy servers can be a firewall blocking traffic based on port number. They can also inspect packets for objectionable or malicious content (malware). They can even work as a cache for frequently visited websites, and since all traffic goes through the proxy server, into and out of your network, they are the default gateway. A spam gateway is software that is used for filtering spam out of email. A load balancer appliance is used in an environment where there are multiple servers to distribute the workload across those servers instead of it all going to one.

9. D. The FF00::/8 range in IPv6 is for multicasts. Remember that IPv6 does not use broadcasts. The closest IPv6 gets is the use of multicast addresses. ::1 is the loopback address for IPv6. IP addresses that begin with 2001 are in the global unicast range, meaning that they are routable on the Internet, and the first 64 bits identify the network. Any number that starts with FE80 is nonroutable and is called a link-local address.

10. C. A personal area network (PAN) is a small-scale network designed around one person within a limited boundary area. The term generally refers to networks that use Bluetooth technology. A local area network (LAN) connects together devices in a small area such as a

house or business or floor of an office building. A wide area network (WAN) covers a very large geographic area, traversing many roads or areas not owned by the entity, and may use leased lines. The Internet is a worldwide WAN, but a WAN can also connect a single company with offices in New York, Chicago, and DC, for example. A metropolitan area network (MAN) is between a WAN and a LAN. It connects devices in a smaller geographic area such as a city or community.

11. A. A wireless locator or a Wi-Fi analyzer can be either a handheld hardware device or specialized software that is installed on a laptop or smartphone, and its purpose is to detect and analyze Wi-Fi signals. A loopback plug is used to test a network interface card (NIC). A toner probe (or tone generator and probe) is used to find a wire out of a bunch of wires, or figure out where the wire runs. A multimeter has many uses, among them testing for continuity, checking power supplies, and checking wall outlets.

12. C. The image shown is a high-definition multimedia interface (HDMI) cable. HDMI carries both audio and video signals in a digital format. A DisplayPort connector is angled on one side, not both. DisplayPort connectors are intended for video only but can also carry audio signals. They are digital connections. A DVI connector is rectangular with 24 pins on the left side in eight rows of three, and four pins on the right, arranged in a square. A digital video interface (DVI) is by definition digital, but there are DVI-A connectors that are analog, and DVI-I that are both, whereas DIV-D are strictly digital. The number and arrangement of pins changes depending on which type of DVI connector is being used. A VGA connector has a total of 15 pins arranged in three rows. VGA is only video, and it transmits an analog signal.

13. A, C. There are several reasons that paper might jam in a laser printer; if you buy the least expensive paper and it's the wrong weight or coating for the printer, debris in the paper path such as dust and pieces of paper, paper with wrinkles or bent corners, too much humidity causing sheets to stick together, and worn paper feed rollers. Ink cartridges are used in inkjet printers, not laser printers, and printheads are found in impact and thermal printers, not laser printers.

14. B. The best option to try first is changing the channel that the wireless access point (WAP) uses to connect. The intermittent connections could be caused by interference with the neighboring Wi-Fi. Turning up the power on your WAP would only make the crossover greater between your Wi-Fi and the neighbor's Wi-Fi. Adding another WAP might help if the problem was too many users, but with only four users in that area, it's not that. You could check the cable from the WAP to the router if changing the channel doesn't resolve the issue.

15. B. An RJ45 connector is used to terminate Ethernet cables used in local area networks (LANs). It has eight wires. An RJ11 connector is more narrow than an RJ45 because it only has four wires. RJ11 is used for landline telephones. An F type connector is used for cable television, satellite television, and cable modems. It has a twist on connector with a solid pin in the middle and is used with coaxial cables. A straight tip (ST) connector has a bayonet-type plug and socket. It is used with fiber-optic cable, and if bidirectional signals are needed, two cables and two connectors are needed.

16. A. DDR3 DIMM's have 240 pins, DDR4 and DDR5 both have 288 pins, and SODIMM is not a type of desktop RAM; it is used in laptops.

17. A. L1 cache is generally the smallest and fastest cache. Therefore, it's reasonable to expect that the computer will have less L1 cache than L2.

18. D. If the device does not produce sound, first make sure that it's not set to silent operation. Most mobile devices will have a switch on the side that sets them to silent or vibrate mode, which will mute the device and keep it from making noises. Also check settings for volume as well as possible redirection of sound, such as an active Bluetooth pairing. If the speakers have failed on a mobile device, it's time for a new device.

19. A, D. A groove or scratch in the EP drum can cause the problem of vertical black lines running down all or part of the page. Because a scratch is lower than the surface, it doesn't receive as much (if any) of a charge as the other areas. The result is that toner sticks to it as though it were discharged. The groove may go around the circumference of the drum, so the line may go all the way down the page. Another possible cause of vertical black lines is a dirty charging corona wire. A dirty charging corona wire prevents a sufficient charge from being placed on the EP drum. Because the charge on the EP drum is almost zero, toner sticks to the areas that correspond to the dirty areas on the charging corona.

20. C. Some motherboards support accessing more than one RAM module at a time. When that is the case, we say that the motherboard has multiple channels. Typically you will purchase identical RAM modules in quantities that match the number of channels there are. In this case, the documentation says to purchase RAM in identical sets of four, so we can assume it is a quad-channel motherboard.

21. B. 802.11ac is in the 5 GHz band, and can be 20, 40, or 80 MHz wide. With the 80 MHz channel width, there are effectively two channels, channel 36-48 and channel 149-161. Since you have three access points, you should use the 40 MHz channel width, which provides four possible channels: 36-40, 44-48, 149-153, and 157-161. The 20 MHz channel width provides nine channels, but you don't need that many, and the narrower channel width would decrease the performance per client. The 20 MHz channels are 36, 40, 44, 48, 149, 153, 157, 161, and 165.

22. A. Memory problems can cause system lockups, unexpected shutdowns or reboots, or errors such as blue or black screen of death (BSOD) in Windows or the rotating pinwheel in macOS. CPUs problems can also cause intermittent rebooting.

23. C. When troubleshooting, always start with the simple things first. It would not be the first time that a display had been inadvertently turned off. If that doesn't resolve it, check the cabling to ensure that nothing is loose, and check any settings on the display to ensure that the brightness isn't turned all the way down and that the display is using the correct input if it has more than one.

24. D. Displays may have their own internal power supply, and they all have internal circuitry, which means they can overheat. Make sure the air vents on the back of the display are dust- and debris-free. In this case, removing the display from the cabinet might help. If the problem persists, it's best to replace the display.

25. A, B. This user needs a virtualization workstation. To ensure that the operating systems have the most resources possible, optimize the processor (the more cores, the better) and memory.

26. A. The micro-ATX form factor is designed to work in standard ATX cases as well as its own, smaller cases.

27. C. Splitters generally have two effects on a coaxial cable: they degrade the signal and limit the distance the signal will travel. Use them judiciously.

28. C. If a computer is a few years old, the BIOS/UEFI may fail to retain your computer's settings, such as time and date and hard drive configuration. The BIOS/UEFI uses a small battery (much like a watch battery) on the motherboard to help it retain settings when the system power is off. If this battery fails, the BIOS/UEFI won't retain its settings. Simply replace the battery with the same type to solve the problem. There is usually a number printed on top of the battery so you know which one to get.

29. D. When the power-on self-test (POST) completes successfully, most motherboards will emit a single beep to let you know.

30. C. If you have a swollen battery, turn the device off immediately and make sure that it's not plugged into a charger. It may be possible to remove the battery, but swollen batteries are more prone to explosions than normal ones because the casing is already compromised, and most batteries in small devices are not user replaceable. The best course of action is to purchase a new device. Take the battery or device to a proper recycling center to dispose of it. Never just throw it in the trash because it can explode and harm sanitation workers as well as cause significant damage to the environment.

31. A, C. The beeps are a BIOS beep code produced because the power-on self-test (POST) routine has found an error. The manufacturer's website will likely tell you what the beep code means, and you can also troubleshoot using a USB POST card. Laptops do not have PCIe slots, and there is no specific tool called a BOOT tester.

32. C. The x8 card won't completely fill the x16 slot, but it will work at x8 speeds if up-plugging is supported by the motherboard. Otherwise, the specification requires up-plugged devices to operate at only the x1 rate.

33. D. The steps of the laser printing process as listed by the CompTIA A+ objectives are processing, charging, exposing, developing, transferring, fusing, and cleaning. In the processing step, data is sent to the printer, where a raster image processor converts it into a raster image (a group of dots) in preparation for printing.

34. B. Currently there are three form factors for SD cards; they are SD, MiniSD, and MicroSD. The cards also come in different capacities and filesystems as follows:

SD: 2 GB or less, FAT12 or FAT16

SDHC: 2 GB to 32 GB, FAT32

SDXC: 32 GB to 2 TB, exFAT

SDUC: 2 TB to 128 TB, exFAT

35. D. If a key on the laptop keyboard is stuck, you need to determine whether the contact is having problems or whether the key itself is stuck. If the key is not physically stuck but the laptop thinks it is, rebooting generally solves the problem.

36. B. The hotspot feature available on virtually all smartphones will enable you to connect other devices to the Internet via the cellular tower system. Typically you turn the hotspot feature on in the phone's settings. It will display a wireless password and allow you to connect wirelessly via Wi-Fi, Bluetooth, or connect physically via USB by connecting a cable between your laptop and the phone. The downside of doing this is that it eats up data quickly and could be expensive if you don't have unlimited data on your cellular plan.

37. A. Most laptop antennas connect to the main board and have wires that run up the sides of the display. Occasionally you may find one on the mainboard. Modern laptops typically don't have removable areas on the bottom/back like legacy laptops do. If a laptop's antenna quits working, one option is to purchase a Wi-Fi network card that plugs into an external port, such as a USB port.

38. C. Microsoft 365 is a cloud application suite that can be accessed from all of your devices and that will synchronize data across them. Among other things, it includes a calendar, contacts list, and mail services.

39. A. Most Internet service providers (ISPs) offer faster Internet access for a premium price, but they also put a cap on that service, and although they won't turn your service off, they may slow it down when you reach that cap.

40. C. To segregate a local area network (LAN) into two virtual LANs (VLANs), you would need a managed switch. Managed switches contain software that allows for port configuration, diagnostics, and monitoring situations such as port flapping. An unmanaged switch is simply a connectivity device. It can't be used to segregate ports into separate VLANs. A bridge is used to aggregate two or more networks into one. A hub is simply a connectivity device that is a single collision domain, whereas each port on a switch (managed or not) is its own collision domain. Hubs are seldom found on networks now, but they are often used to provide multiple ports for a single connection on a computer such as a USB port. Note that some routers have the ability to create a VLAN by using different IP address ranges, but more often a switch is used.

41. A. There are three types of addresses in IPv6: unicast, anycast, and multicast. A unicast address identifies a single node on the network. An anycast address refers to one that has been assigned to multiple nodes. A multicast address is one used by multiple hosts. An anycast message will go to one of the hosts on the list. A multicast message will go to all of the addresses on the list. IPv6 does not use broadcasts.

42. B. Private IP addresses are not routable on the Internet. The following are the IPv4 private address ranges and nonroutable numbers:

10.0.0.0 to 10.255.255.255/8 (Class A)
172.16.0.0/16 to 172.31.255.255/12 (Class B)
192.168.0.0 to 192.168.255.255/16 (Class C)
169.254.0.0 to 169.254.255.255 (APIPA)
127.0.0.1 (Loopback address)

43. C. The range of numbers that can be assigned by a Dynamic Host Configuration Protocol (DHCP) server to client computers is called the scope. Each of those numbers can be leased to the client for a period of time that you choose in the server settings. Reservations are numbers that you set aside for specific devices on the network whose IP address you don't want to change, like a server or IP printer. Automatic private IP addressing (APIPA) addresses are self-assigned by a computer that is set for dynamic IP addressing but that is unable to reach a DHCP server.

44. D. There are advantages and disadvantages to using the unlicensed frequency bands. Advantages include equipment is widely available and inexpensive, there are no fees for using the unlicensed spectrum, and its use is widespread, so information is available to help set one up. The disadvantages of using the unlicensed frequency spectrum are that it is congested (because it's free) and many places regulate how powerful the signal can be.

45. A. The port shown in the graphic is a USB-C port. It is identical in shape to a Lightning port. A Molex connector is a type of 4-pin power connector used for legacy hard drives. The subscriber connector (SC) and Lucent connector (LC) are used for fiber-optic connections. SC is about twice the size of the LC connector. Both have a square housing. The SC uses a small locking tab and the LC uses a locking latch to hold it in place.

46. D. Nonvolatile Memory Express (NVMe) is a driver and communication interface for Peripheral Component Interconnect Express (PCIe)-based solid-state drives (SSDs). It uses the PCIe bus but can be PCIe, M.2, and U.2 form factors. It transfers data much faster than the Advanced Host Controller Interface (AHCI) that was used for SATA. Both AHCI and NVMe SSDs can use the PCIe slot and M.2 connectors on motherboards, so it's important to know whether the M.2 connector supports AHCI, NVMe, or both. U.2 is only NVMe, but it isn't on the CompTIA A+ objectives. SATA will use the AHCI interface, even if it's connected to an M.2 slot on the motherboard. mSATA is a different form factor and can't be used in an M.2 slot.

47. C. Redundant Array of Independent (or Inexpensive) Disks (RAID) level 0 is disk striping and provides improved performance, but no fault tolerance. RAID 1, mirroring, provides fault tolerance but no improvement in performance. Both RAID 0 and RAID 1 require two drives. RAID 5 provides both fault tolerance and enhanced performance, and requires a minimum of three drives. RAID 10 (or 1+0) is a stripe of mirrored drives and provides both fault tolerance and enhanced performance, but requires a minimum of four drives.

48. B. Mini PCIe cards running in PCIe 1.0 x1 mode have a maximum speed of 2.5 Gbps, per lane. Each send and receive pair in PCIe is a lane, and PCIe can have 1, 2, 4, 8, 12, or 16 lanes. PCIe that uses one lane is noted as PCIe x1, two lanes are x2, and so on. Successive versions of PCIe have increased the speed per lane. PCIe 2.0 speed per lane is 5 Gbps, 3.x is 8 Gbps, and 4.x is 16 Gbps per lane. Those speeds are the bandwidth, the theoretical speeds, but the actual throughput will be slightly less.

49. C. If you have scorch marks on a component, say a video card or a motherboard, it could be that the specific component went bad. It could also be a sign of a problem with the power supply. If you see a component with a burn mark, it would be a good idea to test the power supply as well. Not all power supply problems will show up with a tester, so if you replace the component and a similar problem occurs, definitely replace the power supply as well as the damaged component.

50. A. Power supplies convert the volts of alternating current (VAC) from a wall outlet into volts of direct current (VDC) that computers can use. ATX12V power supplies provide the following voltages for the computer: +3.3 VDC, +5 VDC, +12 VDC, and –12 VDC. Older (ATX) power supplies that have a 20-pin main power connector also supply –5 VDC. Power supplies use shapes as keys so connectors can't be plugged in incorrectly. Many companies also have proprietary power supplies, meaning that you must replace their power supply with an identical one, because they don't match the standard.

51. B, C. A local printer can easily be shared with other people in your workgroup. Simply navigate to the Printer Properties, and choose the Sharing tab.

52. C. Platform as a service (PaaS) adds a layer to IaaS that includes software development tools such as runtime environments. Because of this, it can be helpful to software developers; the vendor manages the various hardware platforms. This frees up the software developers to focus on building their application and scaling it. The best PaaS solutions allow for the client to export its developed programs and run them in an environment other than where they were developed.

53. D. Hyper-V is built into Windows 10 and Windows 11, Pro, and higher editions, but it is a Windows feature that is disabled by default. To enable it, open Control Panel, select Programs and Features, and click Turn Windows features on or off. In the resulting dialog box, look for either Hyper-V (Windows 11) or Windows Hypervisor Platform (Windows 10) and select it by checking the boxnext to the option, and click OK. Azure Virtual Desktop is Microsoft's desktop in the cloud, VMware Fusion is virtual machine software for macOS, and VirtualBox is freeware from Oracle.

54. C. Rapid elasticity is one of the greatest benefits of cloud computing. You can add servers or network components as needed, on the fly. Shared resources are what makes rapid elasticity possible. Metered utilization means you pay for what you use, and file synchronization keeps your files up-to-date across different devices.

55. B. The creation of virtual machines (VMs) would alleviate the issue of space, power, and most of the hardware costs associated with maintaining bare-metal systems. VMs can provide much of the same services at a fraction of the cost. Control and management of the machines would not change.

56. A. Before you make any changes to a computer system, you need to consider corporate policies, procedures, and the impacts of your actions. When establishing a plan of action, you need to refer to the corporate policies first. Documenting findings, actions, and outcomes and verifying full system functionality are at the end of the methodology to resolve problems.

57. B. This configuration is a mirrored drive, RAID 1. If one drive fails, you have an exact duplicate on the other. It provides fault tolerance, but it doesn't protect your system against human error, so you still need backups! RAID 0 is disk striping, which enhances performance but doesn't help at all with fault tolerance. RAID 5 is disk striping with parity, so it offers fault tolerance and performance improvement. Data is written on two drives and the third is striped with recovery data. The recovery data is put on each drive in turn. If one drive fails, there is enough recovery data on the other two to rebuild it. RAID 10 is a striped set of mirrors, so like RAID 5 it offers fault tolerance and performance improvement but does so in a different way.

58. D. Nearly every hard drive is built with Self-Monitoring, Analysis, and Reporting Technology (S.M.A.R.T.) software installed on it, which monitors hard drive reliability and theoretically can warn you in the event of an imminent failure. The error ID makes no difference. If it is a S.M.A.R.T. error, it's the hard drive.

59. D. It is normal that a display may have a dead (black) pixel or two. This is not considered a big flaw; there is nothing you as a tech can do to fix it. If there are many dead pixels or you're just not happy with it, your only recourse it to return it for another one, if the vendor will accept it back.

60. A. This is a typical symptom of a loose cable. You need to check both ends of the cable and ensure that they are properly seated. Turning the display or the PC off and back on may also fix it, and checking that someone hasn't bumped or changed the display's settings is a quick fix too. If none of those work, the next step would be to try a known good display on the computer. If the problem still exists, it's not the display. It might be time to get a new graphics card.

61. C. If the phone will charge wirelessly, then it should be fine. If it's not covered by a warranty, the store isn't going to fix or replace it for free. Charging ports aren't normally considered a user-replaceable part. Components like charging ports can be replaced by a service center where there are people trained to work on smartphones. In any case, make sure that person is backing up the data on their phone to the cloud.

62. A. In troubleshooting, try the simple things first. If it wasn't grinding before, and it is since you installed a new toner cartridge, then the problem is most likely the toner cartridge. Take it out and put a new one in. If that doesn't fix it, then look for loose rollers or gears, and jammed paper. Thoroughly cleaning it would be the next step. Chances are that reloading the paper won't help.

63. B. When a Wi-Fi user is getting limited connectivity messages, it means that they are able to connect to the wireless access point but not the Internet. Since other people are getting this error message, we can assume it's the connection between the wireless access point they're connecting to and the wired network.

64. A, C. Biometrics are any device that uses a part of your body to identify you. It's common on modern laptops to have the availability of a face scanner or fingerprint reader to log into the computer. Other biometrics are retina scanners, palm scanners, and voice recognition.

65. B, C. It is likely that the ink on your print nozzles are dried out, or if there is something stuck in the printer, like a piece of sticky label, it could be blocking the ink from going where you want it on the paper. The first step would be to do the nozzle cleaning routine, and you may have to do it more than once. If the nozzle cleaning check printout looks good but you're still having the issue, look inside for something blocking the ink. You may need to replace the ink cartridges. Inkjet printers don't use toner cartridges and the wrong paper would present different problems.

66. A, B. CompTIA's best practice methodology to resolve problems consists of the following steps:

1. Identify the problem, which includes gathering information from the user; identifying user changes, and if applicable, performing backups before making any changes; and inquiring about environmental or infrastructure changes.

2. Establish a theory of probable cause (question the obvious). If necessary, conduct external or internal research based on symptoms.

3. Test the theory to determine the cause. Once the theory is confirmed, determine the next steps to resolve the problem. If the theory is not confirmed, reestablish a new theory or escalate.

4. Establish a plan of action to resolve the problem and implement the solution.

5. Verify full system functionality, and if applicable, implement preventive measures.

6. Document the findings, actions, and outcomes.

67. A, C. Configuring Quality of Service (QoS) to give priority to the Voice over IP (VoIP) phones would likely help the situation, but not as much as putting them on their own virtual local area network (VLAN). Upgrading the cabling to something with more bandwidth might help, but that isn't a quick solution. If you have a managed switch, setting up a VLAN could be done fairly quickly and would segregate your VoIP traffic on its own network so that it isn't competing with computer traffic.

68. B. First, if it is plugged in, unplug it. A swollen phone is usually a sign of a problem with the battery, and batteries that are compromised may explode or burst into flame. Most modern smartphones don't have batteries that can be replaced, so your friend should replace the phone.

69. A, C. Virtualization has many benefits. If you need, for example, Windows 10, Windows 11, and a Linux distro, instead of having three computers you would only need one. Windows 11 could be the host OS and the other two could reside in a virtual machine (VM). This saves power, space, and hardware expense. You would need the same number of licenses whether or not you have the operating systems installed on a VM, and managing the operating systems is simple because they are all in one box.

70. B. If everyone is getting a limited connectivity message, then no one is connecting to the Internet. The place to start troubleshooting is the default gateway, which on many networks could be a router, but it could also be a proxy server, so default gateway is the best answer here. It's not the wireless access point (WAP) because wired users are having trouble too. It's not the switch because switches connect devices on a LAN; they don't connect the LAN to the outside world.

71. C. The vast majority of consumer Bluetooth mobile devices are Class 2 devices, which have a maximum communication distance of 10 meters (about 30 feet.) The maximum communicating distance for near-field communication (NFC) is only about 4 inches, infrared (IR) requires line of sight, and Wi-Fi has a much greater distance depending on the Wi-Fi standard being used.

72. B. OLED displays have many advantages over LCDs. IPS and VA are both types of LCDs, and some displays use LED backlighting. OLEDs don't need backlighting because the carbon-based material they are created from provides the light and color. Fewer layers are needed so OLED displays can be made thinner than LED displays. The color contrast is better than LED displays, and they have faster refresh rates and the unique characteristic of being foldable.

73. A, B. Mobile device management (MDM) and mobile application management (MAM) systems can be used to ensure the security of your company information on employee's personal devices. They can be used to block downloading or printing of certain information and can be used to lock or wipe lost or stolen devices or remove company data from mobile devices when an employee has left the company. A preferred roaming list (PRL) will be updated as needed on a mobile device to ensure that you can roam and connect to the proper cell towers. GSM is the Global System for Mobile Communications and defines how 2G cellular networks work. GSM is used in Europe and much of the world. CDMA (Code Division Multiple Access) is mainly used in the United States and was used on 2G and 3G phone systems. 5G is the current standard in many places.

74. C. Your username is identification—telling a system who you are. Authentication means proving to a system that you are who you say you are, and that is done by something you know, something you have, something you are, or somewhere you are. In a two-factor authentication system, you first identify yourself to the system (username), and provide your first authentication, usually a password (something you know), then you need another form of authentication. A key fob is a small device, about the size of a key chain, that uses algorithms to generate a numeric key that lasts for only a few seconds and is unique to the application and the user. An authenticator app is software on a device that does the same thing, and it is a type of soft token. A key fob is considered a hard token.

75. B, C. Post Office Protocol version 3 (POP3) and Internet Message Access Protocol (IMAP) are used for downloading email messages from a server. The difference between the two is that IMAP allows the messages to remain on the server so they can be accessed from different devices, where with POP3, the email messages will only exist on the device they were downloaded on. Simple Mail Transfer Protocol (SMTP) is used for sending an email. A good way to remember which is for sending and receiving is to remember that S (as in SMTP) is for sending. Server Message Block (SMB) is a protocol for sharing files across a network.

76. D. Address Resolution Protocol (ARP) is responsible for resolving IP addresses to MAC addresses. The Internet Protocol (IP) is used in routing information packets from one Internet location to another. Secure Shell (SSH) is a connection-oriented protocol that is used to securely manage a network and its devices remotely. DHCP is a connectionless protocol that is used to dynamically assign network configuration information to clients that request it on a network.

77. B. If your switch is not Power-over-Ethernet (PoE) compliant, then you can purchase an injector to send power (along with the data) to a PoE device with a single Ethernet cable. The distance is limited by the cable category and Ethernet standard being used.

78. B, D. Only the 802.11n and 802.11ax standards can use both the 2.4 GHz and 5 GHz frequencies, which makes them backward compatible with all the other standards. 802.11a and 802.11ac standards use only the 5 GHz frequency. 802.11b, and 802.11g use only the 2.4 GHz frequency.

79. D. A DHCP server can be configured to provide all required and optional TCP/IP configuration information to clients. This includes an IP address, subnet mask (for IPv4), default gateway, and DNS server address.

80. A, C. Since this computer is not able to reach the dynamic host configuration protocol (DHCP) server, it will self-assign an automatic private IP addressing (APIPA) address. The APIPA address range is 169.254.0.0 to 169.254.255.255. (In the last octet, 0 and 255 would not be assigned because the last number of a range is the broadcast number and the first number of a range identifies the network.)

81. A. Domain Name Service (DNS) servers reconcile human friendly names like Sybex.com to IP addresses so that a browser can find them (not IP address to domain name). A DNS server can be configured on a client computer automatically by a DHCP server, or manually on the Networking tab of a network connection by clicking on either IPv4 or IPv6 properties. DNS differentiates between IPv4 and IPv6 by identifying IPv6 addresses as AAAA records and IPv4 addresses as A records.

82. D. A crimper is a handy tool for helping you put connectors on the end of a cable. Most crimpers will be a combination tool that strips and snips wires as well as crimps the connector onto the end. A toner probe helps a technician to locate a particular wire in a bunch that look the same. A punchdown tool is used to attach wires to a punchdown block on a wiring rack in a telecommunications closet. A multimeter has many uses, among them testing for continuity, checking power supplies, and checking wall outlets.

83. C. The EIA/TIA 568A Standard is green stripe, green, orange stripe, blue, blue stripe, orange, brown stripe, brown. The EIA/TIA 568B standard is orange stripe, orange, green stripe, blue, blue stripe, green, brown stripe, brown. To make it easier to remember, notice that only the green and orange change positions. Blue and brown stay in the same positions.

84. C. Both Cat 6 and Cat 6a will support up to 10 Gbps, but for Cat 6 the maximum distance for 10 Gbps is about 55 meters (165 feet). Cat 6a can support a frequency that is twice as fast, so it can support 10 Gbps up to 328 feet (100 meters.) Since the distance in the question is 200 feet, you would need to use Cat 6a cable. Cat 5e has a maximum bandwidth of 1 Gbps. Plenum simply means that the cable has a coating that is not toxic when burned.

85. D. This isn't memory at all. It is an M.2, which is a solid-state drive (SSD) used for storage. It may look similar to a DIMM, but it's smaller and the connectors are on one (short) end, not on the long edge. ECC is error correction code, a feature of some RAM modules that will detect and attempt to correct errors in storing or retrieving information. ECC is usually found in servers rather than desktop computers and is more expensive. Small outline DIMM (SODIMMs), the memory used in laptops, will have a notch and connectors on the long side as will regular DIMMs, which are used in desktop computers. DIMMs are larger than SODIMMs.

86. A. Duplexing is printing on both sides of the paper automatically, no need to stand at the printer and flip the copies over. Orientation refers to whether a paper is wider than is it tall (landscape), or taller than it is wide (portrait). Tray settings refer to configuration settings such as if the print job is 11 × 14 inches instead of 8.5 × 11, then use tray two. That's just one of many settings. Most printers will have a fast print mode or a quality print mode.

87. D. Thermal printers require a special paper that will turn black when subjected to heat. Inkjet printers use paper that resists colors bleeding into other areas, impact printers often use no carbon required (NCR) forms to make multiple copies of a form when they print, and 3-D printers use a filament or resin to create a three-dimensional printout. The filament is extruded through a hot nozzle and the resin is subjected to lasers that harden it; then the excess resin is washed away.

88. C. CompTIA's best practice methodology to resolve problems consists of the following steps:

   1. Identify the problem, which includes gathering information from the user; identifying user changes, and if applicable, performing backups before making any changes; and inquiring about environmental or infrastructure changes.

   2. Establish a theory of probable cause (question the obvious). If necessary, conduct external or internal research based on symptoms.

   3. Test the theory to determine the cause. Once the theory is confirmed, determine the next steps to resolve the problem. If the theory is not confirmed, reestablish a new theory or escalate.

   4. Establish a plan of action to resolve the problem and implement the solution.

   5. Verify full system functionality, and if applicable, implement preventive measures.

   6. Document the findings, actions, and outcomes.

89. B. Resistive touch screens respond to pressure, and they are highly accurate in detecting the position of the touch. These types of touch screens require the use of a stylus or other hard object, such as a fingernail. Capacitive screens work by detecting interruption in an electric field. You can use your finger with them, but they can't tell how hard you are pressing. Tempered is a type of glass that is very strong, and object-oriented is a type of programming/software.

90. A. The connectors shown are straight tip (ST) connectors for fiber-optic cable. They connect with a BNC-type locking mechanism. The subscriber connector (SC) and Lucent connector (LC) are used for fiber-optic connections. SC is about twice the size of the LC connector. Both have a square housing. The SC uses a small locking tab and the LC uses a locking latch to hold it in place.

91. B. RAID 0 is called disk striping. Data can be written to or read from multiple devices at the same time, increasing data access speed. However, if one drive fails, all data is lost. (Back up early and often!) RAID 1 is a mirror set, which does not increase data access but provides fault tolerance. RAID 5 is disk striping with parity, which provides both speed and fault tolerance but requires three hard disks.

92. C. Generally speaking, you will need a license for each instance of an operating system that is running in your virtual machine.

93. A, C, D. While software as a service (SaaS), platform as a service (PaaS), and infrastructure as a service (IaaS) are widely considered to be the major categories of cloud computing, desktop as a service (DaaS) is not.

94. B. CompTIA's best practice methodology to resolve problems consists of the following steps:

   1. Identify the problem, which includes gathering information from the user; identifying user changes, and if applicable, performing backups before making any changes; and inquiring about environmental or infrastructure changes.

   2. Establish a theory of probable cause (question the obvious). If necessary, conduct external or internal research based on symptoms.

   3. Test the theory to determine the cause. Once the theory is confirmed, determine the next steps to resolve the problem. If the theory is not confirmed, reestablish a new theory or escalate.

   4. Establish a plan of action to resolve the problem and implement the solution.

   5. Verify full system functionality, and if applicable, implement preventive measures.

   6. Document the findings, actions, and outcomes.

95. B. Virtual memory is a paging file on a hard disk that the Windows operating system will use as if it were RAM. Items normally stored in RAM are moved into and out of the virtual RAM as needed. The benefit is that the system can run as if it has more RAM than it does. The drawback is that virtual RAM, because it is on the hard drive, is slower to access than physical RAM. VirtualBox is a computer virtualization software that allows you to run more than one OS in a single PC with each thinking it is controlling the hardware. A small outline DIMM (SODIMM) is RAM for laptops, and ECC is error correction code, which attempts to find and fix errors in memory—it is used mostly in servers.

96. D. The steps of the laser printing process are as follows: processing, charging, exposing, developing, transferring, fusing, and cleaning. It would be a good idea to memorize the order, and remember what happens at each step before taking the CompTIA A+ 1101 exam.

97. B. When wanting to maintain confidentiality, integrity, and availability, security requirements and regulations must first be defined. A company can then consider if an Internet cloud solution would be appropriate.

98. C. For a company needing additional cloud resources on demand, they should request metered utilization, in which a cloud service will bill much like a utility would, as resources are used. Infrastructure as a service (IaaS) refers to hardware and networking in the cloud. Resource pooling is used in cloud computing to mean that resources are pooled and delivered as needed to many clients. Rapid metering is not an IT term.

99. A. A community cloud is the solution for such situations. It allows shared cloud resources to a limited group of people or companies. The group can benefit from economies of scale, but keep their resources separate from other organizations. They could even share in joint projects. Their servers could be in a data center or stored locally by one of the members. The group will have more control than they would over a public cloud but could share the maintenance costs of their cloud. A community cloud is similar to a private cloud but with multiple members.

100. B. A Virtual Desktop Infrastructure (VDI) moves the desktop icons, files, and folders to a server instead of the desktop originating from the local machine. When the desktop experience is hosted on a centralized server location, the icons, files, and folders are the same. With this user working from different offices, the best solution for them is VDI in the cloud. On-Demand Desktop Streaming is a Dell streaming service where the desktops and files are stored on a server that provides them to thin clients without drives over gigabit Ethernet. Desktop emulation is software that imitates a desktop. Synchronized folders means that your documents will be the same whether you log into a desktop, laptop, or other mobile device. Changes on one are synchronized to the other devices.

Chapter 11: Practice Exam 2 (220-1102)

1. A. The quickest way to thwart this would-be attacker is to turn on Airplane mode. This disconnects all of your wireless connections and is usually done by pressing a key or two, such as the Fn key and whichever F key has a picture of an airplane on it. There is no network cable to disconnect if you are on Wi-Fi, and what closing the lid does depends on how the computer is configured. It may do nothing. If you turn the laptop's power off, you will lose whatever you have been working on.

2. A, B. When working with customers, it's important to avoid distractions such as personal phone calls, texting, or social media sites. Exceptions can be made if it's an emergency situation, but in those cases notify the client that you might get a call or text and explain that you will deal with it only if it's the emergency. Otherwise, ignore the personal interruption until you are not working with a client.

3. B, C. The New Technology File System (NTFS) is available with all current versions of Windows. NTFS is an advanced filesystem that includes such features as individual file security, compression, and RAID support as well as support for extremely large file and partition sizes and disk transaction monitoring. In Pro and higher editions of Windows, the Encrypting File System (EFS) is available to encrypt individual files and folders.

4. B. The sudo ("substitute user do" or "superuser do") command is used to run a command with a different privilege level than the current user logged in. Typically this means running a command with superuser or root permissions. The su command switches to a different user, again the default is root, but with sudo you need to enter sudo before each command. With su, you don't. Considering best practices, you would use sudo if you had one command to run and su if you had several. The grep command is used to search for patterns in a file, so if you can't remember the filename but know what is in it, you can still find it. The man command brings up a manual—for example, man grep would show you how to use the grep command.

5. C. Biometric devices use physical characteristics to identify the user. Biometric systems include fingerprint/palm/hand scanners, retina scanners, and anything else that uses part of your body to identify you. To gain access to resources, you must pass a physical screening process. While it's true that guards are humans, they are not biometric devices. Radio frequency identification (RFID) badges have information on them that is read by an RFID scanner, and key fobs generate a new code every few seconds to allow access.

6. B. Many companies rely on digital rights management (DRM) to protect digital assets such as online photos or videos. Unlike an end-user license agreement (EULA) that legally protects software and other objects, DRM will physically protect the information by not allowing copies to be made, printing a watermark on the face of an image or document, or similar measures to prevent use, modification, and distribution of materials that are copyrighted. DRM is not as established as licensing agreements are, but you should still respect the property of the owners of digital content.

7. D. Tailgating refers to being so close to someone when they enter a building that you are able to come in right behind them without needing to use a key, a card, or any other security device. Using access control vestibules, which are devices such as small rooms that limit access to one or a few individuals, is a great way to stop tailgating. A brute-force attack attempts to repeatedly guess a password. Shoulder surfing is just like it sounds—someone looking over your shoulder to gain passwords and logins, and an evil twin is an unauthorized wireless access point that has the same SSID as a legitimate one.

8. A. The `msinfo32` tool displays a thorough list of settings on the machine. You cannot change any values from here, but you can search, export, and save reports. When run from a command prompt, the `/computer` option allows you to specify a remote computer on which to run the utility, and the `/report` option saves the report as a text file. Another option while in the GUI is clicking View ➤ Remote Computer to collect information related to the chosen PC. The `compmgmt` command opens the Computer Management console, `mmc` opens the Microsoft Management Console, and `perfmon` opens Performance Monitor.

9. C. Forensic install is not an option. The easiest way to install Windows 11 on a Windows 10 computer is through Windows Update in the Settings app. If you have a situation where that's not possible, you can create Windows 11 installation media and use it to install the OS. When you launch the installation from within Windows 10, you have three options. The first is Full Upgrade, which will keep Windows settings, drivers, personal files, and apps. The second, Keep Data Only, will keep drivers and personal files but no installed apps or Windows Settings. The third option is a Clean Install, which will wipe out everything on the drive and install a fresh copy of Windows 11. If you boot a computer from the installation media, your only option is a clean install.

10. B. Even if you disable the Service Set Identifier (SSID) broadcast, potential attackers still have many simple tools available to see your wireless network traffic and get the SSID anyway. It is a weak form of security that will keep out only the most casual intruders. Disabling guest access limits who can connect to your network, but if you must have guest access, look for a setting that will isolate the guest network from your network. WPA3 is the best commonly available form of encryption for wireless routers. WPA2 is usually available alongside of WPA3 for networks that are transitioning between WPA2 and WPA3. The router may have an option that says WPA2/WPA3 or WPA3 transitional, which will allow newer devices to connect using WPA3 and older devices to connect using WPA2. Changing the default username and password is always recommended, because those are often easy to find online.

11. B, C. To ensure your personal safety, always remember some important techniques before moving equipment. The first thing to always check for is to ensure that the equipment is unplugged. There's nothing worse (and potentially more dangerous) than getting yanked because you're still tethered. Remove any loose jewelry, and secure long hair or neckties. Lift with your legs, not your back (bend at the knees when picking something up, not at the waist).

12. C. A striped volume is like RAID-0 and will provide a 1 TB volume with a slight performance boost. A simple volume would not be able to combine the two drives. A spanned volume would result in a 1 TB volume, but not the performance boost. A mirrored volume, like a RAID-1 array, will make one of the disks redundant, so in this case it would not give the user 1 TB of storage.

13. A. BitLocker allows the user to use drive encryption to protect files, including those needed for startup and logon. BitLocker can be turned on or off only by administrators, and it's enabled by default in Windows 11. It is only available in Pro or higher editions of both Windows 10 and Windows 11. The Encrypting File System (EFS) can encrypt data at the volume, file, or folder level, but not an entire hard drive. OneDrive is Microsoft's online storage, and ShadowDrive is not a computer term.

14. D. The best way to remove data from the device is to perform a remote wipe. Ideally you have backed up or synced the device before then or you will lose data. Full-device encryption is a good security practice, but that should have been completed prior to the phone being stolen. BitLocker is a Microsoft Windows feature for full-drive encryption.

15. D. When you create a partition in Windows 10, it will ask if you want to create a master boot record (MBR) or GUID Partition Table (GPT) partition. GPT is newer and has far more features. One of those features is that you can create an unlimited number of logical partitions on it. Only the operating system will limit you; Windows 10 will only allow 128 partitions on one drive. Windows 11 supports only the GPT partition type.

16. A. Removing all data on a drive by repeatedly replacing it with binary bits, 0s or 1s, is commonly done using drive-wiping software. This can make the data unrecoverable and make it safe to donate the drives. The format command will erase the file allocation table or master file table, but the files may still be able to be recovered. It is not a secure way to ensure that your data can't be read. Degaussing and incinerating are ways to physically destroy drives. Degaussing works with only magnetic media.

17. C. A battery backup, also called an uninterruptible power supply (UPS), is designed to provide enough power to keep systems running until they can be safely shut down or switched to another power source. The UPS must provide adequate wattage for the devices connected to it as well as sufficient battery capacity. Most also offer protected and unprotected outlets; surge suppression, which protects against power surges; and line conditioning, which improves the quality of power delivered to the device, such as boosting the power when there is a sag on the input side. Power strips only give you a place to plug devices in and turn them all off at once. A smart UPS can notify an administrator that there is a power outage.

18. A, B. There are three tools in Windows 10 and Windows 11 that quickly show you CPU and memory usage in Windows. They are Resource Monitor, Performance Monitor, and Task Manager. Performance Monitor can also be accessed through Computer Management.

19. B. A brute-force attack is an attempt to guess passwords until a successful guess occurs. Because of the nature of this attack, it usually occurs over a long period of time. To make passwords more difficult to guess, longer is better, eight characters being the minimum that should be required. Limiting the number of unsuccessful lockouts may also help thwart this attack, and requiring that passwords be periodically changed will help too. All of these can be set using the Local Group Policy Editor. Navigate to Computer Configuration ➤ Windows Settings ➤ Security Settings ➤ Account Policies.

20. A. Pop-ups are annoying but not necessarily an indication that your computer is infected with anything. Enabling Chrome's pop-up blocker should prevent them. Antivirus and anti-malware programs don't generally deal with pop-ups unless those pop-ups are associated with malware, and most pop-ups aren't—they are just coded into the website. A firewall won't help with pop-ups either.

21. D. Acceptable use policies (AUPs) describe how the employees in an organization can use company systems and resources, both software and hardware. This policy should also outline the consequences for misuse. In addition, the policy should address the installation of personal software on company computers and the use of personal hardware such as USB devices. The AUP is often signed during the employee onboarding process and may be part of an employee handbook but is not required to be. An Android package (APK) is a file for installing an Android app, an access control list (ACL) defines who has what permissions on an object, and an automatic document feeder (ADF) sits atop a copier or multifunction device (MFD) to send a stack of papers through, one at a time.

22. B. This is a form of ransomware, which can be programmed to take control over a user's webcam. It's just another layer of complexity to scare users. Deleting and reinstalling Windows will work, but it's not necessary. The system will be locked, so you can't open the anti-malware software. You can, however, boot to a bootable media from the anti-malware software provider and start a remediation that way.

23. D. While it's possible that the disposal information and risks may be on the container somewhere, you will always find it on the product's material safety data sheet (MSDS). It should be stated that, while CompTIA still refers to these sheets as MSDSs as an exam objective, the name has been changed to safety data sheet (SDS). SDSs include information such as physical product data (boiling point, melting point, flash point, and so forth), potential health risks, storage and disposal recommendations, and spill/leak procedures. With this information, technicians and emergency personnel know how to handle the product as well as respond in the event of an emergency.

24. A, C. When authorized users access devices through unintended connections or unauthorized users access stolen devices, they can access the data on the device. Disable autoconnect to avoid unintended connections and encrypt data on devices to help protect the data on them in the event they are stolen.

25. A. The dir command shows a folder (directory) listing. The /p switch displays only one page at a time. Think of it as the pause switch. The dir /o:s command lists the files in order by size, dir /w shows a wide format, and dir /s includes all the subdirectories. There are many other switches that can be used to modify the output of the dir command. Type dir /? at a command prompt to see them.

26. C. Inheritance is the default behavior throughout the permission structure, unless a specific setting is created to override it. For example, a user who has Read and Write permissions in one folder will have that in all the subfolders unless a change has been made specifically to one of the subfolders. Modify access does not give users permissions to change permissions for others. Only Full Control allows that.

27. D. If you have your policy in place, then your incident response plan should be relatively scripted. Your first priority as the first responder is to identify the improper activity or content. Then you should always get someone else to verify the material or action so that it doesn't turn into a situation of your word against someone else's. Immediately report the situation through proper channels, and secure the drive away from the user.

28. B. Device Manager allows you to manage all your hardware devices, including updating drivers and disabling the device. It is found within the Computer Management console and in Control Panel.

29. D. In macOS, there is a bar of icons that runs along the bottom (or side, if so configured) of your screen. That set of icons is known as the Dock, and it provides easy access to key apps that come with the Mac (such as Safari, Mail, Videos, and Music) or others that you choose to add there. Remote Disc enables Macs without optical drives to use another computer's optical drive across a network. The Finder is similar to Windows File Explorer and enables the user to drill down through files and folders to find what they are looking for. Spotlight is a search tool.

30. D. The purpose of the System File Checker (SFC) utility is to keep the operating system alive and well. sfc.exe automatically verifies system files after a reboot to see whether they were changed to unprotected copies. If an unprotected file is found, a stored copy of the system file overwrites it. The check disk utility, chkdsk, is used to verify the integrity of the filesystem and to identify bad sectors of a hard drive. In the graphical user interface (GUI) it is called error checking. diskpart is the Windows command-line utility that allows you to perform disk partition operations. The tracert utility traces the route a packet takes from one computer to another.

31. B. The user should check to ensure that Wi-Fi is enabled. A common cause for a lack of wireless connectivity is for a device to be in Airplane mode, but since the user has a cellular signal, the phone definitely isn't in this mode. The other wireless signal types (Wi-Fi and Bluetooth) can be individually disabled, so check them both. Adjusting receptivity isn't an available option on smartphones, and resetting to factory defaults will wipe out the phone's data.

32. B. The seven steps of the malware removal process are as follows:

   1. Investigate and verify malware symptoms.

   2. Quarantine infected systems.

   3. Disable System Restore in Windows.

   4. Remediate infected systems.

      a. Update anti-malware software.

      b. Scanning and removal techniques (e.g., safe mode, preinstallation environment).

   5. Schedule scans and run updates.

   6. Enable System Restore and create a restore point in Windows.

   7. Educate the end user.

33. D. The recommended way to assign permissions on Microsoft systems is to grant them to groups. Then, users can be assigned to groups depending on their access needs. This is far less work than managing permissions on a user-by-user basis.

34. A. The `copy` command makes a copy of a file in a second location. It cannot be used to copy folders. To copy a folder, you need to use the `xcopy` command.

35. D. Don't click the buttons! This is some sort of hoax. When you click either button, something bad will happen—something like malware being installed on your computer. Attackers are very creative about making their pop-ups look like legitimate security alerts. Shut your computer down, and after you reboot, run a virus scan, or if possible, boot with bootable media from your antivirus company.

36. A. Keychain is a password management system from Apple. It allows you to store passwords for websites, mail servers, Wi-Fi, and so forth. There is an iCloud variant (iCloud Keychain) that keeps such information as Safari usernames/passwords and credit card information. Mission Control gives you a look at all the open apps, windows, and desktop spaces on your machine. FileVault provides encryption. Terminal is the command-line interface on macOS and most Linux systems. Windows 11 has the traditional Command Prompt and a new tool called Windows Terminal that opens a PowerShell prompt. Unlike the Command Prompt, it allows the user to create multiple tabs. Typing **exit** in Windows Terminal exits the program instead of returning the user to a regular command prompt as it would in the Command Prompt.

37. C. The System Configuration tool allows you to force the operating system to boot into safe mode by clicking the box next to Safe Boot on the Boot tab. The System Configuration utility (`msconfig.exe`) has five tabs: General, Boot, Services, Startup, and Tools. Task Scheduler wouldn't work here because the operating system loads before Task Scheduler could run. Computer Management and Task Manager don't have settings for booting.

38. B. The one big advantage of share permissions is that they can be used if the NTFS filesystem is not in place. Of course, share permissions are in effect only when the user connects to the resource via the network. NTFS permissions are able to protect at the file level. Share permissions can be applied to the folder level only. NTFS permissions can affect users logged on locally or across the network to the system where the NTFS permissions are applied.

39. A. Personally identifiable information (PII) is anything that can be used to identify an individual person on its own or in context with other information. This includes someone's full name, address, and other contact information; the names of family members; and other details that people would consider private. A first name is considered to be generally common enough that it is not PII. A full name, if not common, would be PII.

40. A. No unintended or unauthorized event is a good thing for mobile users. The one that leaves a user most susceptible to an on-path attack is an unintended Wi-Fi connection. This is because the device at the other end that the user is connecting to could be intercepting data or storing it for a possible attack later.

41. C. The way to protect against this is to implement a BIOS/UEFI password. If a user can get into the BIOS/UEFI settings, then they can change the boot sequence, boot to an unauthorized device, and then do some damage to the system. A strong Windows password will help protect Windows but does not protect the computer in general. Autorun is a feature of Windows and does not affect the boot process. User permissions limit what a user can do on a computer system.

42. D. In hibernate mode, the computer saves all the contents of memory to the hard drive, preserves all data and applications exactly where they are, and allows the computer to power off completely. When the system comes out of hibernation, it returns to its previous state. Sleep continues to use a small trickle of power until there is none left, then will go into hibernate mode. Windows 10 and 11 support a feature called Modern Standby. Modern Standby must also be supported by the hardware. It is not the right answer because it also uses a small amount of power. With Modern Standby, the system will wake from the lowest power to allow short bursts (milliseconds) of software execution as the system needs them. The system uses just enough power to process background tasks but still preserve battery life. The result is that when in sleep mode, a computer can stay connected to a LAN and reacts much like a smartphone with instant on/instant off ability.

43. C. A snapshot is an exact copy of a logical volume that has been frozen at a specific point in time. When creating the snapshot, you don't need to worry about users changing files or taking the volume offline. Time Machine, Remote Disc, and FileVault are also features of macOS.

44. A. Windows 10 and 11 both incorporate Windows Defender Firewall with Advanced Security, which can be used to stop incoming and outgoing network traffic. Traffic is allowed or denied by specific rules that are part of an access control list (ACL). By default, Windows Defender Firewall blocks incoming traffic. By creating exceptions, you can configure what incoming traffic you want to allow through. NTFS permissions are used to configure user access to files, folders, and volumes. Local Security Policy is used to configure items such as password policy and account lockout policies. Computer Management is a Microsoft Management Console with several frequently used tools.

45. B. Set and meet, or exceed, customer expectations and communicate timelines and status. Customers want to know what is going on. In addition, giving the customer a choice in repair or replacement options will usually help the customer feel better because they have a choice in the outcome. Remember that if they have called you, their day is already more difficult than normal, so treat customers with kindness and compassion.

46. A, C. If an OS update fails, it could be a configuration issue or simply a one-time glitch in the process. Wait until Windows Update reverts the changes; then reboot and try the update again. If that does not work, you can unplug removable media from your computer and try again, or you can try the Windows Update Troubleshooter.

47. B. Check the simple things first. If the Print Spooler service isn't running, then printers will not show. It's unlikely that you would need to reinstall or repair Windows.

48. C. If you can reach a website using an IP address, then the problem has something to do with DNS settings. The default DNS server can be configured using DHCP settings, but since the other users aren't having this problem, it's not a setting on the DHCP server. That means it must be configured on the local computer. The user is able to reach the file server, and if they're accessing a remote website the problem wouldn't be your company's web server.

49. D. An acceptable use policy (AUP) describes what users are and are not allowed to do on the company's network. Often companies will use a splash screen to confirm that the employee has read and agrees to the AUP or other company policies before they can use the network. In different environments such as a kiosk or app, a splash screen can display while the program is loading, and in those situations, it may be used to reinforce a brand or advertise products. There are ways to track employee time on the network, but that's not the job of the splash screen.

50. B, C, D. Windows 10 and 11 treat these items the same. The difference lies in whether the Home edition or Pro edition is being used. All Windows editions support NTFS file compression. Only Windows editions that are Pro or higher support joining a domain, using the Group Policy Editor (`gpedit.msc`), and Remote Desktop Protocol.

51. B. When a client wants to authenticate to a server over a public network, Kerberos works with an Authentication Server (AS) to ensure that each party to the connection is who they say they are. Multifactor authentication requires two or more methods for the user to prove their identity, such as a password and biometric login. Remote Authentication Dial-in User Service (RADIUS) is a protocol used specifically between a remote connection and a server. It authenticates the remote user, and if the RADIUS server has the remote user configured as a client, it will send configuration information back to the user. RADIUS authenticates the remote user, not both parties. Temporal Key Integrity Protocol (TKIP) was used to encrypt information on wireless networks, but it is no longer considered secure.

52. A. While all four of these options will help to keep a computer system safe, all it takes is one employee who doesn't know how to recognize dangers, and a malicious software can be unleashed on a computer system. Regular user education regarding common threats should be a part of your company's security plan.

53. B, C. If you're running low on memory, you have two options. You can modify the virtual memory settings, or you can add more physical memory if the motherboard will support it. Using Task Manager to close unnecessary programs will help in the short term but not in the long term if you often have those programs running. A faster network interface card (NIC) won't help here.

54. D. There are many settings that can be reached through Settings ➤ Network & Internet. Network Troubleshooter, Mobile Hotspot, and Change Adapter Options are just a few. The main menu items here include Wi-Fi, VPN, Mobile Hotspot, Airplane Mode, Proxy, Dial-up, Properties (for the connection), and Data Usage. There are also Advanced Network Settings, which include Change Adapter Settings, Network Troubleshooter, and Network And Sharing Center. In Windows 10 the Advanced Network Settings are on the same page, but in Windows 11 you'll need to click the Advanced Network Settings option to bring up additional options.

55. B. When configuring a static IP address in IPv6 networking, a subnet mask is not needed, but you do need to know the subnet prefix length. That's the only difference between configuring IPv4 and IPv6. In addition to the IPv6 address and default gateway, you'll need to know the address of the preferred DNS server.

56. C. If they are able to access the Internet using Microsoft Edge, then the issue is with Google Chrome. The most likely problem is that the firewall isn't allowing it. To resolve the problem, go into Windows Defender Firewall, and in the inbound rules, add Google Chrome and allow it to send information through the firewall.

57. D. If you're planning a change to an IT system, it's important to have a rollback plan, in case the change fails, and to test the change in a sandbox before you go live with it. You'll also want to do a thorough risk analysis and identify the systems that will be affected or impacted by the change. Getting end-user acceptance is also helpful, so be sure to explain to them why the change is necessary and involve them in the changes that will affect them, such as user input screens. A kickoff meeting happens after the change board approval and before the change begins to take place.

58. B. The grandfather-father-son (GFS) method of backing up, as described in the question, ensures that there are short-term, medium-term, and long-term backups of a system. You should have backups both on-site and off-site. The 3-2-1 backup rule says you should have three copies of data, using two different types of media, and one should be off-site. A synthetic backup is a full backup created by combining a recent full backup and the changes since then to create new files. It can be done outside the system, so there is no downtime and it's faster than doing a full backup.

59. C. If a problem is beyond your abilities, of course you will follow the company policy, but in most cases you will escalate the problem to someone else who has appropriate training or experience to resolve the issue. Any of the other options might lose a customer permanently.

60. B. It's easy to pick and choose which notifications you want popping up on your screen. In Windows 11, go to Settings ➤ System ➤ Notifications, and there you can choose by application which ones you want notifications from. In Windows 10 the menu option is Notifications & actions.

61. C. FAT32 and exFAT are both compatible with both Windows and macOS systems, but the exFAT filesystem supports files greater than 4 GB; FAT32 does not. NTFS is only compatible with Windows, ext4 is used in Linux/Unix systems, and Apple File System (APFS) is the filesystem for macOS 10.13 and later.

62. A, D. It sounds like the user needs read, write, and perhaps modify to the folder on the C: drive, and they don't need any other access on that drive. The principle of least privilege is one of the most important security rules in computer systems. It says that you give a user only the access that they need and nothing more. If they have access to the entire C: drive, and an attacker gets in on their account, then the attacker will have complete access too and can cause all sorts of trouble. Limiting them to only the folder they need also limits their exposure. The other two options are simply not true.

63. C. The seven steps of the malware removal process are as follows:

1. Investigate and verify malware symptoms.

2. Quarantine infected systems.

3. Disable System Restore in Windows.

4. Remediate infected systems.

    a. Update anti-malware software.

    b. Scanning and removal techniques (e.g., safe mode, preinstallation environment).

5. Schedule scans and run updates.

6. Enable System Restore and create a restore point in Windows.

7. Educate the end user.

64. D. If this is the first time the error has occurred, simply reboot and see if it goes away. Windows is quite stable, but occasionally a blue screen of death (BSOD) occurs, and you need to reboot. If it doesn't happen again, there likely isn't a problem. If it continues to happen, look for any error message on the screen that will give you a clue about what the problem is, and troubleshoot from there. If there is no error message, assume the problem is hardware or a corrupted driver and boot into safe mode to fix the issue.

65. B. If a user profile is very large, it may be slow to load but it should eventually get there. If there is an error message that it is unable to load, suspect a corrupted profile. To verify that's the problem, create a new user and copy the existing user profile to the new user, then try to log on as the new user. If the same error occurs, the profile is corrupted. You'll need to delete the corrupted profile and when the user logs on again, a new profile will be created.

66. C. The first thing to try for an Android-based device that won't load an app is to restart the device and try the app again. If that doesn't work, try each of the following and restart between, then see if the app will launch: First, check for Android updates. Next, check for app updates. Finally, clear the app's data and cache. If none of these solutions work, you may need to contact the app developer.

67. C. When you're installing a new component, the safest place for it is inside (not lying on) the antistatic bag that it arrived in. If an antistatic bag isn't available, the next safest place is lying on a grounded antistatic mat. You would never leave a new card teetering on the edge of a case, and antistatic bags are designed to keep static on the outside, so lying the component on the bag is not a good idea.

68. C. Microsoft Remote Assistance (MSRA) is your best option, and really the only one unless you are a managed service provider (MSP) and already have remote monitoring and management (RMM) set up on their computer. RDP is not available on Windows Home editions, and a virtual private network (VPN) is usually used for connecting remotely to a network as if you were sitting in the office. It also requires some configuration. MSRA allows you to co-control the user's desktop.

69. B. Script files can be used to make repeated tasks much easier by automating the process. PowerShell is a very popular scripting program among network administrators, and Power-Shell files use a `.ps1` extension. A batch file has a `.bat` extension, Visual Basic scripts have a `.vbs` extension, and Python files have a `.py` extension. Others are `.sh`, for Bash (Linux) scripts, and `.js`, for JavaScript.

70. A, C. To add or manage users go to either Settings ➤ Accounts ➤ Family & Other Users, or Control Panel ➤ User Accounts ➤ Manage Another Account. These options are the same in Windows 10 and 11.

71. A. Mapping a network drive for this user will make navigating to the resource much easier. A domain name identifies a Windows Active Directory domain. A subnet mask is used in IPv4 networking, and a gateway is the proxy server, router, or other device that connects a user to other networks, including the Internet.

72. A. The computer is running a virus program before the operating system even boots, which indicates that there is a boot sector virus. The best way to remove this malware is using boot media from your antivirus company to clean the computer. You may need to go into the BIOS/UEFI settings and change the boot order to boot to the anti-malware media. You wouldn't need to repair or replace the operating system yet, although as part of the remediation you may need to. It is unlikely with this scenario that you would be able to boot into safe mode, and even if you did, the malware could be lurking in the restore point. Part of the best practice procedures for malware removal is to disable System Restore in Windows.

73. A, B. Facial recognition and fingerprint readers are common methods of biometric identification on smartphones, tablets, and laptops. A PIN code is a number, which is not biometric. Swipe to unlock offers virtually no security on a mobile device.

74. A. This is a classic symptom of malware. Your first job is to remove it. The seven steps of the malware removal process are as follows:
1. Investigate and verify malware symptoms.
2. Quarantine infected systems.
3. Disable System Restore in Windows.
4. Remediate infected systems.
   a. Update anti-malware software.
   b. Scanning and removal techniques (e.g., safe mode, preinstallation environment).
5. Schedule scans and run updates.
6. Enable System Restore and create a restore point in Windows.
7. Educate the end user.

75. A, C. Possible undesirable outcomes of running or allowing script files to be run are inadvertently changing system settings, browser or system crashes, and unintentionally introducing malware. The other options listed are advantages of script files.

76. D. A 32-bit operating system is a software requirement, not hardware, and it's unlikely that a 32-bit operating system would be adequate for a 3D printer. They typically require a 64-bit operating system and a certain generation, type, or speed processor; some RAM of their own; and space on your hard drive. Some will require that you have a dedicated graphics card rather than an integrated one. The best practice here is to make sure you know what the system requirements are and that everything is compatible before purchasing hardware and software.

77. A. First Aid in the macOS Disk Utility will check and repair the file system, similar to Windows Error Checking. From Disk Utility you can also erase, create, and restore partitions.

78. B, C. For data-at-rest, which means it's on a storage media, your options are Encrypting File System (EFS) and BitLocker. BitLocker is more secure and would be preferred. Kerberos and RADIUS secure information that is moving (data-in-transit/motion) between two points.

79. A, C. Two of the most common, and easiest to fix, problems with AirDrop are if Bluetooth is off or either device is not discoverable. Turning Airplane mode on would disable all wireless communication, and making both phones a hotspot won't help with AirDrop.

80. C. Most laptops, and many commercial desktop computers, will have a recovery partition that can be used to restore the computer to factory defaults. Usually you can get there by pressing a key or group of keys during the bootup. This would be better than using installation media made from the Microsoft website because it will have the proper drivers and other software that came with the computer. There is no need to buy a new hard drive, unless of course the drive is physically damaged.

81. A, B. Many routers that don't have a setting for WPA3 can get it by updating the router's firmware. If some of your devices are older they may not work with WPA3. WPA2/WPA3 Transitional (also known as WPA2/WPA3 mixed mode) is a mode that allows older devices to still work with WPA2, but they should be replaced or updated to WPA3 as soon as practicable. If you choose WPA3 Personal, some devices might not work. If you choose WPA2 Personal, your network is not as secure as it could be.

82. B, D. Creating a screened subnet will protect your network from traffic interacting with the server, and can be done with one router, as long as the web server, outside world, and internal network are on different ports of the router. Incoming requests for HTTPS port 443 should be forwarded to the web server. Universal Plug and Play (UPnP) is considered unsafe, but it is irrelevant to our web server question. You wouldn't forward outgoing requests.

83. A. Always try the simple things first. An invalid certificate warning can come up if your date and time are incorrect, making them fall outside of the time the certificate is valid. That's the easiest fix.

84. C. Jailbreaking does let you do more with your device, but it isn't necessarily safe or legal. Jailbreaking is most commonly done with Apple devices because they are more locked down than Android or Windows devices are. Jailbreaking an iPhone, for instance, allows the user to install apps that are not approved by Apple. When you open the device up for yourself by cracking software or gaining root access, it also opens your device up more for cybercriminals to perpetrate an attack on it. Jailbreaking also voids the warranty on your device. The device may become unstable, and with the warranty voided, you are not likely to receive support in fixing problems. Jailbreaking may be illegal depending on where you are in the world.

85. A, D. There are two places to configure a VPN in Windows 10 and 11. Go to Control Panel ➤ Network and Sharing Center, and select Set Up A New Connection Or Network. or, go to Settings ➤ Network & Internet, and select VPN. The Windows Mobility Center has settings for mobile devices, and Personalization enables the user to change background, lock screen, and color schemes.

86. B. A 64-bit operating system will support both 32-bit and 64-bit applications. A 32-bit application will work on a 64-bit operating system, but it won't take advantage of the 64-bit speed. It will essentially run half as fast as a 64-bit application would. 32-bit operating systems only support 32-bit programs; you can't run a 64-bit application on a 32-bit operating system. Luckily, there aren't many computers with 32-bit operating systems around anymore.

87. C. This is a classic example of multifactor authentication. The username identifies you; the password (something you know) and the authenticator app code (something you have) are multiple ways to prove (authenticate) who you are. The four types of authentication are something you know, something you have, something you are (biometrics), and some place you are.

88. D. The seven steps of the malware removal process are as follows:

1. Investigate and verify malware symptoms.
2. Quarantine infected systems.
3. Disable System Restore in Windows.
4. Remediate infected systems.
   a. Update anti-malware software.
   b. Scanning and removal techniques (e.g., safe mode, preinstallation environment).
5. Schedule scans and run updates.
6. Enable System Restore and create a restore point in Windows.
7. Educate the end user.

89. B, C. No one likes to have changes forced on them, but in IT there are changes every day. When you have a major change, your headaches will be less if you can gain end-user acceptance before the change happens. Two of the best ways to do this are to involve them in the parts of the planning process that affect them, such as user input screens. Have a meeting and listen to input from the people who will actually be using the system. They may have some insight that you don't. Also be sure to thoroughly explain why the change is necessary.

The worst thing to do is spring the change on them by not telling them about it and having them discover it when they log in Monday morning.

90. D. Incremental backups will only back up what has changed since the last full backup or the last incremental backup. An incremental or full backup resets the archive bit, so only Monday's changes will be backed up on Monday, only Tuesday's changed files will be backed up on Tuesday, and only Wednesday's changed files will be backed up on Wednesday. You will need to restore all three backups to get all the changes that occurred since Sunday.

91. A. Secure Shell (SSH) has virtually replaced Telnet as a remote access protocol and program. Telnet is not secure. SSH is. Videoconferencing software allows users to see and talk to one another as if in the same room while they may be thousands of miles apart. File Transfer Protocol (FTP) is used for efficiently transferring files, but it is not secure.

92. B. When an operating system has reached end-of-life (EOL) status, not only are there no more feature updates or support, but there are no security updates and patches, and therein lies the danger. Using an EOL OS may be opening your system up to hackers. When an OS reaches EOL, it's past time to upgrade.

93. A. The Yellowdog Updater Modified (yum) command is used to get system updates automatically, install new packages, and remove old ones. The most similar to yum is apt-get, which is used to install, remove, and update packages. The main difference is that with apt-get, you must tell the command to get all of the updates. In the end, whether you use yum or apt-get may be determined by the Linux distribution that you use. The pwd command prints the working directory, meaning it will display or output the full path to the directory that you are in. The chmod command is used to modify user permissions to a directory or file.

94. C. Following best practices, this user would need two accounts: one a member of the administrator's group and another a standard user. They should be instructed to only log onto the administrator account if they can't do what they need to from their standard user account using features like Run As Administrator or entering their administrator password in the User Account Control (UAC) window.

95. A. The first step for any unresponsive app on your mobile device is to force-close it. How that is done will be different depending on whether it is an Apple or an Android device. If the app is still causing problems, you can try restarting your device, and if that doesn't work, uninstall and reinstall the application. Reverting your mobile device to factory defaults shouldn't be necessary.

96. C. When you tell a client you will do something, you are setting their expectations. The rule is to meet or exceed the expectations that you set. Remember that people like options. Let them know that you're running late, apologize, and give them the option of how to proceed. Be sure to call the other clients scheduled for the day, too.

97. A, C. The exact terms of what you can and cannot do with the software will be spelled out in the license, but it is common that you can use, modify, and share the source code, but not sell it for a profit, and you usually need to credit the original author of the software.

98. B. A case like this is exactly why you have a rollback plan. Occasionally, despite your best efforts, you get into a project and discover that it isn't going to work, or it will take longer than expected. Perhaps if you rework the plan you could make the changes without a big disruption to the business. Involving management in what is going on is always a good idea. The acceptable use policy (AUP) likely doesn't have any bearing here.

99. A, B. Websites store parts of pages in the cache to make loading them faster the next time. If you clear the browser's cache and cookies, then when you access the website, it must download all of the data that was previously cached which means that it will be the updated version. It may take a little longer, but it will be up-to-date. If it's a site where you use cached credentials to log in, you must log in again. Uninstalling and reinstalling your browser isn't necessary. The Ctrl key and F key pressed simultaneously usually bring up a Find dialog box.

100. D. If a battery is very low, the applications can show a slower than normal response time. If this continues when the phone is charged, see how full your phone is. If it's slow when you're saving or reading files, then you may need to clear out some space on the phone. Make sure your phone is updated. If it's an Android phone, ensure that your anti-malware is updated. If the problem is happening with just one app, try updating the app, clearing the app's cache, or removing and reinstalling the app.

Index

ensuring that no data leaves the
    network, 109, 434
exceeding data transmission threshold, 302, 553
increasing data access speed, 357, 586
options for recovering of from failed hard
    drive, 161, 461
preventing loss of if device is lost, 24, 395
protecting against accidental deletion of in
    macOS, 231, 506
protecting from potentially leaking of, 366, 591
protection of company data that is accessed by
    employees, 26, 396
regulated data, 335, 572
risk in exceeding data transmission
    limit, 301, 522
sharing of, 24, 395
software that runs on machine where data files
    to be accessed are housed and controls
    access to those files as requested by
    client, 56, 414
synchronization of, 24, 395
threats to leaking of, 301, 522
tracking boundaries and perimeters of flow
    of, 328, 566
troubleshooting computer that will occasionally
    not read data from hard drive, 185, 467
type of address used by router to get data to its
    destination, 37, 400
data cap, 348, 579
data destruction, proof of, 280, 539
data retention requirements, 333, 570
DB9, 100, 430
DC adapter, 19, 391
DCPS (DC power supply), 70, 94, 418, 428
DDR3, 78, 94, 343, 421, 428, 576
DDR4, 78, 94, 421, 428
DDR5, 78, 421
dead pixels, 140, 449
default gateway, 38, 139, 152, 189, 353, 401, 407,
    448, 456, 471, 583
defragmentation, 134, 445
degaussing, 257, 522
demarcation point, 401
desktop alerts, 306, 307, 556, 557
desktop computer, random reboots of, 344, 577
developer mode, 305, 555
Device Manager, 187, 367, 467, 592
df, 212, 489
DFS (Dynamic Frequency Selection), 57, 414
DHCP (Dynamic Host Configuration Protocol), 42,
    46, 48, 49, 355, 398, 402, 404, 407, 408, 409,
    410, 411, 585
DHCP lease duration, 58, 415
DHCP reservations, 276, 536

dictionary attack, 257, 521
differential backups, 330, 379, 568, 601
dig, 224, 500
digital rights management, 334, 571
digitizer, 11, 12, 14, 143, 387, 388, 389, 450
digitizing pad, 210, 487
DIMM (Dual Inline Memory Module), 69, 385
dir, 202, 481
dir /p, 366, 592
direct burial STP, 103, 432
direct packets out the proper port, 48, 409
Disk Cleanup, 214, 288, 490
Disk Management, 199, 364, 479, 590
disk space, problem with low free disk
    space, 165, 463
Disk Utility (macOS), 202, 481
diskmgmt.msc, 212, 237, 489, 510
diskpart, 185, 467
display privacy filter, 266, 526
DisplayPort, 69, 74, 393, 417, 419
displays. See also screen
    as black, 345, 577
    component of that is capable of discharging
        energy and causing severe injuries, 13, 388
    components of that are often
        connected, 14, 389
    dead pixels on, 351, 582
    flickering of LCD display, 160, 320, 461, 561
    for graphic designer, 82, 423
    green screen with 1s and 0s running
        down, 376, 598
    IPS (intrusion prevention system), 78, 421
    no image on screen with macOS
        desktop, 149, 454
    nothing appearing on screen, 148, 454
    problems with, 157, 459
    problems with dimness on, 166, 464
    problems with LCD display, 143, 450
    problems with on laptop, 162, 462
    shutting down, 345, 577
    strange color on, 351, 582
    that refer to type of backlight being used
        (LED), 26, 397
    that use organic materials, 11, 387
    with wide viewing angle, 78, 421
Displays (MacBook), 206, 483
distributed denial of service, 268, 530
DKIM (DomainKeys Identified Mail), 416
DMARC (Domain-Based Message Authentication,
    Reporting, and Conformance), 416
.dmg extension, 228, 503
DNS (Domain Name System) server, 34, 47, 51,
    355, 398, 404, 408, 409, 410, 411, 585
DNS AAAA address, 58, 415

G

H

M

Online Test Bank

Register to gain one year of FREE access after activation to the online interactive test bank to help you study for your CompTIA A+ certification exams—included with your purchase of this book! All of the practice questions and the practice exams in this book are included in the online test bank so you can practice in a timed and graded setting.

Register and Access the Online Test Bank

To register your book and get access to the online test bank, follow these steps:

1. Go to www.wiley.com/go/sybextestprep (this address is case sensitive)!
2. Select your book from the list.
3. Complete the required registration information, including answering the security verification to prove book ownership. You will be emailed a pin code.
4. Follow the directions in the email or go to www.wiley.com/go/sybextestprep.
5. Find your book on that page and click the "Register or Login" link with it. Then enter the pin code you received and click the "Activate PIN" button.
6. On the Create an Account or Login page, enter your username and password, and click Login or, if you don't have an account already, create a new account.
7. At this point, you should be in the test bank site with your new test bank listed at the top of the page. If you do not see it there, please refresh the page or log out and log back in.